URBAN CHILDREN IN DISTRESS

URBAN CHILDREN IN DISTRESS

Global Predicaments and Innovative Strategies

Cristina Szanton Blanc
with Contributors

HV
873
.593
1994
West

United Nations Children's Fund
International Child Development Centre
Florence, Italy

Gordon and Breach

Switzerland Australia Belgium France Germany Great Britain India
Japan Malaysia Netherlands Russia Singapore USA

Gordon and Breach Science Publishers

Y-Parc
Chemin de la Sallaz
1400 Yverdon, Switzerland

Post Office Box 90
Reading, Berkshire RG1 8JL
Great Britain

Private Bag 8
Camberwell, Victoria 3124
Australia

3-14-9, Okubo
Shinjuku-ku, Tokyo 169
Japan

12 Cour Saint-Eloi
75012 Paris
France

Emmaplein 5
1075 AW Amsterdam
Netherlands

Christburger Str. 11
10405 Berlin
Germany

820 Town Center Drive
Langhorne, Pennsylvania 19047
United States of America

Library of Congress Cataloging-in-Publication Data

Szanton Blanc, Cristina.
    Urban children in distress : global predicaments and innovative
strategies / Cristina Szanton Blanc ; with contributors.
        p.   cm.
    Includes bibliographical references and index.
    ISBN 2-88124-622-2. -- ISBN 2-88124-623-0 (pbk.)
    1. Street children--Case studies. 2. Poor children--Case studies.
3. City children--Case studies.   I. Title
HV873.S93 1994
362.7'09173'2--dc20   94-401
                                                                CIP

The contents of this book are the responsibility of the main author and the contributors, and do not necessarily reflect the policies or views of the United Nations Children's Fund (UNICEF).

Cover photo: A young girl facing the urban jungle in Nairobi, Kenya. *Credit*: Nation Newspapers Ltd., Nairobi, Kenya.

CONTENTS

FOREWORD

By the early 1960s, it was becoming evident to UNICEF and others concerned with the fight against poverty in the Third World that the beginning of a process of rapid and massive urbanization of unprecedented proportions was under way. Barely a generation later, two-thirds of the world's urban population is now concentrated in developing countries. By the year 2000, the developing world's urban population will be twice its 1980 level, and possibly triple by 2010.

During the 1960s, UNICEF assisted children in urban areas through general programmes such as maternal and child health centres, social services for children, the local processing of safe milk, and the provision of low-cost, high-protein foods for children. There was a growing recognition, however, that urban-focused activities were not sufficiently targeted at low-income communities in the slums, shantytowns and squatter settlements, nor was it known how much these programmes actually benefited the women and children of these communities. By the early 1970s, the debate in UNICEF was more clearly focused on the issue of "marginal" children in low-income urban areas who were denied practically all the rights that were ultimately codified in the 1989 United Nations Convention on the Rights of the Child. UNICEF began a search for more realistic approaches. After reviewing a study prepared for the UNICEF executive board in 1971 on problems of women and children living in urban poverty and opportunities for UNICEF assistance, conclusions were drawn that ring with the same resounding relevance today as they did in the early 1970s.

> A number of main points emerge from the study. Although developing countries were still predominantly rural, the urban sector was growing faster; slums and shantytowns were growing still faster than the cities to which they were linked (three to four times as fast), and usually consisted of a young population. Their growth was as much due to natural increase as to the influx from other areas. Slums and shantytowns would continue to exist and to grow at least for the next two or three decades. Slum clearance had not proved to be a practicable or successful solution, partly because of the high cost involved and partly because of the inability to meet the needs of slum people or to control the spread of slums significantly. Therefore, the limited funds available were likely to produce a greater impact upon a larger slum population if they were channeled into slum improvement projects on a self-help basis (para. 119).

It was concluded, furthermore, that "despite widespread notions to the contrary, a majority of the families in slums and shantytowns were stable, well organized and cohesive. Slum people were usually aware of their problems and capable of proposing and participating in practical solutions. There was a basic need to adopt new concepts of slum improvement which were closely identified with the people and laid stress on self-help, mutual aid, local leadership and community participation."

An important period of exploration, experimentation and growth of UNICEF's assistance targeted to the women and children in low-income urban communities began. A new "urban basic services" strategy emerged as an overall approach to development assistance in Third World countries in the mid-1970s. As this strategy developed during the latter part of the 1970s and early 1980s, when I was appointed as UNICEF's senior urban advisor, a comprehensive approach emerged that included:

(1) an emphasis upon social services for the urban poor and linking of social development with infrastructure development;

(2) a multi-sectoral, multi-level approach which respected the fact that urban programmes are area- rather than sectoral-based, and required participation both up and down governmental levels and across governmental sectors;

(3) low-cost and appropriate technologies as an essential part of the approach;

(4) the active involvement of communities in development and residents in community programmes, either as volunteers or paid workers;

(5) a strong focus on women and children.

By 1982, when UNICEF reported to its board on progress in over forty countries in urban basic services implementation, the approach had taken on a strong problem-solving focus on, among other challenges, reducing urban malnutrition; improving the situation of women; supporting a variety of early childhood development services; encouraging responsible parenthood and family planning; improving water and sanitation; and addressing what was beginning to surface as the serious problem of abused, abandoned, working and street children, "children in especially difficult circumstances" (CEDC). Most attentive observers also recognized that institutionalization of these children, whether in prison, welfare centres or orphanages, was not only wrong but it did not work. Solutions had to be sought closer to the roots of the problem, and especially by going back to the families.

At this point in time, in the early 1980s, a clear distinction was beginning to be made between UNICEF's advocacy initiatives and its programme support, each being understood as powerful arms to be used in a pragmatic fashion. As UNICEF expanded its assistance to urban basic services programmes, it also became evident that the most visible and highest-risk urban group were the older children who left their home and community to work in the streets. These were the children who for decades simply had been removed from the streets in many countries by the police, judiciary, and social-service systems and put in institutions, sometimes until they reached legal adulthood. Why? The vast majority were institutionalized because they were poor, not by any stretch of the imagination because they had committed crimes.

The fight for children's rights, in terms of rights, was beginning, even though in the early 1980s the discovery of the legal and legislative world of children's rights "as a field" still lay ahead. UNICEF and other concerned organizations would soon become engaged in powerful ways in supporting the 1989 Convention on the Rights of the Child. It was, however, the activists who, fighting with such determination and commitment against the abuses suffered by street children and other CEDCs, ultimately provided the critical impetus in so many instances which assured that the Convention would become a reality. To this day, this group continues to be one of the major, if not *the* major group that seeks to use the Convention, with national and local legislation, as an important new tool to protect the rights of children and adolescents both on the legal and programmatic levels.

The evolution of initiatives and experiences with CEDC in Brazil is illustrative in many ways of how this issue became a critical one, not only in Brazil but also in other Latin American countries and, more recently, in countries and communities in other regions. From the end of World War II until the end of the 1970s, Brazil's economy underwent a process of accelerated growth, without bringing an improvement in the standard of living for most of the population. By the early 1980s, an economic recession had struck the country, and the positive trends were reversed. From 1980 to 1988, the economy shrank. Average minimum wages declined by one-third. By 1989, 26 million children under the age of 17 lived in families whose monthly per capita income amounted to less than one minimum wage, a euphemism for poverty. The vast majority of these children (71 percent) lived in urban areas, most in subhuman conditions of degradation.

School enrolment rates have increased over time, but this has not brought a corresponding increase in the number of years of study completed. More than half of the children who attended first grade had to repeat the first year or drop out as a result of the inefficiency of the system. In 1989, three out of ten children between the ages of 10 and 17 were working, one in five between 10 and 14, and one in two between 15 and 17. In many cases, they worked more hours a week than their fathers.

The economic reality of poor urban families meant that children worked on the street to help themselves and their families financially, but this was not the only reason. Many were driven out of the home because of tensions, stress and violence, much of this related to the harshness of an economic system which could not satisfy basic family requirements.

Paralleling the Brazilian process of economic growth without equitable distribution of wealth, a social-welfare system was set up to address the problems of children and adolescents that amounted more to social control than to social development. The system, established in the early 1940s, was basically correctional and repressive, viewing poor children on the street as a threat to safety and rehabilitation in institutions as the best solution. In the 1960s, a somewhat more progressive approach was adopted, but it still turned out to be top-down and institutionalization-oriented. In the late 1970s, new legislation was enacted that did not, however, alter substantially the previous law. Children became wards of the court if they were considered in "irregular situations," a category that included poor children who needed help more than anything else, as well as children who had broken the law. A normal solution, typically, was to remove children from their families and communities and commit them to large institutions. Not surprisingly, they learned all the wrong things. Ultimately, the approach continued by and large to be a repressive-correctional one.

Much has been written on the children's rights movement in Brazil, and does not bear repeating here. What is important is to reflect on the characteristics of this effort that are relevant to the search for solutions to the problems of "urban children in distress." Contrary to conventional wisdom, researchers and nongovernmental organization (NGO) advocates were starting to demonstrate in the late 1980s that the vast majority of children working on the streets were not a threat to public society, nor were they without family or community ties. Since then, research, including the major project of the UNICEF International Child Development Centre in Florence described in this book, has shown that a majority of urban poor children on the streets live in parent-headed families, and only a small percentage of street and working children are involved in illegal activities.

Brazil provides an important example of how sectors of a society can mobilize. Among the critical factors underlying change in Brazil were the dynamic role of nongovernmental organizations with support from the academic community, a number of innovative institutions and individuals in government, more relevant basic education and legislation, and their use as instruments of mobilization.

Activist NGOs brought their growing knowledge of the role of law and of the Convention on the Rights of the Child, as well as their experiences working with children in the streets, to the national political and legislative process as the Congress was preparing a new constitution. The NGOs added fresh yeast to the ferment in Brazil over serious violations of children's rights. This, in turn, permitted the promulgation of an innovative safety net in the law to protect the rights of all children, including the very poorest, and those whose rights had been violated by the police and judiciary system.

The academic community, supported by a few creative government institutions, conducted important research that produced a new vision of the street child that helped Brazil change its attitude about street children — a shift away from their being seen as social outcasts to being perceived more as young adults working on the streets and trying to help their families and themselves under very difficult economic circumstances.

Both government and NGOs supported efforts on a small scale that began to bridge the gap between the world of work and the world of education. These efforts showed what the education system could do, when used creatively, to bring to a working child the type of education that strengthens his or her ability to earn more, and with more dignity, on the street. An important objective was to help the child break out of a dependency on street work and reinforce positive coping skills.

This new legislative opportunity, as it was seized in Brazil, resulted in existing NGOs and movements developing a high level of organizational and lobbying skills they did not have before. It also led to new movements that not only played critical roles in seeing laws passed successfully, but set the stage for new institutional solutions developed by NGOs to protect the interests of children and help promote their rights.

Among the most important actors in the process were government civil servants, including youth judges, and some government institutions involved in the process of transformation of institutions to better respond to children as young citizens with their own rights. In some cases, they were as strong in supporting transformation and reform as were the NGOs. Their support was vital to the passing of legislation and their collaboration continues to be vital as Brazilian society transforms its institutions to respond to children's needs in a more humane and effective way.

As part of its collaboration with the government in Brazil, UNICEF supported this process by backing government institutions and NGOs and providing examples of international laws and agreements that were useful in helping to think through new ways to deal with old problems. At times, it found itself cast in the uncomfortable role of go-between among NGOs and between NGOs and government institutions, smoothing the path to continuing collaboration. While this would not be the case in many other countries, the remarkably tolerant spirit of change in Brazil at the time meant that UNICEF was expected to play this role.

Now more than ever, in order to provide effective safety nets for all children, both governmental and nongovernmental organizations have to assume responsibility and work together to ensure the well-being of even the most disadvantaged children. Without this shared responsibility, all the new structures will have little chance of achieving their goals.

Brazilian society has genuinely started to respond in new ways to long-standing problems faced by its children. It has come a long way and recognizes that there still remains much to be done. By *listening* to children, a change of mentality took place. Many Brazilians discovered that children in the street are a major part of the solution and adults are still a major part of the problem.

My family and I had the good fortune, not without its frustrations and disappointments, to be witnesses to the extraordinary transition from the last remnants of authoritarian rule to a still-struggling democratic system in Brazil. My years as UNICEF representative there, from 1984 to 1991, taught me great respect for the Brazilian way of facing intransigent social and political issues with creativity, boundless energy and openness — but also with growing anguish and tensions, felt especially among the poor and particularly among the youth. This experience also taught me to look behind the facades of the social institutions and the false bravado of the street kids and to try to understand what these children and young people in the street need and want most — but still seldom find: solidarity, affection, care, and love. Most difficult of all for adults to understand is that these street and working children need to feel respect — in their own terms, and not in the condescending terms that the adult world often imposes upon them.

John J. Donohue

PREFACE

The Poor Make the City Work:
Can the City Work for the Poor?

Although many of us talk about bettering the human condition — what the specialists refer to as "development" — we are often far removed from the very people to whom development matters the most. Two quickly drawn pictures may help us come closer to their reality.

The first image is of a twelve-year-old girl in Bombay. She migrated to the city with her parents and her four younger brothers and sisters when the possibilities of survival in their home village had run dry. They are homeless and sleep on the pavement. The girl's father wakes up early every morning to look for work, but to no avail. As they were used to doing in their rural community, they share the little they have brought with them, until there is nothing left. The father and mother talk to each other one evening, and the next morning they call the girl, their oldest daughter, and ask her to go out and beg. She is shocked: she has never begged before. But she tries her best and is exhausted when she rejoins her family at nightfall. One evening she does not return. Her father and mother are worried and are about to start looking for her when she appears, smelling of perfume, her lips painted red. She has some money in her hand and holds it out to her parents, saying: "This is so that the little ones won't have to cry any more."

The loyalty and will to help is boundless in children. This young girl has suffered fear and degradation to do whatever she can for her family. Her parents are devastated, but the father reaches out and takes the money.

The other picture is from the West African city of Dakar. In a slum marketplace — euphemistically categorized by the priesthood of economists as the "informal sector" — there is organization in seeming chaos. In one corner, mattress-makers are skilfully recycling scrap metal into ingeniously produced springs. They recently had an important visitor, the Prime Minister of France, who, impressed with their work, offered to help the slum engineers find distributors in Paris — a first step into the profitable French market. The mattress-makers discussed the proposal for several nights but, when a representative from the French Embassy came to finalize the agreement, they declined the offer, saying:

We know we would earn ten times more, and we are grateful for the interest. But there is something we cannot buy, and that is the support and the credibility of our neighbours. Income is vital but, if we lose their support, we will not be able to survive.

Their "development theory" is built not just on technical skills and ability to produce desirable products, but also on the important recognition that a community where everyone works together and helps each other represents their most valuable asset, one that is many times more important than a temporary increase in income. They have learned through hard, day-to-day experience that solidarity and mutual support are the only pillars on which they can hope to build a life that is sustainable, no matter how poor.

The adolescent girl symbolizes the moral and developmental imperative to address the situation of the urban poor and their children. The mattress-makers help us see the possibility of linking up with the people's own strengths, their imagination, their responsibility and vigour. It is from insights such as these that a realistic urban development programme must derive its vision, its energy and its purpose.

The focus must be on the human dimension. The report of the Indian National Commission on Urbanization makes a clear plea for this in its first volume published in August 1988:

> We have spoken much of urban patterns and spatial planning: it is time we turn our attention to the people who inhabit our towns and cities and here, without any doubt, that which is most clearly apparent and which causes the greatest anguish is the starkly visible poverty we see around us. It is, arguably, the worst pollution of all, manifest in the slums which dominate the townscape and in the mass of beggars, petty hawkers and casual workers struggling to eke out a living. The cities have wealth, but the poor who live in them do not share in it. They service the city, they clean the houses of the rich and cook for them, they provide labour for factories and shops, they are the main carriers of goods, and yet they continue to be poor. The transference of poverty from a rural environment, where it is well spread out over space, to a city where it is concentrated, presents perhaps the most horrifying image of independent India.

The urban poor have become an inevitable concomitant of the development path that many countries have chosen or have been forced to choose. The poor in urban areas not only sustain the economy, but they also help city governments make services economical by offering their labour at ridiculously low wages. Imagine the smell of a city without the malnourished loaders, the scavengers and the street cleaners. But we usually forget about them, and act as if their world were not in the same universe as ours.

This book is intended as one vehicle to reach that world, which, I am ashamed to admit, few of us know much about. But the book and its authors cannot achieve this goal alone. They need the participation, the commitment, the compassion and the imagination of the reader who, using all of these qualities to "trade places" with the urban poor and their children, will take part in our discoveries and contribute to our policy discussions.

Researchers have only recently tried to come to grips with how people live in cities and with the realities of urban life. The most comprehensive overviews to date are by Fox (1977) and Hannerz (1980) who discuss some of the pioneering efforts in this field. This book, however, is not a treatise on research. It is principally an attempt to describe and understand — and to some extent analyse — how deprived urban children and their families and communities are trying to cope with scarcity, neglect and discrimination. Although the book has scientific ambitions, its main purpose is to create awareness. It hopes to provide insights into the social and cultural anatomy of cities, but its more deliberate aim is to communicate — often with these people's own words and life stories — the smell, the sweat, the agonies and the occasional triumphs of the poor in their day-to-day struggle for a rightful share of resources and human dignity.

The different authors, each contributing particular knowledge and insights, have together sought to build a convincing case for:

• the importance of a greater understanding of what urban children and their families in difficult circumstances can cope with, what they can achieve and what strategies they adopt to survive;

• the importance of a supportive, cohesive neighbourhood and of a city that provides, in increasingly difficult living situations, a supportive environment and, at a minimum, absolutely indispensable services;

• the importance of analysing examples of successful mobilization of people and resources, particularly the many cost-effective and sustainable initiatives that have attained surprising success despite minimal funding;

• the importance of building on lessons already learned and of transferring innovative approaches across countries.

Underlying these immediate objectives are more elusive and perhaps more philosophical issues that need to be understood. They concern the deeper and, paradoxically, equally pragmatic aspects of the publication.

In spite of increased attention to the problems of urban children and evidence of positive trends during the last decades, results have been slow and limited. What is missing in the chain of translating knowledge into action? Why do the majority of those in power continue to pay lip-service to children, calling them "our most precious resource" and signing progressive declarations, while continuing to permit processes that transform the social and physical environment, especially in urban areas, from life-supporting systems into life-threatening ones? Yes, to be fair, the survival rates of children are improving, but if our aim is for life as it should be — a fulfilling life — for all children, then I maintain that my anxiety is legitimate.

If knowledge of problems and their causes exists but is not acted upon, then it seems to me that we have to ask whether there is a certain *quality* that knowledge has to attain for us to turn it into action. This question touches the deepest level of epistemological philosophy, namely the question of what existence is all about. It forces us to distinguish between what exists because it can somehow be registered and what exists because we give it value, interact with it and in turn are influenced by it. In short, physical existence alone is not sufficient for something to be defined as "real." A quality of "meaning" must be added.

It does not take much reflection to realize that only what we actively assign purpose and meaning to has significant existence. When we discuss the situation of children, it is obvious that the existence of the child and the conditions of existence are totally dependent on what the child means to us. If the child is regarded as expendable — even if an asset — care will be inadequate. This will be reflected not only in high infant mortality rates, but also in other health, education and social indicators, such as the high incidence among children of preventable disease, high dropout rates and high institutionalization rates for juvenile offenders. In rapidly urbanizing environments, and especially in mega-cities, the numbers of abandoned and exploited children who experience with daily monotony the consequences of this attitude are growing. They are treated with abuse precisely because they are not properly valued. To far too many, these children simply represent one more form of unwanted rubbish to be swept off the streets. The challenge is to make knowledge and meaning meet.

The reader will find pictures drawn starkly in this book. They will show *what* some of the problems faced by "urban children in distress" are, *why* the problems exist, and *how* some of them might be reduced or overcome.

Although we seem to have begun to discover our children (even those in our run-away cities), we have yet to realize what to do with our discovery. A major challenge in the next few years will be to give direction and energy to this emerging understanding. Let me venture some suggestions on how to proceed:

- First, we need to take more determined strides in our quest for knowledge about disadvantaged urban children and to step up efforts to convince others that children, apart from representing approximately 40 percent of the populations of poorer countries, are central to what "development" should be all about.

- Second, we need to seize every opportunity to highlight the situation of urban children in an effort to bring together the compassion, experience, responsibility and resources present in both the public and private domains.

- Third, we, and especially public office-holders, need to understand that we must adhere not only to the Constitution of our respective countries, but also to the globally endorsed United Nations Convention on the Rights of the Child. We must also honour the commitments embodied in the National Programmes of Action for Children adopted by individual governments after the first World Summit for Children, held in September 1990 in New York, including the reallocation of human and financial resources.

- Finally, and I feel very strongly about this, we need to recognize the tremendous resource of moral and intellectual energy that exists in young people. This energy must be given meaning and purpose. In a time when ideologies are failing all over the world, we have a rare and even historic opportunity to create a new vision of our future community, whether rural or urban. Children are at the centre of this ideal community. They are surrounded by a supportive physical and social environment and can count on the peace and emotional security they need to develop into creative and confident human beings. Whatever our worldviews and convictions, this vision could give deep meaning and purpose to us all.

Giving words to these possibilities can help us to capture them and use them to build a new solidarity among nations, without which danger and despair will continue to outweigh hope and fulfilment for a large part of the world's population. For this the child might be our finest ally. Solidarity with the child may offer us one of our best opportunities to overcome poverty, ethnicity, and religious fanaticism, those ugly forces that counteract all efforts to join together the nations of the world through knowledge, understanding, and concern. These forces have divided the world into the "them" and the "us": "them" who "we" don't need to care for, and "their" environment that "we" feel free to destroy.

Solidarity with the child may provide us with one of the few bridges left to connect the North and the South. This can help us to prevent the injustice in our own societies and in our own cities from leading to the terrible prospect of not only "two worlds" but of two planets, separated by a widening chasm of difference and disparity.

Furthermore, by viewing our cities from the perspective of the child, we may be able to formulate pragmatic goals, which can inspire and mobilize the commitment and energy of all people and not only the intellectuals and the children of the élite. Equally important, by fostering solidarity with the child and a commitment to a better future for all children, we may be able to organize our cities to support life rather than threaten it. Thus, a movement for a better, more caring city needs the child as much as the children need its help.

Then, maybe, this world can unite, step by step, into a real movement not against something, but *for* something: a popular, professional, and political movement for, with and around children and the cities they inhabit, a movement that future historians will look upon as a major achievement in moral history. Then ultimately it might be the powerless child who will have the power to make our cities safer and better places to live in, enabling them to become environments where new forms of creativity, compassion, and dignity can evolve.

Karl-Eric Knutsson

CONTRIBUTORS

CRISTINA SZANTON BLANC, senior programme officer and coordinator of the five-country Urban Child Project at the UNICEF International Child Development Centre, is an anthropologist with long-term experience in the formulation and assessment of development projects in the Third World. Trained at the University of Chicago and at Columbia University, she has taught at the School for International Affairs, Columbia University, as well as in the Departments of Anthropology at Barnard College and at the New School for Social Research in New York and has published extensively on changing family and gender roles, on ethnic relations and on programme evaluations. She has authored, among other works, *A Right to Survive. Subsistence Marketing in a Lowland Philippine Town* (Pennsylvania University Press, 1972 and 1976) and co-authored with Nina Glick Schiller and Linda Basch *New Perspectives on Transnationalism* (New York Academy of Social Sciences, 1992) and *Nations Unbound: Transnational Projects, Post-Colonial Predicaments, and Deterritorialized Nation-States* (Gordon and Breach, 1994).

FABIO DALLAPE, an Italian sociologist, has been involved in development since 1960. He was the director of the Undugu Society for over ten years and is now the regional representative of Terra Nuova for East Africa. He has extensive experience in working on behalf of street children and other disadvantaged urban children in Nairobi and is the author of *An Experience With Street Children* (Undugu/UNICEF, Nairobi, 1987).

LEONARD J. DUHL, M.D., is a professor of public health and urban health policy at the University of California in Berkeley and professor of psychiatry at U.C.S.F. He helped to develop, and continues to act as consultant to, the Healthy Cities Programme, which started with WHO and now exists in cities throughout the world. He is a practising psychiatrist as well as consultant to government, nonprofit organizations, schools, local urban communities and health systems. His most recent publications are *The Social Entrepreneurship of Change* (Pace University Press, 1990) and *Cities and Health: the Governance of Diversity* (London, Grey Seal Press, 1991). He is strongly committed to the City of Oakland, California, and to the development of their programmes relating to health and the city.

LEO FONSEKA is UNICEF South Asia's regional advisor on Urban Programmes. He has extensive experience in Sri Lanka and India in crosssectoral urban social planning, ranging from micro- to national-level programme and policy development for the low-income urban sector. Recognized for his knowledge and involvement in developing inter-sectoral and community-based participatory approaches to urban primary health care, community education and organization, housing and environmental upgrading, he has served as a member of the WHO/UNICEF Consultative Group, which helped develop the State-of-the-Art Report on Urban Primary Health Care, and of the Consultative Group which guided the ICDC five-country research for the Urban Child Project. He co-authored *Responding to the Child in the Urban Setting* (UNICEF India, 1984) and *Towards a Self-Reliant Urban Low Income Sector in Colombo* (Assignment Children, Vols. 51–52, 1982).

LIDIA GALEANO worked with the Italian overseas development department on strengthening suburban health facilities in Cape Verde in 1987–88 and as an assistant programme officer from 1988 to 1990 in UNICEF Brasilia. She also worked as a consultant at UNICEF ICDC on the organization of the International Meeting of Mayors, Urban Planners and Policy Makers held in Florence in October 1992. She is currently completing a Ph.D. thesis on "Social Policies for Children 1988–1993" at the Ecole des Hautes Etudes en Sciences Sociales, Paris, while engaged in consultancy work for UNESCO.

JORGE E. HARDOY, a valued member of the Consultative Group, passed away in September 1993. He was an architect and urban planner and president of the Instituto Internacional de Medio Ambiente y Desarrollo, IIED-América Latina. He was a full-time researcher of urban problems in Third World countries, and his publications included *Squatter Citizens* and *The Poor Die Young* (Earthscan Publications Ltd., 1989 and 1990), as well as *Environmental Problems in Third World Cities, Historia de Buenos Aires Metropolitano* and *Los Centros Historicos de América Latina,* all co-authored with other researchers in his field.

ROGER HART is professor of environmental psychology and developmental psychology at the Graduate School and University Center of the City University of New York. He is also director of the Center for Human Environments, co-director of the Children's Environments Research Group and editor of the quarterly journal *Children's Environments*. His research focuses on child development in relation to the physical environment and the implications for the planning and design of children's environments and environmental education. Author of *The Changing City of Childhood* (City College of New York, 1987) and co-author of *Getting in Touch With Play* (Lighthouse National Order for Vision and Child Development, New York, 1991), he recently authored an Innocenti Essay on *Children's Participation: From Tokenism to Citizenship* for UNICEF ICDC.

LENNART LEVI is professor of psychosocial medicine and head of the Department of Stress Research (WHO Psycho-Social Center) at the Karolinska Institutet in Stockholm, Sweden. He is also director of the National Swedish Institute for Psychosocial Factors and Health. Author of

Parameters of Emotion (Oxford University Press, 1975) and editor of *Society, Stress and Disease*, Vols. 1–5 (Oxford University Press, 1981), he has published widely on the interaction between environmental, psychological, and physiological processes and health outcomes.

D.D. MALHOTRA, trained at Syracuse University, is professor at the Indian Institute of Public Administration in New Delhi, where he has taught since 1969. He has worked as a national and international consultant on urban poverty, development management, and the universalization of Urban Basic Services programmes in India, and has written numerous articles and reports.

LEOPOLDO M. MOSELINA is programme officer for Urban Basic Services/Street Children Programmes for UNICEF Manila. Before joining UNICEF as consultant on street children in 1986, he was college dean of the Columban College, Olongapo City from 1982 to 1985 and chairman of the Sociology Department of the Asian Social Institute, Manila from 1979 to 1981. An educator and sociologist, his involvement in academia started in 1969 when he joined the faculty of Columban College, where he and volunteer school administrators, faculty and students piloted in 1983–85 a community-based programme for urban poor children, women, and families in Olongapo with funding assistance from UNICEF.

MONICA MUNHOZ-VARGAS, born in Chile, received advanced training in public administration (Chile) and subsequently in urban sociology (Universidade de Brasilia and the Victoria University of Manchester). She worked at the Istituto Nacional de Estudos e Pesquisas, Ministero da Educacao in Brasilia from 1983 to 1985 and as UNICEF project officer for Women's Programmes in Guatemala (1985–89) before joining UNICEF Brasilia as planning officer in 1989.

ROBERTA MUTISO, former associate professor and chairman of the Department of Sociology at the University of Nairobi, has worked as a private consultant since 1990. Her published works include a co-edited book on participatory research in Kenya. She has also contributed to numerous books and has written journal articles on social policy, social work, development, and women. She has a Ph.D. in sociology and a master's degree in social work.

MONICA MUTUKU is a project officer in UNICEF Kenya Country Office where she is responsible for Urban Basic Services and CEDC programmes. Prior to joining UNICEF, Ms. Mutuku worked for the Nairobi City Council in various capacities including assistant director in charge of the Community Development Division in the Housing Development Department, focusing on World Bank and USAID funded projects. She holds a M.Sc. degree in urban development planning from the University College of London.

EMMA PORIO has worked with the Institute of Philippine Culture and is currently teaching in the Department of Sociology and Anthropology at the Ateneo de Manila. She has done extensive work on issues of development and urban improvement policies. She has authored, among other works, *Filipino Family, Community and Nation* (with Frank Lynch and Mary Racelis Hollnsteiner, 1981) and *Partnership with the Poor* (National Economic Development Authority, 1991). She holds a Ph.D. in sociology from the University of Hawaii.

IRENE RIZZINI has been professor of psychology at the University of Santa Ursula, Rio de Janeiro, since 1978 and director of the University of Santa Ursula Center for Research on Childhood since 1984. Trained at the University of Chicago School of Social Service Administration and at the Istituto Universitario de Pesquisa de Rio de Janeiro (IUPERJ), she has written on the history of legislation on children in Brazil and coordinated many research projects on mistreated, abandoned, and neglected children, both nationally and internationally. Her most recent publications are *O Que o Rio Tem Feito Por Suas Crianças?* with F.B. Wiik (Ford Foundation, 1989), *Children in the City of Violence — the Case of Brazil* (The United Nations University, Tokyo, 1991) and *O Estatuto da Criança e do Adolescente Comentado* (UNICEF, 1992).

IRMA RIZZINI is professor of social psychology at the University of Santa Ursula, Rio de Janeiro, and coordinator of Studies on Children at Coordenacao de Estudos e Pesquisas sobre a Infancia (CESPI) at the same university. She has published extensively since 1985 on social policies for poor and marginalized children in Brazil. Her most recent publications are *A Assistencia à Infância na Passagem Para o Século XX — da Repressão à Reedução* (F. Getúlio Vargas, 1990), *A assistencia à Infância no Brasil — Uma Anàlise de sua Construção* (CESPI/USU, 1993), and *O Elogio do Cientifico — A Construção do "Menor" na Pràtica Jurìdica* (CESPI/USU, 1993, prelo).

LAURA SOLITO has a doctorate in the sociology of development and teaches applied research in social services at the University of Florence. She has carried out various research projects and published essays and articles in the field of development and communication. She is the national coordinator of the Italian Urban Child Project at the Istituto degli Innocenti in Florence and author of *Media e Sviluppo* (Ed. Liquori, 1990) and *Alla Ricerca di una Cultura del Servizio* (Adriano Olivetti Foundation, 1991).

ANTHONY SWIFT is a freelance writer and photographer. He has worked independently and with research teams in writing on social and development issues for the non-specialist reader. He is co-author of *Homelessness: An Act of Man* (National Federation of Housing Associations, 1987) and of *Broken Promise — The World of Endangered Children* (Headway-Hodder & Stoughton, 1989), and recently authored *Brazil — The Fight For Childhood in* *the Cities* (UNICEF, Florence, 1991) and *Oxfam at Work in Uganda — Development Against the Odds* (Oxfam, Uganda, 1991).

PETER XENOS is a sociologist-demographer and Southeast Asia specialist at the East-West Center, Honolulu, whose studies of marriage and family systems have led to his interest in childhood and youth under conditions of rapid social change. Co-author with James T. Fawcett and Sien-Ean Khoo of *Women in the Cities of Asia: Migration and Urban Adaptation* (The Westview Press, 1984), he has also recently co-edited *Family Systems and Cultural Change* (Oxford University Press, 1993).

ACKNOWLEDGMENTS

This book has benefited from the contributions of many more people than can be listed here. The initial issues raised and the project design were developed during Consultative Group meetings that assembled representatives/members of the five country teams and from UNICEF headquarters as well as an Urban Child steering committee: Fabio Dallape, John Donohue, Len Duhl, Leo Fonseka, Jorge Hardoy, Jim Himes, Roger Hart, Lennart Levi, Mary Racelis, R. Padmini, Victoria Rialp, Lucetta Tre Re, and Peter Xenos. The main ideas were further elaborated during frequent visits to the four UNICEF country offices and in consultations with the *Istituto degli Innocenti,* UNICEF's collaborator for the Italian project and host institution in Florence. The book is a result of an intense interactive process that has allowed the UNICEF International Child Development Centre (ICDC) to benefit from collaboration with research institutions and children's organizations in each country and city involved in the study.

This project could not have been undertaken without the encouragement of the UNICEF members of ICDC's advisory committee of the time: Richard Jolly, Karl-Eric Knutsson, Nyi Nyi, and Mary Racelis. Numerous other UNICEF colleagues in New York and in the field made important contributions, including Vesna Bosnjak, Clarence Shubert, Bill Cousins, Nazar Memon, Cassie Landers, Agnes Aidoo, Aklilu Lemma, Kimberley Gamble-Payne, Marjorie Newman-Black, Per Miljeteig-Olssen, Emilio Garcia Mendez, and Mario Ferrari. A special word of thanks also goes to the UNICEF country representatives involved at different stages, including Baquer Namazi, John Donohue, Pratima Kale, Keshab Mathema, Eimi Watanabe, Vincent O'Reilly, and Agop Kayayan. Jim Himes, the ICDC director, and Paolo Basurto, deputy director, have offered their valuable comments, encouragement and constructive criticism throughout. The project owes much to their input.

To the teams in the field coordinated by the UNICEF officers for Urban Basic Services and Children in Especially Difficult Circumstances — Leo Fonseka, Jaime Tan, Leopoldo Moselina, Monica Mutuku, Antonio Carlos Gomez da Costa, Ruben Cervini, Monica Munhoz-Vargas, and Gerry Pinto — go my most sincere thanks for their perseverance and good humour. The main team members in each country were: Alda Alves, Luis Basilio, Joao Gilberto Lucas Coelho, Marco Antonio Da S. Mello, Paulo Cesar A. De Mendoça, Wilson Moura, Irene Rizzini, Irma Rizzini, Arno Vogel, and Alba Zalvar in Brazil; A.B. Bose, D.D. Malhotra, O. Mathur, Pratibha Mehta, D. Ravindra Prasad, D.G. Rama Rao, G. Surya Rao, Venkat Rao, and Geeta

Sethi in India; Elena Chiong-Javier, Manuel Diaz, Ana Dionela, Pacifico Maghacot, Lourdes Mamaed, Daisy Noval-Morales, Emma Porio, Pilar Ramos-Jimenez, Aida Santos, and Amaryllis Torres in the Philippines; Fabio Dallape, Victoria Kattambo, M. Manundu, E.K. Mburugu, Samuel Muindi, Roberta Mutiso, Njoki Ndungu, Florence Ombaso, Philista Onyango, Katete Orwa, and Colette Suda in Kenya. With the help of their institutions and of many local collaborators, all generously gave their time and energy to the project, discussed the issues, and produced impressive reports. The UNICEF office staff was also very helpful in each country.

The *Istituto degli Innocenti* team, Laura Solito, Laura d'Ettole, Angela Tonini, Angelica Mucchi-Faina, Sandro Costarelli, and Elena Volpi, under the expert guidance of Lucetta Tre Re and with the support of the two successive presidents, Elvira Pajetta and Francesco Arrigoni, participated in international conferences and in consultative groups and has helped to initiate an important North–South transfer of information and innovative ideas. The *Istituto*'s urban city teams, headed by Luciano Sommella, Angela Di Pasquale, and Anna Lisa Rossi-Cairo, worked with local collaborators and the support of Augusto Palmonari, Carlo Pagliarini, Giancarlo Rigon, and Serena Di Carlo.

To the steering committee members, Fabio Dallape, Len Duhl, Jorge Hardoy, Roger Hart, Lennart Levi, and Peter Xenos, go a special word of thanks for their substantive contributions to specific chapters and for their comments on the final text when our tight deadlines permitted. They provided an important impetus and unfailingly supported the participatory nature of the study. Particular thanks go to Peter Xenos and Roger Hart, who visited the Centre during the production period and were extremely supportive and helpful. Roger Hart also provided extensive comments on many of the chapters.

Colleagues in other internationally known organizations such as the German Development Foundation, the International Labour Office, Childhope, the Population Council, The World Bank, Save the Children, Terra Nova, the Brazilian Centre for Childhood and Adolescence (CBIA), the Mazingira Institute, the International Child Catholic Bureau, Istituto Universitario de Pesquisas e Rio de Janeiro, the Undugu Society, Defence for Children International, the Children's Defense Fund, and the Urban Institute, provided useful information on specific aspects of the study. Maggie Alexander, Stefano Berterame, Susan Bincoletto, Lidia Galeano, Melay Patron, Alice Peinado, Jason Schwartzman, and Monica Von Thun Calderon, always cheerfully supported by Sandra Fanfani and Kathy Wyper of ICDC, helped in coordinating the work with the field and in analysing the reports. Their contribution is gratefully acknowledged.

Finally, a special word of thanks goes to the ICDC Urban Child Team that participated in the production of this book. Diana Saltarelli and, more recently, Richard Dunbar took care of the stylistic editing and text preparation. Their patience and skill in reshaping some of the text, and in dealing with numerous drafts, is sincerely acknowledged. Kathy Wyper and Claire Akehurst untiringly helped to scan reports and provided valuable secretarial assistance, and Paolo Masetti worked skilfully at the computer to construct many of the tables and figures. A special thanks also to Anny Bremner and to Barth Healey who provided expert editorial assistance in the final stages as well as to Patricia Light for her help in managing contacts with the publisher, and to the library staff. The joint efforts of all these people made my task a much more pleasant and productive one.

Naturally, none of the persons mentioned above aside from the authors are responsible for the views developed in this book and for any errors which might have remained.

Cristina Szanton Blanc

ABBREVIATIONS

General

CEDC	Children in Especially Difficult Circumstances
EEC	European Economic Community
GCR	Gini Concentration Ratio
GDP	Gross Domestic Product
GNP	Gross National Product
ICDC	International Child Development Centre
IMF	International Monetary Fund
IMR	Infant Mortality Rate
LDC	Less Developed Country
NGO	Nongovernmental Organization
ORT	Oral Rehydration Therapy
PHC	Primary Health Care
SAP	Structural Adjustment Programme
STD	Sexually Transmitted Disease
UBS	Urban Basic Services
UBSP	Urban Basic Services Programme
UBSP	Urban Basic Services for the Poor
U5MR	Under-Five Mortality Rate
UNDP	United Nations Development Programme

Brazil

FEBEM	State Foundations for the Welfare of Minors
FLACSO	Latin American Faculty of Social Sciences
Forum DCA	National Non-Governmental Forum for the Defence of Children's and Adolescents' Rights
FUNABEM	National Foundation for the Welfare of Minors
OEC	Communal Educational Workshop
PNBEM	National Policy for the Welfare of Minors
SAM	Assistance Service to Minors

Philippines

DSWD	Department of Social Welfare and Development
IAC	Inter-Agency Council
NCSD	National Council of Social Development Foundation of the Philippines
NEDA	National Economic Development Agency
PEPT	Philippines Educational Placement Test
PSSC	Philippine Social Science Council
R&R	Rest and Recreation

India

CCVC	Coordination Committee for Vulnerable Children
CO	Community Officer
ICDS	Integrated Child Development Services
IPC	Indian Penal Code
IUD	Integrated Urban Development
LCS	Low Cost Sanitation
NIUA	National Institute of Urban Affairs
NSDF	National Slum Dwellers Federation
RCD	Rural Community Development
RCV	Resident Community Volunteers
SMTD	Small and Medium-Sized UBS Town Development
SPARC	Society for the Promotion of Area Resource Centres
UCD	Urban Community Development

Kenya

ANPPCAN	African Network for the Prevention and Protection against Child Abuse and Neglect
DELTA	Development Education and Leadership Training for Action

Italy

ADM	Home-Based Assistance Project for Children
CENSIS	Research Centre for Social Investments
ISTAT	National Institute of Statistics
USL	Unità Sanitaria Locale (local public health centre) .

The following conversion rates as of 28 May 1993 are used throughout this book:

Brazil	US$1.00	=	39.93 Cruzeiros
India	US$1.00	=	31.13 Rupees
Italy	US$1.00	=	1,472 Liras
Kenya	US$1.00	=	62.23 Shillings
Philippines	US$1.00	=	26.67 Pesos

Chapter
ONE

Introduction

Cristina Szanton Blanc

INTRODUCTION

Since the early 1970s, recession has severely threatened the welfare of children, youth and other vulnerable groups both South and North. In many developing countries, the effects have been compounded by external debt, declining terms of trade, protectionism in industrialized countries, and excessive military spending. Structural adjustment programmes have failed to respond adequately to the problems.

The State of the World's Children, issued yearly by UNICEF, allows us to monitor across countries some of the major trends in children's welfare, such as mortality, morbidity, school enrolment and gender differentials. Important publications, such as *Adjustment with a Human Face* (Cornia et al. 1987), have clarified some ways in which adjustment policies, requiring governments to concentrate on reducing budget deficits, improving trade balances, meeting debts, and initiating privatization, have led to significant decreases in funding for health, education and other social programmes, especially for vulnerable populations.

While many of these trends have been documented, the complex ways in which they have affected the well-being of our young populations have only begun to be understood. We can often quantify how many children die or become ill, how many finish school, how many become dropouts, and how many suffer from mild or severe malnutrition. It is, however, very much more difficult to demonstrate how existing world conditions and social transformations are creating a relatively unhealthy, disheartened and troubled population of young people who are growing up with more severe problems of social adjustment than ever before.

This social deterioration is chronic in urban areas in the developing world, although it is not always clearly recorded. In most African countries and in many of the developing countries of Asia and Latin America (the Philippines and Brazil, for example), urban children are more likely now than in 1980 to be born into poverty, be born prematurely, die in their first year of life, suffer low birth weight, and have mothers who received late or no prenatal care. They are more likely to have an unemployed or severely underemployed parent, see a parent die or go to prison, live in a single-parent household, endure substandard housing, suffer from child abuse, drop out of primary school, and never attend secondary school, let alone university. They are more likely to be forced to work in an exploitative setting, get involved in substance abuse, enter prostitution, be exposed to violence on the streets, and be affected by armed conflict. In addition, especially in Africa, children are increasingly orphaned by AIDS or die from this disease, which was unknown in 1980.

Problems have been more systematically documented, but hardly eradicated, in industrialized countries. In eastern European countries, infant mortality rates (IMR) stagnated and child poverty registered an often significant increase during the 1980s. The percentage of children in high-risk situations because of extensive alcoholism or conflicts with the law remains cause for serious concern (Sipos 1991). In the United States, since the 1960s, nearly half of the country's black children (4.3 million), one sixth of all white children (8.1 million), and more than one fifth of all American children, including nearly one out of four under the age of six, are poor. Furthermore, children have often become far poorer than individuals of other age groups, in part because policy makers have consistently failed to give this vulnerable group the special attention it requires (Edelman 1987).

Poverty is the greatest child-killer in the highly urbanized United States of the early 1990s. This is a striking consideration. The national death rate for infants between one month and one year — post-neonatal mortality — actually increased by 3 percent between 1982 and 1983. Single adolescent parenthood has also increased in the United States, as jobless or poor adolescent fathers find it increasingly difficult to take on responsibilities. In 1970, three teenage births out of ten were to single mothers; by 1983, that number had increased to more than five out of ten. A single mother under 25 years of age is nine times as likely to be poor as a young woman living on her own without children (Edelman 1987, Weill 1990). The percentage of births to adolescents is particularly high in the United States (52.7 per 1,000 teenagers in 1981), compared, for example, with the United Kingdom (28.6 per 1,000), and Sweden (14.3 per 1,000).

Many other indicators of distress are available. In the United Kingdom, for example, the suicide rate of people between the ages of 15 and 34 years has increased each year between 1975 and 1987 (Lowy et al. 1990). Both obesity and anorexia nervosa, particularly among girls, appear to be on the rise. Racial disadvantage for children is also increasing, especially in the inner-city areas where almost three fourths of the ethnic minority population lives (Bradshaw 1990).

Although, in comparison with the rural sector, the urban sector may appear economically privileged, it conceals severe problems of resource distribution. Urban living is often extremely harsh and exploitative for young people, particularly because of their rapidly rising numbers, the shortcomings of municipal management, and the deterioration of the social and physical environment. The feelings of marginalization of urban poor families are augmented by the stark contrasts with more affluent urban families.

Thus, whether in the South or North, we live in an unequal world and we are faced with interlocking crises. What can we do about them?

Meeting the essential needs of our children and young people, and assuring them their rights, including the right to a better future, requires not only a new era of economic growth for those nations in which the majority of the population is poor, but also a major redistribution of resources so that sustained growth may become a reality for all. Such equity and the sustainable development it would permit require, however, as the World Commission on Environment and Development (1987) powerfully stated, "the cooperation of political systems that would help ensure that the distribution of resources, the direction of budgetary investments, and institutional change are sufficient to meet future needs. Success thus rests ultimately on political will."

Institutions dealing with children often have narrow preoccupations and compartmentalized concerns. The general response of governments to the speed and scale of global changes has been a reluctance to acknowledge the need for institutional change.

The challenges faced today require comprehensive approaches and popular participation. Yet, the institutions which must meet those challenges tend to be independent and isolated from each other, working within relatively narrow mandates and with closed decision-making processes. Institutions concerned with children's problems are cut off from those responsible for handling broader urban problems or for managing the overall economy. Our world is one of interlocked economic and social problems; for significant improvement, the policies, people and institutions concerned must change.

Governments have, in some cases, responded to this newly perceived crisis. They have created new agencies and established ministries. Many have had some success, but much of their work has, of necessity, been after-the-fact repair: rehabilitation and retraining, reeducation and rebuilding urban environments. The very existence of such agencies has given many governments and their citizens the false impression that children are being protected and their conditions improved. Furthermore, the mandates of central economic and sectoral ministries are often limited, too concerned with quantities and with the immediacies of problems, not with their underlying causes and long-term consequences. The mandates tend to be tied to bureaucratic targets and the narrow requirements of management "efficiency." They are based on deep-seated, but often untested, assumptions about what works and what does not work. Broad evaluations to test results against initial objectives are rarely undertaken. Goals are almost never challenged, and evaluations, when carried out, tend to focus exclusively on pre-assigned project aims and their quantitative impact in terms of numbers of beneficiaries and rate of expenditures.

The challenge today is to make the central economic and sectoral ministries assume responsibility for the quality of those parts of society affected by their decisions, and to give agencies providing services to urban children and families more power to deal with the consequences of current urban development. Ultimately, more power, accompanied by appropriate government support, must be shifted to the communities and families themselves.

Municipalities are faced with new institutional opportunities. Ongoing worldwide trends towards democratization, decentralization and privatization, combined with growing urban poor populations have given cities in the 1990s new and formidable tasks, but also new opportunities for leadership in establishing innovative social policies.

There is also a need for change within international development agencies, with more consideration given to the social consequences of their development work on children. Some recognize the pressures exerted by urbanization and are beginning to investigate the impact their programmes have on urban families and communities (UNDP 1991b). The Urban Section of the World Bank, for example, has issued papers on urban poverty and the effects of structural adjustment on families (World Bank 1991a). However, considering that they are the basis of our future, children, and urban children in particular, are not nearly as high on their agendas as they should be.

A significant reorientation of our thinking about urban development in relation to children's well-being is one of the chief institutional challenges of the 1990s and beyond. Meeting this challenge will require major institutional development and reform. Many countries and cities which are too poor, or too small, to have adequate managerial capacity will need financial and technical assistance and training. The changes required involve, by necessity, all countries, large and small, rich and poor, North and South.

THE URBAN CHILD PROJECT

Background and Objectives

The first meetings of the Consultative Group on the Urban Child, organized by the UNICEF International Child Development Centre (ICDC) in Florence in 1988–89, assembled UNICEF Representatives and other professionals from Brazil, the Philippines and India, three countries where the problems of disadvantaged urban children had become particularly pressing; from Kenya, representing the African countries where child-related problems in cities were still relatively minor, but expected to grow during the 1990s; and *Istituto degli Innocenti*, representing Italy, a country whose rapid economic growth in recent decades had not eradicated old forms of poverty, nor prevented the growth of "new poverty" affecting children. The Consultative Group recognized that a fresh and more preventive perspective was needed as a first step towards a reorientation of national policies and institutional commitments towards urban children. This new perspective would acknowledge children as important and creative human beings, as "subjects" in their own right, and would systematically address the roots of their problems.

The Consultative Group was inspired by the experience of Brazil where problems relating to urban children in especially difficult circumstances (CEDC) have been actively researched over the past two decades. Colleagues from the UNICEF office in Brazil described the crucial role that research, linked to action, could play in changing public opinion and ultimately bringing about important policy changes. Research carried out in Brazil during the 1980s revolutionized assumptions about the problems faced by street children; attracted the interest of the media which had previously ignored, or sensationalized, events involving poor urban children; lent authority to arguments presented to policy makers; and helped concerned nongovernmental organizations (NGOs) present their cases.

Since the problems of "street children," a term brought into use by NGOs and UNICEF, were rapidly emerging as a major concern in the other countries represented at the meetings, the Consultative Group proposed that street and working children be the main focus of this first project on Urban Children, and that case studies be prepared, with the close collaboration and supervision of the UNICEF Urban Officers and Representatives, in each of the four developing countries mentioned above. An Italian team, sponsored by *Istituto degli Innocenti*, was also formed.

It was determined that the case studies should: (1) analyse in greater depth the situations of urban children, especially street and working children; and (2) document the innovative policies which had developed in those countries as an initial response to the problems. Although it was suggested that the studies be based as much as possible on secondary material, there was also agreement on using an "action-research" approach and engaging in primary research as well.

The five countries were selected because they face certain common problems, are representative of their region, and/or represent important blocks of the world's population. They have developed, in many cases, particularly innovative programmes at national and municipal levels. Moreover, Country Teams could take advantage of research results which had begun to become available in each of the countries.

Brazil and the Philippines have been heavily afflicted by severely weakened economies and massive debts. Both have extremely unequal income and asset distribution (a deep-rooted characteristic which has become more acute since the Second World War). Both have experienced currency devaluations, soaring inflation and an accelerated erosion of living standards. Economic constraints have been severe in the extensive urban areas of both countries. This has had detrimental effects on the management of cities, the availability of services, and the ability of households to cope. During the protracted period of economic crises between 1971 and 1985, the proportion of people living in poverty in the Philippines rose from 58 to 64 percent in rural areas, and from 40 to 56 percent in urban areas. It was estimated in 1988 that only 48 percent of the households in the vast mega-city of Metro Manila earned incomes equivalent to household expenditure; 35 percent had incomes which fell below household expenditure levels.

Poverty and inequitable income distribution have long been endemic to India, a country which has only recently veered towards more market-oriented policies. This has involved large-scale borrowing from the International Monetary Fund (IMF) and the rigours of structural adjustment. Provisional estimates in this country, where urbanization reached 25.7 percent in 1991, place more than one fifth (20.1 percent or 41.7 million) of the urban population below the poverty line for 1987–88. However, this percentage represented a marked improvement from the estimated 41.2 percent in 1972–73, and even from the 28.1 percent in 1983–84 (Bose 1992).

Kenya, like many other countries in sub-Saharan Africa, has faced very severe economic crises since the 1980s (Cornia et al. 1992). In addition, it is undergoing steady population growth and increasing urbanization, although the country as a whole was still only 17.5 percent urban in 1989. Nairobi registered extraordinary population increases during the 1980s, mainly because of rural-to-urban migration, once again with adverse effects on living standards. The urban nutritional status, especially for children, deteriorated between 1977 and 1982. In 1990, 74 percent of the households in Nairobi were officially classified as poor by the Central Bureau of Statistics. Increasingly, these low- and very low-income households are female-headed.

Such rapid urban growth is straining government planning and management capacities, especially at municipal levels. Even collecting information on the urban poor is problematic. The absence of long-term planning has negative repercussions on basic urban services, as well as on the physical environment, contributing to the deterioration of the quality of life.

Italy, in contrast, represents a very different set of trends. The very rapid economic growth of the last few decades has created a number of social contradictions and dislocations. The nationwide fertility rate is in sharp decline, going from 2.5 per 1,000 in 1960 to 1.4 per 1,000 in 1990, one of the lowest in the world. Currently 68.9 percent urbanized, Italy is facing a recession and must contend with difficult economic and political choices related to its fiscal deficit and the requirements of the European Economic Community (EEC). A rapid influx of immigrants from the Third World, and more recently from eastern Europe, has created mounting social uneasiness.

The management of Italian cities is more structured and better monitored than in the developing world, partially as a result of the increased availability of technology. There has been a trend towards declining sizes of cities and greater suburbanization, without, however, adequate consideration being given to the complex issues regarding the quality of life in today's urban settings. There have been many cases of unauthorized construction and poor urban planning. Moreover, congested streets, air pollution and traffic accidents, especially involving adolescents on motorscooters, are common. Pockets of severe poverty persist in many Italian cities. Italy thus represents the "conscience" of the Project, reminding other countries that economic development alone does not ensure the resolution of all children's problems — and indeed often creates difficult new ones.

By December 1990, a first review of literature had been commissioned in each country, and Country Teams had been selected. Twenty-one cities were chosen in the five countries: São Paulo and Goiânia in Brazil; New Delhi, Bombay, Hyderabad, Vijayawada, Cuddapah, Rahjamundhry and Warangal in India; Milan, Naples and Palermo in Italy; Nairobi, Mombasa and Kisumu in Kenya; Metro Manila (Caloocan City, Pasay City, Quezon City), Cebu, Davao and Olongapo in the Philippines.

The Country Teams were interdisciplinary, including economists, sociologists, anthropologists and psychologists, as well as NGO personnel and urban specialists. Efforts were made to form teams with a good mix of "action people" and academics. All members were nationals of the countries concerned and were provided support by UNICEF Urban Officers. A coordinator was selected for each Country Team, who became responsible for integrating the fact-finding and analytical reports.

Although each project was tailored to the needs of the specific country and UNICEF country programme, all Country Teams had the mandate to document three levels of problems:

(1) the general problems faced by all children in urban areas;

(2) the problems of urban children who live in poverty and deprivation, and who are candidates for more severe disadvantage; and

(3) the problems of urban children in especially difficult circumstances, those who have already "fallen through the cracks" and are facing situations of extreme disadvantage.

Country Teams were requested to analyse the causes of the problems affecting children (with special attention to the crises faced by families and communities), how children were affected, and what policies and programmes had been adopted to address the problems.

The basic steps were as follows:

(1) Reports on different aspects of the problems (demographic, sociological, anthropological, psychological) were prepared by each Country Team;

(2) Meetings and local coordination were provided for by the UNICEF Urban Officer (or the *Istituto degli Innocenti* coordinator) to facilitate the integration of different aspects of the study, and to produce a country report for publication by UNICEF ICDC. A longer local version of some of the reports was also published in the country;

(3) Urban forums were held in each city to discuss the implications for action;

(4) National forums were also held to facilitate a broader review of each country report and its implications for policy changes;

(5) A major international meeting was held in Florence in October 1992 to enable mayors and Country Teams to exchange information and ideas. This meeting is viewed within the context of the support UNICEF is providing to the implementation of the UN Convention on the Rights of the Child and the follow-up to the World Summit for Children, held in New York in September 1990. The goals for children in the 1990s agreed at that Summit include a commitment to "provide improved protection of children in especially difficult circumstances and tackle the root causes of such situations."

Innovative Aspects of the Approach

It was recognized early that individuals work in systems, and that change could best be generated by directly involving a variety of people in the Project. The various reports and meetings sponsored by this first project have, therefore, never been the product of researchers alone. To different degrees and according to the context, UNICEF Urban Officers, practitioners, the decision makers themselves, as well as children and their families, have contributed to the final product.

The approach decided upon by the Consultative Group, and subsequently adopted in the field, was "action-oriented," a term whose origins are worth clarifying. Action research is a concept that emerged in the United States in the 1950s and was taken up with enthusiasm by a number of individuals and groups. The United States Indian Service, which was defined in the early 1940s as a "potential laboratory through which ethnic relations in America could be studied" (Collier 1945), provides one of the first examples. Action research later became, with action-anthropology work in Chicago, a "synergistic collaboration" between social research (in the form of the microscopic analysis of social interaction) and the action agenda developed with the Fox Indians. Lewin (1947) emphasized the "many advances in theory [that] occur by studying social systems in action, and ... [the] danger of sterility in research oriented only to academic publication."

During the 1960s, there was a large governmental use of action research followed by a period of relative eclipse. Assessments in the 1970s emphasized both the pitfalls of action research and its importance. For anthropologists and sociologists, the issues raised were related to the ownership and control of the data and the reconciliation of professional values in anthropology and sociology with "mission-oriented" activities which were often government controlled. Competence in an academic setting was not always directly related to the capacity to negotiate a viable role in what Cora Du Bois (1980) called the "power, managerial administration."

Objective analyses of a number of urban projects in the United States (Szanton 1981, Gerard 1983) concluded that in order to be successful the projects needed: (1) a clear identification of the client, or clients, by all concerned, and the establishment of a relationship of mutual trust with those clients early on; (2) firm and consistent endorsement by those in authority; and (3) appropriate timing in the feedback of data and opinions. But even the more critical observers of the action-projects of the 1970s (Hall 1980, Gerard 1983, Cook 1984) agreed on the importance of encouraging the kind of collaborative research and development work broadly considered to be action research. Today, the concept has reached maturity and is still well accepted, despite some difficulties in its application.

In the Editor's Introduction to the recent book *Children, Youth and Families: The Action Research Relationships*, Robert N. Rappoport (1985) discusses the interplay between research and action in programmes benefiting children and families. Starting with an analysis of the mutually productive interaction between research and action in the hard sciences and technology, he proceeds to analyse the same relationships for the social sciences where scientific knowledge is less developed and standardized, and activities less in the control of the researcher. After discussing some of the very prominent contributions to the book by authors such as Alfred Kahn, Sheila Kamerman and Edward Zigler, Rappoport concludes that "for a productive interplay between research and action, several ingredients are necessary: financial support, an openness to new ways of thinking, competence and public credibility." He also emphasizes that the main problems are often the resistance to new ideas and approaches, as well as inadequate communication.

The action-research orientation of this study provided a challenge to the Country Teams in the five countries, including UNICEF Urban Officers, NGOs and government counterparts who were, in fact, the immediate "clients" of the study. It enabled and encouraged them to: (a) examine what they already knew and to discover what new information was available; (b) define the questions they would like answered; (c) provide continued guidance and ensure the usefulness of what was being produced; and (d) discuss and assess the action implications of the study, rather than just "shelving" the final reports. Ultimately the results were meant to bring improved development for urban children and families in distress.

The action orientation of the study also provided a challenge to academic researchers. They were encouraged to: (a) become more effective collaborators of action organizations; (b) focus on the identification and monitoring of the problems, old and new; (c) keep in mind the project's objective of emphasizing action-oriented initiatives; and (d) produce results which could be used for immediate advocacy with policy makers. This approach was quite new for many team members. Some were able to adapt; others remained more comfortable with traditional academic approaches. In these cases, the reports required substantial editing in order to give them a more decisive policy orientation.

Despite these differences, members of the Country Teams actively collaborated in advocacy efforts being made by the UNICEF Urban Officers in each country. Some of their more extensive reports have been, or are being, published in English or in the local language, usually under the joint sponsorship of the UNICEF country offices and various academic institutions. This is the case of the Brazilian report which UNICEF co-sponsored with FLACSO; the Indian reports, prepared in collaboration with the National Planning Commission; the Philippine reports, co-sponsored with De la Salle and the Ateneo de Manila Research and Policy Centres; and the Kenya report, prepared in collaboration with the University of Nairobi.

Again, the level and type of interaction between Country Team members and other organizations varied, at times protracted and very constructive, and at other times relatively short-lived and specific. Much depended on the personal capacity of each member to collaborate with the others. The interactions in each country had their own particular history, but they always created new connections and a new emphasis on children's problems. They also often prompted new projects at the governmental level, in which team members became centrally involved. The child-focused centres set up by FLACSO in Brazil, the revision of laws relating to children and families being carried out by the Kenyan Law Reform Commission, and the project on children and women implemented by the India National Planning Commission are examples of this multiplier effect.

Approaches and Audiences

The compiled information has come from many sources. The Country Teams have reviewed published articles, university theses or research reports, and analysed the reports of specific organizations. They have identified and interviewed key informants. They have analysed programme evaluations and made rapid assessments of work in the field. They have also interviewed children and their families, discussed issues with street educators and described community and city settings and their modes of operation.

The organizers agreed early that an effort should be made to demystify the research data and make it available to a wide range of people who could help to bring change. The Country Teams have identified, and prepared material for, the following key actors:

- national and international development experts, technicians, academics, and substantive media experts who require more data on project aims and methodology;

- regional and municipal policy makers;

- NGO implementors, staff in institutions, street educators, UNICEF programme staff;

- other audiences, such as National Committees for UNICEF, development educators and academic institutions;

- teachers and school systems, communities, parents and the children themselves.

Occasional papers and technical handbooks have been specifically targeted to one or more of the above audiences. In addition, multipurpose publications, such as the Innocenti Studies, based on the material collected by each Country Team, have been prepared by journalists and writers in collaboration with ICDC (Black 1991b, Swift 1991, Chatterjee 1992, Lorenzo 1992, Munyakho 1992) to provide new insights for readers who might not wish to read a more formal report. Ultimately, some of the results of this book will also be presented as handbooks and summaries to answer the specific questions.

WHY URBAN CHILDREN?: THE DIMENSIONS OF THE PROBLEM

There are compelling reasons for paying particular attention to children in the urban environments of developing countries. Because of rapid urbanization, the number of urban children has been growing steadily over the last few decades, and such growth is likely to continue. According to United Nations estimates (Donohue 1982), there were 369 million children under the age of 15 years living in urban agglomerations in developing countries in

1980. By 2000, approximately 23 percent of the total world population of under-15 children will live in the urban agglomerations of Asia, and 21 percent in those of Latin America (Caritas 1986). It is also estimated that four out of ten children in the developing world will be born in an urban centre by 2000, and six out of ten by 2025, if urbanization trends do not change fundamentally. In developing countries, the young now constitute the majority of the population in many urban areas.

In the heavily urbanized countries of the industrialized North, the situation presents a quite different demographic picture. Because of reduced mortality and fertility rates, the proportion of children 0–18 years of age has been steadily diminishing. In Italy, for example, this age group constituted 29 percent of the total population in 1950, while by 1990 it represented only 21 percent (Lorenzo 1992). However, because industrialized countries are largely urban, most children in those countries do indeed live in urban areas. Thus the pressures and hazards of urbanization affect people whose futures risk being severely compromised.

Urbanization Trends

For centuries, global urban growth rates were modest. Only 3 percent of the world's population lived in cities during the early nineteenth century. However, with industrialization, the pattern changed dramatically. The urban proportion grew from 14 percent in 1920, to 25 percent in 1950, to 43 percent in 1980 (UNFPA 1986), and is projected to reach as high as 60 percent by 2025. Urban population percentages will remain unevenly distributed, however, with the most highly industrialized countries reaching levels of up to 80 percent, and the least industrialized ones, reaching around 42 percent (Hauser and Gardner 1980, Armstrong and McGee 1985, Caritas 1986).

As Table 1.1 shows, the least urbanized countries in the world, which are also generally the poorest, tend to be experiencing the highest urban population growth. This is in part a result of the depressed state of their agricultural sectors which has led to extensive rural-to-urban migration. The situation is expected to continue for at least the next decade.

However, rural-to-urban migration is not the only reason, nor often even the main one, behind urban growth. Another important element is the natural population increase that occurs in some very large cities. Despite declining birth rates and decreases in rural-to-urban migration, the populations of many large cities in Latin America, Southeast Asia and East Asia, for example, continue to grow due to the size of the initial population base (Preston 1988, McGee 1971, Armstrong and McGee 1985). In the developing world, the increase in the total urban population level will not be counterbalanced by a reduction in the rural population, which is actually expected to increase, again largely from natural growth, to 2,868.5 million by 2000, from 1,037.3 million in 1920 (Armstrong and McGee 1985). In turn, the natural

Table 1.1. Trends and Projections in Urban Population by
Region (Urban Inhabitants in Millions and As Proportion
of Total Population, 1950–2000[1])

Region	1950 (% of total)	1970 (% of total)	1990 (% of total)	2000 (% of total)
Africa	32.2	82.7	217.4	352.4
	(14.5)	(22.9)	(33.9)	(40.7)
Latin America & Caribbean	68.6	163.6	320.5	411.3
	(41.5)	(57.3)	(71.5)	(76.4)
North America	106.1	167.1	207.4	227.7
	(63.9)	(73.8)	(75.2)	(77.3)
Asia	265.5	481.1	1070.4	1585.4
	(16.4)	(22.9)	(34.4)	(42.7)
Europe	221.8	306.6	365.9	392.2
	(56.5)	(66.7)	(73.4)	(76.7)
Former USSR	70.8	137.6	189.9	208.1
	(39.3)	(56.7)	(65.8)	(67.5)
Oceania	7.8	13.7	18.7	21.5
	(61.3)	(70.7)	(70.6)	(71.3)
Developing world	285.6	635.8	1514.7	2251.4
	(17.0)	(24.7)	(37.1)	(45.1)
Rest of the world	448.2	698.6	875.5	946.2
	(53.8)	(66.6)	(72.6)	(74.9)

[1]Projected. Source: United Nations (1991).

growth of rural populations will continue to provide the basis for rural-to-urban migrations in the future.

Another important factor is the growth of primate cities. Primacy is measured by the population of the largest centre in relation to the second largest, or the following three (the four-city primacy index), or the following nine (the ten-city primacy index). In the last three decades, Buenos Aires, São Paulo, Santiago del Chile, Caracas, Mexico City and Cairo, followed by Bangkok, Manila, Seoul, Baghdad, Lima and Karachi, and, more recently, Lagos, Nairobi and many others, have grown to dominate their nations' urban systems because of the concentration of economic activities. This primacy resulted in part from the rapid economic growth between the 1950s and the early 1970s, conditions which are unlikely to return in the foreseeable future given the economic recessions, the debt burdens, the protectionist barriers around Western markets, and the inefficient leadership and poor economic performance of most developing countries. Other historical and political factors include the often metropolis-oriented colonial economic organizations, the process of decolonization after the Second World War with the accompanying institutional restructuring, and the removal of colonial restrictions on the free flow of people from rural to urban areas.

The primacy of the largest city in each country seems, however, to be declining in some regions. Until recently in Latin America, the annual population growth rate of the largest city was usually higher than all, or most, other large cities. However, this trend has begun to change in practically all of the more populated countries in the region, with non-primate Latin American cities growing at rates which are relatively higher than their primate cities in many cases. At the same time, medium and small centres (about 50,000 to 500,000 people, and 10,000 to 49,999 people, respectively) are growing relatively faster than rural settlements (fewer than 10,000 inhabitants) in many Latin American countries. The extent to which these changes are indicative of similar transformations in other developing regions needs to be studied.

Latin America and the Caribbean together make up the most urbanized region of the developing world, but different countries have urbanized at different speeds. Declining rural populations have been evident in Argentina and Chile since the 1950s, in Uruguay since the 1960s, in Brazil, Jamaica and Venezuela since the 1970s, and in Cuba since the 1980s (Hardoy 1992).

Asia was relatively late in urbanizing: the transformation of most countries really only began in the 1980s. In the 1950s, nearly all Asian countries were characterized by a low urbanization rate and an urban hierarchy often already dominated by one colonial primate city (for example Manila, Jakarta, Bangkok, Bombay and Colombo). In 1960, the urban populations of China, or even Indonesia, for example, constituted only 19 percent and 14.6 percent of the total population, respectively, while North Korea (40.2 percent) and the Philippines (30.3 percent) had already reached higher urbanization levels (Table 1.2).

By the 1990s, Asia manifested a chequered pattern of urbanization with wide disparities. Rates range from just over 20 percent in Sri Lanka and Thailand to 71 percent in the more industrialized countries. Current demographic trends suggest that Asia as a whole will reach urbanization levels of between 35 and 43 percent by 2000 (Armstrong and McGee 1985, Fawcett et al. 1984, United Nations 1991a). Led by the population giants of China and India, which between them have more than one third of the world's million-population cities, Asia now has more large cities with more people living in them than any other continent (Dwyer 1979).

Africa is not highly urbanized by global standards, but the trend in that direction has been extremely rapid during the last three decades, and the rate is expected to reach 42 percent by 2000. Depending on their economic structure, different countries have reached different levels of urbanization. Africa

Table 1.2. Proportion of Urban Population in Selected Countries
(in Percentages for 1960, 1990, 2000[1])

	1960	1990	2000		1960	1990	2000
Asia				**Latin America & Caribbean**			
Cambodia	10.3	11.6	14.5	Argentina	73.6	86.3	88.8
China	19.0	33.4	47.3	Brazil	44.9	74.9	80.6
India	18.0	27.0	32.3	Cuba	54.9	74.9	79.9
Indonesia	14.6	30.5	39.5	Ecuador	34.4	56.0	63.8
Iraq	42.9	71.3	75.3	Guatemala	32.4	39.4	44.1
Korea, DR	40.2	59.8	63.1	Mexico	50.8	72.6	77.4
Malaysia	25.2	43.0	51.2	Uruguay	80.1	85.5	87.3
Pakistan	22.1	32.0	37.9				
Philippines	30.3	42.6	48.9				
Sri Lanka	17.9	21.4	24.2				
Thailand	12.5	22.6	29.4	**Europe**			
				France	62.4	74.3	76.7
Africa				Italy	59.4	68.9	72.4
Kenya	7.4	23.6	31.8	Netherlands	85.0	88.5	89.2
Morocco	29.3	48.0	55.2	Poland	47.9	61.8	66.1
Nigeria	14.4	35.2	43.3	Portugal	22.1	33.6	39.6
Senegal	31.9	38.4	44.5	Sweden	72.6	84.0	85.6
Tanzania, UR	4.7	32.8	46.5	UK	85.7	89.1	90.0
Uganda	5.1	10.4	13.8				

[1]Projected. Source: United Nations (1991b).

will have an important share of the world's largest cities by 2030–35, since their rates are growing at double or more the world rate. Nairobi is expected to reach 10 million, Lagos 26 million, Kinshasa 12 million; staggering rates considering that no city in sub-Saharan Africa exceeded 500,000 inhabitants in 1945.

Western Europe experienced the rural-to-urban demographic transition much earlier than other regions. Its urban population increased "only" fivefold in the span of 80 years (1870–1950), while it is expected that from 1950 to 2030 the number of urban dwellers in the developing countries will increase sixteenfold (Deelstra and de Waart 1989). The populations of western Europe are now aging (with consequently reduced fertility rates) and demographic projections indicate overall declines starting sometime after 2000. However, estimates may be modified by a number of factors, including the influx of migrants from developing countries and the higher fertility rates among migrant groups.

There has been a recent swing in European patterns of urbanization towards urban-to-rural migration. People are moving away from the city towards suburban areas and into adjacent small towns, which have been increasing in size; commuters repopulate the city during the day. Milan, Turin and other large cities in Italy are showing this pattern very clearly. At times, large offices or businesses are also moving to the suburbs or even into rural areas in search of space and safer surroundings.

Overall projections for the period 1980–2000 show the urban population of the developing world increasing by 1.15 billion people. By 2000 eight of the largest urban settlements in the world will be in developing countries, and only one each in North America and Japan. This exemplifies a worldwide reversal: in 1900, only one of the 10 largest cities was in what is now termed the developing world; by 1950, this number had risen to five; by 1980, of the world's 255 cities of over one million people, almost half (i.e., 116) were in the developing world, as were 15 of the world's 26 cities with over five million people (Hardoy and Satterthwaite 1989, Olpadwala and Goldsmith 1992). According to estimates by the United Nations Development Programme (UNDP), there will be 50 cities of more than four million inhabitants in the developing world by 2000, the number is expected to rise to 114 by 2025 (UNDP 1989).

Such projections do not take into account changing political, environmental and economic factors. Calcutta, for example, received over 2 million refugees after the partition of India in 1947, and this explains projections of up to 40–50 million inhabitants when in fact, it is unlikely that the population of Calcutta will exceed 15 million by 2000. Similarly, droughts or wars have led to the particularly high actual rates of population growth in Addis Ababa, Khartoum, Kampala, Luanda and other cities in Africa. Assembly plants set up by foreign companies in northern Mexico (Ciudad Juarez, Tijuana, Mexicali and others) attracted migrants from rural areas, causing rapid population increases. Growth began to slow down in the 1980s because of changes in the North American market.

It is also unlikely that many primate cities will continue to grow at currently projected rates simply because such growth would be unsustainable. In many cases, the inability of the urban service-oriented economies to develop the complex activities to procure and distribute sufficient food and water for such fast-growing populations is glaringly obvious. Furthermore, many primate and large cities are extending over unsuitable sites, in areas subject to periodical floods (Buenos Aires, Asuncion, Dacca, Bangkok, Calcutta), earthquakes (Mexico City, Lima, Guatemala City, Managua, Santiago del Chile, San Salvador), landslides (Rio de Janeiro, Hong Kong, Quito, La Paz), sea-tides (Guayaquil), hurricanes (Manila), and other natural disasters.

All of these arguments suggest that: (a) the past 30 years provide a poor guide to what will happen in the next 30 years; (b) stagnant or declining economic bases will probably slow the rate of population growth of many large cities; (c) despite this slowdown in the growth rate, the natural increase of the already-huge populations will still add hundreds of thousands of

Table 1.3. Recent and Projected Population Growth Rates (1955–2025)

	1955–60	1985–90	2005–10	2020–25
World	1.86	1.73	1.33	0.98
More-developed regions	1.25	0.53	0.32	0.18
Less-developed regions	2.14	2.10	1.56	1.13

Source: Xenos (1993).

people to primate and other large cities every year, forcing governments to meet unprecedented challenges just to keep these cities functioning and to prevent living conditions from worsening (Hardoy 1992).

Beyond the Numbers

The demographic dimension of the problems of urban children requires special attention. Simply quoting total urban numbers or rates of urbanization does not do justice to the children's situation and may actually be distorting. By disaggregating the age groups, one can get a clearer picture of the urban demographic situation.

Mortality rates decline steadily with economic development and the associated rising standards of living. This usually results in a period of "population explosion" until fertility rates begin to decline, which may be several decades later. Industrialized countries have already experienced this demographic transition, and are currently showing the consequent declines in population growth. In areas of Asia and Latin America, fertility rates have begun to fall as have population growth rates. In most of Africa, on the other hand, while mortality rates are still falling, fertility rates remain essentially unchanged, and population growth is consequently still accelerating, as a comparison of recent and projected population growth rates shows (Table 1.3).

If one focuses on children and youth by world regions, there are still different consequences of the demographic transition in different regions. In Africa as a whole, where fertility rates are still very high and mortality rates are declining only slowly, the child and youth population has reached very high levels, and is still rising significantly. In Latin America, where there has been a decline in both mortality and fertility rates, the percentage of children and youth in the total population began to decrease in the 1970s.

However, even these regional patterns are averages of the heterogeneous experiences of individual countries. The demographic situation in the five countries taking part in the Urban Child Project substantiates these points. In

Kenya, the number of children under 15 years of age exceeds 30 percent, a rate that, even according to the most optimistic projections, will not start to decline until after 2000. The overall number of children has diminished slightly in India, Brazil and the Philippines, but not yet for the 5–14 age group whose numbers are steadily increasing. Italy has experienced low mortality rates as well as a very sharp decrease in total fertility rates during the last few decades of rapid economic development. Its population reproduction rate is negative, and fertility rates are projected to decline still further. Even within Italy, however, there are important north/south distinctions.

These trends also establish absolute changes in population sizes for the relevant age groups.

0–4 age group. The developing countries are the major contributors to increases in this age group. Africa is by far the largest contributor, mainly because of the high fertility rates throughout the region. Asia is also a large contributor, especially East and South Asia, while rates for Southeast Asia are sharply negative, mainly because Indonesian and Thai fertility rates are declining.

5–14 age group. World growth in the number of children in this age group is again dominated by the developing countries, while after 1980, the numbers of children in industrialized countries began to diminish. Growth in numbers of children from developing countries, is, in absolute terms, dominated by the Asian region, with the countries of South Asia contributing dispropor-tionately.

15–24 age group. The patterns are generally similar. The number of youth and young adults is declining in industrialized countries and continuing to grow rapidly in developing countries. Africa and Asia are the major con-tributors, though the Asian net contribution is small because some countries are gaining in this age group while others are losing.

In conclusion, in most developing countries, absolute numbers of children and youth will continue to rise for decades to come, but there will be consid-erable variations by age groups, regions and countries. On the basis of the rather optimistic assumptions about fertility decline made by the United Nations, the numbers of children in all age groups may start falling by 2010–2020. Moreover, the combination of recent fertility and mortality trends has resulted in a dramatic, although temporary, bulge in child and youth numbers. In many societies, such as Thailand or Indonesia, there was a "child bulge" in the 1970s, which "aged" into a significant "youth bulge" in the 1980s. The largest-ever global generation of children will be born in the 1990s.

We are therefore faced with a situation of severe demographic pressure in many countries in the world, especially in cities, and with prospects for rapid rates of growth in the numbers of children and youth for some decades to come. Now is clearly the time to initiate action on behalf of this, and future, generations of children.

Migration

Migration can be from rural to urban areas or between urban areas of similar or different sizes. Rural-to-urban migration is particularly significant when countries are still urbanizing, as is the case for India or Kenya. Frequently, the urban locations to which rural populations migrate are also economically depressed and therefore offer limited opportunities (Preston 1988). Migration can also, as mentioned earlier, become urban-to-rural migration in the very urbanized developed countries.

While the native-born urban, rural and overall populations show more or less the same demographic structure in terms of age composition and sex ratios, the demographic structure of the urban migrant population is highly selective and may vary quite considerably across countries. Distortions in terms of age and sex are thus introduced in the urban demographic structure by these migration patterns.

In much of Southeast Asia, urban migrants have tended since the late 1970s to be predominantly young (adolescents or young adults) and single females (Fawcett et al. 1984). The same is true of Latin America where the shift from a mostly male, to a mostly female, migration pattern occurred earlier, and was already apparent by the 1970s. Throughout South Asia, rural-to-urban migrants are still predominantly young males, both single and married. Similar trends are still being reported for Africa, although there is a significant undercurrent of young women, often with children, starting to move to urban areas.

Migration has potentially important implications for changing gender roles and for household reorganization, with an increased emphasis on the nuclear family and considerable distances separating the extended family. Migration challenges the traditional structural and patriarchal ordering of family authority, particularly in India, and in some cases Kenya. It not only affects male/female relationships within the family, but also female/female ones, especially the relationship between mother-in-law and daughter-in-law in the more emphatically male-centred Indian or Kenyan families, or among sisters in Southeast Asian families. Migration often enhances the position of women within the family, increasing their responsibility towards other family members. Women migrants are given more responsibility within their families. Young girls migrating for work become important family supporters in the Philippines, for example. Subsequent attempts to impose restrictions on them can create the basis for family disagreements.

Conversely, the male position within the family is often diminished by migration. Male authority is undermined by economic insecurity and the male's increasing inability to perform his assigned role as the sole, or at least the main, economic provider. These changing roles create tensions within the family. At the same time, migration can cause changes in the underlying nature of family association. Family ties (husband-wife, for example) become more emotional and voluntary; the conjugal relationship is emphasized at the expense of the consanguineal tie (Kerckhoff 1972). Earlier family relationships may be undermined, and new family and gender relations reconstructed.

GROWING UP URBAN, POOR AND DEPRIVED

From seats of "civilization" to breeding grounds for violence, the city can arouse sharply conflicting images. Cities are commonly identified as modern and technologically advanced. In Europe and elsewhere, they are often considered centres of progress, home to higher learning, knowledge, the media and the arts. They attract migrants with their glitter and liveliness, their potential for improved living standards and entertainment. From this perspective, it is easy to forget that cities are also the breeding grounds for some of the most abject poverty and deprivation.

In the North, there is also a widespread belief that the city and its streets are places of violence and subversion, where people — and children — are prey to abuse, drugs, prostitution and crime. The evidence from the United States, Germany and the United Kingdom, as well as from Brazil would certainly seem to confirm this impression (Hall 1988). Both positions are, however, extreme and potentially distorting.

Worldwide, as we have seen, almost half of the children 0–18 years of age are growing up in cities, and that number is likely to increase. But what does it mean to grow up in today's cities? The Urban Child Project analysed 21 different cities.

The Deteriorating Environment

The current rise in urban populations comes with a host of problems, many of which are closely linked to the environment. Pollution of air, water and land has quite likely reached its worst levels yet in both industrialized and developing nations. In the primate city of Bangkok, where virtually all of Thailand's heavy industry is concentrated (including more than 90 percent of the country's manufacturers of chemicals, dry cell batteries, paints, medicinal drugs, textiles as well as four out of seven lead smelters) without appropriately enforced environment regulations, pollution has recently reached intolerable levels (Hardoy and Satterthwaite 1989). In Cubatao, an industrial city outside São Paulo, or in Mexico City, people are harmed daily by the dense cloud of toxic smoke that perpetually darkens the city.

Air is also polluted by fires used for home heating and cooking. Water is polluted by household sewage and by surface runoff of soil and debris from construction activities. According to UNDP estimates, the number of people without adequate water and sanitation is increasing. When garbage and industrial wastes are collected, they are often not properly disposed of, thus adding to enormous land fills, the multiplication of vermin, and further water and air pollution, including toxic drainage. In Brazil, for example, where less than half of the urban population has its garbage collected, only 3 percent is properly disposed of; 63 percent is dumped in streams and rivers; and 34 percent is left in unprotected open spaces. Much of the time, however, garbage is not collected and runs into streams and rivers, adding toxicity, obstructing water flow and contributing to flooding.

Transportation activities, mainly resulting from the distance between residence and work place, also contribute to the deterioration of the urban environment. Approximately 40 percent of all urban territory may be taken up by the road network. In addition, transportation activities generate considerable solid waste (including metals, plastics and rubber) and cause water damage. The major problem, however, is air pollution from exhaust pipes, as industrialized countries have learned — and developing countries are fast discovering.

Children are the most vulnerable to the effects of environmental degradation. They are more exposed to airborne environmental pollution than adults are because they are usually much more active and inhale greater quantities of pollutants relative to their weight. Their body size and work or play activities bring them into greater contact with heavy pollutants, such as lead close to the ground or in the soil itself. Children are also less aware of environmental dangers, particularly before the age of 12 years, and are therefore developmentally less likely to make a conscious effort to avoid them (Michelson 1984).

Children can be seen playing, washing themselves, and drinking the polluted waters of Bangkok's canals, or roaming through the uncollected garbage in Nairobi and Manila. In 1987, for example, approximately 25 percent of solid wastes generated in the city of Bangkok remained uncollected and were mostly dumped onto vacant land or in canals and rivers and according to Hardoy et al. (1990):

> Only 2 per cent of the population is connected to a sewer system; human wastes are generally disposed of through septic tanks and cess pools, and their effluents — as well as waste water from sinks, laundries, baths and kitchens — are discharged into storm water drains and into canals.

Because of their greater vulnerability to pollution, children have a higher occurrence than adults of respiratory diseases leading to death, even in the highly polluted urban areas of such relatively developed countries as Israel (Goren 1989). Infants and children in developing countries are several hundred times more likely to die from diarrhoea, pneumonia and measles than are children in Europe or North America. In 1986, an estimated 14.1 million children under five years of age died as a result of these illnesses; 98 percent of those deaths were in the developing world (Hardoy et al. 1990).

When they do not die, children living in such extremely polluted environments may grow up stunted and handicapped. Tests in school classrooms in Bangkok showed that noise from traffic, construction and industry reached 76 to 95 decibels (Pathumvanit and Liengcharernsit 1989). The Organisation for Economic Co-operation and Development recommendation is that outdoor noise should not exceed 65 decibels for people's well-being indoors. Research in industrialized countries has similarly shown that high noise levels can have seriously debilitating effects on children.

A definite increase in the incidence of cancer and allergy symptoms has also been detected in the urban areas of industrialized countries, due to air pollution from industrial emissions, vehicle exhausts, tobacco smoke and chemicals from building materials combined with poor ventilation. These factors have been connected with the increase in cases of asthma in large cities (Köhler and Jacobsson 1991). While similar research is less available in the developing world, we should expect these factors to be particularly, and increasingly, prominent there as well.

Many aspects of environmental deterioration affect all the inhabitants of a city. Some, however, are specific to the urban slum and squatter areas. The shortage of water, sewage and sanitation forces parents and their children to use particularly polluted outlets. Overcrowding increases the possibility of the spread of infections and contagious diseases. These problems are usually severely compounded by poverty.

Poverty and Redistribution

Poverty is defined differently in different countries and may change over time. In India, for example, the absolute poverty line is established at the monetary equivalent of 2,100 calories per capita per day in urban areas. In urban India in 1987–88, approximately 42 million people, or 20.1 percent of the total urban population, had incomes falling below the absolute poverty line (Bose 1992). In Nairobi, by 1981, 55 percent of all households were categorized as having low or very low incomes (Manundu 1991). In the developing world, 1.2 billion people (29.5 percent of its population) live in absolute poverty, just barely surviving. About half of them are urban.

During the last three decades, income-growth disparities have been steadily increasing and redistribution has been worsening across the North-South/rich-poor country watershed. The wealthiest 20 percent of the world's population receives on average seven times the income of the poorest 20 percent. Between 1960 and 1989, the countries with the richest 20 percent of world population increased their share of global GNP (Gross National Product) from 70.2 to 82.7 percent. The countries with the poorest GNP saw their share fall from 2.3 percent to 1.4 percent. During 1980–89, the "lost" decade for development, average global growth was higher than during 1965–80, but the developing country share diminished considerably. However measured, the redistribution of resources, already unequal worldwide, has been worsening at alarming rates, particularly in the South (UNDP 1992).

Furthermore, redistribution of resources within developing countries, already inadequate, is, not surprisingly, continuing to show negative trends. In Brazil, for example, the top 20 percent of the population receives 26 times the income of the bottom 20 percent. As a result of urbanization, the urban poor now represent a growing percentage of the global poor. Among them, there are large numbers of homeless and illiterate adults (especially women) and children who do not go to school or who have dropped out of school. A large proportion of Brazilians living in poverty, for example, are children, and in 1989, nearly three fourths (71 percent) of these impoverished children lived in urban areas (see Brazil chapter). In the industrialized North, redistribution within countries has been affected by recession. In Italy, for example, pockets of extreme poverty still exist in Palermo and Naples, as well as in the wealthy northern cities which have attracted a large migrant population.

Lack of Appropriate Shelter

There is no guarantee of a solid roof or appropriate shelter for many of the children of the urban poor. Most are likely to live in shabby tenements or makeshift shacks, as documented by Hardoy (1992):

> A recent report published by the Share and Care Apostolate for Poor Shelters (SCAPS) in Manila reveals the quantitative dimensions of the problem. In 1990, Metro Manila had around 8.2 million inhabitants, 654 officially recognized squatter communities and 3.5 million urban poor (54.7 per cent of the population of Metro Manila) who lived crowded into 5.3 per cent of the land of the metropolis. In Quito, according to the 1982 National Population Censuses, there were 144 precarious settlements with 388,995 people, which represented 47.3 per cent of the population of the metropolitan area. Bangkok had over 1,000 slums and squatter settlements when the city population was 5.5 million in 1985. In 13 selected metropolitan areas of Africa, Asia and Latin America, with a total population of 43.8 million people in the early 1970s, it was estimated that 18.1 million lived in squatter settlements, or 41.2 per cent of the aggregate population. As living conditions for the urban poor in developing countries have apparently worsened, it is quite possible 50 per cent or more of the urban population in developing countries, or at least 600 million urban inhabitants, live in "life- and health-threatening" circumstances. It is also likely that 45 per cent of them are children between 0 and 14 years of age.

Overcrowding is widespread in poor communities. In India, more than half of the urban households occupy a single room, with an average occupancy per room of 4.4 persons (Gilbert and Gugler 1983).

The situation in smaller cities in developing countries is also alarming. Quantitatively, they may have only three or four large squatter or urban poor settlements and these may appear less grim than the settlements in larger cities. Their inhabitants, however, face the same problems of uncertain land tenure, decaying buildings and grossly inadequate services. Many habitations were only meant to be makeshift shacks, but have been used for years. Distances often compound the problems. Schools are so inconveniently located and distant from a long-established squatter settlement in Warangal, in Andhra Pradesh, that flooding prevents children from getting to school during the monsoon season. In Kenya, students living in one neighbourhood of Kisumu risked bad cuts and serious falls if they attempted to reach their school in the nearby wealthier residential area by crossing a small, foul-smelling river usually full of debris, especially during the rainy season.

In general, squatters occupy small proportions of the total urban area, and usually the worst locations, including sites subject to flooding, landslides and high pollution; or sites bordering, or even invading, garbage dumps. Squatter households are often subject to natural disasters (floods and earthquakes, for example), or to man-made ones, such as malicious fires or relocations. Between 1986 and 1990, 19,006 houses were demolished and 27,962 families dislocated in Metro Manila. The Government announced that it planned to demolish 220 poor communities during 1991 because "they are obstructing infrastructural projects" (Porio 1991). Until these communities are demolished, inhabitants live in a climate of anxiety and constant crisis. When families and children are displaced, additional expenses and loss of belongings, familiar surroundings and support systems create new difficulties.

Working in the Urban Informal Sector

Growing up urban for poor children usually means being closely involved in informal-sector activities, on their own or with their parents. Informal incomes represent over 50 percent of all incomes in most cities of the developing world. The urban poor, adults and children alike, are engaged in an apparently limitless number of informal activities in order to improve their meagre incomes.

In the large city of Chonburi (central Thailand), for instance, informal sales of prepared food fed increasing numbers of busy middle-class families of government officials and businessmen and women, and provided the main or supplemented incomes of almost 60 percent of the population. These self-employed poor generated a very sizeable amount of capital monthly at city level (Blanc Szanton 1985).

A National Demographic Survey in the Philippines conducted in 1968 on almost 8,000 households nationwide showed that 39 percent of the urban population 15 to 65 years of age in Metro Manila, and 59 percent in the secondary cities, worked in the informal sector. Of these informal-sector workers, 81 percent in the Manila sample and 64 percent in the secondary city sample were involved in tertiary-sector activities, such as personal and distributive services (vendors, housemaids, barbers, and so forth), rather than transformative or extractive ones (Koo and Smith 1983).

These economic activities are particularly important for women and for migrants. The same study found that approximately half of the recent migrants in Metro Manila (defined as those who have been in the city seven years or less) worked in the informal sector, compared with 33 percent of the native-born. In secondary Philippine cities, the proportion was 64 percent of recent migrants, compared with 39 percent of the native-born. Informal-sector workers were also predominantly female (61 percent) (Koo and Smith 1983). Children often help their mothers, and are thus introduced to the trade (Blanc Szanton 1972).

In Africa, the informal sector represents a very considerable proportion of urban activities. Nairobi was, as early as 1971, characterized as a "self-help" city because, as a result of its rapidly expanding and under-serviced population, one third of all people in the city lived in unauthorized housing and 30,000 jobs were not officially counted (ILO 1972). This self-help economy created more jobs, absorbed more people, and expanded faster than the so-called "modern" economy of the city (Hake 1977). But the problems of that sector are powerfully illustrated in a case study carried out on the *matatu* mode of public transportation, composed of privately owned vehicles. These effectively service the poor, but are constantly harassed by the municipal administration (Lee-Smith 1989).

In India, although child labour in the formal sector of industry has been virtually eliminated, children continue to work in the informal sector, often encouraged by their parents. The typical child worker comes from a poor and large family, and has usually dropped out of school early. Boys work in cottage industries, characterized by non-mechanized, labour-intensive operations, and working conditions which are often hazardous and exploitative. Others are self-employed, selling newspapers, picking scrap or waste material; or apprentices in carpet making or embroidery trades; or, in rare cases, even bonded workers. Girls move in a more protected and restricted environment than boys do. They normally work in their homes, or in all-female units of the weaving and match-making industries, and their wages are consistently lower than those of their male counterparts (Bose 1992).

The important contribution made by informal-sector activities to the economy of the city is rarely recognized by city administrators and planners. The resourcefulness of the urban poor is usually unsupported and often causes them to come into conflict with the law. Children especially are not protected from exploitation by employers.

Exposure to Drugs and Organized Crime

In many poor urban neighbourhoods in Brazil and Italy, and increasingly in the Philippines, Kenya and India, families are being exposed to high levels of violence from local petty drug dealing tied to organized crime. Even worse, many children begin using drugs or become involved in the drug trade, as they are cheaper to hire, are considered expendable and receive less severe legal punishment than adults. The problem of drug-related violence has become so serious in some neighbourhoods that social workers have "given up," and no longer dare to visit families there.

During the 1950s and 1960s, the drug trade was viewed by the industrialized world as a problem confined to the US where drug users had increased from a few thousand in the 1940s to over 250,000 by the end of the 1960s. During the 1970s, however, it became evident that drugs were no longer an exclusively US phenomenon. Drug use had rapidly expanded; first to France, Italy and Holland, and, by the end of the decade, to the rest of western Europe. According to conservative estimates, the number of drug users in western Europe at least tripled between 1975 and 1980, while, in the United States, it doubled between 1977 and 1979 (Arlacchi 1988). Although many Third World countries were drug producers during this period, they argued that their production was mostly traditional and small-scale, and that the use of hard drugs was relatively limited.

In the early 1970s, the Colombian "drug lords" shifted from *marijuana* to *cocaine* production and began to penetrate the US market. By 1982 cocaine was being used by about 4.2 million people in the United States, including the middle classes and young people (N.N.I.C.C. 1984). Its ready availability as well as its cheap utilization as *crack* (a form of free-base cocaine at one tenth of the price) became a cause for great concern. During the 1980s, cocaine production spread to other countries, such as Bolivia, and became semi-industrial. With strong organized crime networks among Italian immigrants in South America (Peru, Brazil, Argentina), Italy has been the almost exclusive European importer of cocaine since the 1980s, while continuing to export Sicilian-produced heroin.[1]

In Italy, the combination of drugs and organized crime was the fifth largest business in the country in 1990, accounting for a yearly turnover of $17.6 billion and "employment" for over 170,000 people. Price markups for heroin can be as high as 3,000 percent between wholesale and final retail; a 1985 study in the region of Campania showed profits ranging from 370 percent for large-scale distributors to 12 percent for user-dealers (Arlacchi and Lewis 1985). Elsewhere as well the drug market involves people at many different levels and has increasingly spawned submarkets requiring cheap labour. According to Kaplan (1977), some 20,000 people dealt daily in drugs on New York streets in the late 1970s. Their risks are high, but the returns are greater than those of being unemployed or severely underpaid in the informal sector.

Developing countries have now become both larger producers and larger consumers of hard drugs. Thailand, with about one sixth the population of the United States, had as many heroin addicts as the US by the early 1980s (Brigantini 1990). In Latin America drug trade and abuse was increased in Mexico and Brazil, as well as Colombia, Peru and Bolivia. Parts of Africa,

South Asia and the Middle East were also showing clear evidence of increasing use (Nigeria, Egypt, Pakistan and Iran, for example).

The use of inhalants and solvents, commonly available products not controlled by international crime rings, rose simultaneously throughout the world. In 1982, studies in the United Kingdom showed an incidence of solvent use ranging from 6 to 8 percent in schools and clubs (but only 1.6 percent nationally). The number of deaths due to volatile substance inhalation (often gas fuels and aerosols) rose in the UK from 12 to 25 per million inhabitants for boys 10–19 years old and from 1 to 4 per million inhabitants for girls between 1983 and 1988 (Ives 1990).

Substance abuse is heavily concentrated among the poor (Le Dain et al. 1973, Cohen 1976, Fauzi 1987, Sing Sandlin 1989, Chambers 1973, Braucht et al. 1973). Inexpensive solvents and other volatile substances are the preferred drugs of young people in their early teen years. In some industrialized countries, solvent use has been reported more frequently among teenage boys (10–14) (Le Dain et al. 1973); with adolescence users often turn to other drugs (Cohen 1976, Korman et al. 1977).

Substance abuse in Brazil among primary school children showed a net increase between 1987 and 1989 (Table 1.4). The use of inhalants by Brazilian children has increased dramatically since the 1970s, and, as a survey of schoolchildren in ten Brazilian cities in 1987 showed, many children prefer inhalants to other drugs. In that survey, 27 percent stated they had used drugs and 19 percent solvents, which are particularly common among 10 to 12 year olds and street children. A 1986–87 survey of street children found that 68 percent of the respondents in São Paulo had used drugs recently, most often solvents (80 percent), and 45 percent used large quantities of solvents daily (Carlini-Cotrim and Carlini 1987).[2]

Similarly, a recent survey in the Philippines showed that about half of the street children (54 percent) and institutionalized children (51 percent) interviewed used drugs. But very few school children report using drugs (Dangerous Drug Board, 1990). In Kenya, street educators have reported apparent increases in drug use, but the phenomenon has not been well documented. However, clear indications of substantial nicotine and alcohol abuse are evident (around 50 percent in rural areas and 2 to 5 admittances per day in some urban hospitals) (Otieno et al. 1979).

Crack and *ecstasy*, used prevalently in northern countries, are also alternatives to costlier drugs.[3] The risk that both will spread to the South is growing; crack has already appeared in the Philippines, brought in by migrants on their visits home.

New Deprivations

Some of the most commonly used indicators for human deprivation include lack of access to health services, safe water, adequate sanitation and other

Table 1.4. Drug Use Among Primary School (Grades I and II)
Children in Brazil (1987 and 1989)

Year	Number of users	Once (%)	Yearly (%)	Monthly (%)	More frequently (%)
1987	16,149	21.2	13.8	5.9	2.7
1989	30,758	26.2	14.3	7.8	3.5

Source: Brazilian Information Center on Drugs (1989).

services. However, deprivation also consists of other more qualitative, and at times subjective, dimensions. New deprivations include the recurrent lack of human concern in the planning of multi-storied tenements on the outskirts of cities both North and South; the loneliness of a child in Milan watching television alone in an empty flat; or the secluded courtyard existence of young girls in India cut off from the world, even through the media. Deprivations also encompass newly created consumer wants and the consequent frustrations of those who cannot afford to satisfy these wants but who see them in other people's hands.

Still only partially analysed, these deprivations seem to be affecting children at many stages and in significant ways. Deprivations become particularly serious when compounded by poverty and economic constraints. Although a complex analysis is required, Country Teams found connections, for example, between these new deprivations and the emergence of street children.

New deprivations tend to fall under at least five main headings:

(1) *A diminishing fabric of social support for children within the family and community.* In developing countries, there is strong evidence of a decrease in the support given by the extended family (grandparents, uncles, aunts and cousins). In some cases, for example in Africa where communities are an important component of social organization, the failure of support systems extends to the whole community.

In the North, the extended family has already lost much of its importance as a system of daily emotional and physical support, and relations within the nuclear family itself are showing clear signs of erosion. Relationships between men and women have become "more fragile, tentative, and insecure" (Bradshaw 1990). In other words, the profound changes that are taking place in gender roles and relationships affect the child's immediate environment and introduce into marital relationships, for instance, the potential for dissension and, ultimately, divorce. New types of households have become widespread, especially female-headed households, which tend to fall more easily into poverty, either temporarily or persistently. The children of these households commonly manifest a range of problems, including low educational achievement and a higher incidence of adolescent parenthood. Many of these problems are cyclical, with adolescents following patterns established by their parents.

According to analysts in the United States, only about 25 percent of children's problems are, in fact, clearly attributable to family income (Danziger and Stern 1990). Recent explanations have also emphasized problems of self-esteem, and the need for meaningful relationships as a form of adolescent self-validation (Musick 1992). Therefore, financial support seems to be less important an element than the development of emotional connections in giving children a sense of security and self-worth (Collins 1991, Lerner 1991). Changed family situations tend to diminish the availability of caring adults.

In the South, gender roles are also changing, and even though this may not result in divorce among the urban poor in India or the Philippines, it does, especially when combined with the pressures of urban poverty, lead to many *de facto* marital separations and breakups. The Country Teams in the Philippines, Kenya and Brazil, and to a lesser extent India, found clear evidence of an increase in female-headed households.

(2) *Decreasing opportunities for socialization.* Interacting with other children and adults is an important component of finding one's adult position in the world. In the North, with the increase of households in which two adults work, there are growing numbers of latch-key children. Moreover, declining family sizes mean that many are "only" children, with no siblings to interact with. The school rarely provides effective alternatives for after-school peer or child-adult interaction, thus condemning only children of busy parents to long hours spent in solitude. A recent study found, for example, that socio-relational difficulties accounted for up to 30 percent of the problems mentioned by children 6–14 years of age in Ferrara, a city in northern Italy (Polletta 1991, see Italy chapter). In developing countries, children's problems are often similarly related to the absenteeism of overburdened working parents and the lack of facilities that can promote safe peer interactions within children's own communities (Hart 1992, Hughes 1990).

(3) *Lack of opportunities to consolidate one's self-worth in the broader societal sphere.* Watching videos or possessing consumer goods has become particularly important as a symbol of social value for adolescents, especially if they are marginalized. When they cannot afford such status symbols, both they and their overworked parents may become extremely frustrated (Jelin 1989). In research carried out in Brazil by FLACSO, the desire to consume, as well as the need for affection and companionship, were found to be two factors "pulling" adolescents towards street bands (see Brazil chapter).

(4) *Experiences of marginalization and uncertainty of the future.* A feeling of not belonging in the present and a fear of what the future will bring are two root causes of urban stress. Children of immigrants in the North are vulnerable to

this kind of stress, especially when their legal situation has not been officially clarified. In the South, recurrent daily crises compound the situation. A major factor is often the inability of individuals, families and communities to control the very events which determine their lives (Duhl 1990); doctors and psychiatrists are increasingly recognizing the negative effects of that lack of control (Levi and Andersson 1974, Levi and Eckblad 1990, WHO 1992, Satterthwaite 1992).

(5) *Poorly planned urban environment.* Urban stress is often due to a lack of social concern in city planning. A poor physical environment can inhibit or damage children's physical and mental development. It may also limit their ability to satisfy their need for social interaction, consistency and predictability in the care-giving environment. Children also need a physical environment safe from accidents or infection and thus suitable for exploring and discovering (Myers and Hertenberg 1987). The children of construction workers in India who are left to roam construction sites while both parents work, and are thus highly prone to accidents and infection, provide a clear case in point. The desolate childhood settings of the poorly built suburban areas of Milan or Naples provide other powerful examples of the effects of poor urban planning (see Italy chapter).

Methodologically, urban stress is due to a complex and dynamic interrelationship of variables: (a) *physical and psychosocial stimuli*, such as high density, pollution, unhealthy housing, lack of safe public spaces, limited adult-child and child-child interactions, and the breakdown of familial cooperation. These elements are dynamically interrelated and in turn interact with (b) *the individual's psychobiological programme*. This includes vulnerability, resistance and certain predispositions related to genetic factors, as well as current and past environmental structures and processes. This interaction, combined with other environmental influences, may set in motion (c) *mechanisms of pathogenic processes*, such as social differentiation, segmentalization, marginalization, segregation, spatial diffusion and child abuse. In turn, (d) *precursors of disease or discomfort*, such as truancy, substance use and petty juvenile crime, may lead to (e) *impaired quality of life*, evidenced by substance abuse, serious crimes, child morbidity (such as obesity, anorexia), child mortality (from accidents or suicide, for example), or inadequate child development conducive to problems in later life (Eckblad 1993).

Such problems have been particularly well substantiated in industrialized countries, but the mechanisms of pathogenic effects can often only be guessed at as they often have not yet been adequately researched. While further research is needed one can only surmise from the growing dimensions of the problems that the effects are considerable indeed.

Warning Signals

Urban children in every part of the world experience difficulties because cities are generally not built with their "healthy, happy growth and development" in mind (UNICEF 1986a). In developing countries, many urban children and families bear the additional burden of absolute poverty, insecurity of tenure, poor or nonexistent infrastructure, and inadequate and diminishing social, educational and health services. This burden increased during the 1980s in almost all countries, but is particularly evident in Kenya and other sub-Saharan African countries where development has been severely curtailed, as well as in countries, such as Brazil and the Philippines, which are struggling with high levels of debt and consequent severe structural adjustment constraints.

In urban environments in the North, children and their families are now experiencing heavy constraints resulting from an extended recession which has eroded important elements of what have long been considered advanced systems of social assistance, health and education. Beyond that, the industrialized countries are also witnessing deep-rooted social changes, which, in extreme forms, are manifested by exasperated individualism and the loss of family support systems. National identities are also in crisis as western Europe approaches unification, and all major industrialized countries experience migration from the South. Italy, a newly industrialized country, exemplifies these trends very clearly. Because of aging populations, children have not been given adequate attention and concern at the societal and policy level.

Media images create a plastic world of mirages and illusions around children and, at the same time, subject them to reality at its crudest. Time and space are telescoped, world events are captured by a reporter's camera and projected into living rooms. Children see wars and killings. They hear reports of atrocities, crime and corruption. They witness substance abuse, suicide and despair, runaways, street children and youth violence. These are indeed the events that journalists are eager to sensationalize. By highlighting the more negative aspects and focusing on extreme cases, the media often compounds the problems and misses the opportunity to analyse deep-rooted causes, and much media reporting fosters discouragement and negative attitudes.

In both the North and South, there has been a noticeable increase over the last two decades in the presence of children in difficult circumstances. Their growing numbers and the extent of the deprivations they experience are striking. Their presence is a warning signal of severe problems and of a deep-seated social malaise.

THE FIVE COUNTRY STUDIES: SOME ISSUES DEFINED

Some of the key concepts and terms utilized in the study warrant further definition.

Childhood

The definition of what constitutes "children" as a category raises some important issues. As Country Teams emphasized, these definitions have been rapidly changing. In the North, childhood became a more clearly conscious construct in the early years of this century after the first phases of industrialization. While young children were previously subjected to the rigours of hard manual labour, with the rise of the middle class, a more clearly defined time span was dedicated to growing up and being educated. Childhood has been codified and extensively discussed throughout the century (Zelizer 1985).

In the developing world, this shift has only partially occurred and the construct is not as consciously a part of prevailing attitudes. Childhood is very short for impoverished urban children forced to work to help sustain themselves and their families. Adult responsibilities are thrust upon these children while they are still young, with no time allotted to them just to "grow up." Adolescent girls are particularly vulnerable; they may shift from being siblings to surrogate mothers (while their mother is out earning a living) to becoming very young mothers themselves, thus never "acquiring the vitally important skills and knowledge [they] need to succeed themselves, and to ensure the adequate development of the children in [their] care" (Musick 1992).

In the Project, children have been defined as being between 0 and 18 years of age. This definition includes adolescents under the category of "children," and thus further expands the usual definition of childhood, both North and South. At the same time, the Project has highlighted, when necessary, the importance of understanding the responses of children and families in relationship to different age groups and genders.

Families, Households and Single-Headed Families

The term "family" has been used broadly by Country Teams to include both the nuclear (husband, wife, children), and the extended (husband, wife, children with parents, siblings or other more distant family members), family. It refers to the bonds of recognized social relationships that exist among people who do not necessarily physically reside together. The term "household," on the other hand, refers very specifically to people, whether related or not, who live together under the same roof. For example, parents and their married sons or daughters may maintain separate households while still being a family.

This distinction between "family" and "household," which is rarely made in development literature on children, is important sociologically because it allows us to identify ongoing aspects of change that directly affect children. Extended family linkages have often dissolved with industrialization, urbanization and development, leaving children without the emotional and physical support of grandparents, or uncles and aunts, and thus too exclusively and uniquely dependent on the care of their often overburdened parents.

The concept (and term) of female-headed households has emerged from attempts to identify broad categories of women (and children) who are especially disadvantaged. Aggregate numbers of female-headed households are thus increasingly quoted to demonstrate family deterioration and diminished support systems for certain women and their children. These aggregate numbers are certainly broadly indicative of ongoing family changes. But there are major problems of definition.

A crude comparison of census data suggests that the overall female headship rates are higher, for example, in European regions than in South or Southeast Asia. The rates are lower in southern Europe (including Italy) than in northern Europe. The Caribbean as well as Norway have very high rates, while Japan's rate is very low. Thus, the female headship phenomenon (as officially defined in censuses) is socially diverse both within and across countries. The determinants of headship and its significance also vary. The economic and social position of such households may vary substantially across countries with similar rates of female headship. The consequences for both women and their children may similarly be quite varied and require further qualification. The United Nations have recognized that the concept, with its implications of authority and economic responsibility, obscures the true picture of household relationships, and have even suggested a new term "reference person." Canada has dropped the headship concept from its census, and has pointed out that in order to identify single parents, or female-supported households or one-wage families, specific terminologies should be used rather than relying on an unclear concept.

The lack of clarity is even greater in Third World countries where there is even less overlap between the legal definition and social or economic definitions of the term. Seniority or legal registration often condition the formal use of the concept by census collectors while family systems may have quite different ways of defining it. Common law marriages and frequent changes of male partners among the urban poor further confuse the issue. The report of a three-year project undertaken by the New York-based Population Council and the International Center for Research on Women (1989) in Washington discusses the problems involved in defining female-headed households, and presents evidence of the prevalence of such family forms, the severity of their circumstances, and the duration of women's tenure as heads of households. Possible impacts on the next generation are also considered.

The concept of female-headed households has been widely used in the country studies. The Country Teams were, however, requested to provide careful definitions of the term "female-headed household" as used in that country as well as qualitative and quantitative assessments about the kinds of household relationships and circumstances that they encountered in their research. They were asked to clarify if the term was used in their country as: (a) a census reference person; (b) the household's chief decision maker; (c) the household's chief economic provider; (d) the person who is entitled to claim certain benefits, such as land or membership in a cooperative on behalf of the household; or (e) the person whose characteristics provide the best indication of the status of the household as a whole. In their own analyses, the operational definition used was *households where women are the sole or primary breadwinner*. The number of women who pass through a phase of their lives as the sole or primary supporter of young children, and the relative length of that phase, were also examined whenever possible and the consequences for children assessed (Bruce 1989).

In the Philippines, the concept of head of household is often related to seniority: the head of household is normally an older male or female relative who happens to live in that household, but is not necessarily, or even normally, its main provider. In Brazil, households legally defined as single-headed usually include a succession of adult males present over the years, as common-law marriages are made and subsequently break down, often after many years. The effects on the children in such households would obviously be quite different in Brazil than in the Philippines. In India, widowed or abandoned women with children usually remarry elderly men in their communities because of social pressures, and the concept of female heads of households, if not better qualified, again provides a distorted image of both adult presences and absences, levels of support offered and the *de facto* incidence of the problem. From the point of view of the child, qualitative definitions that examine the presence or absence of a "husband" and thus potential "father" figure and provider for the children are particularly important.

Coping Strategies of Children, Families and Households

An important element of the study has been the need to gain a better understanding of the survival strategies adopted by urban children and their families in order to: (a) identify their sources of strength and thus be able to devise better support systems; and (b) recognize their resilience and creativity so as to offset existing misconceptions about their ability to confront problems. Different kinds of coping strategies by types of families and households were identified, and their implications outlined and discussed with the aim of formulating specific recommendations.

The process involved recording the particulars of the daily lives of children "coping" in urban environments, and analysing the "coping" strategies of their parents. Poor urban households in all five countries are engaged in a dire struggle to survive. The poor have increased the number of hours they work, explored new niches in the informal sector, tried to use to the utmost all of their available resources. Desperate Kenyan women brew illegal beer, risk six months in prison to sell vegetables on the street or engage in prostitution, often conditioning their young daughters to do the same (Onyango et al. 1992).

Households supported by women in the Indian slums or in poor neighbourhoods of the Philippines are often forced to find outside paid work for their children or rely on them for domestic help within the family. If possible, some children are sent to school. Decisions are pragmatic, but require that meagre resources are maximized which at times means that some children, usually the girls, are "sacrificed" on behalf of the others. Children with a "good head for studying" may be encouraged and their schooling paid for in the hope that an education will help them "make it" so that they can help their parents and siblings later on. Girls in the Philippines have better school achievement rates than boys, but they are often required by their parents to drop out of school as they are considered to be more reliable. Indeed, they do tend to give a larger percentage of their earnings back to the family than boys do. In Kenya, many girls are pulled out of school to be married.

Strategies are only as successful as the family's ability to learn how to deal with the police, school administrators, teachers, medical and emergency personnel, and other representatives of the municipal institutions which have a significant bearing on their lives.

Communities and Neighbourhoods

The use of the terms "urban communities" and "neighbourhoods" has been particularly confusing in the development literature, especially since both terms seem to imply the existence of special relationships linking neighbours without submitting this assumption to the test. Country Teams use both terms simply to denote *a population living within a particular geographical area*. The extent of its social closeness, quality of relationships, level of mobilization and support systems, and potential for unified action are ascertained on a case-by-case basis rather than by assumption.

A qualitative assessment of communities is therefore important, but difficult. How do we measure the apathy of the squatters unless we understand their attitudes as, perhaps, a show of resistance to outside influences? How do we evaluate the sense of frustration and the occasional aggressiveness of many squatters unless we understand their history? They may have been evicted by force from a different settlement because the authorities — often appointed rather than elected — decided to build a new highway or to "clean up" the city for international celebrations and foreign dignitaries. The history of a poor settlement and of its people is very helpful in planning assistance that engages the community itself and its organizations (Hardoy and Hardoy 1991).

Each city is built and rebuilt daily through a multiplicity of decisions. Laws, norms and standards are generally sanctioned on the basis of a fragmented and poorly informed view of the city, with data that is too aggregated to be useful, and without consultation with the different sections of the population. Because all human activities taking place in cities are interconnected, the problems of the modern city in both the developing and the industrialized world cannot be addressed exclusively from a sectoral perspective. Urban change can only be brought about if the city is viewed holistically.

Children in Especially Difficult Circumstances

Within UNICEF, the term "children in especially difficult circumstances" includes "working children, street children, abused, neglected and abandoned children, children in armed conflict and disaster" (UNICEF 1986a).

Working children. Working children are those whose work, part or full time, paid or unpaid, within or outside the family group, is exploitative and damaging to their health and/or development. "Children should be protected from hazardous work, such as mining and quarrying; from inappropriate work, such as lifting heavy weights; from excessive hours of work; from work which may stunt their growth; and from work in harmful environments... [They should be] provided with an environment that fosters their healthy, happy growth and development" (UNICEF 1986a).

Street children. The definition of this category of children is still problematic and in the process of being clarified. It referred initially to all urban children who spent most of their time on the streets, whether working or not. It is progressively being applied to those children on the streets who have only tenuous ties, or no ties at all, with their families, and who have developed specific survival strategies. Research on those children by academics and NGOs, including the research sponsored by this first UNICEF Urban Child Project, has contributed to clarifying the importance of existing — or absent — ties with the family of origin. It has also made efforts to define the extent to which conditions on the streets expose children to specific risks, such as use and abuse of dangerous substances, involvement in the production, processing and trafficking of drugs, exploitative work, sexual exploitation, discrimination, mistreatment and violence.

Children endangered by abuse and neglect. This category refers to those children who are, occasionally or habitually, victims of physical, sexual or emotional violence that is preventable and originates from their immediate environment (UNICEF 1986). It is recognized that there are degrees of child abuse and neglect, and that this is, in significant ways, a subjective category which has been researched only to a limited extent in developing countries. It is also recognized increasingly that abuse and neglect may be inflicted not only from within the family, but also from outside, in some cases directly by the State or by broader societal conditions. Abuses within state-run institutions in Romania and Brazil have recently been examined, and are disturbing examples of ill-treatment inflicted by society (Himes et al. 1991, see also the Brazil chapter). As the Country Teams point out in their studies, institutional abuse exists in varying degrees in all of the countries examined.

Children in situations of armed conflict. This is a growing category of children involved either indirectly as victims, or directly as combatants, in war, civil strife and violence.

Children affected by natural disasters. This category includes those children who experience physical loss or damage, social and/or economic disruption, either by high-impact disasters, such as earthquakes and floods, or by slow-onset events, such as droughts.

These categories are not mutually exclusive. Both street and working children may often also suffer abuse and neglect. Many children in situations of armed conflict or affected by natural disasters become street and working children. All have been "abandoned" in some way. However, the concept of abandonment contains a potential indictment of the family, while very often it is the state and society that have abandoned both the children and their families. Abandonment therefore needs to be explained in terms of broader causalities. Similarly, many of the problems contributing to the children's especially difficult circumstances need to be qualified before these children's predicaments can be understood and broader and more far-reaching strategies devised.

A Comparative Assessment of Situations

The focus of the studies

The Country Teams focused on street and working children on the streets or in the poor sections of the 21 cities selected. Children in institutions were added in the case of Kenya and Brazil. The focus of the study has been reflexive and qualitative and includes:

A. An analysis of the situation of urban children in the five countries, including:

    (a) the types of problems that street or "slum" living creates for urban children, and the children's coping strategies;

(b)   the types of families and neighbourhoods generating urban
       children with problems;

(c)   the broader political, social and economic contexts that af-
       fect urban children and contribute to their situation of rela-
       tive disadvantage.

B.   An assessment in the five countries of:

(a)   policies affecting urban children at the municipal and na-
       tional levels;

(b)   programmes specific to disadvantaged urban children and
       to children engaged in high-risk behaviour; and

(c)   existing coordinated municipal programmes as well as
       processes of mobilization on behalf of disadvantaged urban
       children.

As acknowledged in UNICEF Board documents, and as Country Teams
rapidly discovered, there are generally limited statistical data on children in
especially difficult circumstances. These CEDC are, in fact, an often elusive
population. They are often defensive and resist being interviewed. It is usually problematic to relate the children interviewed with an actual family, and
most existing family or household studies do not contain information about
children. The little existing data are based on limited research and on NGO
estimates, which have often been unsystematic. Definitions and terminologies are not standardized. Furthermore, sociological research has not
developed international standards to the same degree that demography or
economics have. Definitions of abuse, for example, are often culturally relative.

Because secondary data are not evenly available, the Country Teams carefully selected, in many cities, samples of children and their parents to be
interviewed as well as subsamples that were submitted to more intensive
observation and from whom life histories were collected. The intention was
to identify the types of disadvantage that are most frequent, assess the coping
strategies of children and families and analyse the processes that cause some
disadvantaged children to encounter situations of even greater disadvantage.
A multi-method approach, further discussed in Chapter 8 and again in Appendix 1, was adopted in order to "increase empirical and conceptual accountability" (Fielding and Fielding 1986, Kidder 1981). The qualitative
dimensions introduced by the life histories have, when combined with the
more detailed surveys, allowed Country Teams to: (a) clarify and standardize
the categories of especially difficult circumstances across different cultures;
(b) connect the children with family situations; (c) clarify some of the paths
that lead from difficult to especially difficult circumstances, in order to
propose more preventive urban policy approaches; (d) identify recurrent
processes and approximate causal relationships, thus helping to validate and

interpret survey data, facilitate the identification of different levels of causality, decipher puzzling responses and offer case study illustrations (Sieber 1979).

The multi-method approach also included a participation dimension whose aim was to give space to the children's own subjectivities and voices, or, in other words, to make children subjects rather than objects of the research. Country Teams were provided participatory research techniques to help elicit meaningful answers from the children themselves. This involved placing children in play situations that facilitated information-giving in less structured and intimidating ways than by survey or interview which are not appropriate for use with young children, or even adolescents. These techniques have ensured a greater authenticity of the answers. Children, and in particular children who have been emotionally scarred and exposed to exploitative adults, tend to be defensive and conceal the truth about their families and histories. Establishing trust has thus been a very important first step, one which has also had therapeutic effects: telling their stories and being listened to by someone who is genuinely interested in them has helped the children gain new self-esteem.

The assessment of programmes and the documentation of national and municipal mobilization for children have included the analysis of existing reports and evaluations, and interviews with key participants and programme initiators.

The teams were provided with general guidelines. For the situational analysis of the children, the guidelines indicated the areas the Project hoped to shed light on: (1) the everyday activities, time allocation, opinions and personal relationships of children in their immediate physical and social environment; (2) the children and their families: life paths, events, statuses and beliefs; (3) the households' coping strategies; (4) the neighbourhoods and broader city context. It also suggested the kinds of secondary material already possibly available in those areas.

A framework of the elements in the physical and social environment of the urban child and of the direction of causalities was also provided (Figure 1.1). Macro-level contextual trends are major inputs on the left that affect the layered and more immediate environment of the child at city, neighbourhood and household level. From the dynamic interactions that occur between the child and that environment, primarily filtered through the household and the neighbourhood, outputs emerge which may include impaired child survival and development and symptomatic high-risk behaviour. The country analysts were provided with key questions to address for each specific section of the framework. They were asked to provide for each country a brief analysis of contexts, to quantify outputs as much as possible and to illustrate the processes close to — and immediately affecting — the lives of the child.

The initial focus and sampling strategy varied from country to country. The Country Teams in the Philippines and Brazil focused specifically on

CRISTINA SZANTON BLANC

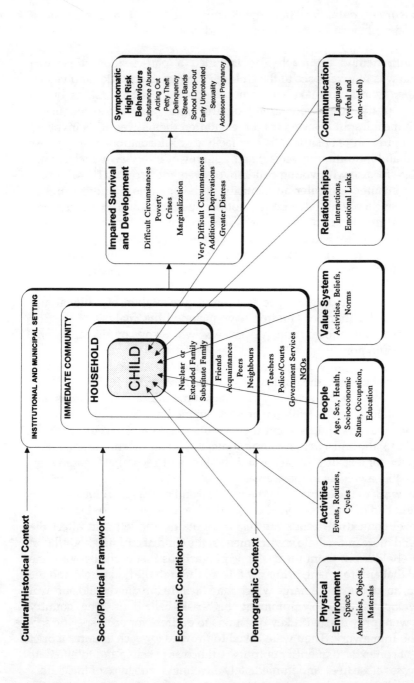

Source: Adapted from International Development Research Centre (1988)

Figure 1.1. Elements of the Environment of the Urban Child.

street and working children, whom they interviewed in their most frequent place of work, the streets. In the process they also explored the children's connection to poor urban neighbourhoods and talked with their families. The Country Teams in India and Italy approached the task inversely, focusing on children and families in poor urban neighbourhoods, but uncovering in the process other categories of children in difficult, or especially difficult circumstances, including many street and working children. In Kenya, the Country Team focused on poor urban communities in three growing cities, and on children in homes and correctional institutions. A major national study on street children, carried out by one of the team members from UNICEF Nairobi on behalf of the Ford Foundation, allowed the Country Team to complete the picture from the point of view of street children.

A greater understanding of "street children"

Street children, a major CEDC category, are basically an urban phenomenon. By analysing the situation of these seemingly faceless children and their relations to their families, the Country Teams have established that only a small number have actually severed all ties with their families. Most still live at home and contribute to the household economy through their informal-sector work. Groups studied by Country Teams in different cities reveal that approximately three fourths of the children on the streets are actively contributing to household economies in the Philippines and in India. In Brazil, where original research was undertaken in Goiânia, it was found that even among street children who had only tenuous ties with their families, 42 percent still sometimes contributed to the family budget. The majority of children live in poor urban neighbourhoods. School attendance varies by country and depends largely on the extent to which children or their parents believe that education can be useful. School hours and fees are also decisive factors.

At the other end of the spectrum there are street children who have no functional family ties at all, and attempt to fill this void by forming "fictive family" relationships and even a strong emotional attachment to the "street." These children are usually completely "on their own," and although they may find some peer support, life for them is a fight for survival. They are also likely to be affected by institutional violence, including, in some cases, police brutality and the harshness of the juvenile court system. These children generally constitute a small portion of the overall number of children on the street. Even in large Brazilian cities, where the phenomenon has attracted broad media attention, the total numbers in each city range from a few hundred to, at most, a few thousand (Blanc 1991, see also the Brazil chapter).

Box 1.1.   Towards an Understanding of
Disadvantaged Urban Children

Country Teams have asked themselves or others (with some variations across countries) the following questions:

- Who are the disadvantaged children of our city? What seems to be the origin of their problems (for instance, in the family, at school, on the streets, among peers, and so forth)? How many are there? Where are they located in the city (communities, ethnic origins if relevant, migration patterns)?

- How do they utilize the city (types of activities, forms of work, conditions of work, peer group relations, play activities) and what kinds of problems do they encounter in their daily interactions (with police, schools, teachers, among others) or in their interactions at home (with parents, siblings, other relatives, neighbours, and so forth)?

- How do their problems relate to other problems in our city, especially urban poverty, new deprivations, abuse, drugs, crime, institutions (schools, health centres), management and tourism? How do their problems relate to broader trends, including industrialization and development patterns, family change, social change, urbanization, migration, global economy, structural adjustment, transnationalism?

- Why do we want to know? Analysing the reasons they need certain information has helped the Country Teams clarify their own definition of the problems.

- How do disadvantaged children perceive themselves and their future? How do they perceive the adults around them (father, mother, teacher, police, social worker, street educator, municipal administrator)? Do they view them as threatening, or as positive or negative influences? Do they see themselves as victims, or as more grown up than their parents?

- How do parents, teachers, street educators, social workers, police and city administrators view the difficulties their children or other children face? How do they evaluate strategies to cope with these difficulties, including those offered by the city or by NGOs or the private sector? How do they perceive disadvantaged urban children, their families and their communities? Under a specific label or social category, such as child, youth, adult, boy or girl, drug addict, worker, squatter, poor? With what characteristics, for example, delinquent, expendable, irresponsible? Are they viewed as positive presences or as liabilities?

- What do these people see themselves doing? What have they done for children recently? Are they part of the problem or part of the solution? What are their limitations? What are their strengths, abilities and commitments?

- Which level of causes can these key people attack and how? How would they define their current and future goals?

- With whom should these key people work? Whom should they consider allies? Whom should they win over?

- What have we all learned so far through our own or other people's experience?

- What would we all like to see happening in the future?

The answers Country Teams have both given and received are not necessarily comprehensive, but have provided insights into the children's and family's relationships and coping strategies. These heightened perceptions have, in turn, helped to shape programme models, future programme directions and mobilization strategies at the municipal and national level.

New views on working children

During the analysis of the lives of children in poor urban communities, Country Teams became aware of the many different categories of working children. Children who work in the informal sector sell items in small quantities (such as newspapers, cigarettes, flowers, food, even drugs), or offer special services (such as shoe-polishing, car-watching, car-washing, luggage-carrying). They work on streets, and in markets, bus depots or railway stations, where there are large numbers of customers. The children can also be found in front of hotels, restaurants or tourist spots. They depend on consignments, work for occasional employers, or are fully self-employed. Children who do not go out on the streets also work, sometimes with adults, as scavengers; these children are often dirty and are thus especially discriminated against. Other children work as part-time domestic helpers, hotel boys or shopkeepers' helpers. Others hold semi-skilled jobs as mechanics or ironsmiths. Still others work at home with their parents or neighbours at local cottage industries (bangle-makers, prepared foods, drug production).

Country Teams analysed these categories on the basis of the life histories and surveys, as well as secondary data, in order to clarify the degrees of exploitative work being undertaken, and provided information on how work can range from constructive, resilient, ego-building activities that make children feel less marginalized (especially when combined with regular schooling) to extremely exploitative conditions.

An important conceptual distinction must be made, with respect to the different categories of urban children in especially difficult circumstances. They may be (1) particularly visible, such as street children and children working on the street, including prostitutes; (2) children who are away from the public eye (working in poor urban neighbourhoods, on garbage dumps, or in secluded places manufacturing drugs), whose problems are publicly recognized but less visible; and most importantly, (3) children whose problems have not been fully recognized, such as the "invisible" girl child in the poor urban settlements of Indian cities, or the adolescent common-law wife and mother in the Philippines, who have very few advocates speaking for them. Because of the different levels of awareness of the problems, these different categories require somewhat different approaches.

A broader view of children in difficult circumstances

The studies carried out so far have allowed us to identify other categories of at-risk children that could either be considered separately or be subsumed into existing categories.

Users and abusers of dangerous substances. This includes drugs, but also in many developing countries, chemical inhalants which are often extremely destructive, such as solvents, adhesives and fuel gases, local drugs (*miraa* in

Kenya, for example), or even excessive alcohol and tobacco (a major problem of youth in the United States and in parts of Europe). The studies reported that 75 percent of street children in Brazil, and increasing numbers of street and poor urban children in the Philippines, Kenya and Italy use dangerous substances (Alexander et al. 1993).

Children and adolescents in conflict with the law. These children are handled, and often mishandled, by the punitive arm of the State (police, courts and the penal system). Abuses and injustice were identified by all Country Teams, although the severity and the numbers vary.

Adolescent mothers. Adolescent mothering is not a new phenomenon. It was actually the norm for centuries in every part of the world. The number of girls involved is exceedingly high in India, where the problem increases rather than diminishes under the pressure of poverty as the country develops economically. Adolescent mothering is surprisingly frequent, but generally unrecognized as a problem, in the Philippines. According to the 1988 National Demographic Survey, 42.5 percent of the ever-married women were already married at 15 to 19 years of age. Live births by adolescent mothers steadily increased during the 1980–87 period from 122,265 to 128,147. Early marriages are often precipitated by an unplanned pregnancy. Adolescent pregnancy is becoming a recognized problem in Brazil.

There has been a rapid rise in adolescent mothering in Kenya, where this phenomenon is considered an urgent problem in both urban and rural areas (Kenyan Ministry of Health 1988). Indian policy makers have been addressing the problem of early marriage and pregnancy, which is related to the high fertility and low educational achievements of Indian women.

Sexually exploited girls. These girls are victims of "a modern form of slavery" which is a considerable problem worldwide. The victims are children and adolescents who are not in a position to defend their most basic human rights. "It is primarily the most defenseless individuals in the community, those with the greatest need for support and care, who are exploited by the sex market" (Naversen 1989). Some of the main factors contributing to sexual exploitation in the South are, according to Naversen, rapid urbanization, the "colonial legacy," a widespread "machismo," foreign military bases, and international trade and tourism. Rapid urbanization and the increasing number of female-supported urban households certainly seem to be a major cause of the still relatively small, but rapidly growing, problem of female and girl-child prostitution in our research in urban Kenya. Naversen also estimated that between 300,000 and 400,000 children engaged in prostitution in India, out of approximately 2 million people involved altogether.

Children and AIDS. This is an increasing problem in the poor urban areas of the cities studied, especially in Kenya and Brazil. There are 6 million cases of HIV infection in Africa, over 50 percent among women, and the numbers are rapidly increasing in other regions. The numbers of orphans and damaged childhoods are rapidly growing. AIDS orphans are often dispersed among members of the extended family living in rural areas, whose resources, however, are severely overstretched. In urban areas, support from the extended family is much less available. Elderly relatives, such as grandparents, are often unable to deal with the situation. Potential foster parents are afraid of being infected. It has been estimated that in the ten worst-affected African countries, between 3 and 5.5 million children will be orphaned by AIDS by 2000 (Black 1991a).

Children of migrants. Children left behind in the large urban areas of the countries of emigration in the South represent a growing problem. Often relatives are nominally in charge of these children, but many, especially adolescents, are largely unprotected. The situation is particularly serious in Manila, for example, because of the number of women who emigrate. Migration is also the cause of particularly difficult problems where migrant families come up against new forms of industrialized urban deterioration and have to compete for diminishing school and health services. The children are often torn between the culture of their parents and that of the dominant society. The increasing numbers of "foreign" youths appearing in statistics on juvenile offenders in Italy or of "black" youths in the United Kingdom may attest not only to the children's coping strategies, but also to fundamental institutional shortcomings in the host society (Blanc and Chiozzi 1992).

Families in peril. Families form a very important context for the child's survival, but also, as powerfully argued by Urie Bronfenbrenner (1986), for the child's human development. The centrality of the family diminishes somewhat, however, as the child moves from early (0–6 years of age) to middle childhood (6–12 years of age) and then on to preadolescence and adolescence (13–18 years of age). The school, peer groups, even work and street settings, acquire increasing importance in the child's life as more time is spent away from adults and in the company of peers. Indeed, the ability of the family to contribute to the child's development in time is greatly influenced by the degree to which other people, policies or institutions function as a support.

In each of the five countries of the study, families of the urban poor are undergoing significant transformations. This is particularly evident in Brazil where the support of the extended family, which was not uncommon in rural areas, diminishes significantly in the urban context. Nuclear households, often female-headed, are becoming increasingly frequent. In Italy, the large families of the postwar recovery period are being replaced by small nuclear families with a rapidly decreasing number of children. In 1981, 53 percent of Italian families were nuclear families. By 1986, the number had risen to 67 percent (ISTAT 1985a cited in the XXI Conference of European Ministers Responsible for Family Affairs). Therefore, even in Italy, which has long been known for its strong family base, the extended family has decreased somewhat in importance in terms of the support it can provide a child, but it is, nevertheless, much more prominent than in other industrialized or post-industrial countries.

In the post-industrial United States, instead, the extended family has largely disappeared, replaced by a type of household that has become both residentially and emotionally nuclearized. About half of all first marriages end in divorce (Cherlin 1988, Danziger and Stern 1990), introducing much instability in the lives of children. However, because black, Hispanic, new immigrant and other poor families each present specific characteristics, generalizations about the family can only be broadly indicative.

While there are comparable tendencies towards nuclearization and some loss of extended family networks and relations in India, the Philippines, and even Kenya, the existing family systems in these countries are still relatively strong and closely connected. This is particularly true in India. Relatives in rural areas may, for example, provide support to young girls who, after reaching puberty, are sent back "home" from the city by their migrant parents to find a husband.

The very different, bilateral family system in the Philippines has remained remarkably close knit, despite the enormous economic pressures on the urban poor. In Kenya, types of families vary according to ethnic background and are changing in somewhat different ways and at different speeds within each ethnic group. However, in general, rapid transformations are taking place throughout the country in family organization, relations and support systems. The community as it exists in rural areas (where support, food and lodging are customarily provided to any person, especially children, asking for help) is disappearing, while households headed by single women, often migrants from rural areas, are rapidly becoming more numerous in the poor urban neighbourhoods of Nairobi or its peripheral towns.

Beyond family and community. The increasing importance, as the child grows up, of other domains, and in particular, of peer socialization and interaction has important implications. Until the child reaches six, immediate family members are the main, and often the only, support system needed to ensure the child's healthy growth and development.

The situation changes in middle childhood when the exposure to external influences acquires increasing importance (Bornstein and Bornstein 1992, Collins 1991, Lerner 1991). It then becomes particularly important to monitor and improve other aspects of the child's surroundings. A careful examination of the life histories of children in especially difficult circumstances collected by the Country Teams provides a clearer understanding of the paths to disadvantage. Their life stories reveal how the broader social environment contributes to urban children's current disadvantaged situation: consistently, the children speak of unproductive encounters with specific institutions and services, such as schools, the police and the transportation system (Blanc et al. 1994).

As the Country Teams highlighted, street children (mostly boys) tend to run away from home in middle childhood, frequently between 10 and 12 years of age. The reasons are complex and highly emotional, but almost always involve the overlap of familial and nonfamilial constraints and opportunities at work, in school or on the streets. From the time children run away, they are exposed to the often violent world of employers, exploiters and police, many of whom worsen the situation. The studies generally made it clear that to reduce the number of children in especially difficult circumstances, interventions need to make a positive impact on family conditions *and* the social environment, city management and institutions that are meant to sustain both the family and their children. These observations have generated specific recommendations for programmes.

A Comparative Assessment of Policies and Programmes

The following considerations were important in the search for innovative approaches to children's problems and an assessment of their validity:

Better diagnoses of children's problems. There is a need to move beyond a vision of "problem children" as isolated, diseased individuals to a larger view which encompasses the origins of their problems in their family, community, school, work and leisure settings. We must take into consideration how institutions deal with children. Children's problems are in part economic, but they are, in important ways, also social, organizational and institutional. Their problems reflect our current limited (and often hurried) approaches, and our often distorted vision of existing problems. Documented analyses of the successes and failures of interventions are rarely available.

The need to gain a clearer awareness of how children's problems relate to broader issues. This must include an analysis of how urban planners and policy makers can create a generally "healthier" environment for urban dwellers, and especially children.

Systematic and integrated planning. Ad hoc and piecemeal responses are often a major part of the problem. To be effective, planning must implement key lessons learned from successful programmes.

The research confirms that most cities in the developing world have been caught between increasing urbanization and decreasing governmental resources. As a consequence, children find fewer opportunities for physical and mental development. This is also the case in the industrialized world whose cities have less money today to spend on social programmes. Lacking sufficient love, care, attention and supportive relationships as families and support systems fail them, children and young people are increasingly vulnerable to street violence and substance abuse.

Many cities which have tried to respond lack the resources to plan effectively. Both municipal and national levels tend to focus only on extreme problems, such as child abandonment and substance abuse, and often offer particularly costly and extreme "solutions," such as institutionalization or imprisonment.

As central planning and administration fall into widespread discredit, cities are faced with new opportunities and challenges; this is increasingly viewed as the level of government best able to respond to the needs of the people. As a result, more and more services that were the responsibility of the central government are being run at the local level. This decentralization goes hand in hand with increased democratization which enables the urban community as a whole to participate in the decisions that directly affect its members. Because of these trends, mayors now have greater potential to bring about real social progress in their communities and to enhance the well-being of the children.

Cities generally assume the responsibility for providing basic services essential for the health and well-being of the inhabitants, particularly children. These include piped water, sanitation, drainage, garbage collection, and sometimes schools and health centres. Municipal governments, however, need funds to permit them to fulfil these, and other, basic responsibilities without continual recourse to higher levels of government. Moreover, they will require additional financial and human resources to meet the many new challenges.

The five Country Teams concentrated on cities that are experimenting with innovative approaches. They assessed each city's potential for economic growth, administrative capabilities, and social conditions of its children. They also surveyed public bodies and NGOs working on children's issues, and assessed their programme approaches and the extent of their coverage.

An initial analysis led the organizers to the following conclusions:

- Although only a minority of the children seen on the streets of major urban centres worldwide are actually living on their own without a family, their numbers are growing. These children are exposed to the street's most exploitative conditions, but they often also respond to them in resilient and creative ways.

- Many of the problems urban children face can be traced to the extremely disadvantaged conditions in which they live. Their families are struggling to cope in a climate of great mistrust and marginalization. Overburdened by the pressures they face within and outside the family, some parents may abuse, mistreat or generally neglect their children. There are growing numbers of children in these circumstances in the poor urban settlements not only in the South, but also — surprisingly — in the more deprived areas of the often declining cities of the industrialized North.

- Worldwide, governmental and nongovernmental programmes benefit at most 10 percent of the total number of children on the streets.

- Worldwide, urban programmes benefit only a limited number of children 0–18 years of age; the gap between programmes and potential beneficiaries is bound to widen given the rapidly increasing size of the urban child population.

- Coverage only increases significantly when municipal governments, NGOs and the city residents themselves — especially the children, families and communities — strike an alliance and jointly seek ways to address the problems. This has been clearly documented by the study teams in Brazil, India, Kenya and the Philippines.

A strategy is needed that will address problems at their source. An overall integrated plan at municipal level is needed that will contain protective and preventive elements, will adopt a new vision of children and families in cities, and will be able to build flexibly on the most innovative actions and strategies developed so far.

CEDC interventions in relation to urban basic services and other urban programmes

An assessment was made of innovative urban CEDC interventions and programmes and their relationship to other programmes. The Country Teams first assessed the overall effectiveness of CEDC programmes, their impact in terms of numbers, and, when possible, their cost-effectiveness. Comparative analyses of goals, resources and implementation were carried out in order to identify consistent patterns across countries. Programmes selected for the study were those considered particularly innovative and effective. Preventive approaches were favoured.

Effective approaches are those which protect the children while providing them with opportunities to learn, to raise their self-assurance, and to develop skills which will enable them to make a better future for themselves. The Urban Basic Services strategy, sponsored by UNICEF since the mid 1970s and implemented in many of the countries and cities studied, is based on a participatory community-based model and on an area-based convergence of service delivery. It has been creatively utilized in some countries to allow for increased city- and even nationwide focus, especially in combination with children's task forces.

In the Philippines, the Country Team assessed street-based, community-based and centre-based programmes for street children in Metro Manila, Cebu, Davao and Olongapo, and looked at their integration with Urban Basic Services (UBS) programmes, which are carried out jointly by government agencies, NGOs, community representatives and municipal authorities. In Brazil, the Country Team analysed innovative governmental and especially nongovernmental CEDC interventions in six Brazilian metropolitan areas. In India and Kenya, the respective Country Teams examined UBS and CEDC programmes. The Kenya Team also observed the Undugu Society, an important Nairobi-based NGO which began as a drop-in centre for street children and enlarged its scope to innovative and preventive work with poor urban communities.

As a second step, the Country Teams sought to identify broader integrated approaches combining citywide emergency support with long-term strategies. Within this framework, the Country Teams assessed the degree of coordination between CEDC interventions and more preventive programmes targeting a broader range of urban children.

In the Philippines, some cities have established multilevel councils or task forces in which government agencies and NGOs join to address specific problems. In Brazil, state governments have organized and funded agencies in Goiânia, São Paulo, Parana and other cities, which provide a flexible system of services for street and working children as an alternative to institutionalization. They have succeeded in obtaining support from the local business community and the police. In Kenya, the Nairobi task force has initiated some important collaborative activities involving city governments, NGOs and disadvantaged urban communities. Examples of this kind of collaboration are being documented and analysed in order to identify the elements that contribute to their success or failure.

Municipal mobilization

In order to learn from existing innovative municipal experiences and make them available to a broader public, the Country Teams documented mobilization on behalf of children within municipalities against the backdrop of national-level mobilization. This documentation has entailed analysis of:

- the information available before municipal mobilization started;
- the extent to which advocacy efforts at the national, state and municipal level have changed public attitudes towards especially disadvantaged children, and how these new perceptions have inspired more effective municipal policies;
- the city's resources — financial and especially human — that have been mobilized, including the children themselves, their families and communities, community-level NGOs, the business sector, academic institutions, the police, and local and national media;
- particularly innovative municipal policies and programmes in each of the five countries.

Importantly, an assessment was made of the strategies and actions that make these programmes particularly effective in each city. Such strategies include: (a) the development of appropriate information; (b) the encouragement of coordinated national and municipal advocacy on behalf of children; (c) a solid base in the community on which to build the programme initially (an organized people's group, a well-established NGO, a forum of NGOs, or an action-oriented academic institution); (d) the creation of representative local councils which maintain an active dialogue on the problems faced by children; (e) the institutionalization of these councils and their programmes within the municipal government; (f) the presence of a coordinating office as a liaison between the municipal departments and the community residents; (g) an appropriate legal framework and provision of legislative powers to the councils in order to ensure long-term effectiveness; (h) improved management, coordination and convergence of municipal activities; (i) the optimization of municipal resources and investments; (j) the empowering of people and communities through effective organization and management of resources; and (k) an increased awareness of the need for a new vision of children, shared by all city residents and reinforcing their sense of joint responsibility.

Finally, an assessment was carried out of the strategies that have contributed to the relative success of these programmes, including, for example: (a) the identification of "change" agents and social entrepreneurs at the municipal level, and beyond; (b) the support of such agents through the provision of a "creative space" which allows them to manoeuvre as they elaborate innovative approaches; (c) the realization of a partnership with poor urban communities based on trust; (d) the utilization of research and of "immersion" (direct personal exposure to the everyday lives of impoverished urban children and families) to engage all city sectors; and (e) the establishment of forums in which various community sectors can discuss the problems of children in the city prior to the consolidation of councils, but also as an ongoing monitoring and mobilizing mechanism.

Again a comparative analysis serves to reinforce the arguments for incorporating recurrent features in other programmes. The common underlying assumption is that a complete transfer of any programme across countries is unlikely to be effective because of the very different subjective and objective contexts in each country, or even each city. However, certain features can prove very useful in bringing about comparable improvements. The Philippine urban programme, whose national advocacy was in part inspired by a similar programme in Brazil but which developed in quite different directions, is a good example of the transference of tested approaches.

CONCLUSION

The purpose of the Project has been to gain a greater understanding of children in especially difficult circumstances and develop ways to better diagnose their problems; to approach the children as whole people and recognize their and their families' resourcefulness and coping strategies; and to analyse innovative municipal policies for urban children. This includes a concern for reducing the number of children who live alone and work on the streets, preventing them from being abused or mistreated, by: (a) creating a healthier environment for them (and their parents); (b) involving children, parents and communities in addressing their problems and carrying out the strategies devised; (c) identifying, and providing assistance to, those children and families most at-risk; (d) suggesting approaches which would better support them in the future.

We are faced with an important challenge. The number of urban children is expected to grow significantly during the 1990s. Worldwide trends towards democratization and decentralization are providing new opportunities at the municipal level. National political leaders have made a commitment to adhere to the standards set down in the United Nations Convention on the Rights of the Child and to fulfil the goals established at the World Summit for Children. There are definite ways in which they can achieve those aims.

We have given the problems of disadvantaged urban children a clearer definition and emphasized the interdependencies among individuals, the environment, lifestyles and children's well-being; we have also learned from the most innovative programmes. In doing so, we hope that this first study will provide a useful starting point in the search for more effective strategies by contributing to the development and expansion of a new vision of children in cities, while helping to engage people at the national and municipal levels in meeting these objectives.

NOTES

1. While *heroin* (refined opium) is produced worldwide, with the heaviest concentration of opium production in Asia, the plant from which *cocaine* derives is native to Latin America and still primarily grown there. The percentage of drug abusers has been growing worldwide. In Italy most of the registered drug users were found to have completed compulsory schooling and a few years of high school, over 40 percent were unemployed, from 16 to 18 percent were underemployed or looking for work, while increasing numbers (27 percent in 1987) were regularly employed. There were 439 drug-related deaths, mostly males, between 1988 and 1989, an increase of 13.7 percent in one year (Ministry of the Interior 1991).

2. The most frequently used solvents in Brazil are glues or mixtures of ether, chloroform and toluene, which have been shown to cause serious brain damage and are potentially lethal. In addition, because they numb the nervous system causing insensitivity to pain, another potentially dangerous side-effect is self-inflicted cuts which can easily become infected, especially in the case of children on the streets.

3. Crack or "rock" was sold in the form of pills in the late 1980s in New York at less than $10 per gram when one gram of cocaine cost at least $100 (Arlacchi 1988). Crack, used as frequently by women and men, is extremely habit-form-

ing and causes progressive brain damage leading to major personality changes and diminished sense of responsibility. "Ecstasy" (Methedrine or MOMA as it is called), a stimulant used by German pilots during the Second World War to improve their aim, provides an instantaneous sense of well-being followed by acute depression. Its use has long-term effects on the central nervous system. In the United States, ecstasy was available over the counter until 1986 and in Italy, it is sold by drug pushers outside discotheques, for example. Fights on the dance floor and fatal car accidents have recently been traced to its use by Italian teenagers.

Chapter
TWO

Brazil: A New Concept of Childhood

Irene Rizzini, Irma Rizzini, Monica Munoz-Vargas and Lidia Galeano

INTRODUCTION

This chapter examines the situation of Brazil's marginalized urban children and their families, as well as the policies and programmes which have affected them over the years. Children who live in São Paulo, with its record population of 17 million inhabitants, or in any of the other cities in Brazil with more than one million inhabitants, share a number of problems. An overview of the current Brazilian social and economic context and the general trends affecting children 0–18 years of age is presented in Section II. Some main social indicators are outlined, with special emphasis on education and employment. Statistics revealing the trends of urbanization during the last decade are also analysed.

An examination of research on disadvantaged urban children and their families is contained in Section III. The first part summarizes the extensive analyses of street and working children carried out during the 1980s. This research provides an insight into the situation and survival strategies of urban children in especially difficult circumstances (CEDC). One interesting aspect of this literature is how it evolved during the 1980s from a superficial categorization of all children seen on urban streets as "street children," with some pejorative connotations, to a fuller understanding of the phenomenon. This research has been especially influential in creating a demand for changes in child-welfare policies. However, it has also had some serious shortcomings, including the absence of an analysis of the relations between street children and their families. The Goiânia study, described in the second part of Section III, is the first systematic attempt made in Brazil to investigate these relations.

Policies and programmes for the protection and welfare of children at risk are discussed in Section IV. The first part focuses on the evolution of social policies, to the embodiment of children's rights in the new Brazilian Constitution and to the creation of institutions which bring the public and private spheres together to monitor and safeguard children's rights. The main points of the legislative and social policy reform are then summarized. The third part includes a discussion of innovative approaches, both public and private, to improve the situation of urban children. The important contribution of universities to the understanding of these children's problems is also analysed.

Because of the significance of the popular movement which led to these legislative reforms, it is fitting that this chapter should end with an analysis of the dynamics of change as it applies to the Brazilian case. This is a pivotal moment in the history of Brazil's children and, in theory, many exciting prospects are opening up.

SOCIOECONOMIC CONTEXT AND DEMOGRAPHIC TRENDS

Immediately following the Second World War and until the end of the 1970s, the Brazilian economy grew rapidly. Between 1960 and 1980, Gross Domestic Product (GDP) rose by 4.1 percent in real terms, and annual growth rates of 10 percent were achieved.

According to Faria (1991), the economic structure of the country was diversified and modernized, causing:

> profound changes in the productive structure — both in the countryside and in the cities — as wage-labour became more common, commercial relations expanded and deepened, national labour markets and consumer markets came into being, and the growth of mass communications changed the structure of employment and of jobs, and changed the class structure.

The living standards of most of the population, however, did not improve. There continued to be wide disparities in the distribution of wealth, with large portions of the population living below the poverty line.

A severe recession struck in 1981–82, heralding what economists have termed the "lost decade." GDP rates, which were 3.2 percent for 1960–70, rising to 5.9 percent for 1970–80, plunged to –0.1 percent for 1980–88 (World

Bank 1990a); the average minimum salary declined even faster, falling 32.9 percent. Investment was at an unprecedented low, inflation soared to 50 percent per month, and the foreign debt and the fiscal deficit had grown to dangerous levels. Moreover, unemployment, a decrease in real income per capita, and reductions in public financing of social services all combined to worsen the situation of the poor (Albanez et al. 1989).

The economic crisis was exacerbated by demographic pressures. While GDP continued downward, population rates climbed. The population of Brazil increased by 25 million between 1980 and 1990, growing from 119 million to 144 million, with approximately 60 million under the age of 17 years. In cities, the population increased because of the continual flow of migrants from rural areas, but mainly because of the high rate of natural growth. The urban population, which before 1950 was less than 19 million and accounted for just 36 percent of the total, by 1980 had risen to more than 80 million, or 68 percent of the total. It is expected to continue to grow through the year 2020 (United Nations 1991a).

Between 1965 and 1980, the urban growth rate was 4.5 percent per year. This fell to 3.6 percent per year during the 1980s (World Bank 1990a). However, even with decreasing annual rates of urban population growth, cities still underwent very large increases in total populations because, according to Hardoy (1992), "once a city has reached several million inhabitants, even a relatively slow rate of population growth can produce annual increments in population of tens of thousands of inhabitants ... and given the current level of poverty, age structure, lack of skills and poor health of most of their inhabitants, this poses one of the greatest challenges." By 1990, the population of São Paulo and Rio exceeded respectively 17 million and 11 million and 14 Brazilian cities had more than 1 million inhabitants (Figure 2.1).

A large proportion of Brazilians living in poverty are children. In 1989, 25.6 million children between the ages of 0 and 17 lived in families whose monthly per capita income amounted to less than one minimum wage, which in October 1990 was approximately $60. Of this number, 43 percent represented children of less than 7 years of age.

In 1989, the majority (71 percent) of these children lived in urban areas. Between 1960 and 1980, the number of children in the 10–17 age group living in urban areas nearly doubled, going from 9.6 million to 18.3 million; in rural areas their numbers increased from 8.9 to 9.5 million, a growth rate of only 7 percent. Because adolescent girls are more likely to migrate to cities than are adolescent boys, there are slightly more girls between the ages of 10 and 17 than boys of the same age group living in urban areas. This phenomenon has been consistent throughout Latin America since the 1970s.

The primary education system, regulated by the Primary School Act of 1946, has experienced considerable growth, reflecting the high priority policy makers have placed on early education. In 1970, roughly 70 percent of 10- to 14-year-olds, and 76 percent of 15- to 19-year-olds were literate. By 1985, the

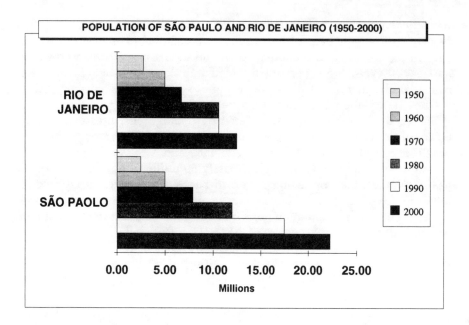

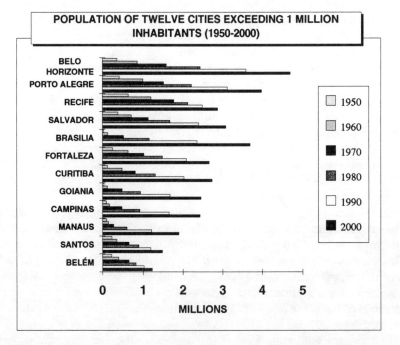

Figure 2.1. Population of São Paulo, Rio de Janeiro and twelve other cities (1950–2000) (source: Hardoy 1992).

rates had risen to 83 percent and 88 percent, respectively. There were no significant differences in literacy rates between males and females (Henriques et al. 1989). The system does not, however, meet the requirements of the Constitution, which foresees preschool services and a good quality of basic education for all.

Although the number of children in the 7–14 age group enrolled in primary schools has increased notably, reaching 89 percent in 1989, many children still remain outside the system. Statistics show that 33 percent of 7- to 17-year-olds who live in extremely poor urban families (whose earnings per capita are under one quarter of the minimum wage) were not enrolled in school in 1989. This indicator rises to 44 percent in rural areas. The increase in enrolment rates, moreover, has not resulted in corresponding advances in terms of the years of study completed. In fact, while the proportion of 7-year-olds enrolled in school increased from 62 percent to 70 percent between 1981 and 1986, this coverage falls dramatically after the first grade when truancy and failure rates ran as high as 50 percent.

According to official statistics, Brazilian children take an average of 12 years, instead of the normal eight, to complete their primary schooling. The main reasons are that many students begin their schooling late, abandon their courses in the middle of the year and later resume their studies in the same grade, or simply fail to pass. More than half the children who enter first grade repeat it the following year. As many as 85 percent of 15- to 17-year-olds, and 78 percent of 10- to 14-year-olds, are in grades that do not correspond to their age group. In the northeast the situation is even more serious, with more than 90 percent of all children over ten behind in their studies.

In the urban areas, 80 percent of the girls and 77 percent of the boys between 10 and 17 years of age are enrolled in school. Of these, 9 percent of the girls and 15 percent of the boys work for a living as well. The higher number of girls in school represents a significant shift in a society where gender differentials in schooling were the norm. Studies that attempt to evaluate the impact of schooling on the labour market have shown that there is generally a close relationship between women's level of schooling and their participation in the labour market. However, higher scholastic qualifications have not, as a rule, translated into significantly better wages or more qualified work when women join the labour force.

There are wide regional and social disparities in the ability of the education system to cater to all children. Coverage tends to be lower in smaller towns. This inequality of distribution also occurs with regard to the quality of teaching, buildings and other facilities.

In 1989, approximately 30 percent of children 10–17 years of age were active on the labour market, 19 percent in the 10–14 age group, and 51 percent in the 15–17 age group. The incidence of working children is higher in rural areas (58 percent) than in urban areas (32 percent). Studies show, however, that for males in both age groups employment rates rose markedly during the 1970s in urban areas, while in rural areas there was no change (Henriques et al. 1989). Work participation rates for girls are much lower: in the 10–14 age group, 9 percent in urban areas and 33 percent in rural areas; in the 15–19 age group, 34 percent in urban areas and 43 percent in rural areas (Henriques et al. 1989).[1]

Studies of types of work carried out by children show a decline over the past few decades in the agricultural sector, and an increase in the industrial and service sectors. Despite this decline, agriculture remains the sector in which the greatest number of children find work. In 1989, 41 percent were agricultural workers, and the proportion rises to 51 percent for the 10–14 age group, and 59 percent for children living in the northeast.

While children generally have low-skilled and low-paid jobs, there is a distinct gender division in occupational roles. Statistics for child workers in the 15–17 age group reveal that boys are more often listed as "other workers" on farms (a category that accounts for 68 percent) and vendors (9 percent), while almost half of the girls (49 percent) find jobs as housemaids. Girls consistently earn less than boys. Statistics for 1989 show that 61 percent of the girls working in urban areas earned less than the minimum wage, while the figure for boys was only 53 percent.

THE SITUATION OF DISADVANTAGED URBAN CHILDREN AND FAMILIES

Review of the Literature on Survival Strategies

Starting from the mid-1970s and particularly in the early 1980s, the growing numbers of poor, marginalized urban children, and more particularly street children, became a matter of great public concern, and the focus of considerable research. From today's perspective, it is evident that the debate had a significant impact on Brazilian society. A new understanding was gained of the problems afflicting the nation's poorest children. It also gradually became common knowledge that inequitable social policies were at the root of some of these problems. This new public awareness in turn created a favourable climate for social change. This section summarizes the results of research undertaken in the 1980s, with special emphasis on urban children who have been forced to make the street their place of work or their home.

Initial research treated "street children" as a uniform category. No distinctions were made between children who work on the streets and children who actually live on the streets; between children who are part of the informal work force and children who engage in illegal activities; between children who maintain family ties and children who have lost all contact with their families; or between children who carve out their own activities and children who work on the street in family "businesses." Research also tended to view street children in a vacuum.

It was only at the very end of the 1980s that there were attempts to distinguish between different categories, identifying a minority of children whose home is the street and who have severed all ties with their family, the *meninos(nas) de rua* (children *of* the street or street children). All other children found *on* the street were *meninos(nas) na rua*, or sometimes "working children."[2] Contrary to what was initially believed, it has been recognized that the vast majority of these children have homes to which they return at the end of the day. Relatively few had abandoned their families, although many studies point to a tendency for family ties to be weakened by the absence of parental supervision and by the relationships the children form on the streets. Most are children who are forced to work to supplement family income.

Street and working children and their families

Research data relating to street and working children are generally not disaggregated by sex, mainly because the children on the streets are overwhelmingly male. Girls are estimated to represent only 10 percent. Research suggests that families try to keep girls at home, either to help with the housework or to avoid their falling into prostitution.

Children are generally initiated into street life between the ages of seven and 12, with an average age of initiation of nine years. Most remain on the streets until they are about 15 or 16. In Rio de Janeiro, only 17 percent of a sample of 300 children were over the age of 14 years (Rizzini 1986); in Fortaleza, 14- to 16-year-olds accounted for only 12.3 percent of the sample (Governo do Estado do Ceará 1988). It appears the older children leave the street to seek greater job security, better wages and social acceptability.

Few studies make any reference to the ethnic origins of the children, but a 1986 survey in Rio found that almost three quarters of the sample (72 percent) were either black or mulatto (Rizzini 1986).

Although most researchers now recognize that the children's families potentially provide an important key to understanding the phenomenon of street children, no studies focusing specifically on their families were found. At best, researchers present an approximate profile of the children's families, obtaining information about them indirectly, and generally from the children themselves. This can lead to a somewhat distorted view, based on the child's perceptions and not counterbalanced by the viewpoint of other members of the family. In a pioneering effort, a research team in Goiânia (FLAC-SO/UNICEF 1991) recently compared a sample of families whose children work on the street with a sample of families whose children live on the street almost permanently, in an attempt to identify differences in the living conditions, structure or dynamics of the families. The results are presented later in this section.

Table 2.1. Urban Children Living with Both Parents, with One Parent or On Their Own[a] (Different Cities In Selected Years, 1979–90)

City	Year	With both parents (%)	With one parent (%)	On their own (%)
Belém	1979	44	39	2
Rio de Janeiro	1986	41	35	6
São Paulo	1988	58	30	–
Fortaleza	1988	52	36	4
Recife[b]	1989	36	33	16
Recife[c]	1989	52	21	5
Goiânia	1990	47	40	4

Sources: Gonçalves (1979), Rizzini (1986), Pires (1988), Governo do Estado do Ceará (1988), UFPE (1989), FLACSO/UNICEF (1991). [a]Children living with other relatives or in other living situations are not included. [b]Based on a random sample of street children. [c]Based on two groups of working children, one assisted by welfare agencies, the other unassisted.

Contrary to popular belief, the majority of urban poor children currently on the streets live in two-parent families (Table 2.1), although not necessarily both their own parents. Research has shown that (1) most children "on" or "of" the street come from nuclear families; (2) a significant number of their families are female-headed; and (3) only a small percentage of these children have severed all contact, or maintain only intermittent contact, with their family. The situation of street children is complex and easily misinterpreted. The families of poor urban children are often considered negligent, but this indictment ignores the social causes that have marginalized a significant part of the urban population and forced them into a full-time struggle for survival. Subsequent stress and adult frustrations often lead to abuse. As can be expected, children usually claim that they "chose" to live on the streets in order to help their families financially. However, other pressures and motivations have also been identified, including the attraction of a freer life with friends on the streets, and, more importantly, conflictual family relationships and a home life marred by abuse and violence.

Family size is another important element. The studies show that the majority come from large families (Table 2.2). These findings may seem to contradict nationwide statistics which document a decrease in family size during the 1980s. It was estimated in 1981 that the average family consisted of 4.3 members; by 1989, it had decreased to 3.9 members. However, lower-income families continue to be large despite national trends.

The available data on family income presented in most research confirm these statements. While researchers usually had difficulties obtaining information on family incomes from the children interviewed, and the figures

Table 2.2. Size of Street Children's Families in Different Cities
(Selected Years, 1980–89)

City	Year	Size of sample	Number of family members
Fortaleza	1980	–	8.2*
Rio de Janeiro	1986	56	4–8
Fortaleza	1988	53	5–8
São Paulo	1989	54	5–7
Recife	1989	45	6–8

Sources: Governo do Estado do Ceará (1988), IPLANCE (1980), Rizzini (1986), Pires (1988), Oliveira (1989). *In the case of this study, carried out by the Government of the state of Ceará, the average size of families is given instead of the minimum and maximum number of family members.

they do show are often riddled with discrepancies, there is a consensus that the majority of children who lead a street life come from poor families, many of which count on their children's earnings for survival.

Daily life on the street

One of the most interesting and revealing aspects of the research on street and working children concerns their day-to-day lives on the busy and often violent streets of Brazil's large cities. The children's accounts reveal how children earn money; what their relations are with each other, with the police, and with passers-by; what dangers they face; and what hopes they hold for the future. Their stories show how mistaken some segments of society are in regarding the lives of these children as worthless.

An "army" of child workers can be found on the streets of Brazil's large cities. Street vending was the principal activity of 64 percent of the sample in Belém (Gonçalves 1979), 40 percent in Recife (Oliveira 1989), 26 percent in Rio de Janeiro (Rizzini 1986), and 21 percent among various groups studied in several states around the country (Myers 1988b). For the most part, the children sell sweets, chewing gum, fruit, biscuits and other inexpensive items for a small profit. Other street occupations, all part of the "informal economy," include shining shoes, washing or minding cars, carrying bags and pushing carts at markets. Usually not captured by the research are the children on the street who are engaged in drug peddling, petty theft or other illegal activities, very often after having fallen into the hands of unscrupulous adults.

The phenomenon of children working on the streets is one dimension of the problem of exploitative child labour. Off the streets, children are often forced to work very long shifts, at low-skilled and poorly paid jobs; on the streets, they are not only exploited, but are also exposed to many types of abuse, danger and violence, without the protection of labour laws.

Most working children are self-employed. A study conducted in São Paulo found that the majority of the working children interviewed had no formal employer (Pires 1988). Similarly, 56.6 percent of the children in Recife were classified as "self-employed," while 22.2 percent were "hired" (Oliveira 1989). A survey in Salvador reported that 1,079 children were self-employed and 481 worked with adults, out of a total of 2,419 children counted on the street in the course of one morning (IBASE 1990). This is one of the few studies that gives an idea, even if only a very rough one, of the disturbing number of children on the city streets of Brazil.

The working day. A survey of urban working children in different states found that 59 percent worked between five and eight hours per day (Myers 1988b), and studies have generally shown that working children work between 20 and 48 hours per week, although a study in Fortaleza found that the work week of roughly half of the sample exceeded 48 hours (Governo do Estado do Ceará 1988).

The significance of school. The children who spend most of their time on the streets see school as important, but quite beyond their reach. It is common for them to claim that they want to study to "be something in life," and to deny that they have stopped going to school, even when questioned by a researcher who knows they have. Most of these children have, in fact, been enrolled in school and at some time attended classes, if only sporadically, but they are unable to reconcile their street occupations with the demands of school. The studies are unanimous in concluding that the time children spend on the streets and the kind of work they do have a negative effect on their school performance and are factors in the high incidence of dropout.

Some urban children maintain that personal and family problems keep them from attending school or have caused them to fall behind in their schooling. When questioned more closely, they explain that "personal" reasons are "the need to work" in approximately 20–30 percent of the cases surveyed, and "financial difficulties" for 10–30 percent. Thus, school difficulties cannot be separated from the wider economic and social reality in which the poorest segments of the population live.

Another important aspect of the problem is the total inadequacy of the public schools in dealing with the needs of urban poor children. The many weaknesses of the national education system have been well-documented, especially its failure to meet the needs of children who lack family support, and the disdain and indifference which often characterize teachers' attitudes towards disadvantaged children. Unfortunately, recent research has seldom analysed the school's response to street and working children, although this was a much-debated issue in the 1980s.

Street and working children's aspirations for the future. It is interesting to note that, despite their difficulties in terms of work and study, a significant proportion of street and working children regard these two activities as the keys to a better future. Their one main goal is to work, but their ambition stops at unskilled or semi-skilled jobs. Only a few have higher aspirations, although they are fully aware of their personal limitations. The following statements made by working children in Rio de Janeiro (Rizzini 1986) are quite typical:

> I must get a job otherwise I'll never manage to get out of this life. I'm young, and I don't want to die early. I'm thinking of going back to school to study. I want to be a jewel engraver. (a 15-year-old)

> I've got no other future and I sell sweets. I want to work and have a job as a porter, a guard at a bank, or maybe an olive box carrier. (a 13-year-old)

> I want to be a doctor in a hospital, or else a driver. I think that would be a nice profession. It's what I'd like. If we have the will to do things then we can succeed. (a 17-year-old)

Urban children's earnings. There is no precise information on how much children earn. Often the children themselves do not know how much they make because their earnings vary greatly. If they do know, they may be reluctant to volunteer this kind of information. It is clear that if children spend long hours working on the street, it is because they have no alternative. Their families often do not simply rely on the children's financial contribution, but are totally dependent upon it.

Research in São Paulo found that working children contribute between 20 and 40 percent of the family income in 36 percent of the families, more than 40 percent in 29 percent of the families, and up to 70 percent in a few cases. Other studies have confirmed that children actively provide financial support to their family (Pires 1988, Silva 1983, Ferreira 1979). One study in Recife concluded that working children contribute approximately half their earnings to their families (UFPE 1989).

It has been estimated that, in their various activities on the street, children earn between one and one and a half times the minimum wage. These earnings, which at first sight hardly seem worth the sacrifice, are in fact vital to the survival of both the children and their families. According to official statistics, 54 percent of Brazilian children 0–17 years of age live in households in which the monthly per capita income is half the minimum wage or less. Of this number, 30.6 percent subsist on one quarter of the minimum wage (IBGE 1989).

"Marginal" activities. The findings presented so far refer to urban children who work hard, often for long hours, sometimes at two or more street jobs, to contribute to their family's well-being. However, some children have chosen other ways to make money. These activities, called "marginal" to distinguish

them from work activities and to underscore the fact that they involve only a small percentage of children, can be divided into offences punishable by law (theft, robbery, prostitution, drug-pushing) and those not punishable by law (begging, vagrancy). Most children will admit to begging occasionally. Others, while too "street-wise" to admit it, are known to "make a little extra" by stealing, pushing drugs or from prostitution.

Very little is known about the "marginal" activities of street and working children or about their links with organized crime. Research suggests that the children involved in organized crime are probably in the 14–18 age group. They have severed all ties with their families and are likely to live on the streets, or to have done so in the past, and have very antagonistic relations with the police, whose brutality they fear (Medeiros 1985, Rizzini 1986, Oliveira 1989).

Most studies concentrate on nonpunishable "marginal" activities. Begging is common. Of 300 urban poor children in Rio de Janeiro, 18 percent admitted to begging a source of income (Rizzini 1986); percentages in Recife and Fortaleza were similar (Oliveira 1989, Governo do Estado do Ceará 1988).

Violence. Official child mortality rates show that homicide and suicide are the main causes of death among adolescents in the cities of Brazil (IBGE 1989). A pioneering study on crimes committed against children on the streets of Rio de Janeiro, São Paulo and Recife discloses that 457 children were murdered between March and August 1989 (MNMMR et al. 1991). Most of the victims (390) were males and most (336) between 15 and 17; only 11 had police records, and 13, at the most, were suspected of drug trafficking. The overwhelming majority had known addresses and lived with their parents. None was known to have ever carried weapons.

These crimes, which resembled executions, are believed to have been committed by hired gunmen. Police are investigating drug traffickers and gangsters who are the prime suspects; individuals who take justice into their own hands ("vigilantes," "death or extermination squads"); and a third group, the military and civil police and private security guards. Few of these cases have been resolved. It is worth emphasizing that the victims are commonly perceived as a social evil which should be suppressed.

A tentative typology

In his 1989 study, which was one of the first attempts to give a typology to what was for years considered a homogeneous group, Mark Lusk differentiates between four main categories in a sample of 103 children found on the streets of Rio de Janeiro: a) family-based street workers; b) independent street workers who have tenuous ties with their families and occasionally sleep on the streets; c) children who live on the streets and have no contact with their families; and d) children of street families.

Family-based street workers. This category represents 21.4 percent of the total; the average age is 13 years, and 90.9 percent are boys. Their families are made up of both parents in 59.1 percent of the cases. Almost three quarters (72.7 percent) claim to attend school and to work on the street out of need. Only 9.1 percent of the group is involved in illegal activities.

Independent street workers. This category represents 50.5 percent of the total; the average age is 13 years, and 73.1 percent are boys. The family ties begin to break down, and these children occasionally sleep on the streets. The families consist of both parents in 61.5 percent of the cases. A much higher percentage of children are involved in illegal activities (44.9 percent) and admit to drug use (61.5 percent). They claim to attend school in 30.8 percent of the cases.

Children of the streets. This category represents 14.6 percent of the total; the average age is 14 years, and 73.3 percent are boys. They live on the streets and do not have contact with their families. Slightly more than half (53.3 percent) report that they come from two-parent households. They tend to be involved in illegal activities (60 percent) and use drugs (80 percent). Only 6.7 percent attend school.

Children of street families. This category represents 13.6 percent of the total; the average age is 10.4 years, and 64.3 percent are boys. These children live or spend their days on the streets with their families, which are usually centred around the mother. They admit to involvement in illegal activities (38.5 percent) and the use of drugs (57.1 percent). Only 14.3 percent of these children claim to attend school.

As may be expected, the children who live on the street with no contact with their families are the oldest; they are also less likely to come from two-parent families. Family-based workers are more than twice as likely to attend school than independent workers, while only 6.7 percent of the children living on the streets attend school. Illegal activities are significantly lower among family-based workers. The high percentage of substance abuse, reaching 80 percent of the children of the streets, is another alarming statistic.

Recommendations for additional research

The categorization of at-risk urban children, as found in the Lusk study, is the exception rather than the rule. Most research carried out in the 1980s focuses primarily on children who work on the streets, but who maintain ties with their families. Less is known about children who live on the streets full-time and who, as has been shown, are the most vulnerable group in terms of schooling, illegal activities and substance abuse. It is essential that in-depth studies be conducted into the living conditions of street children and, with even greater priority, into the factors that have led them to break family ties and "choose" the street life.

The available research on juvenile offenders suggests that only a small percentage of street and working children are involved in illegal activities, although little is actually known about the extent and nature of the problem. The media have been very heavy-handed in their coverage of criminality among "street children," fuelling prejudice against these children and reinforcing the commonly held view that they pose a serious threat to society. "Rehabilitation" for today's juvenile offenders has not advanced much beyond imprisonment. Studies are needed to deflate the myth that every child on the street is a "bandit" or a "pickpocket," to determine the root causes of delinquency, and to investigate and report on the institutional treatment of juvenile offenders.

Data disaggregated by sex are virtually nonexistent. Little attention has been paid to how girls live on the streets or how they were initiated into the street world, despite growing public concern about the phenomenon. A few studies have suggested that girls generally leave home after confrontations with their parents, ending with the girls' refusal to assume the role that the family wishes to impose upon them. Leaving home in the case of girls (in contrast with boys) often implies the total rupture of family ties (Rizzini and Wiik 1990, Fenelon et al. 1992).

The relationships among street-based children also requires further research. Some studies have found that, because of the conditions of violence and insecurity the children face, they tend to look out mainly for themselves (Ferreira 1979). Other studies, in contrast, underscore the support and training functions of street groups, particularly during initiation into street life.

The feelings and emotions of children who are forced from an early age to survive on the streets are also not examined in any depth in the studies. Possibly the more practical questions of living and working on the streets blunt what could be regarded as a more "sentimental" issue.

Families of street and working children also need detailed study. The children's accounts often reveal family conflicts, sometimes so serious that they end with the child leaving home for good. Many children claim that life on the streets is a relief after the violence, sexual molestation, hunger, unstable relationships, or other difficulties they faced with their families. The following research carried out in Goiânia was the first systematic attempt to investigate the issue of the relations between the street child and his or her family.

The Goiânia Study: Children and Families

Goiânia, the capital of the state of Goiás, is in the central-western region of Brazil. In 1989, the state had about 4.9 million inhabitants, of which 2.1 million were children in the 0–17 age group. Approximately 70 percent of the population lived in urban areas.

It has been estimated that 25 percent of families with children have a per capita income of less than half the minimum wage. As a consequence, many children are forced to divide their time between study and work (20.6 percent of the children in the 10–17 age group), or simply drop out of school to work (13.9 percent).

Although school attendance rates are high (70 percent of the 5–17 age group), there is a great discrepancy between students' ages and grades. It has been estimated that 78 percent of the children between the ages of 10 and 14 are behind in their studies.

Child labour has become increasingly common, as figures covering 1980–89 show. Over this period, the number of 10- to 14-year-olds who worked rose from 14 percent to 23.3 percent, while in the 15–17 age group there was an increase from 43 percent to 59.5 percent. Most were "casual labour." Half (50.2 percent) of the children between 10 and 14, and 36 percent between 15 and 17, worked in the informal sector. The number of hours worked per week is another indicator of the difficulty of their situation: 54 percent of the 10- to 14-year-olds, and 81.8 percent of the 15- to 17-year-olds, worked 40 hours a week or more.

The aim of the Goiânia study was to characterize different categories of urban poor children to establish a clearer basis for preventive policies. The study defined two main groups: (1) children who live on the streets and have no, or very few, family links (children of the streets). This category was called "street children," using the term in a specific way, different from its more generalized use denoting all poor children found on the streets. (2) Children who are generally found on the street during the day, but who go home to sleep at night (children on the streets). Because most of the children in this category have street jobs, they were called "working children." The researchers do not mean to suggest that street children never work, nor that all of the working children are actually working.

The study (Alves 1991) sought answers to the following question:

Why is it that, when faced with similarly unfavorable socioeconomic conditions, some children maintain their ties with their families, while others exchange their homes for the streets?

The research was undertaken in Goiânia in 1990 by a multidisciplinary group of researchers from the Latin American Faculty of Social Sciences (FLACSO) with the participation of street educators and the assistance of the Integrated Programme of Support to Children of the Foundation for Social Promotion (hereafter the Foundation) of the Goiás state government, a social service institution for children and their families. The study consisted of quantitative and qualitative analyses of the socioeconomic conditions, structure and dynamics of the families of both street children and working children. Table 2.3 summarizes some of the main findings.

The quantitative survey was of 128 children and their respective families. The survey contrasted three groups: (a) 42 street children who receive assistance from the Foundation; (b) 46 street-based working children who receive assistance from the Foundation; and (c) 40 street-based working children who do not receive assistance from the Foundation. The street children were selected by the researchers on the basis of information obtained from the

Foundation, whereas both groups of street-based working children were selected by an incidental sampling method.[1] The sample was mainly made up of boys (88 percent) because of their higher representation on the streets as well as among the children assisted by the Foundation. The low number of girls in the study made it difficult to make any comparisons based upon sex. The children in the study were between 6 and 17 years of age, with the majority 7 to 14. The study did not compare families across time.

In addition to large-scale interviews, 20 in-depth interviews were undertaken with ten children and their families to explore family relations. Of these children, four were street children (three boys and one girl), four were assisted working children, and two were unassisted working children.

Characteristics of the households of the different groups

Compared with families of working children, families of street children have a slightly younger age composition, having the largest number of children in the 0–7 age range. They are also the smallest, averaging 5.5 persons, compared with the average of 6.6 across all three groups. The majority of all families own their own homes and a few are squatters. Across all groups, an average of 75 percent of the families have migrated from other municipalities or states. One interesting finding is that street children's families have a higher per capita household income than working children's families; 51 percent, versus an average of 45 percent, of the minimum monthly wage.

Thus economic factors cannot be used to distinguish between the families of street children and working children, or to explain why some children leave their home. Poverty alone cannot account for the street child phenomenon.

Both natural parents are present in 49 percent of the street children's families. This is a significant portion and stands in contrast with the popular conception that all street children have been abandoned or come from broken homes. In all three groups the incidence of absent fathers was similar, ranging from 14 to 18 percent.

The illiteracy rate is highest among fathers of street children (40 percent); there is no significant difference in the literacy rates of the mothers, which are between 27 percent and 32 percent. The fathers of street children also have a much lower rate of employment (57 percent); on the other hand, the mothers of street children have a higher rate of employment (68 percent).

The main economic provider in the street child household is the mother; the father is the main economic provider in the unassisted and the assisted working children's households.

These data point to an inversion of roles in the families of street children: the mother takes responsibility for providing for her offspring, thus going against the patriarchal tradition of the Brazilian family. Challenging such deeply rooted cultural attitudes causes both objective and subjective difficulties in the dynamics of the family. Among the objective difficulties are the

Table 2.3. Household Profiles of Street Children and Street-Based
Working Children (in Percentages, 1990)

	Families of street children	Families of unassisted working children	Families of assisted working children
Type of family (C)[a]			
Nuclear	35	57	47
Disaggregated	50	26	42
Extended	8	5	3
Per capita income level (H)[b]			
% of monthly minimum wage	51	46	44
Parental illiteracy rates (H)[b]			
Father	40	33	22
Mother	29	32	27
Percentage employed (H)[b]			
Father	57	92	86
Mother	68	46	61
Siblings	31	54	45
Child	37	65	57
Main economic provider (H)[b]			
Mother	46	13	22
Father	36	50	37
Child contributes to family income (C)[a]			
Regularly	13	69	69
Occasionally	30	17	21
Never	58	14	10
Type of parental relationship (H)[b]			
Married	48	62	52
Cohabiting	32	24	26
Father absent	18	14	17
Duration of parental relationship (H)[b]			
5 or more years	60	80	82
3 to 5 years	26	13	10
Migrated	73	79	77
From where? (H)[b]	Other state	Other city	Other state
Relationships outside of the family (H)[b]			
Relatives	46	58	66
Friends	33	13	11
Neighbours	18	26	19
In difficulty, family turns to (H)[b]			
Family members	72	72	57
Relatives	13	15	14
Main areas of concern (H)[b]	Security: 30 Relationship: 22 Health: 19	Health: 42 Education: 19 Employment: 17	Education: 30 Employment: 24 Health: 10

[a](C) = according to child interview. [b](H) = according to household interview. Source: FLAC-SO/UNICEF (1991).

work overload borne by the mother and how this, in turn, affects her relationship with her children. A long and stressful workday has a negative effect, not only on the mother's relationship with her children, but also upon her ability to control them. A more subjective consequence is the transmission of a weak image of the father, who has difficulty in performing the role that society expects of him. The loss of self-image experienced by an unemployed man who is supported by his wife in a traditionally male-dominated society undoubtedly adds to his frustrations and increases his level of stress. This may cause him to take up drinking or to be abusive. It certainly has a negative influence on his relations with all other family members.

The study suggests that only a small percentage of street children cut their ties with their families definitively. Fifteen percent declared that they had no contact at all with their families, while 70 percent reported maintaining some contact with their families.

The street child's relationships

The study found that the families of street children are more disaggregated and less nuclear than the other families, even though they have a greater incidence of couples who have been together for three to five years. The majority of couples in all groups have been together for the past five years. It should be noted that the relationship referred to does not necessarily involve the child's biological father. Fathers were not found to be more absent in street-child families than in the other two groups.

However, relationships within the families of street children appear to be less caring. Individual members tend not to work together for the betterment of the family group. They are less helpful to each other and to the unit. In comparison with working children, street children report having difficult relationships with parents and siblings more frequently; talking to, confiding in and receiving help from their fathers less frequently; and being subjected to corporal punishment more often. Street children also report having behavioural problems in school more frequently than the other two groups of children.

The picture that emerges is one of street children and their families with strained relationships, no longer operating as a collaborative unit. When families were asked what their concerns were, families of street children frequently mentioned relationships, while families of working children talked about education, employment and health. Despite reported difficulties with their families, more than 70 percent of the street children maintain either regular or occasional contact with their families. Interestingly, all children report that their relationship with their family improved after they had left home for the streets.

Mothers have a central role as decision-maker in the family across all groups. Children in all groups report talking to, confiding in and receiving help from their mother, but street children refer to this slightly less frequently.

On the other hand, they claim to receive this kind of support from siblings and others slightly more frequently than the two other groups.

Family dynamics

Family dynamics can be considered a factor in the attraction/expulsion of the child, as the in-depth interviews with parents and children revealed. An analysis of these interviews shows that a main difference between street children and working children is the quality of collaborative relations within their respective families. Despite the fact that all the families are poor and face many of the same problems, the families of working children tend to be more affectionate, more cooperative, and more actively involved in family life. Conversely, the families of street children are characterized by a lesser degree of family cohesion. Corporal punishment, for example, is much more frequent. In comparing these groups of children, the study suggests that the greater the family cohesion, the more control it exercises over the child, and vice versa.

The absence of a parent responsible for the functioning of the household leads to what has been called the "empty-house syndrome." This is the abdication of responsibility for the affective dimension of the home, which reduces it to a mere sleeping place (Moura 1991).

Even though parental presence is important for family cohesion, the study indicates that physical presence alone is not enough to guarantee the wholeness of the group. Both the quantitative and qualitative aspects of the study detected a climate of violence in a significant proportion of the families of street children. An alarming 63 percent of the street children reported that they had been subjected to corporal punishment before they left home. A more subtle form of abuse is experienced by girls who are invariably charged with the domestic chores and with the care of younger siblings.

From the home to the street

The background of chronic poverty produces a state of permanent tension in these children. The culture of consumerism, to which they are exposed, contrasts with their stark living conditions, creating dissatisfaction. This leads some children to seek alternatives, not just to ensure survival, but also to satisfy their desire to consume. These desires alone, however, are not enough to cause children to abandon their homes. There are vast numbers of children who work on the street and are highly susceptible to its allure, but who, nevertheless, maintain their ties with their families.

Why then do some families lose hold of their children? The quantitative survey detected a high degree of interpersonal difficulties within the families of street children, especially in relation to the father. The qualitative data point to deteriorated household relationships.

The violent environment, the lack of incentive or support, the impotent image of the parents, the daily experience of humiliations (including for many children the threat of punishment if they come home without money), the excess of domestic chores, the absence of free time, and even the lack of food may contribute to the child's decision to leave home. When physical and verbal violence transform the home into a space of conflict, deprivation and loneliness, the companionship of peers on the street may actually hold advantages, not the least of which is freedom from the demands of the family. Moreover, when the family does not inspire trust, communicate a clear set of rules and values, ensure a feeling of safety, or foster warm relationships, it does not compete well with the attraction that the child may increasingly feel for the freedom of the street and the life of the street band.

A street band, a group of street children living together, is a social organization that contributes to making iife on the streets viable. The street band offers such practical advantages as protection from the hazards of the street and psychological support.

Interestingly, the internal organization of the band is modelled upon an idealized view of the family. The group accepts the leader as the father, and the other members as fellow children. It is a model that tries to recreate a nuclear family in which harmony predominates. The leader plays an essential role, which cannot be dismissed as being based solely upon harassment or terror as popular myth would have it. The leader protects and guides the band, and decides who will be admitted to it. The loyalty that the leader commands is not determined by age, physical strength or the length of time spent on the streets.

Households in which interaction has broken down fear the competition of the street band and the potential influence it has on the child. The band may actually take over the social training of children. Under its influence, the child undergoes a subtle process of social reorientation during which new values, based upon begging and predatory behaviour, are inculcated, and the traditional values of the established order — family, school, work and the law — are disdained.

In the seemingly hopeless family situations of many children, the band may appear as the only way that they will ever fulfil their longings for solidarity and protection.

Main conclusions

The statistical data and case studies confirm that economic factors alone are not the cause of the child leaving home. Other factors include hostility, lack of unity, and rejection within the family. The greater the disintegration of the family's ability to cope, the more pernicious are the effects of poverty.

The physical presence of the parents is not enough to ensure the integrity of the family. This explodes the myth that the nuclear family in itself can guarantee that children will remain under the control of the parents. It is the quality of care that makes the difference. In the "empty house," characterized by physically and/or emotionally absent parents and general conditions of stress, interpersonal relationships among family members are weakened and the control mechanisms that govern the lives of the children deteriorate.

It was found that, of the different families, only those of the street children had mothers who were main providers of the household more often than the fathers. This situation represents an affront to the traditional patriarchal values of families in Brazil. It contributes to the father's frustrations and to the strained relationships among household members. Street children have great difficulties in their relationships with their fathers. They do not feel that they can confide in them, or establish a relationship. Street children are also subject to corporal punishment more often than working children.

As the child feels increasingly detached from home, the street band as a social organization becomes more attractive. The street band makes life on the streets feasible, both in terms of practical survival and emotional support.

POLICIES AND PROGRAMMES

The Context of the Reform and its Principal Actors

The situation of disadvantaged urban children in Brazil presented in the preceding sections is in part the direct result of policy decisions. It has also become the determinant of new policies. In 1988, a new Brazilian Constitution was adopted containing "The Chapter on the Rights of Children and Adolescents." Two years later, the National Congress approved the Children's and Adolescents' Act which translates into national law the principles contained in the Constitution. The importance of the recent changes in child-welfare policies can only be understood if they are viewed within their historical context.

Tendencies in social policy, 1930–88

Beginning in the 1930s, public health, education and social-welfare policies increasingly assigned decision-making power and allocated financial resources to the federal level. Beneficiaries had no social or political channel which enabled them to influence the decisions affecting them.

In the 1960s and 1970s, social policies relating to education, health, social assistance, retirement benefits and housing were reorganized in an attempt to overcome institutional and financial fragmentation. In this period, and particularly during the 1970s as a result of rapid economic growth, social policy assumed a more dynamic role. There was an underlying belief that social progress would be closely linked to economic growth and that action was needed to ensure better-qualified human resources. However, in keeping with the free-market ideology, there was also a clear tendency towards the privatization of services, the adoption of self-financing strategies, and a corresponding reduction in government participation, especially in health and education (Martine 1989).

The social programmes were competitive and poorly managed. The over-lap and lack of coordination in health, education and housing eroded resour-ces. Bureaucracy and red tape clogged administration. Large portions of the resources went towards the upkeep of agencies and the remuneration of their staffs.

Public access to social services varied by sector, according to the financial resources available. A lack of state control often led to discrepancies in service provision (Draibe 1989). In the health sector, incentives were offered to en-courage the expansion of curative medicine, with an emphasis on expensive technology and hospital treatment to the detriment of preventive medicine, particularly low-cost primary programmes like vaccination, oral rehydration and prenatal control. In education, while progress was achieved at the primary and university levels, secondary education was practically ignored. The marked increase in enrolments did not improve the quality of teaching, which in many cases even declined because of a lack of resources. Public housing focused increasingly on higher-income groups, to the detriment of the urban poor who crowded into slums without access to basic infrastruc-ture or social services.

Thus an ever-widening gap was created between the basic needs of the poor and the services offered to them. Furthermore, social policy was largely financed by wage earners, but benefited the wealthier segments of society. As Draibe (1989) stated, "it is the principle of merit, interpreted as meaning one's position in the productive, wage-earning structure, which constitutes the basis upon which the Brazilian system of social policy is constructed."

At the beginning of the 1980s, the severe economic crisis led to reductions in government social spending. Large portions of the population began to have only limited access to even the most basic goods and services. The failure of the State to have a positive impact on the well-being of children became increasingly evident, and "problems of governability, the financing of the public sector and the administrative functioning of the State became, as of this point, a constant" (Draibe 1989).

Nevertheless, the process of democratic transition gave new social sectors a voice, albeit a small one, in the decision-making process. Popular move-ments urged the Government to redefine social assistance. In the early 1980s, there were sporadic and only somewhat successful attempts, especially at state and municipal levels, to redefine some areas of social action, such as the right to primary education, to emergency care in hospitals and to social assistance.

Assistance to children in especially difficult circumstances

The following is a brief analysis, partially based on a paper by A. Gomes da Costa (1989), tracing the evolution of the legal position of the Brazilian child from "minor" to "child citizen." It is important to understand the implica-tions of both words. The term "minor" is irrevocably associated with the highly repressive Minors' Code and the abuses of the Assistance Service to Minors which preceded it. The term can no longer be used in the Brazilian context simply to signify a child under the age of 18 years. Similarly, the word "citizen" has a specific cultural dimension in Brazil, expressing the nation's aspirations for economic and social justice. This concept has gained wide consensus.

Up until the end of the nineteenth century, assistance to children who were destitute, abandoned, orphaned or antisocial was carried out mostly through institutions run by religious orders or philanthropic organizations. It was only in the early part of this century that the government established institutions to give these children a "home," and provided noninstitutional assistance in the form of creches, trade schools or extension services to prepare needy children for "introduction into society" (Rizzini, Irma 1989).

In 1941, the Assistance Service to Minors (SAM) was created within the Ministry of Justice. SAM's methods were correctional and repressive, aiming at social control rather than social development. They reflected the prevailing attitude that deprived youths were a threat to public safety and were best rehabilitated in institutions.

Other institutions intended for the welfare of children of the poorer social classes were set up. Priority was given to vocational training in industry, trade, health care (especially to assist mothers with very young children), and rehabilitation of abandoned children or juvenile offenders.

In 1964, the government began to take a more progressive approach that recognized children in especially difficult circumstances. Law 4513 of 1964 designated the National Foundation for the Welfare of Minors (FUNABEM) to replace SAM.

FUNABEM was a top-down and institutionalization-oriented service model first developed in Rio and gradually duplicated in all the states through the creation of State Foundations for the Welfare of Minors (FEBEM). From 1979, under the Minors' Code, children became wards of the court if they were in an "irregular situation," involving need or crime. The court generally "solved" the children's problems by committing them to large institutions.

The legislation of children's rights

The beginning of the 1980s marked the initial phases of a shift in the legal and social position of children. The following steps led to these changes.

Joint efforts. The economic crisis made concerned organizations all too aware of the plight of Brazil's disadvantaged urban children and the need for far-reaching changes. Realizing the important potential role nongovernmental organizations (NGOs) could play, child-welfare specialists from FUNABEM, the Secretariat for Social Action and UNICEF launched the national Alternative Services for Street Children Project in 1982. This project aimed at identifying, analysing and disseminating details of successful community-based projects involving street children.

Grassroots groups connected with the Catholic Church were especially active. Among these, the Minors' Pastorate (*Pastoral de Menor*), created by the National Conference of Brazilian Bishops in 1978, played a prominent role. Differing totally from public institutions in their approach, these groups viewed the child as an active participant in the educational process ("the subject") and not the recipient ("the object") of someone else's effort. Participation in community life was considered of utmost importance to the child's psychological and social development.

The Alternative Services for Street Children Project identified about 400 groups, mainly NGOs, working with urban children, encouraged networking among the groups, and provided support for the training of hundreds of nonformal educators. The project empowered its participants; encouraged leaders to guide the new social movement; and identified resource people, institutions and projects.

Gaining national visibility. The First Latin American Seminar on Community Alternatives for Street Children, held in Brasilia in September 1984, gave the problems of marginalized urban children national visibility for the first time. At a subsequent meeting of the local committees in June 1985, the National Street Children's Movement was officially formed. Less than a year later, in May 1986, the National Movement organized the First National Street Children's Congress in Brasilia, with the participation of more than 500 street and working children.

At that meeting, which attracted wide media coverage, street children spoke out. They were particularly vehement in denouncing the FUNABEM/FEBEM system and demanded an end to institutional and police violence. The children made an impressive public claim for full citizenship, including the right to education and to better living conditions. Their capable presentations had the immediate effect of shattering some of the stereotypes that had grown up around street children, giving these often-despised children a new, more positive public image.

Other democratic forces were at work. A national movement advocating the direct election of the President and the Congress gained wide popular support. The military withdrew from the government in 1985 after 20 years. The ensuing two years, during which the Constitution was redrafted for the seventh time, presented a unique opportunity for discussing urgently needed reforms.

Children's rights and the new Constitution. In September 1986, the Government established the National Commission on the Child and the Constitution, with representatives of the Ministries of Education, Health, Social Welfare, Justice, Labour and Planning. The Commission's role was to receive submissions on the problems of children and to propose constitutional changes. UNICEF was enlisted to provide technical assistance. The Commission also promoted a major media campaign.

Nongovernmental initiatives were an essential factor. Leadership was provided by such organizations as the National Front for the Defence of Children's Rights, the Minors' Pastorate and the National Street Children's Movement.

As a result of this mobilization, two constitutional amendments, inspired by the then draft international Convention on the Rights of the Child, were consolidated in a single submission to the Constituent Assembly, supported by petitions signed by 1,300,000 children and about 200,000 voters, far in excess of the 30,000 voters' signatures needed to ensure the introduction of a constitutional amendment. These proposals became the Constitution's Chapter on the Rights of Children and Adolescents which was approved almost unanimously in May 1988, entering into force in October 1988.

The introduction to the Chapter states that, "it is the duty of the family, society and the State to guarantee the child and the adolescent, with absolute priority, the rights to life, health, food, education, leisure, professional training, culture, dignity, respect, freedom, family and social life, and to protect them from all forms of negligence, discrimination, exploitation, cruelty and oppression" (Art. 227).

Operationalizing the Constitution. The next objective was to incorporate the constitutional principles in legislation. The substitution of the Minors' Code with a new law was the first point on the agenda drafted by NGOs in March 1988. NGOs subsequently established a coalition called the National Nongovernmental Forum for the Defence of Children's and Adolescents' Rights (Forum DCA). Forum DCA united various nationwide networks, including the National Street Children's Movement, the Minors' Pastorate and the National Front for the Defence of Children's Rights. Its broad objectives were to coordinate NGO efforts on children's rights and to promote legislation.

Mobilization was also taking place at the state level, through the creation of joint governmental and nongovernmental fora, and at the local level through other specific initiatives. Some progressive members of the judiciary and of the public sector also publicly expressed their commitment to reforming the law. Further support came from important professional organizations, including the Brazilian Bar Association and the Brazilian Society of Paediatrics. It took more than one year of intensive debate to draft a Children's and Adolescents' Act, which the National Congress adopted as Law 8069/90 in July 1990; it came into effect on Children's Day, 12 October 1990.

During 1991, additional legislation created joint governmental and nongovernmental Councils for the Rights of the Child and Adolescent at federal, state and municipal levels. These Councils institutionalize, for the first time in Brazilian history, the participation of representatives of grassroots groups in setting public policies. The challenge that the Councils face is to transform into everyday practice the nation's commitment towards its children, as expressed in the Constitution.

The full implementation of the rights guaranteed under the Children's and Adolescents' Act is an arduous task, requiring renewed political will at all levels. The extent of the reform is unprecedented. Financial and technical resources must be mobilized in order to extend the coverage of basic social policies, to strengthen community-based preventive interventions and to reform the juvenile justice system. Nonetheless, the existence of a permanent national movement struggling for social and political change and for more equitable child-welfare policies represents an important promise for the future.

The role of UNICEF

In 1982–86, UNICEF Brazil's work for children in especially difficult circumstances was implemented through the Alternative Services for Street Children Project, which it co-sponsored with the national Secretariat for Social Action and FUNABEM. UNICEF's activities included human resources development, communication and information, advocacy and mobilization. These activities constituted an empowerment process, and contributed to creating the initial conditions for a broader involvement of Brazilian institutions and social actors in the promotion of children's rights.

In 1986–90, as Brazil worked towards building democratic institutions, UNICEF faced the challenging task of broadening the scope of its traditional country programmes. In order to take advantage of this unique opportunity to build momentum around children's issues, UNICEF adopted a new advocacy style which made use of different, but complementary, strategies: situation analysis; alliance-building and networking, two activities particularly suited to UNICEF because of its long-standing reputation for non-partisanship; and social mobilization, carried out mainly through social communication campaigns aimed at sensitizing the public about children's issues.

In view of its limited resources, UNICEF Brazil chose to maximize its impact through "a strategy that combines support to effective replicable programmes and projects with well-targeted social mobilization efforts, made possible through a continuous process of situation analysis, and defined by a set of programme goals and lines of action, rather than a set of specific programmes and projects" (UNICEF/IPEA-IPLAN 1990). Through these specific actions, UNICEF was able to play a facilitating role, maintaining a permanent dialogue with the governmental and nongovernmental institutions involved in the children's movement.

The reform period was a necessary step in the process of building up a new social, political and juridical context with more favourable conditions for dealing with children's issues. Since 1990, UNICEF has directed special advocacy and technical assistance efforts towards the restructuring of national institutions, as provided for by the new legislative framework. It has paid particular attention to the process of political and administrative decentralization at the state and municipal levels, and to the creation of Guardianship Councils, described later in this section, and Councils for the Rights of the Child and Adolescent.

New Legal Framework for Child-Related Policies

The legal instruments supporting child-related policies have a common point of departure, namely the acknowledgement of the full citizenship of all children. However, to ensure that this concept would not be just a rhetorical declaration, legislators specified mechanisms for the implementation of children's rights in the Children's and Adolescents' Act. It is recognized that children have a right to protection, and that they have specific developmental needs which must be fulfilled. Because of the participatory way in which the law was written and the mobilization in favour of its adoption, the law was "owned" by individuals and communities, and became a tool which they could use to promote and defend the interests of their children.

The Children's and Adolescents' Act

One of the implicit objectives of the Minors' Code was the social control of poverty and of deviant behaviour through the targeting of "minors in an irregular situation." In contrast, the Children's and Adolescents' Act is a wide-ranging instrument for safeguarding and promoting the well-being of all Brazilian children.

Article 88 of the Children's and Adolescents' Act establishes the following six guidelines:

(1) *Decentralization.* With the political and administrative decentralization established by the Constitution, approximately 4,500 municipalities gain more responsibility for the organization and maintenance of basic health and education services, and the coordination of assistance programmes. Decentralization is expected to result in more needs-oriented policies and increased accountability.

The municipalities can, in principle, draw upon the technical and financial cooperation of both state and federal governments. States are responsible for assisting municipalities in planning and evaluating activities, in developing human resources, in research, and in directly implementing programmes which exceed the demand and the technical and financial authority or capacity of the municipality. The Federal Government establishes the policy guidelines and coordinates programme implementation at the national level. The federal bureau directly responsible for the coordination of the Special Protection Policy at the national level is the Brazilian Centre for Childhood and Adolescence, created in 1990 to substitute the unconstitutional FUNABEM (CBIA 1991).

(2) *The creation of national, state and municipal Councils for the Rights of the Child and Adolescent.* The Children's and Adolescents' Act institutionalizes the participation of NGOs in setting policy and monitoring child-welfare policies and programmes. The Councils consist of an equal number of governmental and NGO representatives who are expected to coordinate policies to eliminate the many weaknesses of welfare programmes, including fragmentation, overlapping and discontinuity of services, and to promote interventions which respond to actual needs.

By early 1992, two thirds of the states (18 out of 27) had created Councils for the Rights of the Child and Adolescent, as had slightly more than one quarter of the municipalities (1,026 out of approximately 4,000).

(3) *The creation of special funds at the municipal, state and national level.* The Councils for the Rights of the Child and Adolescent are responsible for the special funds which are raised in addition to regular financing. The Councils also have the authority to raise any additional funds needed for child-related programmes.

(4) *The operational integration of services for the reception and referral of juvenile offenders.* With this directive, an integrated screening centre is formed, bringing together security forces, the judiciary and the social-welfare system, which together are responsible for the initial reception and referral of juvenile offenders from 12 to 18 years of age. This mechanism serves to coordinate sectors which traditionally worked in isolation. It is meant to ensure that juvenile offenders pass through the justice system as quickly as possible and that their legal rights are fully respected.

(5) *Social mobilization.* Article 227 of the Federal Constitution establishes that the implementation of children's rights is the "duty of the family, the society and the State." The mobilization of different sectors is therefore seen as an indispensable tool.

(6) *The implementation of specific programmes.* The implementation of the new policies will be carried out through a "coordinated system of governmental and nongovernmental actions" at every level. The new policies, therefore, represent a full appreciation of the positive role NGOs can play because of their flexibility, ability to reach difficult groups and cost-effectiveness. One provision of the Act is that NGOs concerned with child-related issues must register with their municipal Council for the Rights of the Child and Adolescent in order to have access to public financing. This helps to avoid overlapping programmes and gaps in coverage.

Policies for the implementation of children's rights

The Children's and Adolescents' Act establishes a three-tiered hierarchy of policies. The Basic Social Policies are for all children; the Social Assistance

Policies are for children in need; and the Special Protection Policies are for victimized children.

The Basic Social Policies are the main instruments for the implementation of social rights, giving all children the right to health care, education, job training, and other basic services.

Social Assistance Policies are not universal. A discrimination, based mainly on economic status, favours underprivileged social groups of children and their families. The objective is to ensure that beneficiaries attain an agreed minimum level of well-being that preserves their individual dignity.

Special Protection Policies are directed towards children at personal and social risk. Beneficiaries include the homeless, orphans, drug addicts, institutionalized children; victims of discrimination, negligence, exploitation and abuse; victims of police or institutional violence; and disabled children. These policies are implemented through the Guardianship system, described below.

The model places an emphasis on the citizenship of those in need of care and protection. Overcoming the paternalistic features of existing programmes and ensuring that basic services of a high standard are made available universally are the main challenges. Improved and increased coordination among basic social and assistance policies is needed, as well as changes in programmatic strategies, administrative decentralization and the promotion of effective people's participation. One step in the right direction is represented by the Guardianship system.

The Guardianship system

The Guardianship system, a municipal office created by the Children's and Adolescents' Act is broadly responsible for monitoring children's rights at the municipal level. The system is made up of a Guardianship Council and Special Protection Services. Each municipality is legally required to create a number of Guardianship Councils, depending on the size of the area and its child population. The rules of operation and the remuneration of professionals vary. The Guardianship Council constitutes the pivotal element of the new social policies relating to children. By May 1992, 406 Guardianship Councils had been created.

Each Guardianship Council is composed of five professionals who must be well integrated into the local community and have prior experience working with children.[3] They are responsible for ensuring that children in need or at risk receive the best possible assistance available. The Guardianship Councils also handle the cases of law infringers under 12, and work closely with families. Anyone (the children themselves, families, teachers, social workers, policemen and other public officials) can request the Guardianship Council to intervene (Box 2.1).

The Guardianship Council is therefore the point of entry into the service system with the role of facilitating the relationship between beneficiaries and existing services.[4] The notion of system is particularly important. Guardianship Councils are components in a broad coalition working for the welfare of children. They must interact with, and complement, other parts of the system. Because they have up-to-date knowledge of the children and the status of the service system, the Guardianship Councils advise municipal governments on budgets and plans of action relating to children. Figure 2.2 shows the terms of reference of the Guardianship Council and the system in which it works.

Reform of the juvenile justice system

The reform brought about by the Children's and Adolescents' Act was radical. From an institution controlling children in an "irregular situation," juvenile justice became an institution responsible for guaranteeing children's rights. This new policy met the standards set down by the United Nations Convention on the Rights of the Child, the Standard Minimum Rules for the Administration of Juvenile Justice (the Beijing Rules), the Guidelines for the Prevention of Juvenile Delinquency (the Riyadh Guidelines), and the Rules for the Protection of Juveniles Deprived of their Liberty.

The jurisdiction of the juvenile court is effectively restricted by the principles of integral protection. The juvenile courts mainly handle cases involving:

Judicial status of the child. When a child is orphaned or abandoned, the judge may place the child under the temporary custody of a guardian or foster parent, or authorize adoption.

Legal offences committed by children between 12 and 18. The juvenile judge has the authority to dismiss a case after a hearing. If a child is found guilty of an offence after legal procedures (during which the child has the right to legal representation), the judge may issue an admonishment or sentence the offender to pay damages, to perform a community service, to parole, to semi-liberty or to deprivation of liberty. The basic criterion is the educational potential in the given social situation. Ideally, the measure should strengthen the child's ties with his or her family and community, and promote the child's personal development and social integration.

Administrative infractions to the norms for the protection of children. In cases of violations (for example, when hotels permit child prostitution on their premises or when restaurants employ children illegally), the judge may apply penalties from fines to the suspension or revocation of licences.

The juvenile courts, together with the prosecutor and the Guardianship Council, also monitor governmental and nongovernmental institutions to ensure, among other things, that they provide adequate and appropriate services, that their staff is trained and that the premises are safe.

Box 2.1   Maringá's Guardianship Council

A town in the state of Paraná with 320,000 inhabitants, Maringá serves as the region's economic pole. Workers from surrounding towns and villages, as well as from more remote rural areas, migrate or commute to Maringá to work on crop or cattle farms or in the food processing industry. With the rapid population growth of the late 1980s, "bedroom" or satellite cities have gradually become part of the urban area of Maringá.

Like many other Brazilian cities, Maringá has a large population of working children who are at risk of dropping out of school, or who have already left school to work full-time, usually in the informal sector. Until a few years ago, there was little coordination between Maringá's welfare institutions. Each was locked in its own specific conceptual, functional and physical spaces. As a result of the effective commitment of local communities, the municipal government introduced a new social policy which is a joint community and governmental effort, coordinated by the public Foundation of Social Development. Its purpose is to promote the social integration of "at-risk" children through improvements in family and community life and, in particular, to ensure that these children have greater access to schools, vocational training and job placement. In keeping with this renewed effort, Maringá was one of the first towns in Brazil to pass the municipal law that created both a Municipal Council for the Rights of the Child and Adolescent and a Guardianship Council.

The Guardianship Council of Maringá is housed in a building in the centre of town and has a car at its disposal. It is open to the public from 8 a.m. to 10 p.m., except for Sundays and holidays. There is, however, always one person on duty. The staff of the Guardianship Council was elected by governmental agencies and NGOs, and consists of two social workers, an education specialist, a psychologist and a lawyer. Essential qualifications for these positions were a university-level diploma, prior working experience in child-related areas, and a proven ability to assess problems and find solutions to them.

In conformity with national legislation, the Guardianship Council is the entry point to the system of social services for at-risk children, which includes, in addition to schools and health care institutions, street education, vocational training and job placement programmes. Depending on the child's needs, he or she is seen by one or another of these professionals who may provide counselling, arrange for the child to attend school or participate in one of the various programmes being offered. Special attention is given to the relationship of the child to his or her family and to their joint needs. Members of the staff may officially request other public agencies (such as health centres, public schools, social services) to provide necessary assistance to children and families.

Public and private institutions make up the 'rear-guard services' of the Guardianship Council. Teachers, policemen, community leaders and the families themselves collaborate with the new office in order to ensure its efficiency. A large media campaign was carried out to inform the public and other institutions about the functions of the Council.

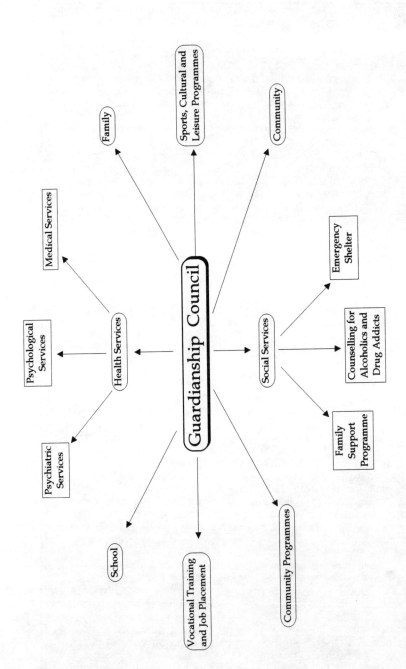

Figure 2.2. System in which guardianship council operates (source: Galeano 1991).

It is very difficult to evaluate the extent to which the Children's and Adolescents' Act has been enforced by the juvenile courts. Factors thwarting the full implementation include: (1) resistance by judges to the new procedures; (2) delays in setting up Guardianship Councils to take over cases previously handled by the juvenile courts; and (3) the existence and efficiency of services and programmes (such as foster care placement and services for juvenile offenders) and their compatibility to the norms contained in the Act.

Innovative Approaches

Brazil has a rich and diversified history of innovative social work on behalf of children in especially difficult circumstances. Lessons learned over the last decade served as the basis for a new social policy, designed jointly by the Government and NGOs. The guiding principles include the need:

- to promote an approach which respects the child's autonomy and dignity, which provides the child with opportunities for individual and social development, and also encourages the child and his or her family to participate in the creation of these opportunities;

- to safeguard the child's right to family and community life; or, conversely, to reject institutionalization as a standard solution;

- to strengthen the family and the community, and to involve them in the search for solutions to their problems;

- to give priority to preventive action;

- to diversify interventions, recognizing the individuality of each child, and especially the specific needs of girls;

- to give top priority to education;

- to protect children from exploitative and dangerous work, and to provide them with job training and employment opportunities;

- to place legal limits on judicial authority.

New social policies and programmes

Already by 1987, programmes had inaugurated a new public approach to children in especially difficult circumstances. In fact, the states of Goiás, São Paulo and Paraná partially anticipated the reform brought about by the Children's and Adolescents' Act, either by intervening in specific sectors or by initiating more comprehensive intervention. Furthermore, when the Act came into effect, these states had less difficulty than others in making the transition to the new system.

In Goiás, the FEBEM, which was considered a tragic legacy of the military regime, was substituted in 1987 by a new welfare agency called the Social Promotion Foundation (Box 2.2). The Foundation, which was given a strong mandate as well as substantial state funding, coordinates and monitors all social action within the state. A comprehensive programme called the Integrated Programme of Support to Children was created to serve "children in need" or "in situations of risk."

One important function of the Integrated Screening Center (CETI) was to monitor the interactions between the police and children. In the past, many children stopped by the police, even for minor infractions and regardless of their age, were institutionalized. Under the new programme, instead, all children stopped by the police must be registered with CETI before further police action. Only children between 12 and 18 years of age charged with serious crimes, including rape, homicide and robbery, are taken to the police station.

Communal Educational Workshops (OECs) are another important initiative in Goiás. Selected children from families whose income falls below an established poverty level receive vocational training in one of six workshops, covering electricity, carpentry, metal work, industrial sewing, beauty and hygiene, and food production. Courses for reintegration in the school system are also provided. Vocational training is however only one of OEC's aims. Based on the principles of "education for and through work," the programme endeavours to teach children the many different aspects of work activities, from procurement of raw materials, to marketing the finished product, and including contractual relations and labour laws. The participation of parents and community organizations is actively sought, to create a network of support for the child and to reach the children most in need.

In São Paulo, the Secretariat of the Child was created in 1987 as an alternative structure for at-risk children (Box 2.3) and was intended to replace the FEBEM. As was the case for the Social Promotion Foundation in Goiás, this structure received a strong mandate and ample funding from the State. By mid-1991 the Secretariat of the Child had served about 270,000 children in the capital city and outlying municipalities. Coverage has been increased to include children in at-risk situations (street and abandoned children, drug users, abused children) and preventive programmes. Some of the state corporations finance the activities of the Secretariat of the Child and also provide job training and opportunities for adolescents.

In response to dissatisfaction with the treatment of youth offenders in FUNABEM/FEBEM institutions, on 12 October 1990, the day the Children's and Adolescents' Act came into effect, the Secretariat of the Child supported the "release" of hundreds of children from the FEBEM, allowing them to return to their families and to society. This highly symbolic event not only testified to the commitment of the Secretariat of the Child to promote children's rights, but also marked the beginning of a new epoch.

Box 2.2 The Goiânia Programme to Support Children and Adolescents at Risk: Learning by Doing

Flexible Programme with Street Educators. The state-funded Goiânia project initially targeted street children, defined as abandoned and runaway children. It rapidly discovered that many of these children had families, that they were predominantly arrested for minor crimes and that there was recidivity. Street educators became a major source of emotional support to these children. Assigned to the different city neighbourhoods where children-at-risk 'hung out', street educators made contact with them and convinced them to participate in specific programmes. In an effort at institutional integration, policemen received training as street educators.

Three centres, with closely-integrated activities, were set up to assist the children:

* *The Integrated Screening Centre* (CETI) functioned as a 24-hour open-door drop-in centre for street children, most of whom were referred by the police or the juvenile courts, or by street educators who then followed their cases. Staff of this first reception centre had progressively learned to show a greater sensitivity towards street children and to make allowances for their initial defensiveness and fears. Street educators collected case histories and made preliminary decisions about how best the child could be assisted. Whenever possible, children were progressively reunited with their families (38 percent of the cases in 1989); most were encouraged to participate in the activities offered by the Training Centre. Eventually, as their personal situation changed, the children moved from one type of activity to another, or out of the programme altogether, while the influx of new participants was constant.

* *The Training Centre* (CFM) offered street-based children a day-shelter and the possibility of participating in educational and training courses and recreational activities. The Centre also coordinated with the juvenile courts and police in cases of juvenile offenders. Depending on their needs and abilities, children either followed a structured course aiming at reintegration into the formal educational system or were channelled, at least temporarily, into alternative educational strategies such as Freire's 'education for and through work'. Children could also learn a trade while earning about half of the minimum wage.

* *The Shelter* (CAM) offered homeless children a safe place to sleep.

Life planning for street-based working children. Street-based working children became a second population progressively targeted by the project. Traineeships and job referrals together with basic life planning and organizational skills were its objectives in the short term, while long-term goals were vocational training and schooling. Education was intended in its broadest sense to mean preparation for full citizenship in the community.

Communal Educational Workshops (OECs), generally located in poor urban communities, were also started for poor 12- to 18-year-olds, who were working, behind at school or drop-outs. Their objectives were to offer extensive vocational training and further life planning to adolescents at risk and to prepare them for reintegration into the formal school system through a two-year basic education course, corresponding to the first four grades of primary school. OECs also offered recreational activities, supplementary feeding, and medical and dental care. Students received a stipend equivalent to half the minimum wage ($40 at 1990 rates) to compensate for income loss resulting from their participation in the OEC and had access to some social security provisions. The participation of parents and community organizations was actively sought, both to create a network of support for children and to reach those most in need.

More than 90 percent of working children between 12 and 17 years of age in the state of Goiás worked in the informal sector in 1991. Of the 4,700 adolescents who participated in the first two years of the project, 213 were incorporated in the formal job market, 193 in vocational training courses, 642 in nonformal schooling courses, and 167 were reintegrated into the formal school system. These results were made possible by a major change in social policy and by *political will*, the determination of the State of Goiás to give priority to children.

Source: Alves 1991.

Box 2.3   Secretariat of the Child — São Paulo

Immediate responses	Protection against violence and crisis management	Preventive approaches
• Drop-in and screening centre • Shelter for homeless youth • Drop-in/rehabilitation centre for drug abusers • Training of street educators	• Temporary shelter for child victims of physical and sexual violence, abandoned children and runaways • Children's hotline • Network of children to combat violence against children (domestic, police, disappearances)	• Youth sports centres • Creches and pre-schools • Recreational activities • Initiation into work • Artistic and cultural activities

Source: Penna Firme and Tonini 1988.

The state government of Paraná developed *SETREM*, an inter-institutional project for young offenders which was a forerunner to Guideline 5 of the National Policy on Children and Adolescents. A technical team, representatives of the social-welfare system, the military and civil police, and the juvenile court worked together on the basis of case histories and personalized counselling to implement a policy incorporating more comprehensive rights specifically for children in conflict with the law. Other cities adopted this model and its principles were subsequently incorporated in the national Children's and Adolescents' Act.

The "education for and through work" method is an example of an innovative approach for working with children in especially difficult circumstances devised within a governmental programme. Influenced by Paulo Freire and Celestin Freinet, this methodology was developed by the pedagogue Antonio Carlos Gomes da Costa while he was working in a progressive FEBEM in the state of Minas Gerais. "Education for and through work" is a didactic method which is based on the principle of the three levels of participation: the management of work; the product of work; the knowledge related to work. Children share in the profits (the product of the work) while learning not only skills, but also how the working world operates.

The Recriança programme, created at the federal level with UNICEF support, has in the course of two years brought sport, recreational and cultural activities to 350,000 poor children in scores of municipalities, especially in suburban areas. Supplementary food programmes, dental and medical care, and income-generating activities were also provided.

In a number of cases, municipalities were able to continue the programme at the completion of federal funding. In Curitiba, the capital of Paraná, for example, a new municipal Secretariat of the Child was created to manage the programme, which changed its name to the Piá programme. In late 1991, this programme was present in 17 decentralized centres in poor suburban areas and served about 4,000 children.

The innovative contribution of NGOs

NGOs active in welfare often provide alternative services to individuals or groups whose needs are not adequately met by existing policies. In Brazil during the 1980s, many NGOs were created to provide social assistance to street and working children. A survey conducted in 1990 in Rio de Janeiro, for instance, revealed the existence of 502 "traditional" institutions for children (social assistance institutions, residential establishments and creches) and 31 "alternative" (community- and street-based) projects for street and working children (Rizzini and Wiik 1990). Not only did many of these NGOs provide services to children who were not eligible to receive public assistance, but they also had a role as innovators, questioning existing practices and developing new intervention strategies, including advocacy and a "fight for rights."

São Martinho "Meet the Street Children" Project. This NGO began very informally in 1984 when a group of former FUNABEM professionals and volunteers began to seek out street and working children in Rio. Rejecting institutional solutions, these volunteers based their actions on solidarity and sharing. In the course of their difficult training on the street, they experimented with a new approach which is now called "street education."

Street educators listen to what children have to say and avoid making decisions for them. In the process, the educators learn how best to help children understand their own reality and to participate actively in their own educational process. As their relationship with the children grows, the street educators provide a more structured environment where education and work problems are faced and met. Support is provided to enable the children to be reintegrated in their family or placed in alternative homes. Some street educators have first-hand knowledge of overcrowding, low earnings and poor health, which are typical of slum families. These educators provide important role models.

One of the first initiatives was to set up a cafeteria for street children and to organize a place where they could meet. An open-access day centre was later established, offering vocational training and, through agreements with local corporations, income-generating opportunities. Programmes now operate in Niteroi as well as in Rio de Janeiro, with a total of about 400 children.

The São Martinho project has also started preventive programmes in five suburban communities, serving about 800 disadvantaged children. The object is to keep the children near home and off the streets, using work as the basic educational principle. In addition, the project set up one of the country's first Defence Centres to prevent police and institutions from violating children's rights, and a programme to train nonformal educators.

The Axé project. This joint effort of the Italian organization for international cooperation, Terra Nova, and the National Street Children's Movement was started in June 1990 in Salvador, Bahia. This NGO coordinates international assistance, provides literacy courses, and distributes food and clothing to street children. Both full-time and voluntary street educators (always a man and a woman who work as a team) take part in the project. The project's philosophy is epitomized in its name. Axé is the Afro-Brazilian greeting which signifies peace, joy and vitality. Central to the project is the conviction that income-generating activities are the key to success in working with street children.

CRAMI Regional Centre for the Abused Children of Campinas. This organization was responsible for a new preventive approach to child abuse within the family. Created in 1985 in the state of São Paulo by a group of professionals, the Centre considers that child abuse is more a social, than a legal, issue; in consequence, the family of an abused child should not be treated as the guilty party, but instead be given support together with the child. The Centre has a hot-line for reporting cases of mistreatment and abuse.

Similar centres are being set up in other cities.

The São Joao Bosco Foundation for Childhood. Formerly involved in community health projects, this organization based in Belo Horizonte, struck out in a new direction in April 1991. Its activities revolve around the promotion of children's rights and support for the implementation of the Children's and Adolescents' Act. Working in one of the poorest regions of the country, the Vale do Jequitinhonha, but also in Minas Gerais and other states, the Foundation offers technical assistance to municipalities, universities and research centres. Its advocacy activities consist of awareness-raising meetings to inform groups about the Children's and Adolescents' Act, to increase the demand for social services, and to mobilize the community in support of the creation of Municipal Councils on the Rights of the Child, Guardianship Councils and, where necessary, Defence Centres. In the first eight months of its new activity, the Foundation held 26 seminars and meetings with the participation of 2,200 people from 158 municipalities.

Defence Centres. These were first created by NGOs to protect children from the institutional arbitrariness and violence and to ensure the legality of procedures used in the handling of juvenile offenders. Defence Centres have undertaken major legal actions against institutions for the violation of children's rights. With the legislative reform and the enforcement of the National Plan to Combat Violence against Children, Defence Centres have diversified their role. In addition to legal action to protect children's individual and collective rights, the Centres provide legal aid to juvenile offenders or victimized children; monitor the implementation of the Children's and Adolescents' Act, paying special attention to the reorganization of the justice system; offer legal advice to NGOs and grassroots associations; provide training in legal matters to street educators; and prepare training and information material. A national network of Defence Centres actively promotes children's rights and plays a central role in the implementation of the National Plan to Combat Violence against Children and Youth.

The two main national-level NGOs working for the rights of the child are the National Street Children's Movement and the Minors' Pastorate. Both are members of the National Council for the Rights of the Child and Adolescent.

The National Street Children's Movement. Established in 1985, this movement grew out of the joint government/UNICEF Alternatives for Street Children project. The national conferences of street children, which the National Movement organized in May 1986 and September 1989 are today counted among the most significant events of the decade in Brazil. The National Movement, basically a network of street children, nonformal educators, and concerned individuals, encourages street children to participate actively in the fight for full citizenship. It coordinates a network of street educators, sets up children's organizations, and delivers specific services to the community, including training courses for street educators and technical assistance programmes.

The National Movement presently has 75 local committees with a membership of approximately 3,000 voluntary educators in about 400 projects. The children who participate are mostly working children and children living in suburban slum areas who spend part of their time on the streets. Only 20 percent of the children are street children.

The Minors' Pastorate of the National Council of Brazilian Bishops. This organization was created in 1978 in São Paulo by the Catholic Church in order to respond more adequately to the needs of the growing number of children living and working on the streets of Brazilian cities. The guiding principle is that "the child is not a problem but a solution." Groups have been created in many of the 300 dioceses giving the Minors' Pastorate national visibility. The Minors' Pastorate is ecumenical; it liaises with other Churches, and organizes a yearly conference in São Paulo, the Ecumenical Week of the Minor.

The Minors' Pastorate actively participates in the Councils for the Rights of the Child and Adolescent, coordinating its efforts with other NGOs and with governmental bodies. More specifically, it publishes and disseminates information about the Councils, as well as training materials to assist communities in setting up new councils. The Minors' Pastorate also organizes special programmes for teenage girls and carries out research on their situation.

The Front of Defence of Children's and Adolescents' Rights. This is an example
of an NGO network at the state level. Formed in the state of Minas Gerais
during the ferment of the draft Constitution period, FDDCA today counts
more than 30 NGOs. In early 1989, FDDCA signed the "Charter of Principles"
which lists as the objectives of the coalition: increasing public awareness of
the rights of children and of the role the Councils for the Rights of the Child
and Adolescent can play in safeguarding these rights; coordinating NGO
efforts; and maintaining constructive dialogue with the Government.
Pluralism is the basic feature of the coalition, and commitment to children's
causes is the only condition for membership.

The contribution of universities

Brazilian universities are involved in action-oriented research and technical
assistance. Throughout the 1980s, research helped to develop and document
a new understanding of the disadvantaged urban child in Brazil. As a result
of the mobilization for children's rights, research centres have been set up in
universities to provide more reliable data on children. The centres are
generally interdisciplinary and encourage close collaboration between
professors and students as a way of breaking down traditional authoritarian
patterns. Research findings have served as the basis for preventive action.

One example is the NUCEPEC Child Research Centre in the state of Ceará,
which was created in 1986. It has a team of 40 researchers, mainly professors
and students, although there are also a number of consultants. One of its
principal activities is to generate and disseminate information. An important
study, conducted in 1988, was the "Profile of Fortaleza's Street Children,"
based on a survey of 1,410 children. NUCEPEC provides technical assistance
to municipal authorities, schools, community associations and NGOs. It also
assists universities in setting up research centres on the child. The Centre is
involved in the systematic internal training of NUCEPEC's groups, including
planning and evaluation of activities, and external training, one example of
which was the training of 57 policemen in 1990.

Networking has made the dissemination of local and regional research
findings possible. Efforts have been made to promote a more systematic
cooperation among the different research centres in order to increase their
technical capacity and political impact, and to establish a national data bank
on the child. However, there are still strong organizational and financial
constraints to these initiatives.

THE SOCIAL MOVEMENT TO PROMOTE CHILDREN'S RIGHTS

Legislative reform in Brazil was brought about by a broad social movement
of people concerned with the alarming situation of the nation's disad-

Street children during the second National Street Children's Congress, September 1989, entered the Brazilian Senate and convinced senators during an emotional encounter to work on behalf of Brazilian "minors." *Credit:* Copyright Paulo MacDowell, Brasilia.

vantaged children. An analysis of how such a social movement is formed and the strategies the movement employed to bring about change are discussed below.

Contemporary analysis has identified a new type of social movement made up of "informal groups of people committed to broad change at the levels of individual behaviour, social institutions and structures" (Jennett and Randall 1989). It has been said that, "social movements aim to reformulate the historicity of a society, that is, the creative work humans perform by inventing norms, institutions and practices to govern and to make predictable their social relations" (Touraine 1973). These informal groups tend to bypass traditional political intermediators and to seek a direct relationship with the ruling class. They are mobilized around specific "themes" (human rights, women's rights, or environmental issues, for example).

The Brazilian movement for the rights of the child certainly should be counted among these new social movements. For the first time in the nation's history, children's issues were included in the national "political agenda," that is, in "the set of problems which are perceived as the object of public debate, if not of active intervention by legitimate public authority" (Meny and Thoenig 1989). The movement has been successful in translating into the national context the international consensus of the United Nations Convention on the Rights of the Child. Moreover, the increased presence of social actors in the public domain is, in itself, an important factor in the country's ongoing democratization and the first step towards participatory democracy. At stake was the "citizenship" of all Brazilian children, defined as their access to full economic, social and cultural rights; also at stake was the "citizenship" of members of the social movement, that is their legitimate participation in decision-making.

The movement was started by community organizations which provided basic services (mainly education) to deprived children. These groups were united by a humanitarian concern for the conditions in which the nation's poorest children lived and by indignation at the State's response. They endeavoured to protect children from police brutality, from harsh sentences, from confinement in massive institutions, and from many other repressive methods. By their daily commitment, they progressively gained respect and credibility and an increasing number of people joined in the public debate.

During the draft Constitution period, characterized by wider participation of nongovernmental groups in national issues and by renewed optimism about the future, NGOs became the driving force behind a mobilization process. Starting with general objectives to promote full citizenship for all children, the movement turned into a broad political strategy aimed at legal and institutional changes.

The drafting of the new Constitution and the Children's and Adolescents' Act served as a catalyst, causing social actors from the judicial, welfare and the education systems, from the private sector, from the Church, and from different professional fields to join in support of the objectives initially proposed by the NGOs. The movement started out as a network of loosely joined groups with multiple leadership. What the movement lacked in formal organization, however, was counterbalanced by its adaptability. Moreover, because its structure was so vaguely defined, the movement had a greater likelihood of recruiting allies from very different social spheres. Cohesion was guaranteed by the movement's respect for the autonomy and identity of each single component. This principle was established as the basis of the coalition of NGOs formed by Forum DCA and was seen as an indispensable condition for achieving the major goals.

The inclusion of the rights of the child in the Brazilian Constitution and the approval of the Children's and Adolescents' Act were fundamental "victories" won by the social movement. To realize these goals, the movement had to overcome the opposition of the more conservative sectors of society. While in-depth research is still needed to understand the dynamics of the movement,[5] some factors which played an important role can be enumerated:

- Empowerment of different sectors was of the utmost importance. Empowerment has been variously defined as the mastery of a skill, the power to participate, and the "acquisition of political competence" which includes the ability to mobilize others.

- Debate was used extensively to forge a common understanding of the many aspects (structural, legal, social) of the situation of children.

- Common agendas were established and disseminated, despite the different origins, identities, beliefs and working methods of the various groups.

- Goals were set for the short and medium term to sustain the movement by a series of small "victories," while it struggled towards more difficult objectives.

- Strategic planning included public demonstrations, legal action, political pressure, lobbying, mobilization of public opinion, and negotiation.

- Ad hoc alliances were formed, facilitating the establishment of very specific goals for different phases. This flexibility gave space to groups with different motivations, beliefs and viewpoints.

- Networking broke the isolation of different groups across the country and led to comprehensive strategies, becoming a main way of achieving global objectives.

- Information dissemination ensured the cohesion of the movement. The intensity of the exchange helped to consolidate a collective identity and increased the members' motivation.

- Political maturity enabled NGOs to go beyond just denouncing and criticizing the Government to establishing a constructive dialogue with decision makers. Eventually very profitable alliances with governmental agencies were formed. Within this political space, the negotiation skills of the movement were of great importance.

- NGOs were empowered through alliances with — and access to — academic knowledge.

- Finally, the support of the media contributed to the creation of a favourable climate for the proposed legal and institutional changes.

This social movement on behalf of children had multiple impacts in the 1980s. Through its alliance with the media, it was able to initiate a process of cultural change by educating the public about the responsibilities individuals and groups have in the promotion of social causes. One promising trend is the widening base of support the movement is receiving, an expression of which is the Pact for Childhood, promoted by UNICEF, and involving entrepreneurs, congressmen, trade unions, NGOs, and policy makers at all levels.

The political competence developed by a number of NGOs has enabled them to move from a simple service-delivery role to one involving advocacy. Some new NGOs were formed specifically to defend and promote children's rights. The intensive "training" they had undergone as part of the children's rights movement increased their ability to negotiate with the State on behalf of children, without losing their autonomy or political neutrality, creating what the German sociologist Claus Offe termed a "non-institutional political space" (Offe 1985).

The movement's most important accomplishment was the pressure it exerted to abolish repressive procedures and to improve child-welfare policies, which led to the slow dismantling of the FUNABEM/FEBEM system, and to the adoption of the more equitable and humane social programmes stipulated in the Children's and Adolescents' Act. The laws have now been written. Implementing those laws to make a real difference in the everyday lives of *all* children in Brazil is the challenge that lies ahead.

NOTES

1. Girls work in the home far more frequently than do boys: in rural areas, 21 percent of the girls compared to 1.8 percent of the boys; in urban areas, 10 percent of the girls compared to 1.4 percent of the boys.
2. Street-based working children will be referred to as working children in the rest of the chapter.
3. Professionals selected for the Councils normally include formal and nonformal educators, social workers, teachers and psychologists who are chosen from within the municipality.

4. For this purpose it regularly receives an updated list of municipal programmes and governmental and nongovernmental services, compiled by the municipal Council for the Rights of the Child and Adolescent.

5. Specific sociological frameworks for the analysis of new social movements are the "resource mobilization theory" which, simply stated, considers the availability of different resources to be the "how" of such movements, and the "relative deprivation theory," according to which the deprivation felt by one group, when it compares itself with other groups, is the motivating force. In order to analyse the Brazilian movement for the rights of the child, a macrosociological approach which takes into consideration historical and structural factors as well as incidental factors, including the availability of human and financial resources, would probably be the most appropriate.

Chapter THREE

Philippines: Urban Communities and Their Fight for Survival

Emma Porio, Leopoldo Moselina, and Anthony Swift

INTRODUCTION

Michael, 9 years old, grain-sweeper:

When I was 4 years old, I was brought here (Pier 6) by my grandmother to help her sweep corn and other grains that drop when cargo is unloaded. This was in 1985 after my father was murdered. He used to work as a stevedore on Pier 5. My mother was too busy with my younger brother to take care of me. She was also pregnant and took in laundry to earn some money. So I was always playing on the streets. This made my mother angry most of the time.

When another brother was born, my mother changed a lot. She either scolded us or completely ignored us, often staring blankly into space. My Aunt, who was working in Manila as a domestic helper, was worried that my mother might be going crazy. In 1987, she came to Cebu and took my mother away with her. I was so alone and lonely. My grandmother urged me to work or else my brothers would starve. My mother had forgotten us. She did not send any money at all from Manila.

Two years ago, she came back to Cebu with her boyfriend. She was pregnant and gave birth here. I hated her boyfriend because he would beat me and
my brothers whenever he was drunk. We quarrelled all of the time. My mother
told me I was a troublemaker. After a while, she sold our house and all our
belongings and returned to Manila with her boyfriend, leaving me and my
brothers behind. After that I felt very bad because my brothers and I were now
truly without a home, even in our hearts. We were left entirely in the care of my
grandmother. Since then I haven't heard from my mother. She has not remem-
bered us at all. She never did anyway, even the first time she went away.

Pier 6, Cebu City, 30 October 1990, nine o'clock in the morning

Ipen, 59 years old, Michael's grandmother:

Michael has to work hard to support his younger brothers, Ryan and Jaime. I
doubt if I can send him to school. In the family, only Michael and I are earning
and there are six mouths to feed. My husband had an accident while he was
working as a construction worker several years ago. His left arm was crushed
so he cannot work any more. He is at home taking care of his grandchildren
and our son. Our son cannot find work because he has only reached grade
three. He also has respiratory problems so he tires easily and cannot do heavy
work. He keeps looking for a job but is always turned down.

I had to leave the family in Naga (a rural area that is a two-hour bus ride
from Cebu City) because we haven't a house here and cannot afford to rent one.
However, Michael and I managed to build a carton shack beside the sea wall,
but even that was a cause for worry. The police told us it was unsafe and illegal
so we had to dismantle it. I give the policeman money when he comes around
so we can have some peace of mind. Michael and I each earn only P15–20 a day
(56–74 US cents). We go home to Naga once a week to take food to our family.
I do not know why my children leave their children with me. I am very old and
very tired. Sometimes I wish I could sit down and truly rest, without having to
think where our next meal will come from.

Pier 6, Cebu City, 3 November 1990, three o'clock in the afternoon

Fely, 39 years old, social worker:

Early this year, our office started an outreach programme in the pier area. When
I came upon Michael sweeping grain under a forklift, I was quite apprehensive
for his safety, but he seemed to be accustomed to the working conditions on the
pier: forklifts wheezing nearby, cargo trucks coming and going, and stevedores
carrying sacks of grain bumping into him. Michael has never been to school
and doesn't know how to read, write or count. He figures out how much
money he has by the colour of the bills and the size of the coins. Vendors and
other children cheat him because of this, and, of course, Michael often ends up
in fistfights.

I invited Michael to come to our tutorial session, which is designed to
prepare children from disadvantaged groups for formal schooling. Initially,
teachers from our programme went to the street and taught children the alphabet wherever they found them, which was quite convenient for the
children. Michael was enthusiastic, but couldn't come regularly because of his
work. Then our office assessed our programmes and decided that it would be

more efficient to hold classes in one place at a regular time. We now teach the children in a more organized manner in the nursery school behind the fire station. Unfortunately, Michael cannot attend any more. The situation of Michael's family is very complicated. Everybody in that family needs help, but we have neither the resources nor the capacity to deal with their problems.

Parian Child Care Center, Cebu City, 1 July 1990, nine o'clock in the morning

During the past twenty years, Philippine cities have undergone rapid changes that have transformed the urban landscape as well as the lives of millions of Filipinos. The impact of these changes has been particularly felt by the urban poor, especially children, as the narratives of Michael, his grandmother and the social worker attest. Michael is one of the many children in especially difficult circumstances (CEDC) in the Philippines today. His story and his words have been included in the firm belief that the voices of the children add an important dimension to the research. These voices need to be heard so that programmes that are fully responsive to children's actual situations can be devised.

This chapter identifies the structures and processes that generate and perpetuate CEDC in Philippine cities, with a particular focus on street and street-based working children. It reviews the limited literature that exists, analyses surveys of disadvantaged urban children dating from the mid-1980s, and presents the findings of the 1989–90 study, sponsored by the UNICEF International Child Development Centre and carried out by the Philippine Social Science Council (PSSC) under the coordination of Dr. Amaryllis Tiglao-Torres, as part of this project. The chapter relates the problems to changing family and community contexts, analysing the survival strategies adopted by urban poor families and households over time, and the children's family, school, peer, community and institutional relationships. The concept of "compounded disadvantage" or "cycle of disadvantage" (Wilson 1989) is used to tie together the sociopolitical and economic processes impinging upon the experiences of these children and their families.

Turning to policy and programme issues, the chapter summarizes tendencies in social policies and provides an in-depth analysis of the introduction of the Urban Basic Services Programme (UBSP) and the National Project for Street Children in three cities — Olongapo, Davao and Metro Manila. The underlying concern was to see the fit between the characteristics, needs and constraints of street and working children, and the city's responses. The analyses have yielded some lessons. One especially important lesson concerns the critical role that can be played by government agencies and non-governmental organizations (often connected with academic institutions), working in partnership, in advancing creative, sustainable and cost-effective solutions, particularly for children in especially difficult circumstances.

SOCIOECONOMIC CONTEXT AND DEMOGRAPHIC TRENDS

New Political and Economic Context

Several interrelated forces operating have contrived to transform the political, social and economic landscape of urban areas in the Philippines into arenas where the urban poor must fight for survival.

On the global level, the Philippines suffers from the impact of external debt and structural adjustment. Current national debt is estimated at about $29 billion. According to figures provided by the Department of Budget and Management, debt servicing absorbed a record 45.1 percent of the national budget in 1987 (compared with 24.5 percent in 1984–86). That same year, public expenditure on health services fell to 2.6 percent of central government expenditures; expenditure on education, to 11.0 percent; and expenditure on housing and community development, to a mere 0.3 percent. Averages for the previous three years were 3.5 percent, 12.7 percent and 1 percent, respectively. Debt servicing therefore contributes indirectly to the deprivation of Filipino children; consequent increases in the cost of these services are particularly devastating for the lower-income population.

The performance of the national economy continues to be poor, basically as a result of structural weakness. The country is heavily dependent on imports, while its exports have very poor competitive status. During the last years of the Marcos regime (1983–85), the national economy shrank, whereas from 1987 to 1989, the economy grew at an average rate of 6.1 percent (IBON 1990). Nonetheless, low agricultural productivity and industrial inefficiencies have yielded high underemployment (31.2 percent) as well as official unemployment of 9.2 percent. It is estimated that 55 percent of the Filipino population lives below the national poverty threshold, P2700 ($73) for 1988.

Regional differences have historically been, and continue to be, marked. The poorest Filipinos are concentrated in Cebu, Leyte, Negros Occidental and Oriental, Iloilo, Bohol, Quezon and Camararines Sur; other regions, including Metro Manila, have relatively low poverty (Jimenez and Chiong-Javier 1992). In 1988, the income share of the bottom 30 percent of the poor, whose average monthly income was P1,260 ($47) per month for a family of six, was estimated at 9.3 percent of the total national income (National Census and Statistics Office 1990).

The Gini Concentration Ratio (GCR) similarly shows the particularly unequal distribution of wealth and income nationwide, a longstanding pattern in the Philippines. A GCR of 1.0 means there is perfect inequality, one person or sector controls all the wealth. The Philippine GCRs for 1961, 1971, 1985 and 1988 were 0.496, 0.480, 0.447 and 0.444, respectively. The GCRs for some other Asian nations were markedly lower: 0.28 for Taiwan in 1972, for example, or 0.36 for Korea in 1982 (Barba 1992).

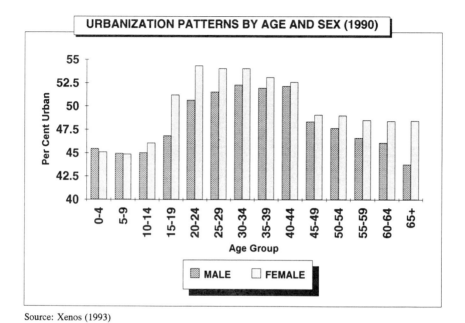

Source: Xenos (1993)

Figure 3.1. Urbanization patterns by age and sex (1990).

Rapid rural population growth, reflecting reduced mortality rates, has resulted in environmental degradation and resource depletion. The very large rural population surplus, which until 1970 was absorbed by the still-active agricultural frontiers of Mindanao in the South and the Cagayan Valley in the North, began in turn to spill into urban areas (Xenos 1993).

The tremendous acceleration of the urbanization process (Table 3.1) beginning in the 1970s, and especially evident from 1975 (see tempo measures, column 5), was partly the result of diminished rural population growth rates (column 8) brought about by fertility declines, but mainly reflected the massive movement from rural areas to cities. Migrants accounted for a large share of the growth of the child and youth urban population (under 35 years of age, but especially under 25 years of age) between 1975 and 1990. These young migrants are disproportionately female, the majority in the 20–24 age group (Figure 3.1).

According to 1990 census data, the urban population was 48.6 percent in 1990, of the total population of 60.6 million. By the year 2000, the urban population is expected to have grown to 70 percent (or close to 50 million). Some 40 percent of the urban population lives in slum and squatter communities (National Census and Statistics Office 1992), and water and housing shortages, uncollected garbage, traffic pollution, electricity failures, clogged

Table 3.1. Urbanization Trends, Level of Urbanization and Size and Growth of Urban Population in the Philippines (1903–90)

Year	Number (in thousands)			Level (4)	Urbanization growth rates[a]				Annual urban growth (thousands) (9)
	Total (1)	Urban (2)	Rural (3)		Tempo[b] (5)	Total (6)	Urban (7)	Rural (8)	
1903	7,635	1,000	6,635	13.1					
1918	10,314	1,294	9,020	12.5	-0.33	2.01	1.72	2.05	294
1939	15,999	3,450	12,549	21.6	3.10	2.09	4.67	1.57	2,156
1948	19,225	5,184	14,041	27.0	3.28	2.04	4.52	1.25	1,734
1960	27,088	8,073	19,015	29.8	1.16	2.86	3.69	2.53	2,889
1970	36,685	12,069	24,616	32.9	1.44	3.03	4.02	2.58	3,996
1975	42,071	14,047	28,024	33.4	0.44	2.74	3.04	2.59	1,978
1980	48,098	17,909	30,189	37.2	3.37	2.68	4.86	1.49	3,862
1990	60,559	29,440	31,119	48.6	4.67	2.30	4.97	0.30	11,531

[a]Instantaneous rates of growth. [b]Tempo measure is the difference between urban and rural growth rates. Source: Xenos (1993), on the basis of Barros for 1903–80, and the unpublished official census returns for 1980–90.

waterways and drainage systems have become routine in the urban Philippines.

Partly as a result of the political and economic crisis, insurgent political movements have repeatedly challenged the State. During the past two decades, the Government has waged a drawn-out battle with the Moro National Liberation Front and its armed contingents in southern Philippines as well as with the Communist Party of the Philippines and its military arm, the New People's Army (a pre-Second World War organization). Every year, military and insurgency operations affect nearly 120,000 children. It is estimated that clashes between the military and rebel forces from 1972 to 1988 displaced 4.5 million children: most fled the terrors of the countryside to the cities, where they try to mend their broken lives. Although some of these young political refugees have been assisted by CEDC programmes (notably in Cebu, Cagayan de Oro and Davao), the majority have received no assistance.

Several major natural and man-made disasters have recently caused inestimable damage to life and property: a major coup d'état in December 1989, resulting in massive capital flight; a sudden crash of sugar prices causing famine and insurrection on Negros; an earthquake in July 1990; killer typhoons in November 1990; and the major eruption of Mt. Pinatubo in June 1991. These calamities displaced large populations, destroyed livelihood bases, and drained public and private resources. The volcano eruption alone affected 500,000 jobs and forced over 100,000 unemployed to migrate to Metro Manila.

Other processes also intrude. Advances in satellite communications have made television widely available. Marginalized populations regularly watch films glorifying consumption habits that are beyond their reach. These have led many young people to raise their expectations, only to be thwarted by poverty. The increasing number of minors involved in violence, crime, substance abuse or prostitution may be, in part, a reflection of the frustrations deriving from these unfulfilled promises.

The dearth of income opportunities in the Philippines has pushed families to look for jobs overseas. During the mid-1970s, the Government adopted a policy of exporting human resources to increase the foreign currency in state coffers. Thousands of contract workers work abroad, as engineers, construction workers, domestic helpers, nurses and midwives. Their remittances account for a higher portion of the nation's foreign exchange earnings than do earnings from agricultural exports. Migrants are often forced to leave spouses and children behind while they attempt to improve their family's situation from abroad. Paradoxically, labour migration has frequently resulted in the erosion of the family base, the neglect of children, and the proliferation of impoverished female- and child-headed households.

Because of the deterioration of urban systems, the physical health of children has also suffered. Infant mortality (IMR) for the capital region —

including Metro Manila, which has the highest percentage of urban population without access to water, electricity, education and health services — is consistently higher than national rates of 32 per 1,000 live births in 1987 (United Nations Statistical Office 1992). Survey data collected by the Food and Nutrition Research Institute from 1987 to 1990 show that 16 percent of Filipino children are moderately underweight. In 1991, 1.7 million preschool children were found to have a very high rate of Vitamin A deficiency. In urban poor communities, children continue to die from pneumonia, diarrhoea, measles, acute bronchitis and other preventable diseases.

Filipinos 0–25 years of age account for 68 percent of the population, and urban deterioration has thus had negative effects mainly on this population, as is evidenced by the following 1990–91 statistics:

- 100,000 street children in major urban centres;

- 3.5 million working children (comprising 28 percent of the 10–19 age group), a large number of whom work in the informal sector;

- 20,000 sexually exploited children;

- 40,000 juvenile substance abusers;

- 4 million preschool and school-age children neglected by their parents;

- 11.7 million children with some form of hearing, speech, physical or emotional disability; and

- 3 million children who live in disadvantaged circumstances in cultural minority communities.[2]

Aware of the deteriorating situation of urban children, civil society has risen to the challenge. Dedicated numbers of the middle class have created voluntary organizations and channelled funds into worthwhile local projects. Academic institutions have started community-based projects. In addition, facilitated by a long history of grassroots movements, there has been an upsurge of urban poor organizations that have at times successfully worked together to pressure the Government for greater attention and resources.

Rapidly Urbanizing Areas and Growing Poverty

Metro Manila, population 7.7 million (1990), also called the National Capital Region, was created in 1975 by presidential decree. The legislative and administrative centre of the Philippines and the foremost destination of rural migrants, it is an expanding conglomerate of four major cities — Manila, Pasay, Caloocan and Quezon — and 13 municipalities. Occupying 636 square kilometres, its population grows 5.5 percent a year — twice the rate of other Philippine cities — and has increased more than fivefold over the last four decades, to 7.7 million, dangerously in excess of its estimated carrying capacity of 3 million. The population density of Manila, currently 40,000 per square kilometre, is almost four times that of Tokyo. The population of squatter/slum areas represents 31 percent of the city's population and approximately one fourth of the nation's urban poor.

There are thought to be from 60,000 to 75,000 street children and street-based working children in Metro Manila. If children working in factories, "job-outs" in homes, commercial and retail activities and domestic-based industries were included, this number could easily exceed 200,000.

Davao City, population 843,600 (1990), capital of the province of Davao, is on Mindanao, the Philippine's second biggest island and one of its richest ones. It has the largest land area of all Philippine cities (244,055 hectares), but only 1.1 percent of this area is actually urbanized; nearly 44 percent is still agricultural, and approximately 55 percent is dedicated to forest reserves. Composed of 171 *barangays* (communities, the smallest administrative units, normally headed by a Council), the city has its principal economic activities and occupations in the agricultural and fisheries sectors.

Davao's large Muslim minority is involved in a continuing armed struggle for an independent state. The communist New People's Army still enjoys high credibility in the city and Davao, in fact, came close at one point to having a communist government. Davao remains a city of deep political division.

The island's agricultural wealth fails to benefit the majority of the population. While landowners operate their plantations — producing pineapples, bananas and rubber — in the service of the multinationals, tens of thousands of peasant farmers have been displaced, many forcibly. Because of the island's wealth Davao has become a commercial growth centre, with big-city aspirations unconstrained by any great sense of history or tradition; it has also become a city of migrants, attracting those seeking business opportunities and poor people from the interior, fugitives of poverty or armed conflict. But some feel that Davao's migrants bring with them the energy to realize aspirations and an openness to new things.

Olongapo, population 197,581 (1989), once a small fishing village northeast of Manila, was subjected to a singular destiny with the defeat in 1898 of the Spanish occupiers of the Philippines. The American victors established a naval base at Subic Bay, imposing their administration on the village. Olongapo grew both in size and dependence on the base (which was, until 1992, the largest US naval base outside of the United States) and the huge dollar spending of military personnel. In 1959, the town was turned over to the Philippines Government and seven years later, in 1966, became a chartered city. But Olongapo remained economically dependent on the base.

The city attracted many migrants looking for work, ranging from tour guides to prostitutes. Street and working children (mostly migrants) thronged the streets. Many were Amerasian, illegitimate children of Filipino women and US servicemen. Business boomed in nightclubs, restaurants, cinemas, beer houses, brothels and elsewhere whenever a ship docked.

The activities, problems and opportunities of street and working children in Olongapo have changed considerably since the data collection in 1990. The eruption of Mt. Pinatubo in June 1991 destroyed property worth millions of pesos, devastated agricultural lands and industrial establishments, and left several hundred thousand people homeless and unemployed. The situation was exacerbated two months later by the decision of the Philippines Senate not to renew the US Bases Agreement, triggering a prompt withdrawal of the military. The base had directly employed some 35,000 Filipino workers, a third of whom were from the communities of the urban poor. Thousands more worked in the R&R industry. The suddenness of the departure left the city struggling to find an alternative destiny, even as it was celebrating.

Cebu City, population 610,000 (1990), is economically a rapidly expanding centre, the commercial, educational and transportation hub of the Visayas and Mindanao regions. With a daytime population of about one million, it is also the second largest city in the country and has the second greatest concentration of street children. It is a historical city, which for decades has been guided by the leadership of the Osmeña family. Under the administration of the current Mayor, Tomas Osmeña, it aims to entice foreign capital and so rival Singapore as a glittering regional free-trade mecca. In 1989, the Department of Trade and Industry attributed Cebu with a 20 percent growth rate.

But there is a shadow: the proliferation of urban poor settlements occasioned by refugees from exploitative rural development practices, poverty, oppression and conflict. They come especially from central Visayas and Northern Mindanao. The city's rapid economic growth — mainly in commerce, the tourist industry and real estate — has generated low-paying sales and services jobs with no fringe benefits and no security. Migrants with low education barely subsist; most can only afford to live in rundown settlements or squat in public areas.

Living and Working Spaces

The urban poor, particularly street and working children and their families, have adapted the little they have and can find into their own living and working spaces, often at great personal risk. Confronted with a shortage of housing and land, urban poor families live in shacks, tents or carton boxes. Often a dwelling is merely a lean-to against a church or factory wall. The poor settle on unoccupied public and private land, next to garbage dumps, beside factories and other work sites, alongside sewers and railroad tracks, in reclaimed marshes, above drainage canals, in parks and cemeteries. Some merely sleep on sidewalks. Others live in old decaying neighbourhoods where dwellings are dilapidated and basic services are inadequate or nonexistent. Few slum-dwellers have access to such basic social services as piped water, sewers, electricity and health facilities. Slum children bathe in polluted canals or with water from burst pipes; they play on the streets in the midst of traffic or in mosquito-infested areas near their homes.

Street-based working children are usually found in crowded areas where they not only try to earn a living, but also interact, play or just while away the time. Usually there is a high degree of fluidity between children's economic and social pursuits. Major streets and intersections, with their constant throngs of people, offer opportunities for children to beg or peddle their wares and services. Both boys and girls sell cigarettes, candy and sweepstake tickets. But vendors obstruct the flow of traffic and are frequently the object of cleanup drives.

Out-of-school youth frequently accompany their vendor-mothers or labourer-fathers; they find work as helpers and vendors or assist stall-owners by grating coconuts, butchering animals, running errands, repacking sugar, flour or clothes, and so forth. Other children come to scavenge or mind stalls after school hours.

Churches are also gathering places for children. Since 85 percent of Filipinos are Roman Catholics, various services attract congregations each day. Child-vendors, mainly girls, crowd around church doors in the hope of selling garlands of *sampaguita* (a white flower resembling jasmine), which are usually offered to the Virgin Mary, roses, small missals, novena prayers and candles. Children offer services ranging from shining shoes to lighting candles and praying on behalf of the customer.

Except for a small number of children, often lone street children, who roam the length and breadth of the metropolis, most children "hang-out" in one area. Knowing the area, its activities and clientele is part of the children's efforts to "stake out" a particular city street or corner, and therefore feel more secure about their environment. Child-vendors, who ply their trade in buses and jeepneys, frequently ride from one transit point to another and back again, and a small number even cruise from one area of the metropolis to another. Aside from the thrill, the adventure and the seeming freedom involved, children move about the city in search of better business prospects.

THE SITUATION OF DISADVANTAGED URBAN CHILDREN AND FAMILIES [1]

The PSSC Study and Related Research

Striving for new typologies and improved enumeration

Until the late-1980s, Filipino policy makers, researchers and the public used "street children" to mean urban children from impoverished families who spent a significant amount of time on the streets, usually not protected, supervised or cared for by responsible adults. Often "street child" was a

Table 3.2. Street Children as a Percentage of Child and Youth Population
(Selected Cities, 1988)

	Urban child and youth population	Estimated number of street children	Percentage
Angeles	71,104[a]	3,000	2.40
Baguio	63,066[b]	800–1,500	1.2–2.38
Davao	208,180[a]	2,600	1.25
Iloilo	102,687[b]	2,500–3,000	2.43–2.92
Metro Manila	3,027,925[c]	50,000–75,000	1.65–2.48
Olongapo	97,674[b]	2,408	2.47

[a]1980 Census of Population and Housing, NCSO. [b]City Situation Studies on Street Children. [c]1985 Philippine Population Projections, NEDA. Source: DSWD, NCSD and UNICEF (1988).

euphemism for juvenile delinquent or vagrant. A 1988 study, *The Situation of Street Children in Ten Cities* (hereafter the Ten-City study) defined the term as "children who had adopted the street as their abode or source of livelihood, or both."

Sponsored by UNICEF in coordination with the Department of Social Welfare and Development (DSWD) and a Manila-based NGO network, the National Council of Social Development Foundation of the Philippines (NCSD), the Ten-City study consolidates analyses undertaken from 1984 to 1987, with a total sample of 3,255 children. It was, however, only able to arrive at very tentative estimates of the street child population (Table 3.2). The information it generated was generally uneven for a number of reasons: (a) the survey was not carried out by one team, but commissioned in each city to a local research team; (b) each team utilized different methodologies (review of secondary data, structured interviews, observations, case studies or interviews with key informants); (c) each team adopted very different perspectives, which affected the gathering and analysis of data; and (d) each team used different measures to summarize the data. The availability of a particularly extensive survey undertaken in Cebu City in 1986 by McGuire (hereafter the McGuire study) made data from Cebu City much more detailed than those available in other cities. All this, as the Ten-City study itself acknowledges, posed severe difficulties in interpreting the data.

In 1989, in a follow-up survey and in line with experiences in other parts of the world, NCSD made the first attempt to distinguish different categories of Filipino "street children." It identified (a) children *on* the streets (about 75 percent of the total urban poor child population), who spend most of their waking hours working on the streets but have a home elsewhere, usually in

Table 3.3. Urban Children Living with One or Both Parents or On
Their Own (Different Cities in Selected Years)

	Year	Sample size	Living with one or both parents (%)	Living on their own (%)
Baguio[1]	1988		92.8	7.2
Cebu[2]	1986	302	37	45
Iloilo[1]	1988		58	42
Metro Manila[3]	1991	208	90	10
Olongapo[3]	1991	40	85	15
Davao[3]	1991	50	94	6

Source: [1]McGuire (1986), [2]DSWD, NCSD and UNICEF (1988), [3]PSSC (1991).

an economically depressed area or community; they were further subdivided according to whether they have adult supervision or not; and (b) children *of* the streets (from 20 to 25 percent of the total) who practically live on the streets and who may be alone, with friends or family members. A third category was also identified, consisting of abused, traumatized and abandoned children (approximately 5 percent of the total), who have been "looped" into drugs and prostitution or caught in abusive and exploitative familial or work relations, including theft and robbery syndicates (NCSD 1989).

In 1991 a PSSC study report sponsored by UNICEF ICDC in four cities made an even sharper distinction between:

- the very small percentage of urban poor children who are actually living alone, away from their parents, whom we shall call *street children*; and

- the other children seen on the street who regularly live with their families, whom we shall either call *street-based working children* or simply *working children*.

If one examines the Ten-City, PSSC, McGuire and other studies from the perspective of a sharper distinction between children regularly living at home and children who actually live fully on their own (even though they may still have occasional contacts with their families), the data forcefully show that, among all children found on the streets by the teams on repeated visits, a very large percentage live with their families (Table 3.3). Conversely, only a small percentage of children live on their own: nationwide, street children are estimated to number no more than 100,000.

On the other hand, because the PSSC research teams could only do sampling based on an often floating and little-known population, their overall estimates can only be generally indicative. The PSSC study tells us that these working children are numerous, that they are mostly vendors of goods and services, that they do not necessarily work for the whole day and that there is constant replacement of the population. Moreover, because vending is an easy-entry occupation, vendors represent an important proportion of all urban children working in the informal sector. However, there are other, less visible working children (listed in part in Box 3.1) who exist in all cities but who are not represented in the sampling. These submerged categories compound an already arduous statistical task.

Characteristics of street and working children

The PSSC study was composed of 298 in-depth interviews of street-based children, not necessarily participants in existing programmes and services, in six cities, and 120 interviews of the households of some of the same children. It provides detailed and consistent information on the children's daily lives and their conditions of work, study and leisure. It also systematically investigates the children's relationships with their families and some of the family support systems.

The PSSC study found that the majority of street children and street-based working children were boys (Table 3.7) and their ages were sharply patterned. Respondents ranged from 6 to 18 years of age; 65 percent were between the ages of 9 and 13 years (25 percent in the 9–11 age group and 40 percent in the 12–13 age group).

Life histories of Filipino children provide some possible explanations of why there is such a large presence of boys of middle years (9–11) and early adolescence (12–14) on the streets. It is at these ages that urban poor children are more likely to be sent out to work or to be required to help their parents who have street-based jobs. Moreover, boys approaching adolescence often start asserting their own self and sexual identity. This leads to conflicts in the families or to the child's refusal to bear difficult circumstances at home. The life histories show that running away from home often coincides with particular moments in the child's development. The markedly reduced presence of girls on the streets, despite the significantly higher number of young female migrants to the cities, has cultural roots to be discussed later.

Education (Table 3.4). The PSSC study found that school participation varied across cities but was generally high even among lone street children. But completion rates were low. Children in all cities were officially behind grade level: most had, once or several times, interrupted their schooling for job-related reasons or because of illness, accident, poverty or unpleasant classroom incidents. Some students could not afford to pay tuition fees, school uniforms, school materials or the daily *baon* (snack or lunch). Many had to work to augment their household income.

Table 3.4. Education Profiles of Street Children and Street-Based
Working Children (in Percentages, 1990)

	Children not living in family (street children)	Children living in family (street-based working children)
Current schooling status		
in school	58	70
out of school	42	30
Schooling interrupted one or more times in the past	45	61
Grade level when schooling interrupted		
1–3	68	45
4–6	26	34
high school	6	18
Combines street-based work with schooling	69	57
Children's main aspirations for next 5 years		
finish studies	80	46
work/find a decent job	14	31
get rich/have a bright future	10	9
Children's main aspirations for next 10 years		
work/find a decent job	53	83
finish studies	10	15
get rich/have a bright future	10	8
Believe aspirations can be achieved mainly if		
finish studies	43	44
persevere	30	30
work hard	13	8

Source: PSSC (1991).

The McGuire survey in Cebu aimed at establishing children's educational attainment rather than their attendance. The most striking finding of this survey, which had a higher percentage of children not living with their families (selected through programmes) than the PSSC study, was that 21 percent of the respondents had never attended school; the majority were girls

Table 3.5. Average Height and Weight of Street and
Street-Based Working Children (Mean) 1991

	Street children (not living with family)	Street-based working children (living with family)
Height (cm)[a]	133.45	136.18
Weight (kg)[b]	32.25	33.96

[a]Height standard for 12-year-olds: 136.4 cm (boys), 134.85 cm (girls). [b]Weight standard for 12-year-olds: 34.05 kg (boys), 37.65 kg (girls). Source: PSSC (1991).

(40 percent compared with 19 percent of the boys). Sixty-four percent had managed to finish grade four, but most were unlikely to continue beyond this level. In contrast, the PSSC study found in the Manila sample that more girls than boys were in school.

There is therefore no conclusive evidence of gender discrimination in education among urban poor families. It should be mentioned that the Philippines has had high national averages for the education of both boys and girls all through the post-Second World War period (Blanc Szanton 1972), and it is estimated that 90 percent of its population is literate (Jimenez and Chiong-Javier 1992). Moreover, functional literacy is higher for women than for men (74 percent versus 72.9 percent), according to the 1989 Functional Literacy, Education and Mass Media Survey. Among the particularly disadvantaged urban poor, however, a tendency persists to teach girls to be fearful of the world outside their home and to exclude them from school.

Health, diet and nutrition. Hixon (1991), investigating malnutrition among urban poor children in Metro Manila, concludes that both girls and boys are underweight and underheight by both international and Filipino standards. When the physical growth of street and working children was measured against mean averages by the PSSC study (Table 3.5), street children, in particular, seemed to have lower-than-average mean heights and weights; they also slept less and ate fewer meals per day.[3]

When asked what common illnesses they had recently had, slightly more children living alone than children living with their parents mentioned (in order of frequency) colds and coughs, headaches, influenza and stomach aches. In Davao, 72 percent of both street and working children had been ill during the preceding three months, but only 54 percent had stopped working. The others continued street work and were therefore exposed to smog, pollution, heat and rain. The incidence of muscular pain and skeletal deformations among baggage boys and skin diseases among scavengers are common.

With regard to access to medical services, from 64 percent (Manila) to 83 percent (Olongapo) of in-school children were aware of the school's health facilities. Only 66 percent in Davao and 60 percent in Cebu availed themselves of these services, mainly for medical consultations and tooth extractions. Most respondents claimed that the school health services were irregular and medical supplies lacking. Out-of-school children, in contrast, hardly ever consulted doctors or took advantage of health services.

Family and household characteristics

Eighty percent of the children interviewed lived in the same city as their families (but not necessarily with their families). Most came from large households (Table 3.6), an average of 6.5 members. Regardless of whether they lived in a single- or two-parent household, children shared living space with relatives and, in some cases, with non-relatives. This finding seems to contradict the popular notion that most urban poor households are exclusively nuclear.

Consistent with earlier research, the PSSC study concluded that members of urban poor households tend to be young and to have low educational levels. The average age of household members in the sample was 23 years with an age range of 0–65 years. Modal educational attainment for adults was grade five.

Children's relationships with their parents varied from "very supportive" to "indifferent" to "very difficult and abusive." This echoes the McGuire study where children often reported that they had run away from home to escape physical abuse and harassment or to find respite from their parents' incessant quarrelling or drinking. More often than their counterparts, street children reported that members of their former households drank, usually the father; they also had more often been punished by their parents.

Migration, residence and family stability

A large number of children in the PSSC study reported having moved, either from the provinces to metropolitan areas or within cities, or both. In Davao, 20 percent had lived in their current place of residence for less than one year, and over 70 percent, less than five years. In Olongapo, nearly 50 percent had lived in their current residence for less than five years. Similar patterns were observed in Metro Manila. Migration to the city was primarily undertaken by whole families. In the McGuire study, 68 percent of the survey sample (both families and lone children) came from depressed rural areas and had transferred their residence within the city several times over the past five years.

Table 3.6. Household Profiles of Street Children and Street-Based
Working Children (in Percentages, 1990)

	Children not living in family (street children)	Children living in family (street-based working children)
Type of Family		
single mother	[15][1]	22
single father	[4]	12
two parents	[18]	65
distant relatives, non-kin	[8]	1
Household average monthly income — overall sample (dollars)	1,285 pesos[2] (US$48.20)	
Average household size — overall sample (members)	6.5	
Percentage employed		
child	87	76
siblings	21	21
Percentage in school	58	70
Percentage siblings in school	28	28
Child contributes to family income		
yes	85	96
no	15	4
Type of parental relationship		
father absent	[75]	23
father sickly	frequent	frequent
Migrated to city (C)	100	81
Migrated to city with family	80	81
Main reasons for migrating		
eviction	50	31
seek better living conditions	19	12
seek education	6	9
seek employment	6	8
family member in trouble	–	2
Household moved within city	60	47

[1]Data in square brackets are from McGuire (1986). [2]Below poverty threshold of 4,037 Pesos (US$151.40), average household monthly income for a family of six. Source: PSSC (1991),

Migration is a constant pattern. Economic pressures, exacerbated by family and community stresses, cause urban poor families to move within cities as a survival strategy. Families were often forced to move to find affordable housing or better livelihood opportunities, or to be near their place of work. Eviction was a common cause for moving. Often the move is to more impoverished neighbourhoods, placing the family at a greater disadvantage.

The children's life histories also reveal that migration gives their families both the hope of new opportunities and disadvantages (Porio 1993). Hope is represented by the greater availability of income opportunities, albeit erratic; disadvantages are caused by the poor environmental conditions in which they live. Migration from province to city and movement within cities increase family stress, often pushing children out of an adult orbit of attention and into risky situations on the streets.

Only a very small percentage of the PSSC sample consisted of children who had run away from home. These children constitute a highly vulnerable group. Many runaways end up living on the streets and usually are "adopted" by older children from whom they learn the ropes, including how to scavenge, "hustle," beg or steal, or by vendors who utilize them as workers.

Work on the streets

Most of the children surveyed were engaged in street-based occupations, mainly vending, hawking and scavenging (Table 3.7). They were recruited and socialized into their street careers by their fathers, brothers, mothers, grandparents or other relatives who were themselves vendors, hawkers or scavengers. A few children not living in a family and a small number of those living with a family and who had been interviewed while running errands for their parents, did not consider themselves working children. The majority of both street children and street-based working children were also studying (58 and 70 percent respectively).

Children in the Metro Manila and Cebu City samples began working on the street as early as four years of age. Initiation into full-time work usually occurred through a combination of circumstances, for example when the child had lost interest or did poorly in school, or when there was an urgent need for another breadwinner in the household. In most cases, both the child and his or her parents thought the situation was temporary; but, as one 17-year-old scavenger said:

> At six, I dropped out of school because my mother was always sick and my father was not bringing enough money for us to buy food. I never thought I would still be doing the same job eleven years later!

Remuneration of street work. Approximately 60 percent of all working children claimed to have employers, and these employers were usually ac-

Table 3.7. Employment Profiles of Street Children and Street-Based
Working Children (in Percentages, 1991)

	Children not living in family (street children) (no. 30)	Children living in family (working children) (no. 268)
Mean age	12.5 years	12.7 years
Gender		
male	63	67
female	37	33
Also studying	58	70
Age started working		
range	3 to 13 years	4 to 18 years
mean	10.5 years	11.4 years
Main reason for working		
insufficient household income	73	61
Main kinds of current work		
vending	50	48
scavenging	33	20
washing cars	8	7
begging	3	7
Employment type currently		
self-employed	40	41
with employer (mostly piece rate or daily rate)	60	59
Employment type at first job		
self-employed	63	60
with employer	37	40
Mean earnings	28 pesos ($1.05)	60 pesos ($2.25)
Child contributes to family income		
yes	85	96
no	15	4
Money earned used mainly for:		
household expenses	30	28
school	23	21
food	17	39
Main leisure activities		
going to the cinema	26	21
none	22	16
playing	22	16
reading comics	11	–
listening to the radio	7	10
telling stories	–	13

Source: PSSC (1991).

quaintances, relatives or friends. Pedicab drivers and haulers usually have employers; the former are paid on a percentage basis, the latter on a piece rate or daily basis. Vendors and hawkers, in contrast, normally have "arrangements" with suppliers and may be paid on a piece rate, percentage commission or daily basis.

Regardless of their working arrangements, children generally earn less than P60 ($2.22) per day. Street children earn even less. Children are regularly paid much less than adults for the same work. In Cebu, it was found that child "barkers," whose job is to shout or announce the destination of jeepneys and buses, earn from 50 centavos to one peso for every vehicle they successfully "bark" to the full; adult male barkers are usually paid twice as much.

Table 3.8 compares the contributions of children and adults to the monthly household income. It shows that, in certain areas, the minimum earnings of an adult are practically equal to those of a child. In Quezon City, for example, the difference between adult and child mean monthly earnings is only about P147 ($5.43). In Caloocan, the difference is even less: P50 ($1.85). In these two cities, adult minimum earnings are either the same or almost the same as the child's. But the highest pay of a child is, across all cities, much lower than the highest pay of an adult. It is also systematically lower for lone street children and for girls.

The majority of urban poor households earn below the poverty line and spend most of their earnings on food and shelter. The child's income usually helps pay for food; it may also be used for matches and cooking fuel, or for the child's school allowance. Poor households are known to spend more than they earn and have to borrow money from "informal sources" usually at very high interest rates (Blanc Szanton 1972, Jimenez and Chiong-Javier 1992).

Adult supervision. Manila and Quezon City had the highest percentages of children claiming to work with their parents. In Cebu, where the screening question for the survey samples was, "Are you with your parent or an adult now?" almost half (45 percent) said no. The children had a very broad definition of "adult supervision": they felt they were supervised — even when they wandered from one end of the street to another, out of the adult's sight — merely because a parent or other adult they knew was working in the immediate vicinity. There are many dimensions to supervision: warning, restrictions, protection and accountability to adult authorities. It is easy to see street scenes of mothers scolding children for not being careful when crossing the street. Children in the company of an adult are considered to be "safe," protected from ill-intentioned strangers. They are, of course, not protected from ill-intentioned friends and relatives who may force children to take or deal in drugs, to prostitute themselves, to perform heavy manual labour or to work for long hours or under very risky conditions.

Hours on the street. In-school children who live with their parents usually spend the afternoon and early evening hours working on the streets. Many

Table 3.8. Range and Mean Monthly Incomes of Metro Manila Households (1990)

	Child			Adult			Combined	
	Income range (peso)	Mean income (peso)	% of combined income	Income range (peso)	Mean income (peso)	% of combined income	Mean income (peso)	% of poverty threshold[1]
Manila	10–1680	421.60	30	50–4500	965.67	70	1386	51
Quezon City	20–1950	690	45	20–3000	836.82	55	1526	56
Caloocan	10–940	102	40	20–2800	152	60	254	9
Pasay	40–900	610	27	100–4500	1650	73	2260	84

[1] In 1988, the poverty threshold for the National Capital Region was established at P2,700 ($101.20) for a family of six. Source: PSSC (1991).

A local community leader demonstrates the use of a self-monitoring board in Little Baguio, Olongapo, Philippines. *Credit*: Dolly Mattosovich.

elementary schools in Metro Manila and other large cities have half-day class schedules to accommodate the large population of children and the limited number of teachers and classrooms. Children, therefore, tend to work longer hours and to work almost every day, while in smaller centres such as Olongapo, children spend longer hours at school and are more likely to work on weekends than every day.

Street children usually follow the rhythms of city life. They wake up at nine or ten in the morning because most snack bars and restaurants where they "hustle" food only open at that hour. After eating, they work until seven or eight in the evening when they have their second meal. Then, they continue working until midnight or later. Children who sleep on the streets have to be on guard from possible dangers posed by drunks, passers-by, security guards or policemen.

Peer relationships

Children surveyed in all cities claim to have many friends of the same sex and acquaintances of both sexes. When together, they tell stories, play basketball, read comics or tease each other. Aside from providing company, friends and peers often recruit children to street careers and to the street life. New arrivals link into a street network, learning from their peers how to protect themselves; how to avoid problems with policemen and drug-pushers, and often how to get "high" on inhalants.

Delinquency and police harassment

Although the children surveyed tended to emphasize the congeniality of their street activities, conflicts and fights among band members, friends and acquaintances were common. From 40 to 60 percent of the sample admitted to having been "in trouble" in the past, to situations ranging from fights and misunderstandings with other street children to police harassment and arrests. The majority were only detained for a day at a youth reception centre or at police precincts.

Cebu City had the highest number of arrests: 45 percent of the total of 302. The main reasons were street fights, suspicion of theft, drug use and vagrancy; only one child was accused of a serious crime, the attempted murder of his stepfather. Sometimes children's arrests were connected with "clean-up" drives carried out by the City Government to "rid the streets" of vendors and hawkers. The Cebu study showed that many of the arrests were unjustified, especially in cases of mass arrests prior to the arrival of visiting dignitaries or during the tourist season.

Family networks and stature in the community

In the Philippines, the family is the most crucial reference group for children, and its prestige and status can open up avenues of mobility and support. Education, business success and kinship ties to people in high places are factors that enhance the position of the family. Child respondents indicated that their families did not enjoy positive status in their neighbourhood and community; nor could they count on an extensive network of friends and relatives there to help them in times of crisis. Most had more friends and acquaintances on the streets.

In Cebu City, families of street children and street-based working children have particularly high levels of mobility so their networks of friends and acquaintances also change whenever they move. They occasionally extend material support to others, but in small amounts because of their own impoverished situation; moreover, their low status and prestige prevents them from generating support from others. Instead, support comes from "caregivers" and "service institutions," which perceive these populations as "wards."

Gender differences

Socialization into gender roles is apparent in the division of household chores. The life histories reveal that both boys and girls are expected to clean, wash dishes and cook. However, boys are usually asked to run errands, to fetch water and to feed the pets. Girls are more often expected to do the laundry and to look after younger children (Torres 1990). This differentiation extends to street activities.

Filipino families tend to define the home and the domestic spheres of social life as the domain of girls. The majority of the girls whom researchers interviewed on the streets were generally there because their parents, brothers or other relatives were also living or working on the streets or in places nearby. Both the family's and the girl's reputation are at risk if the girl is allowed to "roam" without adult supervision. In contrast, it is a popular belief that boys can "claim" the streets as their territories without fear of lurking danger. This is not entirely true, as boys in the study have reported being brutalized by drug-pushers, bystanders and the police.[4]

Work ethics and child labour

Is child labour a part of the Filipino culture? Need we not challenge the presence of large numbers of working children on city streets? Children helping out in household and farm tasks have always been part of the Filipino social organization. However, children who work in rural areas are protected by their family, neighbours and relatives, whereas children who work on the city streets manoeuvre in a more risky situation.

The Labour Code stipulates that children below 15 years of age are not to be employed except under the responsibility of their parents or guardians (Art 139, 1988 Labour Code). In addition, the Child and Youth Welfare Code states that children below 16 may only do work that is not harmful to their safety, health or normal development, or prejudicial to their studies (Art. 197,

P.D. 603). However, the participation of children in the informal labour sector is largely unregulated (Torres 1990).

When queried what the right age to work was, respondents gave varying replies, ranging from age 6 to 18 years. Parents generally stated that children should be at least 15 years old when they started working, but the life histories show us that some were as young as four. Most parents in the survey also argued that they too had had to work as children, in most cases pursuing the same livelihood their children currently pursue. Parents preferred their children to take advantage of work activities that were available close to home, regardless of their nature. Parents in Quezon City who lived near dump sites, for example, surprisingly preferred scavenging to vending or hawking as jobs for their children.

Parents and adults, in general, considered that teaching children to work was an important value and that work prepared them for adult responsibility. Children themselves, when queried about their motives for working, invariably answered that they had to work to help support their family. In fact, children felt very positive about working.

From Visible Street Children to Less Visible CEDC Categories

In 1989, street children formed one general category of "children in especially difficult circumstances," which, however, needed to be reexamined according to the origins and structural bases of the children's difficulties. These difficulties can be of various nature, depending upon the children's economic, work, family and community status. Although this study has focused on a very visible category of CEDC, emphasizing a new and strategically important distinction between street children and street-based working children. The analysis of the lives of disadvantaged urban children has opened a window to other CEDC subcategories, children whose difficulties and circumstances run the gamut from highly visible, to invisible, hidden intentionally or unintentionally and involving exploitative relationships (Box 3.1).[5]

"Invisible" problems are often associated with illegitimate or unethical activities in which the child or the family is inextricably linked with the "broker" or "manager/entrepreneur." Because the activities take place in private, they are beyond anyone's concern. The concept of a continuum of categories of abused and exploited children more or less visible to the public eye has definite programme implications. It relates to where the child can be found, which are his or her problem priorities, and at which level problems can best be addressed.

The risks and threats presented by the city environment are differentiated by occupation, age and gender. More significantly, certain areas of the city pose higher threats than others. These risks increase when children pursue

Box 3.1   From Visible to Almost Invisible Categories of CEDC

Street-based/Visible, Open	Off Street/Often Invisible, Hidden

• Children making a living on the streets
  • Scavengers
  • Beggars
  • Transport 'barkers', conductors
  • Vendors/hawkers of:
    • food, candies, cigarettes
    • plastic, paper bags
    • newspapers
    • religious items, flowers
  • Baggage boys, cargo haulers
  • Grain sweepers (on piers)
  • Car-watch boys, parking assistants
  • Shoe-shine boys
	• Children working behind closed doors
	    • Domestic servants/workers
	    • Unpaid family workers
	    • Children in home-based industries
	    • Children in factories, construction
	    • Children engaged in outwork
	• Sexually abused or exploited children, including child prostitutes
	• Children involved in substance abuse, drug-dealing, theft syndicates
	• Children in homes rife with domestic violence, substance abuse, mental illness
	• Children in situations of armed conflict, refugee children
	• Children in prisons

Source: Prepared by Porio (1992).

their activities alone. Thus, a particular street corner or area may be more frequented by extortionists, gamblers and drinkers, or more carefully patrolled by police authorities. Even if two children engage in the same activity, the locus, their work relations, and the presence or absence of peer, family or adult support can generate different levels of risks and needs. The risks a scavenger runs, for example, apart from being occupation-specific, vary according to age, gender, family support, peer network, areas scavenged, and business relationship with the scrap buyer. The child's progression from selling flowers or cigarettes to selling drugs or his or her body can be determined by adults, syndicates or merely by the opportunity to earn "quick money." Working conditions and family situation are the most important variables in influencing whether a child has the appropriate support to resist this progression.

To reach children in the hidden and invisible categories, current programmes must be reoriented. Moreover, if given a clear understanding of the potential risks and trained to protect themselves, children can be "empowered" to improve their situation. Immediate material relief must go hand in hand with community organization, education, assistance in finding employment and security of housing. Specific potentials for danger may be removed from the environment through the modification of laws, their more attentive implementation and the focused attention of policy makers.

A discussion of the risks that children are exposed to should distinguish between factors propelling children to work and factors posing threats to their physical development. This issue is central to whether children should be allowed to work. Embedded in that discussion are concepts about work, childhood, child development and family survival.

Policy makers and programme directors, generally from the middle class, associate childhood with play, fun and school, and adulthood with work and "breadwinning" responsibilities. Some tend to be prejudiced against impoverished working children, often considering them "hard-core street children" who would have difficulty acting "normally," that is, attending school regularly, leading a disciplined life, and following sound hygienic practices. Many would argue that working on the streets poses risks to children's health, life and social development. For most of the urban poor, however, earning is a matter of survival. As one street hawker in Cebu complained:

> They say we should not let the children be on the streets. But what can we do? Our livelihood is based there. We, including the children, sleep and work there most of the time.

Children thus receive mixed signals. From one side, they are admonished for their street life and made to feel ashamed of their street careers: from the other, they are urged to work and taught that their earnings are essential to their family.

Policy makers and programme actors should distinguish between income-generating activities that jeopardize a child's development (drug-pushing, theft, begging and prostitution, for instance) and those that normally do not (vending, hawking, scavenging or cleaning cars). Equally as important, they should learn to show greater understanding of the economic realities. If they insist on their ideal images, they may end up doing more harm than good.

POLICIES AND PROGRAMMES

Context and Principal Actors

Trends in social policies

The situation of disadvantaged children in Philippine cities has in many cases been the direct result of policy decisions; more recently, this situation has also become, in part, the determinant of new policies. Some of the changes can only be understood if viewed within a broader historical context. The following section contains a brief outline of social trends since the 1960s.

Quite decentralized through most of the post-Second World War period, the Philippines underwent sharp and increasing centralization during Martial Law from 1972 to the early 1980s. Decision-making power and financial resources were primarily allocated from Manila, and recipients had few social and political channels to influence the decisions. The sudden shift to centralization, accompanied by a fast-deteriorating economic situation through the early 1980s, caused a considerable slowdown in social benefits. Social programmes were generally poorly managed. An ever-widening gap was created between the needs of the poor and the services offered. The severe economic crisis made the failure of the State to improve the conditions of the poor all the more evident.

With the political upheaval of February 1986 ending the Marcos dictatorship (1965–86) and initiating the Corazon Aquino administration (1986–92), a new democratic transition began that encouraged rather than constrained nongovernmental and grassroots organizations. The disadvantaged social sectors were allowed a new voice and were able to urge the Government to redefine its approach. The urban sector in particular, thanks to a coalition of grassroots organizations, managed to obtain a special government agency, the Presidential Commission for the Urban Poor, created by executive order in December 1986.

Under pressure from the international financial organizations and the weight of a particularly large foreign debt, the Philippines began to decentralize resources and services. Support to the faltering economy included privatization of state enterprises, financial and fiscal reforms and import liberalization, combined with major social programmes, such as land reform (Nuqui 1991a). Furthermore, even though government expenditure on social services declined from 24 percent in 1985 to 20 percent in 1988, reductions were also evident in economic services and, even more substantially, in the defence budget. Since 1986, education has consistently been allocated the highest share in the social services sector, from 11 to 13 percent (Government of the Philippines and UNICEF 1992).

The Department of Social Welfare and Development (DSWD), created in 1968 by President Marcos and provided with a mandate on poverty and cultural minorities, was the heir of a post-Second World War effort to make social welfare a basic function of the State (de Guzman 1969). DSWD focused primarily on the administration of institutions (centres for the elderly, for women and for disabled, emotionally disturbed or abandoned children and youth). After 1986, DSWD initiated deinstitutionalization policies, with the help of UNICEF, and established the licencing and accreditation of NGOs at regional and national level. With decentralization, DSWD is now also working more preventively with communities and encouraging the establishment of *barangay* committees for the protection of children. It still, however, operates centres for street and abandoned and mistreated children, building on the strength of many NGOs.

Community-based programmes provide real alternatives to the institutionalization of children. While the majority of the CEDC programmes have focused on rehabilitative or curative efforts, such as providing food, shelter and education, there has been a major effort to shift from child-focused services to programmes that give street children and their families access to basic subsistence needs and social services in their place of work and in their communities.

National initiatives: legal and institutional framework (1970–93)

The Child and Youth Welfare Code adopted in 1974 defines the rights and responsibilities of Filipino children and youth. The UNICEF-supported Country Programme for Children and the Philippines Plan for Action for Children, both incorporating principles contained in the Convention on the Rights of the Child, have been included in the Government's Medium Term Plan (1993–98). Moreover, with the presidency of Fidel Ramos (1992–present), the Commission to Fight Poverty has been created and given a broader mandate than the existing Presidential Commission for the Urban Poor. In June 1992, Congress passed the Urban Land Reform Code, to increase the urban poor's access to land and housing; however, the rapidly escalating land values and the failure of the Government to decriminalize squatting, are two major issues standing in the way of effective improvements.

The Child in the Justice System Movement, initiated by a group of concerned judges and lawyers, has also led to several innovative mechanisms to ensure the rights of minors in the courts and police system, and some cities now separate children deprived of their liberty from adult criminal offenders. The Movement has sponsored a series of training workshops for legal workers and police officers. The issue that creates the greatest challenge is, however, preventing cases of child offenders from entering the justice system altogether.

Programme Responses

The National Project for Street Children (1986–present)

The seed of a street children's programme was sown in 1984 when UNICEF hosted the visit to the Philippines of a consultant on Latin American street children, William Myers. He in return arranged a visit to Brazil of key workers of the DSWD, the National Council of Social Development Foundation of the Philippines (an NGO) and UNICEF to study governmental and nongovernmental programmes. They drew up a proposal which became the Philippines National Project for Street Children, begun in April 1986 and developed initially in eight cities.

Programme responses to CEDC problems can be roughly divided into centre-, street- and community-based services:

Centre-based services. Centres or institutions either offer sustained services for child residents or provide a mix, operating, for example, drop-in centres or other temporary shelters, or providing hot meals, counselling or first aid. Although institutionalization permits the close monitoring of children and is particularly useful as an initial response to abandoned children, it is expensive and underutilizes the potential contribution of parents, families and their communities. Consequently, since the late 1980s, there has been a shift to community-based initiatives.

Community-based services. As the vast majority of children on the street have parents and homes to return to, many studies have recognized the importance of community-based approaches which address the disadvantages of parents and communities. Programmes include community organization, housing, early childhood development, women's education, nutrition and feeding, livelihood training and medical services. The programme emphasizes the capacity of urban poor communities to deal with many aspects of their own situation.

Street-based services. Outreach workers go to the children's place of work to talk to them, identify their problems, and start to find ways to solve them. One such initiative, the Brother/Sister Programme for Street Children, in Olongapo, Manila, Davao, Iloilo and Pasay, offers counselling, tutorial sessions and medical attention, and has also organized soup kitchens. This approach was later adopted in other cities. In Cebu City, street education has been expanded from mere tutorial sessions to so-called street schools. An example is a fenced-in corner in the Carbon Market, where Sister Marcia holds lessons for the children of vendors, hawkers and labourers and runs a soup kitchen to ensure that the children's nutritional needs are met.

Training of street educators has become an important programme, supported by the National Project. Because street and working children are often afraid of being victimized by the police, security guards and extortionists, the presence on the street of a *gabay* (guide, big brother or sister) gives these children a much-valued sense of security.

Street-based programmes are able to reach many more children than centre-based activities, at about one fourth the cost per child. They do not, however, replace support networks in neighbourhoods, communities and agencies, but rather complement their efforts.

Street-based services depend on street educators and *gabays* who are in short supply, and not surprisingly so, as the following advertisement of Child Hope illustrates:

> Help Wanted: Street Educators
> Male or female. Low salary, evening hours included.
> Dangerous working conditions — bad neighborhood.
> Work guaranteed to tear you up emotionally.
> Tenuous job security.

Table 3.9. Increase in the Number of Street Children Served
by Programme or Service (1988–89)

Programmes/services	1988	1989	Total	Increase (%)
Health and nutrition	3,742	8,503	12,245	+127.2
Educational assistance	7,577	18,079	25,653	+138.6
formal education	2,789	8,754	12,540	+213.9
nonformal education/alternative education	4,788	9,325	14,113	+94.8
Cultural and recreational activities	5,603	14,120	19,723	+152.0
Value formation/responsible parenthood	4,457	7,083	11,540	58.9
parents	1,370	3,027	4,397	120.9
children	3,027	4,056	7,143	31.4
Counselling	6,177	8,345	14,522	35.1
families	1,988	2,059	4,047	3.6
children	4,189	6,286	10,475	50.1
Livelihood	2,324	3,592	5,916	54.6
children/parents extended skills training	1,151	1,410	2,561	22.5
children/parents extended seed capital for IGP	1,173	2,182	3,355	86.0
Children served in	2,761	2,731	5,492	–1.1
drop-in centres	1,211	1,505	2,716	24.3
temporary shelters	1,550	1,226	2,776	–26.4
Children placed in				
foster care	62	55	117	–12.7
adoption	5	13	18	160.0
Children reunited with their families	1,976	2,398	4,374	21.4

Source: UNICEF Manila (1990b).

Shifts in programme coverage

Cumulatively, the National Project for Street Children reached 30 percent of
the estimated population of 85,000 street children in 17 cities in 1989: 27
percent of the children in Metro Manila, 39 percent in the other 13 cities. Of
the services available in the Philippines as of 1989–90, a high percentage (54
percent) were community-based as opposed to centre-based (34 percent) and
street-based (12 percent) (UNICEF Manila 1990b). By 1990, increases were
especially evident in the number of street children reached by health, nutrition and education programmes as well as cultural and recreational activities,
while there was actually a decrease in the number of children registered in
temporary shelters or placed in foster care as opposed to children in drop-in
centres (see Table 3.9).

Partly in response to the studies carried out by UNICEF Manila and the UNICEF International Child Development Centre, programme thrusts in most cities are continuing to shift towards community- and street-based interventions. A greater effort has also been made to focus on preventive programmes aiming to address rapid population growth, the insecurity of housing and tenure, the inadequacy of urban basic services and other issues at the root of the street children phenomenon.

Most programme actors have realized that trying to meet the immediate needs of CEDC and the poor through assistance in accessing food, shelter, education and income requires both short-term programmes for immediate needs (lone street children) and long-term programmes for the majority of street-based children who are still living with their families, as well as for "hidden categories" of children. Helping street children gain access to shelter will not contribute much unless training, livelihood and credit assistance are also provided. Similarly, unless squatting is decriminalized, assistance at the community level will have only a limited impact. Delivery of social and medical services cannot be sustained when homes are being demolished.

The experiences of the Philippine CEDC programmes suggest that approaches must be multilevel, multifaceted and integrated. For example, "value education" programmes aimed at behavioural changes have limited impact when not supported with changes in children's material situation. It is meaningless to urge children to follow good hygienic practices when their family's access to water and sewers is limited. The legal, social and practical aspects of children's situations must be addressed in a synergistic manner.

The need for this kind of support is clearly expressed in the petitions, drawn up during the 1989 and 1990 regional and national Congresses of Street Children, urging that: (1) police violence towards children be stopped; (2) the incarceration of children in crowded, unhygienic prisons together with adult prisoners be prohibited; (3) paedophiles be severely punished by law; (4) police extortion from children be eradicated; (5) child victims of rape and crime be given adequate assistance; (6) special children's courts be established; and (7) (amidst much controversy) the death penalty be restored, especially for murderers and drug pushers. Adults found it difficult to believe that children had asked for the reinstatement of a severe law on capital punishment. However, as the case studies have illustrated, children on the streets have been victimized or bullied by extortionists, drug dealers and theft syndicates, and, understandably, thirst for redress, if not revenge.

Urban Basic Services Programme (1983–92)

Having long worked in rural areas, the UNICEF Country Office in the Philippines began early on in its Second Country Programme (1983–88) to look for ways to respond to the growing numbers of street children in the city slums and squatter areas. UNICEF believed that NGOs were generally more creative and successful than government agencies. However, because they worked in isolation and were deployed erratically throughout the community, they would never in themselves constitute an effective answer to the problem of poverty. Assuming the role of broker between NGOs and government agencies, UNICEF was looking for opportunities to engage the collaboration of both in piloting child-focused Urban Basic Services Programmes. Pilot programmes were carried out in four cities, two of which are in this study — Olongapo and Davao.

In the concluding years of the Marcos era, such collaboration was not easily secured. Most NGOs and organizations seriously committed to poor people regarded the Government, whose main response to the urban poor was to bulldoze their informal settlements, as serving only the interests of the élite. For its part, the Government was wary of anyone working with oppressed groups, suspecting them of political opposition or subversion.

The "democratic space" created by the fall of the Marcos regime and the first years of the Aquino Government allowed for a flowering of advocacy at national level, which resulted in the new President declaring the year from April 1986 a "Year for the Protection of Filipino Exploited Children" and the revitalizing of the National Council for the Welfare of Children. In the same year, the National Economic Development Agency (NEDA) — the highest economic planning body in the country — and UNICEF agreed that the analysis for the Third Country Programme (1988–93) should include children in especially difficult circumstances — street children, sexually exploited children, working children, children in situations of armed conflict, and other categories. Because at-risk categories of children were so firmly placed on the national agenda, advocacy opportunities were strengthened and programme development better assisted at the municipal level.

In particular, the Third Country Programme proposed to continue the integration of activities for street children into the UBSP through the coordination of the work of the inter-agency working committees on street children, composed of government, nongovernmental, church and civic groups and through close contact with the City Social Development Committees in each city.

Other events had an important bearing on the initiatives being worked out in the municipalities. In 1989, the President set up a fund of P20 million ($740,000) for NGOs involved with street children — an amount raised to P30 million ($1,110,000) in 1990 and P50 million ($1,850,000) in 1991. Also in 1990, the Convention on the Rights of the Child was ratified. This was followed in 1992 by the launching of the Philippines Plan for Action for Children up to 2000 and beyond. The UBSP, including the programme of street children, is seen as having a crucial role in the Plan for Action. The new Local Government Code, enacted in 1991 and implemented in 1992, offers potentially new opportunities for greater local responsibility for — and effectiveness in — the provision of urban services. It devolves resources, manpower and structures to local government, giving it greater capability and responsibility to provide basic services to the people. At least in the wealthier cities, this decentraliza-tion, which allows for the local raising of revenue, should increase resources and the effectiveness of the provision of services.

By 1992, the UBSP was being implemented in 13 cities and involved 130 city government agencies and 140 NGOs. It emphasized: (a) focused target-ing and convergence; (b) decentralization; (c) social mobilization; and (d) sustainability/institutionalization. It has also been adopted as the Urban Pro-Poor Programme of the Philippines Government. Within it, the National Project for Street Children was implemented in 18 cities and involved a national network of more than 300 government agencies and NGOs. A Child Labour Project is also being implemented, primarily in rural areas but also in coordination with the UBSP in two cities and 18 municipalities.

The UBSP and the National Project were conceived of as autonomous programmes, but were pioneered in Olongapo in an integrated way. This convergence of programmes allowed for a high degree of coordination be-tween the support of children on the streets and that of their families and communities and provides the guiding principle for the development of the programmes elsewhere.

Another important principle of the UBSP has been the organizing of deprived communities with the aim of empowering them to gain greater access to resources. The most recent expression of this has been the develop-ment of federations of urban poor organizations, which are beginning to gain direct representation on some UBSP Inter-Agency Committees.

The organization of street and working children has done much to raise their profile and to change public perceptions of them, giving a great boost to pro-UBSP advocacy and publicity. From the initial occupational groups, they have gone on to form a local and national federation (TATAG) which par-ticipated in the first national Congress of Street Children. The Child Protec-tion Act (Republic Act 7610), signed by President Corazon Aquino in June 1992, includes a number of the children's recommendations.

Mobilization at City Level: Process Documentation and Lessons Learned

Three cities have been chosen for an in-depth analysis of the way program-mes were started and the systems developed for coordinating and integrat-ing these programmes at city level: Olongapo, Davao and Metro Manila. The main period under review is that of the Second and Third Country Program-mes for Children of the Philippines Government and UNICEF — 1983–93.

Box 3.2   Community Self-Monitoring

Monitoring boards for identifying families and children at high risk. Halfway up the climb towards the urban poor community of Little Baguio II in Olongapo is a small health clinic with a prominently displayed monitoring board detailing community statistics: number of resident families, number of children under five immunized, number of women in receipt of livelihood loans and number of children enrolled in the scholarship programme that in 1990 kept 39 out of 42 of the community's poorest children in the classroom. The monitoring board attests to the importance the community gives to self-assessment.

Six groups of 15–25 families, each with a leader, were consolidated in 1987 in the Community Development Committee. By February 1988, a Community Council of Leaders had been elected and community committees set up for health, nutrition, income-generating activities, education, water and sanitation, as well as street children. The community identifies high-risk families according to its own criteria: distressed or overburdened households; households with malnourished youngsters; and households with children working on the street. Then the community committees, in close coordination with the UBSP Inter-Agency Council, give these high-risk families first call on social credit, scholarships and special services. The community committees deal with both urgent matters and problems of long-term maintenance (as in the case of community latrines, their first project). They also identify main projects of general benefit to the community, but with special attention to children and women, and coordinate their implementation. Paved pathways, a water pump and retaining tank, washing areas and community toilets were some of their achievements and a source of civic pride.

Street-based children and coordination between city-wide committees and community committees. When street educators identify school-age children on the street who risk becoming street children, they take steps to trace the children's families in the community of origin, often coordinating with *gabays* — community volunteers. *Gabays* supervise the enrolment of schoolchildren (including, when necessary, interviewing their families and assessing the children's attitudes towards being in school) and also monitor all problems. If, for example, a child skips school or misbehaves, a reprimand is given and, in time, scholarship funds withdrawn, as happened to five children in 1990. The school expenses (books, uniforms and school fees) of Reach-up scholars are paid in part by UNICEF and in part by money raised by the community through fund-raising activities. In Olongapo as a whole, by 1992, almost 1,000 street and working children as well as at-risk slum children had been reintegrated into formal education.

The community committees have organized advice and peer support groups for schoolchildren and encourage previous Reach-up scholarship students to help newcomers with exams. They also coordinate special problems through Reach Up, which as a secretariat both for the Inter-Agency Committee and the Working Committee on Street Children, provides an easily accessible liaison office for community committees and leaders within the Municipal Hall. This brokerage has been important, for example, in securing the acceptance by school officials of unofficial versions of necessary documents, such as children's birth certificates, often unavailable to the family. Other committees have also begun to include children as part of their considerations.

Aside from monitoring preschool health, the association leaders hope to put up a playground and basketball court to discourage adolescents from frequenting the Olongapo bars, streets and night spots. A new water system has been built to eliminate the arduous task, usually assigned to school-age boys, of carrying water up the steep hills to households. Through these monitoring systems, the whole community is taking greater responsibility for its children in coordination with the Municipal Hall.

Source: Urban Child Project (1991).

Olongapo

In the early 1980s, Sister Mary Soledad Perpinan described Olongapo's R&R district, as newly arrived US warships disgorged some 5,000 sailors into the town:

> Everything looked plastic under the garish colours of neon and strobe lights. As we wove our way in and out of the disco dens, clubs and bars, everybody appeared like objects of the entertainment world. A certain weirdness permeated the air — of men unwinding after being cooped up in ships and of women, cheap and giddy, prey of pressing economic needs. That night it was the entire sickly system that glared at me — the nauseating dominance of one nation by another. The people in the joints and streets were but pawns playing their pathetic roles.

The person who introduced Sister Soledad to the realities of Olongapo's R&R zones was Leopoldo ("Pol") Moselina. A sociologist and then Dean of Columban College, he had done pioneering research in the 1970s into the R&R industry, revealing the exploitation of young women and even children. The city's dollar glitter attracted a constantly increasing flow of migrants from the interior. Instead of finding a better life, they exchanged the poverty and oppression of the countryside for the poverty and oppression of the town's squatter settlements. These zones of need and desperation furnished the human consumables of the military's R&R. With women entertainers paid only in commissions and tips, the takings went to the city's businesses and so, through taxes, indirectly supported its institutions.

This was the era of the Marcos dictatorship, when community-based, church and NGO responses to people living in poverty sprang up in the absence of any concerted government programme. Columban College and other, mostly private centres of higher learning throughout the country survived as islands of free thought and also became involved in this work. Following his research, Moselina and his colleagues sought to develop an outreach programme to help women entertainers:

> Our idea was to immerse ourselves in the communities and support the people in identifying their own goals and programmes, for which we would then supply the technical support. We started with only one concrete activity. That was nonformal education — our hope was to use it as an entry point through which the women could become conscious of their exploitation and so begin to organize to improve their lives. Even if they had no work alternatives, they had a right to a living wage.

The College organized a team to work full-time in three *barangays*. Through this involvement the team became increasingly aware of the involvement of children in the R&R industry; they also learned of the existence of a few other NGOs working in an ad hoc way in poor communities.

In 1983, when the project, called Community-Based Services for Low Income Communities, was in its early stages, its founders decided to turn to

UNICEF for funding. A disadvantage they saw in working with UNICEF was that it meant taking on a predetermined programme of services that cut across their own more gradual, bottom-up approach. Allowing the community to identify its own way forward provided a formula for a broader programme that promised to equip the community to draw on government and NGO resources.

Columban College framed its application in a way that coincided with UNICEF's aims, and so became the implementing agency for UBSP in Olongapo. The pilot package included primary health care, nutrition, food production, water and sanitation, and early childhood development projects and income-generating activities. These were to be the focus for community organization, and the development of collaboration between government and nongovernmental agencies in the delivery of services. The proposal also recognized the need to pay attention to children involved in the R&R industry.

Building on common interest. The research, exposing the city's R&R industry, had not endeared the College to the authorities. This disenchantment was further aggravated when one neighbourhood targeted by the UBSP was threatened with demolition. The college project suspended the introduction of the UBS programmes in that area and, instead, supported the community deliberations on what action to take. In consequence, it was suspected by the City Government of agitating. When, after two and a half years the community lost its homes, the project showed its integrity and loyalty by following them to their relocation site. The price paid was very restricted opportunity for collaboration with City Hall.

For the period of the land dispute, the project was able to establish working relations only with the City Health Department. This breakthrough was facilitated by the personal friendship and trust between the City Health Officer and Pol Moselina. There was also a coincidence of interests because the Health Department was just starting up a primary health care (PHC) programme.

Community organizing and training of volunteers. Early in their collaboration, the City Health Department recognized that the College had much greater experience in the training of community volunteers. While the Department's principles were impeccable, its training of volunteers was top-down, management-orientated. In contrast, the College regarded the volunteers not as implementors of a programme, but as people serving their own and the community's interests.

The organization adopted was the formation of neighbourhood clusters of 20 or so families who elected voluntary representatives to a Community Development Committee. This committee, in turn, elected office bearers and formed itself into various subcommittees — among them health and nutrition, livelihood, water and sanitation and, unusually, street children. To provide a basis for community action, a situation analysis was made by the college project personnel, and its results were presented to the community for discussion, something that had never happened before.

A subsequent assembly would elicit ideas about what kinds of people would be appropriate as volunteers. At first, candidates were selected by an open show of hands, but later a secret ballot was introduced — an example of adjusting to the needs of the community in an empowering way.[6] The advantage of secret balloting is that it overcomes the problem of people voting for candidates solely out of a sense of personal obligation or for reasons of patronage.

This participative approach helps ensure a high level of community understanding and acceptance of the role of volunteers, and it may partly explain the level of their commitment to the job. Of seven volunteers trained in one *purok* in 1986, four were still active in 1992 — the others had been lost to personal and work commitments.

In addition to providing skills specific to their roles, the College's training provided a framework to enable volunteers to understand the causes of urban poverty. It equipped them to conduct analyses and to draw up and monitor community action plans. Understanding the causes of poverty included a rudimentary introduction to the structural causes at an international and national level, as well as those more directly experienced in the community and within families. This training laid the foundation for the training provided to volunteers today. One of the most ready responses of volunteers to the question of why they volunteer is the quality of the training.

Dismantling suspicion. Despite initial fears that the models of community organizing and empowerment pioneered by the College might somehow be subversive and encourage community leaders to take up radical positions, the City Health Department decided to make use of the College's training and community organization as the basis of its own PHC programme. Fears have gradually been allayed through an intermeshing of strategies:

- the abandonment of a revolutionary posture by community groups;
- actively engaging the Mayor (as the key power figure in the city) in the programme;
- exposing Government to the problems and initiatives of people in poor communities.

Collaboration has also no doubt been facilitated by the fact that no major conflicts of interest have so far surfaced, as has happened in some other centres.

A participatory, action-oriented situation analysis. In 1984, research carried out by Efren Gonzales and students of Columban College revealed that there were 3,000 abandoned and working children on the city's streets, the great majority trying to supplement family income. However, some municipal officials flatly denied the existence of street children, and the Mayor questioned the numbers. In view of the sensitivity of the issue, the College sought to engage as broad a sweep of society as possible in its investigation of the problem. In practice this meant reinforcing the professional research team with a committee representing the churches, academia, relevant government departments, community representatives, and others.

Committee members were kept informed and also invited to accompany the researchers into depressed communities and the streets. This "immersion" became a principle of advocacy and policy-making both in relation to street children and the broader UBS Programme. The College also used this process to establish a frame of reference for the external UNICEF/Government joint monitoring of its programme, insisting that staff at the national and regional levels pay preparatory visits to the poor communities likely to be affected by their decisions.

Implicit in this approach is an underlying optimism that poverty is tolerated by society not so much out of cruelty or indifference as out of ignorance, guilt and fear, reinforced by the stratification of society. It grew out of Pol Moselina's own "participatory research" into the R&R industry, during which he had worked as a nightclub waiter for six months. The experience had radically changed his own perspective, and he believed that exposure to the realities of urban poverty would have a similar impact on others. So successful was this approach with the street children research team that it was later transformed into the country's first intersectoral working committee responsible for piloting an integrated programme for street and working children.

Forging closer links between NGOs, communities and municipal officials. In 1985, the year before the fall of the Marcos regime, various events gave new direction to the development of the UBSP in Olongapo. The project leaders were aware that they lacked the capacity to reach other needy communities in Olongapo and that, even collectively, NGOs could be no match for the growing problem of urban poverty. Only if the plight of the urban poor could be made a central concern of government was there hope of more general progress.

Prompted by UNICEF to transfer the management of the UBSP to the City Government, the project leaders stepped up their advocacy and consultations with key local government officials, particularly the Mayor. The project leaders asked him to become the project's honorary chairman and invited him to attend the UBSP meetings on a quarterly basis. It was felt that if he had a direct role in the project, experiencing the thrust of the work and the response of urban poor communities, his suspicions would be allayed, and he would appreciate the benefits for the city of the UBSP.

During this period, a decision by the Columbans to pull out of the College resulted in its withdrawal of support for outreach work. A new base for the project was needed. With the new name of "Reach the Children of the Urban Poor in Olongapo" ("Reach Up" for short), management was transferred to the municipal Health Department, where it was coordinated by a small but committed secretariat inherited from the College.

Winds of change. The Olongapo research had made it clear that the majority of children on the streets are in fact working children, helping to support their families. A minority are more or less dislocated from their homes. Meanwhile, as elsewhere, it had generally fallen to the police to deal with children on the streets, exposing them to harassment, extortion and beatings. Because vagrancy is a criminal offence in the Philippines, children were — and in many centres still are — arrested and held in cells with adults. The processing of such children by the DSWD generally resulted either in their return to their families (without adequate support that might prevent their going back to the streets) or their placement in an institution.

The key Filipinos invited by UNICEF in 1985 to study approaches to street children in Brazil, including Pol Moselina, were particularly impressed by the role of street educators, the use of open-access drop-in centres, and the mobilization of children themselves to help each other and to identify their problems and possible solutions. The visiting team realized that to be effective, a programme for street children had to have an integrated approach. It needed community-based action aimed at reducing the pressures on children to leave their homes in the first place, a street-level programme offering abandoned and working children better protection and development opportunities, and longer-term solutions for children who were severely emotionally damaged or disadvantaged.

The end of the Marcos regime and the programme changes at the national level helped create a new environment for those wishing to tackle social issues. In Olongapo, it became possible for the first time to talk constructively at meetings about the involvement of children in the R&R industry. The introduction of the National Project for Street Children facilitated this task.

As elsewhere in the country, an interim administration was appointed pending fresh municipal elections. With a strong sense of social conscience, the new Mayor appointed a street educator to develop a street-level programme for children. He first mobilized the street children by taking them en masse to the residence of the new Mayor, who had no option but to acknowledge their existence. The street educator also began organizing street and working children into activity groups — market porters, vendors, plastic bag recyclers. Through these organizations the children were better able to protect themselves from abuse. It also made it easier to communicate with them and for them to communicate their needs.

Some ex-Columban College colleagues established a new tertiary college, Virgen de los Remedios, with the motto of "Education for Liberation." Community outreach work, with a special emphasis on street children, was identified as a college priority. Its Dean, Edgar Geniza, a journalist, became a member of the Inter-Agency Committee for Street Children and an active advocate of the street children, making effective use of all branches of the media. The College also provides community and volunteer training seminars.

Anticipating convergence. In Olongapo, the Inter-Agency Council (IAC) brought together 13 government departments — including Social Welfare, Education, Health, Engineering, City Planning — and 13 nongovernmental social agencies in April 1987 to coordinate services for urban poor women and children. The IAC is made up of steering/working committees on health and nutrition, water and sanitation, livelihood (small loans for such income-generating activities as poultry raising, egg production and candy making), education, community organizing, and services for street and urban working children. The committees, composed of hands-on workers, elect chairpersons and meet once a month. An important new development has been the establishment in Olongapo of a Federation of Urban Poor Associations, enabling community organizations to be directly represented on the IAC.

The Project Director, the Mayor and the heads of the different agencies form an Executive Committee under the chairmanship of the municipal Health Officer. The Reach Up project acts as the secretariat of the UBSP IAC. Reach Up is responsible for financial and administrative matters and for facilitating joint exercises in planning, coordination, advocacy, social mobilization, implementation, documentation and evaluation.

The fruits of collaboration. Perhaps the most important determinant of the successful working of the UBSP, including the street children's programme, has been the seriousness with which the communities and the children themselves have taken up the opportunities afforded them. In Little Baguio neighbourhood, the sense of achievement is almost palpable. Asked what changes had come about through the programme, community volunteer Ramon Jose said:

> This was a very violent place, there was no unity here, everybody thought only for themselves, there was no hope. Now the violence is greatly reduced. The gambling and drug taking is reduced. We are close to each other.

Other community members spoke of having overcome the sanitation problem. "We used to have the wrap-and-throw system — we called it flying saucers. You could smell it the moment you came into community." Now the community has built a public lavatory: the Municipal Engineer designed it and provided the cement, the Sanitation Department inspected it, the Health Department provided the lavatory seats, and the community gave some of the sand and gravel as well as the labour. Private lavatories have also been installed in many homes.

In Little Baguio, as in other neighbourhoods, the volunteers identify "high-risk" families: single-parent families, those with malnourished children, and those of street children. There is a separate subcommittee whose role is to mobilize, administer, monitor and evaluate support to both street children and their families. This support has so far included the selection and training of volunteers, counselling, access to loans for small income-generating initiatives, access to education support, close liaison with the street-level programme and the direct linking of support to the child in the community with support to the child on the street.

One important achievement is the education programme for street and working children. In keeping with the priorities expressed by parents, the programme emphasizes the reintegration of street and working children into formal education, rather than the provision of alternative education, which may be of less value in the job market. As a result, almost 1,000 street and working children in Olongapo, as well as children who would otherwise have gone to the streets, have been reintegrated into formal education. The programme reduces rather than rectifies the underlying inequity represented by children who have to work on the streets in order to secure an education. The overall aim is to increase children's access to full-time education by direct support, and by reducing, particularly during term time, their family's dependence on their earnings.

The programme is an important example of what can be achieved through the collaboration of community, government and nongovernmental agencies. The Inter-Agency Committee for Street Children has contributed to this programme by reducing the costs of education to vulnerable families: books and uniforms are supplied and school fees and "voluntary" contributions are waived by the Department of Education, whose representatives are very actively engaged in the Committee. Through the Philippines Educational Placement Test (PEPT), children are given the opportunity to reenter school at their level of competence, often skipping several grades.

The children themselves have contributed by forming support groups in their communities, which also serve to encourage newcomers to the programme. Schoolchildren commonly help newcomers prepare for the PEPT, for instance.

Bernadet Barbaran, who still works, as she has through the greater part of her childhood, to help support her family, lists the benefits of the Reach Up programme to her:

> First it is giving me an education through the scholarship programme, as well as free immunization and anti-tetanus. Then there are sports activities. But for the programme, I might not be included in the annual sports festival (staged through task-force collaboration) and might not be in school at all. I have my mother, a brother and three sisters. I still have to go to the market to sell eggs but, during term, I only have to go from five to eight p.m. each day. Because I get free education and school supplies, I work fewer hours. But the programme doesn't mean I can stop working.

Could the programme be improved in some respects? She laughs at the audacity of her idea. "Yes, if it paid a monthly allowance it would be good — then I would work only on weekends maybe, but not during school days."

How much would such an allowance need to be? "Three hundred pesos (about $10) would cover the transportation to school and snacks, excluding projects."

Empowerment or exploitation? Among the attractions of the programmes is that, at its best, it is both effective and inexpensive. These attributes are achieved above all through the organization, commitment and unpaid labour of its community volunteers. Elvie Papauran works on a voluntary basis as a guide four hours every morning at Kalingap, a soup kitchen and an important support and first contact point in the city for street and working children. Her husband also volunteers. She has received training in child counselling and is also a trained medical volunteer and community leader, which gives her extra voluntary work in the afternoons. She has been doing the work for three years.

But is this voluntarism of the poor not just a new form of exploitation? Why does Elvie Papauran persevere in her work day after day without financial reward, especially when almost everyone else involved in the programme is getting paid? She says,

> Because I find it more human to serve the children and, as a guide, I learn a lot from them. Through this work, my knowledge has become wider. I can give my time to people in greater difficulty and my life has greater meaning.

Jerome Caluyo, Deputy Dean of Virgen de los Remedios, has been with the programme from the beginning. He doesn't consider the programme exploitative:

> Because you are building people's capabilities to do things on their own, it is not exploitation but liberation. Through the process, they realize they can do something greater, and draw strength and a sense of empowerment from their community achievements because the community improvements are realized by them. It would be exploitation if they were used to provide a health service on the cheap and the credit was taken by the government to strengthen its political base.

The same would apply to the self-promotion of UNICEF and other agencies involved.

Staff and poor pay. The commitment of the volunteers in Olongapo has been matched by that of the Reach Up staff, which government and non-governmental agencies now recognize as a key feature in the programme's success. Their commitment is also marked by the fact that they have received modest UNICEF-financed honoraria without the agreed local government component of their salaries. (The municipal government is due to absorb personnel costs on taking over the running of the programme in 1993–94.)

Changes of heart. Another mark of empowerment is the changing attitude towards people in poor communities. Deputy City Health Officer Dr. Angelina Andrada says:

I used to think of the street children as a nuisance. Then I became involved through the programme and my attitude has changed. I also feel fulfilled in my work, which I didn't before.

Reach Up staff and community members have also felt a significant change of attitude at City Hall. The Mayor, who once regarded NGOs with suspicion, now personally signs the ID cards of Reach Up staff and volunteers, giving them the stamp of his authority. Members of poor communities say they are treated with greater respect at the municipal offices instead of being rebuffed.

Although there has been some inter-agency jealousy, more serious discord on the IAC has almost certainly been avoided by the fact that the programme skirts formal recognition of, or response to, the more structural causes of poverty, including the issues of land and housing rights and security of tenure.[7] Nor does the programme address the gross imbalance of wealth in the region. On the contrary, as a programme for the poorest sectors of society, operated extensively on a voluntary basis, it can be seen by the participants as a means of ameliorating the disparities in wealth.

Clearly the major challenge to the sustainability of the programme, particularly as poor communities gain greater organizational skills, will be its ability to grow to respond to some of the more fundamental concerns of poor communities.

Davao

The UBSP IAC in Davao originated in much the same way as in Olongapo. Here again, an NGO, located in an academic institution and working at community level, provided the entry point. The Davao Medical School Foundation's Institute of Primary Health Care operated PHC programmes, with children as a central focus, in some of the poor communities where no government service was offered. Though the programme was run by doctors, the main movers were community development graduates, sociologists and community organizers. The health concerns had resulted in the identification of a range of related issues that also needed addressing.

In introducing urban basic services, the Institute used the same structures and techniques of community organization that it employed in the development of its PHC work. Its community organizers lived in the communities, getting to know the people and gaining their confidence. Supported by community health volunteers, called "Trustees," their strategy was to encourage the community to discuss its problems in preparation for its participation in a situation analysis.

The situation analysis provided a basis for the community to draw up an Action Plan, prioritizing problems and targets. Once agreed to, the plan was written down by community members — normally unheard of in poor neighbourhoods. In this way there was a building up of capabilities in planning, implementing, monitoring and evaluating action undertaken.

Dr. Jaime Tan, UNICEF UBS Programme Officer from 1986 to 1990 and presently Under-Secretary for Health in the government of Fidel Ramos, was a community-based doctor in Davao and a pioneer of community-based programmes among NGOs. Describing the development of the UBSP in Davao, he explained that the first step in any initiative was to identify the government departments from which services were needed (City Engineer, City Health, Sanitation, for example). The next step was to single out the right official and invite him or her to a community meeting to hear its plans and proposals. Jaime Tan continues,

> So the Institute's activists were power brokers between poor communities and government offices, enabling people from those communities to come face to face with the power structure and facilitating a dialogue between them. Where the government was not capable of helping to implement community proposals, the Medical School went into specific projects.

Projects included credit groups giving women loans for income-generating activities and for water and sanitation, food production, early childhood education and women's literacy.

In the early stages, community efforts to engage government support were hard won. The idea of NGOs working with government was an anathema to both sides. Dr. Tan describes one of the early victories:

> The programme was able to convince the City Health Department that, even though the inhabitants of city slums and squatter areas were not considered legal residents, it had an obligation to provide them with health services. The securing of immunization, maternal health and growth-monitoring services was a great victory for people who said they had never before seen the face of a health worker.[8]

Similarly, the mediating role of the Institute and the development of a community action plan led to an agreement by the authorities to provide piped water to informal communities, which had previously received no water services. For their part, members of the community were all too ready to pay their share for the services. Whereas they had had to pay private water vendors 1 peso (less than 4 US cents) a gallon in the past, the service now cost only 10 centavos, so they gladly paid 25 centavos, 15 of which then went to fund community projects and to pay for maintenance of the water pipe.

Value of mayoral support. Again, as in Olongapo, Davao demonstrates the possibility of great advances with mayoral support. The Mayor of the interim city administration was a progressive human rights advocate who identified closely with the urban poor.[9] NGO attempts to work with government were rewarded with the Mayor first approving the UBSP Inter-Agency Council and then agreeing to its relocation to the Department of Planning and Development. The IAC came under the management of a City Councillor, with the Mayor the titular head.

With its potential for harnessing government, NGO and community resources, the IAC model had enormous appeal given the debt-related spending curbs of the post-Marcos period. Autonomous city departments (Health, Water and Sanitation, Planning and Development, City Education, City Engineer, the centralized DSWD and Education) were represented on the IAC along with various NGOs.

The shift of management from an NGO to the municipality did not take place without problems. In the bigger city environment, particularly one as politically divided as Davao, there were many levels of politics at play both within the NGO fraternity and among government departments. A number of NGOs would not work with the UBSP IAC; others dropped out for various reasons. Nonparticipants included agencies on the left, many with strongly active community-based organizations, and some with sympathies to the armed struggle, as well as agencies on the extreme right.

With the local government chairing the IAC, setting the agenda, calling the NGOs to meetings, controlling most of the UBSP budget and committing more of its own skills and resources to the programme, bureaucracy also increased. Funds flowed more slowly, as did decisions and their translation into action.

Despite these problems, according to Jaime Tan, the central aim of community empowerment has been well served, with different communities giving differing priorities on the basis of their needs. As health targets have been met, the emphasis has slowly shifted to food production and income-generating projects. Community achievements have in turn strengthened the commitment and influenced the attitudes of government partners in the IAC. The biggest breakthrough has been that:

> The city authorities have learned that you really have to dialogue with the urban poor. You should not just plan things without consulting them. When government officials see community credit groups operating one hundred percent, they say, "Well, the poor pay up, even when the rich duck their credit." That has resulted in a real shift in attitude.

The main facilitator of community organization varies: it may be a government agency, sometimes working through an established community organization; it may be the community-based organization itself; or it may be the Institute of Primary Health Care, or another NGO. According to Jaime Tan, where before there was only antagonism, now there is joint planning, a "whole mix of initiating, innovating, creating new approaches." Moreover, government departments have also adopted more community-based techniques. The Institute, for example, was able to convince the Government to adopt Paolo Freire methods in the training of health volunteers. These techniques develop powers of critical thinking and awareness and enable volunteers to operate flexibly. Another lesson learned by Government, according to

Jaime Tan, has been to move out of its static centres and go into the community, and not just as a token pre-election gimmick.

> The one-off high-impact visits have been replaced by a sustained programme.
> Now they have mobile clinics and also include the promotive and preventive
> aspect — they provide immunization, monitoring, health teaching, prenatal
> care. Whereas only 18 per cent of Davao children were immunized in 1986, now
> it is over 80 per cent.

Working to reduce violence. While the programme for street children in
Olongapo developed as an integral component of the UBSP, in Davao, it
came into being only after the 1986 launch of the National Project of Street
Children, when UBSP was already well under way. As in other cities, the
formation of the working committee that established an inter-agency task
force for street children began with a participatory situation analysis. Again
as in the other cities, there was, and remains, a predominance of NGO
involvement.

In Davao, the task force began by focusing on improving provisions for
street children in the centres. They went on to develop alternative education
programmes and, more recently, drop-in centres. There has been a strong
focus on reducing police harassment and violence towards children (police
are represented on the street children's task force) and, because of the ongoing conflict between government troops and insurgents near the city, there
has also been an emphasis on assisting the child victims of armed conflict.

A series of national conferences between 1986 and 1989 has enabled the
task force to draw on the Olongapo experience in the development of its
programme for street and working children. The first conference concentrated on structural analysis and the need to look beyond the individual
child, family and community to wider social issues. The second assessed
what was most valued about the programmes already being carried out. One
interesting conclusion was that children valued education, in whatever form,
above other programmes. Most children said they wanted to work to help the
family and also wanted to continue their studies in order to better augment
family income. Parents most appreciated livelihood assistance that could
make it easier for them to support their children in education, instead of
pressuring them to go out on the street to earn. This was a surprise for some
programme implementors who had employed spiritual and moral instruction without exploring ways to improve the material conditions of families or
the social-psychological aspects of family relationships. At a 1989 conference,
proposals were considered of how best to provide opportunities for children
themselves to speak up and to facilitate the organizing of children in the
cities.

At first, the street children's task force in Davao developed independently
of the UBSP IAC, depriving it of the opportunity to build up an extensive
preventive community-based dimension to its work. As a result of a change

of leadership, the street children's task force is now fully integrated into the UBSP IAC and heads up its subcommittee for children in difficult circumstances. The development of preventive work of the kind pioneered in Olongapo is proceeding, although a remaining challenge is to extend UBSP coverage to all communities from which street and working children come.

Because the UBSP IAC is already under the management of the city's Social Development Committee, which in turn is an arm of the City Development Council, the programme is already well down the road towards full incorporation into the city planning structure. But with Olongapo, a serious shortcoming to date is its failure to address the key issues of housing and land tenure.

Metro Manila

The development of the UBSP in Metro Manila was preceded by a programme for street children. In 1984, there were reports in the international media on the growing numbers of street children in the Philippines and the sexual exploitation of children by foreigners. Teresita Silva set up a department within the National Council of Social Development Foundation of the Philippines (NCSD), of which she was president, to look into the problems. At the time, there were only three organizations in Metro Manila working specifically with street children, two nongovernmental groups and one run by the DSWD.

A small inter-agency committee was formed under the aegis of NCSD and including the DSWD. The committee's role was that of advocacy on the plight of street children and the search for new responses to their problems as well as the building of a network of NGOs.

NGO development. With UNICEF support, NCSD continued its advocacy work and expanded its NGO-development role to build local NGO capacity. It provided training, research support, technical assistance and small grants for networking and education. Some NGOs associated with NCSD replicated this work at the community level. Of special note was the nonsectarian Christian Children's Fund, which undertook advocacy, provided technical and funding support to community projects, and trained parents in leadership and community organizing. Today, the NCSD describes itself as a national network, or federation, of NGOs and community-based organizations.

The capabilities of nongovernmental and community-based organizations involved with street children have been very varied. NCSD has a liberal attitude to new organizations offering services to street children. Silva says,

> As long as they are not damaging to the children, we are happy. Through our network we try to develop the orientation and capability of their staff so as to improve the quality of work. Some church-based NGOs are more intent upon proselytizing and imposing values rather than helping children to clarify their

own values. However, some who begin like that go on to understand and respond to the other needs of children.

A serious impediment to NGO development and to sustaining high-quality work is the low NGO salaries which result in high staff turnover. Silva comments,

> Even in our own council, it has not been easy for us to find good network facilitators. Even where you have trained staff in an organization, the quality of the programme can deteriorate as new untrained staff come into the picture. It's a continuous battle.

As the numbers of child-focused NGOs has grown, the NCSD network has decentralized, forming NGO clusters in each of the four main cities of the metropolis. However, there is still an imbalance in the distribution of NGOs working with children: of a total of 90 or so in Metro Manila as a whole, 50 are in Manila, and 20 each in Pasay and Quezon City. Every year sees three or four new NGOs joining the network in Manila in response to the continuing advocacy work, but the rate of growth in other parts of the metropolis is "much slower." As in other cities, there are also other nongovernmental community-based agencies not affiliated to the NCSD network. Generally they work with the community as a whole rather than specifically with children.

Working with the Government. NCSD has also helped to build government capacity to respond to the needs of street children and their families. From its inception, it has collaborated with the DSWD at a national level and at the local government level within Metro Manila. Because an early emphasis of its work was livelihood and income-generating projects, it has also established contact with the Department of Labour. Only more recently has it begun developing a relationship with the Departments of Health and Education, including the training of staff and volunteers in community organization.

UBSP and problems of convergence. Because of the traditional health focus of UNICEF, the lead agency for the UBSP in any city has tended to be the Department of Health. As this department in the cities of Metro Manila had little experience of networking or working with nongovernmental agencies, the convergence of the UBSP and the street children programme could only take place after some understanding had been established.

In Manila, where the Social Services Department of the local government was selected as the UBSP lead agency, convergence was more straightforward, with the chair of the board of the UBSP IAC going to local government and the vice-chair to Teresita Silva as NCSD President; the street children's network became the UBSP IAC subcommittee for street children. The NGO network has enjoyed good working relations with the Department and has, among other things, trained each of its 100 social workers in working with street children.

In Metro Manila, the UBSP is conducted in selected communities through the Government as well as a few community-based nongovernmental agencies. In Manila itself, four NGOs are lead UBSP agencies. They are established in some of the many slums and squatter areas which lack adequate local government services. Teresita Silva explains,

> Convergence operates in two ways. The four NGOs working with street children select an area in the communities where they are working. They are then allocated UBSP funds to address issues not necessarily included in the street children's programme, such as livelihood, health, training for environmental sanitation, and community upgrading. Another way convergence takes place is in those neighbourhoods where community organization has started with local government introducing UBSP. When they identify street children, the NCSD street children network comes in to help them with the advocacy, training and other technical support to work with street children.

A temporary hitch in securing convergence arose from the determination of UNICEF, with the advent of the UBSP, to channel all its funding through local government, including money intended for NGOs working with street children. NCSD feared that the NGOs would lose their autonomy if such an arrangement were adhered to. Eventually a compromise was reached.

Training and supporting volunteers. The densely populated squatter areas of Metro Manila make community organizing all the more difficult. Most programmes are started by paid professionals. However, as Silva points out,

> In developing the capability of the urban poor to take over the management of their programmes, we have to help them see that they are helping themselves and their communities and that there are almost no resources for their remuneration. Building a sense of community is long-term work, and it is very difficult to find people of the right calibre to do this kind of hard work, which includes working with families living under bridges, or by the railroad tracks. Because of the high cost of living, many community volunteers drift into full-time jobs. Nevertheless, I think the process is very much one of training: part of it is helping people to develop a commitment, and part of that is helping them to feel empowered by the process.
>
> In the 12 barangays where my NGO works, we started by training two community volunteers; now we have 30, of whom 19 are really active. Some are young adults — mostly mothers. We started by organizing groups of 15 for social credit. They repaid their loans very well and, in less than one year, have formed their own cooperative with 150 members and P15,000 ($555) capital. This success was due to the training, support and commitment of volunteers. But if they don't see any improvements in their lives and incomes, and are inadequately supported, commitment cannot be sustained.

The NCSD is currently identifying some of the elements necessary to make convergence of resources work. Silva concludes,

My experience is that as long as volunteers are trained and there is full support from the professional staff and the person in charge of the agency — counselling, training, responding to requests — then, eventually, the people organize other resources on their own.

A drop in the bucket? In its mid-term report to UNICEF covering 1986–90, NCSD estimated that programmes for street children in Metro Manila "reached" in varying ways and degrees about 16,000 out of 60,000 high-risk children. It is clear to some observers that more NGOs and more community-based programmes are needed. Without them, there is little chance to develop a coordinated preventive programme, with effective follow up. Street educators (there are just 60 in the whole of Metro Manila) focus on any children that seem lost, whether they are lone street children or return to their homes every evening. As things stand, Teresita Silva describes the UBSP and the street children's programme in Metro Manila as "a drop in the bucket," and an expanding bucket at that, as the migrant flow continues.

A metropolitan approach. In the Strategy Paper for the Fourth Country Programme (1993–98), UNICEF and the Government recognize the need in Metro Manila, as well as in Metro Cebu and Metro Davao, to achieve wider coverage, improve services and develop referral systems to meet the needs of the highly mobile urban poor. The development to these ends of a metropolitan approach, with strengthened inter-city and inter-municipality management, is earmarked for serious attention. A problem in Metro Manila is the singular lack of a Regional Development Council through which the UBSP, including the street children's programme, could be integrated into mainstream development planning. The recent Strategy Paper of UNICEF and the Government recommends that Metro Manila, having the largest number of urban poor, should be treated as a specific urban region. An effective programme there, it is argued, could galvanize cities throughout the country.

UBSP and the Philippines Plan for Action for Children

The UBSP is seen as having a crucial role in the Philippines Plan for Action for Children. In the Strategy Paper for the Fourth Country Programme, the aims are stated to be:

- enabling families, especially women and children, to have increased access to basic services and increased opportunities in social and economic development;

- empowering people in poverty towards a self-propelling development, especially for women and children;

- raising the capabilities of government agencies and NGOs to address the needs of people in urban poverty;

- advocating the formulation of a comprehensive national urban development policy that will benefit people living in urban poverty.

Most has been achieved so far where the most concentrated investment has been made: at the community level. However, communities' demands for resources from city governments must be matched by responsive city leadership, requiring in its turn technical competence and the ability to respond. Pol Moselina adds,

> We need to enhance the technical skills and competence of the city officials in development management and planning. In fact, a new development orientation is needed. For instance the view of officials of how to deal with the land tenure problem differs fundamentally from what the urban poor regard as real solutions. The kinds of low-cost housing offered are still not affordable by the urban poor.

The major challenge now is to employ the principles of community participation more effectively at city and national levels in order to guarantee sustained support for the communities' efforts. The need to address the challenge is all the more pressing given the devolution of powers to local governments under the new Local Government Code. This should bring resources, manpower and structures to local government, giving it greater capabilities and responsibility to provide basic services to the people. At least in the richer cities, this decentralization should increase resources and the potential effectiveness of the provision of services.

Governors and mayors in the Philippines largely determine city government priorities and policies. Their active support of UBSP has proved highly productive; examples are the dramatically improved immunization coverage, the reactivation of local (*barangay*) Development Councils, the promotion of food production initiatives, and the allocation of funds to children's programmes. However, equally important to their support for the actual programme is their support for the processes involved and their commitment to the underlying principle that the different development aspects of people living in poverty must become an integral part of city development.

However, the support of city leaders who, even if well-intentioned, are uninitiated in participatory and social development may do more harm than good or result in tokenism. It is quite possible, for instance, for a mayor to endorse the UBSP while pursuing development policies that totally confound its goals and gains. City leaders may also promote models of community organization that foster dependency instead of empowerment.

A development orientation towards the urban poor is still generally lacking among local government executives. Many remain mistrustful of the processes involved, viewing empowerment as the possibility to overthrow rather than to participate. There are still city leaders who, with an eye to political advantage, prefer to invest demonstratively in buildings, roads and bridges rather than in human development. Consequently, clarifying the message and getting it over more effectively to city leaders is a key UBSP goal.

A changing agenda. UBSP community organizing has so far revolved around components that are acceptable to government, and are thus able to provide the basis for IAC collaboration. Ultimately, the programme's sustainability depends on its ability to adapt. The direct and effective representation by organizations of the urban poor may help. But though there has been some movement in this direction, it has been slow, and the urban poor are far from being able to mobilize an effective vote. Their organizations have yet to establish federations in most cities, without which representation to the IACs cannot be established. In cities where federations have been formed, the degree of representation they have achieved differs. In Olongapo, for example, direct IAC representation has been attained; in Cebu, representation is only at the level of the area task forces (equivalent to Olongapo's community development committees).

Similarly, the task forces are beginning to benefit from the children's own recommendations. Both developments are flagged for strong support during the next Country Programme. Ultimately, the inhabitants of poor communities can, by collaborative action, counter some of the underlying and more immediate causes of poverty, but the major factors — such as land tenure, inadequate housing, the gross imbalance in the distribution of wealth and cuts in social services — still need to be addressed.

Programme challenges. Through the UBSP, an attempt is being made to systematize and scale up what was pioneered by highly motivated individuals and organizations as intensive, explorative responses to urban poverty. This process, however, requires a more systematic evaluation.

The clearest and most easily measured achievements of the UBSP are found in those components intended to save lives — improved health services and, in some areas, improved sanitation as a result of IAC-supported community action. These achievements are reflected in improved health statistics. However, the returns on the components most valued by parents and children, those intended to secure livelihoods — income generating and education — are not so clear.

While gains have been reflected in strong community support for the programme, no detailed investigation has been carried out on the degree to which families and children benefit. Progress so far has been measured only in terms of the number of families or street children "reached" rather than evaluating the impact of services on their lives.

In a move in this direction, the Strategy Paper recommends a thorough evaluation of income-generating initiatives to identify elements that secure success and sustainability. It also notes the lack of any gender analysis and planning in the formulation and evaluation of the programme, and provides for its introduction.

In the other major livelihood-securing area — education — there is an underlying, unexamined assumption that, despite our technologically rapidly changing world, such provisions will better equip children from poor communities to enter the job market and earn a living. Poor people are either exploited and marginalized, or rejected and excluded by a system that has found little use for them. But if they are not educated because the employment market has seen no reason to invest in them, will an education in itself create better employment opportunities?

The livelihood-securing measure whose practice and potential is most difficult to assess is the community organizing on which the sustainability of the programme also depends. Does the community organizing associated with the UBSP benefit all members of the community? What determines its ability to empower? Does it weaken or strengthen other community-organizing initiatives? In one community in Manila, leaders identified confusion arising from the conflicting organizing efforts of different NGOs as being among the top three problems facing the community (after insecurity of land tenure and employers paying half the minimum wage). An understanding of community participation and empowerment is called for now as the focus of community organizations increasingly shifts from projects to "felt needs."

Finally, no systematic study has yet been made of the motivations of the many volunteers and low-paid development workers. Why and under what circumstances are they prepared to put in the kind of unpaid work the programme expects of them? Community volunteers in Olongapo spoke of their lives having gained more meaning. They both benefited from and took pride in improving their environment. They felt better equipped to procure resources from the authorities and felt that they commanded greater respect. At an inter-city meeting of voluntary workers, those from Olongapo were against being paid, arguing that "prizes" issued as incentives to volunteers missed the point. If there is to be acknowledgement of the role, it must surely come from the communities themselves. In fact, some communities are acting to reinforce the role of the voluntary community health workers. However, the higher turnover of volunteers and low-paid community workers in Metro Manila may suggest that, in bigger cities, non-financial rewards may not be an adequate basis for securing the number and quality of workers needed.

One clear message from community workers is that the commitment of community volunteers, on which all depends, can only be sustained if their efforts are rewarded by continuing improvements in the quality of their lives.

CONCLUSION

The prevailing responses to urban problems have been ad hoc and piecemeal. Moreover, while urban problems are escalating, resources are dwindling.

Policies and programmes designed to alleviate the conditions of the urban poor in general and CEDC in particular have been based on a limited understanding of their situation. Thus, despite the many innovative public and private programmes, only 30 percent of the CEDC population, and a much smaller percentage of the urban poor, have been reached or have benefited substantially. Convergence of services has so far worked most extensively in Olongapo, where there is very strong support from local government; a similar convergence may be difficult in larger cities.

If this situation is to change, some serious rethinking is needed on the following issues:

Interventions in the economy. The high incidence of working children is closely correlated with the poverty of under- or unemployment, the low wages of parents and elder siblings and lives of permanent crisis. Thus, in addition to making the street environment more supportive of working children through media campaigns, training for police forces and other interventions, programme actors must pressure the Government to address these larger economic issues more aggressively. This calls for flexible and well-integrated programming and coordinated interventions.

The family in urban areas. City planners need to recognize that children and their families are affected by industrial location, commercial development, road construction and other events outside their control. Macro-level policies, which often cause displacement of communities or families, should be linked with micro-level programmes, such as family counselling, family support, child care and livelihood assistance.

Development bias. Often the more needy households do not sufficiently benefit from investments in infrastructure and social services. There is a definite bias in favour of middle- and high-income areas to the detriment of impoverished urban neighbourhoods. This must be redressed. To this end, this project has provided useful tools by helping to identify families at risk and to determine how those risks relate to the increased presence of severely disadvantaged urban children.

Developmental role of the poor. The existing and potentially larger role of the urban poor in the development of cities needs to be reevaluated. Their collaboration in monitoring problems and priorities, including the identification of families of potential street children, has proved invaluable — and cost-effective.

Better situational analyses and problem diagnosis. The different categories of CEDC express different dimensions of the phenomenon. A street girl selling cigarettes and candy perhaps occasionally "provides entertainment and fun" to clients recommended by her stepfather, a parking attendant. Because her family's income is so irregular, she may frequently be absent from school and, if no intervention is provided, will eventually drop out. To assure greater assistance and protection to children, programmes must recognize the diversity, complexity and interconnectedness of the children's family, street and school situations. This speaks for flexible and multifaceted responses.

Participation. The participation of urban poor children and their families in decision-making represents a crucial part of effective urban programming. When children and their families have a voice in matters that concern them directly, in collaboration with sympathetic NGOs and municipal offices, programmes achieve larger coverage at lower costs. At the same time, participation raises the children's and families' sense of worth and facilitates effective interventions.

Child care: a responsibility of both parents. An underlying assumption of many programmes is that child care is a woman's main responsibility, whereas most urban poor mothers also work extremely hard pursuing a living on the streets. The need to fulfil both roles puts an enormous amount of strain on these women. Assistance with child care is therefore very important. Daycare centres that double as community centres can be built in partnership with communities. Policies and programmes must also recognize that fathers can play an equally important role in child care. To maximize the impact of health programmes, males and older siblings should be trained in household and community health management, including, for example, oral rehydration techniques to prevent infant deaths from diarrhoea, and environmental and domestic hygiene to limit the spread of sickness.

A clearer vision by teachers and other adults. The emphasis of some programmes on the pathological behaviour of parents and children without looking at the conditions that generate and encourage these pathologies is shortsighted. Continually confronted with severe problems, some individuals adopt inappropriate or antisocial behaviour which needs to be understood. For example, children from urban poor families without adequate basic services, whose parents do not have time to attend to their needs, are unlikely to be clean, well-mannered and orderly at school.

The need for a supportive environment. As demonstrated by some UBSP pilot communities, urban poor families can be mobilized to manage their urban environments, or, as they have always been so creative in doing, to construct housing for themselves. But they need a supportive environment. Thus, the focus should not be on building housing units for them but on assisting them in securing tenure to their home lot.

Interventions at the community and family level should combine immediate, rehabilitative assistance with structural policies that seek to redress resource imbalances between better endowed areas or families and less endowed ones, and with the creation of a supportive legislative and administrative environment at city level. The general aim is to help develop stable and secure families and communities. A strong emphasis should be placed on education for children and on skills training and job creation for parents and adults.

Communities and cities should assume their responsibilities for protecting children and defending their rights. Decentralization is essential in order to enhance responsibility for planning, resource management and implementation at the municipal level. Communities need to become facilitators in the provision of children's priority needs. To do so, civil society needs to mobilize and to help place children on the city agenda. Community monitoring, the utilization of effective change agents, the strategy of "immersion," the emphasis on convergence of programmes and on their better integration are all important and cost-effective means to that end.

NOTES

1. This and the following section are summaries of the situation analyses and evaluations of CEDC programmes undertaken by Dr. Amaryllis Tiglao-Torres of the Philippines Social Science Council, Ms. Ana Dionela of BA Consultancy, Ms. Aida Santos and Associates of WEDPRO, and Dr. Emma Porio of the Institute of Philippine Culture, Ateneo de Manila University.

2. These statistics for 1990–91 were taken from various newspaper and government reports: (a) street children figures, from newspaper reports; (b) working children, from Ministry of Labor 1992 Report; (c) children in prostitution, from newspaper reports; (d) substance abuse, from Dangerous Drug Board; (e) neglected, disabled and disadvantaged children, from UNICEF Manila reports.

3. Most of the children in Metro Manila, Olongapo and Davao ate three to four meals a day at home. For breakfast, they had bread, coffee, plain rice or chocolate porridge; for lunch or dinner, mostly rice, fish or vegetables. Children in the Cebu survey ate only two to three meals, often outside of the home. They also consumed large quantities of high-calorie snack-food with little nutritional value. Other findings were that out-of-school children who have used dangerous drugs are more undernourished than in-school children who have never engaged in substance abuse. Positive family influence was found to be a key factor in both school attendance and avoidance of dangerous drugs.

4. In one case in Cebu City, a child scavenger was circumcised for fun by drunks in a neighbourhood store; in another, garbage haulers destroyed the cart of two scavengers and then beat them up.

5. The authors would like to acknowledge the Brazil study team for introducing this type of conceptualization of CEDC.

6. Because secret balloting is more time-consuming, however, it has not been adopted by other UBSP community-organizing agencies.

7. A community mortgage scheme is only accessible at present to certain communities and then only to the better-off in those communities.

8. Public health resources are much more limited in the cities than in rural areas; they had a health station for every 5,000 population, while in Davao there was one for 60,000 people.

9. During his term of office, Davao was one of several cities to establish a City Commission for the Urban Poor and a City Urban Poor Office, with the inten-

tion of responding seriously to needs of the burgeoning poor communities. Davao was the second city in the country (after Olongapo) to embrace the UBSP IAC strategy. As in Olongapo, the interim government was displaced at the elections, by which time the IAC was nevertheless established.

Chapter
FOUR

India: Urban Poverty, Children and Participation

Leo Fonseka and D.D. Malhotra

SOCIOECONOMIC CONTEXT AND DEMOGRAPHIC TRENDS

Economic Growth

India's overall economic growth was a modest 1.9 percent per year during 1965–90 (World Bank 1991b). It grew by 3.2 percent per year during the 1980s (UNICEF 1993). This huge economy, with a large and generally low-asset agricultural sector, is much less vulnerable than most developing economies to external pressures of trade and finance. Approximately 62 percent of India's total population is dependent on agriculture, which represents, however, only 31 percent of GDP.

World recession and other factors have, however, put heavy pressure on India's economy. In response to a balance of payments crisis, privatization was initiated in 1991, accompanied by economic reforms, including the easing of restrictions on imports; direct foreign investments, subsidy cuts, currency devaluation and tax reform. So far, liberalization has had a positive effect on industrial efficiency thanks to increased foreign investment and the import of higher levels of technology; but it has also provoked inflation, the closure of companies unable to withstand foreign competition, and a decline in agricultural production (UNDP 1993). While the overall performance appears to be encouraging, it is still too early to assess the full impact of liberalization, including the effects on India's vast number of families living in abject poverty. The transformation of such a large and heterogeneous country into a modern economy is certainly very complex, and will continue to be the subject of considerable debate.

POPULATION GROWTH AND DEMOGRAPHIC TRENDS

The already-mammoth population of India continues to grow even though the crude birth rate has decreased as has the total fertility rate, which is nevertheless still high[1] (4.3, comparable to the Philippines) (Table 4.1). A major factor in population growth is the dramatic decrease in mortality rates. The nation's annual population growth rate was estimated at 2.2 during 1960–91, but is expected to decline to 1.8 for the period 1991–2000 (UNDP 1993).

India still has a young population, although the proportion of young people to the overall population fell slightly between 1981 and 1991. It also has a still relatively small proportion of elderly people, despite dramatic increases in life expectancy during the last decades.[2] Given the current population growth rates (Table 4.2), the percentage of children and young people will remain high for at least some decades.

Infant mortality rates (IMR) (Table 4.3), although declining steadily since the beginning of the century, are still quite high (about 84 per 1,000 live births in 1991, according to UNICEF 1993) even with respect to other developing countries. Wide disparities still exist in IMR between rural and urban areas (102 and 62 per 1,000 live births, respectively, in 1988).

Gender disparities in IMR have narrowed since 1979, and a higher male IMR was reported in 1988 for the first time ever. On the other hand, female under-fives suffer higher mortality rates than males, as they have throughout this century, a result of social practices that give lower status to girl children and consider them a drain on the family's resources. Consequently, girl children are discriminated against in terms of both nutrition and health care. Studies have shown that female infants are breastfed less than males, weaned earlier and are less adequately supplemented (Chatterjee 1991).

Another indication of neglect is the much lower life expectancy of Indian women in comparison with women in other parts of the world: despite improvements in the last few decades, their average life expectancy in relation to the male average, which is indexed to equal 100, is only 101, much lower than the world aggregate of 106 (UNDP 1993). Moreover, Indian women in 1990 represented only 93 percent of the male population, an extremely low sex ratio.

Table 4.1. India: Socioeconomic and Demographic Trends

Indicators	1981 (unless otherwise specified)		1991 (unless otherwise specified)	
Total population	683 million		844 million	
children (0–14)	272 million		303 million	
% total population	39.6		37.2	
Natural growth rate	–		2.1 (1980–91)	
Urban population	160 million		217 million	
% total population	23.3		25.7	
children (0–14)	57.6 million		71 million	
% urban population	36.6		33	
females	–		46.7	
Urban growth rate (%)	3.9 per annum (1971–81)		3.1 per annum (1981–91)	
Slum population	32–41 million		65–70 million	
% urban population	20–25		30–32	
Urban poverty[1]	–		41.7 million (1987–88)	
% urban population	–		20.1	
General fertility rate[2]	154 (1976–81)		117 (1986–91)	
Total fertility rate (children per woman)	5.1 (1976–81)		4.3 (1986–91)	
Infant mortality rate (per 1,000 live births)	110		94 (1988)	
Age-specific mortality rate[3]	males	females	males	females (1987)
0–4 age group	39.2	43.3	33.6	36.8
rural	43.1	48.0	37.8	41.8
urban	20.0	20.9	18.1	18.2
5–9 age group	2.7	3.1	2.8	3.9
rural	–	–	3.3	4.4
urban	1.7	1.7	1.3	1.9
10–14 age group	–	–	1.5	1.4
rural	–	–	1.6	1.6
urban	1.6	1.4	1.1	0.9
Life expectancy	51.4	54.7 (1980)	58.1	59.1 (1986–91)
Sex ratio (females per 1,000 males)				
nationally	934		929	
in urban areas	–		878	
Urban demand for labour			2.6% growth rate per annum (1972–85)[4]	

[1]The poverty line is set at the monetary equivalent of 2,100 calories per day (2,400 calories per day in rural areas); [2]Number of children per one thousand women of child-bearing age; [3]Deaths per thousand population per year; [4]World Bank (1989). Source: Bose (1992); Malhotra (1992) (unless otherwise indicated).

Table 4.2. Urban Population in India (1901–91)

Year	Total population	Urban population (millions)	Decadal increase	Urban to total population (percentage)	Decadal urban growth (percentage)
1901	238.39	25.85	–	10.84	–
1911	252.09	25.94	0.09	10.29	0.35
1921	251.32	28.09	2.15	11.18	8.27
1931	278.98	33.46	5.37	11.99	19.12
1941	318.66	44.15	10.69	13.86	31.97
1951	361.09	62.44	18.29	17.29	41.42
1961	439.24	78.94	13.50	17.97	26.41
1971	548.16	109.11	30.17	19.91	38.23
1981[a]	683.33	159.46	50.35	23.34	46.14
1991[b]	844.32	217.18	57.72	25.72	36.19

[a]Includes projected figures for Assam where the census could not be carried out. [b]Includes projected figures for Jammu and Kashmir as given by the Standing Committee of Experts on Population Projections in 1989. Source: Bose (1992) based on Office of the Registrar General (1991a, 1991b).

Urbanization

India has a fairly small urban sector, slightly more than one fourth of its total population in 1991 (see Table 4.2). These low figures, however, conceal enormous numbers of people. Between 1971 and 1981, the urban population grew by about 50 million people, reaching 159.5 million. Natural population growth accounted for 40 percent of the increase; rural-to-urban migration was responsible for a further 40 percent; the remaining 20 percent was the result of the reclassification of rural areas into urban areas (Ministry of Urban Development 1988).[3] According to projections, two thirds of the population increase expected for the 1991–2001 period will occur in urban areas (Planning Commission 1985).[4]

Cities with more than 100,000 inhabitants grew more rapidly than smaller ones: growth was registered at nearly 47 percent between 1981–91 in these larger cities and by 1991 they accounted for nearly two thirds of the nation's urban dwellers (Table 4.4). On the basis of current population projections and urbanization trends, by 2001 the number of million-plus cities will have increased from 23 to 40, accounting for about 50 percent of the total projected urban population of 326 million.[5]

The National Commission on Urbanization (1988) has identified two distinct trends: (a) economic urbanization in response to economic growth momentum; and (b) demographic urbanization in response to population growth momentum. According to the UNDP (1993), declines are apparent in the percentages of the labour force in the agricultural sector (still high at 62.6

Table 4.3. Infant Mortality Rates in Rural/Urban Areas, by Sex (1970–88)

Year	Rural			Urban			Total		
	Male	Female	Comb.	Male	Female	Comb.	Male	Female	Comb.
1970	–[a]	–	136	–	–	90	–	–	129
1971	–	–	138	–	–	82	–	–	129
1972	141	161	150	85	85	85	132	148	139
1973	141	144	143	88	90	89	132	135	134
1974	–	–	136	–	–	74	–	–	126
1975	–	–	151	–	–	84	–	–	140
1976	133	146	139	78	82	80	124	134	129
1977	136	146	140	80	82	81	136	135	130
1978	132	143	137	74	75	74	123	131	127
1979	129	131	130	73	71	72	119	121	120
1980	123	125	124	65	65	65	113	115	114
1981	119	119	119	63	62	62	110	111	110
1982	–	–	114	–	–	65	–	–	105
1983	113	114	114	69	63	66	105	105	105
1984	113	114	113	68	64	66	104	104	104
1985	–	–	107	–	–	59	96	98	97
1986	–	–	105	–	–	62	96	97	96
1987	–	–	104	–	–	61	95	96	95
1988	–	–	102	–	–	62	95	93	94

[a]Breakdown not available. Source: Bose (1992) based on data from Office of the Registrar General of India (1988b).

Table 4.4. Population Share of Urban Agglomerations and Towns (1991)

No. of inhabitants	No. of urban agglomerations and towns	Population		
		In thou- sands	Per- cen- tage	Increase 1981– 91 (%)
1,000,000 and above	23	70,661	32.82	
500,000–999,999	30	20,937	9.72	
100,000–499,999	247	48,132	22.35	
Total 100,000 and above	300	139,730	64.89	46.87
50,000–99,999	345	23,597	10.96	28.14
20,000–49,999	947	28,712	13.33	25.30
10,000–19,999	1,167	16,998	7.89	10.72
5,000–9,999	740	5,644	2.62	–1.27
Less than 5,000	197	0,657	0.31	–21.70
Total	3,696	215,338	100.00	36.09

Source: Bose (1992), Office of the Registrar General (1991b).

percent in 1986–89, but down from 73.0 percent in 1965) and in industry (which absorbed only 10.8 percent of the labour force in 1986–89, as against 12.0 percent in 1965); the share of the labour force in services, instead, increased from 15.0 percent in 1965 to 26.6 percent in 1986–89. If this trend continues, it can be expected that further strain will be put on cities which already have inadequate basic urban services (Ministry of Urban Development 1988).

In 1991, children represented only 33 percent of the urban population compared with 37.2 percent of the national population; similarly, fewer females than males were living in urban areas (Table 4.1). This disparity derives in part from the predominance of single male migrants in the past, a trend which changed during 1971–81 when the proportion of young families migrating to urban areas increased[6] (Office of the Registrar General 1986). In the same period, both *leap migration* (rural-urban) and *step migration* (rural-town, town-city) reached record levels. In general, leap migration is more prevalent in the least urbanized states and is normally confined to the same district or region. When leap migration occurs across state lines, however, it is most often directed (in 80 percent or more of the cases) towards major metropolitan areas, such as Bombay, Calcutta, Delhi or Madras. Indeed, in these large metropolitan cities most migrants arrive directly from rural areas. Step migration, instead, usually takes place in areas where there has been a more generalized process of overall urbanization.

Poverty

More than 20 percent of the urban population lives beneath the poverty line (some claim that the percentage is much higher).[7] This nonetheless represents a significant improvement, given that the percentage for 1972–73 was more than twice as high (Table 4.5). Rural poverty has also dropped substantially from 1972–73 levels. Disparities among states are marked (Table 4.6).

It has been argued that indices of poverty based on calorie consumption alone do not reveal the overall dimension of urban poverty. "Non-food poverty" (that is, the deteriorating physical and social living conditions in slum areas) has a serious impact on family life, even where income levels for households are well above the officially defined poverty line. Several studies have shown that migrants and their children tend to have poorer health in urban than in rural areas, even though they generally eat better and more regularly.

The slum population in Indian cities, particularly in the large ones, is growing between two and three times faster than the overall urban population. However, estimates can only be tentative due to the lack of data. In 1983, a Task Force of the National Planning Commission examined several estimates by official agencies and prepared two sets of estimates — low and high. It concluded that: (a) the slum population of India in 1981 ranged from

Table 4.5. Incidence of Poverty (Percentage of People
Below Poverty Line 1972–88)

Year	Rural	Urban	Total
1972–73	54.1	41.2	51.5
1977–78	51.2	38.2	48.3
1983–84	39.9	28.1	36.9
1987–88	–	20.1	–

Source: NIUA (1988b)

Table 4.6. Urban Population Below the Poverty Line
(Provisional Estimates, 1987–88)

State	Number in millions	Percentage
Andhra Pradesh	4.26	26.1
Assam	0.25	9.4
Bihar	3.61	30.0
Gujarat	1.71	12.9
Haryana	0.47	11.7
Himachal Pradesh	0.01	2.4
Jammu & Kashmir	0.14	8.4
Karnataka	3.37	24.2
Kerala	1.16	19.3
Madhya Pradesh	3.09	21.3
Maharashtra	4.72	17.0
Orissa	1.09	24.1
Punjab	0.43	7.2
Rajasthan	1.90	19.4
Tamil Nadu	3.85	20.5
Uttar Pradesh	7.52	27.2
West Bengal	3.63	20.7
Other States/Union Territories	0.49	4.7
Total for India	41.70	20.1

Source: Bose (1992) based on National Sample Survey data on household consumer
expenditure.

32 million to 40 million, or from 20 to 26 percent of the 162 million total urban
population; (b) approximately 40 percent of the total slum population nationwide was concentrated in 12 metropolitan cities; (c) of this 40 percent, three
fourths lived in the nation's four major cities — Bombay (with the largest

slum population), Calcutta, Delhi and Madras. The same Task Force foresaw that the slum population would reach 45–56 million by 1990 and 62–78 million by 2000, or from 20 to 25 percent of the total urban population, with about 45 percent concentrated in large cities.

These estimates now appear to be conservative. During the 1980s, urban land values increased at a much higher rate than urban incomes, and accessibility to housing further diminished. Consequently, the urban poor population has probably already reached 65 to 70 million, that is, between 30 and 40 percent of the overall urban population.

Urban Poor Neighbourhoods

Urban poor neighbourhoods are not the lawless and depraved places many are led to believe. While a few may contain infamous areas, they are, for the most part, made up of normal individuals who are struggling to make a living, while contributing to the city economy. Many residents are migrants, some more recent arrivals than others. Some manage to visibly improve their lot after working in the city for some time and are able to purchase some consumer items (typically a television set or a motorbike). Others, instead, remain in abject poverty. Most slum-dwellers develop a community life and comply with prevailing social norms. Many slums have local *panchayats* or informal councils formed to resolve specific issues. However, most interactions are informal and are strongly influenced by kinship, caste, language, religion and regional provenance (Bose 1992).

The term "slum" is often used generically in this chapter to describe different types of neighbourhoods or *bastis*: officially notified city slums; industrial housing slums; and squatter settlements. Each neighbourhood has undergone a particular process of growth and decay, and has a way of life distinctly shaped by its own history, age and socioeconomic conditions.

City slums. In many cities, large residential sections of the old city have been officially declared codified slums. Though generally unhygienic and unevenly serviced, most city slums have potable drinking water, paved streets, drainage, electricity, street cleaning and garbage collection. These areas are socially and culturally deeply rooted in the city itself, sharing its customs and traditions. In many areas, the rich and poor live in the same neighbourhood and their lifestyle does not differ much, although caste segregation does exist. However, city slums are slowly being transformed, and are losing their identities and cohesiveness. Factors contributing to this process include: (a) the conversion of buildings from residential to commercial use; (b) the widening gap between the wealthy and the poor; and (c) an urban renewal approach that has tempted those who can to move out, thus causing social conditions to deteriorate even further.

Industrial housing slums. With industrialization, housing complexes, made up mostly of one-room tenements built on private land, were planned for industrial workers and eventually their families. Although basic urban services have been extended to these areas, living conditions, while generally better than in most other poor urban neighbourhoods, have deteriorated in the last 50 years because of neglect. The pressures on social and family life and the risk factors for children have also increased with overcrowding.

Squatter settlements. Since 1951, slum growth has taken place through a process of squatting and land invasion, mainly on public lands. Squatter settlements usually grow near markets, high-income residential areas, construction sites and other areas where there is a demand for casual labour. Initially, a makeshift hut is erected. If the squatter is not evicted, a process of chain migration starts up. When the settlement has grown to about 30 households, little can be done to evict the squatters, and expansion continues unabated. Gradually, some basic services are extended to the settlement and, with security of tenure, the structures begin to show signs of improvement. However, these settlements remain squalid, and do not conform to public health and safety norms. Usually after 15 or 20 years, they reach saturation point and can no longer even absorb natural population growth. With the better areas already occupied by squatters, new slums appear along railway lines or on the slopes of drains (*nallah*). Basic services cannot be extended to these locations, and residents face hostile and often dangerous conditions, which are particularly harsh for women and children.

The 1981 Census reported that 37 percent of households in urban India had no electricity, 25 percent no access to safe drinking water and 42 percent no toilet facilities. Older city slums, however, generally have better basic facilities and services than the newer squatter settlements. Most often, the worst-affected victims of these unsanitary environments are children, who are particularly susceptible to water-borne contaminants.

Pavement Dwellers. As urban lands and housing become more inaccessible, even to those above the poverty line, a minority of the urban poor, especially in large metropolitan cities, are increasingly forced to live on pavements and streets or under bridges. Pavement dwellers officially represent 0.4 percent of the urban population, but their actual numbers are probably much higher. The Municipal Commissioner of Bombay estimated that there were 1.5 million pavement dwellers in Bombay alone, which in itself is more than 0.4 percent of all urban dwellers in India (SPARC 1991).

Pavement dwellers are not an exclusive feature of Indian cities: they have been reported in other large cities. In India, many homeless people put up makeshift huts on the pavements of busy city streets. Using whatever materials can be found — tattered gunny bags, tarpaulin, plastic or polythene sheets, held up by two wooden poles — these constructions provide only minimal shelter. Some homeless merely seek shelter under the staircase of a building or in other covered places. Very few studies have investigated the family life of pavement dwellers (Ramachandran 1972, for example) or the daily lives of their children (SPARC 1991).

Employment

The highest rate of urban unemployment is found among the educated youth. The poor are rarely unemployed, as they have few if any savings and little other support to fall back on. A NIUA (1989) study, based on primary surveys conducted in 20 urban centres nationally in 1987, reported that only 7.6 percent of males and 1.4 percent of females between 15 and 59 years of age were unemployed.

The poor are poor then because they are *underemployed*. They work in marginal occupations and in the informal sector where, because of the excessive supply of labour, they compete against one another and receive extremely low pay. This situation inevitably creates pressures on households to send children to work to supplement the family income. The growth of employment in the organized factory sector has been very slow; demand for labour in urban areas grew at less than 2.6 percent per year during 1972–85 (World Bank 1989), whereas the urban population rose by 3.9 percent per year during 1971–81.

THE SITUATION OF DISADVANTAGED URBAN CHILDREN AND FAMILIES

Growing up in Urban Poverty

As in other developing countries, Indian cities are becoming increasingly younger, a phenomenon expected to continue up to 2000 and beyond. In 1981, 47.1 percent (74.4 million) of India's urban population was in the 0–19 age group. In 1991, it was estimated that of the approximately 69 million children aged 0–14 living in urban areas, 17–20 million were living in slums; of these, it is estimated that 13–14 million were between the ages of 5 and 14 years, assuming the same proportions as found in the Census of 1981. In the 23 cities with over one million populations in 1991, between 5–6 million children lived in very poor conditions, both at the family and neighbourhood levels.

The unhealthy living environment of urban poor neighbourhoods and the lack of basic services are major causes of illness and mortality among young children. According to studies carried out in 1991, the infant mortality rate in some poor urban neighbourhoods reached 123 per 1,000 live births, twice the overall average for urban areas. Twenty-eight percent of infant deaths and 22 percent of child deaths in slums were related to diarrhoea or acute respiratory infections. Apart from being a health hazard, the shortage of safe drinking water also poses other problems for many children who are often given the daily task of carrying heavy loads of water long distances from public taps.

Nutritional status. Although the nutritional levels of children in slum areas have improved, studies have found that about 85 percent of the children were

Many girls are pulled out of school to enable their mothers to work. A young surrogate mother in the slums of Hyderabad, India. *Credit*: UNICEF/Stefano Berterame.

Table 4.7. Urban Children Attending Schools/Colleges
(1981, Percentages)

Age group	Male	Female	Total
0–4	1.9	1.7	1.8
5–9	61.8	55.8	58.9
10–14	77.0	65.4	71.5
15–19	50.1	34.7	43.0
Total	48.4	40.2	44.7

Source: Patel (1983).

suffering from varying degrees of malnutrition in 1991. Four major nutrition-al problems in preschool children have been identified: (1) protein-calorie malnutrition; (2) iron deficiency anaemia; (3) vitamin A deficiency, a cause of xerophthalmia and, in extreme cases, blindness; and (4) iodine deficiency, which is found mostly in the northern and eastern parts of India, and hinders the physical and mental development of children (Gopalan 1984–85). Mal-nourishment among pregnant women can result in the low birth weight of their babies, exposing newborns to greater risks of illness and death. One slum study in 1991 found that about half of the pregnant women were suffering from nutritional anaemia.

School enrolment. Even though enrolment rates have been increasing since 1951, 1981 census data revealed that 82.5 million of 158.8 million children 6–14 years of age were not attending school. In urban areas, only 33 million children, or 44.7 percent of the total 74.4 million urban children 0–19 were enrolled in schools and colleges (Table 4.7).

Figures for enrolment and dropping-out in slum areas compare un-favourably to those for other city areas. For instance, in a study in Delhi, it was found that the non-enrolment rate in slum areas was nine times greater, and the dropout rate 20 percent greater than in non-slum schools (see also Table 4.8).

Working Children. In India, children are not prohibited by law from per-forming certain jobs. However, considerable variations in the estimates of working children exist because of differences in the definitions of "child" (upper age limit) and of "worker." The 1981 Census reported nationally that only 13.6 million children — 8.1 million males and 5.5 million females — in the 5–14 age group were working; work participation rates among urban children, based on 1981 census data have also been roughly estimated (Table 4.9). It has been argued that the census figures essentially account for only those children engaged in the informal sector or formal activities, ignoring the large numbers who are "invisible," working without wages or as domes-tic servants, as well as children who are self-employed. The National Sample

Table 4.8. Literacy Among Children in Urban India, by Sex (1961, 1971 and 1981)

Age group (in years)	Year	Number of illiterates (in millions)			Number of literates (in millions)			Total population (in millions)		
		Male	Female	Total	Male	Female	Total	Male	Female	Total
5–9	1981[1]	4.825	5.017	9.842	5.472	4.684	10.156	10.298	9.701	19.999
	1971	4.062	4.130	8.192	3.627	3.075	6.702	7.689	7.205	14.894
	1961	3.175	3.395	6.570	2.451	1.901	4.352	5.626	5.296	10.922
10–14	1981	1.802	2.483	4.285	8.383	6.778	15.161	10.184	9.261	19.446
	1971	1.370	1.861	3.231	5.789	4.567	10.356	7.159	6.428	13.587
	1961	1.061	1.573	2.634	3.758	2.641	6.399	4.819	4.214	9.033
15–19	1981	1.619	2.257	3.875	7.405	5.538	12.943	9.024	7.794	16.818
	1971	1.028	1.518	2.547	4.935	3.465	8.400	5.964	4.983	10.947
	1961	0.870	1.386	2.257	3.037	1.815	4.852	3.907	3.202	7.108

[1]The 1981 figures do not include Assam where the Census could not be undertaken. Sources: Bose (1992) based on data from the Registrar General and Census Commissioner (1988, 1977 and 1961).

Table 4.9. Work Participation Rates Among Urban Children
(1981, Percentages)

Age groups	Male	Female	Total
0–14	2.6	1.1	1.8
15–19	32.4	7.3	20.8
Total	9.5	2.4	6.1

Source: Office of the Registrar General (1984).

Survey in 1983 estimated that there were 17.4 million child workers, whereas the Operations Research Group (Baroda) arrived at a figure of 44 million.

Estimates of children (age 5–14) working in urban areas are notoriously difficult to make, and they vary nationwide from 1 million to as high as over 9 million (ORG 1988).

In Delhi, it was estimated that there were 400,000 working children in 1988 (Panicker and Nangia 1988). Nearly 80 percent were over nine years of age and illiterate. A recent study in Delhi estimates that 40,000 children work as labourers, 30,000 assist in shops, 30,000 work in eating establishments, and 20,000 in auto-repair shops. Many working children are self-employed as porters, vendors, ragpickers, shoeshine boys, newspaper sellers and beggars. About 100,000 children are estimated to be working as domestic help. Girl children of poor families become surrogate mothers to their younger siblings. Some girls help their mothers in domestic or piece-rate work.

Street children. Detailed information on street children is scarce and defini-tions of "street children" vary substantially. In a broad sense, the term refers to children who earn money, including by illicit activities, on urban streets; in other words, "street-based working children" or "children *on* the street." Among them, however, only a small percentage are actually living on the streets and have weak or severed ties with their families: "children *of* the street." UNICEF, in collaboration with the Ministry of Welfare, sponsored field studies on street children in Bangalore, Bombay, Calcutta, Delhi, Indore, Kanpur and Madras; the studies, however, did not distinguish systematically between children *on* and *of* the streets. Because street children are a mobile group, it is difficult to make even an informed guess about their overall numbers. The Delhi study arrived at a figure of 100,000 by estimating that 25 percent of the working children were street children. Studies in Bombay estimated that about 77 percent of street-based working children lived with their families. Only a minority of these children, almost exclusively boys, live alone; 10.4 percent in Bombay, 7.4 percent in Kanpur and 3.7 percent in Bangalore (D'Lima and Gosalia 1989; Pandey 1989; CWC 1992; Panicker and Nangia 1988).

Table 4.10. Percentages of Young Women Ever-Married, Rural,
Urban and Combined Populations, India, 1981

Age group	Percent married in 1981		
	Rural	Urban	Total
10–14 years	7.8	2.4	6.7
15–19 years	49.5	28.4	44.1
20–24 years	90.2	74.3	86.00
Total			51.30

Source: Office of the Registrar General (1984).

Early marriage. Even though the minimum age of female marriage is prescribed by law as 18 years, the percentage of those marrying before reaching this age, though decreasing, continues to be significant. Census data reveals that in 1961 the percentage of married females in the 10–14 age group stood at 22 percent in rural areas and nearly 8 percent in urban areas. Table 4.10 shows the relative percentages for 1981, which indicate an increase in the female age at marriage. The tendency of early female marriage among migrants from rural poor areas persists.

Early pregnancy and the rapid succession of childbirths following early marriage generally have adverse effects on the health of both the mother and her children (Tables 4.11 and 4.12).[8] Maternal mortality officially accounts for 10 percent of deaths among 15–24 year-old females, although community-level studies indicate that the actual figure may be as much as double the official rate. Nevertheless, the official rate of 460 maternal deaths per 100,000 live births is still 50 times that reported in most industrialized countries. With a high fertility rate, Indian women have about a 300 times greater risk of dying of maternity-related causes than women in industrialized countries (Chatterjee 1991).

Children in conflict with the law. Although both the Indian Penal Code (IPC) and Local and Special Laws define criminal acts, the actual incidence and trends of children coming into conflict with the law are difficult to measure.[9] In 1988, 1.7 percent of all crimes under the IPC were committed by minors and the rate of juvenile crime per 100,000 population was 3.1 (National Crime Records Bureau 1990). The main offences were theft, burglary and rioting, while serious offences such as murder or attempted murder accounted for 3.8 percent of all juvenile offences in 1988. Most cases under Local and Special Laws are related to alcohol abuse and gambling. Of the children apprehended in 1988, most were between 12 and 16 (92 percent for the boys and 83 percent for girls); boys far outnumbered girls. There are some indications

Table 4.11. Infant Mortality Rate by Mother's Age at
Marriage, 1984 (per 1,000 Live Births)

	Rural	Urban	Combined
Under 12	144	61	135
12–14	127	82	122
15–17	112	74	106
18–20	103	62	94
21–23	93	42	78
24 and over	99	35	82

Source: Office of the Registrar General (1986).

Table 4.12. Mean Age at Marriage of Females According to
Educational Level, Rural and Urban India, 1981

	Rural	Urban
Illiterate	16.3	16.7
Literate		
up to 7 years of schooling	17.1	17.4
8–9 years of schooling	17.8	18.1
10–14 years of schooling/college	19.3	19.8
College graduate or higher degree	21.6	21.9
All women	16.5	17.6

Source: Office of the Registrar General (1984).

that the numbers of children in conflict with the law are growing, though
only a small percentage of all children apprehended are actually tried.

Working and Street Children in Perspective: Studies in Six Cities

In order to understand more fully how poor urban children live, how they
run into problems, and how their situations relate to their families' circumstances, the Country Team initiated in-depth surveys in Delhi and in five
Andhra Pradesh towns. The results of surveys on Bombay street children
living "on their own" and children of pavement dwellers, prepared for
SPARC (see Box 4.6) two years earlier, were also analysed, thus widening the
scope of study. Based on purposive rather than representative samples, because of the dimensions of the problem and the difficulties of sampling, these
surveys aimed at identifying key elements for more accurate typologies of
at-risk families and children.

The Delhi researchers interviewed at length 182 randomly selected households in two slum settlements and collected life histories of their children. They also carried out in-depth interviews of a sample of 30 street children "on their own." They were, however, unable to interview their families since most of the children came from rural areas and did not have a family in the city (NIUA 1991b). The Andhra Pradesh study, using the same questionnaire, interviewed 613 children and households in three cities (Warangal, Cuddapah and Rajahmundry) and another 456 street children "on their own" in Hyderabad and Vijayawada (Osmania University Regional Centre 1991). The studies were however analysed somewhat differently.

The two Delhi slums selected (out of over 800 city slums) were: (1) Janakpuri, a 15-year-old settlement with an approximate population of 10,000 migrants, mostly Hindus from Tamil Nadu, Rajasthan, Bihar and Uttar Pradesh; and (2) Nizammudin, an 18-year-old settlement of about 10,030 Muslim migrants from Bangladesh, West Bengal and Bihar. Residents of the first settlement, which was only partly authorized, were engaged in construction work, rickshaw-pulling and domestic services; residents of the second, close to an area where garbage was stored and processed, primarily did ragpicking work which they supplemented with begging. Ragpickers, as evidenced by street children surveys in different Indian cities, represent an important percentage of the street-based occupations carried out by children. At the time of the surveys, both settlements had access to potable water and community latrines, and Nizammudin was slightly better endowed in terms of health and education centres.

Each of the seven Andhra city slums had somewhat different characteristics. They generally tended to be older settlements, ranging from 25 to 100 years old. Respondents were rickshaw-pullers, launderers, porters, construction workers and agricultural labourers, occupations that were more or less similar to the Delhi sample.

SPARC examined four categories of disadvantaged urban children in Bombay: children of pavement dwellers (375 families, 1,200 children); children of construction workers (286 families, 940 children); street children living on their own (over 200); and children working in hotels and tea stalls, whom we shall call "hotel boys" (1,000). The in-depth surveys were carried out by four NGOs in Bombay (SPARC 1991).

These studies, of course, do not claim to represent the universe of Indian street children (intended as children who have severed most family ties) or street-based working children (intended as children who work, many on the streets, but who live with their families). They do, however, provide unique information on the complex processes that lead disadvantaged Indian children to work or to drift into a street life.

How many children work. The number of children engaged in work activities, on the basis of the Delhi and Andhra Pradesh analyses, appears to be higher than the estimates furnished by the 1981 Census of India. According to census data, 6.1 percent of the total number of urban children in the 0–19 age group (4.5 million children out of a total child population of over 74 million) were involved in some form of economic activity. There were large disparities in the participation rates among urban children in the different states, with Andhra Pradesh, Karnataka and Tamil Nadu showing high rates while Bihar and Uttar Pradesh rates were surprisingly lower than national averages. The working children were predominantly male. They were also particularly concentrated in the 15–19 age group, largely because of the way the questions were formulated and the census data analysed. The number of children 0–14 years old who "worked," both "main workers" (full-time) and "marginal workers" (occasionally), represented only 1.9 percent of the total (NIUA 1991b).

The incidence of children working in the two slums in Delhi was much higher. Twenty-two percent of the children in the 5–18 age group worked: 28.7 percent of the males and 15.6 percent of the females. The incidence was slightly lower, but still quite high, in Andhra Pradesh towns: working children were represented in 10.6 percent of the households, with Rajah-mundry reporting the highest incidence (14.6 percent). Furthermore, the ages of the respondents were generally lower than those of working children reported in national census data: more than 80 percent of the children were between 7 and 15, and well over 70 percent between 9 and 15, with an average of 10 years of age.

Main characteristics of male and female working children. Over 28 percent of the low-income households surveyed in Delhi had at least one working child; 6 percent had more than one. In both the Delhi and Andhra Pradesh samples, the eldest child appeared to be most likely to work.

Female working children were younger than male working children (9.5 years versus 10.7 years). Girls had started working earlier in both Delhi (25 percent at 7 years of age or below) and Andhra Pradesh. They also stopped working earlier because of the still prevalent practice of early marriage (the proportion of girls entering the work force tends to decline in Delhi after age 11). Twenty-two percent of the boys entered the work force somewhat later, at eight years of age or below.

Children worked at a surprisingly limited range of occupations. Further-more, these occupations followed some clear gender patterns (Table 4.13). Nearly 50 percent of female children were surrogate housekeepers or sur-rogate mothers. They had often been pulled out of school for precisely that reason. The vast majority of female child respondents worked within the household and were accompanied by mothers, siblings or peers when they went out (usually not too far from home). In contrast, male child respondents worked mostly outside the household and at greater distances.

Most children followed the occupation of the parent of the same sex (60 percent of the cases) and began as their helper or apprentice. This suggests that knowing the occupations of the children's parents may facilitate more

Table 4.13. Gender Differences Among Working Children Living at Home
(Percentages, Unless Otherwise Specified)

	Males (N = 45)	Females (N = 24)
Incidence of work	29	16
Age		
7–8	9	8
9–11	27	46
12–15	46	38
16–18	18	8
Average age (years)	10.7	9.5
Age started working		
range (years)	9–11	6–8
mean (years)	10.7	9.5
6–8	21	59
9–11	63	33
12–15	16	8
Main types of current work		
ragpicking	53	25
construction worker	4	4
shop helper/tea shop	25	4
domestic servant	2	17
surrogate motherhood	0	50
others	16	0
Current employment type		
outside home	100	46 [12][1]
inside home		54
Hours per day		
2–6	0	23
6–8	74	54
more than 8	26	23
Work days per month (25–30 days)	84	85
Educational achievement ages 5–18 (C)[a]		
never attended school	71	50
grades 1–2	25	38
grades 3–5	4	8
still in school	0 [67]	4 [38]
Main reasons for dropping out		
economic	69	0
look after younger siblings	0	100[2]
school-related problems	31[3]	0
Main reasons for working (C)		
parents' wishes	62	75
child wants to	13	18
economic independence	13	7
friends work	6	0
child hates school	6	0

cont'd

Table 4.13. cont'd

	Males (N = 45)	Females (N = 24)
Main reasons for working (H)[b]		
insufficient household income	70	38
father unemployed	20	10
child idle	8	17
child wants to	2	0
mother works	0	35
Child's monthly income		
none	7	58
Rs. 1–250	31	25
251–500	51	13
501–more	11	4
Child contributes to family income		
yes (all)	52	96[4]
yes (some)	41	4
none	7	0
Child started working when h/h size		
4 or less	50	30
5 or more	50	70
Child's attitude towards work (C)		
likes to work	63	58
does not like it	37	17
no choice	0	25
Why does child like to work? (C)		
make money	59	31
work is fun	8	31
make parents happy	14	11
duty	5	27
roam city	14	0
Working child's aspirations[5] (C)		
better job/income	72	25
to study	22	33
to go back to village	3	14
to play	3	14
to be pretty	0	14
Working child's main activities (C)		
work	66	67
work and play	28	8
help mother[6]	3	25
watch movies	3	0
Child (C)		
going out with parents	19	35
activity with siblings		
no time for them	78	50
childcare	no info	50

[1]Numbers in brackets refer to data supplied by Osmania University. [2]Only 12 answers. [3]School was boring, repeated failure, etc. [4]Earnings go directly to parents; girls never receive money. [5]This question allowed for multiple answers. [6]But working children do help out in fact according to interviewers. [a](C) = according to child interview. [b](H) = according to parents' interview. Source: NIUA (Delhi) (1991b); Osmania University Regional Centre (1991).

Box 4.1   Categories of Particularly Deprived Working Children

- Male working children, often first-born, who work throughout their middle years and adolescence to contribute to an overstretched household budget.
- Female working children, also often first-born, who are forced by filial duty to take up the roles of surrogate mother and housekeeper and often become child brides.
- Live-in workers, sent to the cities from rural areas to earn for their destitute households, who are often exploited and abused by their employers.
- Children of pavement dwellers who suffer the physical deprivations of homelessness (including lack of latrines and safe drinking water) and may experience a sense of uprootedness.
- Street children "on their own" who not only are homeless but are also extremely vulnerable to health and psychosocial damage.

---

preventive approaches to improving their situations. The pattern was particularly strong among female children who were frequently entrapped in the same low-status occupations of their mothers (domestic work and rag-picking).

Both boys and girls worked consistently and for long hours. In over 80 percent of the cases, they worked 25 to 30 days a month. Nearly 26 percent of the male children and 23 percent of the female children worked for more than eight hours per day. In addition, children, especially girls, often also performed various household chores which occupied from one to three hours of their time each day.

The earnings of children formed a significant proportion of the household incomes, 25 percent, at times even 35 percent, of the household incomes in Delhi, for example. Whatever the child's share, the loss of the income he or she contributed would have severely undermined the family's ability to purchase basic necessities (Tables 4.15 and 4.16).

There were strong gender differentials: (1) the average earnings of female children were lower than those of male children; (2) a significant proportion of female children in all three locations reported working without any monetary compensation; and (3) female children in almost all cases gave all their earnings to their parents. In fact, those earnings were at times paid directly to the parents by employers (female domestic workers, construction workers, and ragpickers working with their fathers). In contrast, in all samples, male children, especially when earning well, kept a portion of their earnings (Table 4.13).

Surprisingly, given national percentages, more boys than girls had never attended school and slightly more girls than boys were still in school. In all samples, the girls who had dropped out of school had done so to "look after

Table 4.14. Personal Profiles of Street Children (On Their Own)
and of Working Children Living with Family (Percentages,
Unless Otherwise Specified)

	Working street children not living with family	Working children living with family	
Gender	Mostly boys	Mostly boys and girls	
Age (years)			
range	9–17	7–18	
average	13	10	
No contact with family	[74]	0	
Age range started working	12–15	6–15	
Main reasons for working		**Boys**	**Girls**
insufficient household income		76	32
own survival and expenses	100		
Main types of current work			
ragpickers	[55]	57	25
shop helper	0	20	4
domestic servant	0	2	17
surrogate mother	0	0	50
begging	[14]	0	0
Current employment type			
inside home	0	0	58
outside home	100	100	42
self-employed (with parents)	ca. 90	ca. 78	ca. 82
with outside employer	ca. 10	ca. 22	ca. 18

Source: NIUA (1991); SPARC (1991) (in brackets).

younger siblings." Boys had dropped out for "economic reasons" (69 percent
in the Delhi sample) and they worked to generate outside income (62 percent
of the Delhi sample). Sixty-four percent of the Delhi boys aspired to a better
job and income, while Delhi girls tended to want to study (21 percent), go
back to the village (15 percent), play (14 percent) or be pretty (14 percent)
(Table 4.13).

Gender differences were also apparent in the extent of leisure time available or considered appropriate. Indeed, with the same, or often a greater,
work load than boys, girls had much less free time for play. Furthermore,
because of restrictions on their movements outside the house, they had much
less access to videos or cinema and therefore tended to be less exposed to
modern influences. The implications of this isolation emerged with the com-
ment by 35 percent of the Delhi girls that work was fun and this was their

Table 4.15. Household Profiles of Street Children and Working Children (Percentages, Unless Otherwise Stated)

	Children not living with family (street children)[1,2]	Children living with family[3] Working children (N = 54)	Non-working children (N = 128)
Main type of family:			
Single mother[4]	14 [16]	11	2
Single parent	9	22	11
Two parents	>60	66	>80
No parent	[35]	0	0
Mean number of children	no info	2.6	1.3
Average household size	6.9	4.6 [5.84]	3.3
Percentage having children aged 0–4	no info	20	42
Parental illiteracy rates:			
Father	no info	ca. 80	ca. 80
Mother	no info	94	93
Employed:			
Father	87	78	82
Mother	67	52	23
Siblings	no info	6	0
Child	100	100	0
Children aged 5–18 currently in school	3	<2	ca. 30
Main economic provider:			
Mother of two-parent households	[16]	11	8
Father of two-parent households		76	88
Mother of single-parent households	[16]	11	2
Child contributes to family income	occasionally	>90	0
Child's contribution (when paid in cash) to household income	no info	25	0
Effects on household expenditure if not included:			
no effect	no info	19	
survival at stake		11	
no savings		5	
poorer food quality/quantity		62 [61]	
not able to buy clothes		27	
Child migrated to city:	100 [100]	>90	>90
with family or other relatives	30	>90	>90
alone	70	0	0
Household (or child) has been in city:			
less that 5 years	(55)	30	38
6 years or more	(44)	70	62
Contact with relatives in Delhi outside of the household (H):			
frequent	40	58	70
occasional	–	38	24
none	60	4	6

Source: [1]NIUA (1991); SPARC (1991). [2]Data in square brackets is from the Osmania University sample, 1992. Data in parentheses from SPARC (1991). [3]NIUA (1991b). [4]Single-headed households here do not correspond to households with female main earners, of which there are usually a larger number.

Table 4.16. Households of Children Living with Families[1]
(Percentages Unless Otherwise Stated)

	Working children households (N = 54)		Non-working children households (N = 128)	
Similarities				
Parents migrated to city				
over 6 years ago	65		62	
Illiteracy				
father	73		74	
mother	94		93	
Average monthly per capita income				
Rs. 1–500	226		230	
Range (Rs.)	120–643		120–643	
With employed working fathers	78		78	
Differences				
Head of household				
male	78		88	
female	22		12	
Female main earner	50		33	
Estimated mean household size (members)	4.6		3.3	
	[5.58]		[4.3]	
Average monthly household income				
over Rs 1,000	72			
under Rs 1,000			78	
Average number of children	2.6		1.3	
Household with children aged 0–4 years	20		42	
Mother's age at marriage less than 15 years	80		60	
Age distribution of parents	**father**	**mother**	**father**	**mother**
under 30 years			40	54
over 40 years	60	39		
With employed/working				
mothers	52 [31.5]		23 [lower]	
one child	28		no info	
more than one child	6			
Parents' type of work	**father**	**mother**	**father**	**mother**
ragpickers	26	41	38	40
construction workers	29	9	15	24
domestic servant	0	38	34	0
shopkeeper	0	0	8	8
Mother's hours of work, daily 6–8 or more		52		23

cont'd

explicit reason for working (as opposed to only 9 percent of the boys). Young girls, for example, "liked" to work as part-time domestic servants because they could sometimes watch television while doing household chores.

The children's replies made it clear that they felt they had very few options: more than three quarters of the children had friends who also worked and

Table 4.16. cont'd

	Working children households ($N = 54$)		Non-working children households ($N = 128$)	
Some working mothers' strategies:				
take youngest child with her	5		38	
leave child home with daughter	42		8	
leave child with others	3		20	
Children still in school (overall sample)	**boys**		**girls**	
	36		27	
Parents' average monthly income				
Rs. 1–500	19		5	
501–1,000	68		65	
1,001–1,500	9		21	
1,501 and more	4		9	
Household average monthly income				
Rs. 1–500	4		10	
501–1,000	24		70	
1,001–1,500	55		12	
1,501 and more	17		8	
Child's average monthly income				
Rs. 1–301	93		0	
301–500	7		0	
501 and more	0		0	
Age of children				
0–4	13		27	
5–9	37		49	
10–15	37		19	
16–19	13		5	
Educational level of children	**boys**	**girls**	**boys**[2]	**girls**
illiterate	63	52	39	61
literate	5	5	0	1
grades 1–2	14	27	30	18
grades 3–5	13	12	22	17
grades 6 and above	5	4	9	3

[1]Figures in brackets refer to data from Osmania University Regional Centre (1991). [2]Lower ages may also contribute to the lower literacy rates. Source: NIUA (1991b).

most children realistically did not expect anything from their parents. At the same time, they continued to wish and hope for a better future as well as for a better living environment.

What distinguished the working children from street children "on their own," live-in working children or children of pavement dwellers (see Box 4.1). Street children "on their own" came predominantly from large rural households and arrived in the city predominantly by themselves, often with other friends (NIUA 1991b, Osmania University Regional Center 1991, Rao 1989, SPARC 1991). According to the Bombay study, they frequently practised step migration, taking a train to a nearby town and then moving with friends to the big city. They were predominantly boys and somewhat older than the working children (Table 4.14). Over 60 percent of these street children in the Delhi and Andhra Pradesh samples had two living parents. They came from a slightly higher percentage of single-headed families than other working children. Furthermore, they reported having had frequent conflicts with their parents.

Surprisingly, the street children in the samples seemed to have a greater degree of literacy than working children. They had a keen interest in education and had taken advantage of informal educational opportunities provided by NGOs.

However, street children "on their own" often also worked for longer hours than the working children; almost one quarter worked for more than 10 hours a day. They tended to earn variable amounts, not uncommonly earning more than working children living with their families. Live-in working children, including domestic servants and "hotel boys," seemed to work the longest and the hardest of all child workers — for the sake of their families. Respondents in this category were young and predominantly male. Employers preferred to hire 10- to 15-year-olds for the task. "Hotel boys" in Bombay often had completed some years of schooling: 52 percent had completed primary school and 42 percent secondary school; 86 percent currently attended municipal schools, 57 percent studied at the secondary level and over 9 percent were attending night school (SPARC 1991).

Unlike street children "on their own," most "hotel boys" retained contact with their families through visits and regular letters; 62 percent of the boys visited their homes at least once a year.

Live-in working children experienced different degrees of exploitation from their employers. "Hotel boys" in Bombay, for example, were paid very low monthly salaries. Three fourths were paid well below the minimum wage (unlike street children "on their own"). They kept their savings with their employers who had innumerable opportunities to retain their money in unjust ways, charging the children for their use of hotel facilities, for example. More than half of the children bitterly complained about long hours of work, poor wages, inadequate sleeping and bathing facilities and the constant harassment by their employers (SPARC 1991). The situation of live-in domestic helpers, more often female, is no better.

Live-in child workers often changed jobs, rarely staying more than six months in any one place. They found new positions by word of mouth and usually tried to bargain hard for improved work conditions.

The households of pavement dwellers were largely made up of older migrants (45 percent migrated over 11 years ago) with two to four children. Fathers were generally employed but only about 30 percent of mothers worked, much as in the non-working children's households.

Children of pavement dwellers share with street children the physical problems associated with homelessness; such as the lack of common latrines or of safe drinking water. However, the studies also conclude that children of pavement dwellers in no way show the health damage and the potentially serious psychosocial harm manifested by street children fending for themselves on the same city streets.

What characterizes an urban household whose children work? All the households in the samples shared some characteristics regardless of whether the children were working or not (Tables 4.15 and 4.16).

However, a careful analysis of the databases, particularly in Delhi, shows that households without working children had younger parents, a predominantly non-working mother and fewer children. The children, if of school age, more often attended school. In contrast, households with working children (usually one child working while the others go to school) were larger, with more and somewhat older children. They were headed by older parents, and there were slightly more female-headed households. Interestingly, many more mothers of working children were working (both in the Delhi and in the Andhra Pradesh town samples). And more of the mothers had married and started having children before the age of 15 years (80 percent in the Delhi sample). Male children's earnings, and girls' domestic work were needed to support — or care for — younger siblings. Girls most often slid from the role of surrogate mother into early motherhood. The lack of family planning and economic pressures seemed to penalize certain children in the household, especially the eldest ones. All of these factors contributed to the reproduction of a cycle of deprivation.

Some of the patterns — working mothers, early marriage, larger families — are remarkably consistent and suggest the need to focus special attention on those households in which mothers have married particularly early and are currently working.

A systematic analysis reinforces the notion that street children "on their own" are still a reasonably limited, and thus manageable number. It is therefore all the more crucial that city governments collaborate closely with local NGOs and international agencies to address the plight of these children. The analysis also shows that the effort to give a voice to and encourage the actions of communities needs to continue in order to bring real and lasting improvements.

POLICIES AND PROGRAMMES

As in other developing countries, urban poor children in India face complex problems. The continual pressures and hardships experienced by distressed urban families, create a cycle of poverty: sons drop out of school and, like their fathers, take on low-paying, full-time work at an early age; daughters, like their mothers, marry and give birth while still young adolescents; their children are likely to repeat the same patterns. The number of children who fall into especially difficult circumstances is difficult to estimate.

The Government and some NGOs tend to respond in an ad hoc way neither covering a sufficient number of children, nor even always the right children, and usually failing to reach the least visible categories of distressed children. Other NGOs have developed cost-effective approaches which the government can then utilize. As we have seen, effective preventive strategies can only be designed when the processes leading to the children's deprivation are understood.

Policy responses in a country as large as India, comparable to Europe in overall size and with the fourth largest urban population in the world, have, since the establishment of a National Planning Commission in the 1950s, tended to be organized through Five Year Plans and through a proliferation of large, complex and bureaucratic government schemes. These schemes may be coordinated by one or more national ministries or departments; they are then translated into state, district and municipal regulations and implemented at those levels. Public health, sanitation and water supply are more specifically state responsibilities, while education, labour, and economic and social planning are the joint responsibility of the states and the central government which, at least in theory, work together towards agreed aims.

A federation of 25 states and seven union territories since 1950, India has a stable, multifunctional and hierarchical public administration, set up before Independence. Each state has its own legislative, executive and judicial branches of government and is divided into districts (about 450 in 1990, with an average population of nearly 2 million each). Districts are further sub-divided for development purposes into blocks (some 5,000 nationwide) and then into urban municipalities, headed by a municipal corporation (in cities of 500,000 and above), by a municipal council (in cities of less than 500,000) or occasionally by notified area committees or town area committees (representing upcoming or new towns).[10] The potential for confusion of tasks and expensive duplication is very real.

Government Approaches to Children in Especially Difficult Circumstances

During the 1920s, largely as a result of the recommendations of the Indian Jails Committee and in response to public pressure, several states enacted Children's Acts, patterned after newly framed British legislation, that provided for the rehabilitation of juvenile offenders and for the care and protection of neglected, destitute and abandoned children. Children who could not be cared for by parents, relatives or the community were usually taken into children's homes, almost exclusively run by charitable, philanthropic and volunteer organizations, largely Christian.

The Government, which began to provide very limited assistance to private organizations administering children's homes in the 1950s, has only given substantial support to these organizations since the 1970s, initially with an allocation of Rs 20 million ($642,500). By 1980, when there were an estimated 15.7 million orphans nationwide (Pathak et al. 1979), some 40,000 children under 18 years of age were receiving care through government-funded volunteer-run children's homes. SOS children's villages have proven successful but can cover only small numbers of cases. Foster care, started in the 1960s, has not yet taken root.[11]

During the 1940s and 1950s, government efforts instead were mainly directed towards beggar, vagrant and delinquent children. Acts prohibiting begging were passed by several states in the 1940s. The Children Act of 1960[12] was mainly concerned with children in conflict with the law, and provided for the "care, protection, maintenance, welfare, training, education and rehabilitation of neglected or delinquent children and for the trial of delinquent children."

Although the Act foresaw separate institutional services for neglected children and juvenile delinquents, this distinction was not maintained in some state legislation. Moreover, the categorization of children as delinquent or neglected was often merely discretionary. With the Probation of Offenders Act of 1958, probation became, and has remained, an important noninstitutional response to first offenders.

The institutional services under the Children Act consisted of remand and observation homes, children's homes, child welfare boards, juvenile and children's courts, approved, certified and special schools, probation and after-care services, among others. Implementation was generally weak and organizational resources were lacking for individualized attention to single offenders. By 1975, only 12 states/union territories had established 86 juvenile courts/child welfare boards. In the same year, there were only 143 remand homes (87 government and 56 volunteer-run) with a capacity to take in 7,261 children (UNICEF 1990a).

In 1986, the more comprehensive and progressive Juvenile Justice Act replaced the Children Act of 1960 in every state except Jammu and Kashmir. The 1986 Act has provided a new legislative framework for dealing with neglected children and juvenile offenders. It prohibits, for example, the detention of juveniles in adult prisons or police stations, an important gain. However, improvements in services have been slow in coming: juvenile courts and welfare boards have still not been set up in many states; separate handling of delinquents and other children is not ensured; the involvement of voluntary organizations at all stages of implementing the Act is scant; and some states continue to confine children, thousands of them, in prisons (UNICEF 1990a).

The Scheme for the Prevention and Control of Juvenile Social Maladjustment, also started in 1986, extended grants to states to set up institutions prescribed under the Juvenile Justice Act, to upgrade services, to train staff, and to assist voluntary agencies to provide services. The expenditure was shared equally between the central and state governments.

Other government legislation and relevant policies include:

Child Labour. In 1986, the Government passed the Child Labour (Prohibition and Regulation) Act which, by not prohibiting children from working, indirectly acknowledged that child labour will inevitably continue. Indeed, socioeconomic pressures in India, as well as deep-rooted traditions, are such that any legislation simply "outlawing" child labour would still be unenforceable. The Act, however, prohibits children under 15 years of age from working in the more hazardous occupations, and limits hours of work.

The Child Labour Act was much debated and was strongly opposed by a number of groups who believed that merely making child labour less dehumanizing would not address the problem in a serious way.

In 1987, the Government adopted a National Policy on Child Labour, which has, unfortunately, been unevenly implemented. The policy has three components: (1) effective enforcement of the laws relating to employment of children; (2) programmes aimed at improving the socioeconomic conditions of families so that they can afford to send their children to school instead of to work; and (3) projects in selected industries and areas where child labour is concentrated. The projects provide income-generating means to families of child workers, vocational training, supplementary nutrition and other incentives to encourage children to go to school (Bose 1992).

Education. The Directive Principles of State Policy and the Five Year Plans have dwelt on universal primary education, a component of the Minimum Needs Programme for the Fifth Five Year Plan (1975–79).

The new National Policy on Education (1986) gives high priority to Early Childhood Care and Education (ECCE). There are a number of national programmes to improve educational achievement:

(a) *Integrated Child Development Services* (ICDS) include early childhood education centres, nursery/pre-primary schools and creche services. State governments and municipal bodies also provide preschool services, while some voluntary agencies extend free services to disadvantaged groups, mainly preschools, supplementary nutrition and, in some cases, health care.

(b) *Operation Black Board* aims at improving primary school facilities, personnel and teaching materials. In 1989–90, Rs 1,358 million ($43.6 million) was provided to states for primary school infrastructure.

(c) *Nonformal education* schemes, aimed at dropouts, working children and girls who cannot attend school for the entire day were applicable to all children, have been implemented in educationally backward states since 1979–80 to provide a large-scale, alternative support to formal schooling. These schemes could be extended to cover urban slums and projects for working children.

(d) Centrally sponsored programmes to raise *teacher* competence have been implemented since 1987–88.

(e) *The National Adult Education Programme* aims to provide functional literacy to 15- to 35-year-olds, increase their social awareness and thus influence parental attitudes towards the value of child education. The National Literacy Mission was set up for this purpose and has so far obtained the collaboration of teachers, scientists, technologists, ex-servicemen and voluntary agencies. Priority is given to women and disadvantaged groups, and their participation has, in fact, been notable. Seventeen million adults were reached by the programme between 1979 and 1984. A target of 80 million has been set for 1995.

Health care. Schemes devised by the Government are:

(a) *The Working Group on Reorganization of Family Welfare and Primary Health Care Services in Urban Areas* recommended primary health care and family welfare services in areas where at least 40 percent of the population live in slums. This scheme has been implemented in some areas, although initial feedback indicates that it is difficult to find accommodation in or near slum areas and that coordination, integration and training are still weak.

(b) *The Integrated Child Development Services programme*, mentioned earlier, aims primarily at improving the developmental prospects of children aged 0–6 years, but also has "mother-focused" objectives, such as improving the health and nutritional status of women 15–45 years of age and increasing their knowledge of health and nutrition. The programme offers immunization, health checks, referral services, supplementary nutrition, health education for women and preschool education for children. Starting in 1975–76 with only four urban projects, ICDS today is the largest early childhood intervention programme in the country, counting 220 projects.

(c) *A major national immunization programme* to combat childhood diseases. A prototype for ten urban centres is being developed and a National Technology Mission on immunization has been set up.

(d) *Supplementary feeding* of preschool children implemented both by the central and state governments, is very popular, especially in poor communities, and has undoubtedly met a felt need. It does have some weaknesses, however, including low coverage of children under the age of three and little community involvement.

(e) *A national programme of oral rehydration therapy (ORT)* has been established to combat the debilitating effects of diarrhoea, a major health problem. It is estimated that about 10 percent of affected children develop dehydration and about 1 percent are at risk of dying (Ministry of Health and Family Welfare 1990). The scheme has as its main objectives the promotion of homemade ORT and the training of medical and paramedical personnel. Information materials have been prepared explaining how to prevent diarrhoea and how to manage at-home care and treat affected children.

(f) *Multimedia campaigns* cover mother and child health care. The national television and radio network is playing a major role.

Early pregnancy. As already discussed, early marriage and pregnancy can put the health of both the mother and child at high risk. Only a limited number of programmes, however, are specifically aimed at this problem. On the other hand, programmes in a variety of sectors (especially health and education) are starting to consider making their coverage more specific (Chatterjee 1991). Two such programmes are the National Adult Education Programme and the Integrated Child Development Services.

Innovative NGO Approaches to CEDC

Beyond these large government projects, increasing numbers of non-governmental and voluntary organizations have been active in India since the 1960s, but more markedly during the 1970s and 1980s. Two disastrous years of drought in the mid-1960s and subsequent famine transformed these organizations, initially tied to charity work and social services, into relief operations with largely international NGO funding. By the late 1970s, with the growing realization that droughts were recurrent and drought-containment merely an ad hoc response, they shifted their focus to broader development. In this process, early missionary zeal has progressively been replaced by a professionalization of voluntarism. The channelling of public funds through voluntary organizations increased through the 1980s (UNICEF 1990a). The Government has tended to urge voluntary action to fit into its policies and programmes, but this call for concerted action has been in part resisted and hotly debated (Alliband 1983).

Various types of organizations operate in urban and rural India: organizations with a service-delivery model, which also emphasize the use of local resources and skills; organizations that intervene from the outside to help foster self-help strategies at community level; people's organizations; and totally self-generated community self-help efforts (including 350,000 largely rural cooperative societies). With time, the more experienced organizations often shift from service delivery to community-based activities.

In addition, grassroots women's groups, *mahila mandals*, are increasingly linking up with NGOs in what could potentially become a decentralized people-oriented design of development. Furthermore, community-level management of local resources (for example, commonly-owned grazing land, forests, fish ponds and irrigation tanks) is an important local survival strategy and has proven capable of supporting over 40 percent of the needs of the village poor in Rajasthan and Andhra Pradesh, thus preventing more than half of the total village population from falling beneath the poverty line (UNICEF 1990a).

A growing number of innovative urban Indian NGOs have attempted to deal with the special problems of street and working children and other children. The following descriptions give an idea of the range of services offered. Some NGO responses have been very specific, pointing to particular areas where the Government could intervene, but has not necessarily done so. Two insightful organizations which focus on street-based working children, *Butterflies* and *REDS* are described in more detail in Boxes 4.2 and 4.3.

Mobile Creches. This organization provides day care, education, nutrition and training to children of construction workers in many large cities, such as Delhi and Bombay. Despite the advocacy efforts of Mobile Creches, this particularly vulnerable and isolated group of children has generally not been considered in government service-delivery plans. Although the organization cannot envisage reaching all construction sites on its own, it hopes to use its experience to create alternative options.

The National Slum Dwellers Federation has collaborated extensively with SPARC in Bombay. Because several of its leaders are former hotel boys, NSDF has among its objectives increasing public awareness of the plight of this particular category, who remain "invisible" despite unionization.

Don Bosco. Targeting street children and homeless child labourers of Bangalore, *Oniyavera Seva coota*, meaning "an association at the service of the street people of Bangalore," was initiated in June 1980 as a pilot project and soon became a part-time welfare activity of some students of Kristu Jyoti College in Bangalore. It developed into a fully fledged project in 1984, functioning under the auspices of the Bangalore Salesian Society.

This NGO is well known for its work on the street and its overall pedagogical approach which have enabled it to reach, and maintain ties with, a large number of the city's estimated 25,000 to 30,000 street children. Its street workers have helped address the most urgent needs of about 1,500 boys. The organization's overall objectives include: contacting children where they work and live; providing them with personalized care and follow-up; reuniting them with their families, whenever feasible; offering them counselling, a comprehensive educational approach to life planning, and skill training; forming associations of street children and youth to youth programmes. The organization also provides shelter, study and social centres, and advocacy services.

Snehasadan (Shelter of Love), Bombay. Established in 1962 by a group of Indian Jesuit priests, Snehasadan currently provides shelter for 350 runaways and destitute youngsters. The children are divided into groups of 20 to 30, each living in a home supervised by a married couple, some of whom are former street children. There are 15 homes altogether, 11 for boys and four for girls. Most of the Snehasadan children were brought to the organization by children already in the programme. The younger children attend school and the older ones are offered vocational or technical training. The shelter makes every effort to reunite children with their families, even though many children have run away to escape difficult conditions at home. When recon-

Box 4.2   New Delhi's Butterflies

Butterflies is a Delhi NGO which specifically targets street children. One of its most visible activities is a restaurant, opened in 1990 near the Inter State Bus Terminus in New Delhi where the largest numbers of street children are found. The restaurant is currently a "training centre, source of income and home" for eight street boys: they receive training in food preparation; earn Rs 500 ($16) per month working five hours per day; and have free accommodation (in the restaurant itself) food, health care and compulsory education. The assistant cook and the manager earn Rs 300 ($9.60) more. The money is managed by the NGO, and a bank account has been opened where the boys deposit Rs 300 ($9.60) every month, leaving the rest for daily expenses.

Although the children manage every aspect of the restaurant under the partial supervision of a social worker and a cook, they were initially reluctant to show the restaurant's nameboard where "Managed by Street Children" was clearly spelled out. Certain that the sign would deter customers, given the prevailing negative attitudes about street children, they covered it with newspapers for a few days. But finally, after much discussion among themselves and with the social worker, they decided that there was nothing to hide. Rita Panicker, founder of Butterflies, believes that, "unless some status or recognition is given to street children, they will always be looked down upon."

Despite the sign, the restaurant has progressively established a regular clientele, including shopkeepers and policemen who find the prices competitive even if the location is not "choice." The restaurant also provides a service to other street children who can benefit from 40 per cent discounts on meals. About eight to ten street children eat there regularly. A "Meals on Wheels" project is being contemplated that would entail distributing subsidized meals to children on the streets. The boys are receiving good training, and some of them are starting an activity of their own, including consulting for NGOs.

Butterflies has initiated other activities to help street children. By 1992, it had contacted a total of 600 children in Delhi, almost 300 of whom attend regular activities, including a nonformal "school," organized in the playground of a private school in the Chandni Chowk area and in other market places, bus and railway stations, and offering afternoon lessons in basic literacy, health and hygiene as well as sports activities. Butterflies also organized a Child Workers' union to address problems ignored by existing labour unions. The union, after some successful Labour Day rallies since 1988, has been struggling for legalization and has appealed to the Supreme Court. Butterflies believes firmly not only in self-reliance ("the best strategy for the children is themselves," according to Panicker) but also in collective representation to draw attention to specific needs and problems.

Source: Urban Child Project (1992).

Box 4.3   REDS: RAGPICKERS EDUCATION AND DEVELOPMENT SCHEME

REDS, a Jesuit NGO operating in Bangalore since 1979, focuses on the educational and developmental needs of street children who work as ragpickers. It has devised a number of specific programmes for these particularly disadvantaged children:

- *Street work* (now covering about 2,000 children). REDS maintains street-level contacts with the boys in many of Bangalore's slums. Field workers meet with the boys, introduce them to the programme activities and help them to keep in touch with the centre.
- *Retail shop* (1979). The organizers of REDS realized that child ragpickers were easily and frequently exploited because their earnings were determined by middlemen, especially the lorry drivers and wholesalers who paid the boys very little for their scavenged goods which they then sold at a good profit to recyclers or retail shops. A small retail shop was built which purchases waste paper directly and at a fair price, thus eliminating the middlemen.
- *Shelter cum training centre* (1985). The idea of a shelter came from the street children themselves whose major preoccupation was a safe place to stay. Built with West German funds on the parish compound, the shelter works on an open-door basis and can accommodate 35 children. Besides living spaces, there is a workshop for vocational training and area for sorting out rags. Lessons are given for three hours every morning in English, maths and geography. Sports and weekend camps are key components of the programme.
- *Vocational skills*. About 22 boys, sponsored by local families, are paid Rs 50 ($1.60) per month and are undergoing training within the centre as mechanics or tailors.
- *Night shelter.* (1987) a second shelter is rented to accommodate the older boys.
- *Income generation*. An agreement for bulk paper collection has been made with the university and some private businesses. Income from this activity is divided three ways: one third to the boys, one third towards food expenses for the community and one third towards administrative costs. Because this is a "clean" activity (waste paper to be collected must be kept separate from other refuse), it has helped to give a new dignity to the boys' work.
- *Documentation*. Information is kept on all boys staying at the centre and all those who are in regular contact with street workers. Information is also collected on ragpicking populations, retail and wholesale shops and recycling factories.
- *Family reunification*. About 150 of the younger runaways have been reunited with their families. Statistically, it has been found that from 65 to 75 per cent of the boys have run away from families residing in the slums of Bangalore.

REDS is financed by private donations and the Catholic Church. It employs four full-time workers, all male, who divide their time between the centre and the streets. One of its greatest strengths lies in the fact that the boys are paying for their own rehabilitation. Boys staying at the centre have to contribute 50 paise towards lunch every day. Generally, money generated from the sale of paper is enough to pay for their needs at the centre. One of its weaknesses is the total absence of a female figure at the centre. Especially in the case of young runaways, who typically come from violent households with abused and battered mothers, it would be important to provide a more positive idea of male-female relationships so that the pattern is not repeated.

The project has had a significant impact on the lives of street children. Of the 1,000 boys REDS had worked with by 1988, for example, about 200 had given up ragpicking except in times of crisis. Many had gone into construction work. The project has increased their self-respect and confidence; improved the levels of literacy and education of boys staying at the centre; fostered greater community awareness about the problems of ragpickers through talks and slide shows; and promoted publicity and education on the recycling of waste.

Source: Damania (1988).

ciliation is possible, Snehasadan provides counselling and monitors the situation during its initial phases. Occasionally, children leave home again and return to Snehasadan, where they are always welcome. Although its affiliations are Christian, the programme is entirely secular. Its director, Father Placie Fonseca, says, "Our goal is to make these children "whole," not "holy"" (Chatterjee 1992).

The Coordination Committee for Vulnerable Children, Bombay, a coalition of 13 organizations whose programmes reach 800–1,000 children. Through networking, referral and collective fund-raising, the group could eventually have a significant impact on the lives of larger numbers of children. Identity cards have been issued to the children with the endorsement of the Juvenile Aid Police Unit. This gives a relatively small but hopefully growing group of Bombay's street youth a support system and a sense of legitimacy.

NGO Networks and National NGO Forum. Municipal-wide efforts at rallying public attention have been initiated in a number of cities. First started in New Delhi, Street Children's Forums and NGO networks have also been organized in Bombay, Bangalore, Calcutta, Madras and Hyderabad. Composed of resident NGOs and some city officials, they organize rallies and conferences for street children. One goal is to make the children's situation more "visible" and to help the public, officials and media realize that a redefinition of these children's problems is needed. In each of the above cities, city-level plans are being formulated that foresee the collaboration, possibly for the first time, of NGOs, municipal corporations and state governments. A National NGO Forum for street and working children has been set up to coordinate and support state- and city-level fora.

Networking among NGOs has resulted in a number of innovative activities. In Bombay, for example, street-based children are being trained to assist traffic police at pedestrian crossings during peak hours; in Delhi, a local theatre helps street-based children stage mime shows and skits based on the real-life dramas of their situation; in Bangalore street boys run a courier service and an NGO produces a regular news wall-poster for street children.

Despite their growing numbers and their innovative programmes, NGOs have up until now been able to reach only a small number of children — a few hundred or a thousand, when the problems affect millions. NGOs may be particularly effective in dealing with the relatively manageable numbers of street children "on their own" in each city, but they can, for example, barely touch upon such problems as environmental degradation, migration, early marriage and adolescent pregnancy. The dilemma is how to act more preventively while remaining focused on the children at greatest risk. An effective preventive approach requires a much greater and more timely effort at integrated urban planning, such as the Urban Basic Services Programme (discussed in the following section), with the participation of communities and children. A broad coalition needs to be formed involving urban neighbourhoods, NGOs and municipal governments, with a focus on school-age at-risk children, working children and adolescent mothers.

Urban Planning and Development Policies: From Top-Down Investments to Participatory UBS

In India, with industrialization, agricultural surpluses were drawn into urban areas. National planners were aware that public investments in urban areas since Independence had far outpaced those in the agricultural hinterlands. Such glaring disparities fueled the belief that urban areas were being unduly favoured. Phenomenal investments made over the years to build huge institutions for academic, technical and administrative purposes, on the one hand, and an understandable concern for agricultural production, on the other, led to further charges of "urban bias."

At the same time, as in many other countries, national planners long assumed that large-scale investments in urban infrastructure would automatically lead to improvements in the welfare of all urban dwellers. However, not far from the impressive facades of buildings and institutions in India's mega-cities — and yet too far from the concerns of most politicians and administrators — large communities of the urban poor were growing, their residents deprived of the most basic services and opportunities.

The post-Independence phenomenon of outsized slums, fed by formidable migrations of the landless from poverty-ridden rural areas and by refugees from the partitioned west and east of India, now Pakistan and Bangladesh, caught the planners and decision makers unawares. By the mid-1970s, it was clear that a balanced approach to social development in the major cities had become the first victim of large-scale but short-sighted investment in urban areas.[13]

The women and children of the slums suffered the most. Neighbourhoods they had carefully chosen became the dumping yards of the rich; the supportive safety-nets of close relatives and friends, already weak, suffered an irreversible setback with the incoming hordes of new settlers. Their communities had become an altogether new world and they were unsure of their place in it. Caught in this identity crisis, many lost their personality, values and even morals. Privacy, dignity and self-discipline were jeopardized. A lack of sound analysis and effective planning had taken a heavy toll: by the mid-1970s, large numbers of India's urban children and women were destitute or diseased; many had died needlessly.

Urban Basic Services 1975–90: Building on Existing Strengths and Mobilizing Policy Makers

In contrast to these top-down approaches, the Urban Basic Services strategy (UBS) has evolved in India over almost two decades, becoming the key thrust for addressing the problems of India's slum children within a community-focused framework. Unlike programmes that aim to upgrade the urban environment by building expensive infrastructure or by razing the squatter areas themselves, this approach gives highest priority to the needs of the urban poor. It depends on mobilizing the energies of slum residents to help deliver health, education, water and sanitation.

Beyond these basic principles, it is difficult to encapsulate the UBS model because it has evolved and has been adapted to local circumstances. Its major role, however, has always been to facilitate the convergence of government services in particularly deprived areas, while encouraging the active participation of poor neighbourhoods in formulating new approaches to their most urgent problems. In addition, proponents of UBS have acted as catalysts, presenting their cases to bureaucrats while eliciting the support of academic and training institutions, NGOs and the media. Some of the major lessons learned in this process will be briefly outlined.

Urban Basic Services: difficult beginnings (1972–79)

A first urban project, initiated by UNICEF in 1972 with the aim of establishing 12 pilot Integrated Urban Development (IUD) city projects was never fully realized, although studies on the situation of children in slums and shanty towns were produced by UNICEF and the National Institute of Urban Affairs. The results of these studies were later integrated in the Indian Government's Fifth Five Year Plan (1975–79): (a) the Integrated Child Development Services (ICDS), already discussed, which provided a narrower range of urban interventions than IUD; and (b) the Slum Improvement Programme, under the Ministry of Works and Housing, intended to complement the ICDS programmes in a number of cities, including the 12 original ones.

A UNICEF Government agreement in 1978 recommended practical, low-cost models of slum improvement in which people would be seen not as "passive recipients of services, but as partners in development." To achieve universal coverage, several recommendations were made: the effective use of existing resources; interdepartmental cooperation and convergence of services; the integration of voluntary organizations and NGOs into the process; and the integration of basic services with physical and environmental development.

The document further clarified its concern for prevention:

> While never losing sight of the fact that children are UNICEF's basic clients, they must be seen within the context of urban poverty. To improve the quality of their lives, their families must be recognized as the basic unit (of development) and the community as the setting for a joint strategy of change and development.

A more systematic linkage between NGOs and government programmes was particularly important since NGO projects, often excellent examples of community participation but not widely replicated, could help to improve government projects with extensive coverage but limited community participation. Integration needed to occur at an early stage, however, and preserve some of the NGO flexibility.

Building on existing concepts of "community." Even prior to the Second World War, the Government of India had already implemented rural community development (RCD) projects, based on the Gandhian concepts of "community".[14] A number of urban community development projects (UCD) were launched starting in 1958, but by the 1970s only a few of these were still operating (Ramarau 1990). In 1972 UNICEF chose to collaborate with the UCD projects in Baroda, Calcutta, Madras, Ahmedabad and Hyderabad.

Difficulties encountered in initial attempts (1970s) to develop government-NGO partnerships. UNICEF directed many of its early efforts towards forging new partnerships among government offices, NGOs and urban poor neighbourhoods. These partnerships, however, were not always easy to initiate due to the different ways each had of perceiving their roles and of approaching the problems. The poor had been made to feel that their opinions were of little relevance; government officials, in turn, preferred expensive large-scale projects rather than local initiatives. NGOs felt that government officials were generally unsympathetic to their concerns.

To change this, the poor communities needed to mobilize; government decision-making needed to be decentralized and officials trained to look positively at existing local human resources and potential partners; and NGOs needed to adopt a less adversarial stance towards municipal authorities.

In some cases, as in Baroda, an opportunity to create a joint government-NGO project was missed when, after negotiations involving the highly participatory Baroda Citizens Council, the municipal government, the state government, the central government and UNICEF, it was decided to entrust the administration of the UCD project entirely to the municipal government.

In others, agreements died on the vine because of a lack of interest or agreement on the part of potential NGO partners, as in Calcutta and Madras. In Ahmedabad, attempts to establish a low-cost, community primary health care project in the Vasna resettlement colony, sponsored by UNICEF, in cooperation with OXFAM and the Voluntary Health Association of India[15] failed because of divergent views: the project's Health Adviser and the Vasna residents were committed to a physician-centred approach, the residents looked down on a project centred around community health workers. Some community health activity was eventually initiated through the project, but with volunteer physicians and a midwife, rather than the residents themselves.

Negotiations between partners of unequal strengths require an effort towards common understanding, a realistic evaluation of each other's contributions, and flexibility; in other words, it requires the willingness of both government representatives and the community to make adjustments. This was often not achieved at the beginning.

Hyderabad: getting government to work with poor urban neighbourhoods

In Hyderabad, on the other hand, a successful model was developed that emphasized the interaction between the municipal government and the local neighbourhood, but also drew on the collaboration of local NGOs and civil society. This model, which proved what could be done in a large city, was later used in other UCD projects in Andhra Pradesh and Orissa.

By 1977, the project, coordinated by the Municipal Corporation, had already expanded twice and covered three times its original area without any staff increases. This was made possible by the dedication of its Director and seven Community Organizers. A small grant allocated by UNICEF helped it expand further, and reinforced by a new sense of recognition, it became a testing ground for UNICEF's new urban orientation.

The UCD project was based on the assumption that the mere provision of goods or services was not enough; unless people perceived a programme as their own, materials were likely to be mishandled, neglected or stolen, and services inappropriately utilized. The Hyderabad project derived its success from the ability of its staff to convey to the people that the project was theirs.

This task was not easy as the people themselves initially felt that the Government should meet their needs. Community organizers worked intensively with the people in the community to encourage them to articulate their felt needs. Naturally, these reflected their expectations of what the Government could best offer — more water taps, street lights, dust-bins, better drainage, roads and pathways, latrines and income-generation schemes for women. From the outset, the principle of *shramdan* (self-help) was evoked, and it was made clear that the project could help only if local people participated.

Nongovernmental voluntary organizations were encouraged to support community-level *Mohalla* committees, particularly in organizing family welfare programmes such as women's income generation, and in running pre-school day-care centres. The Lijjad Papad Cooperative, for instance, started with a loan from the parent organization in Bombay to purchase equipment for making a popular Indian appetizer. The project supported the cooperative so that women could supplement their family incomes by working from their homes. The cooperative now runs on its own.

Balwadis, or day-care centres, were set up, often with the assistance of voluntary agencies. They continue to be run by women and girls from the neighbourhood, usually high-school graduates, who receive on-the-job train-

---

Box 4.4   Hyderabad — Facilitating Partnerships with
Urban Poor Neighbourhoods

The transition from a squatter's *jhuggi* to a constructed house is not an easy one. In Hyderabad, problems of land tenure, the municipal housing regulations and financing were formidable obstacles that were overcome only thanks to the persistence and creative manoevring of a number of committed individuals who acted as *facilitators*.

The Devnagar Housing Shelter Improvement project (1976) provided a first example of the effectiveness of self-help and showed that community initiatives could correlate with government planning. With the coordination of the UCD project in Hyderabad, 19 initially reluctant families not only became convinced to relocate, but they actually raised Rs 9,500 ($305) towards rebuilding by staging concerts in the vicinity. The project worked with city engineers and the people in the community to redesign some of the physical features of the area, and the Rotary Club helped with the funding.

Based on this successful experience, a more ambitious project was undertaken, initially involving the upgrading of the dwellings of 100 poor urban families. The first step in the process was to obtain a building permit which required inspection by municipal authorities to ensure that the settlement was not located in a prohibited area, such as railway property or other unsafe grounds. The slum dwellers were then helped to apply for *pattas* (land deeds) for the plots ranging from 180 to 280 sq.ft. The transfer of land tenure to squatters was something quite new and actually a feat in itself, requiring the active brokerage role of the UCD project.

The UCD project also worked to generate community interest in the project and managed to obtain financing from several sources: commercial banks provided loans at 6 percent interest (4,000 Rs per house) ($128) with *pattas* as security; the Rotary Club, Lyons Club and Jaycees made contributions (1,000 Rs per house) ($32); and government subsidies were arranged. The Municipality was persuaded to waive contractors' and supervision charges as the residents would fulfil these functions themselves. *Basti Sahayak* or Community Helpers, chosen from among local high-school graduates acted as facilitators between the families and the project, helping people to identify and take action on community needs.

As the project grew in visibility, there was a risk that rules and regulations could be evoked to slow or halt activities. This risk was ably averted by G. Surya Rao, UCD project manager at the time, who contacted municipal offices to receive assurances that the city would not impede the construction work. He also arranged to show photographs of the new area to the state Minister of Housing who was impressed enough to bend a few rules. What was the point, Surya Rao reasoned, of making roads in the slum 30 feet wide (as the regulations stipulated) when the access road to the slum was only 10 feet wide? He also told the Minister that street addresses would be quickly assigned, creating a sizeable pool of new voters.

In the late 1970s, UCD was expanded to cover 300 slums in Hyderabad. It continued to facilitate the transfer of funds and the construction process, and men and women from each community provided labour and helped plan each home. The cost per home was 2,900 Rs ($93), less than usual. In four years 7,000 homes had been constructed, a number that had risen to 13,000 by 1983, many more than the Housing Board had built in a comparable period.

The Hyderabad UCD experience in housing mapped out a course through the maze of practical problems and restrictive regulations and was thus a valuable example to poor urban communities in other towns and cities. It was also a spectacular and visible testimony to the effectiveness of partnerships among urban communities, different sectors of civil society and the municipal government, facilitated by a few effective brokers.

Source: Urban Child Project (1992).

ing and utilize only low-cost handmade teaching materials. To receive project support, communities first had to provide a location for the centre and a list of prospective children, 3–6 years of age. Parents contributed towards the purchase of equipment and a nominal amount was paid to the *balwadi* teachers every month. Within five years there were enough *balwadis* in the city to cater for 2,200 slum children.

The Municipal Corporation of Hyderabad and the state government proposed in the late 1970s that the UCD project be expanded with UNICEF assistance to cover all 300 slums in Hyderabad. By 1981, the UCD project covered 81 percent of the slum population, or an estimated 405,231 people. Its activities included housing improvement, child care, youth clubs and women's groups, training programmes and nutrition programmes.

The Hyderabad UCD Project proved that the classical community development approach can be very effective in providing social services inexpensively while confronting poverty, particularly when effective catalysts (such as community organizers, NGOs and *basti sahayaks*) are involved. It also proved, especially with a highly successful housing scheme that eventually led to the construction of 13,000 new houses (See Box 4.4), that there were enormous resources in slum communities which could be tapped and that the project staff's attitude and approach were key elements. Selection and training of staff is probably the single most important element in any such programme.

The project's most important accomplishment was its capacity to present the urban poor as legitimate citizens who fulfil important functions within the community, rather than as nuisances or recipients of charity (Cousins and Goyder 1986).

The success of UCD attracted new funders. In 1983, the British Overseas Development Assistance (ODA) began contributing, particularly for infrastructure, including health centres, community meeting halls, roads and pathways. Together with HABITAT funds channelled through the Housing and Urban Development Cooperation, ODA assistance opened up a new phase for the urban communities — a phase which, at least initially, had deleterious effects. Large institutional loans were now available, which meant that communities were able to pay housing and other development loans in instalments. Because of the need to disburse these sizeable funds, administrators did not wait for community consensus or readiness before initiating activities. The communities, which had initially been enthusiastic, began to contribute less and less and gradually became passive, reverting to their pre-1976 attitude that the Government should take all the initiatives.

An independent assessment of the project 11 years later pointed out that the main problems were linked to a "too weak investment in the field of social work in the slums. Leaders are able to preserve [if not reinforce] their monopoly on land and housing deals... These [could not] be checked by an internal social control which has not been stimulated and supported by UCD's social workers" (Hennion 1987).

Hennion claimed that the main reasons for this were "the disproportion between the growth of population covered by the programme and the volume of additional staff actually engaged" as well as their commitment to community support. The field staff had not been increased since 1981 but their duties had multiplied, thus leading to a lack of contact with slum dwellers. This was "incompatible with an in-depth supportive work for participation and community development."

Taking note of this retrogression, the ODA and Hyderabad Municipal Corporation introduced many corrective measures. As a result, the Hyderabad UCD has reemerged as a front-runner in urban community development in India.

First expansion of UCD and UBS (1980–84)

Through experimentation, pragmatic planning and the involvement of many government officials, the UBS approach was progressively adapted to other cities. Between 1980 and 1983, the lessons of Hyderabad were successfully adopted by Baroda, Ahmedabad, Vishakapatnam and three other cities. There were also some instructive failures during this period.

Successes and failures of replication. Perhaps the most striking example of UCD–UBS replication in a large city was the Vishakapatnam project. Inspired by the Hyderabad project, the Vishakapatnam authorities established a project independently from UNICEF. Shri Ramarau, an experienced community organizer from the Hyderabad project, was appointed Project Officer. The process was hastened by the results of a recent city election in which an opposition party had come to power and wanted to show what it could do. The Vishakapatnam project, which soon after applied for UNICEF assistance, began with a low-cost, self-help housing activity and gradually added components including nursery schools and health activities. Thanks to these influences, subsequent large-scale ODA funding has remained responsive.

Contrasting and interesting lessons for future work were, moreover, provided by:

The *Kanpur (Uttar Pradesh) UCD project*, originally designed to work with the World Bank-assisted Slum Improvement Programme, had to deal with a too-rapid disbursement of large funds before adequate efforts could be made to create self-reliant and participatory communities. The project struggled with town officials and administrators who were unsympathetic to the participatory approach. The situation degenerated when community organizers were assigned tasks, such as recovering loan instalments from households, which severely damaged their rapport with the communities and their leaders. While the reasons for the municipal attitudes were clear enough, it was evident by 1985 that this collaboration was neither mutually supportive nor harmonious, and UNICEF did not renew its commitment.

The *Jaipur (Rajastan) UCD project* provided a different lesson: the danger of dynamism. Through joint planning and coordination, the project was able to pool eight times the original sum of US$ 180,000 that had been allocated, thus proving the viability of the UCD planning model based on intersectoral convergence. However, after three and a half years of exciting new initiatives, a difference of opinion arose between the director and the authorities in charge. The dynamism of the project's leadership may have been perceived as a threat by the conservative establishment. The director was transferred, the project ground to a halt and was eventually dissolved.

The key elements of the UBS strategy, as evident in the UNICEF–Government agreement, were: (a) small and medium-sized UBS town development programme (SMTD) which represented a major policy effort of the Government at that time to develop satellite towns to attract rural out-migrants; (b) people's involvement at all stages of programme development; (c) the form-ing of neighbourhood *Mohalla* committees; and (d) community organizers for each project town — with salary support from UNICEF — as the main link between the municipal government and the community.

Problems in implementation. The Ministry of Works and Housing had selected 42 towns for UNICEF assistance during the 1981–84 Master Plan period. However, implementation was slow, and by 1985 UBS covered only 16 towns. The problems were mostly administrative and related to the start-up phase. Partners had to be supported and encouraged and outside agen-cies, including the NIUA, had to travel throughout India to assist in the formulation of preparatory studies because most state and municipal authorities had no experience in promoting social development. It is en-couraging that today most have the confidence and expertise to undertake such initial programme development themselves. Even NIUA initially needed UNICEF financial and technical assistance to undertake these studies. A new mechanism of central government "grants-in-advance" was established for "preparatory activities," such as city-level analyses, estab-lishment and training of *Mohalla* committees, the setting up of day-care centres and the provision of latrines and safe drinking water.

The central government also insisted on approving town proposals sub-mitted by the state governments as the states lacked the capacity and exper-tise to guide the city administrations in participatory programme planning. The enthusiasm of the town authorities sagged while awaiting central government approval. During this period of advocacy, mobilization, ex-tended demonstration and replication, further timing problems were caused by the slow flow of UNICEF funds due to various procedural bottlenecks at subnational level. At the time, projects were still almost totally financed by UNICEF grants and community contributions. Even the salaries of frontline staff and the stipends of the volunteer *Basti Sahayaks* were paid from these grants. When the grants were delayed the projects ran into difficulties, caus-ing discouragement among some team members.

Other innovative projects aimed at building openness and flexibility. One such project was Sarjan, a programme of creative activities for children in the

Vasna resettlement colony. Another particularly successful project was the nationwide introduction of the hand-flushed sanitary latrines, promoted by private companies such as Sulabh Sauchalaya Sangsthan in Bihar and Safai Vidyalaya in Ahmedabad. This played a central role in providing a low-cost solution to the sanitation problems of poor urban neighbourhoods.

Box 4.5 Some Lessons from Initial Implementation

- Urban participatory approaches were as effective as rural ones
- Decentralization of project planning at the town and district level was imperative for better timing and effectiveness
- Involvement of all levels of government needed to be ensured
- Bureaucratic tendency towards large disbursements and rapid turnover hindered participatory strategies
- Good planning and carefully timed small amounts of funding were much more effective
- Strategies of community mobilization needed to ensure:
  - more equitable representative participation
  - more women's involvement in decision-making

Lessons at the operational level. Because of this experimentation with multi-level partners, the Government, perhaps for the first time, became convinced that the UBS approach was viable and that people's participation was possible on a large scale in socially and economically heterogeneous urban slum settlements.

Lessons at the operational level, contained in the report submitted to the Planning Commission in preparation for the Seventh Five Year Plan, 1985–89, were: (1) if the programme was to expand rapidly, authority needed to be delegated from the central government to the state governments for approving plans and for allocating funds; (2) since, as the programme expanded, the Government would not be able to commit funds to pay stipends to *basti sahayak*, it was agreed that: (a) the area covered by the full-time municipal community organizer had to be enlarged for this cadre to be cost-effective; (b) additional mechanisms were needed to ensure equitable and representative participation at the community level so that the *Mohalla* committee would not be monopolized by a few powerful residents; (c) because the majority of the organizers were men, women's involvement in decision-making needed to be strengthened; and (d) the monitoring of the programme needed revamping.

Towards universalization (1985–90)

A watershed: the Nagarjunasagar Meeting in September 1984 was a significant milestone in the evolution of UBS. The twelve UNICEF Urban Officers from the different regions of Andhra Pradesh were convened to establish the conceptual framework for the new five-year cooperation with the Government of India. The Joint Secretary of the Ministry of Works and Housing, R. L. Pradeep, was invited to join the last two days of the discussions. Agreement was reached between the Government and UNICEF on both the approach and the operational elements needed to best reach the urban poor and their children in future projects, to be uniformly called the Urban Basic Services Programmes (UBSP):

(a) *Minimum planning perspective of two Five-Year Plans* adopted by UNICEF and the Government in order to give the UBSP a sense of permanence.

(b) *Universal coverage in selected districts* as a step to going to scale in the over 3,800 towns. Districts would be selected on the basis of poverty levels and urbanization, and preference would be given to districts with other UNICEF-assisted programmes.

(c) *Agreement of central government to match contributions* of state or municipal governments and of UNICEF, an essential means to attract national attention and to encourage state governments and local authorities to do the same.

(d) *Use of full-time community organizers (COs) together with resident volunteers* to ensure sustained interaction with the community, greater cost-effectiveness, more equitable community participation. The Government and UNICEF later agreed on a system of resident community volunteers (RCV), preferably women, each representing a maximum of 25–40 households.

(e) *Community participation* was considered an educational process leading to greater self-confidence and self-reliance. Public structures ensuring community participation and a favourable institutional climate were necessary.

To ensure community participation, it was decided that a "social preparation phase" was needed and should include: (i) the recruitment and training of project staff; (ii) the division of project communities into neighbourhood committees of 100–250 households each, which would become the micro units for planning and administration and be expected to submit to municipal authorities and eventually implement a mini-plan; (iii) the selection and training of RCVs; and (iv) community education and promotion of local-level planning, self-help actions and child survival interventions.

(f) *The district would become the planning unit*, eliminating the need to obtain central government approval for town plans. In this way, the time-consuming, nonparticipatory and costly commissioning of outside research agencies to prepare feasibility reports and project proposals at the national level could be avoided.

(g) *Multilevel advocacy.* It was agreed that a conference on Urban Basic Services would be organized for state functionaries to promote the strategy and that states would be encouraged to conduct similar workshops.

Thanks to the Nagarjunasagar meeting and a subsequent brief position paper accepted as the framework for the Government-UNICEF cooperation, a new Master Plan of Operations for the Government and UNICEF was launched for the next five years, and UNICEF was officially invited to future Government National Reviews. The first major breakthrough came when the Ministry of Works and Housing agreed to share the programme costs among the central government (20 percent), state governments (40 percent) and UNICEF (40 percent). About half of the state governments' share was contributed by municipal governments, town-level voluntary organizations and urban poor neighbourhoods. The next challenge was to improve and consolidate the UNICEF-assisted UBS projects initiated under the 1981–84 Plan of Operations by: (a) improving their capacity for convergence; (b) expanding their coverage so as to be efficient and cost-effective; and (c) sharpening their focus on child survival and development strategies.

By 1990 the UBS projects had been expanded to 168 small and medium-sized towns throughout India. The main costs of the programme were progressively shifted from UNICEF to the Government: the UNICEF share of the total programme costs diminished from nearly 100 percent in 1983 to 25 percent in 1990 and became 3 percent with the UNICEF-Government of India agreement after 1990 (see Figure 4.1).

A number of important lessons were learned during this period:

- National government responsibilities were more clearly delineated.

- Planning was decentralized to the district level.

- The importance of partnerships with experienced urban NGOs (see Box 4.6) urban training institutes and academics was confirmed.

- The importance of training the government officials directly involved was recognized.

- Monitoring and reporting remained weak at all levels.

- Better career possibilities needed to be developed for poorly paid community organizers.

UBS gained national attention during this period by showing the efficiency, cost-effectiveness, feasibility and sustainability of certain strategies and approaches. This was done very effectively in Delhi where the areas covered by UBS proved to be the ones least prone to cholera outbreaks during the summer.

In most towns, the community was fully involved in identifying needs, establishing priorities and implementing self-help actions with or without government and other support. The services provided were based on simple technologies affordable to the community; access to specialized services was ensured by linkages with existing formal service systems. The community organizers were partly paid in some states by the urban neighbourhood committees in collaboration with UNICEF and the central government, thus making the urban communities feel that the organizers were in part accountable to them. Resident community volunteers, selected by the community

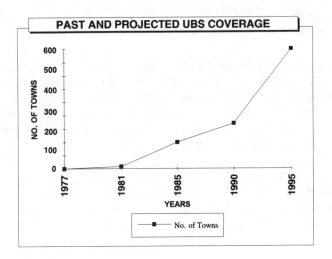

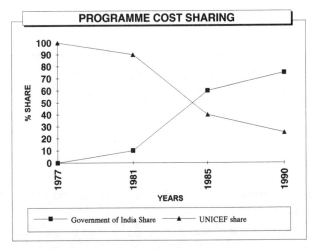

Figure 4.1. Past and projected coverage and programme cost sharing. Source: Fonseka/UNICEF Delhi (1991).

members of neighbourhood committees and trained by the UBSP, were the catalysts in each neighbourhood, promoting the implementation of the activities. Thanks to this combination of sectoral convergence and people's participation, a UBS project cost the Government only 15–18 Rs (48–58 cents) per person per year.

By 1990, a community-level infrastructure had been set up in most project towns, and neighbourhood development committees and trained female RCVs were monitoring health and related aspects of women and children in their immediate neighbourhood of 25–30 households. There were over 25,000 RCVs in 168 towns and each year 8–10,000 women and men were being trained in mother and child care by the UBS functionaries and the RCVs. The learning-aids developed by the programme for this purpose became so popular that almost all other UNICEF-assisted sectors began using them in their community-level operations.

The UBS programme placed emphasis on four main problems of urban poor children and women — namely, malnutrition, diarrhoeal diseases, low family income and low educational attainment. Achievements were obtained in the areas of health and nutrition, water supply and sanitation, and education and skills development.

Health and nutrition. A comprehensive package of child survival and developmental interventions was developed through the close collaboration with the Ministry of Works and Housing, the Ministry of Health and the Ministry of Social Welfare. The package included immunization, improved feeding practices, growth monitoring, diarrhoea management and health and nutrition education. Health volunteers and paramedical personnel were trained to work closely with ICDS and in the Health Ministry's Expanded Programme of Immunization. Traditional birth attendants (*dais*) were trained with the collaboration of municipal health functionaries. In addition to immunization, preventive measures included the provision of environmental sanitation and safe water.

By 1990, the impact was visible. For example, project areas in Kerala, Uttar Pradesh and Orissa reported marked improvements in sanitary conditions and in health and hygiene practices. In some cities, especially the larger ones, there were interventions against gastroenteritis outbreaks, including oral rehydration treatment distribution and demonstration stalls at immunization centres, hospitals and pharmacies. It was estimated that between 350 and 450 gastroenteritis-related child deaths occurring annually in Delhi during the monsoon months were averted after 1988, despite particularly heavy monsoons. This led to even greater government interest in UBS as a strategy.

Water supply and sanitation. To reduce child morbidity and mortality, the programme assisted local authorities in extending drinking water facilities to the poor settlement areas. Low-cost pour-flush latrines were also constructed.

Learning opportunities for women and children. As a means of breaking the reinforcing links between illiteracy, ill-health and poverty, flexible learning facilities were organized. Day-care and preschool centres were also started. These proved very popular and over 1,200 were operational by 1990. Primary schools were helped under the scheme with the provision of water and latrines. They were also helped to promote lessons in health and nutrition education and leadership training through such activities as "Child-to-Child."

Box 4.6   SPARC — Facilitating Other NGOs

One of the most important steps in mobilizing poor communities is ensuring that their inhabitants have access to the resources to which they are entitled. SPARC (Society for the Promotion of Area Resource Centres) was formed in 1984 by a group of social workers, social scientists and researchers in Bombay to help as many as possible of the city's estimated 1.5 million pavement dwellers learn what resources were available to them within the city. Conversely, because little was known about pavement dwellers — how many there were, why and how they lived on the pavements, and how they contributed to the city's economy — SPARC also intended to collect and disseminate knowledge about this highly visible group.

Their first budget expenditures were for four researchers to sit on the pavements and chat to the people about their needs and preferences. Since then SPARC and other collaborating NGOs have conducted extensive research and published several studies on pavement dwellers and other groups of poor people in India's cities, including children, adding a great deal to the understanding of the problems these groups face. Through its activities, SPARC has provided the basis for government and non-governmental projects to improve the pavement dwellers' living environment.

Apart from research and training, the organization acts mainly as a facilitator and network-builder. Rather than designing and implementing projects (like most NGOs), SPARC supports people in setting up organizations and doing things for themselves. It measures its own effectiveness by the extent to which it mobilizes other people and groups.

SPARC has two main partner organizations: *Mahila Mahan*, initially a group of women pavement dwellers who lobbied for their rights to secure shelter, which has now expanded to include other urban poor and has proven the ineffectiveness of planning without women; and the *National Slum Dwellers Federation*, with member federations in various cities in India, which collaborates with SPARC on the basis of an informal agreement and has progressively taken over most of the direct organizational work in the slums.

SPARC puts special emphasis on helping women pursue an active role in community development. All of its activities are directly linked to working for a just resource allocation and access to resources for the poor. To accomplish this, SPARC has set up neighbourhood resource centres where people can obtain information, interact with their neighbours, and eventually learn how to be their own spokespersons. In fact, SPARC works hard to make itself obsolete, eventually entrusting the running of these centres to the users. The centres also generate detailed information about the life, livelihoods and living conditions of local residents, all of which are useful additions to official statistics and can influence development policy.

Since 1988, SPARC has been a member of the Asian Coalition for Housing Rights and has started interacting with groups and movements outside of India.

Source: *Environment and Urbanization* (1990), Urban Child Project (1992).

Women's income generation. Efforts were made to provide greater access to vocational training, skills development, institutional loans for setting up small-scale enterprises, and guidance for marketing. In Andhra Pradesh and Orissa alone, over 30,000 women in 41 towns have benefited from this scheme. The empowerment of the almost exclusively female members of neighbourhood committees allowed for better income generation. In some Andhra Pradesh towns, for example, these women organized training centres for sewing and clothes production and created a service cooperative that allowed them to bypass middlemen for purchasing raw materials and marketing their goods. This has tripled their earnings.

Capacity building and participation. Community organization was promoted in the slums, leading to greater self-reliance, cohesion and responsible participatory action, with special focus on children and women. Key officials of the municipalities and project-level functionaries who visited successful programmes came away convinced that participatory decision-making was a worthwhile goal.

CONCLUSIONS

The discovery that the urban poor (and their children) can be part of the solution rather than a liability was the basis for the adoption of the UBS model throughout India. In 1990, the Government proposed to add to the 168 towns already covered by UBS from 75 to 100 towns each year, bringing an additional 1.1 million population annually under coverage. The UBS programme was renamed the Urban Basic Services Programme for the Poor (UBSP) and adopted nationwide. A first target was set to reach 500 towns by the end of 1992 with about 3,000 community organizers. It was foreseen that state governments could adopt the model, using funds made available by the central government. In financial terms, while the UBS programme was jointly financed during the Seventh Five-Year Plan by central, state and municipal governments, the communities and UNICEF, the contribution of UNICEF greatly diminished proportionally. UNICEF's resources will be targeted to training, communication, NGO support, innovative projects, monitoring, capacity building and advocacy. The Government of India will provide approximately US$35 million to the programme for 1991–95, while UNICEF will contribute another $9 million (an increase in absolute terms but a reduction in percentage terms). A further $10 million is earmarked for supplementary funding, financed by central, state and local government resources, an indicator of the recognition UBSP has gained as an important element of the national poverty alleviation programme. In addition, Government of India resources for two other schemes, the Nehru Razgar Yagana, focusing on employment, and the Environmental Improvement in Urban Slums, will converge in the same cities.

The endorsement of UBS by the Government shows the beginnings of a major change in attitude towards the urban poor and towards NGOs. The urban poor were once only perceived as a problem for urban development. UBS has shown that they are an important element of any low-cost and sustainable urban project.

Similarly, with the changed mood of the 1990s, as civil society acquires a greater say and is increasingly prepared to mobilize for problem resolution, urban NGOs are being officially recognized by the Government as indispensable partners.

There are, however, important challenges ahead:

(a) Deep resistance, anchored in caste and class considerations, persists among local elites and in the bureaucracy against a full acceptance of the urban poor as valued equal partners in development. But experience shows that they can be won over.

(b) The Indian bureaucracy shows recurrent inflexibility and a concern for centralized efficiency rather than decentralized effectiveness, despite continuous advocacy efforts.

(c) Government ability to identify sufficient numbers of NGOs with the appropriate capacity and maturity to effectively reach the urban poor neighbourhoods has been questioned. City-level NGOs have different purposes and organizational potentials and a number of assessments point out that only a few NGOs in each city are mature and developmental (NIUA 1992).

(d) The specialized academic organizations that have provided the staff training will need some additional support to be able to respond to the growing demand. Thus, many of the major partners still require strengthening and encouragement. The momentum will need to be sustained by all involved, including the urban neighbourhoods.

(e) Though quite successful in many medium-sized and small towns, UBS has failed to take off effectively in the huge Indian metropolitan areas. After some attempts, the programme was not pursued in Calcutta, Madras and Delhi. Some of the reasons relate to the lack of community spirit in large multiethnic communities and the fact that municipal administrators did not consider the UBS funds very important because they were only a small percentage of their overall budget (Berterame 1991). The administrative complexities of large cities also made convergence and integration of services more difficult.

(f) Finally, the concern for children needs constant reiteration. While UBS has provided some important services for children in the 0–6 age group, such as creches and preschools, it has rarely addressed the needs of the 6- to 18-year-old school-age children. They still fall too easily into exploitative child labour, leading to a new generation of uneducated, unskilled young people getting married too young and producing too many children. In other words, UBSP has not been able to attack preventively the recurrent cycles that plague poor neighbourhoods.

It has been suggested that UBSP, especially in coordination with ICDS and possibly the urban branch of Development of Women and Children in Rural Areas (DWCRA), could play a much more central role in addressing the needs of adolescent girls and young mothers (Chatterjee 1991). At the same time, a municipal or district focus on children in especially difficult circumstances would help reenergize and focus the networks. UBSP towns and urban neighbourhoods could, with the collaboration of coordinating Urban CEDC task forces, become more responsible for monitoring and curbing exploitative child labour and early marriage of children, focusing in particular on the highly vulnerable middle years and adolescence. This could have long-term preventive effects. It would require strategic advocacy at national, municipal and local levels; the introduction at the community level of other successful role models for girls, boys and their parents; and intensive skill training, possibly through the expansion of existing resources such as young female *balwadi* and *angawadi* teachers or mostly young male community organizers.

Indian society has repeatedly shown its ability to mobilize. NGO growth and community participation in the UBS programmes are two recent and striking examples. These remarkable energies need now to be channelled even more constructively toward children who, while at times uncomfortable reminders of the malfunctioning of society, are also the essence of its future.

NOTES

1. The widening gap between birth and death rates has increased the natural growth rate of the population. By 1986, the natural growth rate was 21.5 per 1,000 population per annum, compared to 6.6 at the beginning of the century.

2. In 1901 life expectancy was 23.63 years for males and 23.96 for females and in 1980, 54.1 for males and 54.7 for females. By the year 2000 the life expectancy is projected to reach 64.9 years for males and 65.1 years for females (Office of the Registrar General 1989b).

3. The term "urban" encompasses all statutory towns (i.e., places with a municipal corporation or board, cantonment board, or notified town area), and places having a minimum population of 5,000, at least 75 percent of the male working population engaged in nonagricultural activities, and a population density of no less than 400 persons per km². Also, cities often have extensions outside their official limits which actually form an integral part of the cities themselves. Sometimes two or more towns are contiguous and should really be considered as a single agglomeration.

4. However, the 1991 urban population falls short of the figure of 230 million projected in 1988 by the Expert Committee on Population Projections, indicating a probable slowdown in the process of urbanization. The Expert Committee also projected an urban population of 326 million by the year 2001, which

would be more than double the urban population of 1981 and more than the total population of the country in 1941. Taking into account the ongoing trends in migration, birth rates and other factors, it is clear that the projections for 2001 need to be reviewed (Bose 1992).

5. Almost 65 percent of the urban population lived in 300 cities with populations of 100,000 and above, and there were 23 metropolitan cities with a population of more than 1 million. Surprisingly, however, the 1991 census data also show a decline in growth rates during the 1981–91 period in the case of 17 out of 23 of these million-population cities, including greater Bombay, Calcutta, Delhi, Bangalore, Ahmedabad, Surat, Patna, Vadodara, but not Visakhapatnam or Hyderabad (Census of India 1991).

6. Marriage remains the main reason for female migration whereas employment and movement of the family are the major reasons for male migration.

7. Quinquennial surveys of consumer expenditure carried out by the National Sample Survey Organization of the Government of India provide the basic data for the measurement of poverty. In India, the official definition of poverty is based on the monetary equivalent of fulfilling the nutritional requirement of 2,400 calories per day in rural areas and 2,100 calories per day in urban areas.

8. In a special national survey (Census of India 1988) to study the interrelationship of fertility and mortality indicators with socioeconomic factors, it was found that the age of females at marriage is of crucial importance. It significantly varies among various groups and states. The survey also revealed that the average number of children born alive per every married woman declines as the age at marriage increases, thus indicating an impact on fertility. In urban areas, 52 percent of currently married women were married before the age of 18 years. About 15 percent got married after 21 years of age. In rural areas, age at marriage is lower than in urban areas. A high proportion of women in urban areas who married before the age of 18 were: (a) Muslims (57 percent), Hindus (53 percent), Christians (33 percent) and Sikhs (33 percent); (b) Scheduled castes (63 percent) as against unscheduled (50 percent); (c) illiterate (66 percent) as against females having matriculation or above levels of education (27 percent).

   The difference between the mean age at marriage of women and their husbands was 4.8 years in rural areas and 5.4 years in urban areas. Mean age at marriage rises with increases in the level of education. Nonworkers, labourers and unskilled workers tend to marry at a lower age, both in rural and urban areas. This has profound effects on the fertility rate, the health of women, household size and the condition of children.

9. In India, the current definition of delinquency is a legal one: the violation of a law by a young person (under 16 for boys and 18 for girls). Figures on juvenile delinquency are published by the National Crime Records Bureau of the Ministry of Home Affairs based on the Juvenile Justice Act, 1986. Many factors may combine, however, to make a reliable measurement of juvenile delinquency difficult. These include: biases in the areas of social class, gender, geography (e.g., regional, urban/rural), as well as changes in laws.

10. These municipal authorities are outside the Planning Framework and by and large do not have a separate capital (plan) budget. Except for health and educa-

tion, for which they get grant-in-aid, municipal authorities have to generate funding for all services.

11. SOS children's villages, an alternative to children's homes, provide more individualized and home-like care. Small groups of children of mixed ages and either sex are placed with a housemother, approximating a family and in net contrast with institutional settings. Foster care, which was an unfamiliar concept in India, faces difficulties in matching children by ethnic group, religion and caste. The scheme started in metropolitan cities and offered limited financial support, which was increased in the late 1970s to Rs 75 ($2.40) per month per child and made payable even to relatives. Foster care remains, however, expensive. Costs, including staff costs, were estimated at Rs 51,000 ($1,638) for 50 children in 1980 (Bose 1980).

12. The neglected child is defined in the Children Act, 1960, as one who "(i) is found begging; or (ii) is found without having any home or settled place of abode or any ostensible means of subsistence or is found destitute, whether he is an orphan or not; (iii) has a parent or guardian who is unfit to exercise or does not want to exercise proper care and control over the child; (iv) lives in a brothel or with a prostitute or frequently goes to any place used for the purpose of prostitution, or is found to associate with any prostitute or any other person who leads an immoral, drunken or depraved life."

13. All large bureaucracies, including the international funding organizations, prefer to invest in large-scale projects requiring the rapid allocation of money rather than small-scale initiatives requiring small amounts of money disbursed at intervals best suited to the needs of the beneficiaries. This tendency is combined with a conviction that "top-down" is best; in other words, that bureaucrats and technical experts know what is needed. Both factors contribute to development projects unrelated to the real needs and concerns of the users.

14. Sriniketan and Shantiniketan programmes for rural development by Rabindranath Tagore in 1914; "Nirmana-karyakramam" for rural reconstruction by Mahatma Gandhi in 1920; the Firka development scheme by Tanguturi Prakasam Chief Minister of Madras State; the Sarvodaya Movement by Jayaprakashnarayan followed by the Bhoodan movement by Vinoba Bhave in 1968, all the way to Community Projects by Jawaharlal Nehru in the First Five Year Plan in 1952. A few British and Americans were also influential in starting community projects in the immediate pre- and post-World War II period (Ramarau 1990).

15. The Voluntary Health Association of India (VHAI) was a response to modern health facilities with limited viability to the surrounding communities. By 1990 it had a membership of about 3,000 organizations (UNICEF 1990a).

Chapter
FIVE

Kenya: The Urban Threat to Women and Children

Monica Mutuku and Roberta Mutiso

SOCIOECONOMIC CONTEXT AND DEMOGRAPHIC TRENDS[1]

Economic Setting

After a promising economic performance in its first decade of independence (1963 to 1972), Kenya, like much of Africa, experienced economic difficulties in the 1970s and has faced economic stagnation and decline since the 1980s. As the country's economic prospects have dimmed, so has its ability to alleviate poverty. Abject household poverty is now on the rise in both rural and urban areas. Kenya in 1993 remains a low-income country[2] with an essentially rural economy based on the export of cash crops and primary products. It is experiencing relatively low capital investments in agriculture, mostly on cash crops that contribute to low yields and an increasingly high land concentration (Gini coefficient of 0.8 for late 1970s and 1980s) together with unequal land ownership and difficult access to land.[3] The numbers of landless or near landless households in the Kenyan countryside, much as in the rest of Africa, are now considerable and, as we will explain, they are mostly headed by women (Cornia et al. 1992).

Like many other less developed countries (LDC) and most other African countries, Kenya is economically dependent on the export of a few primary commodities whose prices have plummeted over the last decade. Between 1980 and 1991, the weighted price index for 33 primary products (excluding energy) dropped by almost 50 percent — from 105 to 57. In Kenya, coffee, tea and horticultural produce accounted for almost half (49 percent) of the export earnings in 1991 (Republic of Kenya 1992). As prices for these commodities declined, the country's terms of trade deteriorated (100 in 1982, 103 in 1986, 71 in 1990), with consequent heavy losses in export earnings (Republic of Kenya 1991).

The Kenyan manufacturing sector has continued to represent a very small share of GDP (just over 10 percent, as in most of sub-Saharan Africa, whereas the figure has risen worldwide to around 24 percent in most middle-income countries).[4] The sector has, however, been able to develop a certain base and bundle of export goods despite its import substitution policy.

Even though Kenya has been able to attract sufficient foreign investment, drawing especially on expatriates, and has registered some improvement in areas such as literacy and secondary enrolment rates, the country is beset with problems. Kenya's relative lack of economic growth is related, in large part, to the decreased domestic demand for products,[5] the world recession, the growing crisis faced by agricultural households, problems of distribution and marketing, sometimes excessive government regulations, and the failure to develop technological skills.[6] Furthermore, government protectionism over time has been problematic.

The deterioration of internal demand has also been attributed to depressed real wages. The official minimum wage fell between 1970 and 1986 in 18 African countries, including Kenya. While teachers' salaries held, other real wages in the Kenyan nonagricultural sector declined (–3.6 between 1980 and 1985) (Cornia et al. 1992).

A number of factors beyond the control of policy makers have also contributed to the deteriorating situation. The oil crisis of 1973 was the first major external shock after Independence. As oil prices quadrupled almost overnight, the world economy slid into a severe recession which persisted into the 1980s. While the import bill shot up, export earnings slackened, causing the new nation to experience unprecedented inflationary pressures and balance-of-payment problems. The yearly rate of inflation rose from 2.6 percent in 1972 to 9.8 percent in 1973 and 15.3 percent in 1975; during the same period, barter terms of trade deteriorated by about 20 percent (Mukui 1992).

A short-lived respite occurred with the coffee boom of 1975–76. However, 1977 saw the collapse of the East African Community, which had been the main market for Kenya's manufacturers. Its collapse was a major blow.

Adverse weather conditions, especially droughts, have been another important factor. Severe droughts in 1975–76, 1984 and 1991–92 wreaked havoc on the economy, which is based on rain-fed agriculture. Declines in crop yields have resulted in lowered export earnings and recurring food shortages. To meet these emergencies, the Government has been forced to import food and to seek foreign aid, further weakening its balance-of-payments and increasing foreign indebtedness.

World political events have also had their influence. The Gulf crisis of 1990–91 adversely affected Kenya's tourist sector (the country's leading foreign exchange earner in 1990); the collapse of the USSR and its satellite eastern European states has led to a shift in foreign aid and capital investment away from sub-Saharan Africa and other poor Third World nations to former Communist countries. Moreover, economic blocs (for example, the recent "Fortress Europe") have increasingly isolated sub-Saharan Africa from world trade.

Among the internal factors contributing to Kenya's dismal economic performance are its economic and political policies. In 1963, immediately after Independence, Kenya adopted an economic development model characterized as "managed capitalism." This model combined the development of a free enterprise system with considerable governmental intervention and an import substitution strategy. The prime objective was the simultaneous attainment of both internal and external macroeconomic equilibria with price stability, based on demand management, price controls and other forms of intervention in the market place.[7] The aim was to stimulate "managed" economic growth in order to fight poverty, disease and illiteracy.

However, managed capitalism has had a number of unintended adverse effects. The economy has acquired structural rigidities and has failed to develop the flexibility needed to adjust to shocks such as the 1973 oil crisis, to droughts and to the hostile international economic environment. The result has been poverty and increasing desperation among Kenyans.

A number of policies have contributed to structural and macroeconomic imbalances. Price controls have led to serious shortages and black markets, and, together with other economic problems, have contributed to systematic impoverishment. The situation worsened dramatically in the early 1980s as shortages of milk, cooking oils and fats, wheat flour, cement, roofing nails and other consumer products became widespread. Inevitably, it is the poor who suffer the most since they are least able to afford black market prices.

The import substitution strategy, established immediately after Independence, has attempted to provide protective walls for domestic industries through high tariff rates and quantitative restrictions.[8] Several problems have, however, arisen. The so-called infant industries, lacking competition from imports, have had no incentives to develop efficiently and have generally produced low-quality goods at exorbitant prices. Moreover, because of their inefficiency, these import substitution industries have tended to use capital, which is relatively scarce, more intensively than labour, which is relatively abundant. (In contrast, production for export, in a neutral policy environment, is often more labour intensive.) Such import-substitution policies have, furthermore, tended to turn the terms of trade in favour of industry and against agriculture.

Since the 1980s, the Government has tended to run up large budget deficits. In 1991, for example, the budget deficit crept towards 7 percent of the country's gross national product. Expenditure has spiralled out of control because of a bloated bureaucracy, a product of the Government's policy of expanded public sector employment in order to reduce unemployment, particularly among university graduates.

With only small proportions of budgetary resources going to development, the civil service has become almost paralysed: transport for extension officers and drugs at health facilities are lacking, roads are poorly maintained and schools ill-equipped. At the same time, the Government has become a major borrower in financial markets, crowding out the private sector. The effects on the economy have been devastating.

Other policies have had disastrous economic consequences. These include regulated exchange and interest rates, government over-investment in the private sector, regulated interest rates, free health services, free primary and university education, and highly subsidized secondary school education.

Apart from policies affecting economic incentives, Kenya has formulated regulatory policies intended to protect the poor, especially unskilled labour. These regulations, including minimum wage legislation and job security, have instead tended to reduce employment in the formal markets and increase income uncertainty. In the midst of this economic malaise, the rich, the powerful and the ruling elite have engaged in an unrestrained plunder of the economy. Their actions have been facilitated by the general absence of good governance associated with one-party rule.

Structural Adjustment and Poverty

By the second half of the 1980s, Kenya, like many other developing countries, had begun a period of structural adjustments. The Government implemented 13 structural adjustment programmes (SAP) in agriculture, trade and industry in the 1980s to restore equilibrium in the external sector, and began to analyse its complex finance sector. These programmes were well supported by external funding, mainly from the International Monetary Fund (IMF) and the World Bank, allowing GDP to recover from its low 1980–85 levels and to reach a 1986–89 average of 5.8 percent per annum (Government of Kenya and UNICEF 1992). A relapse, however, occurred in 1989 when real GDP growth rates dropped to 5 percent, slipping in 1990 to 4.3 percent and further deteriorating in 1991 to 2.2 percent (Republic of Kenya 1992). Because of high population growth rates, the per capita GDP growth rate was negative (–1.3 percent) in 1991. The rate of inflation also rose, from 15.3 percent in 1990 to 19.6 percent in 1991, causing real earnings to fall 8.3 percent.

The basic tenets of the SAPs in Kenya have been: (a) devaluation of the shilling; (b) lifting of price controls and the institution of incentives, especially for agricultural production; (c) removal of subsidies; (d) liberation of external trade through the lowering of tariffs and the elimination of non-tariff barriers to trade; (e) reform of the tax system and increased efficiency in tax collection accompanied by a reduction in budget deficits through cuts in government expenditure; and (f) divestiture of the Government from the private sector and general reform of parastatals.

Generally, SAPs impact negatively on the poor and vulnerable groups by shifting government resources away from social services and poverty allevia-tion (Manundu 1992a). They directly affect the provision of food, shelter, health care, education, water and sanitation, and have forced Kenya and other LDCs to revert to cost sharing with the already overburdened poor.

For this reason, if structural adjustment programmes cannot be eliminated altogether, the pain of adjustment needs to be minimized by assisting those adversely affected by structural adjustment policies. The guiding principle would be to allow the poor to increase their productive capacity as much as possible, and to support them in their efforts to do so.

Some welfare indicators

Health. Infant (IMR) and child mortality (U5MR) rates are steadily declining.[9] Wide geographical disparities and disturbing trends exist, however. The IMR in Nyanza province remained unchanged at 148 per 1,000 live births from 1979 to 1989, while increases were registered in three provinces known in the past for their particularly low figures for Kenya (by 21 percent in Central province, 36 percent in Eastern province, and 75 percent in Rift Valley province). Even when declines are confirmed, IMR rates remain high (139 per 1,000 in Coast province and 126 per 1,000 in Western province). Malaria in low-lying areas and respiratory infection in the highlands together with measles and diarrhoea are the major causes of early childhood death. Some projections suggest that AIDS, as discussed later, threatens to push the U5MR back up to the 1960 levels of 189 per 1,000 live births by the end of the century (Government of Kenya and UNICEF 1992).

Malnutrition. Conservative estimates established that in 1988 at least 5 percent of Kenyans were seriously malnourished and about one third suf-fered from mild forms of malnourishment (Rae et al. 1988). The main causes include poor infant feeding practices, inadequate diets and the high in-cidence of disease. The Government's hopes of improving nutrition for the urban poor through price controls and increased employment opportunities have by no means been fully realized.

Education. Government expenditure policies have generally favoured education and, in fact, Kenya has made exceptional progress since Inde-pendence. The number of primary schools more than doubled from 1963 to 1985, and primary school education is now nearly universal (94 percent). Moreover, with boys accounting for 52 percent of enrolments and girls 48 percent, gender parity in primary school education is close to being achieved. In the same period, enrolment in secondary schools increased nearly four-teenfold, from 36,000 to about 500,000. To broaden secondary education, other institutions have been set up, including technical and vocational schools and *harambee* institutes of technology, built and run on a self-help basis and offering vocational courses for secondary school leavers. Ethnical-ly-segregated schools have been integrated and teaching staff Kenyanized

(Noormohamed and Opondo 1989).

Problems, however, still exist. Enrolment in nursery schools stands at only 21 percent, and there have been drops in attendances in adult literacy classes, according to 1988 data (Noormohamed and Opondo 1989). Despite the rapid growth in secondary and tertiary educational enrolments in Kenya, only about 40 percent of primary school graduates in 1991 gained access to secondary schools. Entry into university is even more limited despite the dramatic increase in student enrolments in recent years (from 8,400 in 1984 to almost 40,000 in 1991).

Girls are underrepresented in terms of literacy levels (27 percent as opposed to 31 percent). They drop out of primary school at a higher rate than boys do, thus multiplying their disadvantages. A recent survey in Baringo, for example, revealed a completion rate of 40 percent for girls and 75 percent for boys. Girls are particularly underrepresented in secondary and higher education enrolment (40 female university students for every 100 males) (Government of Kenya and UNICEF 1992).

Demographic and Urbanization Trends

Since the 1950s, Kenya has undergone rapid population growth, the result of not only high fertility rates but also an improved standard of living and better maternal and child health care. The decline in the overall mortality rate, and especially infant mortality, has been particularly impressive (Table 5.1). With a yearly population growth rate in excess of 3.3 percent since 1962 (reaching 3.8 percent between 1969 and 1979 to become one of the fastest-growing countries in the world), the population of Kenya has more than doubled in the last two decades, increasing from approximately 11 million in 1970 to 24 million in 1990. According to projections, the population will reach 35 million by the year 2000.

Rapid population growth has contributed to the country's decreasing capacity to provide adequate health and educational services (Gachukia 1992). It has also been a factor in environmental degradation and the depletion of the natural resources. Population growth, changes in access and ownership of land, and poor economic prospects in rural areas have resulted in a conspicuous trend towards urbanization. In 1948, the year of the first census, the urban population accounted for only 5.2 percent of the total and was concentrated in Nairobi and Mombasa (73.9 percent). Urbanization increased at a yearly rate of 9.0 percent between 1965 and 1980, due both to natural growth and rural-to-urban migration. With the economic slowdown of the 1980s, the urbanization rate fell to about 7.9 percent (World Bank 1992). In 1989, 23 percent of the Kenyan population lived in urban areas, a percentage that is expected to nearly double by the year 2025. The growing urban population has created serious employment and housing problems and has strained social services.

Table 5.1. Some Demographic, Health and Education Indicators (1960–91)

Demographic Indicators[a]	1960	1990
Population (millions)	8.3	24.0
Urban population (% of total)	7.4	23.6
Age groups (%)		
0–4 years	19.6	19.5
5–14 years	26.0	30.4
15–24 year	15.8	19.3
65+	4.1	2.9
Dependency ratio (/100)		
total	98.8	111.8
aged 0–14	90.6	105.6
aged 65+	8.2	6.2

Demographic Indicators[a]	1960–65	1990–95
Population annual growth rate (%)		
total	3.14	3.74
urban	6.26	6.94
rural	2.87	2.64
Life expectancy at birth (years)		
males	44	59
females	48	63
both sexes	46	61
Crude birth rate (per 1,000 population)	52.8	47
Crude death rate (per 1,000 population)	21.4	9.7
Total fertility rate (per woman)	8.12	6.8
Infant mortality rate (per 1,000 births)	118	64

Education Indicators[b]	Past	Most recent
Primary enrolment ratio (gross)	(1960)	(1986–90)
male	64	96
female	30	92
females as % of males	47	96
Secondary enrolment ratio (gross)	(1960)	(1986–90)
male	–	27
female	–	19
female as % of males	–	70
Adult literacy rate	(1970)	(1990)
male	44	80
female	19	59
females as % of males	43	74
% of grade 1 enrolment reaching final	–	(1988)
grade of primary school	–	62

Sources: [a]United Nations (1991a) and [b]UNICEF (1993).

In 1969, five cities (Nairobi, Mombasa, Kisumu, Nakuru and Thika) had 86.3 percent of the total urban population, a share that dropped sharply in the following decade, reaching 67.8 percent in 1979. This decline coincided with the unusually rapid economic growth in Kenya, which created new opportunities in medium-sized towns (20,000 to 99,999). Large numbers of migrants who would have otherwise gone to bigger cities were attracted to these centres. With the economic stagnation of the 1980s, migrants began to head once more towards the dominant urban areas. Since 1960, over 70 percent of the total urban population has continued to reside in Nairobi and Mombasa.

In the immediate post-Second World War period, most urban dwellers were non-African because of legal and administrative restrictions on the migration of Kenyans. Only young, able-bodied and single men were allowed to migrate to urban areas. Since Independence, rural-to-urban migration has progressively shifted to include both single and married women as well as children. This trend was particularly marked during the late 1970s and throughout the 1980s as the pressures on rural households and families increased. Structural changes (especially changes in land tenure) have also tended to dispossess women from rural areas. Shortages of land related to the introduction of new ownership laws and inheritance practices favouring males have made it impossible for fathers to allot part of the communal land to their daughters, even those lacking other support.

The extended family, facing social, economic and cultural pressures, is no longer able to provide the support it used to ensure to its adult members, both male and female, and to its children. Individual accountability has now replaced collective accountability. General social disruption is also reflected in out-of-wedlock families, especially among adolescents. These young unmarried women, often discriminated against in traditionalist rural areas, find the more tolerant and accommodating urban milieu and the attraction of higher earnings especially inviting. These and other reasons have led to changes in the sex ratios in urban areas. In 1952, for example, there were 169 men for every 100 women in Nairobi, whereas in 1989 there were only 111.

Children (under 19 years of age) in urban areas may number about 3 million, basing calculations on their percentage in the overall population.[10] Children 0–16 represented about 35 percent of the population of Mombasa and Nairobi in 1989 (Table 5.2). Between 1978 and 1989, the overall child population grew by 84 percent in Mombasa and by 57 percent in Nairobi. These are indeed phenomenal growth rates, and carry considerable implications given the special health and social needs of this age group.

Table 5.2. Distribution of Children by Age and Year in Nairobi
and Mombasa (Population in Thousands, 1978–89)

	1978	1979	1980	1981	1982	1983	1984	1989
Mombasa	391	413	436	460	485	512	516	611
0–4 years	50	62	65	69	73	77	78	92
6–12 years	51	54	57	60	63	66	67	79
13–16 years	25	27	29	31	33	34	35	42
Nairobi	818	863	913	963	1016	1072	1054	1286
0–4 years	124	131	139	146	154	162	160	195
6–12 years	105	111	117	123	130	137	136	166
13–16 years	56	59	62	65	69	73	72	88

Source: Population Profiles for the Districts of Kenya. Population Studies and Research Institute (PSRI) (1990).

THE SITUATION OF DISADVANTAGED URBAN CHILDREN AND FAMILIES

Urban Poverty and Deprivation

Estimates made in 1969 and 1982 of the shares of national income accruing to various income groups have concurred on two points: that a small proportion of Kenyans receive a major proportion of national income; and that, at every descending rung of the income distribution ladder, access to national income decreases dramatically. For example, in 1969 the richest 10 percent of the population received 56.3 percent of the national income, while the poorest 10 percent received only 1.8 percent (Morrison 1973). By 1982, the share of the poorest 10 percent had declined to a mere 0.8 percent (Vandemoortele 1982). Thus, while the wealthy few have become wealthier, the poor have become poorer. At the same time, the proportion of those living in absolute poverty has been rising. Between 1984 and 1989, for instance, the proportion of households in the "very low" income group increased from 13.2 percent to 22.1 percent (Republic of Kenya 1990a).

Although poverty affects a larger proportion of the population in rural than in urban areas, the plight of the urban poor remains cause for serious concern. Their situation is often aggravated by municipal authorities who harass street vendors and informal-sector workers in general, destroying their trading structures and dwelling units while providing them with no alternatives. There are signs that the urban poor, increasingly exasperated by the insensitivity of local authorities, have become bolder, better organized and unyielding, characteristics that have transformed them into a powerful political force in urban Kenya. According to Ikiara (1992), the clearest demonstration of this was seen in the confrontation in May 1990 between Nairobi City Commission officials with eviction orders in hand and shanty

Table 5.3. Housing Conditions in Nairobi, Kisumu
and Mombasa (Percentages, 1985)

	Nairobi (778 households)	Kisumu (132 households)	Mombasa (332 households)
Water availability			
use private taps	68	23	41
use communal taps	19	4	10
buy water from vendors		54	49
use boreholes, dams, wells or rivers	1	19	–
Excreta disposal			
flush toilets	69	22	47
pit latrines	30	72	50
no form of waste disposal	1	6	3
Flooring of dwellings			
cement	83	68	75
earth	8	30	14
wood or plastic	9	2	11
Roofs of dwellings			
corrugated iron roofs	59	75	35
tiles or flat cement	40	12	42
makuti, grass thatch or flattened tin	1	13	23

Source: Lee-Smith et al. (1987).

dwellers of the Muoroto slum. The Government and municipal authorities suffered extreme political embarrassment as a result, especially when several people were killed. Such actions exacerbate the already rampant poverty and destitution in urban areas, stretching the poor's coping strategies beyond every reasonable limit.

Poor housing. Although the Government has officially changed its policy from slum clearance to slum improvement, conditions remain virtually unchanged in most squatter settlements.

Most of the urban poor are deprived of a "decent house," defined by the National Housing Corporation as a structure comprising at least two rooms, a toilet, a shower and a kitchen (Odada and Ayako 1988). Data from a 1985 survey in Nairobi, Mombasa and Kisumu (Table 5.3) show that the very poor live in unhealthy and dehumanizing conditions. The poorest urban dwellings have mud floors, roofs made of grass and other low-quality thatching materials, and no provision for the disposal of human wastes. Waste disposal can actually be considered an index of a household's economic status: high-income households tend to have flush toilets whereas low-income households commonly rely on pit latrines or buckets, bushes or open spaces.

In 1985, about 51 percent of all urban dwellers of the nationwide sample did not have flush toilets. The lack of adequate sanitation and safe water is a major cause of water-borne diseases (typhoid and cholera). Access to safe water was particularly limited in Kisumu, where 63 percent of slum dwellers had no access to either private or communal taps and therefore had to buy water from vendors or resort to less secure water supplies, such as wells, boreholes, dams, streams, rivers and the lake. Improvements in the provision of water in slums are hampered by the lack of resources at the local government level. In addition, the uncontrolled growth of slum areas has meant that the worst conditions are found in the newest slums that have sprung up beyond older slums where basic services may have been provided (Government of Kenya and UNICEF 1992).

The inadequacy of garbage collection is also a serious problem. The City Commission charges Nairobi residents K.Sh 10 ($0.16) per garbage bin which each household is supposed to keep. Since garbage collection trucks do not visit some low-income areas, residents do not bother with the bins. Environmental deterioration has reached alarming proportions. Malaria is increasing (Odada and Ayako 1988).

This environment of economic deprivation inevitably breeds a sense of hopelessness and helplessness. The case history of a young migrant family in Nairobi exemplifies the situation of the most severely deprived:

> The family has no source of regular income. The man collects waste materials such as paper and tins for sale, while his wife, who was married when she was 15 years old and is now 27, sells fruit, vegetables, maize and beans outside their house. They live in Kiamaiko, a very poor section of the Kariobangi slum area of Nairobi. They now have five children (ages 8, 5, 4, 3 and 1 1/2 years). They all live in a rented one-room mud-and-wattle house. Three of the children sleep on old rags on the floor while the other two young ones sleep with their parents. The first child is in class one and the second is in nursery school, but most of the time the children are sent home due to lack of school fees.

Limited educational opportunities. Primary school enrolment levels are particularly low in urban slums. Although the Government abolished tuition fees in 1979 and provides free milk, non-tuition fees may still be more than what a poor slum family can afford. Enrolment in Nairobi stands at 63 percent and in Mombasa 64 percent, far below the national average of 95 percent in 1991. This situation is linked not only to an inadequate number of schools and classrooms, but also to the high dropout rates (traced to the inability to pay non-tuition fees, lack of interest, poor health, pregnancy, early marriage or the expectation in some families that children work to supplement the family's income) (Government of Kenya and UNICEF 1992).

Children in Mombasa, multiethnic and largely Muslim, have fared poorly in the national education system at all levels. Only 35 percent of children of nursery school age are in regular schools, a small percentage are in Koranic schools (*madrassa*), while the majority remain at home (Government of Kenya

and UNICEF 1989), often in situations of considerable risk to their health and
safety.

Review of the Literature on Survival Strategies

Children of migrants and refugees. Rural-to-urban migration over the last two
decades has resulted in the proliferation of squalid slums, with large numbers of migrants continuing their lives of abject poverty in the city (see Box
5.1). The urban poor constitute a large proportion of Kenya's economically
marginalized groups (Ikiara 1992). Their desperation is compounded by the
influx of refugees that Kenya has accepted since Independence: first, from
Rwanda and Burundi in the 1960s; then from Uganda and Sudan in the 1970s
and 1980s; and from civil wars and famines in Ethiopia and Somalia.

The majority of refugees are women and children, and most suffer from
chronic hunger and malnutrition. Many children are displaced orphans, and
generally lack access even to basic shelter. Ethnic clashes in Kenya have also
given rise to displaced children, making them refugees in their own country.
The few religious organizations assisting such children with food, clothing
and shelter lack the necessary resources. Without adequate shelter and
schooling, many of the children drift into street life, delinquency, prostitution, crime and drugs, thus swelling the ranks of CEDC in urban Kenya.

The very poor migrant families in urban areas are forced to rely on their
children's help for the economic survival of their households. Therefore,
demands are placed on children (for instance, child prostitution) that would

---

Box 5.1   A Migrant Woman and Her Children

E.W. is a Kikuyu single mother of four children aged 12 to 22. She has never been
married. She became pregnant with her first child while still in grade seven. She
lives in a one-room wood and cement house with three of her children, one of
whom has two small children herself. Her older son lives with friends in the
neighbourhood.

She came to Kangemi from Kiserian in Kajiado where she used to live with her
mother. She moved because her mother's small piece of land could no longer
sustain her and her children. Her mother had 15 children, some of whom live with
her while the others live in various parts of Kenya. E.W. had friends in Kangemi
and thought she could get casual employment there.

She is poor as she only earns about K.Sh. 500 ($8.03) from the sale of produce.
Her daughter, who reached grade seven but could not continue due to lack of
school fees, used to work as a housemaid but stopped when she became pregnant. Her older boy, who dropped out of school in grade six, only rarely finds
casual work as a farm labourer and often gets into trouble with the police.

E.W.'s major concern is that her two youngest children, who are still in school,
might not continue with their education due to her inability to pay the fees. Her
main aspiration is to be able to buy land one day, possibly in Kajiado, where she
could settle permanently with her children.

Source: Ndungu (1992).

not arise if they lived in rural areas. Children in low-income families put up with long hours of parental absence. In Nairobi and Mombasa, cases have been reported of children being locked in crowded rooms overnight in their mother's absence. Many children, especially girls, are denied an education because they are kept at home to cook, fetch water and take care of younger children.

Street children on their own. Compared with other countries, Brazil for example, the problem of street children in Kenya is still limited (Odada and Ayako 1988). Nonetheless, street children are found in most major cities. They fend for themselves, procuring their own food and shelter as best they are able. Most grow up in conditions of poverty and are vulnerable to sexual abuse. Some of these children, especially in Nairobi, come from female-headed households in slum or squatter areas. A number of them, like their parents, have illegal income-earning activities in the informal sector, such as prostitution, unlicensed hawking or brewing and selling of *changaa* (beer) (Government of Kenya and UNICEF 1992).

Working children. Child labour is becoming an issue in Kenya, but precise rates and well-documented knowledge on the reasons leading children to work are not yet available. It is assumed that, given the severe economic problems Kenya is facing, the numbers of children working in cities must be increasing, but only a limited number of case studies have provided detailed information. One problem is the "invisibility" of many working children, especially girls who are not "seen" as working when doing heavy household chores, but rather as carrying out what are traditionally women's activities.

Case studies illustrate that children's ages seem to vary from six to 15 years, and that many work for as long as 14 hours or more daily. The work involves domestic chores (especially for girls), and work in factories or in the informal sector, in food and grocery kiosks, for example, where they are at greatest risk of exploitation and abuse.

Working children generally must work to supplement their parents' income. Some are orphans or neglected children who have to work to survive. For this reason and because many of their workplaces are away from public view, it is not easy to deal with the problem.

Kenyan laws on child labour are vague and do not protect working children adequately. There are also problems relating to enforcement. In addition, most people likely to employ children are ignorant of the provisions of child labour laws (Kattambo 1991).

A study conducted in the Kibera area of Nairobi in 1985 found that of 50 working children, 48 percent were between 14–16 years of age, 36 percent between 11–13 years of age, 14 percent between 8–11 years of age, and only 2 percent between 17–19 years of age. The majority got up at 6 o'clock and went to bed after 10 o'clock in the evening. Asked why they were working, 30 percent replied "lack of money for school fees," 32 percent "poverty at home" and 12 percent "pregnancy."

Because they are dependent on adults, children are the most easily exploited of all workers. They constitute cheap labour since they are usually unaware of their rights and cannot organize themselves to demand better working conditions.

Children of imprisoned mothers. This is a special CEDC category: victims of their mothers' alleged criminality. From the moment a mother is arrested, often for minor infractions like illegal hawking or brewing beer, her child is exposed to abuse or neglect by the criminal justice process (Kattambo 1991). Children below four years of age with their mothers at the time of arrest often accompany their mothers to the police cells, to courts and then to prison. In the police cells, mother and child are often bundled together in filthy conditions with drunkards, prostitutes, thieves and other criminals, many of whom suffer from contagious diseases. There are no facilities away from the prison community where children can be treated as children, and they are often exposed to sexual abuse.

At four years of age, children are required to leave prisons. Where there are no relatives willing to care for them, they often face abandonment, drifting to the streets and into juvenile delinquency. Older children are left to fare for themselves in the slums. These children suffer from loneliness and hunger, drop out of school, and often end up on the streets.

Early pregnancy. Increases in adolescent pregnancies have been linked to a rise in premarital sex among adolescents (in addition to the custom of very early marriage), the erosion of traditional values, a drop in the age at menarche, lack of sex education, the desire of adolescent boys to prove their "macho" image, and so forth.

Most adolescent girls who become pregnant are unprepared for motherhood, leading to a major crisis in their lives. Because of their physical immaturity, they may have health problems and can even risk death. Illegal abortions carried out by unqualified people using crude implements also pose extremely serious health risks.

Pregnant adolescents tend to be stigmatized and even ostracized by their families. They may be forced to drop out of school or refused readmission after the birth. Many suffer from psychological distress. Some run away from their homes to hide in anonymous urban areas where, lonely, desperate and unemployed, they live in abject poverty, drifting all too easily into prostitution. They are thus vulnerable to sexual exploitation and are often exposed to sexually transmitted diseases.

Since the repeal of the Affiliation Act in 1969, Kenyan law does not impose parental duties on men who father children out of wedlock (Kattambo 1991). This leaves the full burden of maintaining children born out of wedlock to the mother, with devastating consequences, especially when the young girl is rejected by her family.

Child brides. Child brides are common among some ethnic groups in the Coast and North Eastern provinces. In the Muslim tradition, girls can be betrothed at birth, usually to a much older man, to be handed over at any time after puberty in exchange for a dowry. When pressure is not needed, it is simply because the girl has been made to understand from childhood that this is her future; thus, alternatives such as education are not taken seriously. Sometimes these marriages end in divorce or separation, leaving the young girl few options beyond the streets and prostitution.

Children and AIDS. According to the National AIDS Control Programme, 11,500 cases of AIDS orphans under 15 had been reported in Kenya by August 1991, a figure that may soar to 300,000 by 1996. It has also been estimated that, because of the number of AIDS deaths among children infected at birth, the under-5 mortality rate in Kenya will increase to 189 per 1,000 live births by the end of the century, the levels prevalent in the 1960s (Government of Kenya/UNICEF 1992) .

AIDS orphans constitute a special category of CEDC. Even when HIV negative, they are rejected by those who fear infection. When HIV positive, AIDS orphans run a higher risk of stigmatization and are neglected by even their closest relatives. Because fostering and adoption without a blood tie is rare, if these children are abandoned, they are unlikely to find the love and care they need, especially during the terminal stages of their illness (Black 1991a).

Children between the ages of 12 and 19 years are also particularly at risk of AIDS infection. Street children, child prostitutes, drug users and others in especially difficult circumstances are increasingly exposed to AIDS. A 1991 study of adolescents in Kenya found that over 50 percent were sexually active, most from the age of 13 or 14. The study also found that 89 percent of these adolescents never used any form of contraception.

There is an urgent need to confront the issue of children and AIDS. Legal provisions must be formulated to deal with problems of discrimination against AIDS victims in educational and other institutions (Kattambo 1991). An institutional framework is also needed to deal with AIDS children abandoned in hospitals. As the growing AIDS problem will put an additional strain on Kenya's already overstretched resources, emphasis needs to be placed on community-based management of AIDS.

Juvenile substance abusers. Kenyan law generally fails to address substance abuse and trafficking adequately, especially with regard to children (Kattambo 1991). Whereas alcohol abuse among children is controlled through the Traditional Liquor Act and the Liquor Licensing Act, statutes concerned with the sale and use of other dangerous drugs contain no provisions to deal with the exploitation of children in the production, sale or use of narcotics.

Drug abuse has been increasing at alarming rates, particularly among street children. This includes sniffing glue, inhaling petrol, chewing *miraa* and smoking *bhang*. Although glue and petrol are not classified as drugs or psychotropic substances, they have similar effects on the user and are often used by children.

The Children and Young Persons Act has conferred powers to the Children's Department and other offices to deal with the drug problem.

However, the Act's measures are at best curative, covering situations where children or juveniles have been caught buying, receiving, selling or in possession of dangerous drugs.

The Nairobi Study

Originally founded by the British during the construction of the Uganda railway in the 1890s and now Kenya's capital, Nairobi experienced explosive growth following political independence, which has resulted in 30 to 40 percent of its residents living in unplanned squatter settlements or slums. Although half of public housing funds are spent in Nairobi, the number of housing units built annually remains insufficient. Most of the shanty dwellers are either unemployed or underemployed.

According to Central Bureau of Statistics data (1992), 74 percent of the households in Nairobi are in either low or very low income groups and are therefore characterized as poor; moreover, the overwhelming majority of urban children come from poor families living in constantly deteriorating slums. Nairobi represents the extremes of Kenyan income groups. In fact "while more people are better off than anywhere else in the country, the poorest are worse off than anywhere else" (Lee-Smith et al. 1987).

When members of the Country Team initially prepared reviews of literature, they discovered that, aside from a few assessments and situational analyses, there was little information on Kenyan urban children in especially difficult circumstances, and what information there was had many gaps. Little was known about where these children came from, what their families were like, what induced some of them to work and others to drop out of school, and what led some of them to the streets or into conflict with the law. Furthermore, no clear information was available on how many such children there were.

The Team needed to document positive and negative coping strategies in order to identify households at greatest risk and be able to suggest preventive interventions. Finally, particularly little was known about the children's daily lives or concerns, or those of their parents.

In coordination with the new Nairobi Task Force for Children in Especially Difficult Circumstances and the UNICEF Urban Programme Officer, the Country Team thus engaged in two additional research projects. A first sample of children and parents was selected, and interviews were carried out in three nonformal schools (selected among the 18 operating in the city). These schools had been started by local women's and/or neighbourhood groups to offset the serious shortage of schools. Built as temporary structures on borrowed land, these schools have succeeded in obtaining government support for teachers' salaries, but their students are not "in the computer"; in other words, they are not officially accepted by the Ministry of Education for entry into secondary schools. In comparison with formal primary schools, which charge exhorbitant building fees in addition to fees for uniforms, books and examinations, these informal schools provide relatively inexpensive education (even though some of them are starting to require uniforms and are raising their fees).

The three schools were in three quite different slum areas. Kangemi, eight kilometres west of the city and only recently incorporated, has good housing in some areas and, because of its proximity to public transport, attracts tenants working in the city. It has a predominantly Kikuyu and Luhya population. Pumwani, in the eastern part of Nairobi, four kilometres from the centre, is Nairobi's oldest slum. Thayu, approximately ten kilometres north of the city, is in a well-established slum community surrounded by an open market and slaughter houses, mainly for goats. Many of the children's parents were vegetable vendors. These slum residents were mainly Kikuyus, but also Luhyas, Luos and Kambas. Together with this informal school sample, a control group of children in formal schools and a group of children from remand homes and approved schools were also selected.

In addition to the survey, a number of children and their parents were interviewed and a smaller number of life histories were collected. This research approach elicited much rich information, the main points of which may be summarized as follows:

- A high percentage of these schoolchildren lived in households with single mothers and with many other children (an average of six per household).

- While more than half of the children in formal schools lived with both of their parents, fewer children in informal schools (35 percent) lived in regular nuclear households, a number which decreased further in the national sample of street-based children or the children in remand homes and approved schools. Also, in the case of children in informal schools and remand homes, a much larger overall percentage of children did not live with their parents but rather with relatives and friends (Table 5.4).

- Similar differences emerged in an examination of who paid their school fees: mainly father or mother in the control group of children in formal schools; a much broader range of people in the other two cases (Table 5.5).

- Parents were predominantly both employed (or one should say underemployed but earning) in the case of the children in formal schools; this was less true in the other cases.

- The children in remand homes and the street-based children tended to be slightly older than the children in formal and informal schools.

- More girl children were still in school; school-leaving and dropping-out tends to be particularly marked in the older age groups.

- Most street-based children were working, the majority as scavengers or beggars. The children in remand homes and approved schools, mostly street-based children arrested for loitering or truancy, had similar occupations.

Table 5.4. Household Profiles of Street Children and Working
and Non-Working Children in Kenya
(Percentages, Unless Otherwise Stated, 1991)[1]

	Street children[2] (N = 634)	Children in remand homes[3] (N = 100)	School children living in family[4]	
			In non-formal schools (N = 284)	In formal schools (N = 30)
Main types of family (%)				
single mother	22.7	36	41	43
single father	6.7	4	7.7	3
two parents	29.5	29.6	35	53
no parent	9.8	0	0	0
friends and relatives	28	24	15	0
Child's average monthly per capita income level (K.Sh.)	493			
modal	300	103	121	0
range	10–3,000	1–1,100	2–400	0
Employed/underemployed (%)				
father	90	73	76	54
mother	73	62	60	64
siblings				
brothers	no info	18	21	20
sisters	no info	17	13	10
child	over 90	18	19	0
School (%)				
currently attending	13	100	100	100
formerly attending	67	0	0	0
never attended	20	0	0	0
Main economic provider (%)				
parents together	0	29	33	53
mother	84	36.7	41	43
father	6	3	8	3
friends and relatives	10	22	16.5	0
Child regularly contributes cash to family income (%)	15	25	57	0
Main types of parental relationship (%)				
married/cohabiting	10	26	35	53
father absent	90	56	51	40
Migrated to city from rural areas				
over last six years	71[5]	34	63	14
7–14 years		51	33	79
more than 14 years		15	4	7
Have relatives in rural areas	no info	73	89	77
Relatives visit household members				
often	no info	9	11	3
occasionally	no info	48	68	63
Household members visit relatives				
often	no info	14	10	3
occasionally	no info	41	56	73

[1]All assessments by child. [2]ANPPCAN (1991). The ANPPCAN large national sample analysed for the Ford foundation did not allow us to systematically differentiate between the street-based children living at home (67%) and those on their own in the streets (27% who live on their own in the streets 80% of the time). It should thus be considered a sample of mostly street-based children. [3]Onyango et al. (1992). Children in approved schools and remand homes often came from very disrupted households and had spent considerable time alone in the streets. The institutions surveyed were located in or near Nairobi. [4]Onyango et al. (1992). School children in three Nairobi urban poor neighbourhoods. [5]No breakdown by years of migration available.
Source: ANPPCAN (1991), Onyango et al. (1992).

- Far fewer of the children in formal or informal schools claimed to work. However, when questioned further, they often admitted to scavenging or begging. Work was increasingly identified as the only way to improve living conditions.

- In a similar vein, the money children earned was used mainly to cover food and clothing expenditures.

- Lack of food and clothing was a frequent complaint, especially in the case of children in formal schools, presumably in part because of the high costs of schooling.

Our research revealed the dark side of life in the slums of Nairobi. Children's basic needs are not met, and they frequently express concern about violence and fights within their households. Evidence of prostitution, a response to dire poverty and often at the instigation of the mother, and the recurrent arrests of mothers or fathers for illegally brewing beer, selling *miraa* or simply hawking vegetables (risking confiscation of wares and imprisonment for up to six months) was also frequently reported (Onyango et al. 1992).

The resourcefulness of both the children and their parents was often striking. A recent survey by the Mazingira Institute points to the persistent and increasing use of urban agriculture and livestock, despite an often unwelcoming municipal environment in which such strategies may be punishable by law (Mazingira Institute 1989). The same was true for the entrepreneurial hawkers arrested for vending in affluent areas where such activities are prohibited. Children do what they can — begging, scavenging in garbage heaps to collect rags, paper, plastic and bottle caps — to earn some money for food and clothing. And they still go to school, contending with double sessions because of severe overcrowding, often even forced to build their own makeshift schools, together with their mothers.

The girls had to cook and take care of younger siblings much more frequently than their male counterparts. In a few cases, they became part-time domestic servants in nearby well-to-do neighbourhoods. With the onset of menarche, they might be given in marriage or become pregnant and leave school. According to a detailed study of 166 schools throughout Kenya, the percentage of young girls getting pregnant and dropping out was particularly high in the urban informal schools (Kenyan Ministry of Health 1988).

The Kisumu and Mombasa Studies:
Helping Children and Families "Own" the Research"

Participatory action-research design

Data collection techniques selected for the Mombasa and Kisumu case studies enabled researchers to see the everyday life of children in especially difficult circumstances through the children's own eyes and from their own

Table 5.5. Employment, Schooling and Police Profiles of Street
Children and Working and Non-Working Children
(Percentages, Unless Otherwise Stated, 1991)[1]

	Street children[2] (N = 634)		Children in remand homes[3] (N = 100)	School children living in family[4] — In non-formal schools (N = 284)		In formal schools (N = 30)	
Range (years)	no info		6–20	6–18		7–13	
Mean age (years)	12.8		12.7	10.9		9.9	
Mode age (years)	12		12.5	12		10	
Gender							
male	91		52	49		40	
female	9		48	51		60	
Working before	0		19	10		0	
Working now	94		18[5]	19[5]		0	
Also studying	10		100	100		100	
Reasons for leaving school							
lack of money	56		N/A	N/A		N/A	
own volition	15						
family-related problem	14						
school-related problem	8						
Age started working (years)	8–13		9–11	9–10		0	
Main kinds of current work							
vending	18		3[6]	2.5		7	
scavenging	46		12	8		0	
washing/parking/ guarding cars	10		0	0		0	
begging	21		14	4.5		0	
Current employment type							
self-employed	ca. 50			ca. 80		ca. 80	
with employer	ca. 50			ca. 20		ca. 20	
Mean earnings (K.Sh.)	493		165	30			
Mode earnings	300		200	20			
Child contributes to family income	15		25	57		0	
Money earned used mainly for:							
household expenses	15		25	57		0	
food and clothing	74		50	43		0	
personal use (leisure/ smoking/drinking/cinema)	2		0	0		0	
Attended rehabilitation programme (remand homes mainly)	17		100	no info		no info	
Who pays school fees							
mother		59	36	45	74	56	96
father			23	29		40	
aunt or uncle			2	7		0	
sibling			2	6		0	
others			28	10		4	
n.a.			9	3		0	
Main types of problems							
food			15.6	19.5		23.3	
clothing			3.9	3.8		3.3	
shelter	60	40.5	10.1	2.8	43.4	3.3	46.5
poverty			10.9	17.3		16.6	
unable to attend school			3.9	5.2		0	
mistreatment			1.5	1.4		0	
missing parents			3.1	4.2		0	
sickness			3.9	0.3		0	

cont'd

Table 5.5. cont'd

	Street children[2] (N = 634)	Children in remand homes[3] (N = 100)	School children living in family[4]	
			In non-formal schools (N = 284)	In formal schools (N = 30)
Has been arrested	frequently	72	5.5	0
Number of arrests:				
1–2 times		85	100	0
3–4 times		13	0	0
5 or more times		2	0	0
Main reasons for arrest				
truancy	mostly	25	8	0
loitering	mostly	27	25	0
disappeared from home		14	33	0
mistaken		2.3	8	0
smoking *bhang*	sometimes	10.5	0	0
stealing	sometimes	6	0	0
vending stolen goods	sometimes	13	8	0
Opinion of neighbourhood	no info			
peaceful		8	22.8	20
violent		42	27	13
safe		8	12	23
unsafe		37.5	35.5	40

[1]All assessments by child. [2]ANPPCAN (1991). The ANPPCAN large national sample analysed for the Ford foundation did not allow us to systematically differentiate between the street-based children living at home (67%) and those on their own in the streets (27% who live on their own in the streets 80% of the time). It should thus be considered a sample of mostly street-based children. [3]Onyango et al. (1992). Children in approved schools and remand homes often came from very disrupted households and had spent considerable time alone in the streets. The institutions surveyed were located in or near Nairobi. [4]Onyango et al. (1992). School children in three Nairobi urban poor neighbourhoods. [5]Work activities including stealing car parts or smoking and selling bhang but not including housework. [6]Most answers in this column obviously refer to the past. Source: ANPPCAN (1991), Onyango et al. (1992).

point of view. These techniques are based on the belief that children can be encouraged to tell their own stories without inhibition once they realize that doing so can benefit them.

Participatory action research has several advantages, including a higher probability of data validity because participants generally express what they feel as they have a greater interest in the research. People can acquire useful skills, change their perceptions of themselves and also change their lives. This leads to higher levels of sustainability in projects.

On the other hand, precisely because participatory action-research can have an immediate and sometimes profound effect on participants, the question of data reliability has to be handled in a different way from survey research. In participatory action research — apart from relatively unvarying personal data such as name, sex or age — it is expected that people's views will change, especially on the more subjective indices the researchers might be interested in. A further difficulty relates to documentation. It is hard to communicate the authenticity of what took place to people who were not part of the process, largely because most of us have been brought up to believe that what can be said and put down on paper is more objective — and hence more accurate — than what may be communicated through less direct means, such as drama, poems or drawings. Nevertheless, it has not been found that these forms of communication require more interpretation than typical survey questionnaires do.

Participatory action research is in some ways the most difficult kind of research to carry out because it is so intense, involving and exhausting for both the researchers and the subjects. Research assistants, for example, need more support from the principal researchers. Yet participatory action-research is far more gratifying because it is truly a mutually enriching process.

The value of community action research and the importance of self-monitoring for communities, families and children

Perhaps the most serious drawback to conventional services for children in especially difficult circumstances is the hierarchical nature of their organization and delivery structures which puts a gulf between service designers and service implementers, and between service implementers and service users. Service implementers expect unquestioning compliance from service users (children and their families) on the assumption that whatever is being offered is for the user's own good. Service users usually do not share this assumption and tend to show their dissatisfaction with authoritarian treatment through resistance, noncooperation and their own styles of counter-exploitation and manipulation.

The researchers in Mombasa and Kisumu decided, instead, to offer children in especially difficult circumstances and their families an opportunity to assume responsibility for their own lives. They were asked, with the help of sympathetic service providers (both governmental and nongovernmental), first to analyse their problems and then to propose interventions, which would be implemented with municipal officials.

Mombasa and Kisumu, both smaller than Nairobi, provided a good opportunity for participatory action research. Their smaller size allowed for easy contacts between people and organizations, openness to new ideas, and thus opportunities for innovation. Moreover, problems in these cities have begun to develop more recently and are less entrenched. In addition, each has a UNICEF-supported programme with sound working relationships.

Mombasa, an island city on the shores of the Indian Ocean, is the second largest city in Kenya. It was known to Phoenician, Egyptian and Greek traders, and was alternatively a Portuguese and Arab settlement from the 1400s. Later the British took control of Mombasa, making it the capital of British East Africa until 1904. The city was occupied by the British until

Kenyan independence in 1963.

Mombasa is multiethnic, with a strong Muslim presence and a flourishing tourist industry. Children living there inevitably come under the influence of activities associated with ports of call: a transitoriness of life; easy money; access to drugs and alcohol; prostitution; exposure to a wide variety of cultures, styles of living, and social and moral values; and a proliferation of gaudy, appealing and not particularly wholesome entertainment.

Kisumu, the third largest city in Kenya, lies on the shores of Lake Victoria and has been an important port and railway staging post. Since the early 1980s, there has been a government policy of industrial investment in Kisumu. The city has a predominantly Luo population.

Three neighbourhoods were selected for research in each city.

Stages of the project

Workshops with service providers. Data collection began with a workshop for street educators, social workers, probation officers and police from the two cities in September 1990, during which instruction was given in conducting participatory action research. Officers and workers shared information on the communities in which they work. This experience formed the basis for the selection of the communities in which to train children.

The workshop was used to explore data collection methods, including drama, interpretation of photographs, focused group discussions, mapping, modelling, drawing and storytelling. Some of these techniques were also later used for the collection of individualized data, both from the 60 children initially selected and from those in the community to whom the researchers gained access.

In order to reach the service users most effectively, subsequent training workshops were also held in each city to teach municipal and NGO staff new approaches to problem-solving and techniques for transferring the skills acquired to those who need it most — namely the children, their families and communities. The emphasis was on ways of facilitating self-education by the children and families.

The purpose of the first workshop was to allow participants to review the situational analysis, which identified the children and the places where they were likely to congregate and provided estimates of their numbers. They were then asked to prioritize the problems and to envision potentials for change. The workshop enabled the researchers (Mutiso and Dallape) to gain an idea of the providers' perspectives and the children's problems. It gave the providers practice on conducting situational analyses, on how to survey the city, and on how to identify key types of problems and key problem children. It also trained them to see children as a source of information and gave them tools to elicit children's opinions.

Workshops with children led by service providers. Subsequently, two workshops, involving children in especially difficult circumstances from selected slum areas, took place in the two cities and allowed the service providers to put the new training into practice.

In Kisumu, the 42 participants, from 10 to 17 years, were asked to talk about what distressed them most. There were some common themes: lack of money for school fees or food, as well as drunkenness, gangs, insecurity, drugs and police harassment. The children saw their families as being very male-oriented: fathers were insensitive and domineering and misused money for drinking, gambling and womanizing, while mothers were generally powerless. The children's drawings presented images of what they wished family life was like — secure, lacking nothing and based on mutual respect. But the parents or other grownups hardly mentioned the children's problems (they had possibly come to take these problems for granted).

In Mombasa, the root problems the children identified were poverty, environmental influence and parental negligence, in that order. They called for more structure from their parents. However, they attributed their parents' negligence to poverty and spoke kindly of them.

The children were sensitive and sympathetic to their own plight and to that of others. They expressed a keen sense of justice and compassion, and generally believed that authorities should provide the necessary economic and physical environment for people to be able to lead decent lives. But they also felt that individuals should be unselfish, mindful of others, and ready to help themselves.

The children's responses underlined the negative effects of broken homes and fragmented families. The children realized that because of their family situation, they had no choice but to make sacrifices, such as working instead of going to school. In the same vein, they condemned the practice of child marriage. Finally, they sought their parents' protection from the corrupting influence of a degenerated social environment and wished their parents could somehow make a better life for themselves.

In both cities, the children also proposed constructive solutions. They selected a special project and made detailed plans for its realization. Projects included building a small bridge over a flood-prone stream so they could go to school without getting hurt on broken bottles and garbage; the allocation and preparation of land for a playing field; and a library. Meetings with the community were conducted by service providers in order to discuss the children's projects. The results were then presented by the children and service providers to local policy makers. These projects have become part of municipal planning and are being accomplished with the free labour of residents, as projected by the children, and with the municipal authorities' support and close collaboration.

Involving street educators and municipal programmers as facilitators

Much was also learned by the service providers who participated in the workshops. During the first workshop, they were required to reflect on what they knew about the children. This was achieved by various projective techniques, such as debates and role playing. Police and probation officers, for example, tried to imagine what it felt like to be a young child being arrested. This exercise allowed them to gain a better understanding of their role as "facilitators" and "enablers" rather than as solely "service providers." They realized that they needed to start trusting children and building upon their resilience and courage.

POLICIES AND PROGRAMMES

Context and Principal Actors

The situation of extreme hardship for disadvantaged children in Kenyan cities has, in many cases, been the result of policy decisions at national and international levels.

As indicated earlier, the progressive deterioration of the Kenyan economy coupled with the impact of structural adjustment policies in the 1980s has created severe pressures at household level and has diminished access to services such as education and health. The societal response — thanks to the still thriving spirit of *harambee* (cooperation and self-help) — has been to mobilize rural and urban neighbourhood groups to unite and contribute funds to put up schools and health centres. Women in particular have mobilized (Box 5.2).

At the political level, civil society is calling for democratization and a reform of the one-party system. People's collective action is increasingly seen as the most effective way of mobilizing the resources needed to counteract some of these downhill trends. Political reforms leading to increased pluralism and multiparty elections, however, face numerous obstacles.

At the same time, decentralization has been promoted since 1983, with mixed results. The district-focus strategy has aimed at integrating ministerial and other local development activities into the projects of the District Development Committees. Despite bureaucratic resistance, new trends have shifted the integration of local development, including NGOs, into elected (rather than appointed) local government authorities that can levy taxes and fees. With a multiparty system, it is hoped that such local governments, properly supported, will be able to provide a more participatory local development strategy.

National Tendencies

Services at the local level are provided by the provincial and district offices of the Ministries of the Interior, Education, Health, Technical Training and Applied Technology, and Culture and Social Services under ministerial

guidelines, as well as by
municipal departments
of Public Health, Hous-
ing and Social Services,
and Education. Fund-
ing is often heavily de-
pendent on the central
government and re-
quires complex coor-
dination across the two
local bureaucracies.

Children in difficult
circumstances are re-
ferred by police and the
justice system to the
Children's Department,
under the Ministry of
the Home Affairs, again
in the provincial offices.
The Children's Depart-
ment provides social

> **Box 5.2   Women's Groups**
>
> Women's groups in rural and urban centres
> of Kenya have been particularly active.
> There were 23,614 such groups in 1991
> whose activities ranged from agriculture and
> livestock production to marketing hand-
> icrafts and social welfare provision. About
> one third of these groups have been helped
> by NGOs, development agencies and other
> voluntary organizations, and many are
> beginning to make use of revolving loan
> schemes. They are also starting to include
> male participants. Quite variable in back-
> ground and composition, and occasionally
> beset by internal conflict, these groups do
> not necessarily include the poorest women
> who are, with their children, at greatest risk.
>
> Source: Palo-Okeyo 1988.

workers who follow up when possible at family level, and, in coordination
with the police, help assign children to juvenile courts or children's homes. In
the case of children in conflict with the law, after the juvenile judge's
decision, children are sent to national referral centres that assign them, according to available space, to the remand homes and approved schools run
by the Government. The children may thus end up far from their original
home, which can impede eventual family reunification.

Coordination between provincial officers and municipal departments is
often uneven and depends on the local good will of all parties involved.

Urban Basic Services

When the Kenya country office of UNICEF was opened in 1989, it started
focusing on urban programmes and progressively introduced, together with
its counterparts in the country, the Urban Basic Services (UBS) model which
had been developed in other countries to address the problems of a rapidly
growing population of urban poor, particularly the increasingly large numbers of deprived women and children. The model emphasizes the integration
of municipal and NGO services and improved municipal planning in collaboration with the urban poor. By 1991 the programme covered Nairobi,
Mombasa and Kisumu, with limited support to Nyahururu, Nyeri, Malindi,
Meru, Isiolo, Nanyuki and Nakuru.

Some crucial issues which hampered implementation of the UBS programmes were: (a) delays in the channelling of funds through the Treasury and

Ministry of Local Government (while rural districts received their grant funds within a month, municipalities had to wait from 8 to 10 months); (b) lack of clarity in the definition of municipal and central government roles in the provision of services, especially in Nairobi and Mombasa where two parallel staff cadres in health and social services operate (a provincial and a city Department of Health, a provincial and a city director of social services or social development officer); (c) lack of clear guidelines on the future of squatter settlements and on the role of major municipalities in the district-focus strategy for rural development; (d) inadequate staff in key areas such as health and financial management.

New opportunities have, however, been created with the establishment of the Department of Urban Development, incorporating a social planning section, within the Ministry of Local Government.

In the area of health, the UBS community approach has helped to increase immunization coverage (especially against measles and polio) in some Nairobi slums as well as in Kisumu. Nutrition programmes have been promoted in most major cities, often in collaboration with women's groups. School health programmes are ongoing.

Initiatives have also been taken to stimulate employment and education opportunities. Income-generating activities for women are being developed, including credit systems. Projects to support the training of preschool teachers in Kisumu and Nairobi and the integration of Islamic and secular preschool education in Mombasa have also been initiated.

Urban Basic Services Task Forces have been organized in Kisumu and Mombasa. In Nairobi, greater difficulties were encountered, possibly because of the size of the city, the numbers of NGOs there, and the political complexity of its slums. Continuing efforts have been made, with varying degrees of success, to facilitate and smooth collaboration between municipal officials, who rotate rapidly in Kenya, and local as well as national NGOs and women's groups. Changing the attitudes of local policy makers about the hidden potential of the human resources within the municipality, including local community resources, and the need to build on people's existing coping strategies and productive efforts, remains a major challenge for the programme.

Children in Especially Difficult Circumstances Task Forces

Soon after the initiation of the UBS programme, a CEDC programme was also launched. It aimed at: (a) improving the availability of information on CEDC; (b) developing a comprehensive national policy for children's welfare and development; (c) reviewing the effectiveness and relevance of existing legal machinery for dealing with CEDC and, when necessary, encouraging the development of more appropriate legislation; and (d) developing mechanisms for a more effective coordination between NGOs, government departments and municipal councils. It also endeavoured to generate ap-

Although the government has officially changed its policy from slum clearance to slum improvement, conditions remain virtually unchanged in most of Kenya's squatter settlements, and children continue to scavenge on rubbish dumps. *Credit:* Copyright Nation Newspapers Ltd., Nairobi, Kenya.

propriate new activities through which children and youth could find gainful employment, and gave support to community and NGO initiatives to establish alternative educational centres for children who could not afford conventional educational institutions.

A very successful CEDC Task Force was established in 1988–89 in Nairobi to coordinate children's services. It included representatives of the national Children's Department, the Law Reform Commission, the Prisons and Probation Departments and representatives of children's organizations such as the Undugu Society of Kenya, the Child Welfare Society, World Vision International and various homes for abandoned children. Very importantly, the Task Force also had representatives from the Nairobi City Commission. A situational analysis identified key problem areas, in part reflected in this chapter. This led during 1990 and 1991 to the beginnings of joint coordinated action and a system of joint referrals among children's organizations, children's institutions, and municipal and national officers, focused in eight city divisions both at community level as well as within 18 nonformal schools.

The joint analysis and planning mobilized Task Force members, who started to address the issues they had identified as urgent, such as the conditions of small children imprisoned with their mothers or of children left to survive in the slums by themselves while their mothers, often hawkers, are in jail. Both the Law Reform Commission and the Prisons and Probation Department initiated actions to deal with these problems. Court clerks, for instance, were trained as judges. Extra-mural penal employment alternatives (community service rather than imprisonment) were also implemented.

The Task Force is continuing, together with UNICEF, to give strong support to the 25 nonformal and community schools in Nairobi by providing books and simple equipment such as benches, chalk and blackboards. Loans are also given early in the school year to poor parents, mostly of street children, which can be repaid slowly.

The Task Force and UNICEF decided in 1992 to form a Children's Advisory Council within each city district as well as divisional and local councils in order to reach children more effectively. By 1993, 21 district children's advisory councils and eight local divisional councils had been formed in close collaboration with the Children's Department. These councils undertake rapid assessments to determine numbers of street children, develop rescue centres and mobilize local organizations and the business community. They are asked to work as much as possible in coordination with the Municipality and the UBS Task Forces (UNICEF Kenya Country Office 1993).

Similar task forces have been initiated in Mombasa and Kisumu with varying success, largely depending on the degree of cooperation they have been able to generate among the various partners.

Cooperation remains a problem. The Mombasa Children's Department, for example, organized a first seminar for street and slum children in 1991 with the local branch of a youth organization affiliated with the Association of

Family Planning of Kenya. The initiative was partially sponsored by UNICEF. However, municipal social service officers did not attend. A few months later, the municipal social services and education officers, challenged by this initiative, organized a special two-day seminar with *maskani* boys (who congregate in poor neighbourhoods, often for mischief) to discuss their special needs. It has since planned activities with the boys thanks to the cooperation of the local chiefs. In this case, officials from the Children's Department did not attend.

Each city has its own children's organizations and activities, often quite innovative. The Kisumu CEDC subcommittee, composed of five NGOs from key central government departments and the municipal council, is chaired by the municipal director of social services and is part of the UBS Kisumu Task Force. It has initiated activities on street children with Pandpieri Catholic Centre and two other NGOs. It is supporting innovative evening classes, similar to adult education classes, for working children, especially domestic helpers, who are mostly female. They had to adapt class timetables to the odd schedules of the girls and obtain permission from their employers, but the classes, established in four centres, are well attended. By early 1993, they had already reached about 200 children, some of whom were adolescent mothers.

To promote greater community empowerment and participation in dealing with CEDC issues and problems, the Mombasa CEDC Task Force formed community-level committees early on, similar to the ones in Nairobi, in close coordination with local community leaders, often Muslim. These committees have undertaken a door-to-door survey to identify out-of-school children, and have convinced local churches and mosques to provide facilities for nonformal schools. Four schools had started by 1993, serving a total of about 200 children.

The mobilization of the Task Forces has been facilitated by: (1) their involvement in the Urban Child Project, (2) the policy discussions during follow-up forums on its findings and (3) the attendance of key municipal and Children's Department officials at the October 1992 International Meeting of Mayors in Florence (UNICEF Kenya Country Office 1993).

The African Network for the Prevention and Protection Against Child Abuse and Neglect (ANPPCAN), a Pan African NGO with its headquarters in Nairobi, has done research and advocacy work related to children in especially difficult circumstances. Recently, ANPPCAN mounted a Community Organization training programme in Nairobi, which targets workers in slum communities. These workers come from NGOs as well as central and local government. The training programme is being carried out in collaboration with COPE and Misereor of Germany. The training programme uses street children as entry points into the slum communities, and it is hoped that it will be replicated.

The Kenyan Law Reform Commission, an active member of the Nairobi Task Force, has taken a lead, in coordination with the Children's Department, in drafting a comprehensive new Child Law in accordance with the Convention on the Rights of the Child. It was ready for tabling in Parliament in 1993. It has also called attention to the lack of implementation of a number of existing laws (Kattambo 1991).

In Nairobi, the work of the largest local NGO, the Undugu Society of Kenya, deserves special attention. Particularly striking for its innovativeness, Undugu illustrates the importance of learning by doing and of continuous experimentation as a way to ensure self-monitoring. The organization, which started as a children's drop-in centre, has moved into community work and has established a record of constructive interaction with different branches of the Government in education (including informal education), housing, community health and street girls. It is now entering a new phase of social mobilization at national level, in cooperation with UNICEF and other partners. It is often called on to provide guidance to NGOs in other municipalities and in other African regions. Its story reflects the potential in many other African organizations.

The Undugu Society of Kenya

The Undugu Society of Kenya (literally the "brotherhood and sisterhood society") was founded in 1975 by Father Arnold Grol, a Dutch Catholic priest in response to the specific problem of Nairobi "parking boys" (boys working on the streets). Initially offering shelter and individual assistance, Undugu has grown in less than two decades into a complex and successful organization, one of the most mature NGOs in East Africa. It now emphasizes improving the living conditions of low-income groups through employment, low-cost housing and community organization. It is dependent on donor funding, but also raises money through its production units and export store, and receives small contributions from local communities.

Adopting a developmental approach, Undugu has continually experimented in new directions and learned through trial and error. In the process, it has pioneered a number of innovative approaches. Its activities can be divided into phase one, 1973–78, typified by a more immediately responsive "curative" and welfarist attitude; phase two, 1979–85, a more preventive and community-based developmental orientation; and phase three, 1986 to the present, a greater emphasis on social mobilization, community empowerment and social transformation. Phase three also coincides with the Kenyanization of the management and staff (Fowler and Mbogori 1993).

Phase one, 1973–78

Street work (1975). In 1973, Father Grol, a keen observer, was struck by the plight of street children, apparently neither working nor attending school. Most of them, he was told, came from extremely poor families living in squatter settlements. To survive, the children begged, stole and engaged in other illegal activities. They were difficult to reach and were left largely to fend for themselves. Realizing that nothing was being done for these children, Father Grol started three youth clubs in the Makadara, Kariobangi and Mathare Valley slums and began generating interest among potential local and expatriate funders (Fowler and Mbogori 1993). In 1975, he was asked by a Dutch organization to help distribute blankets and clothing to these children. The limitations of this welfare approach were immediately evident. The street children took the "hand-outs" and sold them. However, the experience allowed Father Grol to gain the confidence of the children and to devise with them valid strategies (Dallape 1991).

Undugu continues to maintain contact with children on the streets. Some of its street workers are ex-street children (the "Undugu Scouts"), an extremely important resource because they inspire trust and because they have personally experienced a process of change and believe in it.

Reception centre (1976). Father Grol's car was actually the first "reception centre," and there was nothing the street boys liked better than to pile into it for a ride around the city. The car "was crowded, smelly and dirty but full of life and joy. [The street boys] talked freely among themselves and the social workers could learn a lot about them, just by listening and letting them talk. At the end of the tour we used to share a bottle of coke." (Dallape 1987). In 1976, a real open-door reception centre was built which offered children a hot meal, nightly shelter and a sympathetic ear. The children could get involved in recreational and gardening activities and were assisted by social workers who assessed the possibilities of family reintegration.

Basic education (1977). As Father Grol got to know the boys better, he frequently asked how he could best help them. He learned that most longed to go to school. Fabio Dallape, an Italian sociologist who worked with Father Grol and later became the second director of Undugu,[11] writes (1987):

> They see their present situation as a transitional one; they want to be like other people; they need to feel that one day they will have a real job. They don't want to remain the outsiders of society. They would like to join it and to be fully accepted.

While state schools exist in theory for all, most impoverished children are denied access to them. In the first place, many of these children lack the requisite birth certificate: their parents hadn't bothered to keep it, not seeing its utility. Secondly, many poor children cannot afford to pay the incidental expenses involved. In Nairobi, moreover, because of the unprecedented increases in the child population, primary schools are overbooked and families must reserve a place for their child five or six years in advance (in other words, at birth, if not conception)!

Poor children may also be discriminated against at school. They may be dirty and smelly. They may not have a place to do homework. Others are bored by the apparent irrelevance of what they are taught.

Realizing that educational programmes had to be developed that took the special needs of street children into consideration, Undugu started its Basic

Education Programme which by 1978 had already reached about 90 children between 12 and 15 years of age, school dropouts and slum residents. The project is still in operation. The children are taught basic numeracy and literacy skills and given vocational orientation. Called "schools for life," these nonformal schools offer a three-year curriculum with an optional fourth year instead of the regular eight years. Teachers try to make subjects relevant to the daily lives of children. One school, for example, has set up a tea kiosk to give children practical experience in business; others use vegetable gardens to introduce boys and girls to science, carpentry to teach them maths, and crafts to help them learn about the environment. During the fourth academic year (the basic skills year), children are given the opportunity to sample different types of occupations, including carpentry, sheet metal work, screen printing, tailoring, and so forth.

The Ministry of Education has officially approved Undugu's curriculum and pays qualified Undugu teachers. As most of Undugu's teachers are from slums and had no proper qualifications, they have received help in obtaining qualifications through in-service training so that they would be eligible for a government salary.

A Vocational Training Centre was also established in 1976, together with the Government, in Mathare Valley. Courses were given in carpentry, tailoring, car mechanics, handicrafts and masonry. The centre could handle up to 95 trainees and generated some income for the students.

Community Homes (1977). The first "home" was started after the police, in one of their night patrols, netted a number of street boys. Those who "escaped" made it known that they needed a place to stay, away from police harassment. Initially, Undugu thought that all of the children were orphans or abandoned or that they had migrated from distant areas. They later realized that most had some place they could stay, but remained on the streets for many reasons: perhaps because they hadn't made the amount of money expected at home; or because they had late "business" at cinemas; or simply because they enjoyed the freedom of the street and the camaraderie of a gang.

Eventually Undugu established three homes in low-income areas, which, together with the reception centre, had a capacity of 75 to 80 children. More recently it has also added a home for girls. Supervisors were advised to assume a "big brother" rather than a "father" or "teacher" role, and to encourage children to continue managing their own lives. In homes with skilful supervisors, it was found that children acted with a greater sense of responsibility. Thieving, for example, was greatly reduced. Unfortunately, not all supervisors were equally capable.

Many children asked to be admitted to these homes. In fact, mothers encouraged their children to go out on the street so that they could be taken into one of the homes: they had heard that children were given three meals a day (when at home they only had one), sent to school on full sponsorship, and even had their own beds.

But children in institutions lose their sense of individual responsibility and become dependent. Any breakage or loss of property, for instance, is none of their concern. If not watched, some children may eat more than their share of food. If something is missing, most will not ask themselves what to do about it. On the streets instead:

> The children are organized in groups, they suffer and enjoy themselves together, they earn enough to buy the food they like, to go to cinema once or twice a week and to have girl friends. They have to learn how to cope with the police whom they recognize whether they are in uniform or not. Our institutions could not offer those types of advantages, plus the freedom (Dallape 1987).

Another consideration is that most of these children were obliged to contribute towards the maintenance of their younger brothers and sisters. Institutionalizing them and preventing them from working could actually deprive other children of food. Moreover, since there are approximately 30,000 destitute children in Nairobi alone, only an insignificant number of children can be reached by such institutions, and at a high cost. It is also probable, as Dallape points out, that institutions do not reach the children most in need, but rather the children closest to the acceptable forms of social behaviour.

Other activities. Other projects included an adult education project in 1977; a school sponsorship scheme, with foreign donor funding and supporting 400 children at school by 1978; women's groups to foster income-generating activities such as group sewing and marketing; and a loan scheme which financed small-scale youth enterprises, including a jazz band and a radio repair shop, and offered financial and business advice. It is estimated that by 1978 about 1,000 individuals had gained directly and 2,200 indirectly from Undugu's initiatives (Fowler and Mbogori 1993). The activities of this first phase as well as Undugu's later evolution are shown in Figure 5.1.

Phase two, 1979–85

During this period, under the leadership of Fabio Dallape, Undugu retained many of its original programmes while developing a more community-oriented and less institutionalized approach, a dualism which eventually led, however, to financial and organizational problems. Through its contact with young people in slum areas, Undugu became more and more aware of the importance of collaborating closely with families, which led to a change in the organization's approach. It set up a comprehensive community development programme to attack some of the factors that produce street children while helping to upgrade community conditions. This programme included education, work and shelter.

Informal sector training (1982). The experience of the Vocational Centre in Mathare Valley had taught Undugu that its training course, as it stood, had not succeeded in helping graduates to start their own businesses (at the time, less than 20 percent of the centre's graduates were self-employed). The setting was too school-like and did not encourage the students to acquire additional life and business skills, such as the ability to purchase materials, assess the reliability of clients, achieve a cost-effective use of time and materials, control the quality of production, deal with banks, plan for loan repayments, and so forth. In part inspired by an approach pioneered by the Christian Development Education Services, Undugu developed links within the community and made the collaboration of the artisans and parents an important element of their training programme.

At the end of the programme, for instance, the students are given a list of 200 artisans who are willing, for a reasonable fee, to take them on as apprentices. After identifying an artisan to their liking, the children, together with their parents, and often facilitated by the Society, negotiate the fee paid directly to the artisan. Undugu provides financial assistance, if needed (Dallape 1991). The apprenticeship scheme has proved to be an advantageous arrangement for both parties: the artisans have gained prestige, free labour and a modest fee; the children, "hands-on" experience.

The technical support of Undugu personnel has also been very important. Instructors normally visit children in their place of work to prepare them for the state trade examinations. At times, they have suggested, and helped to secure financing for, technical upgrading, such as new tools and the rewiring of electrical machines, which help improve the training conditions. Artisans and apprentices seldom miss a lesson from a visiting instructor. The business skills learned have had a tremendous impact on the development of the informal sector.

A 1986 evaluation traced many of the 66 former apprentices trained during 1984–86 and found that 74 percent were self-employed, a clear indication of a highly successful venture. The numbers of students trained in the apprenticeship scheme have eventually exceeded those trained in Undugu's more formal vocational centre (Fowler and Mbogori 1993).

There were other important initiatives. The Undugu shop (1982) and export unit (1983) were set up to provide marketing outlets for handicrafts, and women's groups were trained. Undugu has helped form a cooperative of metal workers and loaned them the money to open a distributorship through which workers can purchase materials on credit and at a much reduced price.

Another important initiative is the business advisory service (1984) which offers training to individuals by a qualified business educator. It is a common assumption that if people are given capital they can do business, but Undugu has learned that capital is only one element needed. A simple training course is offered, covering such essential topics as public relations, marketing, purchasing of materials, pricing, entrepreneurship, financial management, planning and quality control. Undugu then provides a link to banks, giving references for small businessmen who have attended Undugu courses and thus guaranteeing their loans. A full-time officer is in charge of repayments.

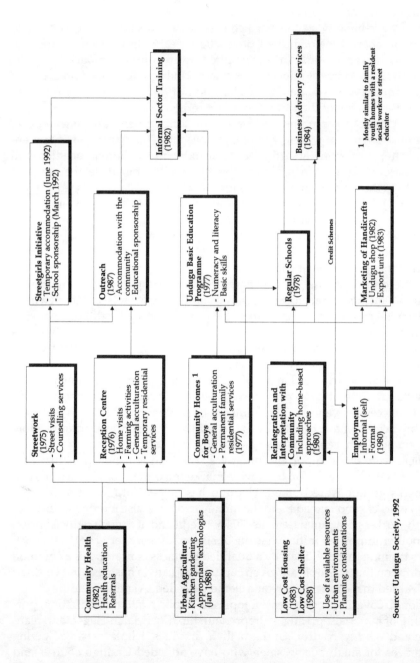

Source: Undugu Society, 1992

Figure 5.1. Undugu Society of Kenya: programme activity chart and dates of expansion.

Low-cost housing (1983) became, during this period, another concern. At first the organization was hesitant about getting involved in housing projects, believing them to be beyond the ken of NGOs. A fire that destroyed over one hundred plastic huts, "igloos" as they are called, in a Nairobi slum provided a unique opportunity to intervene. Undugu, with the consent of the local authorities, organized young people and their families (mainly mothers) to rebuild their houses, not with plastic but with the traditional timber and mud. Undugu offered the basic materials and the people did the work. After the first hundred houses were replaced, other "igloo-dwellers" asked for assistance to build more permanent houses. At this stage, the services of a land economist were procured and every step of the village was planned, from the cluster position of the houses, to roads, water drainage, water points, tree planting, the position of toilets and gardens near the river bank and access for cars and ambulances (often a critical need).

The housing scheme was nominated for an award from HABITAT, the United Nations Organization for Human Settlements, and was considered a valid starting point for slum improvement with people's participation. The University of Nairobi, in cooperation with Undugu and other NGOs, then began studying possibilities of multi-storeyed houses built with locally available, low-cost materials and with the full participation of people. Undugu had learned that a housing scheme in the slums could be viable only if the houses were built on a loan basis and the costs kept low enough to allow people to pay back their loans. By 1986, Undugu had assisted in building 1,068 slum dwellings.

Community health programme (1982). Initially, Undugu social workers could do little more than accompany street children to hospitals to ensure that they were not refused treatment. Trying a more preventive approach, the organization gradually organized one-day workshops on special health problems such as drug abuse, but these were:

> not very efficient (at least from the visible result on the behaviour of the children): many of them knew that the use and abuse of drugs was not good for their health, but they did not care. Whether they had a short or long life did not make a difference to them (Dallape 1987).

Undugu also trained mothers on basic health care. An attempt was made to reach more women by asking participants to share the information they had gained. This project was only 50 percent successful, however, as the mothers, although they learned some important health principles, did not have the time to share their knowledge with others.

Approaching the problem from yet another angle, Undugu began including health instruction in the nonformal schools. Children were taught about common diseases and possible preventions, and it was found that they could learn some of the basics such as the use of rain water, the need to use toilets, protection from insect and mosquito bites and a more balanced diet (in slums, people spend a lot of money on soft drinks). However, it was also found that people feel a sense of powerlessness about disease; they will fight for food, but not to prevent disease. Another lesson learned was that a preventive method works if it is simple, understood by the people and inexpensive. Solutions will be found by the people themselves once they are informed of causes (Dallape 1987).

It has been estimated that in 1986 there were about 2,300 direct and 6,800 indirect beneficiaries of Undugu's work, about 5 percent of the total slum population of Nairobi (Fowler and Mbogori 1993).

Phase three, 1986 to the present

Starting in 1984–85, the organization went through a process of self-analysis. After two expatriate directors, a Kenyan with long experience in the field of development, Ezra Mbogori, was chosen for both symbolic and practical reasons as Executive Director in 1988, and the organization's main base was shifted even more firmly to slum areas.

Overall the Undugu Society of Kenya now aims at:

- raising the socioeconomic status of people in low-income areas through an integrated approach to community and small-scale business development;

- enhancing the sense of responsibility of people in low-income areas for their own development;

- providing non-financial assistance to organizations involved in similar activities;

- progressively reducing dependence on donor funding;

- influencing official policy through innovative approaches that are cost-effective and replicable (Fowler and Mborogi 1993).

The street girls initiative (1992). Reflecting the organization's growing sensitivity to gender issues, the street girls initiative has recently been started to provide temporary accommodation, school scholarships and counselling on sexually transmitted diseases, particularly AIDS, to this most vulnerable group. Street girls, especially if sexually exploited or already mothers, are generally "unmarriageable" and therefore need to learn to maintain themselves financially.

Street girls are often already drug addicts and many have experience of earning incomes of K.Sh. 500–700 a day ($8.00–11.25) through prostitution. The organization initially tried to interest the girls in producing handicraft items for sale, but fast discovered that they were bored by such "tedious" traditional skills as sewing and knitting. Undugu also had difficulty finding markets for the handicraft items.

Special strategies were obviously needed. One successful approach has turned out to be camping excursions involving strenuous activities, such as mountain climbing. This kind of undertaking focuses on character building and restoration of self-worth, enabling the girls to develop a new perspective on their lives.

Community organization. The DELTA (Development Education and Leadership Training for Action) method which was at the core of the "Training for Transformation" methodology provided a structured way[12] to strengthen communication, to stimulate joint problem-solving and to facilitate participatory planning. This generated further efforts to support business development and employment generation.

Loan scheme. Undugu has recently implemented an expanded two-tier loan scheme which requires only 10 percent collateral and relies on a system of local referees (for loans below or above K.Sh. 2,000 ($32) who became social guarantors. Eligibility for higher loans requires participation in a business management course (there is a course for illiterate people as well) and authorization by a Business Review Committee. Loans almost doubled in 1989 (167 loans from 1978 to 1989, for a total of K.Sh. 720,000, $11,570). Loan repayment stands at 75 percent (Fowler and Mbogori 1993).

Urban agriculture. Undugu is currently giving strong support to urban agriculture, arranging for the cultivation of areas along river banks (1 metre by 10 metre strips perpendicular to the river edge, allocated by community committees) and providing small loans for the purchase of tools and seeds. Repayment rates have so far been 100 percent.

Low-cost shelter combined with slum upgrading (sewage, drainage, sanitation, trees, public spaces) has continued to be an important focus. Undugu's staff argue that community-created low-cost shelter is the "mother" of other self-improvement activities.

Throughout, Undugu has remained very innovative, learning by doing. It has acquired valuable experience in developing and financing the business activities of urban poor entrepreneurs; and because of the applicability of its approach, it has been hired by international organizations to help plan projects promoting the urban informal sector. In addition, because of the organization's experience in designing low-cost community-based shelter and coordinating slum-upgrading projects, it has been asked by the Government to recommend new building regulations covering the use of low-cost materials and alternative designs; to make proposals for the reform of land tenure laws; and to suggest approaches to gentrification (Fowler and Mbogori 1993).

The organization has, in its mature phase, also become more independent from international funders and more determinedly preventive. Confident in the expertise it has developed during the years, it is taking a new and stronger advocacy role. Despite growing pains, its various departments remain flexible and committed to the communities for which they are working. Staff members receive DELTA training and head office staff are encouraged, on a rotating basis, to maintain field-level contacts. The point of integration is thus provided by the organization's interaction with communities and individuals rather than by its formal organizational structure.

At the same time, the organization keeps a centralized and stringent order in financial affairs.

CONCLUSIONS

As the research has illustrated, the social and economic conditions of poor Kenyan families and children in rural and urban areas worsened during the 1980s. Larger numbers of poor urban women and their children, often on their own, are now moving to cities where they face seemingly insurmountable problems. Mothers and fathers are forced to leave their children alone in makeshift shelters while they struggle to feed their family. The children themselves share in the work. Responsible beyond their years, they voice concern for shortages of food and clothing and for the deteriorating environment.

The resilience and resourcefulness of families in the face of adversity have emerged as the most impressive finding. Residents of squatter or slum neighbourhoods have developed many coping strategies, including voluntary grassroots organizations that pull together some of the existing resources and address some of the most urgent problems. Civil society is also starting to come to the rescue.

However, the daily needs of the urban poor are still basically ignored. Planning by-laws and other regulations put houses far beyond economic reach. Sanitation regulations forbid the use of pit latrines, even when no healthy alternative is available. Faced with exorbitant water installation fees, poor families must pay for water from a kiosk at rates that far exceed those paid by the better-off city residents and then usually carry it long distances. Vendors regularly have their wares confiscated and are arrested and imprisoned for up to six months. Their children may be left unsupported in the slums. Urban agriculture is outlawed, despite its very real potential for raising the quality of life. In the vitally important area of education, despite a shortage of state schools, especially in large cities such as Nairobi, community and nonformal schools are still struggling for government recognition.

The recently introduced UBS and CEDC programmes have creatively drawn upon existing strengths and entered into effective partnerships with government. Nongovernmental organizations and people's organizations in poor urban neighbourhoods are learning to sustain the efforts of poor urban residents and their children to overcome some of the problems they face. At the same time, mature NGOs such as the Undugu Society of Kenya have developed expertise that gives them an impact even at a legislative level. They have shown how much can be achieved, despite limited funds, by listening to the children and their families, responding to their felt needs and helping them to resolve their own problems. It is hoped that enough of those voices, in a climate of renewed democracy, will help transform the way municipalities interact with their poor residents, be they adults or children.

NOTES

1. Different authors have contributed to this chapter. The section on the Kenyan economy is based largely on papers prepared for the Urban Child Project of the UNICEF International Child Development Centre by M. Manundu in 1991 and 1992. P. Onyango, with a team of skilful researchers, carried out the research and provided the information on Nairobi. She also shared with us the findings of important ANPPCAN studies and made comments on sections of the chapter. The section on the Undugu Society of Kenya draws on two principal sources: (a) a paper prepared for the Urban Child Project by Fabio Dallape in 1992 and his 1987 book entitled *An Experience with Street Children*; and (b) a paper by A. Fowler and E. Mbogori, entitled "A Case Study in NGO Urban Community Development: The Undugu Society of Kenya," forthcoming in 1993. E. Mbogori kindly made comments on the final text.

2. Only nine African countries are now middle-income countries: Botswana, Cameroon, Cape Verde, Congo, Côte d'Ivoire, Mauritius, Senegal, Swaziland, Zimbabwe.

3. These trends have occurred despite the fact that the Kenyan Government has not diminished its capital expenditure in agriculture since 1971 (in contrast to most other African countries) and that Kenya's formal credit institutions are required to advance at least 17 percent of their loans to the agricultural sector (again, unlike other African countries). Yields and inputs remain low, even though slightly higher in estates than on smallholdings and there has been little research on African food crops such as sorghum and millet.

4. In 1965, manufacturing contributed 9 percent of GDP in sub-Saharan Africa compared to 14 percent in South Asia, 19 percent in middle-income countries, 23 percent in Latin America and 27 percent in East Asia. By 1988 the manufacturing portion of GDP had barely risen to 10 percent in most countries in Africa compared to 17 percent in South Asia, 24 percent in middle-income countries, 27 percent in Latin America and over 30 percent in East Asia. At the same time, the share of manufacturing in GDP was stagnant or had declined in a number of African countries during the 22 years from 1965 to 1987, while in others manufacturing registered a larger share only because GDP itself was dropping rapidly, as in Zambia. Generally, the level of industrialization measured in this way has been fairly low in much of Africa.

   In terms of growth rates, African industry did fairly well during the period from 1965 to 1980 (8.8 percent per year). Although the initial base was small, it is clear that the first flush of import substitution that had been built on aid and revenues from the generally booming primary product exports was vigorous. In this period South Asian manufacturing rose at 4.5 percent per year, Latin American at 6.8 percent and East Asian at 10.7 percent. From 1980 to 1987 the growth rate for manufacturing in Africa fell to 0.6 percent, while the rate in South Asia climbed to 8 percent. East Asia kept up a healthy 10.4 percent, but Latin America, beset by debt problems, fell to the same rate as Africa, 0.6 percent. Nor did industry generate much employment. Except for Mauritius, employment in manufacturing accounted for less than 20 percent of all wage employment, which in itself is only a small part of total employment. This share remained constant or decreased during the recessionary years of the 1980s (van Ginneken and van der Hoeven 1989, Cornia et al. 1992).

5. Demand was high in Kenya in 1989, with domestic demand for products constituting 70 percent of industrial growth. The drop in domestic demand therefore had a considerable effect on industrial growth (Cornia et al. 1992).

6. Even a booming export-oriented economy such as that of Thailand has managed well until now by relying passively on imported technology for most industrial needs. It is over the long term, as the industrial infrastructure grows in importance, that research and development becomes a significant factor in competitiveness (Cornia et al. 1992).

7. Politically, this model was inspired by the populism initiated in the KANU manifesto issued immediately before Independence and the Sessional Paper No. 10 of 1965 on African Socialism and Its Application to Planning in Kenya (Manundu 1992).

8 . Generally, the ISI strategy is justified on the infant-industry argument — that is, protection from imports is needed to make it worthwhile for Kenya to establish industries since domestic markets are too small to allow for the realization of economies of scale. Hence, it is assumed that, as the domestic market expands over time, the protected (or "infant") industries will grow, and thus be able to exploit economies of scale and lower costs. As they become more competitive on the world market, protection can gradually be eased.

9. The IMR dropped by as much as 18 percent between 1979 and 1989 and U5MR from 180 (in 1979) to 105 per 1,000 live births in 1989.

10. Because census data are not disaggregated by municipal areas, these calculations are somewhat tentative. We do know, however, that the 0–18 population represented between 40 and 60 percent of the population of urban areas by 1992 and was growing rapidly.

11. Father Grol, a Dutch priest, was assigned to a Nairobi Catholic parish after a brief period in Dar es Salaam, a one-year course in social development in Uganda and about 20 years in the Tanzanian rural hinterland. Fabio Dallape had extensive experience in African development.

12. One initial week with periodic follow-up seminars.

Chapter
SIX

Italy: Where Are Children on the City Agenda?[1]

Laura Solito

INTRODUCTION

The emergence of Italy as a wealthy industrial society has led to significant changes in the living conditions of children. The postwar period has witnessed a considerable decline in the infant mortality rate, broader access to schooling and child care, wider availability of services for families and children, and longer life expectancy. There has also been a continuing decline in the country's birth rate, a phenomenon which has had, as we shall see, both positive and negative consequences for children.

However, despite these overall improvements, there are still troubling levels of hardship and risk. One need not fully agree with the extreme view that "social concern for childhood is more an ideological construct than an actuality" (Sgritta 1988), but it cannot be denied that numerous deep-rooted problems remain unresolved. There are still too many young people in institutions, too many mistreated or neglected children, too many cases of deprivation.

At the same time, new and serious problems linked to the modern urban society are emerging. These include new forms of hardship — particularly of a psychosocial nature — arising from broken families, deepening solitude and lack of social interaction, insufficient services, and a shortage of facilities for recreation and socializing. These hardships and the developmental constraints that Italian children face nowadays are largely unknown or poorly understood.

The media, which could be an extremely valuable resource for promoting awareness of the problems and for shaping public opinion, instead most often offers sensationalist news, providing the public with little more than a partial and superficial picture that overlooks the numerous and increasingly complex difficulties striking at the child's world. A good example is the recent attention directed at violence and child abuse. Though valuable for contributing to the awareness of these issues, it can distort our perception of the problems. Violence is one, but by no means the only one, of the difficult circumstances faced by children, and overemphasizing it risks misconstruing a situation that affects "on the whole, a modest number of children and families in Italy" (Statera 1990). It also shifts attention away from numerous other equally serious problems.

A report by *Centro Studi Investimenti Sociali* (CENSIS — Research Centre for Social Investments) on child-related articles appearing in two leading Italian newspapers (*La Repubblica* and *Corriere della Sera*) in 1988 and 1991 shows that these stories most often contained "hard" or sensationalist news: this was so in 56 percent of the articles in 1988 and 52 percent between November 1990 and November 1991 (Manna 1992). Furthermore, information on existing legislation about children and, even more so, on issues such as health, school and recreation, was seldom reported (Table 6.1).

In order to fill in a more accurate picture of the child's world we must analyse how the issues connect to a broader societal context rather than focus on specific occurrences. We must develop appropriate indicators and an effective, integrated monitoring system that will organize existing secondary data, identify problems, and prioritize root causes. Effective monitoring will then facilitate the search for new approaches and provide impetus for programmes well targeted at solving the most urgent problems. To initiate this process, the Urban Child Project in Italy proposed:

- to study the living conditions of children in urban areas, identify related problems, and propose plans of action;

- to promote social policies and the mobilization of resources at both national and local levels to improve the living conditions;

- to stimulate and influence public opinion on the fundamental problems.

In its first three years, the Project focused first on the analysis of secondary information and the creation of databases on the condition of young people

Table 6.1. Child-Related Topics Most Frequently Reported in Articles from *Corriere della Sera* and *La Repubblica* (November 1990 to November 1991)

Article topics	(N = 667) %	Breakdown of topics relating to difficult situations	(N = 346) %
Children in difficult situations	51.9	Accidents	28.7
Social issues	12.9	Mistreatment	
Culture and school	8.4	by family members	14.7
Children in positive situations	7.4	by outsiders	6.6
Effects of television	5.8	Sexual violence	9.2
Related legislation	4.8	Abduction	9.2
Institutions	4.6	Adoption problems	8.7
Other	4.2	Neglect	7.8
		Psychological abuse	6.1
Total	100.0	Children and drugs	5.5
		Other	3.5
		Total	100.0

Source: CENSIS (1992).

in Italy and in selected cities. Team research was also carried out in specific urban contexts: both old city centres and new satellite housing developments in Naples, Palermo and Milan. The Project is now focusing on facilitating the mobilization of human and institutional resources on children's problems at the municipal (*comune*), provincial and regional level, the three critical administrative levels of intervention.[2]

This chapter presents a summary of the knowledge so far obtained, identifies the pressing needs, and provides the basis for the formulation of a more thorough diagnosis of the problems and an analysis of alternatives. It identifies the current policies in the three cities and the highest priorities for action. It then assesses the effectiveness of some of the most innovative programmes. Particular attention is given to those programmes which: (1) strengthen the ties between children and their families and (2) stress coordination within and among government and nongovernmental services (Section IV). The last two sections illustrate future constraints and opportunities.

GROWING UP IN ITALY: DEMOGRAPHIC, ECONOMIC AND SOCIAL CHANGES

Broad changes and profound socioeconomic transformations have occurred in Italy since the end of the Second World War. Up to the late 1940s, large parts of the Italian population were still rural and only a few concentrated centres of industry existed. Today, according to the Organisation for Economic Co-operation and Development (OECD), Italy has the world's fifth largest economy (OECD 1992). The social benefits of this rapid transformation, however, have not been evenly distributed; indeed, economic development has, in some cases, further widened the disparity between the wealthier North and poorer South. At the same time, industrialization and urbanization have strongly shaped the country's demographic trends. Italy's population is now older and the average birth rate has dipped below zero population growth.

An Aging Population and a Changing Family

The changes that have most affected children concern first and foremost the family. With intensified urbanization and industrialization, extended family relations have diminished in importance and the caring support of grandparents, aunts, uncles or cousins is often less present for the child. At the same time, there has been a steady decrease in the proportion of young people (Figure 6.1). From the late 1960s to the mid 1980s the proportion of young people under the age of 20 fell from around 30 percent of the population to under 20 percent (United Nations 1990). Live births fell from 931,000 in 1960 to 568,000 in 1990.

Between 1951 and 1981 the number of households nearly doubled, to 20,216,000, with an annual increase of 1.53 percent. But the population grew by only 19 percent, an annual increase of 0.58 percent. In other words, households became much more numerous but considerably smaller.

According to the *Istituto Nazionale di Statistica* (ISTAT — National Institute for Statistics), from 1961 to 1988 the average number of household members dropped across the country from 3.6 to 2.8 per household, with families in northern and central Italy in 1988 smaller on average (2.7 members) than those in the South (3.1 members). Similarly, two-person households are the most common in the northern and central regions (25 percent) and four-person households in the South (25.6 percent). Between 1981 and 1988 the number of large families (five or more persons) decreased considerably, from 5.4 percent to 3.1 percent, while one-person households rose from 17.9 percent to 21.2 percent. Again, notable differences separate southern Italy from the North and central regions. Overall, 16.6 percent of southern families have five or more members; the corresponding figure for the rest of Italy is 7.5 percent (ISTAT 1991a).

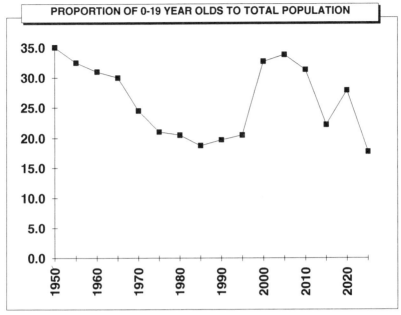

Source: UNITED NATIONS, 1991

Figure 6.1. Proportion of 0–19 year olds to overall population. Source: United Nations (1991b).

These changes in household size can naturally affect the living conditions of young children both positively — by potentially allowing more individual care and attention — and negatively: smaller families and fewer children mean that many children are growing up without siblings. Over time, moreover, a smaller proportion of children may result in reduced political support for them.

The reduction in family size and the changes in types of households are linked to Italy's low birth rate. The decline in the birth rate started some 20 years ago, but has become even more marked in the 1990s. Data from the United Nations indicate that Italy's fertility rate, at 1.3 children per woman, is the lowest in the world (United Nations 1992); if this trend holds, demographic projections suggest that the country's population will decline by 6 percent over the next 30 years. The reasons for this are still being debated.

The higher incidence of women working cannot fully explain this phenomenon; other industrialized countries where women have been active in the labour force over a longer period have not experienced such dramatic declines in fertility. One factor may be the relatively high unemployment rates for young adults in Italy. For this and other reasons, perspectives on marriage may be changing, and less importance attached to raising a family. At the same time, when the decision is made to have a child, even if much later than for earlier generations, greater value may now be placed on establishing a more exclusive relationship between parent and child, with greater emotional investment.

Economic pressures on the family must be viewed in relation to the role of the State. This period of rapid industrialization has been accompanied by reductions in social programmes for families. Expenditures for family-related services compare unfavourably to related expenditures in other European countries. For example, Italy earmarks only around one percent of GDP on family-support programmes; France's share is 2.4 percent. Furthermore, the Italian tax system has shifted back to considering each individual as a taxable unit, thus not providing families — particularly those with children — with preferential tax breaks. Italy is now considering changes in some of these areas to encourage a higher birth rate. Smaller families with fewer children, however, do not provide the public sector an excuse for playing a diminished role. Changing family structures and relationships mean new problems and risk factors. Policy makers, especially considering the severe restraints of public finance in Italy today, must take steps — and soon — to ensure that available resources are not squandered and to respond effectively to the modern dilemmas faced by children.

Income

In the years immediately after the Second World War and in the years following the economic boom of the 1960s, Italian households enjoyed a substantial growth in income, although the benefits were not evenly distributed. The regional differences are especially noteworthy: in 1985, average monthly income for families in northern and central Italy (about 2,400,000 lire or $1,630) was nearly 25 percent higher than family incomes in southern Italy. Given the average larger size of southern families, this gap in family incomes is even more significant.

The 1980s saw a general worsening of the family's economic situation. From 1978 to 1983 the number of families living in poverty increased, particularly for one- and two-person households and households with five or more persons (Table 6.2). In 1983, 20.4 percent of people living below the poverty level were under the age of 14; in the South, the figure stood at 24.2 percent (Commissione Povertà 1985).

Family stability

Despite widespread claims that the family is in danger, statistical data demonstrate that the Italian family is still quite stable, particularly when compared with families in other EEC countries or in the United States.

Table 6.2. Households Below the Poverty Line by Family Types and
Percentage of Total Population[a,b]

No. house-hold members	1978	1980	1983
1	18.1	13.3	15.5
2	12.1	10.1	12.5
3	6.6	4.2	7.0
4	7.7	7.7	9.2
5	13.1	11.3	n.a.
6 or more	18.4	18.0	19.0
Total	11.0	9.4	11.3
Absolute nos. (thousands)	1,918.5	1,680.1	2,114.1

[a]Elaborated on the basis of an ISTAT analysis of household consumption. [b]In order to compare households of different sizes, an equivalency scale was used. Source: Commissione Povertà (1985).

Marriage rates have now returned to the early 1980 levels in Italy, as in all EEC countries, after a slump in the middle of that decade. However, what sets Italy apart, at least for the time being, is the relatively small number of marriages that end in divorce, which was legalized in 1973. In fact, Italy has the lowest divorce rate among EEC countries (Table 6.3), although the number of divorces per one hundred marriages more than doubled between 1980 and 1987 (3.2 to 6.5). Households in which wives did not have an outside job accounted for only 39 percent of the divorces in 1987 (Saraceno 1990).

Legal separations — the first step in filing for divorce under Italian law — nearly doubled from 1975 (19,132) to 1987 (35,205) (Barbagli 1990); here, as well, figures for Italy are lower than in other Western countries — but the gap is narrower than it is with divorce. The ratio of common law marriages, or unmarried couples living together, is particularly low in Italy: only 1.3 percent in 1983 and 1.2 percent in 1987. The highest concentration is in northwest Italy and the women in these relationships tend to have a higher than average level of education. In any event, the trend in Italy is clearly towards an increase in divorce, and thus, more de facto one-parent households.

These changes directly affect children. One-parent families and families in which the adult male is not regularly present appear to expose children to possible hardship due to heightened economic pressures as well as psychological stress. Also, more children are growing up without siblings. As a result, more children are spending time alone and experiencing greater solitude.

Table 6.3. Divorces in EEC Countries (Total Number per
100 Marriages, 1980 and 1987)

European country	1980	1987
Belgium	20.8	n.a.
Denmark	39.3	45.2
France	22.2	30.8
West Germany	22.7	32.2
Italy	3.2	6.5
Luxembourg	27.0	n.a.
Netherlands	25.7	28.6
UK[a]	39.3	41.5

[a] England and Wales. N.B. The indicator gives the rate per 100 marriages that will end in divorce. The method of calculation requires caution in interpreting the results; however, it indicates a trend. Source: Monnier (1989).

Prolonged adolescence

A trend characterizing Italian families which became particularly apparent in the 1980s is the prolonged period in which young adults live in the family home. ISTAT figures on family structure in 1983 show that 76 percent of all young adults resided with their families until the age of 24, a trend not found to the same degree in other European nations.

To understand the situation it is important to consider statistics on education and youth employment. In 1981, 45.4 percent of males and 38.2 percent of females between 15 and 18 were students. Between 1961 and 1981, percentages of the working population between the ages of 15 and 19 fell while enrolment rates in that age group rose: in 1961, 69.2 percent of the males 15 to 19 were active in the work force; in 1981, that figure had fallen to 46.8 percent (D'Alessandro 1990). A similar trend appears between the ages of 20 and 24.

The differences distinguishing Italy from other Western countries lead to further analysis. Although unemployment of young people is a problem in many industrialized nations, the situation in Italy presents some important differences. In the last decade the unemployment levels among young people in Italy have been among the highest in Europe: 39.5 percent for 15 to 19 year olds against the European average of 23.7 percent. Since most of the young unemployed live in the family home, these figures, as Sgritta has observed, show that "in the case of Italy, the cost of youth unemployment, as opposed to other European countries, does not fall on public expenditures but entirely on the families" (Sgritta 1990).

It is therefore evident that if the family has "been restored to playing a determining role at a point of the life cycle [early adulthood] during which, in the past, it had usually been placed in the background" (Scabini and Donati 1988). The trend is not without risks. The growing "privatization of family relations" means the family structure itself can act as a limitation to the external socialization possibilities of its individual members. The child's socialization "is profoundly permeated by how he or she experiences the family, by the relationships and the roles constructed within the family, and by the rhythms and rules that have developed through long periods of living together and which are strongly rooted in the history and socialization patterns of the subject" (Sgritta 1990).

Urbanization in an Industrialized Country

By the end of the 1950s Italy had undergone rapid development and industrialization and large flows of migration had occurred from the still prevalently agricultural South to the more industrialized North (as well as to the rest of industrialized Europe). The new job opportunities in Italy were almost entirely concentrated in and around cities; the 1950s and 1960s also witnessed steady urbanization, again particularly in the North.

In the 1970s the urban growth rate began to wane, falling from 1.5 percent at the beginning of the decade to 0.6 percent at the end of the 1970s. Similar to the phenomenon in other industrialized countries, the urban growth rate tied to the demographic rate is projected to continue falling at least into early next century with projections placing the rate below zero by 2020 (United Nations 1990). The largest Italian cities in the South (Catania, Bari, Naples), in the centre (Rome, Bologna, Florence) and in the North (Genoa, Turin) began recording population declines in the 1980s, due both to diminished rural-urban migration and lowered natural growth tied as well as to the exodus of the middle class from the chaotic and expensive city centres to housing developments on the outskirts of the city and to nearby towns. During that period Palermo was an exception, as it maintained its population of around 700,000, while the city of Milan, more typically post-industrial, lost more inhabitants than any other Italian city.[3] However, the growth of the area around Milan more than offset losses in the city's population: a study undertaken in 1987 found that the Milan "urban agglomeration" had increased from around 6.7 million inhabitants in 1980 to a projected 7.6 million in 1990. Naples and Palermo did not experience similar growth patterns. Palermo has no "agglomeration" to speak of and in Naples the urban agglomeration remained stable during the 1980s (around 4 million inhabitants) while the city's population dropped by around 150,000, to just over 1 million (HABITAT 1987).

In only two decades, Italy has shifted from a predominantly agricultural society with small towns to a fully industrialized and urban society (Silverman 1975). However, while the cities offered work, they often did not provide healthy environments. Urban development was usually chaotic, showing too little regard for the everyday living, work and leisure needs of the inhabitants; huge housing developments sprang up at the edge of the city, poorly linked among themselves and to the city itself, and offering few services. At the same time, urbanization brought on the decline of many of the old, even ancient, city centres. In either case — whether in the decaying, congested city centres or in isolated peripheral housing developments — poor urban planning and neglect helped to create far from ideal environments for growing children, encouraging, if not directly causing, the conditions of hardship that too many children in Italy are still living in.

Fresh attention is now being focused on cities. Large urban renewal projects, aiming to change the face and shape of our cities, are being planned. It is important, therefore, that these plans do not once again neglect to take people's needs into account, particularly those of children and youth.

Societal Changes and Available Services

Health care

On the whole, economic development since the end of the Second World War and the resulting improvements in hygiene and sanitation have produced better guarantees for health. Italy's infant mortality rate has steadily declined (Table 6.4) and newborns appear to be less subject to infectious diseases during their first months of life. In 1970, 3,580 children under the age of one died of pneumonia; in 1984, that number had been reduced to 207 (Pinnelli 1989).

However, significant regional imbalances persist. While lifestyles and economic and environmental conditions are partly responsible, so is often the unequal quality and accessibility of health care. For example, the perinatal death rate in Lombardy, in the North, stands at 9 per 1,000; in Campania, where Naples is located, the rate is 16 per 1,000. Figures for the accessibility of services follow a similar pattern. In 1990, according to Italy's National Health Institute, only 24 percent of the country's 2,474 public family health centres were located in the South. Analogous imbalances are found in services for substance abuse, in the number of hospital beds reserved for children, in health-care education and, especially, in the prevention of childhood accidents. Among the causes of child mortality, traffic and domestic accidents still figure high in all parts of the country.

Education and socialization

Preschool. In 1986 approximately 5 percent of the children under three were enrolled in municipally run nurseries. Although an improvement over the 2.1 percent registered in 1976, these rates are still quite low by most European

Table 6.4. Infant Mortality Rate, Lombardy, Campania and Sicily
(Per 1,000 Live Births, 1980, 1985, 1990)

Region (Admin. Seat)	1980	1985	1990
Lombardy (Milan)	12.5	8.4	6.5
Campania (Naples)	16.6	12.4	10.4
Sicily (Palermo)	18.2	12.8	10.2
Italy	14.2	10.3	8.3

Source: ISTAT (1991a), Ministry of Health (1983, 1986).

standards. The availability of nurseries varies regionally. In some areas of the north-central regions of Emilia Romagna and Tuscany, availability was sufficient to permit 30 percent of the eligible children to use them; in the South the corresponding figure was only 1.8 percent. In the same years, the number of nurseries nearly doubled (1,080 to 1,964), despite a 31 percent decrease in the number of 0–3 year olds (2,555,197 to 1,773,129) (Saraceno 1992). Recently, particularly in those regions where public nurseries are most common, a number of experimental programmes favour a greater diversification of services, including part-time care and meeting areas for those who work in the sector.

The public preschool system, for three to five year olds, is much more extensive than the nursery system. By 1990–91, coverage had reached an impressive 91.6 percent (up from 79.3 percent the previous decade). These preschools, nationally administered since 1968, enjoy a greater recognition for their socialization and educational role, while the nurseries, which are locally run, are looked upon with more ambivalence: their role is most often perceived as one of "assisting" families, such as those with two working parents or single parents, with economic and other difficulties. Regionally, preschool enrolment rates range from 97.9 percent in the northeast to 86.3 percent in the South.

Primary and middle schools. In Italy schooling is compulsory for children up to the age of 14, with the completion of middle school. Thereafter three- to five-year specialized high schools are optional. A significant trend is the decrease in the number of students attending primary and middle schools, due largely to demographic changes. However, there has been an increase in the number of students attending high schools and universities. Fewer students in the compulsory schools has brought about several changes, most notably a lower student to teacher ratio in the classroom and the closing of many smaller schools.

Overall, enrolment rates have been climbing steadily. A 1983 survey (ISTAT 1985b) estimated that 95 percent of children six to 13 were attending school. From 1951 to 1985 the enrolment rate for middle schools rose by 62.7 percent for males and 75.5 percent for females. High school enrolment rates have increased by 39.2 percent for males and 48 percent for females. This growth is especially significant in that it has occurred in all regions. A significant trend is the steadily narrowing gap in attendance between males and females; in fact, girls have overtaken boys in some cases (Dei 1987, Schizzerotto 1988).

Safeguarding the rights of children

The issue of child neglect must be seen in both its traditional sense — severe poverty, illegitimacy and abandonment — and in the broader sense of inadequacies in the family structure and disturbances in primary relationships, which can occur in apparently normal families.

The growing awareness of the children's right to protection and security, and the legal, ethical and social implications of this right, have created a lively debate, contributing to the establishment of new policies and services. Rates of institutionalization provide a good example. In Italy the number of physically abandoned and institutionalized children has fallen dramatically, as has the number of illegitimate children and those whose families are unable to care for them.

In 1971 minors accounted for about half of all institutionalized persons; in 1983 that figure had fallen to 23.3 percent. While reflecting the drop in the birth rate, the decrease is also due to better coordination. One particularly effective example is the placement of children in temporary foster care or in family youth homes and youth communities.[4] These new directives became law during the 1980s. Law 184 of 1983 provided further specifics about the range of needed services for institutionalized children, services often furnished through special agreements with nongovernmental organizations.[5]

Similarly, legislation passed in October 1988 reorganized services for children in conflict with the law, with emphasis shifting away from institutionalization and towards family- or community-based interventions. Again, this was generally achieved through government services but particularly through agreements with NGOs.[6]

A fact-finding study on temporary care promoted by the Ministry of Justice (1989) demonstrates that there has been a definite effort to seek alternatives to institutionalization, although it was still the most common means of family substitution. The study documents that in 1985–86 nearly 20,000 minors (about 1.3 per 1,000) were removed from their families, although, regionally, family substitution was three times more likely in the North-centre (about 1.85 per 1,000) than in the South (.66), or on the islands (.54). Nationally, 54 percent of all cases ended in institutionalization (10,300 children); in the remaining 46 percent (8,762 children), the children were put into foster homes or family youth homes, and in just under half of those cases, the child was entrusted to relatives.

In the past several years, and particularly in certain cities and regions in the North, alternatives to fostering and adoption have been created that offer direct support to troubled families. One example is the Home-Based Assistance Project for Children (ADM) in Milan, whose primary goal is family preservation.

Tightly linked to the decrease of abandoned children are the figures on adoption. The decrease in the number of Italian children put up for adoption has brought about an increase in the adoption of foreign children, who accounted for 46.2 percent of all children adopted in 1987 (Di Nicola 1989).

Children at Risk: an Overview

Children in conflict with the law: drugs and juvenile crime

In 1987, for example, at the national level 0.6 percent of minors between the ages of 14 and 17 were charged with crimes and 0.4 percent were tried. The numbers of children charged with crimes almost doubled between 1986 and 1990 (ISTAT 1991b). The proportion subsequently tried and convicted also rose. The proportion of minors tried in court who were subsequently convicted also rose from 16 percent in 1976 to 19.5 percent in 1985. The most recent figures from the Ministry of Justice (1989–91) show that the number of minors charged before the judicial authorities rose from 29,114 in 1989 to 44,977 in 1991. Increases in certain serious offences from 1989 to 1991 were: homicide, 34 to 56; robbery, 943 to 1,386; extortion, 158 to 257; assault, 1,421 to 2,355 (Ministry of Justice 1991). The problems of organized crime and drug use and drug dealing[7] have also increased and are affecting an ever younger segment of the population. In Naples, the 218 drug-related arrests of minors between July 1990 and July 1991 represented a 30 percent increase over the previous year, in part dictated by the new drug law of 1990. However, most crimes attributed to children and youth are still against property (Figure 6.2). The crimes most often committed — theft, purse snatching and robbery — are those which "characterize urban micro-criminality and for which social alarm is always high, as is the willingness to prosecute and apply legal sanctions" (Faccioli 1990a).

These trends reflect growing hardship and marginalization, as indicated by the schooling level of minors in detention centres. In 1987, 83 percent (up from 76 percent in 1985) of the male and 51 percent of the female minors in penal institutions had not completed elementary school or were illiterate (Faccioli 1990a).

Finally, foreign children and youth also constitute a significant proportion of the juvenile offenders in Italy. Foreign minors most often convicted of crimes are Gypsies and North Africans; the offences they most often commit

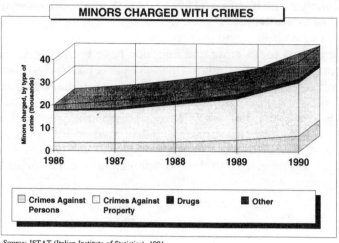

Source: ISTAT (Italian Institute of Statistics), 1991

Figure 6.2. Minors charged with crimes.

are, respectively, theft and drug dealing. However, Gypsy children have been increasingly arrested for robbery, drug dealing and receiving stolen goods. Some of these trends are related to broader changes, such as a tighter enforcement of the 1990 law on drug dealing and drug use (which includes the incarceration of drug users);[8] a sharp increase in foreign immigration, first of Yugoslav Gypsies (beginning in the 1960s) and more recently of Africans (especially from the Maghreb countries), Asians and Latin Americans; and rampant discrimination.

A geographical breakdown for 1987 of accused minors who were eventually convicted shows that the highest rates occurred in Campania (20.8 percent of those charged were convicted), Sicily (15 percent) and Latium (12 percent); Sicily and Campania also recorded the highest percentage of accused minors held in detention centres — 17 percent and 16 percent respectively (Faccioli 1989).

Several factors explain why certain regions are harder hit by juvenile crime. As Chiara Saraceno (1992) points out, "the economic and social instability of the *Mezzogiorno*, the absence of social and educational services, not to mention the often badly functioning schools, are the principal causes of this concentration... Social tensions provoked by persisting class stratification, and the squalor and poverty of the social and environmental surroundings at the cities' peripheries, also help to explain the existence of relatively high rates of juvenile deviance in certain northern and central regions, such as Lombardy."

Dropout and failure rates

Alongside the overall increase in school attendance rates are regional imbalances in the dropout and failure rates. Moreover, problems in quantifying this phenomenon make it difficult to plan effective programmes for prevention.

The dropout rate in middle schools has decreased slightly in recent years — from 3.6 percent in 1984 to 2.7 percent in 1987 — while that in high schools has shown a slight increase. After a somewhat high risk of dropping out in the first year of high school (17.7 percent in 1987), that risk diminishes considerably by the second year (7.4 percent) (CENSIS 1990). In general, failure rates have fallen slightly in primary schools and increased in middle and high schools.

Compared to the national rates of 11 percent for failure and 3.2 percent for dropouts in the first year of middle school, the rates in the South stood at 13.9 and 5.9 percent respectively. These figures are especially worrisome when one considers that in certain areas of the South, situations are far from conducive to stimulating educational achievement. Indeed, Palermo is considered the "dropout" capital of Italy.

A survey on irregular scholastic performance points out several correlations:

- between dropping out and the sociocultural status of the family;

- between dropping out and truancy;

- between dropping out and regressive behaviour which often leads to marginalization and discouragement;

- between dropping out and a lack of sociocultural opportunities (CENSIS 1990).

Children and work

There is a pressing need to promote strategies in Italy that lead to an accurate understanding of child and adolescent work.

Under Italian law (1961), children up to the age of 15 are not permitted to work. This renders data collecting difficult, although indirect indicators, such as school dropout and truancy rates, can provide rough estimates of potential child workers. But the overall phenomenon, in which school and work are often combined from early childhood, is much more complex. Several studies would seem to indicate that many Italian children enter the labour market, usually on an occasional basis, at an early age. Data from a study commissioned by the Ministry of Education on a representative sampling of students in the South, for example, suggested that at least 200,000 children in the South under 14 were working or had worked (Mattioli 1990). Actual numbers, however, and the conditions under which children work are not well known.

Social and economic disadvantage is not enough to explain this complex phenomenon, nor can it simply be considered as a form of neglect. Rather, child labour may also be the result of attitudes that attribute importance to work. It may also reflect the child's strong desire for independence. Usually such attitudes come at the expense of full-time schooling, which often appears unable to motivate young people. The results of a 1978 study in the Naples area are indicative: the main factors leading parents to have their children work were, aside from difficult economic situations in the family, the desire to "keep them off the streets," the chance for them to acquire a trade, and to learn the value of money (Petrillo and Serino 1978).

Weaknesses in the education system, plus economic pressures, though often at the root of the problem, do not provide the sole explanation. Creating or strengthening socializing opportunities, such as cultural, recreational and other activities, "could act as an auspicious counterweight to the problem of child labour" (Mattioli 1989).

New issues: immigrants and Gypsies

Historically, Italy is a land of emigrants. Over the past 20 years, however, Italy, like most other European countries, has slowly started to face the increasingly serious problem of immigration, from much lower-income countries. Growing numbers of foreigners are being attracted not by a real demand for unskilled labour in the Italian job market but rather in response to the deteriorating economic conditions, drought, famine and oppressive political regimes afflicting their homes. Faced with recession and new to the problem of labour immigration, Italy has found itself generally unprepared to confront the needs of this swelling flow of immigrants.

Even today an exact count of immigrants is at best approximate. The latest figures supplied by the Ministry of the Interior show that 844,092 foreigners were legally registered as of mid-1992. Of these, 134,819 were from EEC countries, and 709,273 from elsewhere. Preliminary 1991 Census returns show that immigrants are more prevalent in the North (56 percent of all immigrants), and less in the centre (28 percent) or in the South and islands (16 percent).

Compared to several other EEC countries with longer experiences of immigration, Italy has a relatively small percentage of foreigners (1 percent in 1987 and at least 1.5 percent in 1992); it is behind West Germany (7.6 percent in 1987), France (6.8 percent in 1982), Belgium (8.6 percent in 1987), Luxembourg (26.3 percent in 1981) or even the United Kingdom (3.1 percent in 1984–86). It is followed by newly industrialized countries such as Spain (0.9 percent in 1987) (Blanc and Chiozzi 1992). However, of the EEC countries, Italy has the highest proportion of non-EEC nationals among its foreign population (76 percent). According to ISTAT data in 1989, roughly one third of non-EEC immigrants are from developed countries; the others come from so-called "poor countries."

These figures do not take into account the large numbers of foreigners who are not registered. Indeed, Italy is estimated to have the highest number of illegal or undeclared immigrants in the EEC. Accurate numbers are difficult to ascertain, although in 1990 ISTAT estimated that there were 1,144,000 foreigners in Italy, of whom 963,000 were from non-EEC countries.

Still less complete are the figures pertaining to immigrant children. Foreign children are not accorded an individual legal identity under Italian law, as their status is bound to that of their family. The scant official figures that do exist exclude children born in Italy of illegal immigrant parents and immigrant children who are themselves not registered. Moreover, the official figures do not include children who possess Italian citizenship but who might also be categorized — or stigmatized — as "foreigners" due to their origins. Such is the case of children with one non-Italian parent, although such children are automatically accorded Italian citizenship as a result of a 1983 law.

A recent publication using Ministry of the Interior data has set the number of foreigners between the ages of 0 and 15 in Italy at around 30,000 (Demetrio and Favaro 1992), probably an underestimate. One fact is certain: the number of foreign children in Italy has increased sharply in recent years. The relatively higher marriage and fertility rates of foreign women, together with continued foreign immigration and the more liberal family reunification law (Law 39) passed in 1990, is likely to continue this trend, as in other European countries (Blanc and Chiozzi 1992).

ISTAT figures on school enrolment also show a steep increase in the number of foreign students in Italian schools: from 8,400 in 1983 to 18,400 in 1989. In the 1989–90 school year, the breakdown of overall foreign student enrolment by school type was: 15.9 percent in preschool (probably an underestimate since it does not include private and municipal preschools); 36.8 percent in primary schools; 14.1 percent in middle schools; 17.4 percent in high schools; 5.4 percent in artistic or other academies; and 10.2 percent in technical institutes.

The Ministry of Education has only recently responded to the growing presence of foreign students by issuing two policy statements to broaden the intercultural scope of the schools and promote improved awareness. The circulars make a number of recommendations: periodic training for teachers; training of specialized personnel; appreciation of the various cultures; teaching of Italian as a second language; development of criteria for grade placement; keeping children of the same ethnic origin together; sensitivity to diet and religion; and establishing relations with immigrant families. Characteristically, these two circulars make no mention of funds. At present, teachers specialized in instructing disabled students are called upon to facilitate the integration of immigrant children. The Italian system, nevertheless, with considerable difficulties, is beginning to respond to the needs of immigrant children.

Outside the schools, the situation is more dramatic. Immigrant children must deal with their family's low socioeconomic status, social isolation and prejudice on their path to assimilation. Few foreign children actually live with their families in their own home. The difficulties in finding affordable accommodation, combined with generally long workdays (as is the case for domestics), prompt many parents to repatriate their children or entrust them to religious institutions (boarding schools, orphanages). In Rome, 21 percent of the children living in such institutions are of immigrant backgrounds. Problems associated with contrasting lifestyles, values, child-rearing practices, and divided feelings between the "world of affection" of the family and the broader society already beset children living with their families. Such difficulties are multiplied and intensified for institutionalized children. Psychological, socioeconomic and family problems intertwine, leaving their mark on the children and rendering them more vulnerable to deviant behaviour. Given the numerous hardships affecting many child immigrants and the fact that this phenomenon shows no signs of diminishing, it is imperative that Italian institutions, including the school system, formulate more adequate responses.

DISADVANTAGED URBAN CHILDREN: NAPLES, PALERMO AND MILAN

As we have seen, Italy's rapid development has not been able to eradicate hardship and poverty in all areas of the country; indeed, the very process of development has created new hardships. Naturally, the living conditions of children cannot be defined only in terms of economic indicators; social, cultural and political elements interact to create a more complex picture. However, general economic and social conditions can provide a first indication of the immense differences in the living conditions of children and in the efficacy of the policies that apply to them.

Milan, Naples and Palermo, each very different, provide a clear synthesis of the ambivalence, contradictions and disparities that have characterized recent social and economic transformations. Naples and Palermo demonstrate how areas of entrenched social degradation may constrain the implementation of national social policies. Milan faces different problems, but also possesses greater resources to combat them.

Poverty and Marginalization: Problems Unresolved

Naples

In Naples, sizeable segments of the population suffer particularly acute hardships. In fact, it has been estimated that around one quarter of the children are living in situations of severe, or potentially severe, hardship.

Furthermore, only a very small proportion of these troubled children (around 3 percent) is receiving public support, leaving large numbers marginalized, and often living between legality and illegality (Sommella 1990). The substandard conditions of the impoverished areas have directly impacted the large numbers of children and their families, creating hardships that can be termed as "primary." These are compounded by subsequent health risks, risks of abandonment, abuse, violence, exploitation, crime and child labour, as indicated by the first two parts of Table 6.5.

Despite national industrialization and health improvements, child mortality rates are still surprisingly high in Naples and in southern Italy in general. In 1987 the stillbirth rate in Naples was 8.5 per 1,000, around two points above the national average. In the same year the perinatal mortality rate stood at 15 per 1,000 in the first week of life and 17.6 per 1,000 in the first month; figures on a national level were 12.4 and 15.3 respectively. For the region of Campania (where Naples is located) the infant mortality rate in 1987 stood at 11.5 per 1,000 live births, as opposed to the national average of 9.5.

There are several underlying factors. Low birth weight, which increases the risk of death from diarrhoea and pneumonia, occurs in 8.7 percent of the births in Naples and is often the result of unhealthy practices of expectant mothers, such as smoking and illness during pregnancy. Moreover, health risks and social problems are often linked to the mother's age: in Campania, a higher than average number of pregnant women are under the age of 20 or over 40. A final factor is access to medical care. Around 4 percent of the pregnant women in Campania undergo no prenatal checkup and only 9 percent of the pregnant women use the public family health centres; most women seek care from private doctors.

As mentioned above, dropout rates are an indicator of children's distress and potential involvement in work. Data from CEAPRELDA (a research institute) show that only 65 percent of compulsory school-level students attend classes regularly, 26 percent irregularly and 2 percent do not. Of those who dropped out, around 3,000 children, over half are officially idle or are performing "undefined" activities, and are thus in situations of particular risk. The problem of exploited working children in Naples is great, even if official statistics or estimates are unable to pinpoint the exact number. The large discrepancy in figures for children registered at local employment offices above and below the age of 15 (see Table 6.5) is only indicative. "Whether tens of thousands, as some surveys conclude, or hundreds of thousands, as other sources claim," young child labourers pack the many "large and crowded grounds ... public and private, teeming and heedless, and open for business in Naples, everywhere and at all times" (Sommella 1990).

Naples can be divided into five more or less similar zones, at least statistically. Most of the minors in detention centres come from the zones comprising the city-centre neighbourhoods (33.6 percent), and from the northern

Table 6.5. Social Indicators for Children in Naples

Child population vs. total population by
age group[1] (percentages, 1989)

| | Age group (years) | | | | | | |
| | | | | | | Total | |
Area	0–2	3–5	6–10	11–13	14–18	0–18	19+
Montecalvari	4.3	4.5	8.9	5.3	9.4	32.4	67.6
Scampia	5.1	5.4	10.4	7.7	15.7	44.3	55.7
Other areas	4.2	4.8	9.3	5.7	9.7	33.7	66.3
Naples (total)	4.3	4.8	9.4	5.7	9.9	34.0	66.0

Violence to children[2]

Children's age (%)		Children's gender (%)	
<6	29	Male	47
6–12	39	Female	53
12–18	32		
Main reasons for violence (%)		Main types of family (%)	
physical/psychological abuse	27	both parents	58
abandonment	20	(of which conflictual	29)
mentally ill or substance-abusing parents	17	separated	17
quarrels	13	unmarried	18
irregular school attendance	9	one parent dead	7
poverty	8		
institutionalization	4		
sexual abuse	2		

Working children[3]

Estimated no. of working children	6,000	Type of work[4] (%)	
Children registered at local		assisting parents	15
employment offices:	Total	or relatives	
15 years old and younger	51	shophelpers	14
16–20 years old	36,662	mechanics	16
		other	25
		illegal activities	30

cont'd

outskirts (34.2 percent). Table 6.5 also shows the crimes committed by the youths placed in youth communities and detention centres in 1989–90. A study of 552 Neapolitan minors charged with crimes in 1989–90 indicates several characteristics: 41 percent were 17 years old, 58 percent came from large families; 81 percent had not completed the final year of compulsory schooling.

One of the most alarming aspects for the at-risk children is that most cannot imagine a better life for themselves. The majority receive little or no guidance from their families; those who drop out of school become more exposed to violence and exploitative labour. Poverty, broken families, aban-

Table 6.5. cont'd

Minors in Conflict with the Law				
Distribution of minors entering institutions for criminal charges[5]	Total (552)	%	Types of crime[6] (for 107 minors entering youth communities or family youth homes)	
detention centres	254	46.0		
reception centres	200	36.2		
youth communities or	98	17.8	theft	45
family youth homes			robbery	22
overall			drug dealing	17
boys	528	95.7	carrying arms	6
girls	24	4.3	receiving stolen goods	5
			vandalism	3
			abduction	3
			criminal association	2
			homicide	2
			battery	1
			extortion	1

Sources: [1]Municipality of Naples (1989a). [2]CAM Telefono Azzurro (1990), sampling of telephone reports, 1988 to March 1990. [3]UPLMO (1984). [4]Testa, F. (1982). [5]Office for Juvenile Justice Centres, Campania and Molise, (1990b) (1 Nov. 1989 to 30 Sept. 1990). [6]Office for Juvenile Justice Centres, Campania and Molise, (1990a) (11 Sept. 1989 to 30 Sept. 1990).

donment, abuse, violence, inadequate services, an unreliable job market, the loss of credibility in the school system, the increased involvement with drugs, particularly heroin, and the deep-rooted presence of highly efficient criminal organizations (including the *camorra*) all contribute to the problems of these "wayward" youths.

Indeed, the figures for Naples on health care for children and mothers, on schooling and on juvenile delinquency reveal glaring deficiencies in the organization and availability of the social services. Health care for newborns and expectant mothers represents a major public health problem: the most urgent goals must be the improvement of health services for young children and the better utilization of the municipally run health clinics. For those children involved, or risking involvement, in criminal activity, there is a pressing need to formulate effective programmes of prevention, rehabilitation and reeducation (Sommella 1990), as well as to offer job training and placement possibilities.

Palermo

In Palermo the conditions of severe economic and social marginalization of certain segments of the population, the poverty and degradation of their environment, as well as increased criminality and the more recent phenomenon of the drug trade, fuel particularly precarious living conditions

Table 6.6. Social Indicators for Children in Palermo

Causes of death, by age group and gender, 1988[1]

Cause of Death	0-1 M	0-1 F	1-4 M	1-4 F	5-9 M	5-9 F	10-14 M	10-14 F	15-19 M	15-19 F
Illnesses/various[a]	6	4	10	3	3	3	6	6	18	14
Congenital disease	9	5	2	–	–	–	1	–	–	–
Early childhood diseases	78	55	–	2	–	–	–	–	–	–
Undefined	–	–	–	–	–	–	–	–	2	–
Accidents	–	–	3	1	3	1	3	–	29	7
Total	93	64	15	6	6	4	10	6	49	21

Violence to children[2]
(215 reported cases)

Gender (%)		Age of children (%)	
boys	54.4	0–3	20.5
girls	45.6	3–9	60.9
		9–14	18.6
Perpetrator of violence (%)		Type of abuse (%)	
mother	41.4	physical abuse	45.2
father	35.4	psychological abuse	20.9
both parents	20.9	serious neglect	20.0
peers	0.8	sexual abuse	13.9
siblings	0.5		
other household member	0.5		
teacher	0.5		

Schooling[3] (percentages)

	Primary (48,993 students)	Middle school (37,148 students)
Repeated years	3.3	11.6
Dropout	0.8	2.3
Irregular attendance	1.1	1.7
Total	5.2	15.6

[a]Infectious, parasitic, metabolic, blood, mental, central nervous system, circulatory, respiratory, digestive, urinary, bone, tumours. Sources: [1]Municipality of Palermo (1989). [2]Telefono Azzurro (1988). Data pertaining to first two years of operation beginning in Oct. 1987. [3]Province of Palermo, Office of Education (1990).

for young children (see Table 6.6). Abuse and violence against young children, rampant delinquency, drug use, prostitution, the ruthless exploitation of child workers, and the abandonment of educational institutions are the consequences.

A troubling destiny awaits many of the boys and girls thrust into the environment of poverty and marginalization: the former swell the ranks of petty criminals (purse snatching, theft, drug dealing); the latter are often forced to stay at home and mind younger siblings.

Figures on juvenile crime in Palermo underline several significant factors: in 1986–87, 2,641 juveniles were charged with 1,760 criminal offences. The most common crimes were purse snatching (327), illegal bearing of arms (107), aggravated assault (103), robbery (75), and vandalism (32); the age of minors with criminal records was more or less evenly distributed between 14 and 17, and their level of education was very low, leaving them with few employment possibilities. Interrupted education and unemployment are recurrent problems. Figures from the District Office of Social Services for Youth for the Province of Palermo show that of the 1,777 juveniles charged with crimes in 1987–88, 896 were booked and released, while 465 were detained. Nearly all those held were from the city of Palermo; 33 percent were unemployed, and most had little schooling, with nearly half not having completed primary school.

As the latest report (1991) by the Ministry of Justice points out, many young criminals are themselves victims of exploitation at the hands of organized crime. Indeed, young children and adolescents become preferred "workers" of the *mafia* because of the difficulty in prosecuting minors. The connection between juvenile crime and criminal organizations is often unclear because the data linking certain forms of juvenile crime to organized crime and the criteria for analysing that data have not yet been satisfactorily defined (Ministry of Justice 1991). However, it is known that organizations use children to collect extortion money, to steal, and to pass information. Government action is urgently needed to control such occurrences.

Similarly, figures on child labour are neither exhaustive nor fully reliable, but the problem cannot be underestimated. The accounts of several labour inspectors confirm that child labour in Palermo is extremely widespread. Increasingly larger groups of young children throng at traffic lights and busy intersections to sell fruit, salt, tissue paper and illegally manufactured cigarettes. As many of these children are still in school, the time they spend working is taken away from other activities such as play and socializing. The reasons are complex. On the one hand, many children are forced to leave school in order to contribute more money to their family economies. At the same time, the schools are inadequate to the task, and people are generally disheartened about the ability of the schools to educate children.

Figures on dropouts and truancy for the city of Palermo, though incomplete, are indicative. Studies have uncovered some alarming figures, such as a dropout rate of 30 percent in the Zen quarter. Overall dropout rates in Palermo for the 1988–89 school year were 0.8 percent in primary schools and 2.3 percent in middle schools (Table 6.6). In Palermo more than 16 percent of the children attending compulsory schools are considered "difficult" and the school system is often unprepared to confront this (Cangialosi 1988). "These are children ... with a history, in most cases, of families with serious problems: unemployment, poverty ... young children and teenagers left to themselves, accustomed to living on the streets ... forced to work or steal. For them, school is just a senseless place, uninteresting, where the required rules of behaviour are totally foreign" (Cangialosi 1988). A fundamental problem for the schools is therefore their ability to function effectively in the face of these immense environmental, social and cultural difficulties, and to create educational programmes that help overcome, rather than perpetuate, disadvantages.

The presence of immigrants and Gypsies, while less numerous in southern Italy than in the North, is nevertheless felt in large cities. Many immigrants from both North and sub-Saharan Africa first arrive in southern cities such as Palermo, staying there for some time before they begin migrating to cities in northern and central Italy where better job opportunities are to be found. Also, the situation of Gypsy children in Palermo is compounded by an illegal traffic in Slav children which is practised, it seems, by some Gypsy communities.

Milan

Milan is a large modern metropolis which has undergone many changes. Between 1981 and 1990 the population of the city proper decreased by 300,000, as in those two years births fell from 11,487 to 7,697 (see also Table 6.7). At the same time, single-family and single-person households have increased, as has the number of working women (30 percent of women are now employed). The middle classes are increasingly moving into neighbouring towns, leaving the older sections of Milan to the poor and upper-middle classes. Poorer Italian migrants from the South and immigrants from developing countries continue to arrive; in 1990, 6,187 immigrants entered the city.

In many respects, Milan is a wealthy city, rich in resources and services; on average, the *Milanesi* spent 27.3 percent more per capita than the average Italian in 1987. Overall, children in Milan seem to enjoy access to basic services, especially in health and education. For example, an efficient vaccination programme has substantially reduced infant mortality and morbidity. School attendance also appears to be satisfactory. In 1989–90 the dropout rate for the third year of middle school stood at 0.46 percent.

The number of children in conflict with the law in the Milan area indicates a situation that is not as explosive as that in Naples and Palermo, even though the incidence of juvenile offences may be rising. In 1990, the 314 juveniles charged with crimes represented 32 percent of the charges filed in the district Court of Appeals (Table 6.7). But on closer inspection the data for 1990 supplied by the judicial authorities contain several elements that call for more analysis, particularly in light of a new and growing set of problems

Table 6.7. Social Indicators for Children in Milan

Population, by age group[1]				
	1981	1988	Breakdown of child population, 0–18[2]	
0–17	337,457	225,036	0–3	28,000
18–65	1,041,818	1,004,920	3–6	26,404
Over 65	224,974	233,914	(foreign/Gypsy	1,236)
Total	1,604,249	1,463,870	6–11	50,000
			11–14	38,000
			14–18	99,600

Minors in conflict with the law					
Minors accused of crimes, city of Milan, January to August 1990[3]					
	Italians		Foreigners		
Age	Male	Female	Male	Female	Total
12	0	0	1	1	2
13	0	0	0	1	1
14	17	1	3	13	34
15	35	2	5	12	54
16	80	8	10	9	107
17	80	5	8	7	100
18	11	1	1	0	13
Age not recorded	1	0	1	1	3
Total	224	17	29	44	314

Type of crime, Milan and Province[4]					
Theft/burglary	305	19	51	90	465
Robbery	49	2	4	0	55
Other, against property	118	7	6	0	131
Assault	49	10	1	1	61
Disorderly conduct	27	0	0	0	27
Sexual	2	0	0	0	2
Other, against person	19	6	0	1	26
Abuse/threats	14	2	0	0	16
Drug-related	44	3	7	0	54
Carrying arms	35	1	1	0	37
Resisting arrest/ insulting public official	21	1	1	0	23
Traffic violations	25	0	1	1	27
Other	34	5	10	6	55
Not applicable	1	0	1	0	2
Total	743	56	83	99	981

Sources: [1]ISTAT (1981). [2]Municipality of Milan (1991a). [3]Office of the Prosecutor for Minors (1990). [4]District Court of Appeals (1990).

linked to violence, ethnic tension and drug addiction. A most significant statistic is that of foreign minors involved in illegal activities most are Gypsies, accounting for 84.9 percent of the foreign youths charged with crimes in the city.

In examining the gender and ages of children who have trouble with the law, several important differences stand out. The small number of Italian girls charged with crimes (around 7 percent of all minors) is far below that of foreign girls, especially female Gypsies (who even outnumber their male ethnic counterparts by more than 2 to 1).

On average, Gypsy offenders are younger than Italians and other foreigners: while around one quarter of Italian minors charged with crimes (January to August 1990) were under the age of 16, the corresponding percentage for Gypsies was 63 percent. Ethnic origin also appears to influence the kind of criminal activities that children are involved in. Most of the offences committed by foreign minors are against property; indeed, these are crimes that children are most often associated with. Italian minors, on the other hand, tend to commit a wider range of offences, including those typical of adult criminality (Table 6.7).

However, conflict with the law is only one of the problems related to young foreigners. In 1988 there were 3,734 foreign children between the ages of 0 and 15 living in Milan. Truancy, above-average mortality rates, health problems and abuse also still await solutions. In Milan, studies of the Gypsy population indicate that at least half of all Gypsy children do not regularly attend school or participate in vaccination programmes.

Social Deprivation and "New Poverty"

Overlapping and intertwining with hardships rooted in poverty are several forms of "new poverty," which are also linked to the demographic changes and the process of urbanization. They represent subtle forms of violence that distinctively affect children's development, leading to high-risk situations. Three general causes can be identified.

Frustrated aspirations (psychological and subjective causes)

A bleak future, dashed aspirations and an inability to satisfy material longings can lead to conditions of emotional tension that seriously hinder parent-child relationships, possibly resulting in severe psychological and emotional maladjustment (Palmonari and Rigon 1991).

Recent studies on children undergoing neuropsychiatric or psychological care have signalled a change in the kinds of cognitive and emotional-relational disturbances now being found among Italian children, particularly in the North. An epidemiological study carried out in Bologna (Loperfido and Rigon 1988) indicated that 6 percent of children between 6 and 14 were afflicted with some form of psychiatric disturbance, while a study by the

Children's Neuropsychiatric Service in Ferrara showed that 30 percent of the pathologies diagnosed were emotional in origin (Polletta 1991). The situation in the South is much less researched, but frustrated aspirations are certainly an important element of young people's lives there as well.

Changing family relations within and beyond the family sociological and interactional causes)

Social relations, particularly within the family, represent both the cause and a potential remedy of a great many of the disturbances affecting children and adolescents. Focusing on these relationships highlights the importance of the loving/relating capacities developed in the child-adult relationship and brings out problems that go well beyond those of poverty, even though in part conditioned by it. For the purpose of analysis, one needs to distinguish between the changing relationships of Italian children within and outside the family. While family is the centre of socialization and the source of identity formation for children up to the age of 3, the relational sphere of 6–18 year olds, though still focusing on family interaction, increasingly includes school relationships, peer relationships, leisure activities, and so on. Organizational and environmental features may encourage or inhibit the young person's chances for balanced development (Di Nicola 1990). Changes in family structure and birth rates, both North and South, have led to the growing solitude of the young child. Insufficient social services or areas for play, and difficulty in adapting to school life that may lead to poor scholastic performance contribute to an increase in psychological and psychosocial disturbances.

The importance of well-balanced relationships for children is illustrated by figures on institutionalized children in Milan that attribute 26.7 percent of the cases to bad relations with the family; 28 percent to severe family problems; 12.7 percent to parental work problems; 12 percent to housing problems; 11.5 percent to economic problems; 10.5 percent to school problems; 3.5 percent to disabilities; 2.1 percent to abuse in the family; 1.2 percent to the death of both parents; 1.3 percent to drug abuse; and 12.4 to other reasons.[9] Furthermore, of these children, 33.1 percent have married parents, while 45.7 percent have separated parents, unmarried mothers, unknown fathers, or are orphans. A further illustration of the problems within families comes from a survey on children in institutions in the region of Lombardy (IRER 1987), which showed: (1) a shift from housing mostly young children to adolescents; (2) a shift from housing mostly orphaned and abandoned children to housing mostly children from broken families. As a result of these changes, many institutions were developing new approaches such as joint private and public interventions.

The emergence of these new risk situations linked to relational problems calls for coordinated and comprehensive responses, such as the creation of social support networks that integrate the services of the various agencies and organizations (family, school, social and health services) involved in the socialization and education of children. A primary goal then is to ensure the timely delivery of social, health and educational interventions to the families in need. It is also necessary to move away from a welfare approach in order to create intermediate solutions involving, or patterned on, the family, such as home-based assistance, crisis centres, youth communities, family youth homes and day centres.

Deteriorated urban neighbourhoods (organizational and environmental causes)

Fast-paced and crowded cities are usually not designed with the needs of young children in mind. In fact, such settings can seriously compromise their potential for a healthy and balanced development. Parts of many cities are plagued by an unhealthy environment as well as organizational problems: pollution, traffic, noise, poor housing, insufficient social spaces outside the home and off the streets, insufficient green areas,, and inadequate and inaccessible social services. These factors contribute to the social isolation of children and are thus primary indicators of hardship, if not of actual marginalization.

Differing examples of these problems are found in ancient city centres and in outlying housing developments. Decay, filth and abandonment in the old city-centre neighbourhoods of *Albergheria* in Palermo and the Spanish Quarter in Naples — where degeneration only worsens — create pockets of marginalization in which the considerable hardships drastically reduce any chance for integration and adaptation. Similarly, the quality of life in the tightly clustered buildings found in peripheral housing developments tell of frightening states of deterioration, and of a nonexistent social and cultural identity.

A look at the Scampia area of Naples, a particularly deprived area, illustrates some of these problems (Box 6.1). More than 13 percent of the households settling there from other parts of the city have no fewer than nine members; although apartments are "spacious" by public housing standards (5.53 rooms), the average number of inhabitants per apartment is 7.4 (Municipality of Naples 1981). Around 12 percent of the families do not have a steady income (ISTAT figures indicate that roughly 35 percent of the active population is unemployed); only 37 percent of the population has completed primary school education and there is a high proportion of illiterate persons; and 7 percent of the students in primary schools and 24 percent in middle schools do not attend classes regularly and/or have been held back at least one school year. Finally, nearly one quarter (23 percent in 1983) of all minors held in juvenile detention centres in Naples are from Scampia (Office for Juvenile Justice, Campania and Molise 1983). An insufficient network of basic services and the total lack of spaces for socialization (there are no cinemas,

---

Box 6.1   Scampia (Secondigliano), Naples

Scampia, situated on the northern outskirts of Naples, has been developed over the last thirty years to provide public housing as stipulated by Law No. 167. Occupancy rights for lodgings were assigned by the city of Naples although numerous families have moved in illegally.

The quarter covers an area of 3.3 km². Inhabitants officially recorded at the city registry as of July, 1989, numbered 43,266, giving the area a population density of 13,800 per km² (CRESM, 1989). However, unofficial estimates place the population as high as 100,000. Of this total, over half was 25 years old or younger in 1989, and around 25 percent of the total population was 15 or younger (Municipality of Naples 1990). The crowded conditions in the area have been aggravated by a further proliferation of illegal lodgings made by erecting dividing walls in the large arcades of the buildings or breaking down dividing walls in garage areas.

Large buildings, with an anonymous and impersonal design, are built in clusters, identified by a letter of the alphabet although in some cases the residents have coined more expressive names. Each cluster has its own characteristics. Some are composed of 12- to 13-storey buildings tightly grouped together, around which there is little space or sunlight. Other clusters have lower southern-exposed buildings, creating a more human dimension.

In 1981 there was an average of 1.34 inhabitants per room; by 1984, that average had grown to 1.5. Clusters with illegal lodgings have a particularly high occupant-to-room ratio since in 20 percent of such apartments two family units are housed. In 15 percent of the apartments major repairs are needed due to leaks, damaged dividing walls, faulty or malfunctioning door frames, window frames, fittings, plumbing, and electrical and heating systems.

There is often a deep mutual mistrust among the residents of Scampia, especially between different clusters. Residents do not speak to each other and there is widespread fear of robbery, assault and violence in general that forces many residents to spend their free time — or the entire day for the unemployed — locked indoors. Crime, linked to the *camorra* and drugs, is very common throughout the area.

Most residents are very poorly integrated into their new surroundings. Many families have not yet officially reported their change of residency (mandatory under Italian law) and many families continue to maintain close contact with their former neighbourhoods in the area of work, social services and socializing.

Source: Sommella (1990), Italian Urban Child Project (1992).

---

book shops, playgrounds or shopping areas) reinforce the social and cultural isolation and weaken any sense of belonging. Often, young girls abandon their studies because they fear the many dangers that line the way to school. For many young girls in this quarter, ironically built to favour socialization, the only possible play area is the home, or, at most, the dirty and crumbling entrance yard to their block of flats. Boys are often left to roam the unconstricted open areas, since playing in the courtyard is not allowed. Because of surrounding violence and decay, the use of public areas such as soccer fields, roller-skating rinks and gardens has proven extremely problematic.

In Milan, the situation appears to be somewhat different. There is a greater diversity of leisure-time activities, as well as more accessible public and private services. Nevertheless, the children of Milan pay a price for growing up in a city that was not designed for them. There are few spaces for play, and housing complexes tend to isolate people rather than encourage socializing. Areas abandoned by industries fall into decay. The pace of daily life does not encourage quality contact between children and adults. Consequently, adults often do not understand their children's needs for development, learning and socialization. Services, green spaces and public facilities are not evenly spread throughout the city; thus, those quarters with fewer facilities, such as "Zone 3" in the city centre and Quarto Oggiaro in the outlying area (see Box 6.2), are more exposed to some of the risks of "new poverty" and to the growing marginalization of certain segments of the population.

The diversity of these three cities, with their manifold risk factors, points to the pressing need to reflect on the origins of the hardships. Policies to effectively confront the old and new contradictions in Italy's cities should be based on coordinated programmes that utilize and enhance existing resources, including human resources, and that create partnerships between public and private efforts.

THE PROTECTION OF CHILDREN AND YOUTH AT THE MUNICIPAL, PROVINCIAL, REGIONAL AND NATIONAL LEVELS: A THREE-CITY ANALYSIS

The foregoing analysis has shown bright spots and dark shadows. Despite general improvements in the living conditions of young people, too many children in certain areas are still afflicted by serious hardship. Where risks seem fewer, fast-paced and chaotic urban environments leave too little time and space for play, socialization and the development of caring relationships between children and adults. Children whose only companion is often the television, and whose needs to grow, learn and socialize are being neglected, are increasingly showing signs of emotional disturbances.

In this context the central importance of the family must be emphasized. However, the Italian family is not aided by a sufficiently efficient network of services, nor by policies that place a high priority on strengthening the family as an institution. And the main losers are often children. One objective of the Urban Child Project in Italy has been to analyse and document some of the most effective programmes to help disadvantaged urban children not only survive but also develop. The analysis has focused on (1) the approaches of the government at the national, regional, provincial and municipal levels,

---

Box 6.2   Quarto Oggiaro, Milan

Quarto Oggiaro is a typical housing development located at the northern end of Milan. It is literally on the other side of the railway bridge, which separates it, along with a large refinery, from the rest of administrative zone 20. The area's isolation is heightened by its placement between a railway line and two motorways and by the poor public transportation.

In the 1960s, with rapid industrial development and the migration of workers, Quarto Oggiaro assumed its present form. The population grew from 7,232 to 47,000 and private and publicly funded housing sprung up, consistent with the philosophy that bedroom communities do not require areas for socializing, play, shopping and social services.

In the 1960s, Quarto Oggiaro was a working-class neighbourhood consisting of families arriving from the old city-centre neighbourhoods, the countryside, the northeast region of Veneto and the South. In order to fulfil the requisites for being assigned apartments, families had to have a modest income and numerous children. In recent years the population of the area has aged and declined from around 45,000 in 1981 to 40,000 in 1986. With the economic changes of the late 1970s, much of the second generation has found work in the service economy and moved.

A large number of Gypsies have moved into the area, and there are two officially recognized Gypsy encampments as well as other areas where the migrants illegally camp. Due to their cultural differences, the Gypsies are not integrated into the area; violence has often erupted and residents have long been requesting that the camps be relocated.

Source: IOSA (1975); Consiglio di Zona (1977).

---

and (2) the past and ongoing programmes of the public sector and of non-governmental organizations (NGOs).

National Policy Approaches

Services for children in Italy are characterized by contradictions. Not only are there striking differences from one city to another; within individual cities, innovative interventions based on family involvement stand next to others which fall short in addressing children's increasingly urgent problems in the modern industrial context.

The implementation of laws spelling out child-related policies is overseen by several ministries and is increasingly becoming the responsibility of regional, provincial and municipal administrations. The Ministry for Social Affairs, instituted on 29 August 1987, oversees coordination but has no specific authority or financing power.

In 1985, following the lead of the 1979 United Nations International Year of the Child (though with considerable delay) the Prime Minister decreed the creation of a National Youth Council, composed of representatives from the

Italian children whose needs to grow, learn and socialize are increasingly looking for companionship outside the home and often run into trouble. Quarto Oggiaro, Milan, Italy. *Credit*: Paola Coletti, Milano, Italy.

Box 6.3   The Most Important Recent Initiatives on Youth Issues Being Promoted by Italian Ministries

- The *Ministry of Foreign Affairs* is becoming more involved in adoption cases and the situation of illegal immigrant children, who are often targeted for exploitation, prostitution and criminality.
- The *Ministry of the Environment* is carrying out programmes on environmental education through joint initiatives with the Ministry of Education.
- The *Ministry of Justice* operates an office for juvenile justice which runs programmes for minors in conflict with the law and, more generally, deals with issues concerning young people and the law. In the civil sector it deals with the adoption of foreign children. Internationally, it intervenes in disputes over child custody and visiting rights involving married couples of different nationalities. In the legal sector it regulates all services and structures dealing with minors subject to prosecution.
- The *Ministry of the Interior*, as the general management branch of the civil services, oversees studies and coordinates local projects.
- The *Ministry of Labour and Social Welfare*, because of growing concern about child labour, has intensified work inspections and is promoting investigations on youth labour and the unreported or "black" labour market.
- The *Ministry of Education* is promoting projects on health education, drug prevention, integrating disabled students into the schools and enrolling Gypsies and migrants.
- The *Ministry of Health* initiatives include an information campaign for infant health care, health information in collaboration with the state-run telephone company, surveys on the use and regional distribution of state nursery schools, counselling on abortion for minors, and accident prevention.

Source: Italian Urban Child Project (1992).

Ministries of Education, Health, Interior, Foreign Affairs, and the Treasury, and from regional, provincial and local administrations, as well as ten NGOs working on children's issues. The Council's task was to recommend and undertake studies and projects, and improve sectoral links. It was also to formulate proposals or legislative, administrative and technical initiatives, prepare an annual report on legislative and administrative measures, and recommend directives to be passed from the central government to regional administrations and implementing agencies. After producing valuable work in its first years, several interventions and the publication of two reports on the condition of children in Italy, the Council has recently gone through a period of decline for political reasons. The Council, formerly under the Ministry of the Interior, is now under the Ministry of Social Affairs.

At the same time, there are some indications that Italian lawmakers have greater awareness of policy issues relating to children. One area has been crime and drugs. In the final text on juvenile court procedures, for example, substantial changes have been introduced: "the wheels on which the old system turned (arrest, detention, trial) are set aside in favour of a procedure which is strongly conditioned by social inquiry" (De Nardis 1990). Now included in the evidence examined by the judge are reports by local social-service agencies on the psychological, environmental and sociocultural background of the defendant. Alternatives to detention, such as keeping the minors with their families or sending them to youth communities, have also become more common.

Numerous initiatives now address young people's needs. In the health-care sector, programmes have concentrated on care to newborns, hospitalized children and disabled children. Interventions also assist drug users and improve the mass media's understanding of children's and youth issues. In 1991 the law on drug use was changed, putting greater emphasis on prevention and coordination between recovery and rehabilitation programmes. Law 216, enacted in the same year to support three-year local projects, calls for early interventions for youth risking involvement in criminal activities.

The ministries charged with administering these laws are the Ministry of Justice, which funds projects presented by municipal agencies in high-risk areas of southern Italy, and the Ministry of Social Affairs, which gathers project proposals through the Prefectures. The proposals are evaluated by a special commission on the basis of criteria set by Parliament.

The two laws on drug use and criminality are also significant in that they show a willingness to work with schools, NGOs and local administrations. However, in order to fulfil this potential, links between the projects must be maintained and coordination among the ministries, the regions and local administrations, volunteers and NGOs must be well managed.

In July 1991 Parliament ratified the United Nations Convention on the Rights of the Child; however, it is still too early to foresee its effect. Following elections in April 1992, the new Prime Minister asked Parliament to draw up a Children's Statute of Rights. Here, also, it will take time to see any concrete changes.

Naples

Naples has no comprehensive strategy on child issues. A welfarist approach, which tends to categorize and thus isolate both problems and solutions, has resulted in stopgap measures, fragmented programmes and scattered initiatives, usually rendered ineffective by the inefficiencies of basic services and the chronic lack of communication.

Only rarely do official proposals manage to escape the traditional welfare mentality, like job-placement programmes for drug-dependent youths and minors released from prison. Again, however, concentrating on high-risk subjects comes at the expense of primary prevention programmes.

The Child Research and Documentation Centre of the Municipal Welfare and Social Services Department also goes against the current, promoting "awareness and planning" as opposed to "emergency and improvisation." The Centre, founded by social workers as an experimental project, investigates youth-related problems in areas of social services, health and environment, school, family, criminality, drugs and abuse. It works with juvenile courts, municipal social-service offices, and private and voluntary organizations, and has instituted a child abuse centre and a consultation service, including a library. The Centre also organizes a press review on child-related issues.

However, these few positive examples are exceptions. While there can be no easy excuses for such a state of affairs, many explanations exist: growing economic ills (closely tied to the more general problems of the welfare state and its present crisis); recurring political tumult of local administrations; resistance within the bureaucratic apparatus; and constant clashes between innovative and conservative political forces.

In such a setting it is difficult for the nongovernmental sector to develop a strong advocacy presence. Paradoxically, however, Naples represents a boundless laboratory of social experimentation; indeed, the general immobility of the public sector contrasts with the wide variety of private initiatives that deal with social assistance, disabilities, health, criminality and child care. In 1980 around 600 groups were operating in various ways. Following an earthquake in 1980 the private social sector — particularly church parishes, athletic clubs and associations such as ARCI Ragazzi, Catholic Action and environmentalists — stepped forward to help disadvantaged children. However, these groups are makeshift and are usually not officially recognized, often owing their survival to the good will of individuals.

The myriad of groups and organizations working in certain areas, particularly Scampia, is an example of civil mobilization, but also of a lack of coordination. Beside the eight organizations (three public and five private) counted by the Urban Child Project, a countless number of voluntary groups for after-school activities, Catholic teachings and so on, are involved in bringing together children who spend much of their time on the streets. But the valid experiences of these groups have not been properly documented in most cases, thus preventing a full assessment. And most cover only a small number of children.

Some of the most innovative public and private initiatives are:

The "Ragazzi ancora" project. This project, financed by Law 216, is being set up by the Municipal Department for Social Policies. Though not yet under way, its general goal will be to prevent juvenile crime by offering 11 to 18 year olds social activities as well as job training and orientation.

The project, as planned, features an integration of activities for leisure time, school, family intervention and support, and job training and placement for youth with slight to serious family problems in order to avoid in-stitutionalization and the higher social and economic costs that it incurs.

In more serious cases, these initiatives will be supported by temporary foster care by voluntary agencies. Finally, young people in particularly serious circumstances will be provided entry into family youth homes. Owing to the scarcity of such homes, the project plans to organize coopera-tives to establish and run them. The project plans to use existing structures managed by personnel from the municipal social-welfare offices and stipu-late agreements with organizations that will provide job training, athletics, workshops, family youth homes, neighbourhood programmes, psychologi-cal assistance and teaching.

The project plans to operate in the Flegrea neighbourhood, the city centre and in the eastern part of the city, where children are exposed to the greatest risks. Planned since 1991, but delayed by municipal political in-fighting, it is due to be implemented in 1993.

The Spanish Quarter Association. This group operates in this poor and dense-ly populated city-centre neighbourhood where nearly 6,500 children under 14 live without the benefit of parks or playgrounds. Founded in 1978 by Giovanni Laino, the group's current Director, the Association runs a youth centre and has initiated several projects which have successfully involved local youths. The centre's programmes, such as its photography course, aim to offer children an opportunity to "acquire confidence and skills, to enjoy themselves, to work together with other children and caring adults." Al-though not all the Association's initiatives are exclusively for children, most contribute to children's well-being.

Following six years of experience in providing some youths with employ-ment in a community-based handbag factory, the Association is currently under review by the EEC for special funding to open an expanded plant. If a recent proposal is approved, 300 young people will be trained in a large abandoned shoe factory.

The Association has also been able to utilize state funding (Article 23) to train 162 unemployed youth in "community research and data processing." Called "Butterfly City," the project sent the young people to collect informa-tion on the population, economic activities, housing, services, and so on to create a database. This activity has been useful not only in providing a guaranteed income and experience to unemployed youth, but also for the contribution it makes to the community.

Indeed, this action research encouraged children to use the new youth centre. Hundreds of children and teens, most of whom come from unstable family situations, use the centre each day. Now, in order to encourage other young people from equally poor but more stable families to take advantage of the centre, these children were identified by the database and mailed information on the centre.

The Association is a member of a citywide coordinating group of organizations involved with children and youth, drug prevention and group activities. This group's objectives are to exchange experiences and strategies, elaborate projects across different neighbourhoods, develop awareness and activate public funding.

The broad range of initiatives in Naples — chaotic perhaps, but demonstrating citizens' valid responses to problems — could incorporate new models of social action that tackle child-related problems on all fronts. But in order for this to happen, a coordinated programme of diversified interventions must be formulated, taking full advantage of existing resources and ongoing experiences. A step in this direction was taken in November 1992 with the establishment of a Coordinating Committee for the Municipality and for the Centre for Juvenile Justice of the city. The Committee has the task of planning new policies as well as coordinating existing city policies. The Committee will also stipulate agreements with family youth homes, youth communities and families that provide temporary foster care, and promote professional and vocational courses for teenagers. The first important experimental project is *Ragazzi Ancora* ("Still Children").

Thus, the premise for renewed attention to childhood and for the promotion of more effective and organized policies does exist. "With thoughtful politicians, effective administrators, trained social workers, popular consensus and public participation, it is still possible, here and now, to get back on the right path and face a civil challenge that is both a large gamble and an extraordinarily important social responsibility" (Sommella 1992).

Palermo

The situation in Palermo is not dissimilar to that of Naples, with however a somewhat less broadly mobilized civil sector and a smaller number of very active organizations. At the municipal level, Palermo, much as most Italian cities, lacks a comprehensive strategy for children and youth. The effectiveness of existing interventions is often particularly limited by a welfarist approach and stopgap measures for emergency situations. This has obviously brought about fragmentation, contradictions and ineffectiveness. In such a situation, institutionalization has been the most frequent response to the needs of children with serious difficulties. A further problem is the school system, which is plagued by waste and inefficiency. For example, Palermo lacks new school buildings while the city continues to pay some 18 billion lire (US $12 million) annually on rent for spaces which are seldom adequate.

Yet, from the legislative point of view, the tools do exist; it is at the implementation level that they falter. For instance, a regional law enacted in 1986 calls for the reorganization of the social-welfare services in Sicily. Municipal governments were instructed to institute new services and to set up three-year plans to bring about:

- full-day programmes for preschool, primary and middle schools (there are in fact very few schools in Palermo with full-day programmes);

- nursery schools (only 13 instead of 36, as planned, were opened during the first year);

- social centres (there are no public social centres yet, only several private centres);

- projects to provide alternatives for institutionalized children (no project has yet been designed);

- the creation of services for home-based and daytime assistance (currently none exist).

Even though the city administration has not shown a great deal of interest, there are a number of successful governmental and nongovernmental programmes. Among the most interesting are:

The ministerial project for recovering lost school years. This government action-research project aims to assist disadvantaged students in the schools within high-risk areas. The principle aim is to foster innovation in individual schools through specially trained personnel (teachers with degrees in psychology and pedagogy) and the establishment of close ties with the families in order to involve them in the education of their children.

"Project Childhood." This multifaceted project grew out of initiatives under-taken by the municipal council, the city's women's movement, and numerous voluntary agencies. Implemented between 1987 and 1990, it managed to achieve several significant results despite the city administration's far from progressive approach. Among its many activities, the project established collaboration between the social services and health departments; a shelter for abused children and mothers; a child abuse hot-line; public information programmes; and the rehabilitation and staffing of several older public nurseries.

The project also set up the "Territorial Service for Disadvantaged and Abused Children," coordinating social workers, psychologists, voluntary associations and existing services. A children's workshop was opened in the children's shelter, offering preadolescents the opportunity to take part in creative activities on a regular basis. A drug-prevention programme was also established.

Project for the prevention and cure of substance abuse. This municipal-run project is directed by Professor Luigi Cancrini. The main goals are:

- to integrate existing services;

- to establish coordinated services specifically aimed at recovery program-mes;

- to formulate an information campaign on child health care and health education, school and vocational information and support for youths living in high-risk areas.

The aim is to extend the reach of the municipal social services and draft agreements between the Municipality and private organizations.

The main project has four work units: *the neighbourhood project*; *the services project*; *the family project*; and *two special projects* aiming at pregnancy prevention, an awareness campaign and job training for rehabilitated drug users. However, neither of these last initiatives has been implemented.

Although having the best of premises, the project — still in its early stages — has encountered considerable setbacks due to technical problems, such as inefficiencies in the social services and red tape from the city administration. These problems have created a sense of precariousness and discouragement among personnel; however, the merits of the project deserve recognition. If the project's goals are achieved, the city's social services will be strengthened by the participation of private groups, particularly in health. Also, the focus of the project is on young people throughout the city rather than on specific areas, and it uses a systemic approach that explores the functions of a certain situation and then seeks possible solutions from within the situation itself. Furthermore, the project is designed to coordinate ongoing services, thus profiting from existing resources.

Although these last years have witnessed a growing awareness and increased presence of strongly committed social forces, the movement for children and their rights still lacks a comprehensive plan. There are, however, encouraging signs of change, both in the instruments needed to confront the situation and in the underlying attitudes of officials. The complete picture points to approaches which, if properly developed, could contribute an up-to-date working and legislative tool capable of triggering lasting changes. An example is Law 216, which aims at providing training and employment for convicted minors; however, its overriding goal is prevention. This requires the establishment of structures, like youth communities, trade and vocational schools, support centres for troubled families, and drug prevention centres, which seem to be particularly lacking in the South. But first and foremost it requires the appropriate identification and utilization of existing resources and their coordination in a joint programme.

The preconditions for change exist; it is a matter of transforming ideas into results. A recent statement by the Minister of Justice captures this new political awareness: "We must at last think not of small-scale policies for our young ones, but of broad and ongoing policies for those who will one day be big, and who have large needs and important rights already today."

**Box 6.4   Voluntary Organizations and Volunteer
Group Participation, Milan**

Voluntary work in Milan is regulated by regional law No. 1 (1986) which
provides for the contribution of volunteers in social programmes and for the
registration of voluntary organizations. This law provides for voluntary initiatives to be carried out with the coordination and monitoring of municipal
social service departments. Qualified organizations may gain public financing and work with social service departments in formulating strategies.

Voluntary organizations work together with municipal personnel in various
services, thus providing greater convergence with qualified personnel; in
addition, volunteers can also act independently, working for instance with
children in troubled families and at-risk adolescents. Voluntary organizations
can anticipate municipal services with their own interventions. For instance,
the *Associazione NAGA* provides medical services for non-resident foreigners
and the *Associazione Solidarietà AIDS* promotes many initiatives regarding
this disease. In 1992 there were 1,030 such organizations registered in Lombardy and 111 in the city of Milan.

There are also a great many groups and individuals that carry out informal
initiatives, often with church parishes, area councils and various public services. Informal voluntary activities have been encouraged by the city administration, which has established an office to help connect demand with
supply. While only adults may work as volunteers in the public sector, informal
groups include numerous youths. Thus, voluntary work provides opportunities
for young people, particularly those living in housing developments on the
city outskirts.

Milan

Signs of change towards a more comprehensive approach in programming
for young people are evident in Milan, where policies are primarily preventive, in contrast with the tendencies described for Naples and Palermo. In fact
there has been an increase in recent years of more targeted and better coordinated services — at least in planning if not in implementation. Milan
therefore presents innovative features and a legislative and operational
framework which provides practical guidelines for other cities.

In Milan youth services are managed on the basis of a regional law passed
in January 1986 that calls for the development of a Three-Year Social Welfare
Plan in which general objectives and operational strategies are clearly outlined on the basis of local needs. According to city policy the various departments within the municipal government are to work closely in prevention,
support and family substitution (Figure 6.3).

Joint initiatives between the public health centres and the municipal social
services, for example, are established by formal agreement and call for
municipal personnel and health service personnel to work side by side in

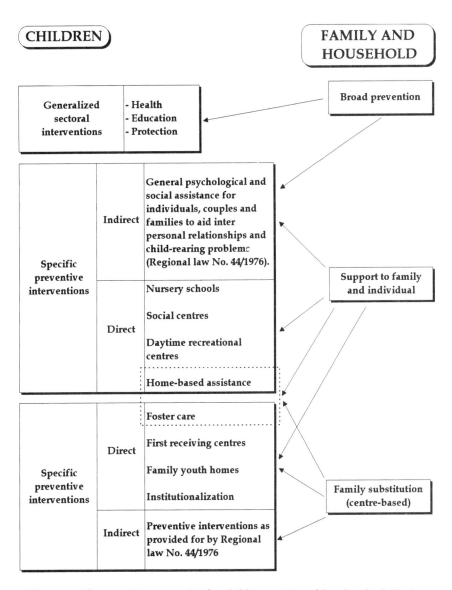

Figure 6.3. Intervention strategies for children, region of Lombardy (Milan).

areas such as foster care, disabilities, family health centres and drug abuse. In the area of schooling, the municipality and the provincial Office of Education collaborate on educational projects for young children that can involve whole classes or individual students. In the past several years the provincial education authorities and the Municipality have taken steps to encourage the attendance and integration of Gypsy children and disabled children and have designed special lesson materials on the prevention of violence, drug treatment and substance abuse. Joint programmes between the Municipality and the juvenile court system involve judges and specialized social-work teams that collaborate in the investigation of alleged crimes, provide home-based family support for the child or, alternatively, foster care or placement in a community.

Of the various bodies working with the Municipality, NGOs play a central role. These organizations operate according to various modalities:

- partial collaboration with private institutions, such as religious institutes, that are also involved in other interventions;

- collaboration with centres that work exclusively with the Municipality (e.g., action and research centres for child abuse victims and their families and several youth communities);

- collaboration with cooperatives on joint projects by the public and private sectors.

ADM — Home-based assistance project for children. An example of such a joint programme is ADM (*assistenza domiciliare minori*, home-based assistance for children), sponsored by the city's Social Services Department. ADM is undoubtedly one of the most innovative interventions in Italy, and it is to be hoped that this approach will be applied in a great many other interventions, and not only those for young people.

ADM provides for home-based support for children and their families who are experiencing a crisis. This experimental project was initiated in 1985 on the basis of work previously carried out by the Social Service Departments: since then it has improved organizationally and made its approach more specific.

The aim is to prevent family breakdown and help individual children remain with their families by developing the potential for cohesion that still exists within the family. The underlying principle is that the home is the setting where the trouble develops, but also contains the best resources for resolving difficulties.

The project operates through flexible individualized interventions aimed at the nuclear family and carried out by social workers and specialized personnel from the public sector, as well as by counsellors and educators from the private sector. Particularly in its early stages, it offers a range of activities to improve the relationships within the family, such as helping with household chores and counselling for the child as well as other family members. The intervention may run from several months up to more than one year.

The key to success lies in the training of personnel, who must be able to manage situations of considerable stress and overcome understandable suspicion from the families.

Some of the most outstanding features of the project are:

- the personalized approach to each case, based on the needs, resources and willingness of the child and his or her family;

- the flexibility and adaptability in addressing the individual cases;

- use of the child's own home as the source of support;

- a direct reading of the child's difficulties without the interference of traditional authority figures;

- the adoption of work methods which, in their approach to the family, differ from both the typical welfare model and the therapeutic model;

- the correlation between the child's troubles and the family's problems as a central working strategy;

- the establishment of an ongoing relationship with the family, rather than relying on an aid model;

- the utilization of the private sector and its coordination with public social services;

- a new emphasis on the role of the social worker, who leads the small ADM team, which includes a counsellor and, at times, other professionals such as psychologists;

- the extension of the concept of "home" to include the broader daily social environment.

The ADM project has grown over the years and is now active in 14 of the city's 20 administrative zones, especially in the outlying neighbourhoods where living conditions are most difficult. The number of children directly involved is continuing to grow, increasing, for example, from only eight children during the last three months of 1985 to 238 children in 1991. From October, 1985 to December, 1991, 519 children and 352 families participated in ADM. Since its outset, 70 percent of the children involved have been males between eight and 15. Many have learning difficulties — 30 percent of the school-age children have been held back in school — and socialization problems. Moreover, the children's families are often large, with financial, employment and housing problems; most families have migrated from other parts of Italy and are thus without the support of the extended family and friends. Nearly half of the children (45 percent) live with one parent, usually the mother, often as a result of divorce (52 percent). Thus, most of these children come from "weakened" families.

The ADM project is funded by the Milan municipal budget. In 1991, for example, it cost just under 1.3 billion lire (around $1 million) (Municipality of Milan 1991b). The project is generally cost-effective as well; in fact, even in lengthy and difficult cases, the per-child cost of ADM is considerably less than maintaining the child in an institution. A limited investment, if well-timed, can be sufficient to prevent painful family situations; a much larger investment, along with the support of other services, is required to keep families with serious difficulties united.

The project is an effective alternative to institutionalization and means of prevention of serious problems. In both cases and through different approaches, ADM is able to provide the instruments to meet temporary difficulties, modify damaging relationships and attitudes, and bring about changes in behaviour, so that the child can attain a greater degree of autonomy and well-being. According to the evaluation provided by social workers of the first 103 completed ADM cases, 64 fulfilled their objectives, 17 partly fulfilled them, 18 had mediocre results and in only 4 cases did the situation remain unchanged.

The project is not without its problems. Foremost is the relationship that often develops between the social worker and the parents, who may believe that they should delegate their responsibility for the child to the social worker. Another is the intense relationship that is often established between the child and the counsellor, which can lead to emotional dependence (of the child) and emotional over-involvement (of the counsellor).

Other problems relate to difficulties that the personnel sometimes have in adapting to work methods based on collaborative effort. It also occasionally requires time to develop good working relations and cooperation within work-teams. Other problems have arisen from the shortage of sites outside the home for activities requiring silence and concentration. Finally, there is a need for an effective information campaign — also reaching out to other services, including schools — to communicate the project's goals, its approach and its criteria for selecting families. Such a campaign would also be a valuable means of tracing children and families in need.

In order to take full advantage of this original and innovative community-based resource and fully utilize its preventive potential, the city administration should act promptly and budget for its expansion. Unfortunately, recent demoralizing budget cuts of 30 percent have confirmed that, in times of financial crisis, the project cannot even count on the financial resources that are available to it today, even in Milan where integrated programming is actively implemented.

Coordination of programmes and services

In Milan, overall coordination occurs at the central level; however, the services are carried out through a network which, in theory, produces coordinated interventions by specialized personnel. One of the most outstanding features of this approach is its flexibility to respond to a broad range of needs while stressing individualized approaches.

Present city policies encourage the increasing delegation of tasks to the private sector so that NGO resources can help broaden and improve the scope of public services. The coordination is provided by the *Consulta Minori*, which allows for NGO input into municipal planning; by the Commission for Community Services, which coordinates the planning and management phases of the interventions carried out by NGOs; and by working agreements with NGOs on the procedures to be followed for individual projects.

Lastly, municipal service departments also plan, coordinate and monitor the activities of voluntary groups and organizations, which can gain official recognition if they meet the established standards (see Box 6.4).

The urban teams in the three cities have identified the existence of numerous resources — sometimes poorly developed or little used — as well as initiatives and ideas that aim to improve the conditions of children. Despite the relative lack of formal evaluations and self-monitoring, an assessment of their strengths and weaknesses, the obstacles they face and their ability to produce positive results makes it possible to obtain lessons for the planning and implementing of future city programmes.

A GLIMMER OF HOPE

Towards a New Italian Social Policy for Children and Youth

On the basis of the initiatives and experiences — both positive and negative — observed in these three Italian cities, it is possible to point to particularly effective strategies, based on the reorganization of existing models and, above all, on a comprehensive and dynamic vision of the problems faced by the younger generations. These trends are:

A shift from welfarist to educational approaches. In Milan, for instance, this has meant going beyond the "shelter" mentality, not only for emergency situations, but also for preschool education, which now aims at developing the cognitive and social abilities of the young child. In the other two cities such a shift is urgently needed.

Also pointing in this direction are programmes to meet the growing demand for skills development, socialization and vocational training, including special courses for school dropouts to complete their education.

A shift from emergency solutions to more preventive approaches. This can be done by creating space for pre-teens in existing services — public family health centres, youth centres, summer programmes — and by creating group initiatives for teens as well as training programmes for parents and social workers. Initiatives with the direct participation and involvement of children can help instil self-confidence and a sense of responsibility. Finally, initiatives that restore the social importance of the schools are necessary.

Coordination of the public and private social sectors. Public and private institutions must work together, since the problems of children cannot be resolved without the participation of civil society.

A shift from institutionalization to a better use of resources within the family environment. A decrease in traditional child abandonment and the rise of new, more complex kinds of hardship have made institutionalization increasingly counterproductive and outdated. New strategies and programmatic responses are needed. When family-based solutions are not possible — often only temporarily — recourse is being increasingly made to alternatives to institutionalization, such as foster care and small youth communities and family youth homes where live-in social workers are the "heads of household." Solutions that recognize the central role of the family and of the home environment require, however, a solid commitment to policies that will properly support the family.

The importance of involving urban neighbourhoods. Developing resources within neighbourhoods is an important step in providing support for families in difficulty.

CONCLUSION

Two closely connected areas need to be examined: (1) a change in the cultural significance of childhood, and (2) technical and organizational improvements that will help ensure more focused and systematic planning for children in cities.

A new cultural concept of childhood in Italy needs to go far beyond "love" and "affection" for children. These sentiments are firmly rooted in Italian culture; indeed, dedication and attachment to children have always provoked strong, passionate feelings. On a much more profound level, this new culture must signify "social responsibility," an awareness of the specialness of the child's world, and, above all, a respect for the ways in which children develop in a complex modern society. A new culture of childhood thus means working towards a fresh perspective of children in society, viewing them, most importantly, in their wholeness, as active members of society and future adults. The Italian public has grown increasingly concerned about child-related issues; however, numerous ambiguities and contradictions persist. The "best interests of the child" (see Article 3 of the Convention on the Rights of the Child) is not always a principle which prevails in social policy considerations.

While Italian laws, as such, may be among the most innovative and sensitive on these issues, this is not sufficient in itself; in our complex and industrialized societies, a political and personal commitment towards children is needed. In Italy, the "passage" from an "enunciation of the principle" to "the declarations of the right and the full implementation of the decree" needs to be made (Palomba 1991).

This points to the need to promote children's issues on the political agenda through mobilization and awareness-building, beginning at the local level. As the leading citizens of their cities and spokespersons for their constituents, mayors can play an especially important role in bringing about changes in the urban fabric, promoting concrete actions and strategies so that our cities can become more liveable. There is, therefore, a need for ongoing commitment at this municipal level to carry on with the work being done, to coordinate and support the different levels of action, while constantly monitoring children's conditions, improving and integrating the projects already underway, and promoting new strategies.

Together with this shift of vision, there is also a need for technical and organizational improvements. The analysis of social services in each city has presented a picture of sectoral fragmentation. This was particularly apparent, together with a lack of political commitment, in the two southern cities. The uncoordinated deployment of resources, the lack of comprehensive plans; and the irregular and casual nature of the interventions themselves, which were often remote from the real problems, represented the most striking problems. At the same time, there were indications of innovation, a sense of transition and a struggling to come of age in each of the cities.

These objectives were restated in the final declaration of the International Meeting of Mayors, Urban Planners and Policy Makers held in Florence in October, 1992 (see Chapter 8). The strategies most urgently called for were: improved organization, coordination and convergence of interests, optimizing resources and investments, and fostering education, social awareness and social mobilization for a new vision of childhood. The development of these strategies is the challenge that awaits Italian politicians and society as they tackle the multifaceted problems still facing their children. The first step, our analysis tells us, is to improve children's living standards. "We cannot demand that the younger generations accept the burden of the errors and encumbrances of a society that they have not contributed to and built, if, at the same time, they have not been granted acceptable living standards and equal rights to citizenship" (Sgritta 1991).

A first concrete result of the Meeting and Project may be seen in Milan, where there are plans for a Council for Child and Family Development, with the participation of the Mayor. The Council will oversee the planning of children's programmes and carefully monitor their rights and assist in the coordination and deployment of municipal resources. In particular, the Council will provide direction for city planning and carry out experimental participatory interventions.

In order to place children's issues more squarely on the city agenda, it is necessary however, that:

- far-sighted preventive approaches replace ad hoc emergency solutions;
- informed analysis replace sensationalism; and
- concrete action replace the glib words of politicians.

The time is ripe for action in Italy. Existing decentralization trends, the ongoing debureaucratization of services, and the growing number of voluntary organizations interested in social issues open the way for change. Politicians are becoming more accountable to the electorate; morality and social responsibility have again become positive attributes. Building on such opportunities should enable:

- the greater involvement of young people in initiatives;
- increased experimentation;
- more effective organization and decision-making regarding goals and resources;
- the tailoring of programmes to specific problems and available resources;
- the evaluation of programmes in terms of cost-effectiveness and social benefits;
- improved coordination of and support for existing human resources (public sector, NGOs, voluntary groups).

To achieve this more comprehensive and coordinated approach we must have "a fuller and more detailed understanding of the child's world. Such knowledge can be obtained by creating a sort of "social ledger," a system of "monitoring" which, through surveys and systematic analyses, can reveal how and where children spend their time as they grow up as well as expose the consequences of the systematic neglect of the needs of children by the institutions, and of the indirect effects of many social, economic and political decisions that are made exclusively in function of the adult segment of society" (Sgritta 1988).

Through substantive changes such as these, and above all through a careful evaluation of the effectiveness of available resources, it will become easier to promote programmes that address the many diverse needs of children. The problems facing children are closely interwoven into the country's social, political and cultural fabric; suitable responses must therefore be solidly grounded in an informed understanding of children, their families and the urban neighbourhoods in which they live.

NOTES

1. This chapter constitutes a synthesis of the most significant results obtained in the first stage of the Urban Child Project in Italy. It has been written from the reports containing data and analyses compiled by the Urban Child Project re-

search teams in Naples, Milan, and Palermo coordinated and directed by, respectively, Luciano Sommella (1990), Annalisa Rossi Cairo (1990) and Angela Di Pasquale (1990). For information on the overall situation in Italy, the report edited by Giovanna D'Alessandro (1990) was used. Data on immigrant and Gypsy children was contributed by Matilde Grechi and the data on psychological and emotional-relational disturbances was furnished by Giancarlo Rigon. Additional information came from Ray Lorenzo (1992). The translation was done by Richard Dunbar.

2. In 1971 the administration of publicly financed institutions providing child services was transferred to the regional governments, which had been created in 1990. In 1977 the responsibility for all youth policy (normatively redefined as preventive and broadly community-based) was attributed to municipalities under the direction of the regional legislatures.

3. While Genoa has experienced an industrial decline (Picchieri 1989) and Turin is a fully industrialized city (Bagnasco 1986), Milan shows signs of post-industrialization. Industries are moving from the city to the 108 municipalities within the metropolitan area and the tertiary service sector is growing (Perulli 1992). Most cities in the South continue to grow in a context of underdevelopment; rather than serving as the centre of regional development, they often can only respond to the immediate needs of the more socioeconomically advantaged portions of their urban population (Crisantino 1990).

4. The terms "family youth home" and "youth community" refer to the experimental structures most commonly called "comunità" in Italian. An unofficial estimate has placed the number of family youth homes in Italy at around 3,000. They create a "family" atmosphere for a small group of children, usually around eight, and trained social workers are the "heads of the household." Ideally, these homes use the services of the surrounding town or neighbourhood and, when possible, maintain ties between the children and their families. In youth communities, larger numbers of children live together in an assemblage of homes, recreating a community atmosphere and a communal way of living.

5. Until the 1960s most NGOs were religious and nonreligious institutions or foundations, usually orphanages and centres for abandoned or sick children, often with attached schools. One exception is the youth towns of Don Bosco, established with a philosophy of full children's participation and education through doing. These have now been replicated the world over.

    During the 1970s many organizations became public welfare institutions with paid personnel; some became youth communities. Especially in northern and central Italy, smaller and largely voluntary associations, such as family youth homes, increasingly obtained funds from the public sector in exchange for services to children.

    In the late 1970s and early 1980s, new forms of associations (therapy centres, youth associations, summer camps, after-school organizations, nurseries, etc.) loosely connected with the public social services, evolved. More recently, "social cooperatives," have been established, concentrated in the areas of employment, social health and education. These are nonprofit, as are the majority of voluntary organizations, but have some paid employees. Law 381 of 1991 (national) recognizes "social cooperatives" as potential partners of the public sector at the local level.

6. The first stop for most accused or suspected juvenile offenders is a reception centre (*centro di prima accoglienza*), housed within the juvenile detention centre. This structure also continues to follow the individual cases after the judge has decided if the youth is to be held in the detention centre, placed in home-detention, given parole, or, more rarely (due to their lack of availability) placed in a family youth home or youth community.

   Daytime centres (*Servizi diurni*) (where available) and part-time penal institutions (*Istituti di semilibertà*) are operated by the juvenile detention centres and provide educational activities and job training in collaboration with local schools and social-service offices. These services are primarily for detainees who are granted day leave, offenders placed in home-detention or in family youth homes and youth communities, or who have been, in general, placed under certain restrictions.

   At present, the Ministry of Justice has agreements with 40 family youth homes and youth communities, generally run by private organizations, for a total of 186 places. In these cases, the juvenile offenders live side by side with the other "members" of the family, i.e., abandoned children, children experiencing serious family trouble, and children whose families are unable to care for them. The Ministry has also set up two family youth homes in southern Italy; these, too, are run through agreements with private organizations.

7. Organized crime in Italy has a long history, in part related to the dependent development of its southern regions and to the generally weak presence of the relatively recent (1870) Italian state. Called *camorra* in the Naples area, *mafia* or *cosa nostra* in Sicily and *'ndrangheta* in Calabria, organized crime has had a somewhat distinct development in each region (Blok 1974, Schneider and Schneider 1976, Figurato and Airolda 1981).

   The existing networks throughout the Mediterranean for the illegal traffic such as cigarettes by the Neapolitan camorra after the war of merchandise, later became useful channels for moving heroin and cocaine arriving in Sicily. Initially, the criminal organizations in the three regions had to rely on each other to assemble the large capital needed for covering the cost of shipments. During the 1970s, they became tied to the expanding industrial sector and moved into international financial networks, money laundering and arms trafficking. Between 1976 and 1980, Sicilian families captured the international heroin market from France; about 30 percent of the heroin needed to satisfy domestic demand in the US was refined in Palermo and distributed mostly in New York City.

   Connections with the Colombian cocaine trade were made during the 1980s, thanks to some Italian immigrants and mafia networks in Latin American. Italian criminal organizations took control of much of the cocaine entering Europe. In Italy, the use of heroin and cocaine has also expanded (Brigantini 1990).

8. The recent "Jervolino-Vassalli Law" made the possession of drugs illegal in Italy, further penalizing drug users by calling for prison terms based on the amount of drugs found on the offender (Article 72, among others). Italian prisons are now filled well beyond capacity (50,000 prisoners in facilities built

to house only 25,000); moreover, from 35 percent to 70 percent of the new prisoners abuse drugs, which are smuggled into prison (Brigantini 1988). The referendum of April 19, 1993, has now abrogated the section of the law requiring imprisonment for drug possession; drug rehabilitation communities and individual medical treatment will hopefully replace imprisonment.

9. The total is greater than 100 because more than one reason can exist for the same case.

Chapter
SEVEN

Some Comparative Urban
Trends: Street, Work,
Homelessness, Schooling and
Family Survival Strategies

Cristina Szanton Blanc

DIAGNOSING DISADVANTAGES OF URBAN CHILDREN

In the preceding chapters, five Country Teams analysed some of the circumstances contributing to the distress of urban children in 21 cities. Detailed life histories and observation of children and their families have added another dimension to the data. What conclusions can we now draw? What have the studies taught us about diagnosis, policy, strategic categories of urban children in difficult circumstances, and the establishment of priorities?

In this chapter, we will compare the reports, prepared under the general coordination of the UNICEF International Child Development Centre, drawing upon additional primary and secondary data. Throughout the analysis, we will emphasize the importance of understanding the ways children, their families, their communities and larger societal problems are interrelated. We hope to suggest ways to diagnose and monitor children's problems and to act upon their causes more effectively.

This will lead us to further questions, which we consider in the concluding chapter of this book. What attitudes are expressed towards children at different levels? How can families be better supported? How can they better support their children? How can resources at the city level be maximized? How can communities and cities be more helpful to their children?

A discussion of the innovative policies and programmes in each of the five countries will help us respond to these questions. We will examine the issues of family preservation, schooling, leisure time, children's work, street life, physical environment and community development, placing particular emphasis on the need for the increased participation of children and their families in all aspects of community life. Specific actions will be recommended. An argument will be presented for integrated responses to children and their families through the fuller utilization of community and city strengths in coordination with national programmes.

Initial Challenges

The Urban Child Project faced enormous challenges, as seen in the Introduction. Furthermore, it was carried out in five countries that span the North/South, industrialized country/developing country divide. They are at different stages of development and at different moments of transition. Two of them, India and Italy, have reasonably strong democratic traditions. Brazil, Kenya and the Philippines have become democracies more recently, after periods of authoritarianism that were sometimes quite severe. Two, India and Kenya, were former British colonies and present some institutional similarities, whereas in the Philippines, the influence of the United States is particularly evident. All five countries face some similar as well as very different crises.

Table 7.1 summarizes some macro indicators and major trends for each country. Despite many limitations, these data provide an overview of the transformations each country has undergone over the last three decades. The increase in GNP, considerable in Italy, has also been reasonably high in Brazil and the Philippines where issues of redistribution are however critical; in contrast, GNP has been stagnating in both Kenya and India since the 1970s. Population densities are highest in the Philippines and higher in India than in Italy, with strong agricultural density in all three countries.

The percentage of population under 15 is conspicuous in all four developing countries but not in Italy, where a steady decline is evident. Crude death rates are highest and life expectancy at birth lowest in Kenya and India. Total gross enrolment rates for secondary school are particularly high in the Philippines for both males and females, even with respect to Italy.

Similarly, the 21 cities ultimately selected for study vary in size and in terms of many other characteristics (Box 7.1). Some are rapidly expanding industrial centres (Cebu, Rajahmundry and Goiânia, for instance). Four were among the world's 30 largest urban agglomerations in 1990: São Paulo was third largest; Bombay, ninth; Delhi, seventeenth; and Metro Manila, twentieth (United Nations 1991a). Others are becoming megacities (Nairobi) or post-industrial service cities (Milan). Large or growing, these cities have attracted people escaping from the lack of opportunities, stagnant development and poor conditions of rural areas.

Within the same country, differences among cities may be striking. Milan and Palermo are historically, culturally and economically worlds apart. Availability of services may also vary considerably. Even when the same social policies are in effect, they may be applied differently because of local conditions (for example, schooling schedules in Manila differ from those in Cebu because of shortages of school buildings and a poor student-to-teacher ratio in the capital city, which in turn affect the quality of education children receive and their ability to combine study with work).

Country Teams (see Box 7.1) sought to understand the extent to which differences among cities might be reflected in the children's conditions or could influence programmes. The strains of a too-rapid economic development were, for example, particularly evident in some Andhra Pradesh cities in India as well as in Cebu and Davao in the Philippines.

Beyond objective indicators of social conditions and degrees of poverty, differences often derived from the "upbeat or downbeat moods" of the different countries or cities, as subjectively perceived. Despite all of these differences, the Project was able to pinpoint some striking similarities in children's conditions, showing that, to paraphrase Kaminsky, the main problems end up being a recurring few.

A generative project. When the Project Coordinator and principal author of this book joined the project in late 1989, the broad objectives had already been decided by a consultative group composed of UNICEF officers and external consultants. These objectives included formulating guidelines for preparing CEDC situational analyses that would lead to more preventive action by reassessing typologies of at-risk urban children and their families and neighbourhoods and paying particular attention to the psychosocial problems disadvantaged children and their families face. It also included making related preventive suggestions.

As a first step,[1] the Project Coordinator visited two countries where particularly innovative projects had been developed, Brazil and the Philippines. She also sought the advice of well-informed people in Kenya, India and Italy. It was immediately apparent that:

- the information available was generally limited;
- whatever information existed was usually not focused on the issues the Project was specifically raising, such as the relationship between children and their families;

Table 7.1. Social and Economic Indicators for the Five Countries of the Study (1960s–ca. 1990)

Indicator	Brazil			Philippines			Italy			Kenya			India		
	1960s	1970s	c. 1990	1960s	1970s	c. 1990	1960s	1970s	c. 1990	1960s	1970s	c. 1990	1960s	1970s	c. 1990
Income[a]															
GNP per capita (at 1990 prices)	270	1070	2680	180	340	730	1260	3700	16830	100	230	370	90	170	350
Natural Resources															
Population density[a]	10	13	17	300	300	300	173	184	191	17	24	40	148	187	253
Agricultural density (population agric. land)[a]	47	50	59	413	526	653	255	316	340	24	34	58	275	339	460
Net deforestation rate (decadal % of change)[a]	-2.0	2.0	-4.0	-0.3	-1.6	-1.9	2.0	2.0	0.0	-7.7	-8.0	-8.0	3.0	-0.2	-2.0
Welfare															
Daily calorie supply (cals./pop.)[a]	2417	2564	2751	1875	2094	2375	3097	3378	3504	2208	2223	2163	2021	2023	2229
Percentage of GDP spent on food[a]	–	24	–	–	–	–	–	20	14	–	28	31	–	43.6	35
Population structure															
Total population in millions[a]	–	108	150	32	43	61	52	55	57	10	13	24	487	613	850
Rate of population change (%) (1)[c]	3.0	2.6	2.1	–	–	2.65	0.6	0.6	0.0	3.0	3.3	3.6	2.3	2.3	2.1
Age dependency ratio (%) (2)[a]	89	78	66	92	83	76	52	57	45	106	112	113	78	77	70
Population under age 15 (%)[c]	43.6	42.3	35.2	44.6	42.8	39.9	24.8	24.5	16.7	45.6	48.2	49.9	40.4	39.8	36.9
Urbanization															
Population urban (%)[b]	44.9	55.8	74.9	30.3	33.0	42.6	59.4	64.3	68.9	7.4	10.3	23.6	18.0	19.8	27.0
Urban population growth rate (%)[b]	5.1	4.6	3.2	3.92	4.03	3.77	1.5	1.4	0.4	5.7	6.9	7.2	2.66	3.27	3.6
Rural population growth rate (%)[b]	1.4	0.2	-0.8	2.39	2.77	1.58	-0.6	-0.7	-0.9	2.8	2.9	2.6	2.17	2.04	1.5
Tempo of urbanization (3) (%)[b]	3.7	4.4	4.0	1.53	1.26	2.19	2.1	2.1	1.3	2.9	4.0	4.6	0.79	1.23	2.1

cont'd

Table 7.1. cont'd

Indicator	Brazil 1960s	Brazil 1970s	Brazil c.1990	Philippines 1960s	Philippines 1970s	Philippines c.1990	Italy 1960s	Italy 1970s	Italy c.1990	Kenya 1960s	Kenya 1970s	Kenya c.1990	India 1960s	India 1970s	India c.1990
Determinants of Population Growth															
Fertility															
Crude birth rate (per 1,000)[a]	39	33	27	41.6	36.6	28.8	19	15	10	52	53	45	44.8	37.5	30
Total fertility rate[a]	5.60	4.40	3.20	6.80	5.46	3.54	2.70	2.20	1.30	8	8.10	6.50	6.23	5.35	3.94
Contraceptive prevalence rate (%)[a]	–	–	65	–	–	44	–	–	–	–	–	27	–	19.5	45
Mortality															
Crude death rate (per 1,000)[a]	11	9	7	11.7	9.7	7.2	10	10	9	20	16	10	20.3	15.1	11
Life expectancy at birth (years)[a]	57.10	61	66.20	55.5	59.1	64.4	70.4	72.60	77.50	47.50	52.20	58.90	45.2	58.4	59.8
Child Health															
Infant mortality rate (per 1,000)[a]	104	84	58	72.4	58.0	40.8	36	21	9	112	92	67	149.8	129.6	91.9
Under-5 mortality rate (per 1,000)[a]	–	–	69	–	–	51.4	–	–	11	–	–	105	–	–	118.0
Children 12–15 months still breastfeeding(%)[d]	–	–	25	–	–	–	–	–	–	–	–	83	–	–	–
Children 0–4 years underweight (%) (4)	–	–	7	–	–	–	–	–	–	–	–	14	–	–	63
Human Investment															
Population per physician[a]	2500	1600	1080	–	9100	6566	1854	–	234	13282	7900	10132	4880	4900	2500
Total gross enrolment rate secondary school[a]	16	26	39	–	113	111	47	70	78	4	13	23	27	26	43
Female gross enrolment rate secondary school[a]	16	28	45	–	107	110	41	66	78	2	9	19	16	16	31
Total literacy rate at ages 15+[a]	–	–	81	–	–	–	–	91	94	20	–	69	–	–	48
Female literacy rate at ages 15+[a]	–	–	80	–	–	–	–	–	–	–	–	58	–	–	34
Newspaper circulation (per 1,000 persons)[a]	32	39	57	17.6	15.9	37.7	112	114	81	10	13	11	13.0	15.3	19.8

Notes: (1) calculated on most recent intercensal interval; (2) ratio of population aged 15–64 to other ages (per 100 persons); (3) difference between urban and rural population growth rates; (4) moderately or severely underweight. Sources: [a]World Bank, *Social Indicators of Development 1991–92*; [b]United Nations (1991a); estimates are for 1960, 1970 and 1990; growth rates refer to 1955–60, 1965–70 and 1985–90; [c]United Nations (1991b); [d]UNICEF (1993).

Box 7.1   The Twenty-One Cities of the Project

BRAZIL

Goiânia (nearly 1.7 million in 1990 from 940,000 in 1980). Capital of the State of Goiás in central Brazil.

São Paulo (nearly 17.4 million in 1990, up from 12.1 million in 1980). Founded in 1554, São Paulo is the largest city in South America, the third largest city worldwide, and Brazil's commercial and industrial centre.

INDIA

Bombay (ca. 18 million in 1991, up from about 8.2 million in 1981). A seaport and capital of Maharashtra, Greater Bombay is the ninth largest agglomeration worldwide and India's largest city. It has an estimated slum population of over 40 percent.

Cuddapah (215,545 in 1991). A medium-sized town in Andhra Pradesh, Cuddapah has low industrial development and low employment rates.

Delhi (up from about 5.7 million in 1981). Delhi (including Old and New Delhi) is the nation's capital and the 17th largest agglomeration worldwide. Its slum population reached 40 percent in 1980.

Hyderabad (4.3 million in 1991, with +24.4 decadal growth rate). The capital of Andhra Pradesh, Hyderabad is the fifth largest agglomeration and the second-fastest growing city (after Lucknow) in the nation.

Rajahmundry (over 403,780 in 1991). A medium-sized city located in the agriculturally prosperous coastal section of Andhra Pradesh, Rajahmundry is an economically expanding centre with a flourishing textile industry.

Vijayawada (845,305 in 1991). A city in Andhra Pradesh, E-SE of Hyderabad, Vijayawada is built on the river Kistna not far from the Gulf of Bengal.

Warangal (466,877 in 1991 and slightly over 335,000 in 1981). A city in Andhra Pradesh, in the less fertile zone of Talangana NE of Hyderabad, Warangal is a transportation centre with thriving textile and rug weaving industries.

ITALY

Milan (ca. 1.4 million in 1991, 300,000 less than 1976). The nation's commercial capital and second largest city after Rome, this post-industrial northern municipality has been losing some of its population to its immediate hinterland. It is losing its industries but has seen an expansion in tertiary sector production (the fashion industry, communications, computer technology, services). Greater Milan on the other hand grew from 6.7 million inhabitants in 1980 to a projected 7.6 million in 1990.

Naples (just over 1 million inhabitants, down 150,000 from 1981). A seaport and the nation's third largest city, Naples, in southern Italy, is densely populated, with chaotic traffic, high pollution levels and few green areas. Its metropolitan population has remained stable at 4 million since 1980.

Palermo (about 700,000 in 1991, roughly the same as 1981). An ancient seaport and capital of Sicily, Palermo was heavily bombed during the Second World War and damaged by a 1968 earthquake. Its growth rate is stagnant.

KENYA

Nairobi (just over 1,5 million in 1990, up from about 863,000 in 1980). Capital of Kenya, Nairobi is also an important centre for commerce and tourism with a rapidly growing population. In 1990, 74 percent of its households had low or very low incomes. It has extensive slum populations.

Mombasa (517,000 in 1989 up from about 180,000 in 1962). One of the oldest cities of East Africa and Kenya's second city, Mombasa is an important seaport with a largely Muslim multiethnic population and a popular tourist spot thanks to its beautiful beaches.

Kisumu (229,000 in 1989 up from about 153,000 in 1979). The third city in Kenya, Kisumu is an important transportation centre situated on Lake Victoria. It has a thriving cotton and coffee market.

PHILIPPINES

Metro Manila (7.7 million in 1990 up from nearly 6 million in 1980). Three of its four cities were studied by the Project: **Caloocan City, Pasay City** and **Quezon City**. Metro Manila is the nation's legislative and administrative centre. In 1987, it had 591 squatter/slum areas with almost 2.5 million inhabitants crowded into its 636 km2.

Cebu (610,000 in 1990). With a daytime population of about 1 million, Cebu is the nation's second largest city and one of its fastest growing. A centre of commerce and tourism, Cebu also has a growing slum population.

Davao (about 844,000 in 1990 from ca. 139,000 in 1960). A seaport and capital of Mindanao, Davao is a sprawling commercial centre, rifted, however, by the continuing armed struggle for an independent Muslim state.

Olongapo (almost 198,000 in 1989). The city's destiny has been radically altered by the 1991 eruption of Mt. Pinatubo and the closure, in 1992, of the US naval base, which directly employed 35,000 Filipino workers and thousands more in the "rest and recreation" industry.

- no general cross-cultural standards were available to determine levels of need;

- the objectives required that Country Teams deal with complex, dynamic levels of causality, different from one country to another;

- the mandate was methodologically complex. Street and working children only partially represented urban CEDC problems and were an entry point to a whole range of other problems. Among their numbers, for example, there were few girls, relatively few drug abusers, and only certain kinds of workers. In order to analyse processes, the children needed to be studied in their various daily environments over time.

The Country Teams focused on street children and street-based working children (a large population of disadvantaged children in the four developing countries of the study, but also a disturbing presence in the southern cities of industrialized Italy). They analysed them on the streets, in institutions (where many from the streets had ended up) and also in the poor neighbourhoods (to identify problems at their origin); they were thus able to establish a broader range of types of children working in the informal sector and to set up both control and reference groups of non-working children.

General guidelines were prepared, focusing the researchers' attention on: (a) the current conditions of disadvantaged urban children, including their work, physical environment, health problems, time allocation, use of the city, and relations to parents, peers and the broader society; (b) the coping strategies, and the processes that lead to abuse, mistreatment, abandonment or other disadvantages; and (c) the levels of risk experienced by young people, including drug use, arrests, imprisonment, exploitation, abuse, AIDS, ill health and accidents. Because many of these elements were generally absent or poorly represented in the secondary material reviewed in each country, the researchers were also asked to undertake primary research.

This approach has allowed us to identify operationally useful categories of children, link children and families, and generate some important qualitative reflections on their levels of risk. It has ultimately yielded suggestions about key monitoring indicators and situational analyses (Appendix 1) as well as policy lessons on addressing the problems of street children, street-based working children and other related categories (Chapter 8).

Methodological Constraints and Opportunities

Secondary and primary data collection. In the four developing countries, the limited literature available focused on "street children"; that is *all* children living and/or working on the streets, with little or no distinction made between children who lived on their own and those who lived with their families. The quality and coverage of the studies available varied greatly. Some good occupational studies of disadvantaged working children had been produced, but they had not specifically investigated the children's living arrangements and their relationship to their families. To compensate for these shortcomings, specific studies to collect additional data were sponsored for this study (see Appendix 1).

The Urban Child Project was particularly aware of the need to balance cross-cultural comparability and the very real risk of imposing alien developmental values on the culture being studied. Because there was not sufficient time to develop instruments that functioned equally in all countries, a compromise was reached. General research and thematic guidelines were prepared and each Country Team developed its own specific instruments, which were thus, to a degree, culturally sensitive.

Still, the research instruments reflected a set of values that were not always made explicit, that varied by team, and that provided few opportunities for the parents or children themselves to frame the questions they thought were important. This is, of course, common to almost all social research with children.

This criticism raises important issues about what it means to interview children rather than adults. There is only limited expertise in this field since social scientists usually interview adults. The Country Teams used techniques appropriate to children, especially deprived, marginalized and generally disadvantaged children. Nonetheless, the researchers encountered difficulties because these "streetwise" children are known to be defensive and elusive, especially when talking to strangers. As confirmed by all NGOs on the teams, the children's initial stories often contradicted the subsequent versions pieced together by a street educator or social worker.

The *life histories* allowed us to analyse ongoing processes and thus better interpret the more quantitative data. However, collecting life histories is time-consuming and expensive. A total of 120 life histories of children and families have been collected in the five countries: 7 in Brazil, 33 in the Philippines, 17 in India, 45 in Kenya, and 18 in Italy. The children were selected on the basis of a certain degree of representativeness. The interaction with the children was, in the best of cases, established over time and provided authentic exchanges of information.

In addition to interviews with children and their families, the Country Teams, the Project Coordinator and various consultants interviewed some of the principal actors directly involved in making decisions about children. At the municipal level, informal in-depth interviews were carried out with mayors and their staffs, members of inter-agency committees, heads of city agencies and voluntary organizations, street educators, service operators, academics, urban planners and trainers; and at the national level, with key representatives in ministries, special commissions, urban planning institutes and UNICEF country offices. District- or state-level officials were at times contacted, especially in India, Brazil and Kenya, where they play special roles.

This study has used the information gathered not in a strictly comparative way, but rather, in conjunction with in-depth life histories, to illuminate quantitatively and qualitatively some recurrent patterns. The consistency of the patterns, especially in the street-based Philippines and Kenya data, is particularly impressive given the methodological limitations.

Objectives. The members of the Country Teams had different objectives: the focus of the project reflected the reigning preoccupation of collaborating agencies. The studies were, in part, also tailored to the programmatic needs of the UNICEF country offices, which provided their own guidelines on what they wished to see done. The Country Teams were multidisciplinary. Each team looked at the project from a different perspective and each had its own history, misunderstandings, politics and achievements. Important lessons were learned along the way.

The Project Coordinator gave suggestions and corrected parameters whenever possible. Even though the project was designed to be generative rather than strictly comparative, efforts were made to ensure some basic similarity in approaches and definitions while preserving the richness of each country's testimony. And we can now hope that the results of this vigorous effort will be useful to the broader academic and programming world and that it will raise new hypotheses and generate better informed future studies on urban children in distress.

How a Problem is Defined Conditions the Search for Solutions

From primarily normative categories (focused on problems) to more operational categories (describing a range of populations). International organizations have defined CEDC normative categories, each based on one specific problematic circumstance: labour, street life, armed conflicts, abandonment, imprisonment or abuse (with the exception of disabled children). Although these categories effectively identify problems in need of immediate attention, they identify the child only on the basis of a single difficult circumstance.

Broader *risk indicators* indiscriminately combine poverty, school dropout, single parenthood, displacement, violence, conflict with the law, substance abuse, neglect, homelessness and minority status. They monitor the progress in "tackling root causes" at the country level. They refer to types of potential risk, indicating certain characteristics that represent early symptoms and that may lead to still higher risk. Some represent the high-risk behaviour of the children themselves (substance abuse, for example); others characterize the families children are born into (single parenthood or minority status) and are part of a societal environment; still others occur over the course of time (neglect).

The CEDC categories assume that the particular circumstance in question (street life, for example) represents a danger, without actually assessing the problem. Similarly, risk indicators are based on risks whose effects have been assumed rather than documented. These effects have not been ordered sequentially according to levels or degrees of risk (see Figure 7.1) that would then point to levels of action. Finally, any given child is almost always facing a number of these risks simultaneously. Neither CEDC categories nor risk indicators should, therefore, be used as if actually different populations of children were being discussed. If the aim of policy makers is to find a single indicator in order to establish "a total estimated number of CEDC," they must be particularly careful of "additive numbers" based on these categories, which are actually "overlapping" (Manganhas 1992).

Normative categories are important for advocacy, whereas operational categories serve programming purposes. It is important, especially at the municipal level, to establish baseline populations of children-at-risk; locate them geographically (slums, urban peripheries, streets); determine where they can be reached not only at present, but also as their problems begin; prioritize their problems; and then outline interventions that would best respond to those problems. In other words, for interventions to be appropriately protective and preventive, they need to start from the children themselves rather than from the problems they face.

This approach does not exclude the use of secondary material from specialized sources, including the courts, street educators or social workers. It allows better decisions to be made about interventions likely to have the greatest impact. Once these steps have been taken, it is then possible to address each problem individually with specific interventions, which should be assessed, when possible, from the point of view of sustainability, cost-effectiveness and capacity to grow to scale.

The need to establish cross-cultural standards sensitive to children's developmental needs. Research findings must be measured against standards. In other words, before we can assess the situation of children, determine the effectiveness of past interventions and propose new interventions, we must have an explicit concept of what constitutes a healthy childhood, physically and psychologically. This raises a central question of values:

> Who decides what a healthy childhood is and, hence, what should the developmental goals of childhood be?

One important "guide to standards" and "framework for action" is the Convention on the Rights of the Child.[2] Because children's rights are codified in an international Convention:

> Governments, UNICEF and others working to achieve human development goals now have an even greater responsibility to ensure that children are protected from preventable diseases and malnutrition, that they have access to basic education, that they are protected from exploitation and from the effects of wars and natural disasters, and that they are enabled to participate in the life of their communities (Newman-Black 1991).

The Convention was carefully elaborated to be acceptable across political boundaries and to take into account cultural differences the world over. More culture-specific developmental goals of childhood can be found in anthropology and developmental psychology. Cultures have for generations defined what a healthy childhood is, and there remains much in parents' child-rearing practices that comes from this wisdom. However, with increased urbanization in all cultures, most local child-rearing practices have been adapted and transformed, while preserving some important core elements. At various points in this chapter, we will turn to some basic principles of child development and child-rearing that appear valid across cultures as possible sources of insight for guiding parents and for developing appropriate policies and programmes for children.

A working definition of child development emphasizes that development: (1) is multidimensional, including a physical, mental or broadly cognitive, emotional and social dimension (the ability to relate to others); (2) is integral, in the sense that these several dimensions are closely interrelated and affect each other; (3) occurs continually (throughout life) with some changes in emphasis at different ages; (4) occurs in interaction, on the basis of initiatives taken by both the child and the social environment; and (5) is patterned, but with a certain degree of variation by culture or individual. Its goal is adaptation to, and mastery (and transformation) of, one's surroundings (Myers 1991) and the achievement of full, responsible adulthood (Lerner 1991, Collins 1991).

At different ages, the four dimensions of physical, mental, emotional and social development acquire different emphases as children move from their immediate families to a broader social context that increasingly shapes their mental, emotional and social development. The study focused on the 6–18 age group, when children are most at risk in terms of work and street life. The importance of the distinction between the middle years (6–12) and early adolescence (13–15 years of age) has emerged in each study. These are two critical times in the child's schooling, street and work life, and thus provide the basis for a discussion of standards in the light of the child's developmental needs and rights (Lerner 1991, Collins 1991).

Similarly, some sharp gender differences appear, which are being emphasized especially by informed NGOs. Since the development of children occurs over years and differs by gender — aspects which the Convention, because of its global concerns, does not elaborate upon — we will continue to give special attention to the most critical transitions in the life paths of boys and girls, to provide a more informed discussion of their needs in specific settings.

Enumeration and Diagnosis

Identifying the CEDC population. From a policy and programming point of view, the first problem was one of defining urban children in distress and identifying their locations. This is the first issue government and non-governmental programmers have to face.

A rapid survey of the literature in each country revealed how remarkably little was known until recently about the real conditions of many of the children seen on the streets of Northern and Southern cities. As discussed at length in each chapter, no one seemed to know where the children came from, how often they were on the streets, for how long every day and what they did when they were not on the streets. This growing phenomenon, however, could no longer be ignored, not only because of media coverage but also because of pressures exerted by service sectors, the public and, increasingly, international organizations such as UNICEF or Save the Children.

The numbers game. The Project developed different strategies for estimating the numbers within each problem category. The country chapters present some of those estimates, but also refer to estimates from other sources (quoted from newspaper articles, for example, or obtained from NGOs), which are even less certain. The UNICEF urban officers in each country are constantly faced with the problem of providing figures, either for their own presentations or when they interact with NGOS, who tend to rely on large numbers to stress the importance of advocacy. Large estimates emphasize the importance of the problem, but can make it seem so overwhelming that policy makers are discouraged. Action in fact is more likely to be initiated when numbers are manageable.

Accurate estimating is an overwhelming task because some of the problems are not immediately visible, as has been explained, and it is often impossible to determine how many children in one given location experience a particular problem. It was assumed that some children, because of their visibility, could be more easily counted. This was true in the case of children in institutions, whose numbers are relatively low, but whose problems deserve special attention, as will be discussed later. In the case of the street-based children, Country Teams readily agreed that the count needed to be at the local, municipal level in order to be reasonably reliable. They also agreed that even municipal counts were essentially imperfect and that the numbers could shift greatly from one year to the next depending on circumstances. Much could be learned in trying to develop a reliable estimate.

The first step in producing such a count was to define "street children" more accurately and to establish a methodology. City-level analyses were often based on a one-day head count in smaller cities, such as Mombasa and Kisumu in Kenya, or, as in Manila, Nairobi and other large cities, on estimates derived from NGO statements. Even Brazil, relatively advanced in this regard, had not, by early 1990, elaborated a satisfactory methodology for establishing overall numbers, and was struggling with problems of diagnosis (Myers 1991, see also Brazil chapter). Other enumerations have been based on short, exploratory, survey-like questions (for example, the 1988 Ten City Study in the Philippines). The experience of the Project has allowed us to develop guidelines for establishing counts (see Appendix 1).

The second step was to determine where to find the children. As discussed in the Philippines, Brazil and Kenya chapters, street-based children usually assemble daily in certain areas for work and other activities. They are seen at busy intersections; in commercial areas, especially near markets and shopping centres; in parking lots, railway and bus stations, and areas outside international air terminals; on wharfs; in squares and parks; and in front of churches, hotels, entertainment places or tourist attractions. In these crowded locations, they encounter potential customers for their wares or services. An initial census found as many as 515 "hang outs" in the large and sprawling city of Mexico City (COESNICA 1992). Similar numbers were reported in Nairobi (Onyango et al. 1992) and in Manila by the PSSC survey.

Children tend to "stake out" locations for their income-generating activities with a certain regularity. In Cebu, out of a sample of 302 street-based children, 91 percent returned to the same places every day (mainly for work) and another 7 percent returned to the same places at least a few times a week (McGuire 1986). The same regularity was noted in other studies, regardless of the country.

The "work places" are not necessarily close to the children's homes, although both children and their parents would prefer them to be. Opportunities are difficult to find in the labour-abundant, informal urban sector of most developing countries. The children find what work they can through relatives, friends and word of mouth, as revealed in the life histories.

However, the children we see in the streets predominantly come from poor urban neighbourhoods and spend portions of their day in other locations. Other less visible children work within those neighbourhoods or alternate between different occupations. Thus an exclusive focus on work places in the street is inappropriate and street-based children should be traced back to their families and neighbourhoods for follow-up.

CHILDREN IN RELATION TO THEIR FAMILIES

Street Children

The Preamble to the Convention on the Rights of the Child recognizes,

> that the family, as the fundamental group of society and the natural environment for the growth and well-being of all its members and particularly children, should be afforded the necessary protection and assistance so that it can fully assume its responsibilities within the community ... [and] that the child, for the full and harmonious development of his or her personality, should grow up in a family environment, in an atmosphere of happiness, love and understanding.

The Convention also reinforces the concern that the family be helped to assume and carry out its responsibilities fully, unless proven unable to do so.

Such a consideration requires knowledge about the families of children in difficult circumstances. Similarly, programming at city level requires knowledge about where children are. How and when do family supports fail in each country? When does a child voluntarily sever ties with his or her family? What triggers this reaction? The information presented has allowed us to establish some surprisingly similar patterns concerning what happens to poor urban children as they face the uncertainties of city life. A key variable has been the presence or absence of caring adults (perhaps themselves overburdened but usually committed — with only limited but notable exceptions — to the children's welfare).[3] These trends, in turn, suggest shifts in definitions as well as the need for a reorganization of programming.

The total disadvantaged urban child population (including children living on the streets, in the slums or in institutions) represents a considerable proportion of the urban children in each age group.

"Real" street children live on their own on the streets. They are, by our definition, the roofless and rootless who live alone or with children like themselves. They sleep under bridges or in railway stations and eat with the money they earn during the day. Often they own only what they have on their backs. They are difficult to locate, let alone count, because of their wandering. Families may be in the same city, but frequently have limited (sometimes no) contact with the child. Many analysts have pointed to the importance of isolating this "much smaller" and "extremely vulnerable" group (Myers 1991. See also Kaminsky and Wright 1992, Lusk 1989, Childhope 1993).

"Real" street children represent only a small percentage of the total disadvantaged child population: 11 percent of the total national PSSC sample in the Philippines; 27 percent in Nairobi; 2 to 16 percent in Brazil; 23 percent in Vijayawada, India; even fewer in Italy where they may be in serious trouble, but still live at home. Surveys of street children in other countries substantiate these findings: about 10 percent in Mexico; about 20 percent in Honduras, and small percentages in Nigeria and in Senegal have little regular contact, or have severed all ties, with their families.

Street children are generally voluntary runaways. When surveys tried to establish why children run away, replies were often simplistic and unreliable. Running away is usually a result of complex circumstances. Children have been made to feel that their household is a less appropriately supportive place for them. They may be indignant because they are not properly appreciated or given adequate emotional support, despite their contributions (monetary or other) to the household. Often adults take from children without giving back enough, especially in terms of care, affection and love. School or work may make children feel marginalized. Harsh punishment or fear of punishment is frequently the last entry on the runaway's long list of grievances.

Of the street children interviewed in Bombay, 39 percent had left home because they faced problems with their parents, whereas 21 percent had left to escape acute poverty and to earn money (SPARC 1991).[4] The role of friends already on the streets may be significant (as documented in the Brazil and Philippines chapters). Across all countries, very limited numbers of street children had left their families involuntarily: some had been separated while travelling (India and Philippines); some had been deserted; the parents of a small number had died.

Street children on their own as well as street-based working children are mostly boys. Comprehensive censuses found that girls numbered one out of every three or four children in the Philippines (PSSC 1991) and in Mexico (COES-NICA 1992), while there was only about one girl for every 10 boys in many Indian cities (SPARC 1991, Panicker and Nangia 1992, Rao 1989).

Live-in working children are a different, although often equally deprived, category of children. Live-in restaurant, hotel and shop helpers and domestic workers, mostly girls, have fixed places to live; and many still have ongoing, and possibly even strong, relationships with their families and may, in fact, be in the city for the sake of their families. They were, however, often interviewed while surveying street children,[5] as they are living away from their families and are frequently found on the streets. Their special problems will be discussed further.

"Real" street children, because of their still relatively small numbers, represent a manageable problem. At present, the numbers of children living on the streets in small cities may not exceed a few hundred; even in larger cities, their numbers generally range from 1,000 to at most 3,000. Estimates, however, are complicated by the different definitions of street children.

Although a small population now, street children may become more numerous. Observers who work closely with these children have seen their numbers swell as the economic situation worsened, as happened in the early 1980s in Brazil and the Philippines. Poverty is increasing in many Third World countries, while cities are expanding. Armed conflict is recurrent in some areas. In such circumstances, family crises augment, migration to escape problems increases, more families face crises and sink into severe stress, and the number of street children can be expected to increase.

Most street children on their own also work and are thus also "working children." In Nairobi, 95.8 percent worked, but this included 21 percent who begged and loitered. In Vijayawada, 79 percent worked (14 percent of whom begged). In the PSSC survey in the Philippines, 94 percent of the street children worked, and less than 5 percent of the sample were beggars. Country Teams, following the example of most existing studies, considered begging work.

On the whole, the income-generating activities of street children and street-based working children are similar. From the surveys, vending and scavenging appeared to be the principal occupations for street children on their own, only few of whom sell services or beg: in the Philippines sample, for example, 50 percent were vendors; 33 percent, scavengers; and only 17 percent, beggars, car washers, car minders or other workers. Street-based working children in the Philippines were also predominantly vendors (48 percent) and scavengers (20 percent), but they tended to have wider work activities, including driving pedicabs, shining shoes and stevedoring. In Kenya, scavenging and vending were still the principal occupations of street children, although the surveys reported larger numbers of car parkers and washers. In India, the street child population included primarily scavengers (known as "ragpickers") as well as tea and juice shop helpers, mechanics-helpers, and a relatively smaller number of vendors.

In general, street work as vendors (including the sale of illegal items), scavengers, service providers or beggars provides the main source of independent earnings for urban poor children aged 5–18 years, whether still living at home or living on the street. The street is also where most of their parents, especially the mothers, make their living. Part-time domestic work, some home-based crafts (pottery, bracelets), food production (local sweets), prostitution, and the illegal preparation and sale of drugs or beer are some of the main income-generating activities of children working from the home (Table 7.2).

Given the surprising similarities in the activities carried out by street-based children the world over, the relatively small variations noted seemed to depend on the general level of economic development reached by the country (India and Kenya are more agriculturally based, for example) and the characteristics of the city under study, which ranged from industrializing (as in the case of Rajahmundry) to service-oriented (Olongapo or Mombasa) or post-industrial (Milan). Scavenging appeared to be a major occupation in many large metropolises (Bombay, Delhi, Nairobi, but interestingly not in Mexico City[6]).

Vending was somewhat more prevalent in the Philippines and Mexico and not uncommon in Italy, especially in the poorer South. Apprenticeships in trade occupations played an important role in India (where they are still tied to caste) and — in very different ways — in Italy where it is one way for a 14 or 15-year-old to start learning a saleable skill and earning a living.[7]

The earnings of street children are often higher than those of street-based working children. In India, in the Andhra Pradesh towns, 45 percent of the street children earned 300 to 900 rupees a month ($9.64–28.90), while the average monthly earnings of 55 percent of the working children living at home amounted to less that 150 rupees ($4.82). This trend was also evident in Delhi and in Bombay. In the Philippines, on the other hand, street children earned less than street-based working children: an average of 28 pesos a day ($1.05) as opposed to 60 pesos ($2.25). However, averages may be tilted in favour of working children because a few have better-paying jobs (as shop helpers or drivers, for example).

The higher earnings of street children on their own are a measure of both their needs and their survival skills, whereas the lower incomes of working children may be indicative of their greater family commitments (in terms of caring for younger siblings and doing housework) or school commitments. Furthermore, the earnings of street-based working children often constituted one third of the household income. This was true in the Philippines, India, Brazil and Kenya, but it has not been confirmed for Italy; and even when their earnings are low (half the minimum wage or less) they still represent a significant portion of the family's income (see also Wright et al. 1992). Highly remunerative occupations such as prostitution or drug peddling may become all the more attractive in situations of severe economic need; shop lifting of food and stolen goods for resale is another survival strategy.

Both street children and street-based working children tend to work for employers. They sell items on consignment, work as apprentices or receive salaries.

Street girls alone on the streets are heavily exposed to the multiple risks of street life and sexual exploitation. They all too often use prostitution initially as a survival strategy and subsequently for money. The small numbers of street girls on their own in all countries normally "gang up" with boys of their own age. Teams in Brazil and India noted that street girls tended to protect themselves by deemphasizing their gender and dressing and acting like boys for as long as they could. In Delhi, young girls, after 10 or 11 years of age, were sometimes taken off the streets by pimps and others and kept in private dwellings or sold to brothels (Panicker and Nangia 1992). This was also true in Manila, where, in addition, street girls were frequently arrested for vagrancy or forced to pay policemen to "look the other way." Street girls run the risk of being doubly exploited — at work and sexually. Rape and sexual molestation are not infrequent, sometimes even at the hands of the girl's street-boy companion, especially when he is high on solvents. He may also initiate her into prostitution (Childhope/NCSD 1989).

Street children on their own are more likely to have been apprehended by the police. In Bombay, 39 percent had been subject to routine arrest under the Vagrancy Act; of this number, 81 percent had been released automatically. Only few children of construction workers (1.2 percent) had been arrested (SPARC 1991). Harassment by police was also frequently mentioned as a problem in Brazil and Kenya.

Street children frequently come from households which have broken down or have suffered a recent loss of support, even though both of their parents are usually alive. Many have left families whose members were overstressed, overworked and increasingly unable to collaborate or even to relate emotionally or constructively with one another. These households were more frequently than others composed of recent migrants. In Delhi, however, there was a higher incidence of street children who had migrated from rural areas to the city alone, leaving families behind. The families of street children had often been evicted from their homes (Philippines, Italy). They had lost support systems of extended families and neighbours. The households had experienced repeated crises of health, employment and, in some urban areas, criminality.

Table 7.2. Work Activities, Place and Structure of Work of Street
Children and Working Children Living at Home

Sector	Street children (on their own)	Working children (living at home)	
	On streets	On streets	Not on streets***
Vendor			
Lottery tickets	▲	▲	
Newspapers	▲	▲	
Food (sweets, peanuts, candy)**	●▲	●▲	●
Other small items**	●▲	●	●
Flowers** (F)		●	
Pottery and other handicrafts**	●	●	●
Illegal items (drugs,** home-brewed beer,** contraband cigarettes, counterfeited or stolen goods)	●▲	●▲	●▲
Services			
Car washer, windshield cleaner (M)	●	●	
Parking attendant (M)	●		
Shoe shiner (M)	●	●	
Shop helper*	▲	▲	▲
Stevedore (M)	●▲	●▲	
Delivery boy (M)	●		
Scavenger and garbage sorter (steel, plastic, paper, rags, bottles, etc.)	●▲	●▲	
Mechanic (M)		▲	●
Domestic worker (F)*		▲	
Surrogate mother (F)			●
Prostitute (M/F)*	●▲	●▲	●▲
Other			
Member of crime syndicate	●▲	●▲	
Pickpocket and purse snatcher	●▲	●▲	
Beggar	●	●	

* = Activity usually carried out in the homes/work places of other people; ** = also home-based production (including piece work); ***activity carried out in the home and immediate community; (M) = prevalently male occupations; (F) = prevalently female occupations; ▲ = predominantly with employer; ● = predominantly self-employed. Source: Country studies.

They often had fewer employed fathers and more working mothers, and thus tended to be female-supported households. In general, they had created a less emotionally supportive, more conflictual environment for the child to grow up in. Other studies of street children in Brazil, Honduras, Bogota, Guatemala City and elsewhere have started to suggest that weak or disorganized family structures lie at the core of the "street children" problem (Aptekar 1988, Connolly 1990, Janowsky 1991, Wright et al. 1992, Lucchini 1993).

Street children show clear signs of greater health problems and high-risk behaviours than working children living at home. In the Philippines, children on the streets were generally found to be underweight and underheight, but street children were more markedly so than the working children living at home. Out-of-school children who engaged in substance abuse appeared particularly undernourished. In India, where malnutrition is still rampant, local Indian researchers in Vijayawada and Hyderabad found that about 5 percent of the street children appeared to be severely undernourished. Another 5 percent seemed to suffer from tuberculosis. They also presented scars and signs of accidents. The rest of the street children appeared malnourished.

Because of their life outside a family structure, street children engage in more health-threatening activities than working children. Not surprisingly, substance abuse is frequent,[8] especially glue and petrol sniffing, with the possible exception of Kenya where alcohol and cigarette abuse appears particularly high instead, and Italy where cigarettes and hard drugs offered alternatives. Across all surveys, street children on their own were more frequently involved in street violence and prostitution, and were more often malnourished or subject to diseases (including AIDS). This is fully confirmed by a World Health Organization study of homeless teenagers in Honduras (Wright et al. 1992)[9] and by studies of homeless teenagers in the United States (Wright 1991).

Street-Based Working Children

Most street-based working children come from poor, stressed, but still reasonably supportive households. Like street children, street-based working children are mostly boys (two thirds to three quarters). They came from two-parent families in 57 percent and 47 percent of the samples in Brazil, 50 percent in Kenya, 65 percent in the Philippines and the overwhelming majority in India. In most households, the mother also worked. There were only low percentages of single-headed households (that is, formally headed by a single woman or man). In many households, women were the main, or in the case of India very significant, economic providers (52 percent in India, 62 percent in Nairobi, over 50 percent in the Philippines and Brazil). In other words, the need for the additional earnings of the child (usually only one in India, or more than one in the Philippines) was a clear sign of economic stress in these families.

Family members may feel the strain of long working hours and the lack of time spent together or for leisure, but they still essentially form collaborative household units. Children, even though they have friends, still turn to their parents, especially mothers, for advice; they still feel their parents have a right to scold them; they still feel a sense of responsibility towards their siblings and spend varying amounts of time playing with them; and they still feel a strong attachment towards some household members. In comparison with the often deteriorated and uncooperative households of street children, these are still reasonably supportive settings for children.

Street-based working children's contribution was generally quite important to the household (see country chapters and later in this chapter).

In all countries these children appeared relatively less subject to severe problems. They presented a significantly lower incidence of malnutrition, substance use and abuse, and had experienced less family violence. They had also been arrested by the police far less often.

They have varying degrees of schooling, but in the best hypothesis, are behind in their studies. In India, 60 percent of urban children (and an even higher percentage for girls) have never attended school; in Kenya, three fourths were out-of-school, most had dropped out at primary level when they reached urban areas, and they are presently illiterate; in the Philippines, more than half are in school but often lagging behind; in Brazil, three fourths are in school but severely behind in their studies; in Italy, they are mostly in school but behind official grade level, and school dropout is frequent.

Street-Based Working Children on their Way to Becoming Street Children

Among the street-based working children, a relatively small number were found to be showing signs of greater stress. They do not return home every night, they sniff glue and petrol, they may have dropped out of school or turned to illegal activities, and they may be arrested more frequently (Box 7.2).

Immediately responsive and protective interventions for *street children on their own* should include:

- mapping their presence and conditions;
- establishing safe temporary shelters;
- establishing drop-in centres;
- providing medical care and psychological assessments;
- providing specialized support for advanced cases of drug abuse, AIDS and criminal behaviour;
- providing support for children, especially girls, exposed to sexual abuse;
- identifying and supporting households and families of origin;
- arranging for progressive and monitored family reintegration and family counselling; and
- creating better alternatives through schooling and vocational training.

**Box 7.2   Recurrent Similarities and Differences in
Street and Working Children**

Street-based working children (still living with their families)	Children on their way to becoming street children (still in families)	Street children on their own (not living with a family)
• Predominantly 8–9 to 14 years old with concentration in 10–12 age group (middle years)	• Same ages and gender	• Slightly older, i.e., predominantly 13–15 (early adolescence)
• Predominantly boys	• Predominantly boys	• Predominantly boys
• Predominantly from migrant families but not necessarily recent migrants (over 6 years in India or Kenya, mostly over 4 years in the Philippines with one fourth over 10 years)	• Majority living with two-parent families (parents or other adults)	• From households of recent migrants, often evicted (Philippines, Kenya)
	• About 1/3 living in single-headed households	• Separation from parents occurred when already in the cities with their families (Philippines, Brazil, Kenya); in India, high incidence of boys migrating to city alone.
• Considerable variations by countries in levels of school attendance, but generally behind grade level	• Over 2/3 with both parents alive	
	• Sleep irregularly at home	• From slightly larger percentages of female-supported households; majority have parents alive
• A higher proportion from two-parent households, both parents usually working, even in India.	• May be out of school already or in process of dropping out	• Households show greater signs of disaggregation and loss of cooperation, thus providing a less supportive, more often conflictual environment
• Contribute regularly to family, and their earnings represent on average about 1/3 to 1/4 of household income	• May resent portion of earnings given to family	• In some countries, a majority attend school, in others only a minority
• Come from poor, already stressed, but still reasonably supportive families, but with limited extended family support	• Exposed to some drugs, illegal activities, glue sniffing, street companions	• Only a minority contribute to the income of their households of origin, and usually sporadically
	• Family discord more evident	• More heavily exposed to and more likely to be abusing drugs, alcohol and solvents or to be involved in early unprotected sexuality and violence

In order to reinforce the resilience and coping strategies of street children, interventions should, beyond addressing immediate problems, recreate appropriately supportive environments. Institutionalization, which tends to destroy the children's spirit of independence and gives them little in exchange, should be avoided and, instead, ways devised to reinforce the children's self-esteem and enlarge, through their families, their range of opportunities.

For street-based working children still with their families, the largest number in the streets, the effort needs to be both protective (by improving their working conditions) and preventive (by helping and sustaining families and abolishing the need for excessive work). While some immediate supports such as specialized services may be appropriate as well, programmes that aim to stem the flow of children taking "refuge" on the streets should direct their main efforts towards the children's families.

Institutionalized Children

Institutionalized children include orphans, abandoned or destitute children living for extended periods of time in children's homes, and children living in prison or in special homes for juvenile offenders. The placement of a child in the latter kind of institutional care rather than in prison is usually in part regulated by law and in part at the discretion of judges.

The number of children in institutions is rarely large, especially in the developing world, because only proportionately few children can be reached through such a staff-intensive system. In India, it has been estimated that, at most, there are 200,000 to 300,000 children in institutions in a country of millions. Kenya has been facing severe space restrictions because of a lack of appropriate institutions. In the Philippines, less than 100,000 are institutionalized. In Italy, approximately 21,000 minors are arrested each year. But thousands of destitute or problem children are placed in mainly church-run boarding schools.

According to our research,[10] the majority of children who go through these referral systems have been charged with minor infringements (typically petty theft or lack of a vending licence). In Setrém, Brazil, in one year, only 2 to 3 percent of the cases involved major crimes (homicide, rape); most internments were for theft (40 percent); and 17 percent were for lack of a licence.

In Kenya among 100 children mostly between the ages of 10 and 14 years in two approved schools, a children's home and a remand home, one fourth had been arrested for loitering, one fourth for truancy, one fourth for stealing, and the rest for smoking *bhang* or just by mistake (Onyango et al. 1992). In Italy, between January and August 1990 in Milan, 47 percent of the arrests of children under-18 were for theft and burglary; other infractions included robbery, damage to property and assault; 5 percent of the arrests were drug-related, almost 3 percent were for traffic violations; no homicides were reported and sexual violations (unspecified) accounted for only two cases out of 981 (Table 6.7).

Inspired by the work carried out in Brazil on the conditions of children in approved schools and remand homes (the FEBEM and FUNABEM types of institutions), Country Teams explored in various ways the situation of such children, discovering serious violations to their rights. Because of mismanagement, some juvenile offenders convicted of only minor crimes lived for years behind bars, often in close contact with "hard core" delinquents.

The extremely poor conditions inside some institutions, notably the FEBEM/FUNABEM ones in Brazil, have been well documented. The

Country Teams heard descriptions of "parked" lives: whole days for the imprisoned youth consisting of waiting in line for baths, meals, services, toilets and activities. A brief visit to a juvenile home in Andhra Pradesh showed that, despite the police director's statements to the contrary, as many as one fourth of the children between 12 and 14 years of age were still imprisoned one or two years after the court had freed them simply because their rural poor families had been unable to collect them, and the state institution did not have the money or personnel to accompany them home. These children had been arrested for such minor infractions as taking a bus or train without a ticket. As we discussed their cases, they refused to sit down again after their turn was over, in silent protest. In these cases, the infringement of the children's human rights was blatant and requires urgent attention in each country.

The conditions of children in children's homes, schools for orphaned and abandoned children and other residential institutions are too often given uneven personalized care and handled in authoritarian ways, creating dependency. In India and the Philippines, poor, mostly rural, parents use these institutions as costless boarding schools by officially "abandoning" their children (Himes et al. 1991).

Compared with other CEDC categories, institutionalized children are relatively easy to enumerate, even though in the more active and innovative institutions (the ones actively promoting family reunification, for example) or in referral organizations that shift children to other support systems according to their needs and ages, the numbers may fluctuate greatly from one month to the next.

Suggested interventions include:

- improving implementation of existing laws for the arrest or referral of children under 18 years of age;

- eliminating bureaucratic loopholes and suggesting needed changes in the law;

- training personnel to take decisions in the best interests of the child, including important child development support strategies and a concern for enabling the child to grow into a responsible adult decision maker;

- harmonizing referral systems with other programmes for children in especially difficult circumstances at municipal, regional or national level; and

- mapping distribution of institutions and children, and analysing samples of case histories.

Some Other Important Populations of Working Children

Not all urban poor children work on the streets. Many have jobs in other sectors of the huge informal economy operating in most Third World cities.

The more qualified are mechanics or ironsmiths. Others work at home with their parents or neighbours at cottage industries (jewellery-making, prepared foods, clothing) or in marginal or illegal occupations. Surrogate motherhood occupies many young girls. This list does not claim to be exhaustive since other kinds of work are dynamically created by local circumstances as we write. Previous types of work reemerge under new guises. Home-based piece work in India, for example, has increased for some traditional handicraft activities (lace and jewellery-making), but is now serving a new and often international clientele (Mies 1982).

Three particularly exploitative categories of child workers deserve special attention: live-in working children (shop helpers and domestic workers); child prostitutes; and children of construction workers. The first two categories are on their own and, as a result, especially vulnerable.

Live-in working children on their own

Live-in shop helpers are a growing category of working children in Third World cities. Often recent migrants from rural areas (and in India, prevalently older sons), they have usually been placed at a young age by their families and are likely to be under the control of exploitative employers. They work all day serving clients, running errands and guarding the premises; after closing hours, they prepare food or other goods for sale, clean the shop and finally sleep there at night. Generally, shops have no toilets and sometimes not even running water. Many are only flimsy constructions with one whole wall open to the street and wares displayed on the pavement. Because the distinction between "on" and "off" the street is particularly unclear, the children were sometimes mistaken for street children and interviewed by Country Teams.

Often the children give their employers their savings (destined for the family) for safekeeping, and so are easily cheated. In addition, they may be charged for food and lodging, heavily penalized for breakage or accidents, or encouraged to borrow from the shopkeeper at high interest rates (to repay their arrival ticket, to send gifts to parents or to raise money for their family in emergencies). Some end up in quasi-bondage. In some countries, live-in shop helpers are only or predominantly males (India). In other countries, they may be either male or female (Philippines, Kenya). Females generally earn less than males. Whether male or female, most are not officially registered as workers (Bose 1992).

Live-in domestic workers contribute to the high incidence of young female rural-to-urban migration in Latin America in general and in the Philippines, for example. Country Teams in Brazil, the Philippines and Kenya found that domestic workers were predominantly female; in India, instead, more males were found in this kind of employment. Young Indian girls from poor neighbourhoods are, however, extensively engaged in part-time domestic work (NIUA 1991b).

In Nairobi, 95 percent of the 521 domestic workers aged from 7 to 17 years interviewed by the University of Nairobi were female (Bwibo and Onyango 1985). Often school dropouts and many times the "poor country cousins" of their employers, they generally work only for food and lodging, and occasionally for a small wage to be sent back home. Most are supposed to be just child-minders, but end up shouldering a significant proportion of the housework. They are also treated more like slaves than members of the household. Many of these girls are in a pathetic state (Mutiso 1989, University of Nairobi 1987). According to one research study (Onyango and Kayongo-Male 1982), they "would prefer to return home to their poverty and family's relative care rather than to be overworked and degraded in a situation from which they feel there is no escape."

Older domestic workers may be more demanding and thus run into problems with their employers. They sometimes try to attract household male attention or steal small things either for direct use or for resale (Achola 1989). Some leave domestic service hoping to improve their situation, but instead begin a downward spiral, frequently leading to prostitution (Achola 1989, University of Nairobi 1987).

In Bombay, the Domestic Worker Movement, headed by Sister Jeanne Devos, has established contact with 12,000 female household helpers aged 9 to 18 since 1984. Ninety percent are from rural areas and Adhevasi; some come all the way from Nepal. They are poorly paid with no legal protection, work for long hours, have no free time and usually sleep in makeshift quarters. Many are physically debilitated and feel abandoned. Because most have had little schooling, they generally lack self-esteem. These young girls may be exposed to sexual harassment or turn to prostitution (5 percent). The luckier ones are able to return home (40 percent) or to pursue an education in the hope of improved employment (15 percent) (Bruce 1991).

Interventions for such girls can occur at many levels. At a more global and preventive level, interventions to improve the family conditions that forced children to be sent out would be needed. Generally protective as well as immediately responsive interventions for both live-in shop helpers and domestic workers would require:

- mapping to establish numbers, gender and living and working conditions (best done in a participatory manner with the help of NGOs);

- formation of support networks among the children and a service centre for backup support;

- encouraging unionization to press employers to provide better living conditions, more reasonable working hours and appropriate social benefits;

- better enforcement of the minimum wage laws;

- formal and informal education.

Children in prostitution

Prostitution is a largely urban phenomenon. In all the countries in the study, the potential for young girls (and boys) to be forced, to slide, or to be enticed into prostitution is a very real one (Box 7.3).

The extent to which prostitution represents a "solution" for urban poor children and their families varies from country to country because it relates to a complex cultural package of gender ideologies. Some countries have also had a longer tradition of urban poor prostitution than others (White 1990).

The presence of large military contingents in Korea, Vietnam, the Philippines and Thailand has encouraged a sex industry which has now become an adjunct to the tourist industry. Olongapo, until the 1992 closure of the US naval base, was a good example of a town geared to the "Rest and Recreation" of soldiers. Most female prostitutes were 14 years old or older and had migrated from rural areas for economic reasons. Many were sponsored by their families who expected to receive part of the proceeds. Variations of this kind of family-ingrained and family-supported prostitution were found in India and Kenya where girls enter the profession immediately at adolescence and boys in their middle years.

Dasgupta (1990), in a survey in Calcutta, counted 6,698 prostitutes in eight brothel areas in the city.[11] The survey found that a good number were daughters of former prostitutes who had worked in Calcutta as part of traffic initiated in the early 1950s under the impetus of rural poverty. From castes once heavily dependent on local feudal lords, they were brought up recognizing their master's prerogative to exercise feudal rights on his women. Young girls take over their mothers' jobs in the Calcutta brothels to support them in their old age. Arrangements are worked out by the mothers before the onset of the girls' puberty.

Prostitution of young girls in the poor urban neighbourhoods of Nairobi presents some of the same elements.

Prostitution offers a good income, around 500 rupees ($16.06) per month in 1990 in India, for example, after the cuts for brothel operators and pimps. However, timing is often more important than money. A moment of crisis may create the opportunity for the child's enlistment, as the case of a Kenyan girl points out:

> Anne, who is now 16 years old and lives with her grandmother, was a good student and enjoyed going to school. Two years ago, because of her grandmother's illness, Anne had to leave school because she couldn't pay her school fees. Unable to pursue her studies, she slowly started to entertain male customers, much as her mother had done before her. Last year, with the money she had earned she went back to school, but soon became discouraged because she couldn't catch up with her class and finally dropped out. Her teachers felt she deserved better.

To be effective, interventions would require:

- an alternative income-generating activity for the girls, which should possibly be carried out collectively in order to enable the girls to develop a collective identity that will help them to stand up against the moral coercion exercised by parents;

- a shelter or home for temporary transitional periods for sexually exploited girls, and for ex-prostitutes and their children;

- the availability of specialized (but not coercive) health facilities; and

- emergency support to the family and to reinforce other alternatives, such as education and job training, to promote opportunities for better jobs.

Children of construction workers

Construction work is an important source of unskilled employment in expanding Third World cities. Construction sites are normally on open areas. Most construction workers are young migrants from rural areas. In India, Thailand and Kenya, extensive cases have been reported of young construction worker families which move from one site to another. Because the pay is so low, usually both husband and wife work, leaving their children to roam about the site, unsupervised and prone to dangers of all sorts. Often dirty and unkempt, these children are frequently scoffed at by passers-by.

Interventions range from preventive to immediately curative. Ideally, highest priority should be given to employment and improving opportunities in rural areas. Interventions in urban areas should address why parents are living as they are and provide them with increased alternatives. More particularly, immediately responsive as well as generally protective interventions would require:

- mapping of numbers, major sites, moves;

- provision of and support for on-site child care;

- first aid in emergencies;

- nonformal and on-site schooling at the pre-primary and primary level, with the possibility of lateral entry into the formal system;

- support activities to ensure follow-up when children move to another site;

- advocacy for better enforcement of existing laws when these are adequate; and

- legislation guaranteeing a minimum wage and welfare provision.

Working and Non-Working Children Living in Poor Urban Neighbourhoods

Beyond street-based children, Country Teams also examined other children from some poor urban neighbourhoods to determine the less visible work

activities of children, establish some control
groups and analyse
household coping strate-
gies. Particular attention
was paid to the family
reasons leading boys and
girls to work and/or to
study.

Surrogate motherhood

More than half of the
female working children
in the households inter-
viewed in Delhi slums
had no monetary earn-
ings (as opposed to only
7 percent of the male
working children) These
unpaid workers were
predominantly surrogate
mothers and house-
keepers and occasionally
helpers in family enter-
prises. They were often
taken out of school,
specifically in order to
help a working mother.
They worked hard in the
dreary slum environ-
ment (as opposed to the
more pleasant court-
yards in rural areas) with
little entertainment and
no time for themselves.

Box 7.3   Child Prostitution

- Child prostitution is rampant in Colombia, Brazil, Benin, and especially Thailand and the Philippines where the marketing of sexual services is on an industrial scale.
- 800,000 adolescent and girl children work as prostitutes in Thailand.
- 10,000 boys or more between 6 and 14 years of age work as prostitutes, mainly serving foreign men in Sri Lanka.
- Boys and girls from Bangladesh and India have reportedly been sold by their families and taken to the United Arab Emirates, Oman and elsewhere in the Middle East to work in brothels or appear in pornographic films.
- Physicians in Asia, Latin America and the United States report treating many more children under 14 years of age for sexually transmitted diseases.
- Virginity fetches high prices which means 10- to 12-year-olds but even children as young as 8 are in demand.
- Fear of AIDS is one reason for this trend: children, perhaps naively, are considered "safer."
- The multi-billion dollar sex industry, which has "normalized the open buying and selling of sex and ... eroded taboos against sexual exploitation of children" is a second reason.
- Also implicated are the "sex tours" of Asian and Latin American cities, marketed in the West and often involving adolescent girls.

Source: The International Herald Tribune of 10–11 April 1993, reporting conclusions of a UNESCO conference on the sex trade and human rights held in Brussels.

Surrogate motherhood is a direct response to the need to work of mothers who may be the family's main breadwinner or an essential auxiliary earner. Large families of usually illiterate rural Indian migrants with both parents working cannot manage without a surrogate mother: at least one of the daughters, sometimes a succession of them as the older girls are lost to early marriage, is sacrificed to the task. Surrogate mothers are generally between six and 14 years of age. They have limited educational opportunities; the skills they have acquired relate only to their probable future roles as mothers and housekeepers and are unlikely to enable them to improve their situation. This pattern will eventually influence the young girl's own children.

Part-time domestic work

Part-time domestic work is another characteristically female occupation, but, unlike surrogate motherhood, it is remunerated. Part-time domestic work is growing in importance among poor urban families in the Third World (but not in Italy where domestic service is now practised increasingly by immigrants from developing countries, among whom a large percentage of Filipinos). Part-time domestic helpers often follow a pattern established by their mothers. They then return home, usually to find not a well-deserved respite but rather more housework to do and perhaps siblings to care for. Generally, they automatically hand over their earnings to their parents, unlike almost half of the male working children in India, for example, who kept all (17 percent) or part (33 percent) of their earnings. Girls are expected to have a higher sense of filial duty and obligation towards their households than boys are in most of these societies. Furthermore, especially in India, but also in the other countries (with the partial exception of Italy) poor urban girls did not have the same right to leisure as boys did. The situation of Indian girls in some samples was particularly disadvantaged because they were not allowed to wander far from home if not in the company of adults.

Family enterprises

Both male and female children may work as unpaid labour in family enterprises. Ragpicking, handicrafts, sweets-making, beer-brewing, prostitution, the production and dealing of drugs, even stealing for resale, were examples of home-based family businesses which utilized children. However, despite being carried out in a family environment (usually more protective than other environments), some of these businesses can be extremely detrimental to the children's future.

STREET LIFE AND HOMELESSNESS

The Dangerous Street

In large cities throughout the industrialized world, the street has come to represent lurking danger and violence. In inner-city ghettos, social life is fast deteriorating under the impact of rampant drug problems and crime. The influence of the street extends beyond the slums to middle-class neighbourhoods where inhabitants, exposed to the stealing and scavenging raids of burglars and crack addicts, have adopted a quasi-siege mentality. In the

United States especially, large cities are open to riots, crime, racial violence and drug and gang wars. In Italy, the presence of organized crime and violence is felt in inner cities and new tenement areas.

The street is also feared in the Third World where urban poverty has in many cases worsened during the last two decades and where laws are less enforced. Children who work on the street report being victimized. Violence can be fatal, as in the case of the 457 street-based children murdered in three Brazilian cities between March and August 1989. Children in Kenya who live in poor neighbourhoods, even in secondary towns, are troubled by the violence and environmental deterioration they see.

In these contexts, society at large often attributes the problems to the "street kids" whom they perceive as being ruthless young criminals (Anderson 1990). These children's origins and circumstances are usually inadequately analysed. Schools, the justice system and other institutions often "give up" too quickly on the "troublemakers" who are instead the most in need of support (Inciardi et al. 1993).

To counter these perceptions, a new anthropological literature has emphasized the positive aspects of the street experience for young people in the slums, and the new pride and confidence street work gives them (Anderson 1990, for example). The literature calls for ways to channel the children's creative energy into constructive projects.

Not only is the street becoming more dangerous but it is also generating dangerous scapegoating at the expense of children and young people who are often the most deprived. However, analysing children in terms of the street is grossly insufficient: the street is only one of the problematic areas in their lives; the real cause of their distress originates elsewhere.

Homelessness

Homelessness in the sense of not having a physical abode is not uncommon in Third World countries. Street families are a well-documented phenomenon in large Indian cities (where they are called "pavement-dwellers"). They have become increasingly present in the Philippines and Brazil since the 1980s. In Kenya, where it is against the law to sleep on the streets, homeless families create make-do shelters with three sticks and a plastic bag on the outskirts of cities. Paradoxically, despite constant exposure to street dangers, children living in street families are still relatively immune from the severe risks of substance abuse or illegal activities.

In a study of pavement-dwellers in Bombay, of 1,130 homeless children whose parents had migrated to Bombay from 11 to over 25 years ago, 35 percent were students, 35 percent were temporarily employed or seeking employment, and the rest were too young to work. They enjoyed studying and helped their parents. Only a few smoked *bedis* (cigars), gambled, used drugs or consumed alcohol, in contrast to samples of street children from the same city (SPARC 1991). The same observation was made in the Philippines and in Brazil. The children of street families give the most striking evidence that it is the presence of caring adults, in this case family members, overburdened and stressed as they may be, that still shelters them and provides them the emotional and crisis support they need.

Homelessness in the United States is not a new phenomenon: homeless families were known during the depression years (1929 through the 1930s). Homelessness has increased during the last decade in large urban metropolises.

Homeless runaways represent a much smaller population of children permanently away from home, only 50 percent of whom eventually return home or find placement in an institution (Chelimsky 1982). They are children who choose the street as an alternative to what they perceive as intolerable living conditions at home. Homeless runaways were not unknown in the past and articles on "little street Arabs" or "street waifs," appeared in *The New York Times* all through the late 1860s and into the late 1880s (Rivlin and Manzo 1988). Their number has increased under the pressure of the strained economic conditions of the 1980s (Edelman 1987, Battle 1990). In poor health (Wright (1991), they are prone to additional dangers of exploitation, lack of support, substance abuse and other high-risk behaviours.

Homelessness in the United States means poor living conditions and street exposure but is compounded when it also entails the lack of a caring family.

WORK AND WORKING CHILDREN

Policy Perspectives

This Project has analysed many different categories of working children on the basis of the primary and secondary data to clarify the degrees of exploitative work in urban areas of five countries. We have not sought to be comprehensive but rather generative. It has been shown that work can range from meaningful and constructive activities that make children feel less marginalized (especially when combined with regular schooling) to extremely exploitative conditions.

Globally, policy makers must identify which activities constitute a danger for children in terms of health, education or development. They must determine what work is appropriate at what ages in societies with different cultural and social histories.

In many developing countries, men have been assigned, within their respective cultures, the main breadwinner roles outside the home; women are less likely to work in the paid labour force and more likely to be relegated to unpaid household work. They still, of course, work hard at reproductive tasks (giving birth, feeding, raising children) or on the family fields and in other income-earning enterprises.

The definition of what constitutes work as well as the issues of the appropriateness and extent of women's work, long discussed by feminists in the North, have now become subjects of active debate in the South. Women's movements, initially inspired by northern models, are now struggling to arrive at definitions that are meaningful in their cultural context (Mohanty et al. 1991, Ong 1988).

The issue of children's work has not yet provoked the same level of intense discussion. Furthermore, the extent to which children should work and at which ages are matters that are often not clearly regulated. Immediate circumstances determine parental attitudes towards child labour. Children are expected, in all cases, to obey parents and elders. Adults, on the other hand, are assumed to act in the best interests of the child and for the overall benefit of the household. The State determines the general context in which the decision to send a child to work is taken. However, the State is itself subject to processes at global economic and political levels.

There are some recent indications that the issue of child labour is coming to the fore and may be widely discussed in the 1990s. It has been given new prominence in many countries in part as a result of the ratification of the Convention on the Rights of the Child and in part because of the obvious increase in working children, a trend connected with the global economic crisis of the 1980s. Some insightful writers in countries where the problem is prevalent have already addressed the issue (Bequele and Boyden 1988, Myers 1991, Weiner 1991, Goonesekere 1993). If child labour indeed moves into the forefront of policy-making at the country level, it will raise as many questions as were raised about women's work in the past. What types of child labour should be abolished? At what age and for how many hours a week should a child be allowed to work? Should there be different standards for girls and boys?

The debate will also centre on which are the most appropriate local standards and to what extent international standards, largely based on Western concepts, should apply. It should be noted that States that adopt international standards also commit themselves to intervening much more directly in the lives of their citizens. This interventionist approach will, however, only be valid if States realistically assess the situation of families and children and devise ways to provide adequate support.

Child labour needs to be addressed from many fronts. The families of working children need to join with rights advocates in the search for approaches that are most advantageous to children. Particular care must be taken so that state efforts to abolish child labour do not become a means to blame and punish impoverished urban families and children. Penalization of families in the supposed best interests of children is a major recurrent problem at the local level.

Size and Definition of the Problem

Country Teams have provided statistics on the extent of child labour in each country. In India, government and NGO estimates have ranged from 17.36 million (National Sample Survey Organization 1988) to 44 million (Burra 1986a) to 100 million, depending on definitions (paid versus unpaid, ages 5–15 versus 5–18, employed versus self-employed, formal versus nonformal sector, "main" or full-time workers versus "marginal" or sporadically employed workers). Percentages in urban areas appear to be increasing. Based on census findings, which are, however, only partial, child participation in the most hazardous industries (aside from home-based work and construction) had already increased from 308,000 in 1961 to 671,000 in 1981 (Ramaswany, Dave and Kashyap, 1987).

Recent nationwide estimates of child labour are 7 million in Brazil, 3.5 million in the Philippines, a smaller number in Kenya, and a surprisingly high figure of 200,000 children under 14 years of age in southern Italy. Estimates are only partially reliable and vary according to the kinds of work included and definitions of child labour.[12]

The four developing countries in the study have only prohibited some forms of child labour by law. In India, the 1986 Child Labour (Prohibition and Regulation) Act, which defines a child as being under 15 years of age, prohibits child labour in the more hazardous occupations and regulates it in others, thus acknowledging that "child labour will continue to be a reality in Indian society for some time and that legislation attempting to prohibit all of its forms would be unenforceable" (Bose 1992). In Italy, it is, with few exceptions, illegal for a child under 15 to work because it means the child's family is not complying with national laws on compulsory education. This has had two results: younger child workers are not reported; as a consequence, although child labour is still common and extensive according to both NGO and government reports, it is hidden and unregulated, leaving children vulnerable to exploitation.

In terms of the size of the population involved, child labour is probably the issue that involves the largest number of children worldwide. Speaking to this problem, Article 32 of the Convention on the Rights of the Child recognizes:

> the right of the child to be protected from economic exploitation and from performing any work that is likely to be hazardous or to interfere with the child's education, or to be harmful to the child's health or physical, mental, spiritual, moral or social development.

The definitions of "work," "labour," "exploitation," "hazard" and "developmentally damaging" require special attention. A rapid glance backward shows that historically, in North and South, children working is not a new phenomenon or even unusual. We must, in fact, be careful not to "cry wolf."

What constitutes a child is already defined differently in different societies. Age may not always be a sufficient base, since the fulfilment of certain rites may be more important. In addition, as our data have strongly substantiated, because of children's early involvement in socioeconomic life, the threshold between adulthood and childhood may not be clearly marked.

Existing child labour legislation has been slow (1) in developing an appropriately broad but informed set of definitions; and (2) in finding means to implement legislation. International standards have been unsystematic. Attempts to reduce child labour in the formal sector have so far produced inadequate laws, weak or no enforcement, and too many exceptions, leaving too many children unprotected. States have not yet addressed many of the main "new" problems of child labour that have emerged from our close analysis, including domestic service and drugs, prostitution and petty theft. They have also not yet made sufficient efforts to uncover the multiple dimensions of invisible work, within the domestic realm or in secluded courtyards, behind mud walls and in windowless sweat shops. Invisibility actually has two dimensions: work that is acknowledged as such but carried out in isolated environments; and work that is not officially acknowledged as such. The second category is, as we will see, particularly insidious.

The Convention on the Rights of the Child provides an important new way to approach these issues. However, because of its aim to be a document for governments, the Convention has had to avoid the politically delicate gender and age issues and thus sets standards for the protection of all children under 18.

In general the issue of working children has often been effectively presented as a dichotomy (Myers 1991):

> Some feel that the crux of the problem is in the fact that children are allowed to engage in economic activity. They argue that childhood should be reserved primarily for study and play, with work consisting (only) of light chores in the home. They maintain that even when children are not mistreated, their participation in the work force weakens adult wages and employment and is thus a factor in generating the very poverty that forces them to work. Virtually all working children are considered by definition to be at risk and, therefore, ... the ultimate goal of action should be the elimination of all child labour.
>
> A different position is taken by those who point out that work, under appropriate protection and supervision, is an essential vehicle of juvenile socialization, training and self-esteem. They hold that the economic participation of children is acceptable as long as it is consistent with healthy development and that the real problem is the special vulnerability of children when they enter the labour market. Although they support the elimination of child participation in hazardous work, they feel that youngsters wishing to work should have the right to do so and that the scarcity of employment oppor-

tunities suitable for minors is as much a problem as is the existence of exploitative working conditions. Proponents of this view claim that prohibiting child labour without first raising family real income from other sources will invite tragedy for the poor, creating even more destitute children. To them the central issue is how to protect the safety and development of children who work.

These dichotomies, while they help to locate the arguments more sharply, also tend to unduly exaggerate them. As Myers himself states in reference to child labour (Myers 1991):

> Effective programming depends on being able to comprehend the problem from a variety of perspectives, including some that appear contradictory. Without such comprehension, there is a risk of launching simplistic actions that are not only ineffective, but perhaps even detrimental to the welfare of the children involved. Unfortunately, this very situation has often occurred.

Myers also suggests the need for a "situation diagnosis" that will provide policy and programme planners with "detailed information about how children enter and perform their work, the occupations they follow, the conditions under which they labour and how they are supervised and remunerated ... (in other words) an understanding of the labour market systems through which children work." He emphasizes that systematic diagnoses of working children are surprisingly scarce, especially in developing countries, and that the problems most frequently encountered concern how to: (a) "operationally identify those in special need and estimate their number and distribution; (b) determine the actual effects of work on children; and (c) identify the causes of child work problems and potential points of intervention to stem them" (Myers 1991).

Effects of Work on Children

Developmental psychologists tell us that the middle years of childhood (6–12 years of age) — often thought of as a quiet, uneventful period between early development and the more turbulent years of adolescence — are a time of intensified social interaction at school and outside the home, when peer and non-parental adult relations become more important. This is also the time of exploration, of early independence and risk-taking. In addition, from seven years onwards, children can be considered responsible, they know when they do wrong, they have *bu-ot* as the Filipinos call it (Collins 1991, Bronfenbrenner 1989). Children from five or seven exhibit certain abilities and a greater maturity, which cultures universally recognize by giving children more independence and greater responsibility.[13] They are assigned new roles that sometimes take them outside of the home and away from direct adult supervision. Children may be asked to take care of younger siblings, tend animals, carry out household chores and run errands. This new stage is usually marked by rites of initiation. The full acceptance into adulthood, however, occurs after adolescence.

To what extent is work in the middle years and early adolescence detrimental? It has been argued that participation in economically productive activities before 15 deprives children of opportunities for meaningful relationships with family members, peers and others; deprives them of time for play, exploration, spontaneity, rest and even moments of irresponsibility and indecision;

Box 7.4   Some Positive Aspects of Children's Work

Work can:

- increase children's sense of responsibility
- build their self-esteem and confidence
- enhance children's status as family members and citizens
- provide them with an opportunity to learn the skills of their parents and neighbours
- make children feel less marginalized, especially when combined with regular schooling
- provide an important and gradual initiation into adult life

and, in a sense, deprives them of their childhood (WHO 1988). On the other hand, some child advocates argue that work is not necessarily negative for children, and may be meaningful and constructive (Box 7.4). They point out that urban working children appear to be carrying heavy family responsibilities with considerable cheerfulness, good will and enthusiasm, that the children's contribution should be more widely appreciated and more opportunities made available for them to develop their talents (Myers 1991).

Issues to be addressed include: (a) the size of the child's contribution; (b) the extent to which that contribution is appreciated by others, including the parents; and (c) the extent to which the child engages in such work willingly and feels that positive outcomes (greater independence, heightened sense of responsibility leading to enhanced self-esteem) outweigh negative outcomes (poor working conditions, excessive responsibility).

Children nine to 10 had different attitudes towards work across the countries of the study. Filipino children, more often than others, viewed their street work (often combined with schooling) positively, as did their parents. In Brazil, street work was, in general, also viewed positively. In India, reactions were mixed; children in this age group, generally ragpickers or part-time domestic workers, more often felt that they had been forced by their parents to work, claimed they were unhappy about working and would have preferred to go to school instead. Similar reactions were found in Kenya.

When does work become unacceptable and exploitative? There are some indications that work thrust suddenly upon children in their middle years through dire need may have a somewhat more negative impact on them. In an empirical study of the effects of the Depression in the United States during the 1930s, Elder (1974) found that younger children were more negatively affected than adolescents because they were more liable to suffer the strains that their parents endured, but also less able to feel that they contributed significantly to the alleviation of economic stress.

As discussed in a recent ILO publication, work turns into exploitation for children when it threatens their welfare. In other words, when children (Bequele 1991, Fyfe 1993):

- *work too young*: for example starting factory work at six or seven years;

- *work too long hours*: in some cases 12 to 16 hours a day;

- *work for too little pay*: as little as $3 for a 60-hour week or no pay as in agriculture;

- *work in hazardous conditions*: in mines, quarries, plantations, sweatshops or even on the streets;

- *work under slave-like arrangements*: an estimated 20 million child-bonded labourers in South Asia.

Each point needs further qualification in individual settings, as will be discussed in the next section.

An attentive look at the lives of working children has shown that work becomes detrimental to different degrees and in different ways depending on the age and gender of the child. It has also been seen that there may be real advantages in engaging children in a certain work and that not doing so may actually cause just as much, if not greater, harm (see Italian chapter, for example). Labelling working children "disadvantaged" needs careful qualification in order to avoid it being grossly misinterpreted.

In the life histories, children themselves have indicated a number of reasons for working (Box 7.5). The progression is from motivations contributing to a child's development to those which actually work against it. The first reasons for working are positive and desirable for children; the last negative and unacceptable, but unfortunately not infrequent. In the Philippine sample, for instance, about 18 percent of the children claimed to work for one of the last three reasons listed in the box. The responses in the middle of the list, reflecting the temporary or regular need of a child to help support the family, are by far the most frequent. In India, for example, over 60 percent of the boys compared with 40 percent of the girls claimed they worked to contribute to the household income. The same reason was given by over 60 percent of the street-based working children in the Philippines, regardless of gender. It was also clearly a main concern in the samples in Brazil and Kenya.

Although children may derive pleasure from helping others, this may still be psychologically harmful if it involves them in exploitative labour that compromises their future. However, this generalization needs to be measured against the family's economic situation. If children understand that both they and their families are being forced to work — in excess of what is considered normal or desirable — by forces beyond their control, then the

---

Box 7.5   Why Children Work

- Because they derive personal satisfaction from testing their abilities against new tasks; acquiring new skills, insights or knowledge; doing a job well
- Because they like helping others and being considered competent or helpful by them
- Because they want to earn extra money for personal use (snacks, leisure activities, consumer goods) or to cover their own school expenses
- Because they have to contribute to the basic household income. This may be temporary (caused by parental illness, absence or unemployment) or it may be more permanent. It may be done in ways that are positive or potentially negative
- Because their families see the need to supplement the household income to permit purchases beyond basic requirements, including school expenses of siblings
- Because they have become their family's main breadwinner as a result of the death, illness, chronic unemployment or absence (imprisonment, abandonment) of a parent
- Because they are compelled to work by adults who exercise various forms of "enslavement" over them, including forced prostitution or labour
- Because they have to support themselves after the death of their parents, the collapse of their family or after having been rejected by the family

---

psychological impact on the child and the child's sense of resentment may be less.

The position of the children in many households changes after they start contributing to household expenses. Surveys have shown that child bread-winners have fewer conflicts with their parents and are less frequently punished than their non-working siblings. The higher respect they have earned is reflected in their generally positive attitudes towards work (PSSC 1991). In India, although children may not be very pleased about the work *per se*, their earning activity gives them a purpose away from the drudgery of daily life in the slums, a boredom which may be relative idleness for boys and hard and repetitive domestic work for girls (NIUA 1991b).

From the point of view of child development, it has been shown that children during the middle years, whether attending school or not, acquire a stronger sense of self by contributing to the family's well-being, especially in a collaborative family atmosphere. This situation tends to change as children enter adolescence and start to reevaluate their lives in the light of future plans. Boys and girls may then bitterly regret having left school or having fallen behind in their schooling. They may blame their parents or bad luck for their life circumstances (Moura 1991, Arellano-Carandang 1987, Schwartzman 1992). From age 15 on, adolescents, and especially boys, tend to move progressively towards independence from the family, and thus reduce the amount of money they contribute to the household (even though they may be earning more), as shown in the Philippines survey.

In summary, to evaluate the impact of work on children we must weigh the importance of their contribution to family survival and the self-esteem they gain, especially in the middle years, against not only the children's hopes for the future but also against the "real" advantages education would provide them in the Third World economies they live in. We must understand children's resilience and strength in the face of family adversities and propose balanced rather than simplistic solutions.

Main Characteristics of Street-Based Work in the Five Countries

The Urban Child Project has found striking similarities in the main characteristics of street- and slum-based work across the five countries, and some significant differences as well.

Age of initiation

In any discussion of the age most urban poor children begin work, it is necessary to specify "outside the house." As the life histories have shown, children, especially girls, work from an early age in the house — cooking, fetching water, watching younger siblings, doing the housework, helping to prepare items for sale and contributing to the household in many other ways not generally recognized as "work."

Country Teams have found that children usually start working on the street early in their middle years (seven to 10). Work is continued through adolescence and adulthood, although the types of work undertaken may change over the years. Girls in some countries (India, for example) generally started working on the street well before boys. In Delhi, 25 percent of the girls started working at seven, or even younger, but their numbers declined after 11, while boys started working between eight and 10, with a current mean age of 10.7 years for boys and 9.5 for girls (NIUA 1991b). In Hyderabad, children generally initiated work between eight and 10, although starting work at six was not infrequent. Again, girls started and stopped working on the streets earlier than boys.

The Philippine survey presents comparable information. Again 68 percent of all street-based working children were between nine and 13, with an average of 12.6 years. They had started to work on average between 10 and 11, slightly later than the Indian children. In Brazil, street surveys showed that children are generally initiated into street life between the ages of seven and 12, and most remain on the streets until 16. It appears that, as they get older, children leave the street to seek better-paying and more socially acceptable employment. The average age of the sample in Kenya was 12.8; the mode age, 12; the average age of initiation, 10.

Large numbers of children in the Third World, but also smaller numbers of children in the pockets of poverty in the industrialized world, start working in their middle years, often despite regulations. In fact, the age of initiation into employment for children is likely to decrease under economic pressures, affecting their school attendance and reducing the number of years dedicated purely to growing up. As clearly illustrated in the life histories, much of the child's future may be determined by the time he or she reaches 12 years of age. A failed attempt to juggle school and work at that age may, for instance, sentence a child to a life without an education, which will influence the type of work undertaken and age of marriage. It is therefore of critical importance that appropriate schooling support and alternative family support be preventively devised for this age group.

Hours of work

Street-based working children's answers about numbers of hours must be considered cautiously since they often have only approximate notions of time, and the number of hours on the streets often does not reflect the number of hours working. Country Teams in the Philippines and India found children who worked up to 12 hours a day, alternating housework with the preparation of food for sale (chapati, sweets) and with actual selling. The average in Hyderabad and Delhi was 6 to 8 hours a day. However, since children do not necessarily work every day and do many things in a day, it is more appropriate to focus on: (1) hours per month (seasonally) and (2) ratio of hours to different activities.

Data from the Philippines, for example, show, again with respect to children in the middle years, that working children living with families spend between one and 16 hours daily, with an average of six hours, working on the streets.[14] They are in school from one to eight hours per day, with an average of six hours. They sleep an average of nine hours per night and do varying amounts of housework. A main difference is that working children carry out these street-based activities for fewer days each month, an average of 10 days as opposed to 22 days for street children. These averages show that when working, even children with families may be under considerable time pressure, with limited availability for rest or leisure. About 20 percent of the PSSC sample, and especially girls, explicitly stated they had no time for leisure, a complaint echoed in the life histories. They sometimes stole "free time" away from other activities, but it was stolen rather than allotted time, and often provoked punishment.

In India, a slum child in Delhi may spend three hours in school, three and a half hours ragpicking, four hours sorting, and, if she is a girl, another three to four hours doing housework, including the hard task of fetching water. Time for leisure and creative growth becomes very short indeed.

Clearly, researchers trying to calculate the developmental effects of work on children need to measure the child's deprivation not only by the number of hours at work, but also the free time that he, or especially she, has left for personal growth.

Pay

Across all five country studies, children earned less than adults, even when performing the same work. One example was the child "barker" in the Philippines, who managed to fill up buses as rapidly as his adult counterpart but was paid far less for his efforts.

Gender discrimination is also evident, and in all countries, including Italy, girls earn far less than boys. Children who have had little schooling are easily cheated by their employers. The life histories have revealed extremely exploitative pay levels.

Hazards

The hazards vary according to the type and conditions of work. The hazards listed in Box 7.6 serve to highlight those dimensions of child labour that are frequently noted by children, parents and programme operators, but sometimes overlooked by international organizations and missing in the standard discussions. The psychosocial risks to children's welfare are especially important. Such considerations as the effects on children of being separated from supportive adults for

Box 7.6 A Comprehensive Range of Hazards Faced by Working Children

Physical Hazards

- Inadequate and irregular meals (snack and other high calorie food)
- Physical tiredness
- Strenuous efforts
- Lack of sleep
- Exposure to the elements
- Unhealthy, airless environments

Psychosocial Hazards

- Lack of sufficient:
  - parental love and care
  - interaction with peers
  - interaction with meaningful adults
  - control over decisions
  - leisure time
  - variety in work activity
  - personal satisfaction from work
  - stimulation or pleasure from work environment

Occupational Hazards

- Malnutrition leading to stunted growth
- Susceptibility to diseases
- Skeletal deformations (porter)
- Danger of accidents (street vendor)
- Scarring, infections (scavenger)
- Sexually transmitted diseases (prostitute)

Danger of Abuse

- Psychological (exploitative employers, municipal authorities, teachers):
  - sense of marginalization
  - loss of self-esteem
  - sense of indignation
  - extreme frustration
- Sexual (clients of prostitutes)
- Physical (peer groups, hoodlums, police)

Bondage

- Various forms of coercion, seclusion and exploitation of children as prostitutes, factory workers, live-in domestic and shop helpers and surrogate mothers long hours or — in the case of domestic work away from home — even for months or years at a time, need to be given more prominence.

Bondage

This term usually refers to children kept away from sight, in secluded environments and without freedom of movement. Some children in bondage may have been sold, even internationally. The term could easily be applied to prostitutes or to young victims of paedophiles. Children are held in quasi-bondage to work in factories, often manufacturing goods for export, as was documented during the 1980s in Thailand and in India, among others. Bondage is, in many ways, also an appropriate term for the many young surrogate mothers kept at home in India by traditional parents, and weighed down by culturally patterned gender roles. The Filipino girl working as a live-in domestic worker against her will and with no control over her earnings, and the Brazilian girl forced to become the household's main supporter through prostitution, are both in a kind of bondage.

Additional Policy Considerations

Beyond concerns about age, hours of work, pay, hazards and bondage already considered, two other main types of concern should enter much more explicitly in future policy considerations about children's work.

Gender differences

Girls' experience is often considerably different to boys'. For one, the impact of puberty on girls is socially greater in the sense that it often entails their sudden seclusion. Work activities also differ by countries and by age groups. A comparison of boys and girls in their middle years shows divergent work experiences, daily schedules, degrees of independence and levels of self-esteem.

In India, girls in their early middle years (6–8) may already be working while boys continue to go to school or are idle (NIUA 1991). By the time Indian girls are 11, they slowly withdraw from work. In rural areas and in migrant families, there is a tendency to seclude girls at the onset of puberty to prepare them for early marriage. Often young urban girls are sent back to rural areas to stay with grandparents.

Age of marriage is low in India, particularly in the poorer rural areas, but also among migrant families in cities. According to 1981 census data, 2.4 percent of urban girls aged 10–14 years, 28.4 percent 15–19 years, and 74.3 percent 20–24 years were married. (Relative national figures of 6.3 percent, 44.9 percent and 86 percent show that the situation is even worse in rural areas.) More recently, a five-state study found that between 56 and 64 percent of all girls 15–19 years of age were married, and most had children (Chatterjee 1991).

The family's decision to invest less in the girl child while utilizing her informal domestic labour, their need to protect her chastity to ensure a "good match," and the process of preparing her for home-making may also mean that she drops out of school early or never attends. One of every two Indian girls surveyed in urban areas had no schooling and only about a quarter were still studying, as opposed to 36 percent of the boys (NIUA 1991). Control over a girl's sexuality is particularly important in India, where parents regularly send daughters back to rural areas, away from the male-centred and violent cities, to preserve virginity. In Kenya, the growing wave of adolescent pregnancies in urban areas, linked to school dropout, is cause for alarm.

In the Philippines, this type of control is less rigorous, although an interesting finding of the PSSC report was that 33 percent of the girls surveyed were accompanied by a relative when on the street compared with only 6.5 percent of the boys. Moreover, in distinct contrast with India, more girls than boys are in school nationally (68 percent versus 55 percent). Poor urban girls, however, often drop out and, like Indian girls, tend to marry early. In the Manila slums, the average age at first pregnancy was between 17 and 20 years (Jimenez et al. 1986). There is also evidence that adolescent pregnancies and births for girls below 15 increased between 1980 and 1987. Married girls represented more than 7 percent of the entire under-18 female population in 1989.

Thus, the street, working and, in some cases, educational careers of girls in all countries of the Project differ from those of boys, and these differences must be taken into account.

Informal-sector careers of boys and girls

Recently, attempts to distinguish the formal from the informal sector by types of activities (traditional technology, scale of operation or localization) or forms of employment (self-employment as opposed to wage employment) have been criticized as being partial or arbitrary, since these typologies overlap and are closely interrelated. A more essential difference appears to be the overall mode of operation and the nature of contractual relations (Bose 1990). The informal sector is characterized by: (a) a wide variety of self-employment (artisanal production, small manufacturing, petty trade, construction, transportation); (b) opportunities for wage employment (but usually not government-regulated or covered by trade unions, and thus low-paying and unprotected) in some of those same activities as well as in services (repairs and servicing workshops, shops, domestic service); (c) outwork, which, it has been argued, has emerged in different forms throughout the Third World in the course of the displacement of handicrafts by capitalist manufacture; (d) apprenticeship; and (e) unpaid family labour (Scott 1979, Pineda-Ofreneo

1982). The types of occupations that become available in the informal sector vary continuously and dynamically in each of these categories.

Most children start off their street careers as self-employed vendors or, in the case of girls, family-employed vendors. However, from self-employment, boys in the Philippines, for example, progressively shift into working for others (64 percent were working for mostly non-related employers) and into a broader range of occupations (only 36 percent were currently vending as opposed to 75 percent of the girls). Girls, on the other hand, either remain in self-employed vending (28 percent) or family-employed vending (51 percent).[15] As in other countries, girls who work on the street start at an earlier age and consistently earn less than their male counterparts (Xenos et al. 1986).

Jobs carried out are all easy-entry occupations. Boys progressively explore wage work in mechanics workshops, stalls or shops; learn to sort garbage, scavenge and stake out scavenging territories; become drivers' helpers, pedicab drivers, or bus ticket vendors; and thus move into various forms of apprenticeship. Girls remain much more entrapped in unpaid family labour, domestic work (part-time domestic work in India and Kenya, in particular) or even family-sponsored prostitution. By adolescence (ages 13–18) and usually after 16 years of age, boys have moved away from vending and the street into other occupations.

Furthermore, beyond the general patterns emerging from the surveys, the life histories show us some of the processes which lead boys or girls into their first working experience (often helping a close relative) and then into their first earning occupation (Blanc et al. 1994). They reveal how children, and especially boys, are actively on the lookout for better work possibilities, shift occupations according to what is available and make able use of networking, as shown in the excerpts of a family history provided by the Brazilian team (FLACSO/UNICEF 1991).

> Evandio was nine years old when he started selling sweets prepared at home by his mother. Now 11, he continues to sell, working at the bus terminal in Goiânia where he has established his clientele. He is in grade four and does well in school. His older brother Rosario, aged 17, started off as a messenger in a downtown office, a job he left when he was 14. Then he and his cousins sold sweets that his mother and Aunt Rogeria made, working mostly outside of the airport. Now Rosario works with their father as a mason's helper for a construction company. Their sister, who is 18, used to "take care of everything in the house" (including her many siblings) while doing part-time work as a domestic helper. Now she has little time to help because she works all day in a small shop near home. After work she and Rosario go to a school downtown, some distance away and don't come back home until after eleven o'clock.

Information about children's careers and life paths is thus important for policy makers.

As we have seen, work *per se* is not necessarily negative for children. It should not be banned *a priori* but rather qualified from the point of view of the child and then carefully regulated. Special attention needs to be paid to children during their middle years. Although still expected to attend school, the majority of poor working children first begin to work outside the household between the seven and 10, and for the most part in order to supplement the family income. Many struggle to stay in school, but too often drop out.

Similarly, educational programmes must be designed on the basis of an assessment of: (a) the alternatives realistically open to the child; (b) the understanding the child and family have of the "tradeoffs" entailed in the choice of work vs. schooling; (c) the immediate problems faced by the working child (including how his or her time is allocated and not just the number of hours at work); and (d) the extent to which certain occupations are hazardous or exploitative, not only physically, but also psychosocially. Finally, gender and age considerations are essential to an understanding of the problems across cultures and to any search for viable approaches.

When work descends into drudgery and when its advantages in terms of the child's survival, development and future health and happiness are outweighed by its disadvantages, then we need prompt and determined intervention at various levels.

Protective laws and regulations should also be devised with these considerations in mind. Setting 14 or 15 years as a strictly held minimum age for employment, while well-meaning, deprives the child of income, jeopardizes the family's ability to provide psychological support, and thus ends up punishing rather than protecting the child.

The Impact of the Place of Work on Children

An important theme in the child labour debates of nineteenth century Britain was the impact of the place of work on a child's working conditions. The power of steam-driven weaving machines, for example, pulled children out of homes where they had worked on hand-looms, to work in factories. E.P. Thompson (1963) describes the relative advantages of family work as opposed to the work of children in factories:

> Weaving had offered an employment to the whole family, even when spinning was withdrawn from the home. The young children winding bobbins, older children watching for faults, picking over the cloth, or helping to throw the shuttle in the broadloom; adolescents working a second or third loom; the wife taking a turn at weaving in and among her domestic employments. The family was together and however poor meals were, at least they could sit down at chosen times. A whole pattern of family and community life had grown up around the loom-shops; ... By contemporary standards work was ... arduous, even brutal... But, when compared with the factory system, there are important

qualifications. There was some variety of employment (and monotony is peculiarly cruel to the child). In normal circumstances, work would be intermittent: it would follow a cycle of tasks, and even regular jobs like winding bobbins would not be required all day unless in special circumstances (such as one or two children serving two weavers). No infant had to tread cotton in tub for eight hours a day and for a six-day week. In short, we may suppose a graduated introduction to work, with some relation to the child's capacities and age, interspersed with running messages, picking blackberries, gathering fuel, or playing. Above all, the work was within the family economy and under parental care.

In the five countries of this study, children working as apprentices in the home were found to be better protected from the abuses of wage labour or the dangers of the streets. The problem of working on the street does not relate so much to monotony, since the street environment is quite varied, but rather to the fact that it exposes children to physical dangers and exploitation and does not provide them with the constructive structure provided by a caring adult.

Although we were able to hear only relatively few voices of parents, we know that mothers generally fear that if their children roam the streets, they may be enticed into vices. They worry especially about children in their middle years who may begin progressively to abandon school and take up street jobs. Italian mothers are generally overprotective: they "imprison" their children in the home, depriving them of social interaction and often generating rebellion. Kenyan or Philippine mothers often cannot control the circumstances that lead children out of the household to work, at least part-time, but they have also expressed their concern.

This does not, of course, imply that families never involve their children in abusive work situations. We have recurrent examples that they do when pressed by circumstances (see cases of family-sponsored prostitution in Chapter 5 amd Blanc et al. 1994. for instance). However, the family is the institution primarily responsible for child-rearing throughout the world and should be given greater support so it can balance its income needs with its own ideas of what constitutes healthy development for its children. While protecting children from abusive family situations through its laws, the State can best help the child by helping the family, affording it "the necessary protection and assistance so that it can fully assume its responsibilities within the community," to repeat the words of the Preamble to the Convention on the Rights of the Child.

Where children are so extensively engaged in outside work that their development is jeopardized, it is usually, as the Project reports reiterate, because their parents feel that they have little choice economically. Increasing support systems for families in crisis and strengthening their economic situation should therefore be the first object of a preventive strategy. Family planning workshops are needed so parents can receive sound advice on family size and household management. When the child's earnings are not essential to the family's survival, parents, and particularly those who have not benefited from formal education, should also be helped to weigh the long-term benefits of the child's schooling against the short-term advantages of the child's earnings. State-run schools need to consider such counselling as part of their mandate.

The Relationship of Schooling to Work

Sending the child to school is primarily a way for the family to provide for the social reproduction of its members (by educating the children to the level achieved by the parents) or — if a child can achieve a higher level of schooling — to improve the overall status of the household. One way to obtain greater educational achievements for children is to build on the household's coping strategies and hopes for improvements by helping the family overcome its continuing crises; by helping it to avoid incurring debt at high interest rates when a crisis does occur by making available some capital for production; and by supporting its ongoing productive efforts, such as urban gardening or food vending.

Low school enrolment is often a rough estimate of economic activity at different ages, as shown in Table 7.3. However, as the country studies pointed out, such tables are fraught with problems. Data are often missing. Italian children below age 14 work, for example, but are not included in the census because their work is illegal. Similarly, Kenyan children are not listed as working even when they are. Those who both study and work are not included. Furthermore, the problem is generally viewed as a dichotomy, with the assumption that if a child is working he or she is not studying. Two obvious alternatives for policy makers are to create incentives for the child to go back to school or to enforce legislation on compulsory education (Weiner 1991, Goonesekere 1993). The State clearly has the responsibility to define child labour, when excessive, as a problem, and to create conditions which encourage children to attend school, including incentives for parents. The issue is, however, not so much the unwillingness of the household to send its children to school, but its inability to do so, and the causes must be removed. Simply issuing a law on compulsory education is not enough. Policy makers need to understand the context in which such decisions are taken at family level and turn the problem around, asking themselves how they can collaborate with a family to help it achieve one of its own goals. How can conditions be improved for schooling (fees, payment schedules, accompanying school costs, registration requirements, school hours, reception by teachers and school administrators)?

Interviews with families show that in most countries parents are aware that schooling is valuable for their children but do not feel they can afford it. Parents of working children in Brazil, for example, placed education second

Table 7.3. Economic Activity Rates in the Five Countries of the Project (1989)

	Brazil			Italy			India			Kenya			Philippines		
Age	0–9	10–14	15–19	0–9	10–14	15–19	0–9	10–14	15–19	0–9	10–14	15–19	0–9	10–14	15–19
Economic activity															
Male	–	25	73	–	–	25	–	7	55	–	–	–	–	13	48
Female	–	12	42	–	–	21	–	3	16	–	–	–	–	8	30
School year	1st	2nd	3rd	1st	2nd	3rd	1st	2nd	3rd	1st	2nd	3rd	1st	2nd	3rd
Gross school enrolment rate[1]															
Male	101	31	12	96	78	29	112	54	8	96	27	2.20	111	72	27
Female	97	36	12	96	78	28	82	31	4	92	19	1.00	110	75	28

Economic activity rates are taken from the *International Labour Yearbook of Labour Statistics* (1992), Table 1. Data are not collected for under age 10 in Brazil and the Philippines and age 15 in Italy. Data under age 10 are collected but not analysed in India. Gross school enrolment rates are taken from: World Bank, *Social Indicators of Development 1991–92*. All data are for 1989, except for Brazil (1980); the Philippines 3rd level data are for 1980; and India 3rd level data are for 1985. [1]Ages 0–14. Sources: Prepared by Peter Xenos (1993).

only to health on their list of concerns for their children. This was even more true in the Philippines, while in India (and Kenya) there were differences by gender.

The surveys, reports and life histories also show that, in most countries, street-based working children, as well as street children, are struggling to stay in school. And in India home-bound adolescent girls were resentful because their parents had constrained them to leave school. Schools in the Philippines were generally accessible — at most a 10- to 15-minute walk — while schools were often distant and difficult to reach in Goiânia, and in many cities in India and Kenya. School fees, often concealed under other headings, are a major problem in most developing countries. They may require one single payment, often quite steep for a Kenyan or Filipino family when added to other expenses like uniforms, books and examination fees.

When working children do attend school, they do so with a number of disadvantages that inevitably lead to discrimination. Lack of materials, delayed enrolment, poor clothing, low-status jobs that affect their appearance (scavenging or begging) are all factors that handicap and discourage working children. Uneven school attendance compromises their school performance still further and almost inevitably many drop out.

Key characteristics of interventions could be:

A more client-focused school system that would:

- allow for payment of school fees in instalments;

- establish forms of credit for crisis situations, including repayment by especially disadvantaged families in labour or kind (cleaning classrooms, repairing school property, preparing school meals, and so forth);

- adapt school schedules to students' needs, establishing alternative and flexible hours in public schools, and increasing the availability and access to night schools;

- make the teaching more relevant; by redefining "basic education";

- make the classroom more welcoming to marginalized children by emphasizing their creativity and positive contributions;

- offer incentives to children, such as scholarships and meal programmes;

- link schools with on-site income-generating alternatives for working children.

Nonformal schooling for working children that would:

- provide alternative or on-site schools for certain child occupations (the building sites in Delhi and "street schools," for example);

- establish community schools that are integrated with other community development efforts and services to achieve integrated child, family and community development.

Other training and community efforts could include:

- teacher training for special needs of working, minority and migrant children, including anti-discrimination teaching;

- children's rights education of working children: empowerment/consciousness-raising;

- local committees in support of action for children's rights, modelled on similar initiatives in Brazil.

HOUSEHOLD AND FAMILY COPING STRATEGIES

Reference Groups and Issues of Poverty

Concerned policy makers seek an understanding of the characteristics of families that generate street and street-based working children (Box 7.7). Do they belong to the "poorest of the poor," defined in terms of income? Is this only a question of structural poverty, which Third World countries themselves often feel they cannot resolve? Are other important causes also evident? Is there something the countries can really do about it? The results of the research, thanks in part to the use of reference groups, can contribute important elements to this discussion.

Country Teams established reference groups in Kenyan, Brazilian and Indian urban poor neighbourhoods among households with and without working children. This allowed them to examine why certain households, even though in comparable economic conditions, fare better than others. The objective was to discover the key ingredients of their success in keeping their children off the streets. As illustrated by the life histories and substantiated by street and slum surveys,

> **Box 7.7   Main Characteristics of Families of Street and Working Children**
>
> - They are often migrants, evicted from their homes, and uprooted many times
> - They live below the poverty line
> - They are often incomplete households that have lost a main household member
> - They may have lost critical family support by moving
> - Their diminished family strength is often related to loss of parent's employment
> - They continually face special crises:
>   - eviction
>   - migration
>   - lack or loss of parent/illness
>   - loss of parent's employment
>   - parental frustrations
>   - alcoholism/family violence
>   - overburden and stress
>   - total disintegration of cooperation within family
> - Many have given up trying

households, defined as the residential unit where people live, had the following characteristics:

(1) All families interviewed in the slums of the four Third World countries appeared to be below the overall poverty level; those in Italy lived in seriously deprived pockets of poverty.

(2) The families of street and working children were often migrants. Frequently, they had been evicted from their homes. Some families had been uprooted many times. Their situation was not necessarily due to poverty, as such. They tended to move during moments of family crisis, as a result of job loss or eviction, or with the hope of improving their situation — a hope that had only occasionally been realized.

(3) The families of street and working children were also quite often incomplete households where only one adult was available or able to work. Such households had lower adult earnings and their children were more likely to have to work. Single-headed or single-supported households were a frequent occurrence in all four developing countries, but were not yet prevalent in Italy.

(4) Other working children lived in particularly large households where both adults, generally older, were working but where there were also more children to support. This was particularly the case of the poor urban households in India. The adults of these households had similar jobs, earnings and levels of schooling to the adults in households without working children, but they were at a later stage of their life cycle and had more children.

(5) Across the countries of the study (with the partial exception of Italy), working children's contributions amounted to about one third to one fourth of total household income. Because of these contributions, the overall income of the working children's households was equal to and often higher than that of the non-working children's households.

(6) Since many households had lost critical family support, for example by migrating, they had difficulty finding a helping hand in crisis. Brazilian households relied heavily only on themselves. Italian, Filipino, Indian and Kenyan families complained about lost networks.

(7) This diminished family strength was often related to the loss of a parent's employment. Ensuing economic difficulties often led to frustration within the family. The loss of face of the unemployed father in Brazil as well as the changing roles, particularly of males, within the family were found to be serious causes of personal frustration. The parent often then escaped into alcoholism or family violence.[16] A child may then be asked to start working and was also likely to enter in conflict with his or her father.

(8) In the strained family climate, family members at times ceased to cooperate. This was particularly true in the families of street children. Family members showed little affection for one another or understanding of each other's problems. Some families had given up trying. Although these ex-

treme cases exist and contribute to the number of boys (and few girls) who sever all ties with their families, we generally found that most families were at earlier stages of deterioration, struggling hard to overcome the crises they constantly face. On the whole, Indian and Filipino families appeared to be stronger and more cohesive; Brazilian and Kenyan families were more disrupted or disintegrating.

(9) Most households face, beyond urban poverty *per se*, a life of permanent crisis, involving loss of employment, eviction, migration, arrests, and so forth, which progressively undermine their ability to manage. If the household has no one to turn to for help, each crisis may cause it to sink further down. It is likely to have to borrow money at high interest rates, for example; the child may drop out of school to work; the parent may lose his or her means of livelihood. Thus weakened, the household may not be able to avoid further deterioration.

Children are central to the coping strategies of poor urban households. In a household, the skills, capacities and resources of all members, including children, are usually combined for productive and distributive tasks, which are always closely linked to — and affected by — wider social, economic and political processes and policies. Cooperation within a household is based on a shared ideology of family. Household members share production and reproduction interests and have their own internal power structures and lines of authority (Jelin 1991).

Their strategies generally aim at three main goals: (1) the production and immediate survival of household members; (2) their social reproduction and long-term maintenance; and (3) their improvement and household/family social mobility.

The urban poor households appeared generally resourceful and surprisingly resilient, given their troubles. When still stable, their members cooperated, following an established pattern of activities, responsibilities and authority. They organized production, reproduction and consumption activities, married, had children, worked to support dependents, transmitted and inherited cultural and material resources, and deployed financial and labour resources according to existing opportunities in family enterprises, outside work, small-scale self-employment or complementary activities such as urban gardening or urban livestock-raising (Kenya).[17]

To achieve these three main goals, urban poor households constantly used a number of strategies (Box 7.8), adapting them to their needs and to the crisis at hand. The extent to which they were able to utilize these strategies depended, however, on their resources and other variables, such as their living arrangements; the specific moment in their life cycles; their current level of earnings; and their particular cultural, family and gender ideology, which helped establish roles and levels of authority within the household itself. The timing in the household's life cycle, the number of siblings, and the respective ages of the mother and the father had an important bearing on why children worked.

In Delhi, for example, by contrasting the households of working and non-working children, we discovered that the households of working children usually had more adult and child members working. Fa-

> **Box 7.8 Main Strategies of Uran Poor Households**
>
> • Diversification of activities to diminish risks
> • Greater reliance on women's earning capacities
> • Deployment of children into income-generating activities
> • Use of education to raise the child's job market value
> • Attempts at increased income-earning through national and international migration
> • Creative utilization of urban environment (urban gardening and livestock-raising)
> • Timing of marriage of daughters (for dowries)

thers in both kinds of households were in similar positions in terms of educational level, type of occupation (mostly ragpickers and construction workers) and migration status, but were older in the working children's households (60 percent were 40 years old and above); 39 percent of the mothers in the working children's households were also older and the majority worked. In these large households, the additional income of usually only one working child considerably increased the overall household income. In contrast, the smaller and younger non-working children's households (usually about 42 percent with children under the ages of four and parental ages from 19 to 29) earned as much with only the father working. In other words, as households grew older and larger, the father's earnings alone were often not sufficient to maintain the household, causing the mother and initially the eldest child to seek paying work. The third income produced by the working child generally covered the expenses of the additional children (food as well as schooling). The mother's ability to work because of time freed by the girl child acting as a surrogate mother was also valuable. Most children gave as a reason for dropping out of school the need to work or to help an overburdened mother with child care; most also claimed their parents wanted them to work. Another way children help households is to contribute their labour to produce food (urban gardening) or items for sale (sweets, handicrafts), which they then help to sell.

Across all five countries it can be said that:

- the coping strategies of urban poor households involve their children centrally;

- their responses to difficult circumstances tend to be creative and enterprising;

- under economic pressure, these responses tend to emphasize immediate survival but include concerns for education;

- children and their families usually do not receive much support in their endeavours; and

- they are, instead, much more likely to be penalized by municipal officials for working on the streets or on open lands.

PREDICTORS AND INDICATORS

Having examined street children on their own, street-based working children and other working and non-working slum children in relationship to their families, we can now isolate some major causes of their problems (Fig. 7.1).

"Initial characteristics" are structural givens which allow us to catalogue the neighbourhoods, households or individuals most likely to generate street or working children. They are related to broad economic, social and demographic trends. "Situations" are more immediate descriptors of current conditions and trends. "Levels of cooperation," "degrees of marginalization" and "coping strategies" are related to the management of social relationships. "Crises" are unexpected occurrences.

The evidence that the problems faced by urban children in distress have some recurrent and common antecedents is, as we have seen, substantial. While all of the antecedents listed in Figure 7.1 have proven to have important effects on the child, seven characteristics appear to be *primary predictors* at the household level respectively of working children, street children on their own and children manifesting high-risk behaviours. These predictors, summarized in Table 7.4, are recurrent in all five countries. Points 6 and 7 characterize all children; points 1 to 5 are specific to certain categories. The model shows how certain household factors indicate quite systematically a potential of progressive deterioration in the child's life.

These predictors represent in most cases the end results of a succession of crisis events (parental loss of employment, marital separation, illness and early pregnancy or marriage), as already mentioned. When one household is characterized by most or all of these predictors — in other words, when the predictors are compounded — the household is likely to sink into deeper stress and aggravated frustrations. It is precisely in order to avoid the effects of such negative circumstances that preventive action needs to be taken. It is important to point out that predictors at one level are usually caused by antecedents at previous levels. Thus again both this analysis and Figure 7.1 show clearly how preventive action needs to occur at family, neighbourhood and higher levels so that problems can be avoided at the level of the child.

Finally, if one wished to select a single common indicator for all CEDC (abused or abandoned children, street children, children in conflict with the

Major Categories	National/International	City/Society	Neighbourhood/Community	Family/Household	Child
Initial characteristics	- economic development status - development indicators	- size of city - type of city (e.g. expanding economically or not)	- composition (age median, gender, education, ethnicity, migration history)	- education of parents - household composition, lifestyle, size and age - adult employment status - migration status - ethnic status	- age - gender - ethnicity - education - birth order - health/disability
Situations Level of cooperation Degree of marginalization Positive and negative coping strategies	- structural adjustment - economic development - inadequate funding - structures of services in health, education, welfare, employment, etc. - level of intersectoral structured cooperation - negative biases in national legislation - overall policy directives	- low degree of decentralization - high degree of bureaucratization - inefficient local structures of services - low intersectoral cooperation - employment conditions - negative biases in local legislation - high degree of punitive action exercised - limited overall city planning (for local development and for intersectoral cooperation of services)	- poor neighbourhood quality (shelter, water, sanitation, green spaces) - lack of services (telephone, health centres, schools, police) - exposure to 'new' poverty (consumerism, TV, drugs, solitude) - poor school quality - poor street quality - low level of cooperation and degree of community mobilization - exposure to marginalization - available strategies of income generation	- high level of income poverty - exposure to 'new' poverty - parental expectations of education for children - low level and degree of family cooperation - high level of family conflict - poor quality of parenting - exposure to marginalization - positive and negative coping strategies (increases in work burden, deployment of children)	- low expectations for education - negative perception of life options (including employment) - poor sense of self (self-esteem) - poor sense of competence - low level and quality of social relationship (with adults, with peers) - awareness of marginalization - positive and negative coping strategies (work, street, high-risk behaviour, reliance on street educators)
Crises	- world recession - economic and political crises - natural disasters - security emergencies	- city budget crises - local economic and political crises - local natural disasters - local security emergencies	- neighbourhood crises (eviction, relocation, fire, famine, contaminated or insufficient water, epidemics) - level of violence	- unexpected crises (illness, death, migration, eviction) - family member involvement in high-risk behaviour (substance abuse, crime, etc.)	- unexpected crises (illness, death, migration, eviction) - involvement in high-risk behaviour (substance abuse, crime, etc.) - physical/sexual abuse

Figure 7.1. Levels and types of antecedents.

law, children in situations of war), the most encompassing would be "children who are relationally deprived," that is, children who experience serious privations and problems in social relationships.

PREVENTIVE AND PROTECTIVE APPROACHES

The Preservation of Families and Communities

The research has clearly revealed that economic pressures on the family and family crises can plunge children into difficult circumstances. The family continues to serve as the principal child-rearing agent throughout the world and provides the child's immediate environment. It is thus an obvious focus for preventive CEDC policies and initiatives. Although government agencies, NGOs and international organizations may consider this to be an expensive level of action, it is surely the most cost-effective in the long term.

We must, however, look beyond the family system to the surrounding community in our approach to family support (Bronfenbrenner 1978). The community, social networks or other social contacts can help families under stress weather a crisis by offering valuable material and psychological support to both the child and his or her parents (Whittaker and Garbarino 1983, Munger 1991). One key finding from the life histories and surveys is the potentially destructive effect migration has on the family's relationship with a surrounding social support network. Migrant families, often forced to leave their community of origin by economic hardship, family deaths or other precipitating crises, find themselves in an alien community with neither members of the extended family nor friends to turn to. Most are reluctant to turn to institutions for help. Even in the United States and other industrialized countries, where social services abound, research has clearly revealed that migrants first seek information and help from friends, relatives, neighbours and other nonprofessional "helpers" such as bartenders and beauticians before turning to social service agencies (Whittaker and Garbarino 1983, Cowen and Gesten 1978, Gottlieb 1981).

Research in the United States (Box 7.9) has characterized at-risk families in much the same way as highlighted by Country Teams. These families need strategic support to prevent them from falling into a downward spiral. Garbarino and Sherman (1980) conclude from research in the United States that "high-risk families are most likely to live in high-risk neighbourhoods both because their personal histories incline them to do so and because the political and economic forces that shape residential patterns encourage them to form clusters." Some of the residential patterning is also determined by municipal planning. Such "high-risk" communities are likely to be much less responsive to families that find themselves in crisis. These communities need to become the priority targets in strategies for developing family support programmes.

Table 7.4. Main Household Predictors of Children's Work, Street Life and High-Risk Behaviours

	Non-working poor urban children	Working children (living with families)	Street children (on their own)	Children with high-risk behaviour
1. Migration status	Some migration	Migration status of parents, fewer supports for emergencies	(+recent migrant status, low family supports)	(+marginalization)
2. Household life cycle and size	Younger, smaller household	Older, larger household	(+diminished sense of belonging)	(+low sense of competence, low expectations)
3. Parents' employment status	Father working	Mother working (father not always working)	(+lack of caring adult support)	(+low resistance to peer influence)
4. Household composition	Two-parent household, predominantly natural parents	Incomplete household	(+low level of cooperation, high level of conflict)	(+antisocial behaviour)
5. Education and age at marriage	Some education and later marriage	Uneducated parents, married early	(+evidence of abuse)	
6. Environment	Living in deprived neighbourhood with poor access to services		(+evidence of violence and illness)	
7. Level of poverty	Below poverty line			

Source: Urban Child Project (1992).

For families newly
arriving in a city, these
problems are further
exacerbated. If they
find a home, it is often
with other migrants
who are also struggling
to find resources to sur-
vive; it may take them
many years to replace
old social networks
with new ones. These
high-risk communities
demand our special at-
tention: we need sup-

**Box 7.9   Families at Greatest
Risk of Disintegration**

- Migrant families that have not yet established
  links with the surrounding social support network
- Families that are not socially well-integrated and
  that have low levels of support from friends and
  relatives
- Families that live in inner-city ghettos or other
  neighbourhoods that are unlikely to be responsive to families in crisis

Sources: Belsky 1978, Horowitz and Wolock 1981,
Polansky et al. 1985.

port strategies uniquely tailored to the requirements of migrant families,
including advice to replace what they have lost.

Given what we know about the nature of community support for families,
it is clear that family preservation is a natural by-product of what would
appear to us to be the most fundamental preventive strategy: facilitating
action at community level.

Facilitating Action at the Community Level

Some of the different types of urban poor neighbourhoods have been briefly
described. These neighbourhoods have their own characteristics and histories which influence the way residents relate to one another. Some are
economically, politically, socially and ethnically heterogeneous, composed
not only of well-established long-time residents, but also of migrants, whose
position is less secure. The migrants themselves often come from different
regions and tend, at least initially, to relate along ethnic, regional or linguistic
lines. This diversity, of course, complicates effective local organization.

The degree of cooperation and mobilization within these neighbourhoods
varies. Some have a long history of social mobilization and interact actively
with other city sectors. They have strong and skilful representatives who can
speak on their behalf, if necessary. One community organization may cover
the entire area or, more commonly, a number of distinct or often overlapping
organizations may exist. At the other extreme are neighbourhoods where
internal factionalism or external political manipulation have effectively discouraged joint social action; and others still where residents face serious
problems of basic survival and health, leaving no energy to organize. Those
are the neighbourhoods that appear to have given up!

Collective solidarity often conflicts with highly individualized survival
strategies. The different socioeconomic status of families within a neighbour-

hood also creates divisions. Local factionalism may be accentuated by the many national and international, government and nongovernmental, projects which now interact in various, and usually uncoordinated, ways with urban residents and existing local organizations. Other divisive forces invading neighbourhoods are drug dealers and organized crime syndicates. *Favellas* in Rio and poor urban sections of Naples are being devastated by local criminality. These new challenges require both community and extra-community action.

In general, however, as Bose (1992) points out, poor urban neighbourhoods are neither filled with criminal elements nor as dangerous as is commonly believed. They are made up of hard-working families and individuals struggling for survival and betterment. Another myth is that the poor automatically organize themselves into communities. This romantic notion was created in part by the highly publicized protests of squatter communities facing demolition. Actually, the residents of most low-income communities are more often divided by conflicting interests.

Conflicts are especially frequent among resident homeowners, renters and squatters. Top-down projects usually include, for example, only home owners, while renters and squatters are at times reluctant to involve themselves in bottom-up mobilization unless they can clearly see how it will benefit them. In fact, communities usually only organize themselves when there is a clear common interest, frequently involving land, tenure and housing — all major problems in rapidly expanding and densely populated Third World cities or in changing northern cities (Moser 1989).

UBS projects in India, Philippines and Kenya have repeatedly shown how a common interest can consolidate communities and help to create supportive networks around at-risk families. A shared concern for sustaining school-age children, especially those from at-risk families, brought about effective community action in the Philippines, for example. Mobilization is most likely to occur when community members feel a project is especially needed and when they can work constructively with municipal officials to realize their goals.

When neighbourhood residents, encouraged by interest from outside the community, start monitoring their at-risk children and planning constructive responses, they lay the foundation for collective solidarity. Positive inputs from the outside and concrete help, such as business loans or scholarships, help them feel reinvigorated.

Thus, by directing attention to the children and families at greatest risk, collaborative programmes can activate and reinforce the support systems of urban poor neighbourhoods. The more dynamic neighbourhood members will begin to take it upon themselves to analyse problems and to suggest ways to reduce them. Deprived and overburdened households will begin to feel less marginalized and may derive comfort from the knowledge that others are concerned. Overburdened children will begin to feel that adults wish to help them and care enough to try. All are potential partners in making the programme a success.

Analyses in India, Kenya and the Philippines have shown the remarkable effects that self-monitoring and community action-research can have on women, households and children. And as urban neighbourhoods continue to be involved in the realization of plans they have contributed to formulating, new and stronger partnerships can also be forged, not only among residents but also and importantly across neighbourhoods as well as with municipal authorities and business sectors.

The dynamic potential has been emphasized by research in other contexts as well, and has some strong advocates in the development community. The country studies, especially in Brazil and in the Philippines, have also clearly emphasized that action (including action research) at community level contributes to the creation of a more positive environment for the children of urban poor families at other levels as well. People in authority have changed their attitudes about poor urban families by visiting them, listening to what they say, working with them to find appropriate ways of dealing with problems that the families themselves felt were important. This process of "immersion," especially when combined with well-documented research, has led not only to changed attitudes but also to greater social mobilization and coordination among initiatives at all levels.

Thanks to many efforts in this direction, to which the Urban Child Project has also contributed, a major shift has been taking place in some countries in the way social-service providers view children in especially difficult circumstances. This change in perspective comes from the recognition that the desire for competence is a fundamental urge in all children. Even the language used to describe social service agencies and social service professionals changes when it is recognized that children need conditions that allow them to develop: not paternalistic welfare but support, not handouts but resources. Many children show extraordinary competence through their survival on the streets or at work. Yet such children are commonly considered by policy makers as the problem rather than the solution. The problems, of course, are the conditions which led them to be working, to end up alone on the street, or to engage in high-risk behaviour. The children themselves are part of the solution. Social-service support agencies need to recognize this and to redefine their work as participating with each child, family and community in the creation of choices to transform the lives of children in distress.

A most useful part of the research has been the life histories. They have not only revealed how, in certain families, difficult conditions accumulate and lead children to work or even to be abandoned to the streets; they have also shown us how, with the critical support of a certain person or programme at a particular time, a child's own aspirations can lift him out of great difficulties (Blanc et al. 1994).[18] The life histories thus illustrate the positive energy of urban poor residents, tell us about their aspirations, and remind us of their humanity.

Regrettably, such life history research is extremely rare and considered by most social scientists as simply illustrative of children's lives rather than of unique substantive diagnostic value.

There needs to be a paradigm shift in thinking about research with children to match the shift taking place in outreach programmes for CEDC children. Research needs to be conducted with children and families to enable them to articulate their own unique aspirations. This is the level at which situation analyses must be conducted in order to create suitable and effective plans of action. Quantitative analysis is excellent for discovering the nature and scale of the problem but cannot, by itself, guide us in the design of interventions because it does not tell us how the many important variables interact to affect families and children. This can only be seen by looking at the "whole child." In short, to maximize support to children at risk, research and action need to be carried out at the community level and involve the collaborative efforts of families, children and outsiders alike.

CONCLUSIONS

The Urban Child Project has examined reports, analysed surveys, collected data and talked with children and neighbourhood residents in five countries; it has attempted to obtain more accurate estimates of numbers; it has investigated children's work, analysed how it is defined in different contexts and proposed concrete standards against which it can be measured. The Project has identified root causes — the indicators and predictors of children's problems — and constructed typologies of families likely to produce children in distress; it has documented the importance of family and community support; and it has also developed interesting hypotheses.

At the same time, the Urban Child Project has documented how the very gathering of information on at-risk urban children and families is an important way to focus the attention of neighbourhood residents, programmers and policy makers on children and to encourage these different groups to collaborate. The action-research strategy employed by the Project, therefore, not only provided data but also generated, and became part of, the action itself.

Furthermore, the Country Teams have suggested that to have a greater impact on policy makers at national and municipal levels, it is also important to improve the quality of the data. Census bureaus should disaggregate their large databases to municipal levels to enable more careful computations of urban populations of all ages, and more specifically of the urban poor within each municipality. While administrative and political decentralization is gaining momentum the world over, census bureaus have tended to make their information available in an increasingly aggregate manner. This process needs to be reversed as much as possible.

More child-focused data sets could also be constructed at low cost from already collected national censuses and household surveys with some changes in coding. The relationship between household life cycles and working children below and above 15 could be potentially quantified and mapped at city level, thus allowing for more informed municipal planning. A number of countries in Latin America and Asia, including Brazil and the Philippines, have started to involve census bureaus in improving databases for children. Such efforts should be encouraged because, combined with constructive interaction with the child, family and community, they can provide the basis for more effective future planning and action in urban areas.

NOTES

1. She was asked to start coordinating the project immediately in each country. The UNICEF International Child Development Centre, itself barely established, did not yet have a reference library or a systematic reference system on the topic, and was in the process of moving into new offices.

2. Of particular relevance to children in especially difficult circumstances are the articles that oblige the State to protect the child from violence, abuse and neglect by parents or others responsible for their care (Article 19), from economic exploitation (Article 32), from drug abuse (Article 33), from sexual exploitation (Article 34), from sale, trafficking and abduction (Article 35), from all other forms of exploitation (Article 36), from torture, the death penalty, life imprisonment and unlawful or arbitrary deprivation of liberty (Article 37); and articles that provide for the rights of a child to an adequate standard of living (Article 27), and to special protection if an asylum seeker or otherwise affected by armed conflict (Article 38) or if disabled (Article 23).

3. The recurrent patterns have been established on the basis of: (a) the results of the primary research done by the Country Teams in different cities; and (b) the findings of additional surveys reviewed by the Country Teams. The latter include the DSWD, NCSD and UNICEF Ten-City study in the Philippines in 1988, the 1986 McGuire study in Cebu, the 1989 Rao study in Vijayawada, the 1992 Panicker and Nangia study in Delhi, the 1992 Arimpoor study in Madras, and the 1991 SPARC study in Bombay. We will refer to these surveys often only with the name of the city or country to avoid constant repetition of citations. We will also frequently refer to: the 1992 studies by Oloko and others of some major Nigerian cities; the 1992 Commission for the Study of Street Children (COESNICA) summary report on Mexico City; the 1992 Kaminsky report and the 1993 Proyecto Alternativas (a and b) on Tegucigalpa, Honduras; and the studies in Latin American cities and countries published in Series on Children in Especially Difficult Circumstances 1988–91 by Francisco Espert and the UNICEF Latin American Regional Office. However, since most surveys beyond the country studies do not distinguish systematically for most variables between the populations of street children and street-based working children nor between

households with working children and non-working children, they will be referred to only when relevant. Citations for the many other both general and specific reports utilized in this synthesis will instead be given in full.

4. Forty-five percent of the 50,000 cases of people reported missing yearly from their homes in Bombay are children and young people (and an estimated 50,000 cases are not reported).

5. Variable numbers of live-in hotel and shop helpers and domestic helpers were included in many of the street-based surveys. They represented almost one third of the NIUA Delhi sample, 14 percent of the Delhi study (Panicker and Nangia 1992), 16 percent of the Madras study (Arimpoor 1992), possibly over 14 percent of the Mexico city census, 1 percent in the Philippines national sample, 3.5 percent in Vijayawada. The Nigeria study included them as one of the purposeful categories they interviewed (Oloko et al. 1992).

6. This is presumably an issue of sampling procedures. Similarly, Italy did not have ragpickers or scavengers as such. Begging, on the other hand, was found to be a common occupation among Gypsy children.

7. In Italy, Law No. 25 of 19 January 1955 specifies that apprentices must be at least 15 years of age and no more than 20. An exception is made for 14-year-olds who have already received their middle school diploma. Their employers are required to give them rest periods during the day, time off for relevant courses, paid vacations, and should not request the apprentice to work on a piece-rate basis, or for more than a certain number of hours per week (depending on the trade) and never at night. Often apprenticeships are found through relatives or acquaintances.

8. The abuse of different substances seems to follow gradients and availability in the different countries and may be in part interchangeable. Drugs and solvents satisfy similar needs and offer the illusion of an escape from similar problems. While hard drug use is said to be increasing (although the trend is poorly documented so far) and the use of inhalants is reported by NGOs working with street children, our analysis both in slums and in institutions revealed a very active use of cigarettes and alcohol (we learned, for example, that institutionalized Kenyan youth have organized illegal beer brewing inside the juvenile homes themselves). In Italy, much as in the United States, young substance abusers prefer cigarettes and hard drugs. The United States has, in addition, serious problems of alcoholism among its youth.

9. Compounding the health and emotional difficulties of the abandoned street children many of them (44 percent) are sexually active (compared with only 5 percent of the market children). Almost all of the sexually active children "of" the street (85 percent or 47) have been treated for sexually transmitted diseases at least once (compared with only 40 percent of the sexually active market children). More than one fifth of the sexually active children "of" the street have also engaged in prostitution. At the Tegucigalpa health clinics, one client in six was thought to suffer fair to poor mental health, more than one third were assessed as being in fair to poor physical health, and over 40 percent were found to have significant nutritional problems. In most cases, these assessments

were more negative for the children "of" the streets than the market children (Wright et al. 1992).

10. Analyses of the case histories collected in all five countries, secondary data in Brazil and Italy, short studies in India and a survey by the Urban Child Project in four institutions in Kenya.

11. They work as call girls in hotels, rooming houses and about 50 brothels scattered through the various low-income and industrial areas of the city. Predominantly from an area of West Bengal known as Radh and from families who are landless, female-headed, or belong to obsolete occupational castes, they are not accustomed to agricultural work, nor socially accepted as agricultural labourers. Many of the young girls are destitute brides (Dasgupta 1990).

12. The recent attention given to street children has enabled NGOs to raise, if not the issue of working children in general, at least the issue of street-based working children. Up until now, many of the estimates quoted combine both street and working children. It is clear that a more careful set of definitions by different types of working children needs to be developed in order to facilitate the understanding of the problem and thus permit appropriate protective action to be taken.

13. A review of 80 cultures by Rogoff et al. (1975) as well as observations by Kuznesof (1991), Harkness and Super (1991) and Gibson (1991) in articles respectively on Brazil, Kenya and Italy and by Whiting and Edwards (1988) on Kenya, Philippines and India.

14. Average time is obviously an unsatisfactory concept since it does not sufficiently give a sense of the median and of the range of possibilities. We need to focus on children spending over eight hours a day working and studying in order to assess the extent of the problems they potentially face. These difficult calculations could not be finished in time for this book, but will follow in subsequent publications by the main author.

15. Both the self-employed (buying or producing items for resale) and the employed (who take items on consignment or are paid by the piece or by wages) sell a wide range of products, some of which are ultimately controlled by larger enterprises, including at times criminal organizations. These children are therefore often the last rung of a whole system of marketing.

16. Drug abuse among parents was not extensive in the developing countries of the study; nor was it in Italy, although it was more of a problem there.

17. Kenyan urban households did not receive much support in their creative endeavours. In fact, they were most often penalized, together with their children, by municipal officials for working on the streets or on open land (Mazingira Institute 1989).

18. A chapter on the life histories collected in each country during the project was prepared for publication in this volume but had unfortunately to be cut out because of space constraints. It will come out as a separate publication.

Chapter
EIGHT

Innovative Policies and Programmes: Lessons Learned

Cristina Szanton Blanc

MODELS OF CHANGE

Policies and programmes aimed at reinforcing positive trends and modifying negative ones are based on explicit and implicit models of behaviour. The model used by this Project highlights the relationship between children and their wider social, economic and physical context, at the family, household, community, city and national levels; and it stresses the importance of influencing all these domains (see Figure 1.1). It is based on a theory of change that emphasizes causes rather than immediate symptoms. It is also based on a theory of change that looks at development as the "process of enlarging the range of choices — increasing the individual's opportunities for education, health care, income and employment," as defined by the *Human Development Report* (UNDP 1992). However, the Project interprets the phrase "enlarging the range of choices" to mean more than merely handing out ad hoc resources (a utilitarian view of social change) and emphasizes the importance of *behavioural changes* which could allow all participants to manage existing resources more wisely and in a way that is self-sustainable, with long-term effects. As the Project has argued, the issue of how to achieve change needs to be squarely addressed and new models developed, especially in view of the global crises of poverty, environmental destruction and social deterioration.

We have documented the growing numbers — and the situations — of urban children in advanced distress in four developing countries and one industrialized one from the perspective of the children themselves, their families and their communities. In Chapter 7, we analysed trends in the five countries, identified some major causes, and made suggestions about appropriate preventive and protective responses as opposed to curative ones.

Urgent action is required to help the small numbers of children already manifesting symptoms of advanced distress, but also to foster change in the lives of the much larger numbers of children in danger of falling into greater distress. How can needed changes be achieved? One approach is to change the structural causes that limit Third World development by, among others, improving the growth potentials of these countries and giving development strategies a more human face. Concomitantly, however, an approach needs to be devised to improve resource management and to encourage social programmers to take fuller advantage of the resources and people available.

The fact is, however, that most people do not spend much time reflecting on abstract issues of change. In order to affect change, one needs to reach people where they are, in their immediate worlds and personal circumstances and at their level of concern. Once a broad social problem has been identified (in our case, urban children in distress) behavioural changes can then be brought about by:

a) *convincing people about the advantages of one approach over another*. Discussions on effectiveness, sustainability, costs, replicability as well as goal attainment are an integral part of rational arguments; and

b) *changing people's perceptions and circumstances through their personal exposure to first-hand experiences of change, including the people's own organizing; allow people to speak for themselves*. This can be particularly effective, as highlighted by the country chapters. Behavioural changes have both psychosocial and cultural dimensions, and involve feelings, emotions and patterned expectations of behaviour that are central to the individual's sense of self and thus to his or her ability to change. Culturally patterned behaviour is extremely dynamic and constantly in the process of reformulation. Culture as it is lived (and before it is encoded and systematized in the writings of anthropologists and sociologists) is continually changing and contains its own constantly renewed contradictions.

When opportunities and situations change, or new approaches are emphasized, individuals often change their behaviour and attitudes, filtering them through previous cultural understanding and progressively modifying this understanding as they go along. The most recent literature also sustains that attitudinal changes tend to last longer when associated with emotions, feelings and personal experience. Thus, the importance of the concept of participation, for it entails personal voluntary action and involvement.

Culture is not necessarily a stumbling-block to change, as is often argued. Change and new opportunities are most effective, however, if they are presented in ways appropriately tailored to the individual's or community's knowledge, felt needs and expectations, a fact powerfully illustrated in the extensive literature on the shortcomings of the rural and urban development projects of the 1960s and 1970s (for example, Moerman 1968, Bose 1980, Palmer 1983, Hill 1986). An understanding of people's culture, daily situations and expectations provides a unique opportunity for ensuring long-lasting and constructive behavioural changes. It is a very powerful tool for making a difference!

This perspective implicitly acknowledges that actors and decision makers at all levels can, if adequately supported, bring about change. Because individuals tend to have not only rational and pragmatic but also emotional responses to situations, tied to their experience and culture, this Project has presented and developed approaches that take into account both dimensions.

MAIN CHALLENGES FOR POLICY MAKERS

Country chapters have emphasized the innovative aspects of policies on behalf of children as well as the many challenges and difficulties that had to be overcome before such policies could be enacted. In Chapter 7, the importance of recognizing and supporting the creativity and resilience of disadvantaged urban children was stressed. The chapters also show how essential it is to create a supportive environment in policy and organizational terms (that is, both at the legislative and administrative levels) in order to increase the competence of families and communities to build on their existing strategies. The principle is to support families and communities so that they are better able to support children.

Country Teams have also highlighted shortcomings in national policies: they are often established on an *a priori* basis, without a careful analysis of the felt needs of the populations. Moreover, policies are frequently based on biased assessments of the problems rather than on informed planning. Because politicians and government officials are often in "crisis management" situations, there is also little time and little money available for serious planning. Thus policy makers, both North and South, pressured by their constituencies to solve immediate problems at city or national level, too often revert to ad hoc responses that are costly in both monetary and developmental terms. Typical of these are the institutionalization of "street children," the criminalization of drug use or truancy, and the imprisonment of "delinquent children."

In each country, there was an awareness that new ways of perceiving and responding to the situation were urgently needed. Innovative approaches are emerging in some countries and generally involve local action as well as the identification of new change agents.

Important Elements of a Country Diagnosis

The first step of a social planner is the identification of conditions, resources and partners. However, the most effective urban/CEDC programmes have gone beyond a listing of problems, potential partners (with their relative strengths and weaknesses) and resources, and have been able to diagnose the country's potential for change and build upon it.

In addition to the standard statistics planners always seek, a thorough diagnosis should also answer more qualitative questions: How have issues been defined historically? To what extent is the country bureaucratized and the policy-making top-down? To what extent, even under authoritarian regimes, is there a basis for democratic trends and impulses generated at the grassroots level? What is the state of mind of civil society? What level of indignation is felt towards current economic and social constraints? What is the country's "pulse"? Which opportunities are feasibly available? Which potential partners are or could be a driving force for change?

> **Box 8.1   Some Important
> Elements of a
> Country Diagnosis**
>
> - Social, economic and political conditions
> - Democratization trends
> - Decentralization trends versus centralized bureaucratic presence
> - Existing legislation for children and levels of implementation
> - Historical definition of issues
> - Level of community and grassroots participation and mobilization
> - Civil society's "mood"
> - Potential leading partners for new initiatives

Each country had different responses, related to their historical trajectories towards development. Some were able, through a sensitive diagnosis, to identify new human, economic, political and organizational resources. As each Country Team discovered, the skilful utilization of existing strengths was the key to a successful urban/CEDC programme and determined its ability to grow to scale, if necessary. In many cases, the people's responses to their country's problems were transformed into programme opportunities. Brazil, India and the Philippines are particularly good examples of a skilful employment of local resources and good timing:

Brazil was ready for change and increased democratization by the 1980s. There was widespread public indignation at the State's authoritarian and sometimes violent response to the rising number of children drawn to the streets by dislocations of the economy. An NGO-led social movement was able to pressure the Government to make changes in the Constitution that were then translated into a three-tiered hierarchy of policies at national, state and municipal levels: basic social policies for all children; assistance policies for children in special need; and special protection policies for victimized children. How these policies will respond to the most urgent needs in urban neighbourhoods remains to be seen.

> **Box 8.2   Neighbourhoods and Communities in the Countries of the Project**
>
> * Brazil: highly politicized urban neighbourhoods and communities
> * India: strong community focus historically
> * Italy: limited mobilization of local neighbourhoods within a city (issue has become part of political ideology)
> * Kenya: strong community and grassroots organizations, often occupational and based on women
> * Philippines: strong grassroots movements historically

The Philippines, like Brazil, was afflicted in the 1980s by severe economic dislocations, tied to problems of structural adjustment. Rampant civil discontent eventually contributed to the overthrow of an oppressive regime. In the ensuing "democratic space," civil society mobilized en masse in support of the urban poor. NGOs multiplied, and voluntary urban grassroots organizations also began applying pressure on the Government. Committees at local or municipal level joined for more effective action. The Government progressively learned how to collaborate with voluntary groups and NGOs, and effective partnerships were formed.

India had a very powerful top-down bureaucracy in the 1980s, a problem that has persisted into the 1990s. Support to an immense and growing population of urban poor has been provided through an intricate system of overlapping schemes, unevenly implemented. Specific support to children has similarly occurred through nationwide, centrally planned programmes, such as the Integrated Child Development Service, which, however, are not always well coordinated. A new attempt at integration has taken place recently with the expansion of the UNICEF-supported Urban Basic Services Programmes (UBSP) to the whole country. Community participation, now with NGO support, has been the cornerstone.

Kenya is characterized by popular trends towards democratization, though resisted by the current Government, and a situation of rapidly growing urban poverty with evidence of family disaggregation. The emphasis has been on building upon strong urban grassroots movements to help those movements interact with municipal and national officials.

Italy, already urbanized, has in the past few decades undergone an extremely rapid process of industrialization and further urbanization, going from a prevalently agricultural economy to the fifth largest industrialized country in the world. Policy makers have tended to focus on the problems of

an ageing population, leaving
families to struggle, largely unassisted, with the problems of
children. Recent new political opportunities (a rejection of some of
the negative elements of the existing political system), a growing concern for the uneasiness of
its youth, an unusually high rate
of unemployed young adults,
and a growing number of immigrant children from the Third
World and central and eastern
Europe, are factors that may
begin to shift neglect into real
concern.

> **Box 8.3   Child-Related
> Legislation in the Countries
> of the Project**
>
> • **Brazil:** until recently repressive and
>   correctional, now more progressive
> • **India:** ambitious laws, often poorly
>   implemented
> • **Italy:** generally progressive legisla-
>   tion, but poorly implemented
> • **Kenya:** fragmented colonial and
>   post-colonial legal structure
> • **Philippines:** mild and moralistic ap-
>   proaches to law formulation and im-
>   plementation

Interacting Processes and Levels of Action

The Project has documented multiple interrelated processes (Table 8.1) contributing to the distress of urban children. Some of these processes affect
children directly; others indirectly, through the social and physical environment. These divisions are inevitably artificial, but they are convenient for
analytical purposes and suggest areas for intervention, which have in many
cases only been partially explored by NGOs and governmental agencies:

(a) *Macro processes*, interaction of national and international levels of
decision-making, is one level where action should be taken. The aim would
be, for example, to affect unequal trends in economic development, structural
adjustment and its policies or the globalization of ills (the drug trade, for
one), as well as the political responses to those trends, through international
pressure on donor countries and large funding agencies, regional associations of NGOs, transnational planning and international scientific or legal
collaboration. A supportive international and national policy influences and
greatly facilitates actions at meso and micro levels.

(b) *Meso-level processes* involve municipal-level policies and practices,
which are influenced by national or international trends. The lack of coordinated services, people-oriented planning and appropriate community support can undermine the most earnestly pursued survival strategies of poor
urban families. At the same time, the potential for positive action is considerable. The decentralization of resources and responsibilities, better coordination of services and support, a more people-oriented focus and more con-

Table 8.1. Levels of Causality Pointing to Important Levels of Action

International and national level	State and city level	Community and family level
Macro processes	**Meso processes**	**Micro processes**
Structural adjustment	Large-scale planning	Conflicts with parents
Uneven balance of power	not connected with	Lack of cooperation
Insufficient democratization	people's needs	within family
and decentralization	Inadequate policy	Lack of shelter
Inadequate planning and	formulation and	Parental illness, death,
policy formulation	implementation	imprisonment
Transnational migration	Lack of coordinated	Evictions
Globalization of ills	services and support	Degraded community
(drugs, AIDS)	Urban migration	environmental conditions

structive interactions with urban poor communities are some of the responses documented by the Project.

(c) *Micro-level processes* provide an assessment of the social conditions surrounding the child from the point of view of family/household and urban neighbourhood/community (see Figures 1.1 and 7.1). All five country studies found that high-risk behaviours, such as running away from home, substance abuse, petty crime or early unprotected sexuality, were largely the result of the child's emotional reaction to unsatisfactory conditions in the home or the immediate environment. Irrespective of culture, these emotional reactions manifested themselves in middle childhood and adolescence, but somewhat differently according to gender. Often the child was reacting to the emotions, frustrations and loss of self-esteem of family members, and especially parents. At other times, as found in northern Italy, the precipitating factor was the solitude and lack of social interaction of the "latchkey kid" or "only child."

The life histories have also revealed the extent to which factors outside the child's control play a significant role in maladjustment. Child victims in all five countries had been incarcerated for minor infractions, abused sexually by family members or others, exploited on the job, or exposed to excessive work. They had to cope with eviction, homelessness, street life, parental incarceration, illness or death.

Of the many actions that can be taken to change the situation at the micro level, the provision of stronger support to children, families and communities; the provision of basic resources (shelter, water and sanitation); and protection from major medical, legal, political and economic constraints are some of the most obvious. The Country Teams have also repeatedly made a strong plea for ensuring the active involvement of children, families and communities in planning as one of the most constructive responses. One especially significant instance is the street children's movement in Brazil that eventually led to modifications in the Constitution.

New resources and new partners can be identified at each level. However, at times the programmes put more emphasis on one level than another, often to the detriment of their effectiveness. The emphasis may also shift over time. A shift from a national- to a city-level focus in Brazil, and from a city- to a national-level focus in the Philippines has occurred. Indian planners have worked primarily at connecting national macro and community micro levels in an attempt to attenuate the exceedingly centralized aspects of decision-making. Kenya, like the Philippines, has primarily supported grassroots efforts and linked them with municipal, and only more tentatively with national, levels of action. Italy has given priority to building up collaborations at meso and micro levels where programmatic strength is located and where party ideologies are somewhat less influential. A multilevel approach often indicates a more mature programme.

Issues of Transfer and Replicability

Given the differences among the five countries, policies clearly cannot be transferred automatically. Indeed, country-level policies and programmes are never "transferrable" in a strict sense. When the Brazilian approach to the street child phenomenon, for example, served as a "model" for the Philippines Government/UNICEF Country Programme for Children in the 1980s, the programmes that emerged were quite different. The Philippines programme adopted the idea of national street children's congresses and other participatory techniques; it also took up the idea of forming partnerships with umbrella NGO networks for advocacy purposes. But these concepts were substantially adapted to the Filipino reality.

However, as the Project has shown, some key elements of the most innovative policies recur and suggest principles of broad applicability. Moreover, clear patterns help account for their success or partially explain their shortcomings. Similarly, experiences at the programme level provide many examples of what has worked and how, and what could be adapted in new settings.

MOBILIZING PARTNERSHIPS AND MAKING THEM WORK

Initial Constraints

As illustrated in the country chapters, government resources for social services during the 1980s were generally diminished, sometimes drastically, in most developing countries as a consequence of macro-level constraints. Very modest funds are available from international agencies (Hardoy 1992). After households, governments remain, of course, the largest provider of funds for social services. Thus, governments must not be "let off the hook," but rather ways need to be found to increase their sense of responsibility. At the same time, in a context of growing needs and diminishing resources, it becomes especially important to mobilize a wider array of partnerships and to make these partnerships work. Existing policies, as we have seen, sometime encourage, but frequently discourage, development of new partnerships.

Partnerships in each country were remarkably similar in many respects. Each approach emphasized disadvantaged urban children in different ways: some placed more emphasis on families and communities (India, Kenya and the Philippines); others, at least initially, on the broader civil society (including the media, the church, associations of lawyers, and so forth); others still, on the private sector (Brazil). In all countries, it was found that to be effective programmes needed to involve communities, NGOs, voluntary grassroots organizations, academics, media and public officials (including the police).

Action must start with an understanding of current attitudes. In order to draw a larger range of people into partnerships, the perspectives and constraints of potential partners need to be understood; then, some common agreement needs to be reached about the problems faced by urban poor children and their families and the most appropriate approaches; and finally, various partners need to be convinced by being shown concrete examples of the advantages of working together.

During interviews with government officials and representatives of the private sector, Country Teams regularly encountered negative attitudes, which create serious constraints to real change for the urban poor. The most common are:

- Stigmatizing: impoverished children are seen as diseased individuals to be cured, dangerous individuals to be constrained, or polluting and dirty individuals to be removed from sight.

- "Scapegoating": children's families and immediate urban poor neighbourhoods are blamed for not controlling their children better. Fining families of children found earning a living on the streets, as happened in some Philippine cities, is one manifestation.

- Moralizing: a judgmental finger is pointed at the poor, who are assumed to be the cause of their own distress.

- Stereotyping: poverty is attributed to cultural beliefs that need to be eradicated, or to their ethnic origins (rural migrants in India, Gypsies and ethnic minorities in Italy, Afro-Brazilians have all been affected).

- Patronizing: the urban poor are viewed as unable to manage their lives or to understand their own problems. Programmes that provide an external assessment of needs and, if something goes wrong, assume that "they" misused or mismanaged what was given to them, are expressions of this attitude.

The analyses of programmes and of the poor's resilient coping strategies point out the inaccuracy of these views and emphasize the importance of countering them (Box 8.4). A renewed vision of the urban poor is not only the basis for effective partnerships, but should become one of the main goals.

NGOs as "New" Partners

There is also a general lack of clarity about who exactly NGOs are. If NGOs are indeed going to become increasingly prominent counterparts to social planners, much more needs to be learned about who they are, what they represent, and how they might contribute, on a more sustained and systematic basis, to programmes addressing the problems of urban children and families in distress.

Box 8.4   Renewed Vision of the Urban Poor as the Basis for All Partnerships

- Raise public awareness about the situation of the urban poor and children at risk, and inform communities, including children, about their rights and the city services to which they are entitled.
- Require the staff of all municipal agencies to use language adapted to this new vision of childhood to reduce stigmatization.
- Work with academics and the media to project an informed and non-sensationalist picture of children in difficult circumstances.
- Strengthen capacities of municipal service providers to be more open to participatory ways of solving problems.

Source: Meeting of Mayors, Urban Planners and Makers, 1992.

In their broadest definition, NGOs include all the many types of organizations that are not governmental, from small-scale people's organizations to large public service contractors and major humanitarian institutions and international organizations (Box 8.5). Some people's organizations are anchored in one section of an urban slum. NGOs are constantly being transformed: voluntary organizations may become public service contractors, for example. The vital role NGOs have played in different contexts needs to be better understood.

During the past decade, partly as a reaction to a threefold global crisis of poverty, social deterioration and environmental degradation, the strength and numbers of NGOs, and particularly voluntary organizations and people's organizations, have grown surprisingly in the four developing countries under study, usually immediately preceding or accompanying democratization trends (Berg 1987, van Til 1988). In these countries, NGO networks have performed pivotal roles in advocacy, whereas both voluntary organizations and people's organizations have provided a strong basis for joint project activity, primarily at municipal and local level.

Local nongovernmental programmes are often very small and are managed by NGOs operating at international, national, regional, municipal and neighbourhood levels. Many NGOs have limited funding, depend on public or private sources, or both, and must grapple with difficult decisions about how and where to expand (Box 8.6). These decisions often require striking a balance between the management requirements of their local programmes (if the NGOs wish to continue to provide important local services) and the need to attract funds by becoming well-known nationally, or even internationally.

Even at the local level, they often have to respond to the guidelines established by funding agencies, which thus potentially constrain and direct their decision-making. Since the late 1980s, large international NGOs (such as Save the Children, CARE) and government-funded international agencies (such as UN agencies), have had to respond to increased numbers of emergencies, especially in Africa.

> **Box 8.5   Main Types of NGOs**
>
> • **Voluntary Organizations** that pursue a social mission driven by a commitment to shared values, such as citizens' action groups. They may represent a variety of conflicting commitments and perform an important role in a democracy. They could include welfare organizations and children's homes.
>
> • **Public Service Contractors** that function as market-oriented nonprofit businesses serving public purposes usually defined by their specific private contributor or government agency.
>
> • **People's Organizations** that represent their members' interests, have member accountable leadership, and are substantially self-reliant. Because of their essentially democratic structure they are more likely to serve their constituencies consistently and exclusively. Community and grassroots organizations often fall under this definition.
>
> • **Quasi-public Nongovernmental Organizations** that are creations of government and serve as instruments of public policy. They represent a means for the government to channel back to itself the funds international organizations direct to NGOs.
>
> **Source: Korten (1990).**

International funding sources are, in fact, spread thin, with immense tasks. As a result, relief operations have often had to take priority over local community development.

Furthermore, international funding agencies operate in ways that are often incompatible with the survival strategies of disadvantaged urban households. National agencies for international development (the US AID, the Italian Cooperazione, the British ODA, the Swedish SIDA, their French and German counterparts, among others) have generally moved into large-scale development rather than community support. When offering funding to local voluntary organizations or people's organizations, they have tended to impose increasingly stringent conditions, which small citizen's groups are unable to meet and which, if accepted, would destroy their potential for meaningful local impact.[1]

To become national from
a local base, an NGO must
make considerable changes,
including bureaucratiza-
tion. A mature and highly
respected East African
NGO, the Undugu Society
of Kenya, for example, has
adamantly refused to ex-
pand to other Kenyan cities
despite strong encourage-
ment from the international

> **Box 8.6 Some
> Constraints of NGOs**
>
> * Funding for NGOs is limited.
> * NGOs can provide quality coverage but
>   usually only to small populations.
> * NGOs face considerable problems of lack of
>   coordination not only with other NGOs but
>   also with governments.
> * The extent to which NGOs can grow to scale
>   is debatable and involves compromises.

funding community, including UNICEF. It has been involved in training
NGOs in Kenyan cities as well as in other African nations, often in coordination with ENDA, a very strong West African NGO, initially established and
still based in Dakar, Senegal, but with branches throughout Africa. Nonetheless, the Undugu Society has insisted on remaining Nairobi-based and service-oriented rather than establishing a national or international network. It
is, at the same time, moving into a broader advocacy role and forging
partnerships with other sectors of society and government.[2]

Being an NGO is thus a complex enterprise, and, because of their social
mission, this is especially so for voluntary organizations and people's organizations. Some succumb to the funding temptation; others remain true to
their initial charter. All urge international funding agencies to make greater
efforts to understand the complexities of local long-term development and of
their beneficiaries.

Civil Society Cannot Afford To Sit Back and Watch

In each of the countries, under the impact of this threefold global crisis, civil
society has mobilized in various ways (Box 8.7). Many lawyers and other
professionals, academics, and elements of the new middle classes have begun
to realize they can no longer "sit back" but must, for both humanitarian and
pragmatic reasons, become more actively involved in addressing growing
problems. The mass media have sometimes taken on new roles, including
local and national advocacy. Size makes a difference: in a small city, where
face to face interaction is frequent, a key journalist befriended by an NGO or
UNICEF programmer may be extremely helpful at critical moments in influencing politicians; at the national and international level, the media's
contribution is somewhat more dispersive but still extremely influential.

The private sector, as a major employer with increasing interest in
humanitarian causes, can lend critical support to the fight against exploitative labour. Employers are especially important interlocutors in improving
child labour conditions or eliminating child labour altogether, at least for

certain age groups. At the national level, employers' unions and interest groups often interact with the International Labour Organisation to formulate and enact broad legislation. However, employers have even more to offer at the local, mostly city, levels. When mobilized, they can contribute funds (as they did for the drop-in centre in Cebu) and, even more importantly, provide jobs for young people. In Maringà, a wealthy city, companies that offer apprenticeships to adolescents are

> **Box 8.7   Level of NGO/Government Partnerships in the Five Countries**
>
> • **Brazil:** primarily oppositional during the 1970s, but more closely allied with the Government, at least on children's issues, during the 1980s.
>
> • **India:** primarily oppositional but recently adopted as allies by the Government for UBSP.
>
> • **Italy:** more oppositional in the South, more often contracted in the North.
>
> • **Kenya:** largely oppositional.
>
> • **Philippines:** largely allied (but also critical).

given tax rebates amounting to half the trainee's salary. In Goiânia, labour leaders and professionals volunteer their time at communal educational workshops to advise participants on workers' rights or to discuss basic economic principles, such as production costs, pricing and marketing.

Partnerships with Churches and Religious Bodies

In countries where religious groups are particularly progressive, their interest in children has provided a strong impetus for specific projects and for advocacy in general. In Brazil, for example, the Minors' Pastorate has been an influential source of support to street educators, not only providing training materials but also protecting street educators with the weight of its authority. In the Philippines, research teams discovered many more programmes for street children at the parish level than they had been aware of. In Kenya, the support of local Muslim leaders has been critical in many urban neighbourhoods of Nairobi and Mombasa.

Other Advocacy and Action Groups Should Join Forces

In a democratic world of electoral accountability, pressure groups represent an important element, positive and negative, that allows for the venting of particular humanitarian, social, or just self-serving interests. They exemplify one way to apply pressure on governments and to ensure some measure of consideration for the rights of specific groups. Lobbying can be instrumental in bringing about redistribution of resources, depending on who is conducting it. As countries move more towards democracy, advocacy and action groups become particularly important allies of poor children.

Human rights organizations are the most obvious partners. Many other groups are potential partners but have as yet shown only halfhearted interest in children's issues: environmental groups, for example, could easily add a strong child dimension to their arguments for a better quality of life and for the preservation of natural resources. Such a dimension would contribute an even greater sense of urgency to their cause since it is the children's future that is being mortgaged.

Groups speaking on behalf of the poor, including some urban neighbour-hood groups, have started to adopt a child's angle in some countries. In contrast, trade unions have been particularly uninterested. NGOs in India, for example, after trying to create a partnership with labour unions, are now supporting the creation of children's labour unions in order to enable their special problems to be voiced. The Italian trade unions, long courted by youth associations such as ARCI Ragazzi, may have occasionally funded activities on behalf of children, but have recently been so caught up in changing political and economic realities that they have found only limited time to support children's causes.

Women's organizations in the five countries have generally not espoused children's issues *per se*. The more radical women's groups, such as Gabriella in the Philippines, have set up committees for women and children, but usually these groups seem to believe that helping poor women sufficiently helps their children. Middle-class women's groups have rarely rallied to the support of child domestics and have generally offered only misguided and overly moralistic concern for child prostitutes and pregnant adolescent girls. Despite repeated efforts by the Undugu Society, street and working children have not yet been placed on the agenda of the Kenyan Women's Movement.

Women's groups generally have a defensive attitude towards children's advocacy groups, claiming that they are insensitive to women's concerns and more ready to blame women for being inadequate mothers than to under-stand their problems. At the same time, the children's advocacy groups depend on women volunteers, thus further taxing the already overburdened urban poor female population. A well-balanced focus on women and children that acknowledges the importance of the healthy development of both and encourages greater male involvement and responsibility could do much to correct this lack of strong cooperation and unite two potentially powerful lobbies towards common aims.

Getting Government Officials to Work for Children

Government officials as major organizers of services and disbursers of funds are obviously critically important partners. They can do — and sometimes have done — much for disadvantaged children. In all five countries, however, the negative attitudes and apathy of some public officials are a major obstacle. Especially in Brazil, Kenya and India, law enforcement officers are sometimes hostile and occasionally brutal towards impoverished children. Public officials should start "seeing" children less as a nuisance (to get rid of) and more as an opportunity for gaining political support. They should be trained to understand that a better city for poor children is a more liveable city for everyone. Personal contacts between disadvantaged children and public officials, for example, during the Street Children's Congresses in the Philippines and in Brazil, as well as the "immersion" of public officials into community problems as in the Philippines, have proven to be particularly rewarding. Some police officials have learned to appreciate the capabilities and spirit of initiative of urban poor children. A husband and wife police team in Cebu, for example, has created an innovative drop-in and work centre where street children can now earn money by capping bottles or making jewellery, and also administer the profits. Similar initiatives have been undertaken in India. These successes attest to how powerful personal contact can be in changing people's perspectives.

More broadly, the concern of social planners has been to achieve greater coordination of government departments involved in children's lives and to counter the tendency of each department to think about its own objectives and budgets. This convergence needs to be at ministerial and national levels, but operationalized at local levels. Convergence is not sufficiently practised, often because of the sectoral biases and political ambitions.

Convergence, however, may yet prove to be an especially effective method for achieving the major health and education goals for children in the 1990s.

Involving Urban Poor Communities and Families

Communities and families need to be more closely involved in problem-"solving" and problem-monitoring attempts, which give communities, families and children a sense of heightened self-esteem and importance; and create a feeling of connectedness in strife-ridden neighbourhoods, as vividly portrayed in the Philippines and India chapters. This involvement presents challenges, however, and needs to be carefully monitored. It may be useful to cite a few brief examples of problems identified:

Resentment of men who feel excluded. In India and Brazil, a certain resentment by male local leaders for the exclusive focus of UBSP on their women and children has been at times forcibly expressed. In Hyderabad, for example, during a reception for the Country Team in a community house, newly built expressly as a preschool for children and a place for the income-generating activities of women, drunk men hovered at the door apparently disturbed at not being more centrally a part of the intervention. Similar reactions occurred in Brazil. The Indian programmes are now studying ways of including men, while continuing to provide special support for women and children.

Resentment of women volunteers who feel exploited. The Brazilian feminists we met in São Paulo and women volunteers involved in community health projects openly doubted that their efforts — the long hours worked without any recompense in addition to regular activities — were sufficiently appreciated. Some feminist groups claim that volunteer work perpetuates societal expectations that women's work should be unremunerated. Paying volunteers, on the other hand, often raises issues of commitment and participation as well as the problem of "poor pay." High turnover of volunteers, especially in large cities (see discussion of the UBSP in Manila in the Philippines chapter) is a related difficulty. A feeling of "ownership" can offset resentment as can the realization that the project is making a qualitative difference in the volunteer's personal, family or community life.

Government fears of manipulation of votes by volunteers. This issue, evident in countries with highly politicized systems, requires careful monitoring, with the help of government officials knowledgeable on the project. In Delhi, when UBSP first started, some of the hundreds of community volunteers initially assigned were forced to resign just before elections because they ran into problems with the local grassroots party organizations.

Concerns of community members that their organizations will be manipulated by political parties or by government officials more for their own purposes than for the benefit of the communities. This concern was frequently expressed in Brazil and is very common in Latin America (Hardoy 1992). The Project encountered it in all countries, not least in Italy.

Children as Potential Partners in Their Own Development

The role of children as potential partners in their own development has been widely underestimated. They can make valuable contributions to situational analyses by indicating what troubles them most. A careful analysis of a family situation may uncover many problems affecting children, but their own life histories — especially those of children at risk of running away or who have already severed all family ties — show us indirectly but vividly the importance for their emotional development, especially in their middle years, of caring relationships with adults and peers. It is when these children seek street bands or attach themselves to a sympathetic street educator in order to obtain the emotional support they lack that their voices are the loudest. The particularly severe psychological problems faced by the "only child" in northern Italy also shows the importance for children of meaningful interaction: trapped alone at home by overanxious but emotionally, and often physically, absent parents, with no structured safe interaction with peers because of excessively bureaucratized and unresponsive schools, they have difficulties learning how to become adults.

Not only are they their own best spokespersons, children can also be good researchers. They often have a good sense of what the key problems and

Box 8.8 What Children Can Do About City Planning

"Kid's Place," a programme that started in Seattle, Washington, and that is now present in other cities in the United States as well as in Canada, Europe and Australia, illustrates the importance of involving children in city planning. A number of local business and political leaders at an informal gathering began talking about the deteriorating city environment and how it affected their children. They decided something had to be done. In a stroke of brilliance, they drafted a one-page questionnaire, containing only 16 adjectives, asking children to identify the "dirtiest," the "cleanest," the "happiest" and the "saddest" places in the city. The questionnaire was an immediate success. Over 9,000 children responded and their projections, by way of this simple survey, were as effective as a sophisticated and costly urban planning project. The children identified places where accidents were likely to happen, where violence took place, where it was safe to play, and much more.

A televised press conference was organized to publicize the results of the survey and, for the occasion, a child Mayor was elected for the day. She was 11 years old and no more than 4'3" tall. A journalist winked at her sweetly and asked, "What does it feel like to be a little girl and a Mayor?" This young girl drew herself up to her full height, looked around and said, "Next question, please." Someone else asked her what her long-range plans for the city were, and she replied that she had no long-range plans yet, but a number of "short-term problems." One of these involved shopping. Children, she reported, were always served after adults, even if they "got there first." Hearing this, the owner of a large chain of department stores spoke up and said that he intended to make non-discrimination of children an official policy of his stores. Other department stores followed suit, first in Seattle, then in neighbouring states and now throughout the United States.

Transportation was another problem children faced because city buses did not go where they wanted to go. Because of this complaint, the "real" Mayor decided to assign three children to the transportation board. They rode all the buses and subsequently redesigned the bus routes to go to parks after school. The rerouting actually increased the bus company's profits because buses were being used at a time they had previously been empty.

The survey revealed that environmental degradation and security were high on the children's list of critical problems. The majority liked school even if it was boring. Confronted with that finding, the school board agreed to appoint a student/teacher committee to investigate how school might be made less boring. The police, surprised to learn from the survey that children "liked" them, decided to work more closely with children.

Children also began organizing themselves. Deciding that some places in the city were unfriendly to children, they handed out stickers stating, "This is a kid's place" to restaurants, stores, businesses, museums and every other place they felt welcome. Within a few months, everybody was competing to attract children and many things had changed, including opening hours at the aquarium, the museums and the zoo.

The Kid's Place movement has made some exciting and significant changes in how the city of Seattle is run. Children are now included on the boards of all commissions and help make decisions on expenditure priorities. The movement has also shown that children can become an important influence on local elections. With children's issues on the political agenda, mayoral candidates campaign declaring that they can do more for children than their opponents can. Children can also have an impact nationally. Conferences organized by the Kid's Place programmes are well attended by Mayors from different parts of the United States and also from Canada. As politicians, they realize that this is a great political game and they want to be in it.

Source: Duhl (1990).

those of their neighbourhood and city are. Children are also often eager to help adults resolve these problems — and proud when they succeed in doing so. They respond systematically and with a sense of responsibility — from their viewpoint — to serious questions the world over (see Boxes 8.8 and 8.9). Questionnaires sent out by the Mazingira Institute to Kenyan schoolchildren about their problems elicited a surprisingly high number of carefully worded, thoughtful responses. A citywide drawing competition for children on the theme of the Mafia/Camorra in Naples in 1991 generated sharply evocative images of growing violence, its connection with the Italian State, and the overwhelming presence of organized crime, especially in inner-city areas.

Parents and other adults often represent a major constraint to children's open involvement in assessing problems. They may be hesitant about — and even feel threatened by the idea of — allowing children to become self-suffi-cient individuals, often because they are unaware of the children's capabilities. This is reflected in the observation that, in the four developing countries, the best examples of children's participation invariably involve street children: they have already had to learn to take decisions in order to survive.

Children, if taken seriously, can give important suggestions for improve-ments in city living. Project members witnessed a meeting in the small city of Fano, Italy, in the autumn of 1991 when schoolchildren aged 9–14 years presented their plan for an urban renewal project, drafted during an intense meeting with an educator, to a surprised but sympathetic Mayor and his council. The plan incorporated the children's concerns not only for them-selves but also for adults and especially for the aged. It was well defended by articulate young advocates in a meeting that lasted well into the evening in an atmosphere of enthusiasm. The most surprised observers were the parents, who were seeing their own children in a new light as city planners.

It has been shown that children can be indispensable collaborators with city governments. The New York City Parks Department has learned that it is valuable to plan and design new recreation facilities with the involvement of local neighbourhood groups, including children. They have discovered in some urban neighbourhoods that the only way to create safe spaces is to plan them with neighbourhood parents and children (Hart et al. 1992).

When Kenyan children in Mombasa and Kisumu were asked by the local Project team what their major problems were, they spoke about the deteriora-tion of their physical environment and lack of security. They were especially worried about the violence they saw growing around them, already taken for granted by their parents (who did not mention it in the interview). They had specific suggestions for improvements, including a bridge across a dangerously polluted stream on their way to school, playing fields and a lending library. When Filipino children in Olongapo were taken by a street educator to meet the Mayor, they spoke very frankly with him about their

---

Box 8.9   Listen to the Children

About 500 schoolchildren of a disadvantaged urban neighbourhood in San Salvador of Bahia, Brazil, have over the years been involved in collective efforts to improve their community. They participate in yearly debates on community issues, including housing, health, ecology and sexuality. During these debates, children as young as nine years of age speak out, not hesitating to make their opinions known, even though between 50 and 100 people are often present.

These children have also initiated some projects of their own. One of these projects grew spontaneously as a result of repeated incidents of police harassment. The children realized they were being treated unfairly because of their neighbourhood, which was considered a blight by the more affluent residents of adjacent areas. The police seemed to be looking for scapegoats and were clearly at the beck and call of the wealthier community. The children first discussed the problem at school, relating the numerous incidents of police violence and discrimination. Anger at this unfair treatment grew. Finally, a protest march was staged, which wound its way from one end of the community to the other, gathering people dressed in white to show their adherence to the children's stand. After circling the wealthy zones, the marchers had a meeting with the police chief, during which it was decided that the community should have its own police post.

A community-wide meeting was then held to decide the location of the police post and the duties of the policemen. The children actively participated in the meeting, contributing their unique knowledge and making useful suggestions. The outcome was that a trailer was brought into the community to serve as the police post and full-time police staffing was ensured.

Source: Hart (1991).

---

problems at school and in their neighbourhood. This was an important turning point in securing municipal support. Indian children, interviewed by the Country Team, repeatedly complained about difficulties at school, including school expenses, school location and the absences and insensitivity of school teachers.

A turning point in action on behalf of children in Brazil took place in 1988 when petitions signed by 1,300,000 children in support of a new children's rights chapter of the Brazilian Constitution were presented to the National Assembly by a delegation of street and working children in an emotion-filled event.

These are only a few examples of the positive contribution children can make as participants in community projects and even as initiators of them.

The Project has been advocating a much more active involvement of children in city planning and a greater recognition of their largely untapped potential (Box 8.10). This kind of involvement is not only helpful to policy makers but it also gives children an important opportunity for personal growth, as pointed out by Hart (1992):

> Children need to be involved in meaningful projects with adults. It is unrealistic to expect them suddenly to become responsible, participating as adult citizens at the age of 16, 18 or 21, without prior progressive exposure to the skills and responsibilities involved. Children's participation does not, however, mean supplanting adults. Adults ... need to learn to listen, support and guide, and to know when, and when not, to speak.

In other words, children are not to be considered adults: they grow into adulthood, feeling gradually more competent to enter the world of adults. Their value judgments

Box 8.10   Ways to Support Participation

- Expand training for all (including children, youth, teachers and community leaders) in the skills of community participation

- Establish Children's Assemblies and Youth Councils as ongoing mechanisms for involving children and youth in community development and community management.

- Support associations of working adolescents to provide protection and improve communication and understanding between the children and city agencies.

- Improve urban planning and design for children and families by involving the community directly in the process.

Source: Meeting of Mayors, Urban Planners and Policy Makers, 1992.

about their own self-worth are largely based upon their sense of competence in doing things and upon the approval of others, especially peers. Low self-esteem can easily be generated in children by repeated negative experiences and by their own perception of marginalization, a situation that occurs frequently to children from disadvantaged urban neighbourhoods the world over. Involving children, especially disadvantaged children, in situations where they can demonstrate competence can contribute to their heightened self-esteem. It can also serve to raise their status within the family and enable children and their elders to collaborate productively towards their future joint improvement, while continuing to respect their past.

SITUATIONAL ANALYSES AS A MEANS TO AN END

The potentials for action stemming from situational analyses on urban children in especially difficult circumstances have been greatly undervalued.

They provide a means (a) to engage a sector of society that may otherwise remain indifferent or uninformed, including academics and journalists;[3] (b) to create important new partnerships among researchers, journalists and other sectors; (c) to facilitate continuous monitoring of the conditions of disadvantaged urban children and of programmes for them; and (d) to develop, as a result of the writing of academics and other professionals, a broader and better informed base for advocacy and a new relationship with the media.

As the Project has asserted and the country studies have shown, situational analyses should be prepared in partnership with the very people who will be an integral part of the future programmes. Without their partnership, programmes cannot be successful since they alone can provide insights about problems they face. Their perspectives and their strengths and weaknesses need to be determined before any effective programme can be carried out. Secondly, programmers and educators close to the children (the implementors, already knowledgeable about children) as well as municipal and national policy makers (the overall decision makers), can each contribute directives about what they feel are important issues. These concerns are an important element of any policy since they will need either to be supported or to be counteracted, which can best occur in the very process of developing the situational analysis.

Finally, as the Project repeatedly found, all of these people are usually too intensely engaged in action to have time to write extensive reports. Thus, while helping to shape those reports, many rely on trained researchers and writers used to managing words and clarifying concepts. It should, however, be made clear that these writers are not "experts" on the topic but only, possibly, experts in putting findings into writing. In other words, it is essential that the product be "owned" by all contributors, including as much as possible the people who have provided key information, such as community members and the children themselves.

Finally, census bureaus, research centres, international development agencies and potential funders need to become active partners of situational analyses. This is especially important with regard to agencies not yet directly concerned with children's issues because it is a way to place children on their agendas. The situational analysis should thus not be viewed only as an end product but as a means to an end — effective partnerships for change.

The importance of partnerships with academics was raised in the country chapters. In Brazil, NGOs allied themselves with social scientists and other scholars early in the 1980s to help change the concept of "delinquent minors" and relied on their research and writing to give "authority" to their claims, to influence lawyers and policy makers, and to attract the attention of the media and the public. Children have become an issue of concern for major university departments such as the Latin American Faculty of Social Sciences (FLACSO) or the Research Institute of the University of Rio de Janeiro. The

Census Bureau has started to dedicate a special section of its report to children and families.

In the Philippines, although few centres are exclusively involved in research on children, partnerships among academic institutions engaged in community action, municipal officials, communities and UNICEF played a critical role in generating joint situational analyses, in giving "authority" to disadvantaged children and community issues, and in facilitating the institutionalization of the UBSP projects inside the municipality.

In India, urban research institutes played an important role as monitors of UBSP programmes and trainers of government officials, and in facilitating partnerships between communities and municipal governments. In Kenya, partnerships among NGOs (such as the community-based Undugu and the child advocacy group ANPPCAN), journalists and researchers were reinforced through their participation in the Project.

In Italy, the Istituto degli Innocenti, inspired by these examples, has successfully initiated partnerships with local universities with the long-term objective of monitoring the problems faced by Italian children, improving the analytical quality of media reporting, and sponsoring training of government officials and programmers.

ASSESSMENT OF PROGRAMMES FOR URBAN CHILDREN IN DISTRESS

Some Important Concepts

A number of complex concepts, each of which is the subject of extensive literature, are briefly discussed here to give the reader an idea of the many elements policy makers must take into consideration when evaluating the situation of disadvantaged children and assessing the efficacy of programmes devised to address their plight.

Preventive as opposed to compensatory and curative interventions. It is important to reflect on the degree of prevention or compensation that each intervention offers. In the Convention on the Rights of the Child, for example, numerous provisions refer to "protection rights," but only a few articles specifically refer to "preventive measures" (Article 19, for example, mentions social programmes to protect the child from abuse and neglect by providing necessary support for both care-givers and the child and "other forms of prevention.") Compensatory or curative measures are often introduced by the phrase "special protection and assistance" (as in Article 20 relating to children without family, Article 22 for refugee children and Article 23 for disabled children). In general, however, a combination of preventive and rehabilitative dimensions is implicit in many of the protective actions the Convention suggests.

Interventions on behalf of urban poor children tend to focus on children engaged in high-risk behaviours. According to our definition, these are: (1) children who are already in serious conflict with the law; (2) substance-abusers; (3) children practising early unprotected sexuality; (4) school dropouts; (5) family dropouts; and (6) any other children who are "acting out" their deep-seated uneasiness by engaging in forms of behaviour that are detrimental to their development or health. These children are found in poor urban neighbourhoods and on city streets both North and South.

The main antecedent of their high-risk behaviours is often that they face the complex tasks of self-development with too little family and external support: in other words, they lack emotionally supportive relationships with a caring adult or with peers; they are marginalized (at work, in school or on the street); they perceive themselves as having few options; and they are vulnerable to exploitation. An early predictor of high-risk behaviour could be relationally deprived children (deprived of appropriate social relationships).

A curative, compensatory intervention addresses the problems of those already manifesting high-risk behaviour (drug users, for example) and attempts to cure the problem (through rehabilitation programmes, institutionalization or imprisonment). Instead, a more constructive intervention tries to reach the child before he or she engages in high-risk behaviour (through job training, information campaigns, community monitoring of neighbourhoods or control of drug trafficking, for example). In other words, it exerts a positive influence on the various domains of the child's life, tries to diminish marginalization and relational deprivation, and reinforces the child's and the family's positive coping strategies. Such action would prevent the kinds of severe deterioration that are much more difficult and expensive to cure.

Some analysts argue that programmes should just target children-at-risk and their families and try to change their behaviour. Others, instead, believe that major institutional and organizational changes in the economic, social and policy systems are required in order to respond to problems of severe disadvantage.

In general, theories on the prevention of high-risk behaviour have ranged from simple cause-effect that identify one or two powerful antecedents of problem behaviour on which programmes could focus, to complex risk assessments that call for an array of interventions.

In the United States, the research of Jessor and his colleagues has focused on the clustering of adolescent high-risk behaviours (for instance, drinking, smoking marijuana, early unprotected sexuality) and claim that these are "an organized constellation of behaviours rather than a collection of independent activities." According to Jessor, these behaviours have to be addressed simultaneously in order to change the children's life trajectories. He suggests that in each area, "health compromising" behaviours need to be discouraged and "health enhancing" ones rewarded (Jessor et al. 1977). The research findings of Hawkins and Weis (1985) stress the critical importance for a healthy childhood experience of strong social bonds to individuals exhibiting pro-social behaviours.

In the specialized areas of substance abuse or adolescent pregnancy, similar conclusions are being drawn. Botvin (1985) believes that adolescent high-risk behaviours stem from complex factors: social influences from parents, peers and the media; personality characteristics; and values. Thus interventions must address these multiple factors by dealing with social influences and by teaching coping skills. Schorr (1988) has developed a strategy based on the links between high-risk behaviour and poverty, and emphasizes the importance of going beyond the individual and personal aspects of children's lives to larger-scale social responses (for example, family planning to avoid early pregnancy). Ginsburg et al. (1988) call for the establishment of a more protective and supportive environment. Again in the United States, Dryfoos (1990), reviewing a broad range of reports on high-risk behaviour, identifies a number of main antecedents, such as low resistance to peer influences, lack of parental support, and living in a deprived neighbourhood. He then outlines a prevention strategy constructed on: "the interrelatedness of problems, and the need for early sustained interventions; the importance of a one-to-one intensive attention, and the importance of basic educational skills, social skills, and experimental education for gaining the necessary competencies to function in the adult U.S. urban world" (Dryfoos 1990).

Similarly, the Country Teams have generally shown that a narrow focus on changing the high-risk behaviours of the individual alone is less effective than changing negative behaviour (and attitudes) and building on positive ones *at many levels*, including the institutional level. They have stressed the importance of creating a more supportive environment for the poor and disadvantaged, rather than viewing them as being exclusively at fault.

After ascertaining at which point in the cycle of disadvantage they intend to intervene, policy makers must then address cost-effectiveness, replicability and sustainability, and, when problems of coverage are raised (How can we affect the largest number of children?) also issues of growing to scale.

Cost-effectiveness. A cost-effective programme makes the best use of available resources and seeks options that yield the highest degree of effectiveness for the lowest cost. However, both the effectiveness and the costs have complex parameters, difficult to define and even more difficult to assess. Furthermore, most social goals are not easily measurable in standardized ways.

As evaluators have pointed out, an analysis of costs and effectiveness: (a) depends on a convincing assessment of goals, as well as some standardized ways to determine the costs;[4] (b) must take into account accompanying unintended positive and negative consequences, and (c) should carry a time dimension, which introduces the issue of sustainability.

The financial feasibility of a programme in its initial period depends on the objectives assigned, the priority it is given and the way funds are allocated. Costs alone may not be the most relevant criterion since a less expensive programme may also be less effective or less likely to be continued. Moreover, costing resources in itself often requires complex measurements; because of the large variety of resources, standardized measurements are often not available. Furthermore, effectiveness is often subjective. It is, for instance, difficult to measure the level of "improvement" achieved by remedial or curative interventions; it is even more difficult to measure the number of people who, because of developmental or preventive measures, have not slid into higher risk conditions. Moreover, arguments are raised about the extent to which empowerment can be measured.

Sustainability. Programmes are sustainable only if they can be continued following the end of temporary external support. This is a major challenge for most programmes, since they tend to require inputs, in terms of human and financial resources, that are often not available or affordable at the local level. For instance, the urban poor may be so busy earning a living that they are unable to assume responsibility for the project unless it responds to their own high priorities. In other words, the organizational constraints of sustainability at all levels, starting with the household (time availability, opportunity costs) are just as important as the financial and technical ones, but too often neglected.

Replicability. Finally, since a major reason for conducting cost-effectiveness analyses is to recommend the intervention for other sites, clients and times, this immediately raises issues of replicability. In other words, can the results be generalized and transferred? The presence of key agents of change makes that a debatable issue as well.

More comprehensive cost-effectiveness analyses, however, even though difficult or tentative, should be developed whenever possible (and new approaches to them worked out) because they force programmers to evaluate all the elements of their interventions; they introduce some elements of accountability; and, they can provide effective advocacy tools for convincing decision makers that shifts in policy can also be justified by financial considerations (such as the shift from institutionalization to out-of-home and home-based assistance).

It is important, at the same time, that an overriding concern for cost-effectiveness not end up limiting the scope of programmes and the creative search for effective approaches. That would be self-defeating.

Evaluations. A recurrent theme is the absence of conclusive evidence on the effectiveness of programmes (aside from the fact that findings are usually published at least five years after the end of the project). This problem is particularly evident in Italy and other southern European countries, but has also been identified in a country as research-oriented as the United States.

A review of 5,000 reports on various educational programmes in the United States found, for example, only 28 with valid evaluations that included achievement test results and programme costs (Phi Delta Kappan 1983); out of a review of 350 school-based drug education programmes, only 126 had some kind of evaluation data, and, of those, only 33 entries were acceptable (Bangert-Drowns 1988); a review of dropout prevention programmes found only 20 rigorous evaluations out of 452 programmes surveyed; 6,000 abstracts on delinquency prevention yielded only 96 with empirical evaluations. A similar search in developing countries would elicit a far shorter list of systematically evaluated programmes.

The issue here is what constitutes sufficient documentation. Prevention programmes, for example, direct interventions toward the common antecedents of certain problem behaviours, such as running away from home or dropping out of school. Many evaluations may then show changes in knowledge or attitudes, but these are not sufficiently predictive of behavioural change to accept as evidence that a programme "works." Ideally, the evaluation should demonstrate that, in aggregate, more of the participants changed to the desired behaviour than matched controls. It is, in fact, very difficult to prove that a programme "causes" a change in behaviour, that the change is, in other words, exclusively attributable to the programme.

Assessments of effectiveness have more recently been elicited through systematic interviewing of programme participants (and participatory assessments), external observers, and relative assessments of coverage, retention rates, and so on. While the Project could count on a few systematic evaluations from industrialized countries, most programmes of the developing world were too recent to have been formally assessed. However, according to informed observers, the impact they have had in mobilizing people and changing their behaviour and world views appears to be quite impressive. The relative lack of strictly scientific evaluation data should, thus, not keep societies from moving ahead to develop strong programmes to help children in distress. As the reader has seen, there is much that we know already, certainly enough to proceed.

Going to scale. In developing countries, because of the numerical dimensions of the problems, priority is necessarily given to programmes likely to reach the largest number of children at risk. "Scale" — or substantially increased coverage — has important financial and managerial implications. It usually requires the involvement of the government, generally the largest welfare provider, since NGOs have so far only been able to aim at "quality" coverage of small numbers of children. In its documentation of programmes, the Project has identified options available for extensive quality coverage and the means to achieve expanded coverage through government involvement. A key challenge may be how to get governments involved in expanding coverage without discouraging the participation of local community organizations and NGOs, important both in terms of financial feasibility and the quality of work. Two approaches — pilot models in India and in the Philippines, and legislative change in Brazil — will be discussed later. Another way to "reach scale," and an important alternative for community programmes, is to multiply smaller programmes until considerable coverage is reached. Teaching could then occur through direct transfer (and adaptation) from one community to another. Even in those cases, a supportive external environment remains an important element of success.

Offsetting High-Risk Behaviour

A large number of interventions both North and South have been specifically targeted to particular CEDC categories, e.g., a programme aimed at an abstract category of "drug abusers" rather than at the actual population of urban children who may be abusing substances, including drugs, but who are often also in conflict with the law, pregnant or school dropouts. In this section, we will focus on such "categorical" interventions. We will examine current knowledge in both industrialized and developing countries on the most effective interventions in these areas and the consensus about what has proven most useful.

"Delinquency"

Policy analysts both North and South use the term "delinquent" to categorize children involved in behaviour ranging from misdemeanors (truancy, petty theft, vandalism) to increasingly serious violations (car theft, burglary, rape, homicide). Social analysts also include forms of "acting out" (frequent fights, damaging property, bullying) which may be precursors to more serious problems. Legal systems have developed different ways of handling these problems, either through specific laws or through the implementation of existing broader laws. "Truancy" or "vagrancy," for example, are poorly defined but legally punishable in some countries. Because of the way laws are interpreted, children and young people may also be imprisoned for such minor infractions as riding a bus without a ticket, loitering or petty theft. State interventions targeting "delinquent children" usually expose children, regardless of their offences, to the severity of the criminal law enforcement process (police, lawyers, probation officers), and sometimes to confinement with other "delinquent" children and, in some countries, with adults. The experience often erodes the young people's self-esteem and increases their feelings of rebellion, especially when they feel they have been punished unjustly for minor "crimes," as often happens to children on the streets of Third World countries.

Imprisonment and institutionalization neither "cure" antisocial behaviour nor prevent future problems: in fact, these measures usually reinforce negative behaviour because they expose children to models of negative behaviour. The stigmatization of having been institutionalized, moreover, leads them to further life deterioration. The ineffectiveness of correctional institutions has been repeatedly confirmed by research in the United States (Leitenberg 1986, Lundman 1984, Rabkin 1987, O'Donnell et al. 1987, among others) and in other industrialized countries, including Italy. The issue has been less systematically researched in developing countries, with the possible exception of Brazil.

As an alternative, the *screening and referral centres* that grew with government support in many Brazilian cities (the Secretariat of the Child in São Paulo, the Social Promotion Foundation in Goiânia) deal with juveniles who have been arrested, usually for minor offences, and referred to them by the authorities. Attempts have also been made to humanize existing services or to offer multicomponent services as alternatives to institutionalization. Some screening centres are involved in advocacy and offer training programmes to government and NGO staff who work with juvenile offenders, following a pattern increasingly favoured in Italy. Others have created or contracted *residential communities* or *family youth homes* to provide safe harbours for small numbers of young offenders, away from the street bands and the temptations of their urban neighbourhoods. In an often strongly democratic context, children are made to feel like members of a family and are expected to contribute to the running of the household and encouraged to be active participants in the community. Advisory staff help them reestablish contacts with their families, and work to facilitate family and school reintegration. Employment trainee positions at local businesses are often available.

This solution is particularly appropriate in urban neighbourhoods already heavily penetrated by organized crime and drug dealing, as in many cities of Brazil and Italy. In India, Philippines and Kenya, residential communities and family youth homes are used primarily to provide temporary shelter and support to young people during reintegration into the community.

Programmes for "street children" are another approach, particularly effective when: (a) they succeed in improving the children's relationship with the police; (b) they offer these often emotionally disadvantaged children stable contacts with a caring adult who acts as a role model or advocate; and (c) they provide employment-related activities. The four developing country studies have paid particular attention to the role of street educators and to innovative ways of involving the police in helping these children. In Brazil, the local private sector plays an important role in training street children for jobs.

The possibility of using dedicated trained volunteers to achieve individualized approaches has been explored by Feldman (1988) and O'-Donnell et al. (1987). Multifaceted community outreach to high-risk adolescents, implemented by local clubs and carefully monitored, has also proven quite effective in limiting exposure to crime (Boys Club of America 1986–87). In the United States, neighbourhood watches fostering partnerships are also thought to reduce robberies, sexual offences, incidents involving drugs, and assaults on teachers and other school staff (National Crime Prevention Council 1987). Targeted outreach programmes that encourage young people in their own decision-making about drugs, sex or illicit activities or involve them in creative responses, have been highlighted as particularly promising (Dryfoos 1990).

Thus, both North and South, the most effective programmes are pointing in similar directions. They emphasize broader goals than "delinquency" prevention *per se*, as well as comprehensive coverage, since no single component has proven to be the "magic bullet." One approach that appears underutilized in Italy and the United States, not to mention the developing world, is upgrading the quality of education and of school environments to engage the interests of the child and discourage negative behaviour (Greenwood and Ziming 1983). The potential for greater school and community collaboration for outreach has still only been partially explored in the five countries of the Project.

Drug and substance abuse

The growing numbers of drug users worldwide is tied to global changes in supply and demand and to the globalization of organized crime. It is also an indirect consequence of the economic crisis that affected most of the world in the 1980s, leading more people to turn to drugs to "forget their troubles." Similar trends are found in the use of solvents, the "poor man's drugs," less well-known but often equally damaging.

A number of legislative responses have been devised to counter these trends, including laws making drug possession and trafficking a criminal offence. Programmatic responses, both North and South, include a proliferation of governmental agencies attempting to cure or prevent the problem. The emphasis has been on rehabilitation, although various attempts have been made to deal with prevention as well.

Programmes specifically addressing the high-risk behaviour of substance abuse usually fall into a small number of rehabilitative categories and one or more of five categories for prevention. Rehabilitative programmes in countries where drug possession is illegal may utilize, at the discretion of the courts, institutionalization. In Italy, for example, the Government's initial response was to leave largely to rehabilitative services those drug users arrested with "moderate amounts" (undefined) of substance for personal (but not therapeutic) use (Law 685 of 17 December 1975, Art. 80). With a new law of 13/6/1990, individuals found possessing any amount of illegal substances were automatically liable to imprisonment, which could be avoided only if they were willing to be rehabilitated, normally in a group home, and if the judge consented. However, this penalization of the users (whom many consider as victims) was again abolished by the referendum of 18 April 1993, although drug trade and use remained illegal. It has been shown that imprisonment or obligation to enter a centre has actually hindered the rehabilitation process, which requires willing participation. Furthermore, prisons often allow continued use of drugs or a shift to alternative substances[5] (Brigantini 1988 and 1990). Such curative measures beyond imprisonment may become an extension of government services but are often now administered by NGOs.

Prevention strategies, on the other hand, usually include one or more of the following elements:

- information campaigns, usually using instructors, limited group participation, scare tactics;

- affective strategies aiming at social growth, self-esteem building, and values clarification (without reference to drugs);

- social influence (peers) and life-skills strategies, including instruction on resisting social pressures and developing better communication, coping and other skills;

- alternative strategies, based on the assumption that changes have to be made in predictors or correlates of drug use, such as school failure and delinquency, by replacing negative behaviour with positive activities (recreation, jobs and volunteerism) and by developing competence in high-risk youth through basic skills training and individual attention.

Evaluations of 143 drug prevention programmes in the United States (Tobler 1986, 1987) showed that two strategies — social influence/life skills and alternative strategies — have been particularly effective. Another recent large-scale review of 350 school-based drug education programmes has reached similar conclusions (Bangert-Drowns 1988). Though some programmes succeeded in increasing knowledge, the impact on substance use was minimal. Peer-taught programmes appeared more successful than adult-taught ones. The evaluation did not examine any life-skills programmes. Bangert-Drowns concluded that school-based drug education was not an effective means of shifting drug-use patterns. Its primary function was to reassure parents that schools were taking action. Other extensive evaluations are currently under way.[6]

The history of substance abuse prevention is replete with failed models. Very few among the many preventive programmes can show actual changes in behaviour. The more successful preventive programmes in the United States, in Italy and in the Third World countries tend:

- to address risk factors, such as lack of family support and poor school achievement, rather than the high-risk behaviour *per se*;

- to direct their efforts simultaneously at all the major social influences and institutions;

- to emphasize social skills (coping and resistance);

- to be peer-led (using positive role models);

- to include media analysis;
- to be school-based and focus on middle years, while involving parents and the surrounding community.

The emphasis on the middle years is important. Research in the United States has found that drug use started in the 6–12 age group is much more difficult to eradicate than drug use by adults (Palmonari, personal communication).

The Cancrini approach to drug use and abuse, developed in Italy and aimed at Palermo, contains many of the same elements and a similarly strong emphasis on neighbourhood participation. Evidently successful (but un-evaluated) examples in the developing countries combined parental educa-tion with peer support groups and, in the same spirit, preventive counselling with treatment of high-risk users.

Drug abuse treatment is much more developed than drug abuse preven-tion in Third World countries. The Project, however, discovered that im-provements in the physical environment of urban slums accomplished by UBSP may represent an important prevention strategy. According to con-cerned mothers in one inner-city neighbourhood in Metro Manila, a major deterrent of drug use has been the construction of a multipurpose cemented area for community use. In those crowded and unsanitary neighbourhoods, the availability of a space for play and interaction, both important develop-mental needs for children, has encouraged children to stay near home rather than roam the streets. Again young people are telling us with their actions what can help them.

The problem of substance abuse in Brazil and the Philippines is still much more confined to the increasing use of easily available solvents and inhalants. The most effective rehabilitative responses have included group homes com-bined with family counselling. In São Paulo, street educators work in new recreation centres, where they are able to make contact with drug users and eventually channel them to rehabilitation centres. An interesting therapeutic approach was developed by a Don Bosco organization in Récife which found that caring for animals, especially ones as naturally playful as goats, in-creased an addict's sense of responsibility and encouraged responsive inter-action.

Urban at-risk neighbourhoods, families and schools can play an important role in providing early detection and in creating a supportive environment around the child, with relevant government and nongovernmental institu-tions, some additional help from agencies, social workers, the police, lawyers and the courts.

Early unprotected sexuality

Early unprotected sexuality is a high-risk behaviour with potentially dangerous consequences, in both the short and the long term, for female adolescents and for their children. The health risks include: (a) sexually transmitted diseases (STDs) and related disorders (infertility, cervical cancer, infections passed on to newborns); (b) AIDS, the most life-threatening of the STDs; (c) pregnancy complications, including ectopic pregnancies, toxaemia, anaemia and prolonged labour (the younger the mother, the higher the risks of morbidity and mortality); (d) for the child, prematurity and low birth weight.

The risks can be defined for preventive action at three points: initiation into sexuality, the use of contraception, and the birth (and parenting) following an early pregnancy. Responses at each point need to include both medical and psychosocial dimensions because they involve complex decision-making (or lack of decision-making) by the adolescent and his or her family. This decision-making is largely shaped by cultural considerations, family and the adolescent's perception of his or her place in society. However, striking similarities are also found.

Prostitution and other forms of sexual exploitation, very prevalent in many cities, require special attention, but include all the preventive and curative points mentioned above.

Programmes specifically aimed at adolescent girls and early pregnancy are few, and informed evaluations of the effectiveness of such programmes are even harder to find. In a recent report by the U.S. National Academy of Sciences, an expert panel on adolescent pregnancy and childbearing concluded after two years that substantive proof of "what works" was still lacking because of the dearth of evaluations (Hayes 1987). While information about births is relatively easy to collect, abortion rates are elusive because of underreporting and because the issue of sexuality carries loaded meanings (moral, customary and religious) in different populations. These difficulties are further compounded in Third World settings where sexuality is considered a very private matter.

As analysed in Chapter 7, the problem of early unprotected sexuality is tied in complex ways to early menarche, marriage patterns, dowries, religion (especially the Catholic religion, which maintains an official stand against contraceptives) and practices within a particular culture.

Another study by the UNICEF International Child Development Centre in collaboration with the German Foundation for International Development and the World Bank investigated programmes for adolescent girls/mothers in the Philippines, Kenya and India. It has provided the following preliminary results.

In the Philippines, most programmes are sectoral and come under the Health, Education, Labour or Welfare Ministries and the Commission on Population. In general, adolescent mothers and their children are not specifically targeted, but are only incidental beneficiaries of more general programmes. Early unprotected sexuality and pregnancy, although already potential problems, have not yet emerged as a major policy issue (Palattao Corpus 1992). The few programmes specifically for this category, such as family planning for young mothers or temporary shelters for unwed mothers just before and after childbirth, are NGO-run with limited budgets and outreach.

In Kenya, where church and NGO programmes for children and adolescents are more prevalent, few programmes were specifically targeted on adolescent mothers and even fewer were community-based, despite the documented increases in the incidence of adolescent pregnancies (Gachukia 1992). Some innovative peer-group approaches to sex education have been developed by nongovernmental youth groups in Kenya.

In India, similarly, existing large sectoral programmes and schemes only benefit young women and children incidentally. Family planning programmes, after the negative government experience of the 1970s, are not well developed (Chatterjee 1991).

The issue of delayed sexuality and/or marriage is critical in the Third World, as we have seen, both for the urban girls caught in cross-generational cycles of early marriage and disadvantage in Brazil, Philippines and Kenya (see Chapter 7 and Blanc et al. 1994) and for the Indian (and at times Kenyan) girls married early by their families, in part because of dowries. India, in particular, has been struggling to delay age at marriage and encourage education, thereby offering urban poor girls and their parents alternative opportunities. The adolescent section of the Integrated Child Development Scheme (ICDS) is developing an innovative programme which involves periods of training for unmarried girls, aged 11 to 18 years, with an *angawadi* (village centre) worker, usually a woman and a literacy teacher, who serves as a role model.

As Marian Wright Edelman, President of the Children's Defense Fund, has often stated (Schorr 1988): "The best contraceptive is a real future."

Various approaches have been devised to accomplish these aims.

Clinics and counselling centres. Obviously, in order to ensure contraception, contraceptive methods must be available to adolescents at risk. However, the extent to which counselling centres will be successful depends on moral, customary and religious variables. School-based contraceptive clinics have met with controversy in the United States. Some groups feel that by eliminating fear of pregnancy and by putting the school's "stamp of approval" on contraceptives, such clinics will increase early sexuality. Specific research on the question, however, has shown mixed evidence. A three-year study in two Baltimore schools found that, in comparison with students in a control group, students with access to a contraceptive clinic delayed first intercourse by seven months, had a higher utilization of contraceptives when first intercourse did occur, and had significantly fewer pregnancies. The success of the programme was attributed to the amount of attention the students had received (Zabin et al. 1986). In contrast, other studies sustain that adolescents may have all the information they need about contraceptives, but there is no guarantee they will buy or use them (Kirby 1984, Dawson 1986).

Group counselling sessions have met with positive results (Philliber et al. 1988, Stern 1988).

Adolescent peer counsellors were successful in combination with community awareness-building in a programme in South Carolina: estimated pregnancy rates among 14- to 17-year-olds in the area dropped significantly (Vincent et al. 1987). Emphasis on peer models also proved effective in a study of 200 male high school students in North Carolina (Jalloh and Alston 1988). Informed peer exchanges on the potential problems of unprotected sexuality are often a good way to ensure a culturally sensitive approach.

Voluntary community work. An interesting project sponsored by the Eleanor Roosevelt Foundation in New York has shown that the insights gained by young volunteers while babysitting for schoolmates who are adolescent mothers can often have considerable impact.

Life-skills and life-planning approaches to sex education in schools are based on the recognition that changes in behaviour, especially in sexual matters, are rarely obtainable through rational means alone. The individual must also be affected emotionally. This is particularly true of adolescents, whose efforts to find their place in an adult world make them particularly self-centred. This accounts in large measure for the relative success of approaches emphasizing decision-making skills (obtaining information and using it in making effective decisions) or life-planning (such as worksheet exercises designed to lead to more rational decisions in school, social and family settings).

These new curricula involve adolescents much more personally and have been rated higher than other approaches by students, parents and school administrators. Furthermore, follow-up research has shown a shift towards more protected sexuality among students for up to one year immediately following the programmes (Schinke et al. 1981, 1984; Hunter-Geboy et al. 1985; Dryfoos 1990).

Multiple-goal programmes, usually including educational enhancement, job preparation and family planning, are gaining momentum. These programmes view early child-bearing as only one symptom of disadvantage, and assume that more comprehensive approaches are necessary to help children and adolescents achieve their life goals. Typical of these programmes is the five-year-old Harlem programme sponsored by the Children's Aid Society, which has both a community and a school base. The programme offers primary health services, performing arts, coaching in sports, college admission programmes, job clubs, family life units and individual counselling. Although not yet formally evaluated, the programme shows great promise. Compared with surrounding areas, the target area has a much lower pregnancy rate and a lower dropout rate (Carrera 1987).

The creation of a network of supportive relationships is the guiding principle of the Ounce of Prevention Fund,[7] a joint public-private agency in the United States that believes programmes should go beyond family planning *per se* and focus instead on the central role that relationships play in fostering healthy adolescent development. The Fund maintains that adolescent girls have children because they want to: pregnancy gives them emotional fulfilment and makes them feel less lonely. Adolescent mothers are often already particularly disadvantaged and can count on few support systems. Pregnancy becomes a kind of coping strategy because of a lack of appropriate alternative opportunities and emotional supports. The strong relationships that adolescent girls and young mothers form with staff members and counsellors is, in fact, a good measure of their emotional needs. One interesting lesson was that, by promoting a network of supportive relationships for adolescent mothers, the Fund was obtaining considerable delays in subsequent pregnancies (Musick 1992).

School and family dropout

These two high-risk behaviours need to be qualified before a North/South comparison can be attempted. Dropping out of school in industrialized countries is a major handicap since education is an important precondition for most kinds of employment. In contrast, in Brazil and, even more so, in India, the Philippines and Kenya, the only kinds of work available to large segments of the population are in unskilled or semi-skilled occupations where educational qualifications are usually superfluous. Education has indeed become a prerequisite for a better career in these countries, and children and families go to great lengths to pursue schooling even when education is not compulsory; however, schooling does not determine post-school opportunities to quite the same degree. Furthermore, in developing countries, children more often drop out of school for "family" (economic and/or cultural) reasons than by personal choice.

Family dropouts or runaways in the North also differ in important ways from those in the South. In the United States and even in Italy, the typical runaway apparently comes from a fairly well-off family and leaves home for personal and emotional reasons. In the developing world, the growing wave of family dropouts is an indication of deep-seated social and economic problems, tied to broad international and national trends. In both cases, however, dropout behaviours are related to the initiation by those children of other high-risk behaviours, which are early responses to urban (or even rural) stress.

Programmes devised in the four developing countries to prevent school dropout present some interesting contrasts to programmes in industrialized countries. One major difference is that the latter tend to emphasize elaborate and personnel-intensive interventions, such as early-childhood education, curriculum revisions, school counselling and schools for gifted children. However, programmers in the North, like their counterparts in the South, have also recognized the effectiveness of community-based multicomponent programmes where the key word is flexibility. Integration of the school in the community has been considered essential, the community taking responsibility for the complete package of educational, family, social, health, as well as job placement services (Pennsylvania Department of Education 1987, Vallejo 1987, Designs for Change 1985).

Elements of Effective Interventions

Effective interventions addressing each of these high-risk behaviours or conditions point with somewhat different emphases to comprehensive, flexible and multifaceted approaches, best located where the child actually lives, but also where the child studies and works (Box 8.11).

The most successful programmes both North and South provide individualized attention to children. The "intensive care" of a responsible adult and a focus on children's specific needs have been shown to be of utmost importance. Such programmes also seek to affect the immediate environment of the child by providing counselling and other support to families.

Successful programmes for disadvantaged children are usually based on a multicomponent network of protective interventions. Multicomponent methodologies appear to be more effective because the different elements reinforce each other. The same network may also be extended preventively to other disadvantaged children at risk of faltering, as some programmes have shown by moving from rehabilitation to prevention.

Box 8.11   Lessons from Specific Interventions

The most effective results for children already involved in high-risk behaviours have been obtained through:

- Individualized attention
- Creation of a supportive immediate environment around the children
- Greater support to families
- Multicomponent rather than unimodal approaches to these children's problems
- Active participation and involvement of children, families, neighbourhoods and the broader community in programme activities
- Collaboration among different components at all levels
- Recognition of the potential of the school as the locus for interventions
- Recognition of the advantages of locating programmes in urban neighbourhoods
- Careful use of peers in interventions
- Some arrangements for training

The active participation and involvement of children, families, neighbourhoods and the broader community has also been emphasized by successful programmes. However, the kinds of participation vary, from joint planning to specific moments of involvement or just presence at training sessions. Some of the more effective programmes have included actual planning collaboration.

The potential of the school as the locus for interventions is important because it is there that children in their middle years and adolescence can easily be reached when they first show signs of high-risk behaviour. Moreover, a healthy school climate contributes to the prevention and control of such behaviour. Alternative schools have demonstrated improved behavioural outcomes for high-risk youth both in the South (Brazil, for example, or Kenya) and in the North.

Schools can provide space and maintenance, and facilitate coordination between outside and school personnel. The personal involvement of the principal is often a key element. In Third World countries where school counsellors are a rarity, teachers are often valuable sources of information about children showing early signs of difficult home situations. However, schools have their own objectives, capabilities and bureaucratic procedures, and it is unrealistic to think that they can take the place of outside organizations in developing and administering effective programmes for at-risk children. Studies have shown that most successful programmes in schools are administered by external organizations which provide support (training, special curriculum materials) and help to coordinate collaboration between school and community. By being anchored in urban neighbourhoods rather than in schools, programmes can also reach dropouts, truants and children generally "turned off" by the school system, an important consideration in Third World countries where the numbers of such children are high.

Using peers in preventive and protective interventions produces mixed results, especially when peer-exchange programmes are too narrowly focused. The most successful approaches both North and South seem to be the use of older peers: first, to influence or help younger peers, as classroom instructors, role models, tutors and mentors; second, to attract children to programmes; and third, in group analysis of problems.

The principles underlying effective interventions for these high-risk behaviours can be summarized as:

- a better understanding of what children most lack by listening to what they tell us;

- an understanding of the multiple components that may help to improve or prevent the situation; in other words, a valid theory of what brings about change;

- the realization that, because children's problems come from many sources, no long-term results can be achieved without the mobilization of a broad range of people and institutions. A few programme personnel cannot change conditions sufficiently (although the importance of dedicated quality personnel coming close to the child has often been reiterated);

- the need for a "quality jump" at both the municipal and national levels in the understanding of — and responses to — specific children's problems, and in the overall environment surrounding the child.

Lessons from Innovative Municipal and NGO Programmes

The importance of prevention cum protection: learning by doing

Urban children in the Third World and in industrialized countries are increasingly engaged in street-based work and exposed to exploitation, physical and health risks, and other hazards. The inner cities where most live are sometimes infiltrated by drug and crime syndicates. Children living in these deteriorating environments develop all kinds of coping strategies. When left without nurturing family relationships and personal supports, they become particularly prone to high-risk behaviours. Street children on their own manifest many of these high-risk behaviours, but no urban poor child, whether working on the streets or in the slums, still attending school or out of school, is immune.

Many government agencies and NGOs in the 21 cities of the research have taken steps to address the situation, despite diminishing budgets and other crises. A few have some particularly important lessons to share. The most innovative have engaged in a constant process of self-monitoring and self-renewal, and, in that process, have identified problems and sought creative approaches. Starting from the most urgent problems (such as institutional violence towards the "delinquent" child in Brazil and the plight of the street child in the Philippines), they have progressively developed more preventive approaches, which emphasize the importance of:

- discovering effective ways of making contact with children-at-risk;

- operationalizing flexible approaches to the wide range of problems;

- shifting from an exclusive focus on "the child" to a broader focus on the child, family, school and community, reinforcing their coping strategies, and involving them in the elaboration of more affordable approaches to family preservation, and school and community development;

- seeking alternative approaches to education in order to facilitate reintegration;

- forming constructive linkages with the world of work;

- developing broad partnerships and self-managing networks.

For that purpose, these government agencies and NGOs have mobilized substantial funds and obtained large-scale impact. In Brazil, state-funded programmes, as in Goiânia and São Paulo, were the precursors of the more developed system of Guardianship Councils and Councils for the Rights of the Child and Adolescent legislated in 1990 and now being implemented, after state approval, throughout Brazil. Together with the pioneering work of Brazilian NGOs, these early programmes provided a first experience to local governments of a system that protects and serves children and families rather than penalizes and punishes them; moreover, by showing what was feasible and effective, they served as an initial model for the institutions subsequently set up.

Reaching children. Innovative programmes in all cities have started to use other ways to reach children in distress besides existing referral structures, which are usually remedial and limited in reach. The Secretariat of the Child in the State of São Paulo, the Goiânia Social Foundation and SETREM all initially received children primarily through court, police or welfare agency referral (see Boxes 2.2 and 2.3). By mid-1991, the São Paulo Secretariat had also developed large youth recreation centres, rapidly built in poor urban neighbourhoods and conspicuous in the surrounding drabness. These centres offered art and sports activities and arranged for special events, including seven circuses with four performances per day (for a daily total of some 1,500 to 3,000 children each). These activities acted as a pole of attraction for street-based and other disadvantaged children and enabled educators to make contact with them off the street.

Similarly, the Goiânia Social Foundation, inspired by the NGOs, realized that, beyond referrals, children needed to be reached on the streets.[8] A key role was assigned to street educators (Box 2.2) who identified children on the streets, invited them to the open-door screening centre, and followed up with visits to homes and neighbourhoods.

SETREM in Curitiba did not set up a new way to reach urban children, but it was very effective in providing technical assistance to the local court, police and welfare institutions and helping them to address children's problems with greater sensitivity, utilizing existing mechanisms. It thus humanized and energized existing networks. The new Brazilian system of Councils for the Rights of the Child and Adolescent have similarly "energized" all the networks already engaged in helping children in distress by providing them with increased resources and encouraging new partners to join. The same was true of all the more innovative municipal-level programmes, not only in Brazil, but also in the other countries, although to a lesser extent in Italy.

Decentralized and diversified care. Programmes in Brazil, as well as some of the more innovative ones in the Philippines, India, Italy and Kenya, progressively realized that the children's problems needed to be addressed in comprehensive and flexible ways. Through its system of daytime centres with street-based extensions (the street educators), the Goiânia Social Foundation, for example, was able to innovate in a number of important directions, summarized in a "pedagogical" model that included a comprehensive approach to education, career planning, community involvement and family preservation. This was translated into a system of specialized services made available at state level. It emphasized *alternative education*, combined with *formal education* and *vocational training*. Innovative alternative education, such as the culturally-sensitive one proposed by the Axè project, allowed for individualized attention and was considered particularly appropriate for adolescents already engaged in high-risk behaviours. It provided new entry into the formal school system as well as into vocational training. Brazil has been particularly innovative in developing an overall "pedagogical" approach to children-at-risk, especially those engaged in drugs and solvent sniffing or in conflict with the law (Gomes da Costa 1989, de Florio La Rocca 1992).

Another innovation of the Social Foundation was the importance given to *life skills* and *life planning* (including career planning) for young people. Although the Social Foundation focused primarily on rehabilitation, it was moving towards prevention by establishing contact with families, coordinating with local schools and communities, and liaising with other city sectors, especially the business sector for promotion of work opportunities for urban poor children. It was learning through follow-up studies that rehabilitation was difficult to accomplish and that the key was to create an overall supportive environment since more than half of the young people relapsed into minor trouble. It was, moreover, learning the importance of establishing closer contacts with the urban neighbourhoods in order to reduce the time and effort of street educators and social workers in community outreach and home follow-up activities.

The importance of prevention cum protection — that is, reaching urban children in distress before they engage in high-risk behaviours has been discovered as we have seen over and over again by large developmental urban NGOs concerned with children.

Coverage versus effectiveness. Coverage was found to be quite extensive in all cases. The São Paulo state programme reached the largest numbers (about 270,000 children by 1991) but was not always able to follow them over time to test the effectiveness of its efforts. By its presence, however, it gave new energy to other pro-children activities in the city and state. Goiânia reached over 5,000 children, was able to follow up carefully and provided them with long-term life opportunities. It served as a good test of what could be done with job training and education. SETREM in Curitiba was able to handle 1,912 cases between January and September 1991, or an estimated 2,554 cases a year, almost exclusively (99 percent) referred to them by the court, police and welfare agencies. One of its offshoots, the Pià Programme, with decentralized centres in poor urban neighbourhoods, was serving about 4,000 children in late 1991.

Coverage *per se* serves little purpose if it is not accompanied by effectiveness: the ability to change positively the lives of an increasing number of children. Many projects have proven their ability to reach thousands and make a difference. In Brazil, thousands have been moved out of FEBEM/FUNABEM and into much better municipal and state programmes, all through the country. In the Philippines and increasingly in India, Kenya and Italy, thousands have found new opportunities away from institutions. These achievements need to be monitored on a continuing basis.

Key role of dynamic leadership. Political will and innovative leadership were very important in generating the funding needed to make these efforts successful and to bring them to national attention. Until the end of the 1980s, social policy in Goiânia, for example, was characterized by wasteful overlap. The lack of administrative flexibility in the public sector hindered structural modernization. Governmental agencies also covered some of the same grounds that private child welfare organizations did. Each sector worked in isolation without the benefit of coordination. Disadvantaged urban children were primarily identified by the court and police and institutionalized in national centres.

After a careful review, the Governor of the state of Goiás, in the midst of an electoral campaign, proposed a new policy, strongly influenced by the debate on the draft Constitution and particularly on the proposed chapter on children's rights. The Social Promotion Foundation was created in March 1988 with the main goal of "formulating and executing the state government's social policy, giving priority to proposals and activities aiming at the constant improvement of the population's quality of life, particularly of its poorer segments" (Alves 1991). A very efficient staff was selected with a mandate to focus on children. Similar stories characterize many innovative national and citywide programmes.

Growing to Scale. The Brazilian system of Councils developed a multicomponent, citywide approach to planning and acting on behalf of children which reinforced existing city networks, structured their collaboration and introduced new partners. From the point of view of reach, it goes beyond exclusive reliance on institutional referrals and provides for the institutionalized coordination of referrals from NGOs and additional coverage through recreational and street education programmes. However, there are limits to how much even NGOs can accomplish. They cover only small populations and often reach children when the more serious problems have already manifested themselves. The new Brazilian system thus remains focused on the identification of high-risk behaviour patterns or severe exploitation, which characterize most of these referrals, and has not formally enlisted the help of neighbourhoods and communities. However, by creating a protective environment, it has also been generally preventive. The challenge now lies in its full implementation.

Alternatively, programmes in the Philippines, Kenya and India, where family support systems are still relatively sound, have worked at developing innovative forms of cooperation between the government and poor urban neighbourhoods, thus attempting to reach preventively, but much more specifically, a broad range of children and families at-risk (school dropouts and street-based children in Kenya, poor urban children, often working, and street children on their own in India). In Kenya and India, these urban neighbourhood and CEDC programmes are often not closely integrated. In contrast, in the Philippines, a particularly interesting integrated programme has been developed at municipal level. It elicits the full cooperation of urban poor communities, but also utilizes citywide street educators and has forged an impressive network of partnerships (see Philippines chapter).

Urban poor neighbourhoods as indispensable partners

Referral systems also exist in the Philippines for children in conflict with the law and children with special needs (mentally retarded, emotionally disturbed or physically disabled, abandoned or orphaned children). In the past, they were usually placed in institutions. Since 1969, however, legislation also permits government departments to contract special services or residential care from local nongovernmental organizations.

In order to respond to the escalating problem of children on the streets, Philippine city governments, in collaboration with NGOs, DSWD and UNICEF, have, since 1988, progressively organized municipal-level inter-agency committees for especially disadvantaged children in order to coordinate municipal action (including NGOs) and provide overall planning. These committees, working with the help of street educators as well as through coordinated referrals, identify problem families and children. Local social planners have linked the CEDC committees with the broader municipal inter-agency council that plans improvement projects in poor neighbourhoods. The urban communities have set up committees for street children, which focus on the problems of disadvantaged school-age children and have now become active partners of the citywide CEDC (and UBS) inter-agency committee in planning how to best provide preventive help (see Box 3.2).

The advantages of Olongapo's approach to community-building is that the community itself can now monitor the situations of its older at-risk children and not only those 0 to 3. Duplication of effort by voluntary organizations and government are greatly diminished. The programme uses local resources, but deploys them better. The analysis of the children's and the families' problems is much better informed and less costly. The responses at all levels, including the community level, are flexible and comprehensive. The children can be referred for special services to urban NGOs or technical support staff, if needed. Furthermore, as discussed in chapter 7, this approach encourages inter-family interaction and joint community responsibility. The programme has already proven successful in a number of other Philippine cities.

The Undugu Society, an experienced NGO in Nairobi that started out working only with street children, has similarly learned how important it is to engage the local urban communities in support of their own children as part of community-building activities. It has fostered greater school-community interaction and has also developed an interesting informal education curriculum now accepted by the formal school system, as well as special projects for adolescent girls, community health, urban agriculture and low-cost shelter. Its pioneering efforts in the slums, based on continuing self-assessment, and on playing a facilitating role for the community, have been recognized throughout Africa. Having established very solid partnerships with government agencies in the past, it is now increasingly moving into citywide social mobilization strategies as well (Mbogori, personal communication).

In India, community-based activities, even though not specifically focused on school-age children, have shown the potentials and strengths of urban neighbourhoods. In Kenya, it is at the level of urban neighbourhoods that the most active grassroots movements are emerging in urban areas.

Cost-Effectiveness, Sustainability and Growing to Scale

Policy makers must ask themselves how to address the problems of the largest possible number of children at the most reasonable financial and social cost and with the most effective results.

The key elements of specific approaches have been quite similar across North/South borders: (1) alternatives to institutionalization such as out-of-home placement or foster care; (2) family, community and peer monitoring and support with the involvement of schools; and (3) citywide systems of problem identification, collaborative support, and flexible specialized service centres. On the other hand, interventions that try to reach families and children preventively, *before* they engage in high-risk behaviour, have been identified as: family preservation; community construction; and citywide systems of collaborative support that establish more protective networks around children and families. The potentials for development of these different approaches vary, however, between North and South.

In industrialized countries where, in comparison with developing countries, the numbers of children to be reached are far fewer and welfare services are better developed (although not always sufficient to the task or well-implemented, as in many instances in Italy and the United States), there has been an increasing reliance on out-of-home placement for children at high risk (Bruner 1988, Johnson 1987).[9] Youth homes or residential communities are used to recreate some of the support systems of a family or neighbourhood. Foster care has also been increasingly practised, for example, in Italy, although recent publications question whether, as practised, it actually serves the best interests of the child (Arrighi 1992, Moro 1989).

Family support is now being increasingly approached through family preservation interventions, such as the intensive home-based family assistance proposed by programmes in the United States (Wells and Biegel 1991) and in Italy (Gardini and Tessari 1992). These programmes have proven to be quite cost-effective.

Family preservation through intensive home visits, as is carried out in the Homebuilders project, the longest running family preservation model in the United States,[10] can prevent out-of-home placement in a large number of cases for a considerable length of time. Evidence has also been collected which demonstrates that the per family costs are much lower than the costs of foster care or especially of institutionalization (half and one thirteenth, respectively, in the particular study carried out on the Homebuilders project), assuming, however, that the various conditions determining costs and placement rates — including court and community attitudes and behaviours, prevalence of drug abuse and the supply of placement resources — remain the same (Nelson 1990).

The long-term advantages of family preservation in terms of cost-effectiveness are clear and their replicability has been confirmed, but research still needs to elicit documented answers to issues of long-term sustainability, tied to problems of recidivism. To what extent can programmes invert the deteriorating path on which these often dysfunctional families are set? The answer to that question is generally not encouraging. Remedial interventions after household relationships have severely degenerated are often a formidable task.

The more comprehensive approaches advocated aim at modifying elements of the environment that cause family dysfunction. They focus on communities and cities and suggest strategies and actions to make these environments more supportive. They are thus both generally protective (reinforcing the potential long-term efficacy of home-based assistance, for example) and also preventive (limiting the potential increase in the family's and child's problems).

Placement in institutions, until recently the main approach to the growing numbers and problems of children in Third World countries, was repeatedly documented by the Country Teams as being less effective, both in the short and the long term, and is definitely more costly.

Other forms of out-of-home placement, similar to the youth homes and residential communities described earlier (SOS villages, Don Bosco institutions), appear reasonable options for children already engaged in high-risk behaviours who cannot be immediately reintegrated into their families. These therapeutic centres, however, cannot reach enough of the children-at-risk; moreover, governments will need to support many more such institutions, either directly or by subcontracting NGOs, unless they take timely preventive action. Foster care, possibly because of the numbers involved and the poor economic conditions in many developing countries, has not been widely adopted in the Third World as an effective solution.

Improving the quality of schools, lowering their costs to the families and improving local neighbourhoods for children are thus much better investments than building and maintaining more institutions. Preventive approaches, such as the reinforcement of existing family and community support systems, including schools, are also much more appropriate in the Third World where governments could not easily afford to staff large welfare systems for intensive home-assistance to children, for example.

In order to achieve coverage, affordability and sustainability, and allow such programmes to grow to scale, the following elements are important:

A new role for urban neighbourhoods and families. Urban neighbourhoods must monitor the conditions of children, especially on the preventive level, and identify families in distress in coordination with the citywide referral systems. Technical advice, whenever needed, should be provided by social workers and street educators. It has been clearly shown that only with the active involvement of urban communities as full partners can large numbers of children both North and South be effectively reached and monitored.

New roles for nongovernmental organizations. Nongovernmental organizations have very important roles to play in growing to scale as: (a) providers of quality services for out-of-home placements in order to expand their reach and coverage and to improve the quality of existing government rehabilitative services for children; and (b) facilitators of relationships between urban poor neighbourhoods and local governments. As local governments take a leading role in, and form partnerships with, urban neighbourhoods, they will need sympathetic brokers, provided that the neighbourhood organizations are able to remain in control of their decision-making process.

Coordinating activities through inter-agency and citizens councils that work in close collaboration with families and communities. UBS has had an impact on national and municipal governments and has occasionally successfully mobilized municipal business sectors. It has provided the basis for all the programmes in most of the countries of the study. The whole system needs to be provided with an appropriate system of checks and balances, in order to avoid monopolization or distortions, and to foster instead balanced cooperation.

UBS has proven to be a particularly helpful model. It has generated numerous examples of authentic neighbourhood participation (Hyderabad, Olongapo), and has responded to the need for the intersectoral convergence of municipal and NGO activities as well as the direct collaboration of urban neighbourhoods, families and children. Intersectoral convergence represents an important strategy for diminishing costs and obtaining maximum impact in the most cost-efficient way.

In order to be fully effective, it needs, however, to achieve a greater child focus that includes school-age children and to involve a larger number of municipal departments beyond Social Welfare and Health Departments. Citywide planning for children needs to be institutionalized into a citizens council for all the children and families, which would make it possible to mobilize broader resources.

The model projects in Brazil, the Philippines, India, Kenya and Italy are important because they provide examples of what can be made to work and how. With appropriate transformations and the provision of necessary checks and balances, these models can be replicated and adopted on a large scale, in a committed effort to reach more urban children in distress nation-wide.

MAJOR CONSTRAINTS: ORGANIZATION, FUNDING AND UNEQUAL PARTNERSHIPS

Lack of Government Intersectoral Coordination and Convergence

The complexities of the national, regional and state systems are reflected at the local level. Since urban and CEDC programmes are usually implemented at the city level, they have to struggle with a lack of coordination within both national ministries and existing municipal services. The initial lack of cooperation among municipal health, welfare and local development officials in the Philippines clearly illustrates the difficulties. For another example, the municipal Welfare and Education Department in Mombasa has no official links with the National Children's Bureau. In many countries, officials rotate frequently, sometimes changing assignments every two years. When an individual has started to understand the programme and its intricacies, he or she is transferred, thus jeopardizing a project's success. In India, the administration of often complex schemes creates a maze of overlapping responsibilities and much potential for bureaucratic inefficiency and or waste.

Furthermore, government funding usually follows the sound managerial principle of large allotments for rapid turnover. Energies are mostly consumed, however, in seeking to ensure that these large amounts of money are earmarked and spent on schedule and according to procedure rather than on the more time-consuming effort of increasing local capabilities for more sustainable, self-reliant development. Moving money or just handing it out is antithetic to building capacities and tends to generate unrealistic expectations while often unleashing negative local forces.

However, many of the innovative projects described in this book have been able to offset those negative tendencies, transforming relatively small amounts of public money into highly constructive self-help efforts.

Local Nongovernmental Organizations

There are often many NGOs working on the same issues at both the national and the municipal level. The local branches and main offices are usually engaged in a wide range of activities; but they have rarely been systematically counted, nor have their capabilities been assessed. NGOs thus face considerable problems of lack of coordination, both with other NGOs and with government agencies. For instance, there is normally no structured provision for interaction between community-based NGOs and institutional NGOs, such as homes for abandoned children, street-based drop-in centres, or for that matter, with the local social welfare and juvenile justice system. They are therefore unable to contribute to efforts of social reintegration and family preservation by the organizations dealing directly with the child, even though they may have valuable information about the family and neighbour-hood. Such information is usually gathered by social workers in visits to the child's household. However, because social workers are much less integrated in the community, the information they collect is often incomplete and a costly duplication of previous efforts.

Furthermore, fund-raising is a time-consuming concern for municipal NGOs, with uncertainty the only constant. They can usually only provide quality coverage to small populations, and, as we have seen, they cannot easily grow to scale. They are dependent, beyond government subcontract-ing, on international development and humanitarian assistance which repre-sents only a very small percentage of the overall funding for social services provided by governments.

Unequal Partnerships

The many different partners whose mobilization we urge also have very different political and economic strengths and belong to very different sec-tors of society. This is indeed a major part of the issue. Given the complexities of the organizational and funding problems they face, collaboration is indis-pensable. However, such collaboration needs to be constructed with many built-in checks and balances in order to ensure that (1) no one party can manipulate the situation, but, instead, that (2) each party, whatever its strengths or weaknesses, is able to realize its potential.

TODAY'S CHILDREN, TOMORROW'S CITIES: HOW TO PLACE CHILDREN ON THE CITY AGENDA

A first and major message from the country studies was the importance of decentralizing responsibilities and resources to the municipal level. Both North and South, it is increasingly in cities that children's prospects for survival and for physical and mental development are determined. It is in cities that significant numbers of today's children are facing street life and harsh working conditions, sometimes within overburdened family settings, often after migratory moves that have deprived them of family support systems. Globally, it is in cities that the highest concentration of children with high-risk behaviours are found. And it is in some rapidly growing cities that the shortage (Nairobi) or poor distribution (Delhi) of municipal primary schools create special problems.[11] Thus, cities are a vital focus of any effort to improve educational attainment and reduce the numbers of children in especially difficult circumstances.

Our research and existing evaluations of CEDC interventions all strongly confirm that to be effective, programmes need to reach children where they live; it is the city, and city neighbourhoods, with their households, schools, playgrounds and streets, where attention needs to be sharply focused.

Our analysis, as well as the participatory research with children and their families, have all shown us the importance of combining a citywide approach to children's problems with focused, community-level interventions. Urban families living lives of permanent crisis need flexible support systems, often best achieved through community and neighbourhood projects. They also need a supportive social environment in which, to begin with, they are no longer marginalized by municipal officials, uncaring school teachers and police officers.

It is at city level that this approach can best be operationalized, because of the direct accountability of municipal politicians together with current trends towards decentralization of resources and greater democratization. Finally, it is in cities that the personal leadership of a committed and caring leader can achieve some of the most tangible results for the urban children in greatest distress, directly reaching them and their families. Initiatives at the municipal level need to be strongly supported and guarded from the repercussions of declining national budgets, especially for social services.

As part of the Urban Child Project, policy meetings to discuss municipal planning were organized at city and national levels. They called attention to many of the citywide programmes already emphasized. Some of the most innovative City Teams were then invited for further comparative discussions at the International Meeting of Mayors, Urban Planners and Policy Makers in Florence in October 1992, under the joint sponsorship of the UNICEF International Child Development Centre, the Istituto degli Innocenti and the Municipality of Florence. The aim of the Meeting was to establish a new North/South understanding on how to effectively place children on city agendas — and keep them there. As a basis for discussions, the Project synthesized the various successful city-level initiatives and drew up the following guidelines, which were then discussed:

- Change can only occur when different sectors of society have achieved a new vision of children and families living in urban poverty;

- Decentralization of responsibilities and resources to the municipal level needs to be encouraged and continued;

- New partnerships and key municipal actors for change must assume responsibility for the creation of a more supportive environment for urban children and families in crisis;

- Government officials and NGOs as well as Mayors must increasingly view themselves not only as *providers* but also as *facilitators* of services to families and children in distress;

- A citywide municipal council should help coordinate different sectors in order to avoid costly duplications and improve performance;

- Large physical infrastructures are often not the most cost-effective investments;

- Improved division of tasks, coordination and intersectoral convergence among government agencies and NGOs at municipal level make demonstrably more effective results possible in shorter times;

- Full partnership with the city's human resources (including distressed children, families and communities) increases affordability, sustainability and coverage.

Examples of these interrelated points were provided by each Country Team. In many of the cities examined, some progress has been made (in some instances with the direct contribution of the Project) towards creating a new vision of both the disadvantaged child (Brazil, Philippines) and urban poverty (India, Kenya, Philippines). Key decision makers have begun to recognize the urban poor's positive contributions, resiliency and sense of responsibility. These changes were acknowledged quite candidly by decision makers.

New partnerships have also been created in which key participants have become not only the providers of services, but also *facilitators* and *catalysts* at municipal level. City residents concerned about children (lawyers, judges, professionals, NGO programmers, municipal and state officials from different departments) participated at regular meetings of newly created municipal councils on children and families, learned about each other's capabilities and constraints and listened to reports on municipal interventions with a variety of other partners, including urban neighbourhoods. In that process, they progressively learned how to work together, and with new partners, to ensure that children are increasingly placed on the "agendas" of all city residents.

Key Structural Elements

These new partnerships are often based on key structural elements. In Brazil, for example, the new policy for translating children's rights into services and responsibilities is a "coordinated system of governmental and non-governmental actions of the federal government, states, federal district and municipalities." This policy implies among other things a system of municipal registration of NGOs. Besides being a condition for public financing eligibility, this provision helps to coordinate efforts and to avoid programme overlaps and gaps in coverage. Italy, Brazil and the Philippines now register their urban NGOs at the national level and are starting to do so at the municipal level as well. well. India has recently decided to use NGOs to reach urban communities, and as its Urban Basic Services Programme goes national, the issue of recognition and coordination will become important there as well. This new recognition of NGOs as partners has been followed by NGO municipal subcontracting. Furthermore, the Brazilian Councils of the Rights of the Child and Adolescents at federal, state and municipal levels and the municipal Guardianship Councils have also been formally given responsibility for reviewing budgetary requirements of social policy for children, in coordination with municipal authorities. Additional efforts are nonetheless needed, even in Brazil, to improve access to public financing, to ensure the continuity of state support to overcome political party favouritism and clientelism in the distribution of resources, and to adjust the procedures of financial transfers to actual economic conditions (through price indexing, for example, in order to maintain the real value of grants).

The participation of urban neighbourhoods, following the guidelines of the UBS model, has played an important role in the Philippines, India and Kenya where, together with inter-agency and intersectoral collaboration, it has ensured cost-effectiveness and coverage. At the beginning of the pilot UBS project, the city of Davao, for example, had limited public health resources — one urban health station for every 60,000 inhabitants as opposed to one for every 5,000 in rural areas. A community-based project, initially run by a local university-based NGO, became the basis for a UBS programme. An inter-agency committee was set up bringing together representatives of urban NGOs and different city departments (Health, Water and Sanitation, Education, City Engineer), and is now the responsibility of the municipal Department of Planning and Development. As a result of this collaboration, the municipal government has a less bureaucratized approach, using mobile clinics and more community-based promotive and preventive techniques. Immunization coverage increased from 18 percent in 1986 to over 80 percent in 1990.

In Kisumu, a city in Nyanza province in Kenya, immunization was found to be most efficiently carried out in areas where UBSP had encouraged intersectoral integration and community participation. This contributed to lowering the IMR for the province from the 1985 rate of 199 per 1,000 live births to 133 per 1,000 in 1992 and increasing immunization coverage in the city from 25 percent in 1985 to 50 percent in 1992 (against a national average of 67 percent, but a marked improvement over the generally low immunization coverage for most of the western part of Kenya). In Andhra Pradesh, India, cost-sharing with UBS partners has allowed everyone to have a stake in the project. In 1990, the UBS model received 40 percent of its funds from state and municipal governments, town-level voluntary organizations and slum communities; 40 percent from UNICEF and the remaining 20 percent from the central government. The salaries of community volunteers and of *balwadi* teachers were paid in part by the government and UNICEF and in part by the community, through its Neighbourhood Committees. The community thus felt accountable and responsible for the project. Costs were lower for the government and the results were better. A UBS project, for example, costs the government 15–18 Rs per person per year ($0.48–0.57), a minimal sum with respect to other urban schemes.

In Visakhapatnam City, India, close coordination between social programmes and urban infrastructural projects has proven vital to their success. The UCD–ODA (Urban Community Development and Overseas Development Agency) programme, launched in 1988, was consolidated from 1982 to 1987 when the UBSP was in operation. Strong and motivated Neighbourhood Committees have organized active literacy programmes and their own engineering and water section. Most of the positive results of the programme have been attributed to this integrated organizational scheme.

Additional Strategies

An analysis of the process in the different cities has also pointed to other actions needed to ensure both effective implementation and sustainability:

- Exposing key actors and potential partners at the municipal level to the problems of the urban poor — the process of "immersion" — and encouraging them to participate in planning increases their sense of responsibility towards children in distress and leads to changes in attitudes.

- Involving families and communities more centrally and supporting their survival strategies heightens their sense of responsibility and leads to higher income generation, lower incidence of school dropout, fewer defaults in loan repayments, infrastructural improvements (such as water tanks, playgrounds) and a more rational utilization and better maintenance of municipal resources.

- Involving children in this process increases their sense of responsible citizenship.

Joint planning by all new partners and "immersion" have meant that the urban poor and their children are much more widely seen as the "solution" rather than the "problem." In India, as a result of the direct exposure of bureaucrats and NGOs to the realities of urban neighbourhoods and thanks to the universalization of the UBS programme, national, regional and local bureaucracies no longer view the urban poor (and their children), as "standing in the way" of urban development, but have now realized that they are actually a key element in sustaining that process. In the Philippines, this view is now shared by different sectors of society, including the government bureaucracy, and has allowed for the adoption of new municipal policies for disadvantaged urban children in more than 15 cities in coordination with over 300 NGOs. In Kenya, a national survey (Mazingira Institute 1987) on food production in 1985 showed that almost two thirds of urban dwellers in the sample (64 percent) grew some of their own food, while over half kept livestock (51 percent). Urban agriculture encounters problems of land disposition and availability. However, when this important coping strategy is supported by the municipal government, it gives the urban poor a way to survive and generate income, keeps the air clear and channels the energies of families and children into productive enterprises.

A particularly strong shift in cultural attitudes towards children in Brazil has been promoted as a result of partnerships among the media, academics, NGOs, lawyers, officials and UNICEF. The word "minor," which had become a disparaging term, has been banished from the legal code, from official documents and from the language of NGOs. Emphasis is now also being placed on "children"s rights' rather than only on "children's needs," and on children as subjects rather than as objects.

Child-specific statistics are being compiled yearly by the National Statistical Office and the media, in partnership with academics, NGOs and UNICEF, have played a central and controlling role in the dissemination of this new vision of the child. The National Advertising Council, for example, actively promotes campaigns in favour of children. Rede Globo, the world's fourth largest TV network, dedicates ample network time to children's issues during the yearly "Week of the Child." It has campaigned actively against violence towards children and for the establishment of Municipal Councils on the Rights of the Child and Adolescent. In Salvador, a weekly column contributed by the State Forum on the Child and the Adolescent in the regional newspaper *Tribuna da Bahia* gives press exposure to child-related experiences, programmes and ideas.

Similar partnerships have influenced decision-making in the Philippines and India. In Italy, the Italian Committee of UNICEF and other child-focused organizations work efficiently with the media in education for development initiatives at national, regional and municipal levels, and the Istituto degli Innocenti has recently drawn the media into advocacy efforts.

At the International Meeting of Mayors, Urban Planners and Policy Makers, City Teams discussed innovative programmes for children on the basis of documents provided by the Urban Project and their own examples. Three cases generated particularly lively discussions: the municipal programmes for children and families in Maringà (Brazil), in Vishakpatnam (India) and in Cebu (Philippines), each vividly illustrating different types of private-sector involvement and the attempted integration of infrastructural and qualitative community-based projects.

After a week of lively discussion, meeting participants agreed upon a municipal framework for action and main strategies for providing a more protective environment for urban children in distress, which contained many of the elements already presented by the Urban Project (Box 8.12). Within each of those strategies and on the basis of their own experience, they also identified a first detailed list of actions (see Appendix 2) which incorporates some of the more general recommendations that had already emerged from the country studies. At the end of the Meeting, the Mayors also drafted a strong global appeal (Box 8.13).

The Meeting participants included numerous important national and city-level actors who had participated in the Project from its start as well as some who had recently joined the effort. Some were also representatives of large mayoral organizations, such as the 3,500-strong organization of Brazilian mayors. Many of the mayors and high-level national and municipal officials were nearing the end of their terms. Some have moved to national-level leadership. Limited terms of office, elections and shifts in party leadership dictate frequent changes of personnel in municipal and national offices.

Nonetheless, these mayors wanted to leave a mark and allow other cities and countries to learn from their experience. They thus sat patiently (*unexpectedly patiently*) for a whole day without reprieve, painstakingly checking, analysing further and ultimately approving each item in the long framework of strategies and actions that had been formulated. And they appeared very satisfied with the job done when they left. The results have since been utilized at national and international level to mobilize other cities and energize their networks while providing strategies and guidelines for action; they are being included on the agendas of mayors and cities worldwide; and they have provided new encouragement and recognition to those who have already significantly contributed towards making children's lives better in the 21 cities of the Urban Child Project.

Box 8.12   Strategies for Implementing the New Urban Vision

Mayors and urban residents should become partners and assume responsibility for the disadvantaged children and families of their cities. Working together they should:

- **Collect better information for advocacy and monitoring**
- **Improve municipal management, coordination and convergence**
- **Implement stronger legislation for children**
- **Optimize resources and investment**
- **Empower community members through community participation and organizational development**
- **Increase public awareness of the problems urban children in distress face and the range of possible approaches to these problems in order to reinforce a new vision of childhood.**

Box 8.13   Letter from Florence

Recognizing that the worldwide economic crisis is provoking serious consequences which directly affect the welfare of our children and families,

We (Mayors and City Teams), must take increased responsibility for preventing the deterioration of the quality of life of our populations and the accentuation of social inequities, and we must ensure that others, including representatives of national, state or municipal governments, nongovernmental agencies (NGOs), community-based organizations, and the private sector, join in our efforts.

We must insist that municipal governments, which are on the front line, be given legal instruments and economic resources so that they can implement social policies which guarantee the full citizenship and rights of all children and families.

We must guarantee that citizens, including children according to their capacities, be given the opportunity to participate in a genuine, and not just a token, way in the definition of priorities for municipal action, and that institutionalized channels (committees, task forces, and councils) be established at the municipal level for this purpose.

We must ensure that the accounting of the use of public resources be transparent to the public.

We must strive for greater coordination within government agencies and among these agencies, the private sector, NGOs and community-based organizations, in order to implement integrated plans of action which promote the rights of all children and families in the city.

We therefore call upon Mayors worldwide to make a decisive commitment to protect the rights of our children, to achieve the Summit Goals, and to ensure, by making our cities more humane, that all children have a better future. We call upon you to involve all citizens of our cities in this alliance, to encourage others by your example and to share, at future meetings, your accomplishments on behalf of children.

> "The future of our children begins today!"

FINAL REMARKS

We have covered much ground with the Urban Child Project and this book: starting with an analysis of the difficult conditions of specific disadvantaged urban children in five diverse countries and twenty-one cities, we moved on to assessments of programmes and processes, and finally to suggestions for specific key actors within cities — all on behalf of children.

We may have included at times too much detail for some readers, too little for others. We do hope a few broad messages stand out. We have witnessed and reported the commitment of many active supporters of children, each with specific tasks, and have built on their knowledge, experience and expertise to present alternatives that may enable us to protect today's and tomorrow's urban children more effectively. We have suggested how these alternatives could be realized and have shown some of the important elements that have allowed others in those many cities to begin a process of innovation that will ensure better prospects for their children.

We have shown how the time is ripe, both North and South, for change and for new approaches that include broad partnerships and build on the brokerage capacities of municipal decision makers, politicians and technical advisors.

Caring is the first step needed to bring about change, although caring alone is not enough. We, like the innovative mayors and municipal actors who have inspired some of the pages of this book, need to see the problem as a whole and then break it into manageable pieces for action. And we need to understand HOW that action can be successfully carried out.

An important accompanying realization, and one emphasized by all Country Teams, is that effecting change requires a long-term commitment and hard work: without thorough homework, appropriate fact-finding and careful analyses over time — *with the active collaboration and the direction of the people and children in distress themselves* — the problems will remain and may, in fact, multiply. Simplistic remedies, as the Project has amply illustrated, often create more problems than they "solve." Unfortunately, no cure-all has been found to the complex social and economic problems affecting urban children worldwide. Perseverance and follow-up, collaboration and the building of partnerships, are some of the essential elements of successful interventions. We need to offer constructive alternatives, both broad and specific, and be willing to adjust them according to need. And, most of all, although we are living in a tormented and often tragic world, we need to be more visionary and daring, willing to dream of a better future. As powerfully argued by Marian Wright Edelman, a prominent advocate for children in the United States (Edelman 1987), "the tragedy of life does not lie in not reaching your goal but in having no goal to reach ... (It is) not failure but low aim."

NOTES

1. A small people's organization in Cadiz, Philippines, for example, primarily involved in providing limited capital to urban slum-dwellers for small-scale animal husbandry (pigs, in particular) and proud of its record of high return

rates and good money management, found itself in the late 1980s in the improbable position of having to refuse large international funding already assured them. The reason for this painful decision was that the funding would have forced them to change their lending methods in ways that would not have been manageable by their beneficiaries (Franco, Administrative Director, personal communication).

2. The Undugu Society has also been particularly concerned about the increasing lack of interest shown by some of its international funders for the complexities of urban community development and institutional change, which has a less immediate funding appeal. It has therefore created an independent funding endowment that makes the society less dependent on fluctuations in the interests and priorities of international funders.

3. Journalists and academic researchers offer different strengths. The first usually excel in impressionistic writing. They give a vivid sense of the immediate and work at making an impact on the reader. Only few among them have developed systematic analytical skills, for which they usually have, as journalists, little time or space. Researchers, in contrast, often interact too exclusively with the theoretical arguments currently developing within their own discipline and can thus appear esoteric. If, however, properly guided by programmers and willing to abandon their "expert" stance, they can become useful collaborators of government agencies and nongovernmental organizations. Articles written by substantive journalists on the basis of research analyses can have a great impact on the general public.

4. When a specific intervention is assessed — a family preservation programme in urban poor neighbourhoods, for example, aimed at reducing the numbers of runaway children present on the streets — several questions arise, including: (a) the statistical validity of quantitative measurements of outcomes (How many children did not run away? How many ended up on the streets? Are there more or fewer runaways from one neighbourhood or control group than from others? Is this statistically significant?), presuming, of course, that such measurements exist; (b) the internal validity of the assessment (Did the programme actually cause these effects?); (c) the identification of elements of the programme that produced those effects (construct validity); and (d) the assessment of the costs of each key element as well as accompanying costs for setting up and carrying out the intervention.

The results of such an analysis should then be measured against the costs of other interventions addressing the same problems (welfare agencies deploying a wide network of social workers or the institutionalization of these children either as law offenders or as effectively abandoned and endangered children). There, costs are somewhat easier to calculate, but problems of objectives emerge. Institutionalization, for instance, is usually effective primarily in removing a child from the street but not in giving the child hope and realistic options for a better future. The issue then becomes the long-term effectiveness of institutionalization (How long will the child be institutionalized? How much recidivism is there?).

5. Solvents are commonly utilized in Italian prisons when drugs are not available (Brigantini 1988).

6. A particularly successful US programme has been a drug abuse prevention and research project in 100 middle schools in Kansas City and Indianapolis with five main elements sequentially introduced: (a) school-based curricula (ten school sessions on drug resistance skills and ten homework sessions with interviews and role-playing with family and others); (b) parent programmes (parent-student-principal groups) promoting a drug-free environment in the school; (c) community organization in which community leaders are trained in drug prevention strategies and encouraged to develop agency task forces, media appeals, community events, awards ceremonies, networking and referrals; (d) health policy change with government officials to promote anti-smoking policies, enforce drunk-driving laws and create neighbourhood watches; (e) mass-media efforts with press kits, commercials, news features and television used to promote drug prevention. After 18 months, the prevalence of cigarette, alcohol and marijuana use (a likely precursor of other drugs) was significantly lower in those schools than in control schools. Pentz et al. (1989) attributed the project's success to the support of the power élite and the strong commitment and involvement of the communities, as well as to agency cooperation.

7. The Ounce of Prevention Fund was created as a joint public-private agency in 1982 in Chicago, but has now expanded and offers a state-wide and inter-state system of preventive services, research, training and technical assistance to preadolescents, adolescents at risk of early parenthood and disadvantaged parents and their young children. Partially funded by the State of Illinois Department of Children and Family Services and a private foundation, it has also extended into other states and is now receiving some federal aid as well as funds from private foundations and corporations.

8. All three state-led programmes discovered by monitoring their case histories that the children referred to them by the courts were mostly accused of minor offences. In Goiânia in 1989, for example, 27 percent were accused of burglary; 19 percent, vagrancy; 7.9 percent, drug use; 16 percent of the children were runaways. There was a high degree of recidivism. Serious crimes against life and homicides accounted for only 1 percent and 0.4 percent, respectively, and involved predominantly males (Alves 1991). Similarly, in Curitiba between January and September 1991, the children exclusively referred to the centre by the courts, police and welfare agency were generally older (15–18 years of age), had not finished primary school (68.5 percent) and had been arrested for such "crimes" as petty theft or lack of a vending permit in 60 percent of the cases rather than for serious offences.

9. Since the mid-1980s, US federal spending under title IV-E and Medicaid has grown at an ever-accelerating rate, reflecting, in part, this increasing nationwide reliance. However, despite repeated assertions, there has been virtually no national leadership in providing states with the fiscal incentives or supports to develop alternatives to placement. A cost-effective argument would suggest that other courses of action need to be taken (Nelson 1990).

10. The Homebuilders project was first initiated in Tacoma, Washington in 1974, then reproduced in many other parts of the United States. It has been ascer-

tained that the children of families targeted would indeed have most likely undergone out-of-home placement without the project's presence and that such placement was avoided in a majority of cases, sometimes as many as 90 percent, for a considerable length of time (as much as over a year) (Nelson 1990).

11. It should also be noted, however, that the quality of schooling in cities is generally higher than in rural areas where expenditure per student is often far inferior, especially in more remote regions.

Appendix
ONE

Primary Data Collection and Secondary Data Analysis

Street children are a highly mobile population, not census-assessed, whose living arrangements were poorly known. We did not know: (a) where the children seen on the streets of the major cities or even of the smaller centres of the developing world came from; (b) what kind of household they went back to at night; (c) whether they were on the streets working every day; (d) whether they had other activities; or (e) more generally, what the reasons for their being on the streets were.

As a result, we could not reach them and interview them at home or through their other activities, nor could we construct a sample based on households. At best, we could adopt purposive direct samples of children that contrasted street children with other kinds of working children on the streets and with working and non-working children in the slums. When households could be reached, we lacked appropriate population descriptors.

We knew that samples of other severely disadvantaged urban children could be found in slums and poor neighbourhoods or in institutions. However, again they were a large population, and not specifically enumerated by problem areas, except in the case of institutions, and were thus difficult to sample properly. In many developing countries, little information is available, beyond age and gender, on overall city-level populations, which makes estimates of slum populations difficult. In addition, slums and poor sections of the city, even when settled by long-time residents, often witness rapid changes because of evictions, relocations, fires and floods. Moreover, slum areas are subject to inflows of new populations, from other slums, from rural areas, or as illegal settlers chased by war and illness from neighbouring countries (Ugandans moving to Nairobi for example). Thus, the following methodology and sampling techniques were adopted:

(a) *Using the street as the reference point and then finding the households.* The teams in the Philippines and Kenya identified meeting places where the children were known to congregate. They then selected some such places in each city, usually on the basis of the size of the congregation. A special effort was made to ensure some randomness by interviewing either all or every third child encountered who agreed to be interviewed (with replacement of those who declined). In the Philippines, the interviews were carried out at different times of the day (PSSC 1991, McGuire 1986), and depended on sighting on the street rather than inclusion in an initially demarcated "universe" of street children. However, since sighting occurred at different hours but usually not late at night, certain categories of children beyond those sampled — children who spent longer hours on the streets working, who went to work irregularly, or who only appeared early in the morning or late at night — were probably not reached.

Most Filipino children had heard little or nothing about any of the service organizations for them (except in Olongapo and Davao, where the children interviewed were selected from the areas covered respectively by the popular Reach Up programme and by the City Interagency Working Committee on Abandoned and Street Children).

In Kenya, the University of Nairobi, under the sponsorship of the Ford Foundation, had recently carried out a nationwide survey of children on and of the street (ANPPCAN 1991). Five cities were selected for study because of size, location, types of population and types of problems faced: Nairobi, Mombasa, Kisumu, Narok and Kitui. Researchers mapped out the sites that the street-based children seemed to visit on a regular basis. From these, the 74 sites (38 in Nairobi, 13 in Mombasa, 11 in Kisumu, 7 in Kitui and 5 in Narok) with the highest populations of street children were chosen, and all street-based children presenting themselves to those sites were interviewed, a sample of 634 children. Subsequently, 32 parents (selected from a list established on the basis of their presumed willingness to be interviewed, according to the children) and 80 individuals who had some relationship with street-based children were also interviewed. This type of sampling provided information about a broad range of street children beyond the limited number usually reached by government departments and NGOs.

In the case of Brazil, the researchers from FLACSO (1991) decided to rely on samples of street and working children suggested by the resident and very successful state-run Goiânia Foundation. Assisted street and working children were contrasted with unassisted working children. The suggestions for selection were purposeful and established through informal networking with street educators who were well acquainted with the children, rather than by street-based surveys striving towards randomness. We were aware, however, that the state-run organization utilized in this case — as so often happens — only managed to reach a small percentage of all street and working children in the city of Goiânia, which meant that the sample was only partially representative of the overall street and working children population.

(b) *Using the slums as reference points and discovering how many of their children work on or are of the streets.* In the case of India, the sample was drawn randomly from pre-selected slums (every other home from pre-drawn blocks of 200 homes located in those slums). In Delhi alone, which has over 800 slums, the interviews took place in three slum areas where children were selected on the basis of their different religious affiliations, places of origin, and types of occupation. Interviews covered 182 households in depth. Consequently, these interviews may well represent a reasonably random picture of those particular slums, but not necessarily of the universe of all slum working and non-working children, since we have no statistical assurance that analogous pictures would emerge in other slums. The interviews included working and non-working children who lived with their families. A small sample of 30 street children, selected with the help of NGOs located in Delhi, was also interviewed in depth.

The same procedure was adopted in two slums for each of three cities of Andhra Pradesh around Hyderabad, Warangal, Cuddapah and Rajhamundhri, for a total of over 500 households. A sample of 400 street children was interviewed directly on the streets of Hyderabad and Vijayawada.

Italy, because of more limited resources and the greater availability of documented city-level information, did not engage in primary data collection. It relied on the extensive information provided by practitioners and field workers.

(c) *Interviewing slum children selected on the basis of case histories provided by service organizations and community schools.* In Kenya, the Nairobi sample was drawn from three "informal" schools located in the slums of Thayu, Pumwani and Kangemi (pre-selected on the basis of programme concerns), in five children's homes, remand homes and approved schools. With a methodology similar to the one in Brazil, the project established a baseline population of 1,000 children on the basis of case histories provided by headmasters and teachers of the informal schools, directors of the approved schools and other individuals whose daily activities involved close interaction with the children. Institutional records and registers were used to complete the information. The basic indicators used to establish that baseline population related to indicators of stress and risk (health-related, financial, psychosocial). Again, the selection was purposive rather than exclusively random.

Out of that baseline population, which in this case had a residential base, an actual purposive study sample of 220 children was then drawn: 25 children across the four institutions (since institutionalized children seemed to manifest similar problems and needs) and 30 children in each of the three informal schools, together with a control group of 30 children in regular public schools. The survey thus included both working and non-working children in the slums as well as institutionalized children. These children, who came from poor urban households, were considered to be at particularly high risk, financially at least, since they were in informal schools and had not been able to attend the more expensive public schools. We later discovered that there were other children in those slums who could not even attend these less expensive informal schools and had, despite their eagerness, no access to education due to a severe shortage of schools.

(d) *Interviewing children's households. Samples of households of the children interviewed were also systematically reached in the Philippines, India, Brazil and Kenya.* These interviews provided additional information on sibling sets and household coping strategies. The survey samples were drawn somewhat differently in each country because we were dealing with populations that were difficult to reach and not well known, and because the Project was structured from the beginning with a mandate to satisfy local programme needs as well. The samples do not randomly represent a probability universe (to do so would have required a much greater investment in research and funding in order to first define the universe and then interview an appropriate sample from that universe), but rather a purposive sampling. The samples therefore can not be used for straightforward quantitative, cross-national comparisons, although they do provide valuable information on populations at risk.

The interviews were carried out with both structured and unstructured questionnaires. The same questionnaires were used, as far as possible, for children and households in each country, even when different, and at times competing, research teams were involved. Similar questions were often asked across all countries, but because they had to be translated into local languages, their comparability is not fully ensured.

SECONDARY DATA ANALYSIS

Because of the lack of coordination among the studies, the reports on street and working children undertaken during the late 1980s and early 1990s in the countries under study, as well as a number of other large-scale reports that were part of important long-term studies in particular countries, reflect the concerns of the authors and of their sponsoring organizations (often NGOs) at the time:

(a) *Most studies focused on "street children"; that is, ALL children living and/or working on the streets with no distinction made between children who lived on their own or those who lived with their family* (McGuire 1986, DSWD, NCSD and UNICEF 1988, Rao 1989, ANPPCAN 1991, COESNICA 1992, PSSC 1991). Although the studies may have asked where the children lived and thus provide some information on the topic, they never organized the data along those variables. As a result, they generally lumped together children who needed to be reached, strategically, in altogether different ways. In some cases, however, the Urban Child Project was able to obtain the original computer diskettes and reanalyze the data on the basis of this distinction.

The emphasis on street children came about after this term came into use in Brazil as a potentially neutral term that could define all disadvantaged children roaming the streets even if their occupational affiliation was uncertain. It was created to offset terms such as "delinquent minors," most commonly used in Brazil, and to generate a more sympathetic — and less penalizing — view of the children's problems on the part of policy makers (Myers, personal communication). The term "street children" became useful for initial advocacy and was adopted by important child-advocacy organizations such as Child Hope and Streetwise International.

(b) *Studies on specific street or working children identified occupationally.* In the introduction to the report prepared by SPARC on Bombay 1989–90 (1991), a distinction is made between studies focusing on street children, irrespective of where they lived, and studies focusing on specific occupations typically engaged in by many vulnerable migrant children in Bombay, as indicated by NGOs. Those studies, as defined, could not tell us much about the ragpickers or scavengers who actually lived with their families in the slums, and gave only partial, though important, insights into why some children had left their families and entered those occupations and about their life careers (children do not necessarily always remain in the same occupation). The studies were able to provide great insights into the occupational conditions of children engaged in particular activities, their daily schedules and the lives of the selected children themselves at any point, but told us little about other children roaming the streets.

The SPARC report focused on four categories: children of pavement dwellers; children of construction workers; street children living by themselves on the street (with a special emphasis on ragpickers); and "hotel boys" or children working in hotels, eating establishments and tea stalls. "Hotel boys" tend to live where they work (although it depends on the size of the tea stalls and on their private arrangements). They have usually migrated from rural areas, but close to 70 percent are in the city with their families' consent to earn money.

An excellent report on live-in domestic workers in Kenya, sponsored by the Undugu Society (Mutiso 1989), tells us much about that group, which also emerges occasionally in our sample of children on the streets. It does not give as much information, however, on part-time domestic workers living in the slums. Similarly, Oloko et al. (1992) provides vaulable information on different types of working children in Nigeria.

(c) *Studies on street children with special attention to whether they live alone or with a family, and their relationship to their family* (NIUA 1992, Osmania University Regional Centre 1992, Lusk 1989, FLACSO and UNICEF 1991, Kaminsky and Wright 1992, Wright et al. 1992). Most of these studies were sponsored by the UNICEF International Child Development Centre. They allowed us to contrast street children, that is children who lived on the streets on their own, and street-based working children; they often also compared their results with those of control samples of poor urban non-working children regularly living with their families (FLACSO and UNICEF 1991, NIUA 1992, Osmania University Regional Centre 1991, Onyango and Dallape 1992, Mutiso et al. 1992). In a few cases, the studies also established contrasting samples of assisted street children or of child offenders in reform school (predominantly lone street children) (McGuire 1986, Onyango et al. 1992, FLACSO and UNICEF 1991).

(d) *Studies on children in poor urban neighbourhoods with special attention to their working and schooling patterns and with control samples of non-working children and/or children in regular government schools* (as opposed to children in the less expensive "nonformal schools" of Nairobi) (Porio 1993, NIUA 1992, Osmania University Regional Centre 1991, Onyango et al. 1992), Mutiso and Dallape 1992, Sommella 1990, Rossi Cairo 1991, Di Pasquale 1990), all sponsored by the International Child Development Centre in coordination with UNICEF country offices or, in the case of Italy by the Istituto degli Innocenti).

In each country we were able to utilize reviews of literature on other working or disadvantaged urban children.

Appendix
TWO

A New Vision for Urban Children and Families: Strategies and Actions for Transforming Cities

Prepared by the participants of the International Meeting of Mayors, Urban Planners and Policy Makers: Today's Children, Tomorrow's Cities

I. PREAMBLE: THE NEW VISION

This document is based upon a radically new vision of childhood and youth which has been developing throughout the world and was formalized by the signing of the Convention on the Rights of the Child. Fundamental to this new vision is the assertion that children are citizens who have rights and the capacity for improving their own lives and the communities[1] in which they live. Furthermore, all citizens should become jointly responsible for creating and acting on this new vision of the urban child.

Our future vision of the city is a city where:

- Love and care of children underlie all policies and actions.

- Analysis, action and evaluation are based on a holistic view of the child and environment.

- All children — and especially those who are poor or under stress — are given care, protection and opportunities for development.

- Poverty reduction and full and equal access to social services are seen as crucial to child, family, community and city development.

- Urban interventions to support children are aimed at the community level, empowering and strengthening family and community support networks.

- People no longer stigmatize, marginalize or victimize children, their families and poor urban communities; a more inclusive definition of children at risk and children in difficult circumstances has been accepted;[2] a new language and terminology is used to describe children and the urban poor.

- A new dual role of municipal governments has emerged, which has been formally recognized and strengthened. Municipalities are not only the exclusive providers but also facilitators of services to families and children. Consequently, the role of Mayor has been redefined and enhanced. The Mayor[3] is now the defender of children's rights and facilitator of child and family development. Mayors are recognized for their concern for children and families, not only for building bridges and roads.

- There is a long-range plan for addressing child and family needs and the commitment to the plan extends beyond the Mayor's political term of office.

- All citizens are treated equally, given equal protection under the law, and provided with equal opportunities to develop to their highest potential.

- Democratic processes involve all citizens, including the poorest.

This document offers a flexible system of strategies rather than a fixed plan of action. We hope it will serve as a set of guidelines for cities to develop their own strategic plans uniquely adapted to local conditions.

II. MAYORS SHOULD ASSUME RESPONSIBILITY FOR THE CHILDREN OF THEIR CITIES

Mayors and heads of local government are a focal point for changing cities because of their leadership role. It is proposed that they use this leadership position to mobilize the extraordinary strengths of existing communities in combination with the coordinated energies of existing government and non-governmental organizations and of civil society. Children provide a unique opportunity to achieve widespread social mobilization to create cities that are humane for all. Women's groups have particularly important roles to play in this regard. A fundamental change in the way most cities work with poor urban communities is required to support this effort. Service to communities is replaced by empowerment of, and collaboration with, communities.

III. STRATEGIES FOR IMPLEMENTING THE NEW URBAN VISION

A. Collecting Information for Advocacy and Monitoring

- Help communities to conduct their own situational analyses. Such analyses should be conducted at regular intervals and not be limited to experimental and special project areas. They should also involve residents from different communities in order to develop general citywide social responsibility for children and families between, as well as within, communities.

- Ensure greater use of universities and research centres in collaborative research and community service with communities and in coordination with municipalities.

- Experiment with and develop community-based monitoring systems utilizing tools such as "community balance sheets" that can be easily understood and used by the community. Particular attention should be given to a system for identifying high-risk families and involving them in the monitoring process.

B. Improving Management, Coordination and Convergence

- Establish a Council for Child and Family Development at the city level comprising representatives of NGOs, grassroots organizations and heads of all municipal departments, including finance. The Council should be permanent and its continuity guaranteed across administrations. Its functions should include advice on the coordination, planning and monitoring of all programmes to defend the rights of children. A strategic plan, incorporating the strategies described in this document, should be formulated and administered by The Council for Child and Family Development.

- Instal mechanisms facilitating community-based planning at different levels by the residents themselves. "Community planners," and other community-level workers not tied to any particular agency, would facilitate collaboration with, and between, different sections of communities under the coordination of the Council for Child and Family Development.

- Create a new framework of agency responsibilities which identifies roles and responsibilities for all levels of government.

- Identify new roles for agencies not traditionally concerned with children. Agencies such as transportation and sanitation departments should be given technical assistance/training to help them understand: (1) how their activities have an impact on children, and (2) how they can work better with other agencies to serve families and children.

- Encourage pilot participatory projects in order to foster the self-initiating and self-monitoring capacities of communities.

- Place families and children on municipal council agendas. A report from the Council for Child and Family Development on progress made in programmes should be an item on the agenda of every municipal council meeting.

- Provide coordinating mechanisms so that the energies of international agencies, which often work independently of one another in the same community, do not overlap and compete.

C. Strengthening Legislation

- Make legislation as flexible as possible to give municipalities freedom to apply funds in accordance with community needs and priorities.

- Work towards the implementation of a legal framework based on the international Convention on the Rights of the Child.

- Shift more economic power, and hence political power, from the national to the municipal level. Mayors can join with other mayors to lobby for this change.

- Undertake an early review of all local legislation (by-laws and ordinances), and amend and expand legislation to maximize conformity with the Convention on the Rights of the Child.

- Ensure that equal rights are administered to all children and families (including refugees, migrants and other disadvantaged groups).

- Create necessary legislative instruments to broaden people's rights to the use and ownership of land.

- Encourage and support the establishment of independent committees for the Defence of Children's Rights in each city. These committees would perform legal surveillance of conformity with the Convention on the Rights of the Child.

D. Optimizing Resources and Investment

- Establish community-based decision-making processes including micro-planning, to facilitate the transfer of decision-making on funds and resources to the lowest feasible operational level, i.e., the community.

- Review and, where necessary, restructure municipal revenue and expenditure patterns in order to improve revenue collection and ensure judicious management of expenditures and thereby to release enhanced financial support for child development programmes.

- Integrate sectoral services, streamline the bureaucracy and avoid overlapping of actions in order to prevent waste of scarce resources. Aim for more cost-effective responses (i.e., better and increased services at reduced costs).

- Intensify lobbying for greater debt-reduction and "debt swaps" aimed at promoting child development programmes at municipal and national levels.

- Make more effective use of tax rebate incentives to encourage profit-sharing for child development by city-level industrialists and business establishments. Consider the feasibility of setting-up a city-level Special Fund for Child Development, to be administered by the Council for Child and Family Development and to be used for the voluntary sector to develop programmes for children and their families.

- Encourage optimum use of public facilities, such as schools and community centres, by opening them up for multiagency use.

- National and international agencies should provide municipalities and community organizations with technical advice and guidance on how to involve the local business community in child development.

- Publish annual citywide reports of expenditures on children and on the progress of programmes for children.

- Establish a minimum permissible share of the municipal budget for child development purposes.

- Lobby at the national level for greater political, legislative and resource support to translate the new vision of childhood into action.

E. Empowering People Through Community and Organizational Development

- Expand training for all (including children, youth and community leaders) in the skills of community participation. This should include curriculum development and teacher training to enable schools to work with planners to involve children in the analysis of problems in their communities, particularly those which directly concern them. Provide training opportunities for municipal officials who desire to enhance their abilities in participatory decision-making.

- Provide opportunities for adolescents' and women's participation in income earning and decision-making by ensuring that operational guidelines exist for the implementation of suitable municipal programmes.

- Establish Children's Assemblies and Youth Councils as ongoing mechanisms for involving children and youth in community development and community management.

- Ensure that community-based organizations have unhindered access to all levels of decision-making.

- Support associations of working adolescents, including working children, to provide protection and improve communication and understanding between the children and city agencies. Arrange for statutory provisions to channel municipal resources to strengthen their work.

- Ensure that all children who work due to economic and social circumstances have access to formal or nonformal educational facilities and supportive services which will enable them to acquire an education and vocational skills.

- Improve urban planning and design for children and families by involving the community directly in the process. This will involve the design or redesign of residential areas so that children are not isolated, can socialize with others, and have access to a diverse physical environment for play and recreation.

F. Increasing Public Education and Awareness of the New Vision of Childhood

- Ensure universal primary education for all children and promote adult literacy.

- Raise public awareness about the situation of urban poor and children at risk, and inform communities and children about their rights and the city services to which they are entitled.

- Introduce the use of the "new vision of childhood" language among all the staff of all municipal agencies to reduce the stigmatization of the urban poor and children-at-risk.

- Work with the media to project a realistic picture of children in difficult circumstances; these children are law-abiding but often unprotected; when some of these children become deviant it is due to compelling circumstances which need to be addressed.

- Strengthen capacities of municipal service providers to be more understanding and open to participatory ways of solving community problems.

NOTES

1. The term "community" is used throughout this document to refer to the smallest possible geographical area with which people identify. The relevant term in the Philippines is "barangay," in India it is "ward level," and in many English-speaking countries it is "neighbourhood."
2. The definition includes: street and working children; abused, abandoned, neglected and mistreated children; children affected by armed conflict and other disasters; substance users and abusers; adolescent mothers; children and AIDS; disabled children; children exchanged for money; urban children in poor urban communities; and children deprived of love, care, attention and supporting relationships.
3. The term "Mayor" is used in this document to refer to all heads of municipal governments.

Bibliography

Achar, D.P., et al. (1988). *Immunization Coverage Assessment in New Modi-kanna Area of Pune.* MJAFI, 44:2, April.

Achola, M. (1989). "Houseworkers in Nairobi: Background and Related Issues." Unpublished report. University of Nairobi.

AIIMS (1985). *Integrated Child Development Services, Annual Surveys, 1979–1982.* New Delhi: Central Technical Committee.

_____ (1990). *ICDS — Evaluation and Research 1975–1988.* New Delhi: Central Technical Committee.

Albanez, T., E. Bustelo, G.A. Cornia, and E. Jespersen (1989). "Economic Decline and Child Survival: The Plight of Latin America in the Eighties." *Innocenti Occasional Papers,* Economic Policy Series, no. 1. Florence: UNICEF International Child Development Centre.

Alexander, M., M. Brigantini, and E. Mendez (1993). "Coping: Substance Use and Abuse with a Special Focus on Inhalants" (forthcoming).

Alliband, T. (1983). *Catalysts of Development, Voluntary Agencies in India.* West Hartford, Conn.: Kumarian Press.

Alves, A. (1991). "Meninos de Rua e Meninos na Rua: Estrutura e Dinâmica Familiar." Report prepared by FLACSO for the Urban Child Project, UNICEF International Child Development Centre in coordination with UNICEF Brasilia, and subsequently published in Fausto, A. and R. Cervini, *O trabalho e a Rua.* São Paulo: Editora Cortez.

Anderson, E. (1990). *Street Wise: Race, Class, and Change in an Urban Community.* Chicago: University of Chicago Press.

ANPPCAN (1991). "Research on Street Children in Kenya." Unpublished report of a study on street children in Kenya, prepared by P. Onyango, K. Orwa, A. Ayako, J.B. Ojwang, and P.W. Kariuki for the Ford Foundation, May 1991.

Antler, S. (1985). "The Rediscovery of Child Abuse," in: *The Social Context of Child Abuse and Neglect*, ed. H.L. Pelton. New York: Human Sciences Press.

Aptekar, L. (1988). *Street Children of Cali*. Durham, NC: Duke University Press.

Arellano-Carandang, M.L. (1987). *Filipino Children Under Stress: Family Dynamics and Therapy*. Metro Manila: Ateneo de Manila University Press.

Arimpoor, J. (1992). *Street Children of Madras: A Situational Analysis*. Uttar Pradesh: National Labour Institute.

Arlacchi, P. (1984). *La Mafia imprenditrice*. Bologna: Il Mulino.

_____ (1988). *Droga e grande criminalità in Italia e nel Mondo*. Caltanissetta-Rome: Salvatore Sciascia Editore.

Arlacchi, P., and J. Lewis (1985). *I Profitti della Camorra nel Mercato Campano dell'eroina*. Studio effettuato per conto della Commissione Parlamentare sul fenomeno della mafia: Roma.

Armstrong W., and T.G. McGee (1985). *Theatres of Accumulation: Studies in Asian and Latin American Urbanization*. London: Methuen & Co.

Arrighi, G. (1992). "Per esempio ... esaminiamo il rapporto fra volontariato e servizi territoriali." *Comune Aperto*, vol. 2.

Bagnasco, A. (1986). *Torino: un profilo sociologico*. Turin: Einaudi.

Baguioro, Bing et al. (1992). *Help Wanted: Street Educators. A Primer on Street Education*. Prepared by the Children's Laboratory for Drama in Education for the National Project on Street Children.

Bangert-Drowns, R. (1988). "The Effects of School-Based Substance Abuse Education: A Meta-Analysis." *Journal of Drug Education*, vol. 18.

Barba, A. (1992). "Income Distribution in the Republic of the Philippines." *ASIA, Manila Bulletin*, April 4.

Barbagli, M. (1988). *Sotto lo stesso tetto: mutamenti della famiglia dal XV al XX secolo*. Bologna: Il Mulino.

_____ (1990). *Provando e riprovando: matrimonio, famiglia e divorzio in Italia e negli altri paesi occidentali*. Bologna: Il Mulino.

Battle, S.F. (1990). "Homeless Women and Children: The Question of Poverty," in: *Homeless Children: The Watchers and the Waiters*. ed. N.A. Boxill. New York: The Haworth Press.

Belsky, J. (1978). "Three Theoretical Models of Child Abuse: A Critical Review." *Child Abuse and Neglect*, vol. 2.

Bequele, A. (1991). "Emerging Perspectives in the Struggle Against Child Labour," in: *Protecting Working Children*, ed. W.E. Myers. London: Zed Books Ltd.

Bequele, A., and J. Boyden (1988). "Child Labour: Problems, Policies and Programmes," in: *Combating Child Labour*, eds. A. Bequele and J. Boyden. Geneva: International Labour Office.

Berg, R.J. (1987). *Non-Governmental Organisations: New Force in Third World Development and Politics*. East Lansing: Center for Advanced Study of International Development, Michigan State University.

Berterame, S. (1991). Report on a trip to India, prepared for the Urban Child Project, UNICEF International Child Development Centre, Florence: Italy.

Bhatnagar, S. (1986). *Health Care Delivery Model in Urban Slums of Delhi*. New Delhi: National Institute of Health and Family Welfare.

Black, M. (1990). *Children and AIDS: An Impending Calamity*. New York: UNICEF.

_____ (1991a). *AIDS and Orphans in Africa*. New York: UNICEF.

_____ (1991b). "Philippines: Children of the Runaway Cities." *Innocenti Studies*, Urban Child in Difficult Circumstances. Florence: UNICEF International Child Development Centre.

Blanc Szanton, M. C. (1972). *A Right to Survive. Subsistence Marketing in a Lowland Philippine Town*. University Park, Penn.: The Pennsylvania State University Press (reprinted by Ateneo de Manila Press 1976).

_____ (1985). "Street Food Demand and Consumption in Chonburi Town." Report prepared for a meeting with Bangkok Municipal Authorities and Representatives of the Ministry of Interior, sponsored by the Equity Policy Center, Washington, DC and the Ford Foundation, Jakarta, and held in Bangkok, Chulalongkorn University, Social Science Research Institute, Spring 1985.

_____ (1990). "Collision of Cultures: Historical Reformulations of Gender in the Lowland Visayas, Philippines," in: *Power and Difference: Gender in Island Southeast Asia*, eds. J.M. Atkinson and S. Errington. Stanford: Stanford University Press.

Blanc, C.S. (1991). "Street and Working Children — Field Perspectives." *Innocenti Update*, no. 10, December. Florence: UNICEF International Child Development Centre.

Blanc, C.S., and P. Chiozzi (1992). "Children of Migrants and Ethnic Minorities: An Overview and Conceptual Framework." *Innocenti Occasional Papers*, Urban Child Series, no. 5. Florence: UNICEF International Child Development Centre.

Blanc, C.S., E. Porio, P. Mehta, and W. Mouru (1994). "Life Paths: Off and On the Street." UNICEF International Child Development Centre (forthcoming).

Blanc Szanton, C. (1992). "Urban Children in Distress: An Introduction to the Issues." *Innocenti Occasional Papers*, Urban Child Series, no. 2. Florence: UNICEF International Child Development Centre.

Blok, A. (1974). *The Mafia of a Sicilian Village, 1860–1960*. New York: Harper and Row.

Bornstein, M.H., and H.G. Bornstein (1992). "Infancy," in: *Development of Children from Infancy through Adolescence*, eds. C. Landers and C. Blanc. New York: UNICEF.

Bose, A.B. (1980). "Welfare of Children in Need of Care and Protection," in: *Profile of the Child in India*. New Delhi: Government of India, Ministry of Social Welfare.

_____ (1990). "The Urban Informal Sector Revisited; Some Lessons from the Field." *Discussion Paper*, no. 276, July 1990. Brighton: Institute of Development Studies.

_____ (1992). "The Disadvantaged Urban Child in India." *Innocenti Occasional Papers*, Urban Child Series, no. 1. Florence: UNICEF International Child Development Centre.

Botvin, G. (1985). "The Life Skills Training Program as a Health Promotion Strategy: Theoretical Issues and Empirical Findings," in: *Health Promotion in the School*, ed. J. Zinis. New York: Haworth Press.

Boxill, N.A. (Ed.) (1990). *Homeless Children: The Watchers and the Waiters*. New York: The Haworth Press.

Boyden, J., and P. Holden (1991). *Children of the Cities*. London: Zed Books.

Boys Club of America (1986–87). *Targeted Outreach Newsletter*, vols. II-1 and III-1.

Bradshaw, J. (1990). "Child Poverty and Deprivation in the UK." *Innocenti Occasional Papers*, Economic Policy Series, no. 8. Florence: UNICEF International Child Development Centre.

Braucht, N., et al. (1973). "Deviant Drug Use in Adolescents: A Review of Psychosocial Correlates." *Psychoanalytical Bulletin*, vol. 79.

Brazilian Information Center on Drugs (1989). *Encontro de Centros Brasileiros de Tratamento de Dependência de Drogas*. Edited by Centro de Pesquisa em Psicobiologia Clinica do Departamento de Psicobiologia da Escola Paulista de Medicina. São Paulo: CLR Balieiro Editores Ltda.

Brigantini, M. (1988). "Imputato speciale: genesi della giustizia minorile in Italia." Unpublished thesis in sociology. University of Rome.

_____ (1990). "Primo rapporto di ricerca: diffusione ed uso di sostanze stupefacenti, con particolare rilievo al 'solvent abuse,' in alcuni stati del mondo." Report prepared for the Urban Child Project, UNICEF International Child Development Centre. Florence.

Bronfenbrenner, U. (1978). *The Ecology of Human Development*, Cambridge: Harvard University Press.

_____ (1986). "Ecology of the Family as a Context for Human Development: Research Perspectives." *Developmental Psychology*, 22/6.

_____ (1989). "Who Cares for Children?" Paris: Unit for Cooperation with UNICEF and WFP, UNESCO.

Bruce, F. (1991). *L'Exploitation Sexuelle des Enfants: Analyse du Problème-Des Solutions Courageuses*. Paris: Fayard.

Bruce, J. (1989). "Homes Divided." *World Development*, 17/7.

Bruner, C. (1988). *Family Preservation Services in Iowa: A Legislator's Perspective on Key Issues*. Washington, DC: Center for the Study of Social Policy.

Burra, N. (1986a). "Child Labour in India: Poverty, Exploitation, and Vested Interest." *Social Action*, vol. 36.

_____ (1986b). "Glass Factories of Firozabad, II: Plight of Child Workers." *Economic and Political Weekly XXI* 22/47:2033–2036.

_____ (1987). "A Report on Child Labour in the Gem Polishing Industry of Jaipur, Rajasthan, India, New Delhi." Mimeo.

_____ (1988). "A Report on Child Labour in the Pottery Industry of Khurja, Uttar Pradesh." Paper presented at the Second Asian Regional Conference on Child Abuse and Neglect, 8–13 February 1988, Bangkok.

Burt, M.R., and B.E. Cohen (1989). "America's Homeless: Numbers, Characteristics, and Programs that Serve Them," in: *Urban Institute Report 89-3*. Washington: Urban Institute Press.

Bwibo, N.O., and P.P.M. Onyango (Eds.) (1985). "Children in Especially Disadvantaged Circumstances," in: *Proceedings of the Regional Pre-Workshop on Children in Especially Disadvantaged Circumstances* (Nairobi, Kenya, 10–11 April 1985, Sponsored by UNICEF in collaboration with the University of Nairobi).

CAM Telefono Azzurro (1990). *Campione delle denunce telefoniche sulla violenza sui bambini*. Naples.

Cangialosi, M.R. (1988). "Come i monelli diventano gangster." *Cronache parlamentari siciliane*, September.

Caritas (1986). "The City of the Poor." *Caritas International Quarterly*, no. 1, March.

Carlini-Cotrim, B., and E.A. Carlini (1987). "O consumo de solventes e outras drogas em crianças e adolescentes de baixa renda na grande São Paulo, Parte II." *Revista de ABP/APAL*, no. 9.

Carrera, M. (1987). "Multi-Service Family Life and Sex Education Program." Report from Children's Aid Society, New York.

CBIA — Centro Brasileiro para a Infância e Adolescência (1991). *Vale a Pena Lutar. Diretrizes Basicas e Missão Institucional*. Brasilia: Federal Government of Brazil.

CENSIS (1990). "Analisi sulla dispersione scolastica in Italia in aree di rischio e disagio educativo." Rome: CENSIS

_____ (1991). *Analisi di dati nazionali sulla sanità*. Rome: CENSIS.

_____ (1992). *Dossier Infanzia: Il Bambino come Soggetto, Note e Commenti*, Anno XXVIII, no. 5. Rome: Stampa Edigraf.

Central Bank (1991). *Central Bank Notes*, 2nd quarter. Manila: Central Bank.

Central Bureau of Correctional Services (1970). *Juvenile Delinquency: A Challenge*. New Delhi: Department of Social Welfare.

Central Bureau of Statistics, Republic of Kenya (1992). *Economic Survey 1990*, Ministry of Planning and National Development.

Centre for Juvenile Justice, Molise and Campania (1983). Report prepared for the Region, Naples. Mimeo.

Chambers, C. (1973). "An Assessment of Drug Use in the General Population," in: *Special Report No. 1 Drug Use in New York State*. NY State Narcotic Addict Central Commission.

Chatterjee, A. (1992). "India: The Forgotten Children of the Cities." *Innocenti Studies*, Urban Child in Difficult Circumstances. Florence: UNICEF International Child Development Centre.

Chatterjee, M., and V. Kapoor (1990). *A Report on Indian Women from Birth to Twenty*. New Delhi: Women's Development Division, National Institute of Public Cooperation and

Child Development.

_____ (1991). "Towards the Development of a Programme for Adolescent Girls and Young Mothers in India." Report for the UNICEF ICDC Urban Child Project presented at the planning workshop "Meeting the Basic Learning Needs of Adolescent Girls/Mothers," 9–11 March 1992, Florence, Italy.

Chelimsky, E. (1982). Statement before the Sub-Committee on Human Resources in the Runaway Homeless Youth Program. US House of Representatives on Education and Labor. Washington, DC: US Government Printing Office.

Cherlin, A.J. (1988). "Introduction," in: *The Changing American Family and Public Policy*, ed. A.J. Cherlin. Washington, DC: The Urban Institute Press.

Childhope/NCSD (1989). "The Street Girls of Metro Manila: Vulnerable Victims of Today's Silent Wars." *Research Series*, no. 1. Manila: Childhope/National Council of Social Development Foundation of Philippines, Inc.

Childhope (1993). *The Street Children of Asia: A Profile*. Manila: Childhope Asia.

Children's Environments Quarterly (1988). *Street Children and Children in Homeless Families*, vol. 5, no. 1, Spring.

CINI (1988). *Situational Analysis of Women and Children in Urban Areas of West Bengal*. Daulatpur: CINI.

COESNICA, Commission for Study of Street Children (1992). *Mexico City: Street Children Study*, Executive Summary. Mexico City.

Cohen, S. (1976). *Why Solvents?*, A research report presented at the First International Symposium on the Deliberate Inhalation of Industrial Solvents, Mexico.

Collier, J. (1945). "The United States Indian Service as a Laboratory of Ethnic Relations." *Social Research*, vol. 12.

Collins, W.A. (1991). "Development During Middle Childhood," in: *Development of Children from Infancy through Adolescence*, ed. C. Landers. New York: UNICEF.

Commissione Povertà (1985). *La povertà in Italia*. Rome: Istituto Tipografico di Stato.

Connolly, M. (1990). "Adrift in the City: A Comparative Study of Street Children in Bogota, Colombia, and Guatemala City," in: *Homeless Children: The Watchers and the Waiters*, ed. N.A. Boxill. New York: The Haworth Press.

Consiglio di Zona (1977). "Guida alla zona 20." Milan.

Consiglio Nazionale dei Minori (1988). *I minori in Italia*. Milan: Angeli.

Cook, S. (1984). "The 1954 Social Science Statement on School Desegregation: A Reply to Gerard." *The American Psychologist*, 39/8.

Cornia, G.A. (1990). "Child Poverty and Deprivation in Industrialized Countries: Recent Trends and Policy Options." *Innocenti Occasional Papers*, Economic Policies Series, no. 2, Florence: UNICEF International Child Development Centre.

Cornia, G.A., R. Jolly, and F. Stewart (Eds.) (1987). *Adjustment with a Human Face*, Vol. 1: *Protecting the Vulnerable and Promoting Growth*. Oxford: Oxford University Press.

Cornia, G.A., R. van der Hoeven, and T. Mkandawire (Eds.) (1992). *Africa's Recovery in the 1990s: From Stagnation and Adjustment to Human Development*. London: The Macmillan Press.

Costarelli, S. (1992). "Il bambino migrante a Firenze." Unpublished research paper, Urban Child Project, Istituto degli Innocenti, Florence.

Courier, J. (1988). "Structural Adjustment." *Structural Adjustment*, no. 111, September/October.

Cousins, W. J. and C. Goyder (1986). "Hyderabad Urban Community Development Project," in: *Reaching the Urban Poor — Project Implementation in Developing Countries*, ed. G. Shabbir Cheema. Westview Special Studies in Political and Economic Development. Boulder, CO: Westview Press.

Cowen, E. and E. Gesten (1978). "Community Approaches to Intervention," in: *Handbook of Treatment of Mental Disorders in Childhood and Adolescence*, eds. B. Wolman, J. Egan, and A. Ross. Englewood Cliffs, NJ: Prentice-Hall.

CRESM (1989). "Domanda di concorso del programma comunitario per una integrazione economica e sociale dei gruppi meno favoriti." Naples.

Crisantino, A. (1990). *La città spugna: Palermo nella ricerca sociologica*. Palermo: Centro siciliano di documentazione Giuseppe Impastato.

CWC, The Committee for Working Children (1992). *Street Children of Bangalore: A Situational Analysis*. A study conducted for the Ministry of Social Welfare, Government of India and UNICEF. New Delhi: National Labour Institute.

D'Alessandro, G. (1990). "La condizione dei minori in Italia." Unpublished research paper, Urban Child Project, Istituto degli Innocenti, Florence.

Dallape, F. (1987). *An Experience with Street Children*. Nairobi: Undugu Society of Kenya.

_____ (1991). "Undugu Society of Kenya." Paper prepared for the Urban Child Project, UNICEF International Child Development Centre, Florence.

Damania, R. (1988). *Reaching Out to Street Children: The Programme Strategies*. Unpublished Report for UNICEF, New Delhi.

Dangerous Drug Board (1990). "Study on the Nature and Characteristics of Solvent/Inhalant Abuse in the Philippines." Report for the World Health Organization (WHO), December.

Danziger, S., and J. Stern (1990). "The Causes and Consequences of Child Poverty in the United States." *Innocenti Occasional Papers*, Economic Policy Series, no. 10. Florence: UNICEF International Child Development Centre.

Dasgupta, A. (1990). "Causes of Prostitution and Methods of Prevention." *Social Welfare*, June. Calcutta.

Das Gupta, M. (1987). "Selective Discrimination against Female Children in Rural Punjab, India." *Population and Development Review*, 13/1.

Dass, J.R. and V.P. Garg (1985). *Impact of Pre-Primary Education on Drop-Out Stagnation and Academic Performance*. New Delhi: Education Department, Municipal Corporation of Delhi.

Davidson, J. (1988). "Reducing Adolescent Illiteracy," *TEC Networks*, 18.

Dawson, D. (1986). "Effects of Sex Education on Adolescent Behavior." *Family Planning Perspectives*, 18.

Deelstra, T. and J.P. de Waart (1989). "The Concept of Resourceful Cities Fit to Live In: Outline of Problems, Points of Discussion," in: *The Resourceful City: Management Approaches to Efficient Cities Fit to Live In: Proceedings of the MAB-11 Workshop* (September 13–16, 1989), ed. E.M. Deelstra. Amsterdam: Royal Netherlands Academy of Arts and Sciences.

de Florio La Rocca, C. (1992). "Oltre l'indignazione," in: *Axe*. Rome: Terra Nuova.

de Guzman, L. (1969). *The Philippines Department of Social Welfare, Its Establishment and Historical Development*. Manila: Department of Social Welfare.

Dei, M. (1987). "Lo sviluppo della scolarità femminile in Italia." *Polis*, no. 1.

Demetrio, D. and G. Favaro (1992). *Immigrazione e pedagogia interculturale. Bambini, adulti, comunità nel percorso di integrazione*. Florence: La Nuova Italia.

De Nardis, P. (1990). "La normativa: dal garantismo all'indagine sociologica," in: Consiglio Nazionale dei minori, *I Minori in Italia*. Milan: Angeli.

Department of Education (1986). *National Policy on Education, 1986*. New Delhi: Government of India.

_____ (1990). *Annual Report 1989–90*. New Delhi: Government of India.

Department of Social Welfare and Development (DSWD). National Council of Social Development Foundation of the Philippines (NCSD), and UNICEF (1988), *The Situation of Street Children in Ten Cities*. Manila: DSWD, NCSD and UNICEF.

Department of Social Welfare (1968). *Report of the Committee for the Preparation of a Programme for Children*. New Delhi: Department of Social Welfare, Government of India.

Designs for Change (1985). *The Bottom Line: Chicago's Failing Schools and How to Save Them*. School Watch, Report no. 1, Chicago.

De Souza, A. (1979). *Children in India: Critical Issues in Human Development*. New Delhi: Manohar.

Di Nicola, P. (1989). "Famiglia, infanzia, adolescenza," in: *Primo rapporto sulla famiglia in Italia*, ed. P.P. Donati. Milan: Paoline.

_____ (1990). "I minori tra famiglia e Welfare State," in: Consiglio Nazionale dei Minori, *I Minori in Italia*, Milan: Angeli.

Dingwaney, M., et al. (1988). *Children of Darkness A Manual on Child Labour in India*. New Delhi: Rural Labour Cell.

Dionela, Ana (1992). "Assessing Interventions: Myths and Realities." Evaluation report prepared for Urban Child Project, UNICEF International Child Development Centre and UNICEF Manila.

Di Pasquale, A. (Ed.) (1990). "La condizione dei minori nella città di Palermo." Unpublished report, Urban Child Project, Istituto degli Innocenti, Florence.

Direzione Generale dei Servizi Civili, *Politiche sociali per l'infanzia e l'adolescenza*. Milan: UNICOPLI.

District Court of Appeals (1990). "Reports, Jan.–Aug. 1990." Milan: District Court of Appeals.

D'Lima, H. and R. Gosalia (1989). *Situation Analysis of Street Children in the City of Bombay*. Bombay: College of Social Work.

Donohue, J. (1982). "Facts and Figures on Urbanization in the Developing World." *Assignment Children*, nos. 57/58.

Donzelot, J. (1979). *The Policing of Families*. New York: Pantheon Books.

Draibe, S.M. (1989). "As Políticas Sociais Brasileiras: Diagnósticos e Perspectivas," in: *Para a Década de 90: Prioridades e Perspectivas de Politicas Publicas*. Brasilia: IPEA/IPLAN.

Dryfoos, J.G. (1990). *Adolescents at Risk. Prevalence and Prevention*. New York: Oxford University Press.

Du Bois, C. (1980). "Some Anthropological Hindsights." *Annual Review of Anthropology*, vol. 9.

Duhl, L.J. (1990). *The Social Entrepreneurship of Change*. New York: Pace University Press.

Dwyer, D.J. (1979). "The Problem of In-Migration and Squatter Settlement in Asian Cities: Two Case Studies, Manila and Victoria-Kowloon," in: *Changing Southeast Asian Cities*, eds. Y.M. Yueng and C.P. Lo. Singapore: Oxford University Press.

Edelman, M.W. (1987). *Families in Peril: An Agenda for Social Change*. Cambridge: Harvard University Press.

Ekblad, S., et al. (1991). *Stressors, Chinese City Dwellings and Quality of Life*. Stockholm: Swedish Council for Building Research.

_____ (1993). "Urban Stress and Its Effects on Children's Lifestyles and Health in Industrialized Countries" (forthcoming).

Elder, G.H. Jr. (1974). *Children of the Great Depression*. Chicago: The University of Chicago Press.

Ennew, J. (1993). "Maids of All Work." *New Internationalist*, February.

Environment and Urbanization (1990). "SPARC: Developing New NGO Lines," 2:1, pp. 91–104. London.

Faccioli, F. (1989). "Devianza e controllo istituzionale," in Consiglio Nazionale dei Minori, *I Minori in Italia*. Milan: Angeli.

_____ (1990a). "Devianza e controlli: tendenze e antinomie dell'intervento penale," in Consiglio Nazionale dei Minori, *I Minori in Italia*. Milan: Angeli.

_____ (1990b). *Secondo rapporto sulla condizione dei minori in Italia*. Milan: Angeli.

Family Planning Foundation (FPF) (1987). *Report on Slum Areas of Bombay*. FPF Project on Infant Mortality in Relation to Fertility. New Delhi: FPF.

Faria, V. (1990). "Cinqüenta Anos de Urbanização no Brasil. Tendências e Perspectivas." Mimeo.

_____ (1991). "A Montanha e a Pedra. Os Limites da Política Social Brasileira e os Problemas da Infância e da Juventude." Mimeo.

Fauzi, M.T. Haji (1987). "Report on the Inhalant Abuse Problem in Sarawak East Malaysia." Pemadam, Malaysia.

Fawcett, J.T., S.E. Khoo, and C. Peter (Eds.) (1984). *Women in the Cities of Asia. Migration and Urban Adaptation*. Boulder, CO: Westview Press.

Feldman, L. (Ed.) (1988). *Partnerships for Youth 2000: A Program Models Manual*. Norman, Okla.: The University of Oklahoma, National Resource Center for Youth Services.

Fenelon, G.M., L.C. Martins, and M.H.S. Domingues (1992). *Meninas de Rua: Uma Vida em Movemento*. Goiânia: CEGRAF/UFG.

Ferreira, R.M.F. (1979). *Meninos de Rua: Valores e Expectativas de Menores Marginalizados em São Paulo*. São Paulo: Ibrex.

Fielding N.G., and J.L. Fielding (1986). "Linking Data," in: *Qualitative Research Methods Series*, Vol. 4. Newbury Park, CA: Sage Publications.

Figurato M. and F. Airolda (1981). *Storia di Contrabbando Napoli 1945–1981*. Naples: Pironti.

FLACSO/UNICEF (1991). "Identification of Characteristics of Family Dynamics of Street Children and Underemployed Families." Research reports prepared for the Urban Child Project, UNICEF International Child Development Centre in coordination with UNICEF Brasilia, some of which were subsequently published in Fausto, A. and R. Cervini, *O Trabalho e a Rua*. São Paulo: Editoria Cortez.

Fonseka, L., and UNICEF Delhi (1991). Reports prepared by UNICEF Delhi for the Urban Child Project, UNICEF International Child Development Centre, Florence.

Fowler, A. and E. Mbogori (1993). *A Case Study in NGO Urban Community Development: The Undugu Society of Kenya*. Report prepared for Undugu Society, May. Nairobi: Undugu.

Fox, R. (1977). *Urban Anthropology*. New York: Prentice Hall.

Fyfe, A. (1993). *Child Labour: A Guide to Project Design*. Geneva: International Labour Office.

Gachukia, E.W. (1992): "Integrated Child Development Programme for Adolescent Mothers in Kenya. A Situation Analysis." Report prepared for the Urban Child Project, UNICEF International Child Development Centre and presented at the planning workshop "Meeting the Basic Learning Needs of Adolescent Girls/Mothers," 9–11 March 1992, Florence.

Galeano, L. (1991). "O Direito da Criança à Proteção Especial." Mimeo. Brasilia: UNICEF.

Garbarino, J. and D. Sherman (1980). "High risk neighbourhoods and high risk families: the human ecology of child mistreatment." *Child Development*, vol. 51.

Gardini, M.P. and M. Tessari (1992). *L'assistenza domiciliare per i minori*. Rome: La Nuova Italia Scientifica.

George, K.N. (1975). "Child Labour in the City of Madras." Report prepared for the National Seminar on Employment of Children, 25–28 November 1975, New Delhi.

Gerard, H.B. (1983). "School Desegregation: The Social Science Role." *The American Psychologist*, 38/8.

Gibson, M. (1991). "Italy," in: *Children in Historical and Comparative Perspective: An International Handbook and Research Guide*, eds. J.M. Hawes and N.R. Hiner. New York: Greenwood Press.

Gilbert A. and J. Gugler (1983). *Cities, Poverty and Development. Urbanization in the Third World*. Oxford: Oxford University Press.

Ginsburg, E., H. Berliner, and M. Ostow (1988). *Young People at Risk: Is Prevention Possible?* Boulder, CO: Westview Press.

Goldstein, S. "Glue Sniffing: The Volatile Solvents." *Public Health Review*, vol. 2, 1973. Why Solvents? A Research Report presented at the First International Symposium on the Deliberate Inhalation of Industrial Solvents, Mexico 1976.

Gomes da Costa, A.C. (1989). "De menor a cidadao. Cidadao-criança e cidadao-adolescente." Brasilia: UNICEF. Mimeo.

Gonçalves, Z.d.A. (1979). *Meninos de Rua e a Marginalidade Urbana em Belém*. Belém: Salesianos do Pará.

Goonesekere, S.W.E. (1993). *Child Labour in Sri Lanka: Learning from the Past*. Geneva: International Labour Office.

Gopalan, C. (1984–85). "Maternal Nutrition: The Foundation of Child Health." *Future*, vol. 13.

Goren, A.I. (1989). "Environmental Health in Towns in Israel: Tools for Improvement," in: *The Resourceful City: Management Approaches to Efficient Cities Fit to Live In: Proceedings of the MAB-11 Workshop* (September 13–16, 1989), eds. E.M. Deelstra et al. Amsterdam: Royal Netherlands Academy of Arts and Sciences.

Gottlieb, B. (1981). "Social Networks and Social Support in Community Mental Health," in: *Social Networks and Social Support*, ed. B. Gottlieb. Beverly Hills, CA: Sage.

Gouveia, A.J. (1983). "O Trabalho do Menor — Necessidade Transfigurada em Virtude," in: *Cadernos de Pesquisa*. São Paulo: Fundação Carlos Chagas.

Government of Kenya and UNICEF (1989). *Children and Women in Kenya: A Situation Analysis 1989*. Nairobi: GOK/UNICEF.

_____ (1992). *Children and Women in Kenya: A Situation Analysis 1992*. Nairobi: GOK/UNICEF.

Government of the Philippines and UNICEF (1992). *The Situation of Children and Women in the Philippines*. Manila: UNICEF.

Governo do Estado do Ceará/Secretaria de Ação Social (1988). "Perfil do Menino e Menina de Rua de Fortaleza." Fortaleza. Mimeo.

Greenwood, P., and F. Ziming (1983). *One More Chance: The Pursuit of Promising Intervention Strategies for Chronic Juvenile Offenders*. San Diego: Rand Corporation.

Gupta, J.P., and I. Morali (1989). *National Review of Immunization Programme in India*. New Delhi: National Institute of Health and Family Welfare.

HABITAT (1987). *Global Report on Human Settlements*. New York: Oxford University Press.

Hake, A. (1977). *African Metropolis*. Sussex: Sussex University Press.

Hall, P. (1980). *Great Planning Disasters*. New York: Penguin Books.

_____ (1988). *Cities of Tomorrow. An Intellectual History of Urban Planning and Design in the Twentieth Century*. Oxford: Basil Blackwell.

Hannerz, U. (1980). *Exploring the City: Inquiries Towards an Urban Anthropology*. New York: Columbia University Press.

Hardoy, A. and J.E. Hardoy (1991). "Building Community Organisation: The History of a Squatter Settlement and its own Organisations in Buenos Aires." *Environment and Urbanization*, 3/2.

Hardoy, J.E. (1992). "The Urban Child in the Third World: Urbanization Trends and Some Principal Issues." *Innocenti Occasional Papers*, Urban Child Series, no. 4. Florence: UNICEF International Child Development Centre.

Hardoy, J.E., S. Cairncross, and D. Satterthwaite (Eds.) (1990). *The Poor Die Young. Housing and Health in Third World Cities*. London: Earthscan Publications.

Hardoy, J.E., and D. Satterthwaite (1989). *Squatter Citizen: Life in the Urban Third World*. London: Earthscan Publications.

Harkness, S. and C.M. Super (1991). "East Africa," in: *Children in Historical and Comparative Perspective: An International Handbook and Research Guide*, eds. J.M. Hawes and N.R. Hiner. New York: Greenwood Press.

Hart, K. (1973). "Informal Income Opportunities and Urban Employment in Ghana." *Journal of Modern African Studies*, vol. 11.

Hart, R.A. (1992). "Children's Participation: From Tokenism to Citizenship." *Innocenti Essays*, no. 4. Florence: UNICEF International Child Development Centre.

Hart, R.A., Iltus, and R. Mora (1992). *Safe Play for West Farms: Play and Recreation Proposals for the West Farms Area of the Bronx, Based Upon the Residents' Perceptions and Preferences*. New York: Children's Environmental Research Centre, University of New York Graduate School.

Hauser, P.M. and R.W. Gardner (1980). "Urbanization, Urban Growth and Intermediate Cities: Trends and Prospects." Paper prepared for East-West Population Institute Workshop on Intermediate Cities, Honolulu, Hawaii.

Hawes, J.M., N.R. Hiner and Schulz C.B. (1991a). "The United States," in: *Children in Historical and Comparative Perspective: An International Handbook and Research Guide*, eds. J.M. Hawes and N.R. Hiner. New York: Greenwood Press.

Hawes, J.M. and N.R. Hiner (Eds.) (1991b). *Children in Historical and Comparative Perspective: An International Handbook and Research Guide*. New York: Greenwood Press.

Hawkins J. and J. Weis (1985). "The Social Development Model: An Integrated Approach to Delinquency Prevention." *Journal of Primary Prevention*, vol. 6.

Hayes, C.D. (Ed.) (1987). *Risking the Future: Adolescent Sexuality, Pregnancy and Childbearing*, Vol. 1. Washington, DC: National Academy Press.

Hennion, M. (1987). "People's Housing Cooperatives in Vishakapatnam." Report prepared for ORSPOM, Paris: France.

Henriques, M.H., et al. (1989). *Adolescentes de Hoje, Pais de Amanhã: Brasil*. New York: The Alan Guttmacher Institute.

Henry, P.M. (Ed.) (1990). *Pauvrete, Progres et Developpement*. Paris: UNESCO/L'Harmattan.

Hill, P. (1986). *Development Economics on Trial: the Anthropological Case for the Prosecution*. Cambridge: Cambridge University Press.

Himes, J.R., S. Kessler, and C. Landers (1991). "Children in Institutions in Central and Eastern Europe." *Innocenti Essays*, no. 3. Florence: UNICEF International Child Development Centre.

Hixon, M. (1991). "Report on Health and Malnutrition." Report prepared for UNICEF, Manila.

Horowitz, B and I. Wolock (1981). "Maternal Deprivation, Child Maltreatment, and Agency Intervention among Poor Families," in: *The Social Context of Child Abuse and Neglect*, ed. L.H. Pelton. New York: Human Services Press.

Hughes, B. (1990). "Children's Play — A Forgotten Right." *Environment and Urbanization* 2/2.

Hunter-Geboy, L., et al. (1985). *Life Planning Education: A Youth Development Program*. Washington, DC: Center for Populations Options.

IBASE (1990). "Contagem de Crianças de Rua no Municipio de Salvador/Bahia." Mimeo.

IBGE (1989) *Familia: Indicadores Sociais*, vol. 1. Rio de Janeiro: IBGE.

_____ (1990). *Síntese de Indicadores da Pesquisa Básica da PNAD de 1981 a 1989*. Rio de Janeiro: IBGE.

IBGE/UNICEF (1989). *Crianças e Adolescentes — Indicadores Sociais*, vol. 1. Rio de Janeiro: IBGE/UNICEF.

IBON (1990). "Facts and Figures." *IBON*, October. Santa Mesa, Manila.

Ikiara, G.K. (1992): "The Challenge from Kenya's Economically Marginalized Groups." Paper presented at the Law Society of Kenya Conference on The Rule of Law and Democracy in the 1990s and Beyond, March. Nairobi.

ILO (1972). *Employment, Incomes and Equality: A Strategy for Increasing Productive Employment in Kenya*. Geneva: International Labour Organisation.

Inciardi, J. A., R. Horowitz and A.E. Pottieger (1993). *Street Kids, Street Drugs, Street Crime: An Examination of Drug Use and Serious Delinquency in Miami*. Belmont, CA: Wadsworth Publishing Company.

Indian Council of Medical Research (ICMR) (1974). *Studies on Pre-School Children*. ICMR Technical Report Series No. 26. New Delhi: ICMR.

_____ (1989). *Epidemiological Survey of Endemic Goitre and Endemic Centrism*. New Delhi: ICMR.

_____ (1990). *A National Collaborative Study of Identification of High Risk Families, Mothers and Outcome of their Offsprings with Particular Reference to the Problem of Maternal Nutrition Low Birth Weight Perinatal and Infant Morbidity and Mortality in Rural and Urban Slum Communities*. New Delhi: ICMR.

Institute of Psychological and Educational Research (IPER) (1989). *Situation Analysis of Street Children in the City of Calcutta*. Calcutta: IPER.

International Development Research Centre (1988). *The Learning Environments of Early Childhood in Asia.* Bangkok: UNESCO.

Iosa, A. (1970). *I quartieri di Milano.* Milan: Centro culturale Perini.

_____ (1975). *Rilevazione statistico-sociografica a carattere esplorativo sul quartiere Q.O.* Milan: Centro studi PIM and Centro culturale Parini.

IPEA/IPLAN (1989). *Para a Década de 90. Prioridades e Perspectivas de Políticas Públicas: Políticas Sociais e Organização do Trabalho.* Brasilia: IPEA/IPLAN.

IPLANCE (1980). *O Trabalho do Menor no Setor Informal.* Fortaleza: IPLANCE.

IRER (1987). *Gli istituti per minori in Lombardia.* Milan: Angeli.

ISTAT (1981). *Censimento 1980.* Rome: ISTAT.

_____ (1985a). XXI Conference of European Ministers Responsible for Family Affairs (1990) Report. Paris: OECD.

_____ (1985b). *Indagine sulla frequenza scolastica.* Rome: ISTAT.

_____ (1988). *Indagine sulle strutture ed i comportamenti familiari.* Rome: ISTAT.

_____ (1989). *Rapporto sull'immigrazione extra-comunitaria in Italia.* Rome: ISTAT.

_____ (1991a). *Censimento 1990.* Rome: ISTAT.

_____ (1991b). *Elaborazione dei dati dell'Ufficio di Giustizia Minorile.* Rome: ISTAT.

_____ (1991c). *L'Italia in cifre.* Rome: ISTAT.

Ives, R. (1990). "The Fad that Refuses to Fade." *Druglink*, Sept.–Oct.

Jalloh, M. and S. Alston (1988). "Mantalk: A Pregnancy Prevention Program for Teen Males." Paper presented at the Annual Meeting of the American Public Health Association, Boston, November 1988.

Janowsky, E. (1991). *Street Children and Street Education in Guatemala City and Tegucigalpa, Honduras.* Unpublished thesis, Tulan School of Public Health.

Jazairi, N.T. (1976). *Approaches to the Development of Health Indicators.* Paris: OECD.

Jelin, E. (1989). "Buenos Aires: Class Structure, Urban Policy and the Urban Poor," in: *Cities in Crisis*, eds. M. Edel and R.G. Hellman. New York: Bildner Center for Western Hemisphere Studies.

_____ (1991). "Everyday Practices, Family Structures, Social Processes," in: *Family, Household and Gender Relations in Latin America*, ed. E. Jelin. London: Kegan Paul International/UNESCO.

Jennett, C., and G.S. Randall (1989). *Politics of the Future: The Role of Social Movements.* Australia: MacMillan.

Jessor, R. and S. Jessor (1977). *Problem Behavior and Psychosocial Development: A Longitudinal Study of Youth.* New York: Academic Press.

Jimenez, P., and E. Chiong-Javier (1992). "Philippines Urban Poor Situation." A Post-EDSA Analysis. Paper presented at the UNICEF International Child Development Centre Urban Child Project Meeting, March 1990, Manila.

Jimenez, P. Ramos, E. Chiong-Javier, and J.C.C. Sevilla (1986). *Philippine Urban Situation Analysis.* Manila: UNICEF.

Johnson, K. (1987). *SRS Substitute Care and Intensive Family-Based Services in Vermont.* Montpelier: Vermont Coalition for Runaway Youth Services.

Kambargi, R. (1988). "Child Labour in India: the Carpet Industry of Varanasi," in: *Combating Child Labour*, eds. A. Bequele and J. Boyden. Geneva: International Labour Organization.

Kaminsky, D.C., and J. Wright (1992). "Project Alternatives Comprehensive Health Services for Children 'of' and 'in' the Streets of the City of Tegucigalpa and their Families: Preliminary Report." Unpublished paper.

Kaplan C.D. (1977). "The Heroin System: A General Economy of Crime and Addiction." *Crime and Justice*, November.

Kattambo, V.M. (1991). "The Needs of the Urban Child in Especially Difficult Circumstances — A Case Study." Report prepared for the Urban Child Project, UNICEF International Child Development Centre, Florence. Mimeo. Nairobi.

Kenyan Ministry of Health (1988). *Schoolgirl Pregnancy in Kenya. Report of a Study of Discontinuation Rates and Associated Factors.* Nairobi: Ministry of Health, Division of Family Health.

Kerckhoff, A. (1972). "The Structure of the Conjugal Relationship in Industrial Societies," in: *Cross National Family Research,* eds. M.B. Sussman and B.E. Cogswell. Leiden: E.J. Brill.

Khatu, K.K., et al. (1983). *Working Children in India.* Baroda: Operations Research Group.

Kidder, L.H. (1981). "Qualitative Research and Quasi-Experimental Framework," in: *Scientific Inquiry and the Social Sciences,* eds. M.B. Brewer and B.E. Collins. San Francisco: Jossey-Bass.

Kirby, D. (1984). *Sexuality Education: An Evaluation of Programs and Their Effect.* California: Network.

Köhler, L. and G. Jakobsson (1991). *Children's Health in Sweden: An Overview for the 1991 Public Health Report.* Stockholm: The Swedish National Board of Health and Welfare.

Koo, H. and P.C. Smith (1983). "Migration, the Urban Informal Sector and Earnings in the Philippines." *The Sociological Quarterly,* vol. 24, Spring.

Korman M., et al. (1977) *A Psychosocial and Neuropsychological Study of Young Inhalant Users. Preliminary Findings.* Dallas: University of Texas Health Science Center.

Korten, D.C. (1990). *Getting to the 21st Century: Voluntary Action and the Global Agenda.* Connecticut: Kumarian Press, Inc.

Kothari, S. (1983). "There's Blood on Those Matchsticks — Child Labour in Sivakasi." *Economic and Political Weekly,* 18/27.

Kuznesof, E.A. (1987). "Perspective on Children." Final Report of the Child Labor and Health Research, WHO and the University of Nairobi.

_____ (1991). "Brazil," in: *Children in Historical and Comparative Perspective: An International Handbook and Research Guide,* eds. J.M. Hawes and N.R. Hiner. New York: Greenwood Press.

Le Dain, G., et al. (1973). "Final Report of the Commission of Inquiry into the Non-Medical Use of Drugs." Ottawa: Information Canada.

Lee-Smith, D. (1989). "Urban Management in Nairobi: A Case Study of the Matatu Mode of Public Transport," in: *African Cities in Crisis. Managing Rapid Urban Growth.* eds. R.E. Stren and R.R. White. Boulder, CO: Westview Press.

Lee-Smith, D., M. Manundu, D. Lamba and P. Kuria Gathuru (1987). *Urban Food Production and the Cooking Fuel Situation in Urban Kenya.* Nairobi: Mazingira Institute.

Leitenberg, H. (1986). "Primary Prevention in Delinquency," in: *Prevention of Delinquent Behavior,* eds. J. Burchard and S. Burchard. Newbury Park, CA: Sage Publications.

Lerner, R.M. (1991). "Development in Adolescence," in: *The Development of Children from Infancy through Adolescence,* eds. C. Landers and C. Blanc (forthcoming).

Levi, L., and L. Andersson (1974). "Population, Environment and Quality of Life." A Contribution to the United Nations World Population Conference, Royal Ministry for Foreign Affairs. Stockholm: Göteborgs Offsettryckeri AB.

Levi, L., and Eckblad, S. (1990). *Environment, Life Conditions and Human Needs in Latin America: Their Dynamics and Psychosocial and Health Implications, A Call For Action.* Montevideo, Uruguay. November 2–15, 1990.

Lewin K. (1947). "Frontiers in Group Dynamics: Social Planning and Action Research." *Human Relations,* vol. 1.

Lewis, O. (1979). *The Children of Sanchez: Autobiography of a Mexican Family.* New York: Random.

Loperfido E., and G. Rigon (1988). *Prevalenza dei disturbi psichici nella popolazione infantile della scuola d'obbligo (6–14 anni).* Bologna: Università di Bologna.

Lorenzo, R. (1992). "Italy: Too Little Time and Space for Childhood." *Innocenti Study,* Urban Child in Difficult Circumstances. Florence: UNICEF International Child Development Centre.

Lowy A., et al. (1990). "Increasing Suicide Rates in Young Adults." *British Medical Journal,* vol. 300, March 10.

Lucchini, R. (1993). *Enfant de Rue: Identité, sociabilité, drogue.* Geneve: Droz.

Lundman, R. (1984). *Prevention and Control of Juvenile Delinquency.* New York: Oxford University Press.

Lusk, M.W. (1989). *Street Children of Rio de Janeiro: Preliminary Issues and Findings.* Rio de Janeiro: Mimeo.

Majumdar, T.K. (1983). *Urbanizing Poor.* New Delhi: Lancers.

Malhotra, D.D. (1992). "A Flicker of Childhood." Report prepared for the Urban Project, UNICEF International Child Development Centre, New Delhi.

Malin, A.S., and R.W. Stones (1988). "Nutritional Anaemia in the Urban Poor: A Community Based Study of Under Fives in an Indian Slum." *Journal of Tropical Paediatrics,* 34, October 1988.

Manganhas, M. (1992). "Indicators for Children in Especially Difficult Circumstances," in: *SEAPRO: Proceedings of the Meeting on Children in Especially Difficult Circumstances.* Bangkok: SEAPRO.

Mangiarotti-Frugiulese, G. (1992). *Sulle tracce dell'infanzia.* Milan: Vita e pensiero.

Manna, E. (1992). "La costruzione sociale dell'infanzia." CENSIS, *Note e commenti,* no. 5.

Manundu, M. (1991). "The Kenyan Urban Case Study of Children in Especially Difficult Circumstances: Economic Aspects." Report prepared for the Urban Child Programme, UNICEF International Child Development Centre, Florence.

_____ (1992a). "Structural Adjustment Programmes in Emerging Democracy — The Case of Kenya." Paper presented at the Law Society of Kenya Conference on The Rule of Law and Democracy in the 1990s and Beyond. Nairobi, March, 1992.

_____ (1992b). Preliminary Report for the Urban Child Programme, UNICEF International Child Development Centre, Florence.

Martinatti, G., et al. (1988). *Milano Ore Sette: Come Vivono i Milanesi.* Milan: Maggioli.

Martine, G. (1989). *A Resolução da Questão Social no Brasil: Experiências Passadas e Perspectivas Futuras.* Brasilia: IPEA/IPLAN.

Mattioli, F. (1989). "Quale lavoro," in Consiglio Nazionale dei Minori, *I Minori in Italia.* Milan: Angeli.

_____ (1990). "Il lavoro rinviato," in Consiglio Nazionale dei Minori.

Mazingira Institute (1989). *Urban Food Production and the Cooking Fuel Situation in Urban Kenya.* National Report, Results of a 1985 National Survey, August 1987.

Mbuguru, E.K. (1992). "The Kenyan Urban Case Study of Children in Especially Difficult Circumstances: Demographic and Migration Aspects." Report prepared for the Urban Child Programme, UNICEF International Child Development Centre, Florence.

McGee, T.G. (1971). "Catalysts or Cancer? The Role of Cities in Asian Society," in: *Urbanization and National Development,* eds. L. Jacobson and V. Prakash, Newbury Park, CA: Sage Publications.

McGuire, T. (1986). "The Situation of Cebu City: Three Hundred and Two Street Children." Research report submitted to UNICEF Manila. Mimeo.

Medeiros, M.S.F. (1985). *O Trabalhador Infantil — Estudo Sobre o Trabalho Autônomo do Menor de Rua.* Master's dissertation. Rio de Janeiro: IUPERJ.

Meny, Y., and T.C. Thoenig (1989). *Politiques Publiques.* Paris: PUF.

Michelson, W. (1984). "Consulting with Children for Urban Planning and Management," in *Collected Reports* (1988), vol. 2. Proceedings of the International Experts Meeting on Ecological Approaches to Urban Planning, sponsored by UNESCO-MAB and UNEP in cooperation with the USSR Commission for UNESCO and the USSR Commission for UNEP, September 24–30, 1984. Moscow: Centre of International Projects of the USSR State Committee for Science and Technology.

Mies, M. (1982). *The Lace Makers of Narsupar: Indian Housewives Produce for the World Market.* London: Zed Press.

Miller, B. (1981). *The Endangered Sex: Neglect of Female Children in Rural North India*. Ithaca: Cornell University Press.

Ministry of Health (1983). *Relazione sullo stato sanitario del Paese 1981–1983*. Rome: Ministero della Sanità.

——— (1986). *Relazione sullo stato sanitario del Paese 1983–1986*. Rome: Ministero della Sanità.

Ministry of Health and Family Welfare (1990). *Annual Report 1989–90*. New Delhi: Government of India.

——— (1991a). *Annual Report 1990–91*. New Delhi: Government of India.

——— (1991b). *Health Information in India*. New Delhi: Directorate General of Health Services.

Ministry of Home Affairs (1983). *Survey of Infant and Child Mortality 1979*. New Delhi: Office of the Registrar General.

Ministry of Justice (1989). *Prima indagine sull'affidamento familiare in Italia*. Rome: Ministero della Grazia e Giustizia.

——— (1991). *Rapporto al Parlamento sulla criminalità giovanile*. Rome: Ministero della Grazia e Giustizia.

Ministry of Labour (1979). *Report of the Committee on Child Labour*. New Delhi: Government of India.

Ministry of Programme Implementation (1989). *Report 1988–89*. New Delhi: Government of India.

Ministry of the Interior — Direzione Generale dei Servizi Civili (1988). *Report of the Permanent Monitoring Centre on Drugs*. Rome: Ministry of the Interior.

——— (1991). *Politiche Sociali per l'infanzia e l'adolescenza*. Milan: Unicopli.

Ministry of Urban Development (1988). "Report of the National Commission on Urbanization," Vol. 2. New Delhi: Government of India.

MNMMR, IBASE, and NEV/USP (1991). *Vidas em Risco: Assassinatos de Crianças e Adolescentes no Brasil*. Rio de Janeiro: MNMMR.

Moerman, M. (1968). *Agricultural Change and Peasant Choice in a Thai Village*. Berkeley: University of California Press.

Mohan, N.C., and S.A. Aiyer (1991). "Poverty: Gap between Myth and Reality." *Economic Times*, 13 September, 1991. New Delhi.

Mohanty, C.T., A. Russo, and L. Torres (Eds.) (1991). *Third World Women and the Politics of Feminism*. Bloomington, Ind: Indiana University Press.

Monnier, A. (1989). "La conjoncture démographique." *Population*, no. 4–5.

Moro, A.F. (1989). *Erode fra noi: La violenza sui minori*. Milan: Mursia.

Morrison, C. (1973). *Income Distribution in Kenya*. Washington, DC: World Bank.

Moser, C. (1989). *Community Participation in Urban Projects in the Third World*. Oxford: Pergamon Press.

——— (1992). "Report on the Effects of Structural Adjustment in Urban Poor Households." Mimeo. Washington, DC: World Bank.

Moura, W. (1991). "A Família Contra a Rua: Uma Análise Psicossociológica da Dinâmica Familiar." Report submitted by FLACSO for the Urban Child Project, "Identification of Characteristics of Family Dynamics of Street Children and Underemployed Families," sponsored by the UNICEF International Child Development Centre in coordination with UNICEF Brasilia and subsequently published in Fausto, A. and R. Cervini, *O Trabalho e a Rua*. São Paulo: Editoria Cortez.

Mukui, J.T. (1992). "Kenya: Economic Performance and Future Prospects." Paper presented at the Law Society of Kenya Conference on The Rule of Law and Democracy in the 1990s and Beyond, March. Nairobi.

Munger, R.L. (1991). *Child Mental Health Practice from the Ecological Perspective*. Lanham, Maryland: University Press of America, Ltd.

Municipality of Milan (1991a). "Analisi di dati anagrafici." Milan: Comune di Milano.

Municipality of Milan, Settore Servizi Sociali (1991b). "Progetto di Assistenza Domiciliare ai Minori." Milan: Comune di Milano.

Municipality of Naples (1981). *La popolazione nei quartieri di Napoli*. Naples: Comune di Napoli.

_____ (1989a). *Elaborazione su dati CED e CEAPRELDA sulla dispersione scolastica a Napoli*. Naples: Comune di Napoli.

_____ (1989b). "Special Report from Registry Office Data." Naples: Comune di Napoli.

_____ (1990). *Rapporto sulla popolazione nei quartieri del comune di Napoli*. Naples: Comune di Napoli, Ufficio Anagrafe.

Municipality of Palermo, Department of Statistics and Census (1989). *Statistiche sulla mortalità infantile/giovanile a Palermo*. Palermo: Comune di Palermo.

Munyakho, D. (1992). "Kenya: Child Newcomers in the Urban Jungle." *Innocenti Studies*, Urban Child in Difficult Circumstances. Florence: UNICEF International Child Development Centre.

Musick, J.S. (1992). "Creating Effective Intervention Programs for Adolescent Mothers: Lessons from Research and Practice." Report for the UNICEF ICDC Urban Child Project presented at the planning workshop "Meeting the Basic Learning Needs of Adolescent Girls/Mothers," 9–11 March 1992, UNICEF International Child Development Centre, Florence.

Mutiso, R. (1989). *Housemaids in Nairobi: A Review of Available Documents on the Subject of Female Domestic Workers in Nairobi*. Report prepared for the Undugu Society, April.

Mutiso, R., and F. Dallape (1992). "UNICEF Project on the Urban Child in Especially Difficult Circumstances: Mombasa and Kisumu." Research report prepared for the Urban Child Project, UNICEF International Child Development Centre, Florence.

Myers, R. (1992). *The Twelve Who Survive: Strengthening Programmes of Early Childhood Development in the Third World*. London: Routledge.

Myers, R., and R. Hertenberg (1987). "The Eleven Who Survive: Toward a Re-Examination of Early Childhood Development Program Options and Costs." *Discussion Paper, Education and Training Series*, Report no. ECT69. Washington, DC: The World Bank.

Myers, W. (1988a). "Alternative Services for Street Children: The Brazilian Approach," in: *Combating Child Labour*, eds. A. Bequele and J. Boyden. Geneva: ILO.

_____ (1988b). "Characteristics of Some Urban Working Children: A Comparison of Four Surveys from South America." Stanford University Law School. Mimeo.

_____ (Ed.) (1989). "Protecting Working Children." *Staff Working Paper*, no. 4. New York: UNICEF.

_____ (1991). "An Agenda for Action," in: *Protecting Working Children*, ed. W.E. Myers. London: Zed Books.

Nangia, P. (1987). *Child Labour: Cause-Effect Syndrome*. New Delhi: Janak Publishers.

National Census and Statistics Office (1992). *Population Census: Advanced Report*. Manila: National Census and Statistics Office.

_____ (1990). *Survey of Income and Expenditures, 3rd Quarter*. Manila: National Census and Statistics Office.

National Centre for Human Settlements and Environment (1987). *A Study for the Formulation of Poverty Alleviation Programmes for Urban Slums*. Bhopal: NCHSE.

National Commission on Urbanization (1988). *Report of the National Commission on Urbanization*, vol. 2. New Delhi: NCU.

National Council of Educational Research and Training (NCERT) (1980). *Fourth All India Educational Survey: Some Statistics on School Education*. New Delhi: NCERT.

_____ (1989). *Fifth All India Educational Survey: Selected Statistics*. New Delhi: NCERT.

National Crime Prevention Council (1987). "The Success of Community Crime Prevention," in *Topics in Crime Prevention*. Washington, DC: National Crime Prevention Council.

National Crime Records Bureau (1990). *Crime in India 1988*. New Delhi: Ministry of Home Affairs, Government of India.

National Institute of Health and Family Welfare (NIHFW) (1986). *Demographic Situation and Utilization of Health Services in Bihar — A Baseline Survey Report*. New Delhi: NIHFW.

National Institute of Public Cooperation and Child Development (NIPCCD) (1989). *Research on ICDS: An Overview*. New Delhi: NIPCCD.

National Institute of Urban Affairs (NIUA) (1988a). *Dimension of Urban Poverty: A Situational Analysis*. Research Studies Series no. 25. New Delhi.

_____ (1988b). *State of India's Urbanization*. New Delhi: NIUA.

_____ (1989). *Profile of the Urban Poor: An Investigation into their Demographic Economic and Shelter Characteristics*. New Delhi: NIUA.

_____ (1991a). *India's Urban Profile*. New Delhi: NIUA.

_____ (1991b). *Urban Child: Factors and Processes of Marginalisation*. Report prepared by P. Metha for the Urban Child Project, UNICEF International Child Development Centre. New Delhi: National Institute of Urban Affairs.

_____ (1992). Preliminary Report and Analysis of Bangalore Urban NGOs. New Delhi. Mimeo.

National Project of Street Children (1989). *Proceedings of the Third National Street Children Conference*, Manila.

_____ (1992a). *A Primer on Street Children*. Manila.

_____ (1992b). Unang Pambansang Congress ng mga Batang Lansangan (Proceedings of the First National Street Children Conference), Manila.

National Sample Survey Organization (NSSO) (1988). *Tables with Notes on Particulars of Dwelling Units*. 38th Round (January–December, 1983). New Delhi: NSSO.

_____ (1990a). "A Profile of Households and Population by Economic Class and Social Group and Availability of Drinking Water; Electricity and Disinfection of Dwellings," 42nd Round (July 1986–June 1987), in *Sarvekshna*, vol. 13, no. 4, April–June, 1990. New Delhi: NSSO.

_____ (1990b). "Results of the Fourth Quinquennial Survey of Employment and Unemployment (All India)," 43rd Round (July 1987 to June 1988), in *Sarvekshna* (Special Number). New Delhi: NSSO.

_____ (1991). "Participation in Education," 42nd Round (July 1986 to June 1987), in *Sarvekshna*, vol. 14, no. 3, January–March, 1991. New Delhi: NSSO.

Naversen, O. (1989). *The Sexual Exploitation of Children in Developing Countries*. Stockholm: Redda Barna.

NCSD National Council of Social Development Foundations (1989). *Report on Street Children*. Manila.

Ndungu, N. (1992). "Kangemi In-Depth Case Study." Report prepared for the Urban Child Project, UNICEF International Child Development Centre, Florence.

Nelson, K.E. (1990). "Program Environment and Organization," in: *Preserving Families: Evaluation Resources for Practitioners and Policymakers*, eds. Y.T. Yuan and M. Rivest. Newbury Park, CA: Sage Publications.

Newman-Black, M. (1991). "The Convention: Child Rights and UNICEF Experience at the Country Level." *Innocenti Studies*. Child Rights. Florence: UNICEF International Child Development Centre.

N.N.I.C.C. National Narcotic Intelligence Consumers Committee (1984). *The Supply of Drugs to the US Illicit Market from Foreign and Domestic Sources*. Washington, DC: US Government Printing Office.

Noormohamed, S.O., and F. Opondo (1989). "Education," in: *Report of Proceedings of the Workshop on The Impact of Structural Adjustment Policies on the Well-Being of the Vulnerable Groups in Kenya*, eds. J.E.O. Odada and A.B. Ayako. Nairobi, November 3–5, 1988. Nairobi: UNICEF, Kenya Country Office and Kenyan Economic Association.

Nuqui, Wilfredo G. (1991a). "The Health Sector and Social Policy Reform in the Philippines since 1985." *Innocenti Occasional Paper*, Economic Policies Series, no. 12. Florence:

UNICEF International Child Development Centre.
_____ (1991b). "The Urban Poor and Basic Infrastructure Services in the Philippines," in: *The Urban Poor and Basic Infrastructure Services in Asia and the Pacific*. Economic Development Institute and the Asian Development Bank.

Oda, M., et al. (1989). "Effects of High-Rise Living on Physical and Mental Development of Children." *Journal of Human Ecology*, vol. 18.

Odada, J.E.O., and A.B. Ayako (Eds.) (1988). *Report of Proceedings of the Workshop on The Impact of Structural Adjustment Policies on the Well-Being of the Vulnerable Groups in Kenya*, Nairobi, November 3–5, 1988. Nairobi: UNICEF, Kenya Country Office and Kenyan Economic Association.

O'Donnell, C., M. Manos, and M. Chesney-Lind (1987). "Diversion and Neighborhood Delinquency Programs in Open Settings," in: *Behavioral Approaches to Crime and Delinquency*, eds. E. Morris and C. Braukmann. New York: Plenum Press.

OECD (1992). *Development and Cooperation*. Paris: Organisation for Economic Co-Operation and Development.

Offe, C. (1985). "New Social Movements: Challenging the Boundaries of Institutional Politics." *Social Research*, vol. 52, no. 5.

Office for Juvenile Justice Centres, Campania and Molise (1983). "Report on minors held in juvenile detention centres." Naples. Mimeo.
_____ (1990a). "Minors placed in youth communities, by type of crime." Report on the period of 11 Sept. 1989–30 Sept. 1990. Naples. Mimeo.
_____ (1990b). "Minors placed in institutions, receiving centres and youth communities." Report on the period of 1 Nov. 1989–30 Sept. 1990. Naples. Mimeo.

Office of the Prosecutor for Minors (1990). *Segnalazioni di minori nel comune di Milano*. Milan: Procura dei Minori.

Office of the Registrar General (1981). "Internal Migration in India 1961–81 — An Analysis." *Census Monograph No. 2*. New Delhi: Government of India.
_____ (1984). *Census of India 1981. Series V*. New Delhi: Government of India.
_____ (1986). *Sample Registration System*. New Delhi: Government of India.
_____ (1988a). "Census of India: Advance Report on Age at Marriage Differential in India — 1984." *Occasional Paper No. 2 of 1988*. New Delhi: Government of India.
_____ (1988b). *Report of the Expert Committee on the Population Projections*. New Delhi: Government of India.
_____ (1988c). *Sample Registration System*. New Delhi: Government of India.
_____ (1989a). "Negative Aspects of Urbanization A Study of Civic and Other Amenities Available in Notified Slums of Class I and II Towns." *Occasional Paper No. 3 of 1988*. New Delhi: Government of India.
_____ (1989b). Vital Statistic Division, *Occasional Paper 1 of 1989*. New Delhi: Government of India.
_____ (1991a). "Census of India 1991, Provisional Population Totals." Series 1, INDIA, Paper 1 of 1991. New Delhi: Government of India.
_____ (1991b). "Census of India 1991 — Provisional Population Totals: Rural-Urban Distribution." Series 1, INDIA, Paper 2 of 1991, New Delhi: Government of India.

Olga Tellis vs. Bombay Municipal Corporation (Pavement Dwellers' Case) AIR (1986). S.C. 180. A published judgement of the Supreme Court of India.

Oliveira, C. de F.G. (1989). *Se Essa Rua Fosse Minha — Um Estudo sobre a Trajetória e Vivência dos Meninos de Rua do Recife*. Recife: UNICEF.

Oloko, S.B.A., et al. (1992). "Situation Analyses of Children in Especially Difficult Circumstances (CEDC) in Nigeria — Summary." Unpublished report prepared for UNICEF Nigeria Office.

Olpadwala, P., and W.W. Goldsmith (1992). "The Sustainability of Privilege: Reflections on the Environment, the Third World City, and Poverty." *World Development*, vol. 20, no. 4.

Ong, A. (1988). "Colonialism and Modernity: Feminist Re-Presentations of Women in Non-Western Societies." *Inscriptions* vol. 3, no. 4.

Onyango, P., and N. Bwibo (1987). *Final Report of the Child Labour and Health Research.* Nairobi: WHO.

Onyango, P., and D. Kayongo-Male (Eds.) (1982). *Child Labour and Health.* Proceedings of the First National Workshop on Child Labour and Health, December 2–3, 1982, Nairobi. Sponsored by WHO in collaboration with the University of Nairobi.

Onyango, P., K. Orwa, C. Suda, F. Ombaso, and N. Ndungu (1992). "A Report on the Nairobi Case Study on Children in Especially Difficult Circumstances." Prepared for the Urban Child Project, UNICEF International Child Development Centre, Florence.

Operations Research Group (ORG) (1988). *Accessibility and Utilization of Basic Services in Selected Urban Slums with Special Reference to Women and Children* (Summary Report), Baroda: ORG.

Osmania University Regional Centre (1991). *Children and Families in Urban Poverty: A Study in Andhra Pradesh.* Research report prepared by P.V. Rao and D.R. Prasad for the Urban Child Project, UNICEF International Child Development Centre. Hyderabad: Regional Centre for Urban Environmental Studies.

Otieno B., J. Owola, and P. Oduor (1979). "A Study of Alcoholism in a Rural Setting in Kenya." *East African Medical Journal,* December.

Palattao Corpus, L. (1992). "Situation of Adolescent Filipinos, 1991: Focus on Teenage Mothers." Paper presented for the Urban Child Project at the planning workshop "Meeting the Basic Learning Needs of Adolescent Girls/Mothers," 9–11 March, Florence, UNICEF International Child Development Centre.

Palmer, I. (1983). *Rural Urban Migration Patterns in North East Thailand,* Special Series. New York Population Centre.

Palmer, J.L., T. Smeeding, and B. Boyle Torrey (Eds.) (1988). *The Vulnerable.* Washington: Urban Institute Press.

Palmonari, A., and G. Rigon (1991). "Servizi socio-sanitari e prevenzione delle situazioni a rischio," in Ministero dell'Interno, Direzione Generale dei Servizi Civili (ed.), *Politiche sociali per l'infanzia e l'adolescenza.* Milan: UNICOPLI.

Palomba, F. (1991). "I diritti del bambino: sistema sociale e azione politica," in Ministero dell'Interno, Direzione Generale dei Servizi Civili (ed.), *Politiche sociali per l'infanzia e l'adolescenza.* Milan: UNICOPLI.

Palo-Okeyo, A. (1988). *An Assessment of Functional Literacy, Non-Formal Education and Community Development in Relation to the Health of Women: A Study of Two Divisions in South Nyanza, Kenya.* Nairobi: Ministry of Health/World Health Organization.

Pandey, R. (1989). *Street Children of Kanpur: A Situation Analysis.* Kanpur: Indian Institute of Technology. Mimeo.

Panicker, R., and P. Nangia, (1988). *Situation Analysis of Children in Specially Difficult Circumstances in the Union Territory of Delhi with Special Focus on Working and Street Children.* New Delhi. Mimeo.

——————— (1992). *Working and Street Children of Delhi.* Uttar Pradesh: National Labour Institute.

Patel, S.P. (1983). *Equality of Educational Opportunity in India: A Myth or Reality.* New Delhi: National Publishing House.

Pathak, K.B., et al. (1979). "Projections of Orphan Children in India: 1971 to 1991," in: *Demographic and Socio-Economic Aspects of the Child in India,* eds. K. Srinivasan, P.C. Saxena, and T. Kanitkar. Bombay: Himalaya Publishing House.

Pathumvanit, D., and N. Liengcharernsit (1989). "Coming to Terms with Bangkok's Environmental Problems." *Environment and Urbanization,* vol. 1, April.

Patil, B.R. (1984). *Problem of School Drop-Outs in India: An Annotated Bibliography.* New Delhi: Council for Social Development.

Pelton, L.H. (Ed.) (1985). *The Social Context of Child Abuse and Neglect.* New York: Human Sciences Press.

Penna Firme, T., and A. Tonini (1988). "Avaliacâo dos Programmas da Secretaria do Menor do Estado de São Paulo." Report prepared for UNICEF Brasilia in collaboration with the

Secretariat of the Child of São Paulo, Brasilia.

Pennsylvania Department of Education (1987). *Achieving Success with More Students: Addressing the Problem of Students at Risk, K–12*. Harrisburg: Pennsylvania Department of Education.

Pentz, M., J. Dwyer, D. MacKinnon, B. Flay, W. Hansen, E. Yang, and C. Johnson (1989). "A Multi-Community Trial for Primary Prevention of Adolescent Drug Abuse: Effects on Drug Prevalence." *Journal of the American Medical Association*, vol. 261.

Pentz, M., et al. (1990). "Effects of Program Implementation on Adolescent Drug Use Behavior: the Midwestern Prevention Project (MPP)." *Evaluation Review*, 14/3.

Perulli, P. (1992). *Atlante metropolitano: il mutamento sociale nelle grandi città*. Bologna: Il Mulino.

Petrillo, G., and C. Serino (1978). "Scuola e lavoro minorile in un'indagine nel centro storico di Napoli." *Inchiesta*, no. 35–36.

Phi Delta Kappan (1983). 64:339–347.

Philliber, S., et al. (1988). "Teen Outreach: A Three-Year Evaluation of a Program to Prevent Teen Pregnancy and School Dropout." Unpublished report to the Association of Junior Leagues.

Phillips, W. (1989). *Child in Blind Alleys: A Situation Analysis of Street Children*. Indore: Indore School of Social Work. Mimeo.

Picchieri, A. (1989). *Strategie contro il declino in aree di antica industrializazione*. Turin: Rosenberg and Pellier.

Pineda-Ofreneo, R. (1982). "Subcontracting in the Philippines: Domestic Outwork for Export Oriented Industries." *Philippines Labour Review*, 7/2.

Pinnelli, A. (1989). "La sopravvivenza infantile," in: *Demografia e società in Italia*, ed. E. Sonnino. Rome: Riuniti.

Pires, J.M. (1988). *Trabalho Infantil: A Necessidade e a Persistência*. São Paulo: USP/FEA. Master's dissertation.

Planning Commission (1968). *Report of the Working Group on Policy and Programmes for Destitute Children*. New Delhi: Government of India.

_____ (1980). *Sixth Five Year Plan 1980–85*. New Delhi: Government of India.

_____ (1983). *Report of the Task Force on Shelter for the Urban Poor and Slum Improvement*. New Delhi: Government of India.

_____ (1985). *Seventh Five Year Plan 1985–90*. vol. 1. New Delhi: Government of India.

Polansky, N., P.W. Ammons, and J.M. Gaudin (1985). "Loneliness and Isolation in Child Neglect." *Social Casework*, vol. 66.

Polletta, G. (1991). "Registro neuropsichiatrico del servizio infantile della USL di Ferrara, 1991." Ferrara: USL.

Popenoe, D. (1977). *The Suburban Environment: Sweden and the United States*. Chicago: University of Chicago Press.

Population Council and International Center for Research on Women (1989). "Notes from Seminars I, II, and III, 1988–1989, on The Determinants and Consequences of Female-Headed Households." Special Reports. New York.

Population Studies and Research Institute (PSRI) (1990). *Population Profiles for the Districts of Kenya, 11 and 30*. University of Nairobi, Nairobi: Kenya.

Porio, E. (1990). *Becoming and Being a Streetchild: Survival Contexts, Strategies, and Interventions*. Report prepared for the Urban Child Project, UNICEF International Child Development Centre, Florence.

_____ (1991). "Urbanization and Urban Children." Mimeo. Report prepared for the Urban Child Programme, UNICEF International Child Development Centre, Florence.

_____ (1993). *Children of the Streets: Surviving Urban Poverty in Cebu City*. Report prepared for the Urban Child Project, UNICEF International Child Development Centre, Quezon City: Institute of Philippine Culture (forthcoming).

Preston, S. H. (1988). "Urban Growth in Developing Countries: A Demographic Reappraisal," in: *The Urbanization of the Third World*, ed. J. Gugler. Oxford: Oxford University Press.

Province of Palermo, Office of Education (1990). *Rapporto sulla frequenza nelle scuole d'obbligo*. Palermo: Provveditorato agli Studi.

Proyecto Alternativas (1993a). "Presentacion de los Resultados de una investigacion de Variables Relacionadas con el Abuso de Sustancias por Menores 'en' y 'de' la Calle." Preliminary report prepared for symposium, 5 Feb. 1993. Honduras.

_____ (1993b). "Servicios Comprensivos de Salud Para Ninos 'en' y 'de' la Calle y sus Familias en la Ciudad de Teguigalpa." Informe Semestral Quinto Semestre Julio-Dicembre, 1992. Paper prepared for Tulane University, Programa Colaborativo Tulane-Honduras.

PSSC — Philippine Social Science Council (1991). "Situation Analyses for the Metro Manila cities, Olongapo and Davao." Report prepared by A. Torres for the Urban Child Project, UNICEF International Child Development Centre, Florence, and UNICEF Manila.

Rabello, A.M., et al. (1989). *Sistema Educativo-Cultural: Uma Visão Prospectiva*. Brasilia: IPEA/IPLAN.

Rabkin, J. (1987). "Epidemiology of Adolescent Violence: Risk Factors, Career Patterns and Interventions Programs." Paper delivered at the Conference on Adolescent Violence, Stanford University, California.

Rae, G.O., M. Manundu, and F.V. Mondia (1988). "Health Care Delivery," in: *Report of Proceedings of the Workshop on The Impact of Structural Adjustment Policies on the Well-Being of the Vulnerable Groups in Kenya*, eds. J.E.O. Odada and A.B. Ayako. Nairobi, November 3–5, 1988. Nairobi: UNICEF, Kenya Country Office and Kenyan Economic Association.

Ramachandran, P. (1972). *Pavement Dwellers in Bombay City*. Bombay: Tata Institute of Social Sciences.

Ramarau, D.G. (1990). "Urban Community Development Programme. Its Origin and Growth." Unpublished Report prepared for the Urban Child Project, UNICEF International Child Development Centre, Florence.

Ramaswany, S.S., S.K. Dave, and S.K. Kashyap (1987). *Status Report on Child Labour*. Ahmedabad: National Institute of Occupational Health.

Rane, A.J., et al. (1986). *Children in Difficult Situations in India: A Review*. Bombay: Tata Institute of Social Sciences.

Rao, K.S.J. (1986). "Urban Nutrition in India, II." *NFI Bulletin*, 7/1.

Rao, P.V. (1989). *Street Children: A Study Conducted in Vijayawada*. Municipal Corporation of Vijayawada, sponsored by UNICEF, Southeastern India Office, Hyderabad.

Rappoport, R.N. (Ed.) (1985). *Children, Youth and Families. The Action-Research Relationship*. New York: Cambridge University Press.

Reddy, V., and K. Satyanarayana (1991). "Nutritional Status of Indian Girls," in *Proceedings of the Workshop on Improving Young Women's Health and Development Sprinagar*, 1989. New Delhi: ICMR.

Regione Campania, Assessorato alla Sanità (1990). "Relazione sanitaria 1985–1989 della Regione Campania." Naples: Assessorato alla sanità.

Report on Drugs and Organized Crime, (1993). Rome: CENSIS.

Republic of Kenya (1984). *Situation Analysis of Children and Women in Kenya Section 1: Some Determinants of Well-Being*. Nairobi: Central Bureau of Statistics, Ministry of Finance and Planning and UNICEF.

_____ (1990a). *Economic Survey 1990*. Nairobi: Central Bureau of Statistics, Ministry of Planning and National Development.

_____ (1990b). *Statistical Abstract 1990*. Nairobi: Central Bureau of Statistics, Ministry of Planning and National Development.

_____ (1991). *Economic Survey 1991*. Nairobi: Central Bureau of Statistics, Ministry of Planning and National Development.

_____ (1992). *Economic Survey 1992*. Nairobi: Central Bureau of Statistics, Ministry of Planning and National Development.

Rivlin, L.G. (1990). "Home and Homelessness in the Lives of Children," in: *Homeless Children: The Watchers and the Waiters*, ed. N.A. Boxill. New York: Haworth Press.

Rivlin, L.G., and C. Manzo (1988). "Homeless Children in New York City: A View from the 19th Century." *Children's Environments Quarterly*, 5/1, Spring.

Rizzini, Irene (1986). *A Geração da Rua: Um Estudo sobre as Crianças Marginalizadas no Rio de Janeiro*. Séries Estudos e Pesquisas-1. Rio de Janeiro: USU — Universidade Santa Ursula/CESME.

_____ (1989). *Levantamento Bibliográfico da Produção Científica sobre a Infância Pobre no Brasil*. Rio de Janeiro: USU — Universidad Santa Ursula/CESME.

_____ (1992). *Children in the City of Violence: The Case of Brazil*. Tokyo/Lima: The United Nations University/APEP.

Rizzini, Irene, and F.B. Wiik (1990). *O que o Rio tem feito por suas Crianças?*. Rio de Janeiro: Universidade Santa Ursula — USU/CESME/IBASW/Ford Foundation.

Rizzini, Irene, Irma Rizzini, M. Munoz, and L. Galeano (1992). "Childhood and Urban Poverty in Brazil: Street and Working Children and their Families." *Innocenti Occasional Papers*, Urban Child Series, no. 3. Florence: UNICEF International Child Development Centre.

Rizzini, Irma (1989). "A Assistência à Infância no Brasil. Uma análise de sua construção." Rio de Janeiro: CESPI/FINEP. Mimeo.

Rogoff, B., M.J. Sellers, S. Pirrotta, N. Fox, and S.H. White (1975). "Age of Assignment of Roles and Responsibilities to Children. A Cross-Cultural Survey." *Human Development*, vol. 18.

Rojas-Aleta, I., et al. (1978). *A Profile of Filipino Women: Their Status and Role*. Prepared for the United States Agency for International Development. Manila: Philippine Business for Social Progress.

Rossi-Cairo, A. (Ed.) (1991). "La condizione dei minori nella città di Milano." Unpublished report, Urban Child Project, Istituto degli Innocenti, Florence.

Saraceno, C. (1990). "Child Poverty and Deprivation in Italy: 1950 to the Present." *Innocenti Occasional Papers*, Economic Policies Series, no. 6. Florence: UNICEF International Child Development Centre.

_____ (1992). "Trends in the Structuring and Stability of the Family from 1950 to the Present: The Impact on Child Welfare." *Innocenti Occasional Papers*, Economic Policies Series, no. 27. Florence: UNICEF International Child Development Centre.

Satterthwaite, D. (1992). "The Impact on Health of Environmental Problems in Urban Areas of the Third World — An Overview." Paper prepared for the International Workshop on Planning for Sustainable Urban Development: Cities and Natural Resource Systems in Developing Countries, Cardiff, July 13–17.

Scabini, E., and P. Donati (1988). *La famiglia lunga del giovane adulto*. Milan: Vita e Pensiero.

Schinke, S., B. Blythe, L. Gilchrist, and G. Burt (1981). "Primary Prevention of Adolescent Pregnancy." *Social Work with Groups*, vol. 4.

Schinke, S., and L. Gilchrist (1984). *Life Skills Counseling with Adolescents*. Baltimore: University Park Press.

Schizzerotto, A. (1988). "Il ruolo dell'istruzione nei processi mobilità sociale." *Polis*, no. 2.

Schneider, J., and P. Schneider (1976). *Culture and Political Economy in Western Sicily*. New York: Academic Press.

Schofield, C.J., and G.B. White (1984). "House Design and Domestic Vectors of Disease." *Transactions of the Royal Society for Tropical Medicine and Hygiene*, 78/285.

Schorr, L. (1988). *Within Our Reach: Breaking the Cycle of Disadvantage*. New York: Doubleday.

Schwartzman, J. (1992). "Developmental Tasks and Social Support for Children of Low-Income, Urban Families in Developing Countries: Life Histories of Middle Childhood and Adolescence." Unpublished paper prepared for the Urban Child Programme, UNICEF International Child Development Centre. Florence.

Scott, A. MacEwen (1979). "Who Are the Self-Employed?" in: *Casual Work and Poverty in Third World Cities*, eds. R. Bromley and C. Gerry. Chichester: John Wiley and Sons.

Sen, A., and S. Sen Gupta (1983). "Malnutrition of Rural Children and the Sex Bias." *Economic and Political Weekly*, Annual Number, May 1983.

Sgritta, G.B. (1988). *La Condizione dell'infanzia*. Milan: Angeli.

_____ (1990). "L'adolescenza tra familiarizzazione e socialità limitata." Paper presented at the Convegno dell'Università Cattolica del Sacro Cuore, 27–30 October 1990, Rome.

_____ (1991). "Iniquità generazionale e logica delle compatibilità," in Ministero dell'Interno — Direzione Generale dei Servizi Civili.

Sieber, S. (1979). "The Integration of Fieldwork and Survey Methods." *American Journal of Sociology*, 78/6.

Silva, A.R. (1983). *Um Estudo Preliminar sobre o Menor Carregador em Feiras-Livres*. São Paulo: Cadernos PUC.

Silverman, S. (1975). *The Three Bells of Civilization. The Life of an Italian Hill Town*. New York: Columbia University Press.

Sing Sandhu, N. (1989). "Social Consequences of Glue Sniffing and Inhalant Abuse." Report on the National Campaign Against Glue Sniffing and Inhalant Abuse, Singapore.

Singh, A.M. (1978). "Women and the Family: Coping with Poverty in the Bastis of Delhi," in: *The Indian City: Poverty, Ecology and Urban Development*, ed. A. de Souza. New Delhi: Manohar.

Singh, A.M., et al. (1980). *Working Children in Bombay*. New Delhi: National Institute of Public Cooperation and Child Development (NIPCCD).

Singh, A.M., and A. Kelles-Viitanen (Eds.) (1987). "Invisible Hands: Women in Home-Based Production," in: *Women and the Household in Asia*, Vol. 1. New Delhi: Sage Publications.

Singh, K.P. (1989). "Green Revolution and Child Survival in the State of Punjab." Paper presented at the International Population Conference, 20–27 September 1989, New Delhi.

Singh, M., V. Kaura, and V. Khan (1980). *Working Children in Bombay — A Study*. New Delhi: NIPCCD.

Sipos, S. (1991). "Current and Structural Problems Affecting Children in Central and Eastern Europe," in: *Children and the Transition to the Market Economy*, eds. G.A. Cornia and S. Sipos. London: Avebury Academic Publishing Group.

Solito, L. (1992). "La condizione dei minori in Italia" (forthcoming).

Sommella, L. (1988). "I minori tra marginalità e devianza. Un case study," in Consiglio Nazionale dei Minori, *I Minori in Italia*. Milan: Angeli.

_____ (Ed.) (1990). "La condizione dei minori nella città di Napoli." Research paper for the Urban Child Project, Istituto degli Innocenti, Florence.

_____ (Ed.) (1992). "Le mille bolle blu — Napoli: storie di vita dei ragazzi di strada." Research paper, Istituto degli Innocenti, Florence.

SPARC (Ed.) (1991). *Waiting for Tomorrow: A Study on Four Groups of Vulnerable Migrant Children in the City of Bombay 1989–90*. Bombay: Department of Social Welfare, Government of Maharashtra/UNICEF.

Statera, G. (1990a). "I minori in Italia alla soglia degli anni '90," in Consiglio Nazionale dei Minori, *I minori in Italia*. Milan: Angeli.

_____ (1990b). *Secondo rapporto sulla condizione dei minori in Italia*. Milan: Angeli.

Stern, M. (1988). "Evaluation of a School-Based Pregnancy Prevention Program." *TEC Newsletter*, vol. 19.

Swift, A. (1991). "Brazil: The Fight For Childhood in the City." *Innocenti Studies*. Urban Child in Difficult Circumstances. Florence: UNICEF International Child Development Centre.

Szanton, P. (1981). *Not Well Advised*. New York: Russell Sage Foundation.

Tapan K.M. (1978). "The Urban Poor and Social Change: A Study of Squatter Settlements in Delhi," in: *The Indian City: Poverty, Ecology and Urban Development*, ed. A. de Souza. New Delhi: Manohar.

Telefono Azzurro (1988). *Campione di denunce telefoniche sulla violenza infantile*. Palermo: Telefono Azzurro.

Testa, F. (1982). *I cento mestieri dei ragazzi di Napoli*. Naples: Lampo.

The Committee for Working Children (CWC) (1989). *Situation Analysis of Street Children in the City of Bangalore*. Mimeo.

Thompson, E.P. (1963). *The Making of the English Working Class*. London: Gollancz.

Tobler, N. (1986). "Meta-Analysis of 143 Adolescent Drug Prevention Programs: Quantitative Outcome Results of Program Participants Compared to a Control or Comparison Group." *Journal of Drug Issues*, vol. 16.

_____ (1987). "Adolescent Drug Prevention Programs Can Work: Research Findings." Paper presented at the Parsons/Sage Fall Institute, Albany, NY.

Torres, A.T. (1990). "The Urban Child and Family in Especially Difficult Circumstances — The Case of Metro Manila." Mimeo. Preliminary report prepared for the Urban Child Project, UNICEF International Child Development Centre, Florence.

Touraine, A. (1973). *Production de la Société*. Paris: Sévil.

Trivellato, P. (1990). "L'istruzione scolastica." ISTAT-AIS, *Immagini della società*. Rome.

UFPE — Universidade Federal de Pernambuco (1989). "Trabalho e Menor: Contradiçes, Perspectivas." Recife. Mimeo.

UNDP (1989). *Urban Transition in Developing Countries. Policy Issues and Implications for Technical Cooperation in the 1990s*. New York: United Nations Development Programme.

_____ (1990). *Human Development Report 1990*. New York: Oxford University Press.

_____ (1991a). *Cities, People & Poverty — Urban Development Cooperation for the 1990s*. New York: United Nations Development Programme.

_____ (1991b). *Human Development Report 1991*. New York: Oxford University Press.

_____ (1992). *Human Development Report 1992*. New York: Oxford University Press.

_____ (1993). *Human Development Report 1993*. New York: Oxford University Press.

UNESCO (1988). *The Learning Environments of Early Childhood in Asia*. Bangkok: International Development Research Center.

UNFPA (1986). *The State of the World Population*. New York: United Nations Fund for Population Activities.

UNICEF (1986a). "Children in Especially Difficult Circumstances." Document based on Executive Board Resolutions E/ICEF/1986/CRP 33 and 37, and distributed as CF/PD/PRO-1986-004, October 31, 1986. Mimeo.

_____ (1986b). "Exploitation of Working Children and Street Children." UNICEF Executive Board 1986 Session, Document No. E/ICEF/1986/CRP.3. New York: UNICEF.

_____ (1986c). "Overview: Children in Especially Difficult Circumstances." UNICEF Executive Board, 1986 Session, Document No. E/ICEF/1986/L.6. New York: UNICEF.

_____ (1990a). *Children and Women in India: A Situation Analysis. 1990*. New Delhi: UNICEF India Office.

_____ (1990b). "1990 Mid-Term Review Project Document." Manila: UNICEF.

_____ (1990c). *The State of the World's Children 1990*. New York: Oxford University Press.

_____ (1992a). "Menores en Circunstancias Especialmente Dificiles, La Paz Bolivia." *Analisis de Situacion*, No. 8. Bogotá: UNICEF.

_____ (1992b). *The State of the World's Children 1992*. Oxford: Oxford University Press.

_____ (1993). *The State of the World's Children 1993*. New York: Oxford University Press.

UNICEF/IPEA-IPLAN (1990). *The Child in Brazil: What to Do?*. Brasilia: UNICEF/IPEA-IPLAN.

UNICEF Kenya Country Office (1993). *Donor Report to Netherlands National Committee for UNICEF*. Nairobi: UNICEF.

United Nations (1990). *World Urbanization Prospects 1989*. New York: United Nations.

_____ (1991a). *World Urbanization Prospects 1990*. New York: United Nations.

_____ (1991b). *World Population Prospects 1990*. New York: United Nations.

_____ (1992). *World Population Monitoring 1991*. New York: United Nations.

United Nations Statistical Office (1992). *Child Mortality Since the 1960s*. New York: United Nations.

University of Nairobi (1987). *Final Report of the Child Labour and Health Research*. Nairobi: WHO.

UPLMO (1984). *Rapporto sul lavoro minorile nella provincia di Napoli*. Naples: UPLMO.

USAID (1990). "Women in Development: A.I.D.'s Experience 1973–1985," in *Ten Field Studies*, Vol. II. Washington, DC: USAID.

Valladares, L., and F. Impelizieri (1992). *Invisible Action: A Guide to Non-Governmental Assistance for Underprivileged and Street Children of Rio de Janeiro*. Rio de Janeiro: Instituto Universitario de Pesquisas do Rio de Janeiro.

Vallejo, E. (1987). "How to Curb the Dropout Rate." *School Administrator*, September.

Vandemoortele, J. (1982). "The Public Sector and the Basic Needs Strategy in Kenya: The Experience of the Seventies." *World Employment Research Working Paper*, No. 38. Geneva: ILO.

van Ginneken, W., and R. van der Hoeven (1989). "Industrialization, Employment and Earnings (1950–1987): An International Survey." *International Labour Review*, 128/5 (September–October).

van Til, J. (1988). *Mapping the Third Sector: Voluntarism in a Changing Social Economy*. New York: The Foundation Center.

Vijayalakahmi, S. (1984). *Working Conditions of Children Employed in Unorganized Sectors Study in Sivakesi*. Madras: Centre for Social Research. Mimeo.

Vincent, M., A. Clearie, and M. Schlucheter (1987). "Reducing Adolescent Pregnancy through School and Community-Based Education." *Journal of American Medical Association*, vol. 257.

Vogel, A., and M.A. Mello (1991). "Da Casa à Rua: A Cidade Como Fascínio e Descaminho." Report prepared by FLACSO for the Urban Child Project, International Child Development Centre in coordination with UNICEF Brasilia and subsequently published in Fausto, A. and R. Cervini, *O Trabalho e a Rua*. São Paulo: Editoria Cortez.

Wainana, J. (1977). "Life Histories of Parking Boys in Nairobi." Unpublished B.A. Dissertation, Department of Sociology, University of Nairobi.

WCED — World Commission on Environment and Development (1987). *Our Common Future*. Oxford: Oxford University Press.

Weill, J.D. (1990). "Child Advocacy in the United States — The Work of the Children's Defense Fund." *Innocenti Essays*, no. 2. Florence: UNICEF International Child Development Centre.

Weiner, M. (1991). *The Child and the State in India*. Princeton: Princeton University Press.

Wells, K., and D.E. Biegel (1991). *Family Preservation Services: Research and Evaluation*. Newbury Park, CA: Sage Publications.

White, L. (1990). *The Comforts of Home: Prostitution in Colonial Nairobi*. Chicago: University of Chicago Press.

Whiting, B.B., and C.P. Edwards (1988). *Children of Different Worlds: The Formation of Social Behavior*. Cambridge: Harvard University Press.

Whittaker, J., and J. Garbarino (1983). *Social Support Networks: Informal Helping in the Human Services*. Mew York: Aldine.

WHO (1981). *Development of Indicators for Monitoring Progress Towards Health for All by the Year 2000*. Geneva: World Health Organization.

_____ (1988). *Urbanization and its Implications for Child Health: Potential for Action*. Geneva: World Health Organization.

_____ (1992). *Our Planet, Our Health*. Geneva: World Health Organization, Commission on Health and Environment.

Wilson, J. (1989). *The Truly Disadvantaged*. Chicago: University of Chicago Press

World Bank (1984). *Towards Sustained Development in Sub-Saharan Africa: A Joint Programme of Action*. Washington, DC: The World Bank.

_____ (1985). *World Development Report 1985*. New York: Oxford University Press.

_____ (1989). *India: Poverty, Employment and Social Services*. Washington, DC: The World Bank.

_____ (1990a). *Informe sobre el Desarrollo Mundial. Indicadores del Desarrollo Mundial*. Washington, DC: The World Bank.

_____ (1990b). *Structural Adjustment and Sustainable Growth: The Urban Agenda for the 1990s*. Washington DC: The World Bank.

_____ (1990c). *World Development Report 1990*. New York: Oxford University Press.

_____ (1991a). *Urban Policy and Economic Development: An Agenda for the 1990s*. Washington, DC: The World Bank.

World Commission on Environment and Development (1987). *Our Common Future*. Oxford: Oxford University Press.

_____ (1991b). *World Development Report 1991*. New York: Oxford University Press.

_____ (1992). *World Development Report 1992*. New York: Oxford University Press.

Wright, J., D. Kaminsky, and M. Wittig (1992). "Health and Social Conditions of Street Children in Honduras." *American Journal of Diseases of Children*.

Wright, J.D. (1991). "Health and the Homeless Teenager: Evidence from the National Health Care for the Homeless Program." *Journal of Health and Social Policy*, vol. 2, no. 4.

Xenos, P.S. (1993). Report and Compilation of Data for Urban Child Project, International Child Development Centre, Florence, Italy.

Xenos, P.S., and Koo, H. (1983). "Migration, the Urban Informal Sector and Earnings in the Philippines." *The Sociological Quarterly* vol. 24, no. 2.

Xenos, P.S., et al. (1984). "The Migration of Women to Cities: A Comparative Perspective," in: *Women in the Cities of Asia: Migration and Urban Adaptation*, eds. James T. Fawcett, Siew-Ean Khoo, and Peter C. Smith. Boulder, CO: The Westview Press.

Zabin, L., M. Hirsch, E. Smith, R. Streett, and J. Hardy. (1986). "Evaluation of a Pregnancy Prevention Program for Urban Teenagers." *Family Planning Perspectives*, 18 (May–June).

Zelizer, V.A. (1985). *Pricing the Priceless Child. The Changing Social Value of Children*. New York: Basic Books.

Street children's resilience against significant odds constantly surprises street educators and outside observers. Here a group is playing joyfully in the main fountain of Praca da So, São Paolo, Brazil. *Credit*: UNICEF/Claudio Edinger.

Index